Education and the State
Volume I

Schooling and the National Interest

Education and the State
Volume I

Schooling and the National Interest

Edited by
Roger Dale,
Geoff Esland,
Ross Fergusson
and
Madeleine MacDonald

The Falmer Press
A member of the Taylor and Francis Group
In association with
The Open University Press

First published 1981

ISBN   0 905273 15 x Limp
        0 905273 16 8 Cased

Cover design by Pedro Pra Lopez
Printed and bound in Great Britain by
Taylor & Francis (Printers) Ltd.,
Basingstoke, Hampshire for
The Falmer Press
(*A member of the Taylor & Francis Group*)
Falmer House,
Barcombe, Lewes,
Sussex   BN8 5DL
England

This reader is one part of an Open University integrated teaching system and the selection is therefore related to other material available to students. It is designed to evoke the critical understanding of students. Opinions expressed in it are not necessarily those of the course team or of the University.

ACKNOWLEDGEMENTS

We are grateful to the following for permission to reproduce copyright material:

The Open University Press for HALL, S. 'Schooling, state and society – review of the Course' Unit 32 of E202 (The Open University Press 1977), copyright © 1980 The Open University Press.

Elsevier Scientific Publishing Company for HOGAN, D. 'Capitalism, liberalism and schooling' in *Theory and Society*, Vol. 8, 1979, pp. 387–413, Elsevier Scientific Publishing Company.

The Falmer Press for GINTIS, H. and BOWLES, S. 'Contradiction and reproduction in educational theory' in BARTON, L., MEIGHAN, R. and WALKER, S. (Eds) *Schooling, Ideology and the Curriculum*, 1981, The Falmer Press.

Archives Européennes de Sociologie for MACPHERSON, C. B. 'Do we need a theory of the state?' reprinted by permission from *European Journal of Sociology*, XVIII, 1977, pp. 223–44.

The Editor, New German Critique for OFFE, C. and RONGE, V. 'Theses on the theory of the state', *New German Critique* (6) 1975, pp. 137–47.

The Centre for Policy Studies for WILKINSON, M. Introduction from *Lessons from Europe*, 1977 Centre for Policy Studies, pp. 1–14.

The Editor of Screen Education for DONALD, J. 'Green paper: noise of crisis' 1979, *Screen Education*, (30).

Basil Blackwell for McCANN, P. 'Trade unions, artisans and the 1870 Education Act', *British Journal of Educational Studies*, Vol. XVIII, No. 2, June 1970.

The Editor, Monthly Review Press for BRAVERMAN, H. Chaps. 4 and 12 from *Labour and Monopoly Capital*, 1974, New York, Monthly Review Press.

Routledge and Kegan Paul Ltd. for HUSSAIN, A. 'The economy and the educational system in capitalist societies' *Economy and Society*, Vol. 5, Number 4, November 1976.

Dr D. A. Reeder for REEDER, D. A. 'A recurring debate; education and industry' in BERNBAUM, G. (Ed) *Schooling in Decline*, 1979, Macmillan Publishers Limited.

Routledge and Kegan Paul for SANDERSON, M. Chap. 9 from *The Universities and British Industry 1850–1870*, 1972 Routledge and Kegan Paul, pp. 243–75.

BARKER, J. and DOWNING, H. 'Word processing and the transformation of the patriarchal relations of control in the office', 1980, copyright © 1980 J. Barker and H. Downing.

The Open University Press for WILLIS, P. 'The class significance of school counterculture' from HAMMERSLEY, M. and WOODS, P. (Eds) *The Process of Schooling*, 1976, Routledge and Kegan Paul, copyright © 1980 The Open University Press.

Contents

SECTION THREE: EDUCATION AND NATIONAL DEVELOPMENT

Introduction

This collection of readings is the first of two volumes compiled as a component of the Open University course *Society, Education and the State*.[1] It is our hope that these two volumes will be of interest not only to Open University students, but also to a much larger group of readers who are interested in the sociology of education.

In terms of its overall structure and content the course and this Reader have been conceived as being in two parts. The first – as represented in this volume – examines elements of the large-scale political and economic structures which affect educational provision, and the second – represented in volume two – is concerned with more specific areas of social policy and political practice. Correspondingly, Part One of the course considers the relationship between the economy and education, the nature of the nation-state, and the part played by education in national development; in Part Two, the topics include the politics of school culture, sexual divisions and patriarchy, the social construction of the child and the family, and the politics of schools and teaching.

Volume I: Education and the State: Schooling and the National Interest

Since the publication of Bowles and Gintis's *Schooling in Capitalist America* (1976), debates about the political economy of education have given rise to a number of criticisms of its early formulations. The most important perhaps relates to the oversimplified portrayal of the relations between education and the economy. The educational system is seen as taking its form directly (and by implication, wholly) from the functions it performs for the economy – these are to supply an appropriately skilled, socialized and hierachized workforce. This not only entails a restricted view of what education involves, but it fails to clarify just how the needs of the economy are conveyed to, and imposed on, educational institutions. This approach also has rather pessimistic connotations. It was not clear from Bowles and Gintis's analysis how education systems and schools could be changed because it was not clear just how they were controlled by the capitalist class. Much of the subsequent effort in sociology of education has been directed at elucidating the relationship between the economy and education in capitalist societies through a focus on the relation of each of them to the state, which is the immediate provider of education and controller of education systems. It cannot, of course, be inferred from this emphasis that there is a single state policy on education which it is the task of the sociology of education to discover. The state is not monolithic: there are major differences of content and method both within and between its various apparatuses. And its influence on educational practice by no means wholly results from consciously planned educational policy.

The focus on the state informs both volumes of this reader, in more or less direct ways. It is most directly evident in the first section. Here, the major criticisms and developments of the political economy approach are set out in the pieces by Hall, Hogan and Gintis and Bowles. The piece by Stuart Hall is an extract from his review unit in *Schooling and Society*[2] where he demonstrates some of the main ways forward to a fuller understanding of schools which had been opened up by that course; this extract draws on the sections of that unit which develop and extend the 'political economy' approach and paradigms of social and cultural reproduction in the sociology of education.

The critique of *Schooling in Capitalist America* by David Hogan, an historian of education, is, in our view, the most comprehensive and constructive yet available. The extract published here, while sharing the book's critique of liberalism, points out its historicism and economism and identifies shortcomings in Bowles and Gintis's 'correspondence thesis'.

The article reprinted here by Gintis and Bowles themselves is their first major contribution to the analysis of education since *Schooling in Capitalist America*. In it they acknowledge the criticism made above and suggest instead that in the education system three major discourses, based on property rights, personal rights and gender rights co-exist in shifting and contradictory relationships; it is these contradictions, and not merely the needs of capitalism which shape education.

An emphasis on the state has become more prominent within social and historical studies in recent times. A concise review of pluralist and Marxist theories of the state is provided by MacPherson. Few of these contributions however, have referred to education; one which does, is the piece by Claus Offe and Volker Ronge. This work sees the state not as representing the interests of a particular class or group but as guarding the general interests of all classes on the basis of capitalist exchange relationships. One instance of this is that the education system serves the economy not by providing pupils with particular skills but by maintaining labour in the commodity form.

The challenges to the apparent functionalism and determinism of the political economy approach also open up the possibility of examining the processes of policy formation and implementation. They therefore provide greater purchase on contemporary political matters. In the late 1970s the Great Debate and the Green Paper on education were major events which it is essential for sociology of education to be able to interpret. The article by Max Wilkinson gives a flavour of the arguments about the structure and content of education which eventually gave rise to the Great Debate and were very influential in laying down its agenda. As education correspondent of the *Daily Mail* during much of that time, Wilkinson was a major contributor to those criticisms. James Donald's article examines in detail the assumptions and representations of the 'national interest' in the text of the Green Paper itself. The analysis reveals the discourses which the text exploits to convey its own particular ideology of education and construction of the terms of the debate.

The first section concludes with an article by McCann who documents the progress of Forster's 1870 Education Act in terms of the policy and demands made by trade unionists and skilled artisans. The historical account of how this educational Bill was contested and affected by trade union campaigns and debates reminds us that state policy is not adequately explained as solely an 'imposition'. The struggle over education is one in which the labour movement has not only participated but also helped to define.

The readings in *section two* focus on the relationship between the economy and education. They are grouped around two broad themes: the changes in the labour process which have occurred with the emergence of monopoly capitalism during the twentieth century, and the entry of school-leavers into work. With regard to the first theme, the readings concentrate primarily on manufacturing industry, in that it has been this sector which has attempted to exert the most strenuous pressure for more vocationally-relevant types of education.

During the two main phases of industrial merger and concentration – primarily the 1920s and the 1960s – the drive for more efficient production led to the substantial internal rationalization of companies as well as investment in new technology and the adoption of methods of 'scientific management'. These changes had far-reaching effects on the composition and deployment of the labour force. As Braverman has documented, the restructuring of production, supervision and management gave rise to entirely new areas of managerial and professional work which became adjuncts to the production and distribution processes – among them, personnel management, industrial psychology, research and development, advertising and marketing.

The evolution of the large corporation and the industrial significance of new forms of labour are examined in the extracts from Braverman's book *Labor and Monopoly Capital*. Here, Braverman considers both the tendencies behind the concentration of production and the importance within 'scientific management' of the principle of separating the *conception* of work tasks from their *execution*. An important feature of this process has been the growing importance of science and technology to industrial production and the enormous increase in the number of scientific and technical workers.

A discussion of the relationship between the education system and the economy is developed in Hussain's paper which consists primarily of a critique of the market conception of labour held by economists of education working within a neo-classical framework. He argues that they have typically portrayed the relationship between the economy and education as a technical one in which 'educated labour' is simply a 'factor of production'. In doing so, they have ignored the *relations* of production which are crucial to an understanding of the hierarchical structures of the labour market.

The article by Reeder shows that historically the debates over education have involved a concern about the validity of technical and vocational curricula within educational institutions. On the one hand, there is the recognition of the need for industry to recruit a technically competent work force in order to ensure 'national efficiency'. On the other hand, there are pressures to ensure the autonomy of education as a 'cultural force, monitoring social and economic developments'. The present debate, Reeder argues, is another example of a recurring conflict as to how the education system should relate to industry. Relevant to this discussion is the work of Michael Sanderson, who, from the standpoint of the economic historian, analyses the role played by British industry in the expansion of the universities. The chapter from his book examines the ways in which industrial promotion of university education took place during the inter-war years. One of the important features of this study is the light which it throws on the attempts of certain sectors of manufacturing industry to incorporate 'intellectual labour' within its domain.

The paper by Barker and Downing addresses issues raised by Braverman and provides a number of important theoretical developments of his thesis in the context of a particular empirical case. These writers are concerned with the structural changes taking place in the work of secretaries through the introduction of the word processor, and argue that the continuing subordination of women workers is maintained through both patriarchal forms of control and the use of a technology 'which embodies the social relations of capital's dominance over labour'.

The remaining article in this section – that by Paul Willis – deals with aspects of school education in relation to work. In this chapter, Willis explores the continuity between counter-school culture and shop-floor culture and sees each in relation to more pervasive elements of working-class culture. In terms of 'job choice', suggests Willis, 'it is the "lads" culture and not the official careers material which provides the most located and deeply influential guides for the future'.

One of the features of the move away from the 'pure' political economy approach has been an increasing emphasis on the importance of historical and comparative studies of educational provision. Some aspects of the comparative approach are found in the articles included in *section three*. In the first, Randall Collins sets out his theory of cultural markets and their influence in educational provision; cultural markets are formed by a range of groups (not only social classes) competing for status through possession of educational credentials. This theory is related in Alan Pomfret's paper to Immanuel Wallerstein's theory of a single-world system. Pomfret brings about this union between the two theories because he feels that Collins' theory cannot explain why particular kinds of cultural market are formed. He suggests that Wallerstein's concept can help account for variations in the formation and growth of cultural markets and examines this theory through a consideration of the development of education in Southern Ontario, New England and New-foundland.

While comparative studies emphasise differences in educational provision between different societies, the cataloguing of such differences is not their sole or even their main rationale. Similarities between different education systems and the sources of these, are at least as significant as the differences. One particularly important similarity between education systems is the view of education as a crucial provider of appropriately-skilled human resources: this is frequently taken to be its universally pre-eminent function.

The technical-functional theory on which this approach is based is examined and criticized in La Belle and Verhine's contribution. They see it as underpinning a pervasive 'credentialism' which effectively marginalizes alternative forms of schooling. Further implications of the technical-functional theory are examined in the papers by Ann Wickham and Stephen Stoer. Wickham's paper has as a major task the demonstration of the importance of the international context in the analysis of the education policy of any nation state. The example she chooses is Ireland whose education system is shown to have been significantly influenced by supra-national organizations like the World Bank.

Stoer's paper on recent developments in Portugese education shows first of all how the leaders of that country's education system attempted to base it on a form of technical-functional theory, and, secondly, how, after the 1974 revolutions, attempts were made to implement a socialist education policy. A major feature of this paper is that it argues that 'socialist education' does not consist of a single homogeneous package (solution to all social ills), but that it contains many often conflicting strands.

Most current work in the sociology of education is about education in capitalist societies. The critical approach adopted in much of this work has led some commentators to assume that this *ipso facto* entails approval of education systems in non-capitalist countries. The final two articles in this section, focusing on education in Russia and Cuba, show that such inferences are hardly valid. Westoby's paper provides a critical account of the historical relationship between education, property and class in the Soviet Union, while the article by Carnoy and Werthein gives a brief history of pragmatic and ideological changes in education since the revolutions in Cuba.

Acknowledgements

In compiling this Reader we would like to acknowledge the help of the other members of the *Society, Education and the State* course team, particularly, Heather Cathcart, Dan Finn, Simon Frith, Richard Johnson, Charles Posner, and Ann Wickham.

We are grateful to Olive Banks for her comments on the development of the Reader.

The editors would also like to thank Denise Hamilton and Tracey Lenton for their secretarial assistance.

Notes and References

1 OPEN UNIVERSITY (1981) *Society, Education and the State*, (E353), Milton Keynes, Open University Press. This is a third level course produced by the Faculty of Educational Studies.
2 OPEN UNIVERSITY (1977) *Schooling and Society*, (E202), Milton Keynes, Open University Press. This is a second level course in the sociology of education.

I

The State and the Politics of Education

1   Schooling, State and Society

Stuart Hall

[...]

The current crisis about education is quite unprecedented, at least for the post-war period. Through looking at education we can examine many of the major issues and problems – social, moral, economic – which Britain is facing at the present time. The urgency and extreme nature of the debate, and the spectacular treatment it is accorded in the media, suggest the beginnings of what has been called a 'moral panic' about educational questions. In this debate the protagonists of discipline, authority and traditional 'standards' in education – contrary to the prevailing educational trends of the 1950s and 1960s – are decisively in the lead. They are setting the pace, defining the issues, establishing the terms of reference for the debate. The forces of 'progressivism', so long in dominance in educational thought and policy-making, are now in retreat. My view is that the later 1970s may well see a reversal of many of the trends that have defined the whole period of post-war education from the 1944 Education Act to the present. The irony is that, in conditions of economic recession and social crisis, the Labour government (which is usually seen as wedded to reformism and educational expansion and, through its advocacy of the comprehensive system, as the apostle of a more egalitarian and 'permissive' educational philosophy) is itself beginning to adopt many of the traditionalist arguments. So gradually in the country at large, a traditionalist consensus on education is shaping up, replacing the 'progressive' consensus which has dominated British educational policy since the coming of the welfare state.
[...]

Education is a major sphere of public expenditure. This becomes particularly important in a period of economic stagnation. Britain, it is said, simply cannot afford to sustain costly and 'unnecessary' major educational expansion. The political and economic circumstances thus exert a direct constraining force on the capacity and the resources with which to expand and reform the educational structure; they define the outer parameters of expansion and reform.

Source: This is an abridged version of HALL, S. (1977) 'Review of the course' unit 32 of course E202 *Schooling and Society* Milton Keynes, Open University Press.

Moreover, education is seen as a process which affects everyone – parents and children – so it is of universal concern. Everyone has a major interest in it; and thus educational issues can be used to highlight the issues and terms of a more generalized ideological conflict. Even those who do not take a 'sociological' view recognize the centrality of education in shaping future generations and their outlook. Education has therefore become a major way of regulating the balance between traditionalist and 'permissive' outlooks in society. The basic direction of schooling has thus become a moral and ideological test-bed for the wider society. The trigger-events of Tameside and William Tyndale School [. . .] show in practice what is often denied in theory: that the ideological balance within education and the ideological struggle outside are inextricably linked.

The basic point is clear. If one looks at the evidence on the front pages of newspapers it is possible to see writ large something that is often and systematically denied: the crucial relation between schooling and society; between – in the British case – the structure and kinds of education we are said to 'need' and the needs of a capitalist economy in crisis. This connection is once again apparent, not in theory but *in practice*. [. . .]

[We] should also try to analyse the nature of that *dominant consensus* in education which the 'return to discipline and authority in the classroom' is replacing. For the crisis in education arises not only from the effect of these multiple pressures and forces operating on education from the outside, but also from certain internal contradictions and limits in the 'reformist' approach which had earlier prevailed within education. What was this approach? How was it formed? What social forces were behind it? How did it win general consent, and why did it lose its legitimacy? What underlying societal and economic needs did it serve? What kinds of society did it regulate, service and support? [. . .]

The Problem of the Reformist Consensus in Education

[. . .] There are three basic aspects [of post-war educational reformism] which should be borne in mind.

a It is not difficult to see how a traditionalist and conservative practice in educational policy would have the general effect of conserving the social system, defending and reproducing its class nature, preserving and legitimating its existing structure. But the problem is quite different with a *reformist* strategy, which has the ostensible aim of modifying and improving the existing structures of educational inequality and class relations in society. An analysis of the reformist consensus would entail looking at the schooling-society relationship through its contradictions, its unintended consequences and effects.

b The second aspect of the problem has to do with the nature of the social and economic system which, it is claimed, education preserves and reproduces. The social functions of education before and after the inception of 'mass schooling' cannot be exactly the same. We are dealing with a changing and developing form of society; each change brings in its wake new needs, new means of 'conforming'(*) society to its basic needs and tendencies; it creates new mechanisms, requires new functions. [...] The effects which schooling has on the maintenance and reproduction of capitalist social relations are *specific* to a particular phase and stage of their development. Social functions and effects are always historically specific in this way. But this means we must specify more exactly why and how a reformist practice in education comes to be the form of educational practice most adaptable to the task of 'conforming' society to the fundamental needs of its economic and productive system, especially in the post-war period.

c The third aspect concerns the nature of the account we give of the various specific means by which this 'conformity' between the two spheres is achieved – an account which should be convincing, without falling into a blind and simple 'functionalism'. Unless we believe that society is an organism with universal 'needs' and 'requirements', and that education is always and necessarily in a smooth functional 'fit' with those needs, we must find an account of the way the mechanisms of conformity operate which allows for contradiction, discrepancy and internal conflict between them.

Can it be shown that reformism, which is a strategy designed to change and modify prevailing conditions, in fact serves to perpetuate them?

[...]

The conditions for understanding the establishment of a reformist consensus in education in the post-war period involve coming to terms with the nature of *social democratic* practice and ideology in education, for this is the political configuration that supported and defined reformism in Britain. The question has been fully discussed in a recent paper, 'Social democracy, education and the crisis' by Finn, Grant and Johnson,[1] [...] [who] begin with a definition of the relationship between a political party and the class forces which form its basis. They note, following Gramsci, that parties are not the direct and unmediated expression of the interests of the classes they represent. Parties have a shaping, educative, controlling – as well as a representational – relationship to their class base. Everything turns on how parties operate to represent (re-present) the classes and interests which form their basis, on the political scene. They point out that, though the Labour Party, since the early years of this century, has been the major organizational political form of the working classes, throughout this period it has had a very specific representational relationship to those social forces.

Throughout its history the Labour Party has sustained, in its actual political practice, an unswerving commitment to the parliamentary road to power and the parliamentary system. It has aimed to win electoral power, and then to use the state and the machinery of government to legislate reforming measures on behalf of its working-class constituency. It has never adopted an educational-agitational role in relation to working-class struggle. The Labour Party has seen itself, instead,

---

*Here I use 'conforming' in Gramsci's sense, to mean the process by which civil society and the state are drawn into line with the basic tendencies of the mode of production.

as the legitimate representative of that interest on the political (parliamentary) stage. At the same time, it has aimed to be a 'national' party of government, improving the conditions of working people whilst also governing in the national interest – representing all the people. It has consistently taken the administrative rather than the class-struggle route in British politics. This administrative use of the machinery of government has been strengthened by the influence within the ranks of the Labour Party of Fabian reformism, with its philosophy of 'the inevitability of gradualism' and 'piecemeal social engineering'. Fabianism has been not the exclusive but the principal and dominant social democratic tendency, especially in the areas of social legislation like welfare, social and legal policy, education, etc.

In the post-war period, the Labour Party committed itself to making improvements within the broad framework of a 'mixed' capitalist economy. But as the economic position of Britain has worsened, Labour has seen itself as obliged to 'govern' in the national interest, often at the expense of the immediate interests of its own working-class support. Time and again, Labour in office has been caught between these conflicting tendencies. Where its educational thinking and policy has been concerned, Finn, Grant and Johnson note that:

> It did not have a starting-point in some conception of socialist education. Nor did it set out from the cultural and educational resources of existing working-class communities. Its educational policies, like its general politics, were posited instead on a pre-existing machinery – in this case, a structure of state schools and a particular distribution of formal 'educational' opportunities. It was these that the party set out to reform. Thus the party began as and remained an educational *provider* for the popular classes, not an educational *agency of* and *within* them.[2]

The authors then examine the precise nature of these internal tensions in the relation of party to class, through a detailed examination of one of the most formative documents of Labour educational policy, Tawney's *Secondary Schools For All*, published in 1922.[3] Already, many of the main tendencies noted above are clearly registered in this seminal policy document, even though, within the constellation of ideologies which make up the complex strands of social democratic thinking, Tawney was not a Fabian, and had pertinent things to say about the differences between 'equality' and what he called 'mere equality of opportunity'.

The tendencies described above were reinforced and strengthened in Labour's first post-war period in office, 1945–51. In this period, the two faces of 'Labourism' become clearly apparent. Important reforms were initiated which had the aim of improving social opportunities for the poor and the disadvantaged, protecting the working classes against unemployment and destitution, and creating a more humane society. The consolidation of the welfare state was the principal achievement of this period, and the reforms of the education system formed an important part of the legislative programme. On the other hand, these reforms were all designed to operate within a 'mixed' capitalist economy; one which should be better and more humanely managed, but which was not to be dismantled. This settling for the terms of the existing system set crucial limits to the extent of reformism, even in the immediate post-war period when the tide of popular reformism was running high. When the Conservatives returned to power they had to commit themselves to the main elements of Labour's reforms – the welfare state and full employment – before they could win a mandate to govern. Then, on the basis of these reforms and the establishment of a consensus between the two major political parties, the full return to a peace-time economy was made. During this period, Labour's reforms which were once seen as making direct inroads into the capitalist system were gradually absorbed by it, becoming the key supports of a 'reformed capitalism'.

As the economic problems began to accumulate in the late 1950s and 1960s, the Labour Party found itself increasingly tied to this logic – constrained by the limits within which it had resolved to operate. Further reforms could therefore only come by expanding growth, making capitalism more efficient, increasing the size of the cake so that further benefits could be drawn from it to sponsor further reforming measures. This was the period of Labour 'revisionism' – with its new emphasis on modernizing society, improving the conditions for technical innovation and efficiency. As Harold Wilson said in 1963 in his famous 'science' speech at Scarborough: 'If there had never been a case for socialism before, automation would have created it'. Growth, not redistribution or structural change, became the lynch-pin of Labour's strategy. Further reforms had to be sponsored by means of producing more, rather than by redistributing what already existed. In any case, the backward, archaic and underdeveloped nature of Britain's economy set very firm limits to any redistribution.

To put it crudely, these circumstances brought to the fore what Finn, Grant and Johnson call Labour's 'dual repertoire'. Already the case for increasing equality of access through educational expansion was supported, not in terms of shifting power from one class to another but in terms of eroding class differences *in general*. But under the pressures of maintaining a weak and failing economic system, the ambiguities become sharper. Educational expansion had to be more selective, more carefully controlled, more slowly introduced. Also, the traditional aim of helping to erode class differences through the expansion of educational opportunities had to be legitimated in terms which justified these measures in terms of national economic efficiency and growth. Finn, Grant and Johnson call this persistent contradiction in aims and practice a 'duality of ideas'. The shift from 'equality' to 'equality of opportunity' was accomplished in this period, under these conflicting pressures. This weakened the radical side of the Labourist repertoire, and considerably strengthened its Fabian, social-engineering, national efficiency and meritocratic emphases. The authors quote an apt example of Labour's 'dualism' from another speech by Harold Wilson in the run-up to the 1964 election, in which we can hear the emphasis in Labour's electoral rhetoric changing from egalitarianism to efficiency, growth and the 'white heat of the technological revolution':

> ... we cannot afford to force segregation on our children at the 11 plus stage. As socialists, as democrats, we oppose this system of educational apartheid, because we believe in equality of opportunity. But that is not all. We simply cannot as a nation afford to neglect the educational develop-

ment of a single boy or girl. We cannot afford to cut off three-quarters or
more of our children from virtually any chance of higher education. The
Russians do not, the Germans do not, and the Japanese do not, and we
cannot afford to either.[4]

Finn, Grant and Johnson add two other important factors to this analysis. The
first is the professionalization of teachers – a trend which was also apparent in other
professions. This growing professionalization was fully in line with the general
expansion of the intermediary, white-collar and supervisory social strata, and the
growth of the welfare-state and other non-commercial professional classes and their
growing unionization. But this new base and expansion of numbers gave teachers
a structural interest in 'teacher autonomy' – in improving their professional status
and powers of decision and in winning greater rights for teachers over classroom
and curriculum innovations. The growth, for example, of the teachers' unions as
an independent professional voice for teachers in this period is, again, part of a
longer-term trend – the unionization of the white-collar sectors – with very specific
consequences in the educational sphere, in terms of winning space for teaching
expertise as against the guiding hand of the educational administrators. The second
factor concerns the growth of the supporting research fraternity, but more especially
of a body of 'experts' in the sociology of education, who provided most of the
evidence for particular kinds of reforming strategies in education. Many of these
experts were Fabians, which is not surprising, given the influence of Fabianism
in British sociology both before and after the war.

Against this background, it becomes possible to understand why reformism
assumed the peculiar shape that it did in the 1950s and 1960s – why it was riven by
internal contradictions, long before it was assailed from outside. In sum, Finn,
Grant and Johnson argue, the reformist strategy could not succeed. First, it was
beset by contradictions – contradictions not only in terms of the 'logic' of the
structure in which it was operating, but also in terms of the material interests upon
which its dual repertoire was founded. The rhetoric of 'egalitarianism' represented
a real but subordinate tendency within Labourism as a political formation; it was
required whenever Labour had to make its populist appeal and mobilize the working-
class vote for electoral purposes. From time to time it became one of the bargaining
points in cementing the party-union alliance. 'Labour's Fabianism, on the other
hand, reflects quite directly the party's structural and historical commitment to
managing and reforming a capitalist society.'[5] Second, they argue, the elements of
the strategy were incompatible in practice. Since Labour basically put national
growth ahead of the redistribution of wealth and power, the pace of reformism had
constantly to be limited to the capacities of the system, which were declining. By the
1970s, the case for sustaining the momentum of reformism against the background
of a deepening economic recession had lost all claim to political credibility. In the
educational sphere, this credibility gap has been quickly and successfully occupied
by the 'retrensionist' wing – those who argued that egalitarianism had advanced
at the expense of 'standards'. And Labour has been forced by its own political logic
largely to follow suit and accept the 'discipline' of the situation. Third, Finn,

Grant and Johnson argue that the policies were, in any case, bound to fail politically. 'Equality of opportunity' as an educational programme was neither successful enough in delivering the goods to win the support of the expansionist and mod-ernizing elements of the middle class and employers, nor radical and popular enough in character to mobilize working-class support. The authors argue that it was intrinsic to the basic practice of Labourism to seek to implement educational reforms *for* the working class through what it conceived of as the neutral machinery of the state. But, as they remind us: 'this state is not the neutral "machinery" which Social Democracy takes it to be: it systematically transforms the political demands that are made on it ... '[6] And here we are at the very nub of the contradictions of reformism.

> What is claimed [of the state] 'as of right', returns [to the claimants] in unrecognisable forms. Of this process education is the best example. In a general sense, pressure for the extension of social rights and for greater 'equality' has fuelled the long-term growth of the state system. But in practice this process has been inflected and given its content by specific features of the state in the educational region. The key features have been the structural separation of the schools from other kinds of learning and their tendency to monopolise the whole notion of education; the profes-sionalisation of the teachers and their pursuit of sectional interest within the apparatus; and, above all, the structural necessity for educational policy-makers and administrators to take account of capital's interests. So it happens that, as in production so in school, a nature-imposed necessity – to learn – is experienced as something quite alien. School becomes moreover the site of class struggle. The divisions of parent, teacher and child, barely disguised antagonisms, are intrinsic to the apparatus itself. The general tendency of Labour's policy in concert with the teachers, moreover, has been to exalt the 'experts' of the region over the mere parent and to devalue the common sense of the parental culture. The social reforming tendency in the party's ideology does this in an absolutely insulting way, scarcely compensated for by a romantic opposition. ... At the same time progres-sivism has rendered schooling more and more esoteric. In this way, Labour's whole educating stance, not only vacating the ground of agitation, but actually sponsoring new forms of oppression, has opened up massive opportunities for a demagogic, anti-bureaucratic, anti-statist Toryism.[7]

Schooling and which Capitalism? Whose 'State Education'?

The analysis by Finn, Grant and Johnson goes some way towards exposing the political conditions in which the reformist consensus in education became established in the two decades following the second world war, and also why it has been driven apart by its own internal contradictions. It also suggests one framework in which to draw together the disparate aspects of 'reformism' in education. [...] Reformism, in the context of the post-war development of capitalism, turned out to be a very *particular* kind of social configuration: a specific set of practices and aims, based on certain specific educational ideas and assumptions, supported by a certain quite specific alliance of social forces, and constrained in very definite ways by the logic of the economic structure and the social and political system in which it was set to work.

[...]

Reformism did command wide assent in the years after the second world war. It set the terms in which educational practice developed. [...] It established the framework for the educational debate in the mid-1960s. It initiated the move towards comprehensive schooling. But it also presented itself as an educational programme appropriate to a modern capitalist economy, a modernizing society. It set out to win for itself 'national' support. It forged a particular consensus. But not everyone could benefit from it equally, and by no means everyone favoured or supported it. Progressively, as its basic assumptions have been challenged, so contrary forces – with other social interests – guided by a different social and educational philosophy, have increasingly placed their stamp on education, shifting the terms of the debate and changing its emphases. This analysis of reformism should undermine the notion that there is *one* national educational strategy or consensus on education which can benefit everyone equally. It does suggest how deeply education is shaped by the general relations of social and political forces at any one time. It also shows how, in broad terms, education is changed and shaped by the overall logic of the structures of the society in which it operates.

However, this political foregrounding may not take us far enough. For the argument is not simply that education is always shaped, in one way or another, by specific political and ideological forces. The argument is that, so long as the fundamental social and economic relationships of a society remain intact, education will tend to obey the 'logic' of that system. Education will tend to be harnessed and made to conform, by means of certain specific mechanisms, not simply to the interests of particular groups or classes, but to the dominant tendencies *of the whole system*. It is not enough to show that education did not accomplish the reforming work that it was intended to do in the 1950s and 1960s. It remains to show that, by means of some of the very distortions and contradictions which we have briefly analysed, education *did* perform a critical kind of 'work' for society – for a society which, despite all the changes after the second world war, remained fundamentally capitalist in its form. [...]

How, then, did reformism specifically relate, or contribute, to the maintenance and development of a particular stage in the capitalist relations in Britain in the post-war period? What was it about the capitalism of this period which 'required' a reformist educational strategy, of the kind we have outlined, to complete and sustain its logic?

[...] [We can] conceive of two main phases in industrial capitalism: (a) the period in which the whole productive basis of society was transformed by the introduction of the factory system – industrial capitalism – and when the main social and political structures were gradually moulded to the needs of a new social order. This was the phase of entrepreneurial or *laissez-faire* capitalism. (b) The second phase, starting in or about the 1860s, saw a massive transformation in the internal organization and structure of capitalism, based on the growing concentration of capital, the revolutionizing of production through the application of science and technology and the regime of 'scientific management', spurred on by the intensification of rivalries between the industrialized capitalist states. This is the stage of corporate or 'monopoly' capitalism.

The schema employed here is basically one which follows Marx's analysis, and which theorists like Lenin and Hobson were to develop (Lenin, for example, in his theory of 'imperialism', the 'highest stage of capitalism'). It is also a schema which is widely employed – but with some significant differences – in much of recent economic history. The changes in the structure and organization of capitalist societies entailed in the shift from the first to the second phase were profound. The transformation affected, at different rates, all the capitalist societies. In the course of that transition, the global hegemony of capitalist trade and production passed from Britain (which led the first phase) to other countries which developed later but more rapidly: Germany, Japan, and, above all, the United States. This whole period is conceived as a long transitional phase, lasting well into the present century, and in many ways the transformation is still incomplete. It was particularly slow and uneven in Britain – slowed down by Britain's 'early' industrial start. Though the signs of developing monopoly forms were certainly present in the British economy in the inter-war years, corporate capitalism was not fully established in Britain until the post-war period. Thus, it is to the phase of the transformation of Britain into a (not very successful) 'corporate capitalist' society in the post-war period that reformism as an educational strategy belongs. It is to this kind of capitalism that, partly through education, civil society and political life are 'conformed'. This is the particular 'logic' to which, it is argued, educational reformism is linked. It is by means of reformism, specifically, that – in this particular period – the attempt was made to make education do certain kinds of work for a relatively new kind of capitalism: the capitalism of large-scale production, high technology and the mass-market. [. . .]

Some of the pertinent features of corporate capitalism which relate to the argument about education can now be summarized as follows:

a There has been a decline of small and independent capital, and the growth of the concentration and centralization of capital – the capitalism of the large, corporate organizations.

b There has also been a massive application of scientific and technological development to production in order to increase the productivity of labour. Marx called this the harnessing of science and technology by capital 'as a material force'. This was necessitated, he argued, because capitalism had reached the limits of its expansion on the earlier basis of its organization; especially because reformers and working-class organizations had forced the introduction of the factory reforms in the mid-nineteenth century, limiting the degree and length to which capital was permitted to go in exploiting labour power. The intensification of labour, not through lengthening the working day and employing women and children, but through the application of machinery and the revolution in techniques, was capital's way of overcoming this barrier. This shift from what Marx called 'absolute' to 'relative surplus value' was the originating point of the long transition to the 'monopoly' phase.

c Capitalist production has increased in scale, requiring a great expansion of non-productive, supervisory and managerial workers and staffs to superintend the workforce, supervise and support the new tasks of co-ordination and control, marketing and planning.

d As a consequence of a, b, c above, there have been major changes in the organization of production and the labour process itself. Old skills disappeared, and new skills were required, as well as new technologies of work and new techniques of co-ordination in production. The recomposition of the working class, in terms of its occupational skills, traditions, etc., took place, in a long and uneven way, throughout this phase. But the 'skills' required were also differently composed – advances in technology involved the transfer of many 'human' skills to advanced machinery itself; and thus there developed a greater gap between 'conceiving' work-related tasks, and 'executing' them, [. . .] or, as it is sometimes put, a sharper division between mental and manual labour.

e There were parallel shifts in what we might call the modality and ideology of societies undergoing such a transition. In productive work, control became more 'rationalized', and the organization of tasks was more 'hierarchical', more, 'technocratic' and 'managerialist'. The disciplines of production were less overt, more covert and indirect. In the *laissez-faire* stage, the new industrial work-force had to be actively disciplined to factory labour; in the later phases, labour was 'cultivated' to disciplined productive work.

f Outside the workplace, consumption – especially on a mass scale – is absolutely crucial for maintaining large-scale capitalist production. In the monopoly stage, capitalism came to depend more than ever before on steady consumption by the great mass of the population. Earlier ideologies of thrift and saving were transformed, in these conditions, into new 'market' ideologies of consumption and spending.

g In corporate capitalist societies there has been massive expansion of the state, its structures and apparatues – in contrast to the *laissez-faire* period (when the state was not supposed to intervene directly in production but to 'leave well alone' – *laissez-faire*). The state becomes generally more active and interventionist. It developed a role in ensuring the general conditions for the favourable accumulation of capital. Many tasks and areas of responsibility which had previously been left to private institutions were brought into the orbit of an expanded state and administrative system (for example, social welfare, the family and schooling). The direct intervention of the state in economic affairs was another, related dimension: the ownership by the state of certain basic industries; the state as a large-scale employer of labour; the management of employment, investment conditions and even wage levels by the state; the use of fiscal and other 'Keynesian' methods of regulating the way the economy works by means of government intervention.

h Such societies tend to be ones in which the state also acts to ensure minimum conditions of life for everyone. The active production of wealth and goods is left to private capital, but the *conditions* necessary for that productive work to proceed have become increasingly the responsibility of the state. So has the establishment of certain minimum levels of social provision, and protection against severe and unrestricted deprivation. In this period, corporate capitalist societies have also become 'welfare states'.

i These are societies in which the great mass of the population has won formal political representation – they are societies of near or complete 'universal suffrage'. This means that citizenship is universal as all classes have won some degree of formal political representation and 'rights' within the political framework. Now, major legislative and administrative initiatives of the state have to favour the expansion and growth of the economic system *and* win majority 'consent'. So the production or construction of popular consent to the imperatives which the system must meet in order to survive has become, itself, a major social task; this has been called the new task of the 'engineering of consent'.

j Finally, of course, such societies have remained complex class societies, in the sense that the ownership and control of the means of production, and the power to put machinery and labour to work remain in the hands of capital, or under its superintendence and management, while the great majority of wage-earners, whether in productive or other kinds of work, are expropriated from possession and control. That is, corporate capitalism is a *class* system – even if the composition of the classes is more complex and varied, and the lines of class division, class struggle and conflict are less clearly delineated than in the *laissez-faire* stage of capitalism. Thus there must also be ways in which society 'works' so as to sustain the hegemony or domination of the leading classes, *within* the framework of the 'consent to power' by the great majority.

This is a very over-simplified and condensed sketch of some salient features of post-war corporate capitalist societies. But it is sufficient to make clear a central line in the discussion. In sum, I would argue that education is not simply shaped in a general way by the imperatives, arrangements and logic of the capitalist system. Education is *specifically articulated* with this system in certain very definite ways. It plays a role in sustaining and reproducing, within a structure of capitalist relations, each of the dimensions or features listed above. [. . .]

The distribution of skills and abilities within the schooling system replicates, in microcosm, the general system of inequalities in the social structure of society at large. [. . .] Different features of the education system have the overall effect of maintaining this internal-external link. [. . .] The schooling process also includes the whole system of grading, testing for abilities, streaming, tracking, qualifications etc. Moreover, the education system also contributes to aspects of [. . .] 'socialization': transmitting the self-evaluations, maintaining the distinct cultures, teaching and regulating the moral attitudes and rationales appropriate to the various positions in the occupational and authority hierarchy. At the level of knowledge transmission itself, there is the ordering, structuring and hierarchization of knowledge through the curriculum. These are all very general ways of suggesting how schools serve to support and maintain the social system. However, it is more important to see these as very different effects, sustained through several different mechanisms, at several different levels. It is not enough to argue that there is a simple replication of the large structures within the smaller one, accomplished, so to speak, at a stroke.

But class relationships are not only sustained and reproduced through the preparation for, and the assignment of, the youthful population to positions in work. Just as important are the 'ideological' skills and dispositions: the dispositions of command and obedience, problems of discipline and control, of regularity and regulation, of consent (see points **i** and **j** above). Many of the interactions and regulations which organize schooling as a process have the overall effect of harnessing the school to society through the moral and ideological 'cultivation' of labour – the engineering of the appropriate modes of consent and control in the social classes which will be dominant and subordinate in adult society.

Along another dimension, [we can] think of the modalities and ideologies characteristic of an advanced capitalist system, and then of the organizational, managerial, technocratic ethos of much of 'mass schooling' today, and the importance of these aspects in the perspectives and the professionalization of teachers, and the work they do in classrooms.

In another sphere, [we can] think of the expansion of the state, and its advance into areas of civil and social life hitherto reserved for less public bodies, the related rise of the welfare professions in an expanded state sector, and the role of 'expertise' in the management of social problems. Within this framework [we can] look at the character and the consequences of the advance to mass schooling, the organization of a universal state education system, and the attitudes of the professionals who service and the experts who administer this new, expanded function of the state. One might argue that part of the reason why the state has expanded its role in the 'corporate capitalist' phase is that only in this way can the general social conditions in which production takes place in an increasingly complex economy be ensured – a function which can no longer be left either to private initiatives or the whim of individual entrepreneurs. If this is so, then the massive involvement of the state in the detailed administration of a state education system, maintaining certain 'universal' standards right across the complex structure of schooling, begins to take on that double-edged character which we spoke of earlier. We begin to see now to what, and by what, Labour's 'dual repertoire' was harnessed.

Here I have been looking at the schooling-society relationship historically. In the following sections I turn to an examination of some of the current ways in which the question has been posed theoretically.

[. . .]

Parallels, Fits, Correspondences, Homologies

The general assumption that there is a relation of some kind between the principal aspects of the schooling process and various dimensions of the class structure and economic order of modern societies makes sense as a general proposition, and has provided the basis for much of the sociological research on educational systems. As Bowles and Gintis [...] observe: 'No sophisticated educational theory has overlooked the fact that schools prepare youth for economic life'. An examination of this feature of the educational process has formed an important element in each of the major reports that has framed educational policy in Britain since the second world war. However, 'Approaches to educational reform have differed ... in the way they view the demands which this role imposes on the schools' (Bowles and Gintis). It is the *nature* of this 'connection' that accounts for the substantive distinctions between different approaches. [...]

In many traditional approaches, a broad 'functional imperative' is seen as providing the main link between the *technical* needs of an advanced industrial society (the 'industrial revolution') and the elaboration of its education structures. This is usually predicated on a particular reading of the history of the impact of industrialization, as a general process, on society as a whole. Broadly speaking, as society has become more complex in its structure, and as industrial processes have become more technically sophisticated, it is assumed that there will be a corresponding development both in the scale of mass schooling, and in the expansion of the different types of educational provision. An advanced industrial society 'needs' a literate population, a skilled workforce, technically and managerially equipped strata, those capable of taking broad, strategic decisions about the general allocation of resources. The rise of mass schooling, of technical education, of more specialized schools and colleges and the expansion of higher education are all seen as features related in some general way to the requirements of a developing industrial society. The articulations between the two are not thought of as very 'tight' – indeed, problems are seen as arising only when the divergencies between them become very wide, for example, when society needs applied scientists but the bulk of the university population opts for humanities and social science courses. However, a broad correspondence between the two is assumed. No doubt, some of the connections pointed to here are real and important; though we should beware of reducing the complex *social* articulations between an industrial system of a specific type (e.g. advanced capitalism) and an educational system of a particular kind to the technical necessities of 'industrialism'. In this context, [...] Johnson argues that the attempts to ' ... link education and industrial revolution through some notion of the "need" for labour skills (for literacy or a technical know-how) have produced, so far, mainly negative results'.[8] At least for the mid-nineteenth century period which he is examining, Johnson argues, there was little stress, before 1850, on the teaching of *specific* occupational skills; the industrial revolution was often parasitic upon skills learned not in school but in the family, neighbourhood and through the trade itself; strictly-defined 'occupational' schooling was often reserved for poor, orphaned or pauperized children, who were destined for unskilled labour; and the main stress in the educational reforms of the period fell, not on the passing-on of occupational skills but on the moral 'cultivation' and disciplining of the working class as a whole: ' . . . habits, attitudes, the general "moral" orientation of the child, were of more concern than either the development of skills or the transmission of knowledge'.[9]

A traditional concern in post-war 'sociology of education' has been a recognition of the *parallels* between the structure of social, economic and occupational disadvantages in one generation and in the succeeding ones. Since young people are recruited into the occupational structure after the completion of a period of required schooling, and attainment or success in school has come to provide one of the principal criteria for allocating youth to jobs and positions in the occupational hierarchy, it has been assumed that the school must play a part in mediating and *maintaining* this structure of disadvantage, *transmitting* it (with due allowances for a limited degree of social mobility between generation.) from one generation to the next. This body of research also drew attention to the broad correspondences between the different grades of schooling, the different strata of occupations, and the structure of status and rewards for different jobs. The school was thus seen as playing a function of maintaining and transmitting the unequal distribution of opportunities and rewards: generally, as performing the role of helping to fix, for each generation, the general structure of social class (i.e. class differences principally linked to inequalities of income, jobs and the distribution of opportunities and resources, and to the restriction of inter-class mobility).

It was the very recognition of this class-maintaining function which made the school a potential site for *reformist intervention*. Schools were to be reformed in such a way that they could serve as instruments for evening up 'educational opportunities', redistributing them more effectively and fairly. Both words are important. 'Fairly' meant that schools should provide the means whereby a measure of redistribution of educational chances among social classes could be effected. 'Effectively' meant that this redistribution would enable the recruitment of able students from the existing 'pool of talent' wherever in the social-class structure it existed, for the benefit of society at large. This double goal gave rise to the demand for – and the development of educational strategies designed to effect – a greater measure of 'equality of opportunity in education'. [. . .] Note the presence, here, of what we have called (following Finn, Grant and Johnson) the 'dual repertoire': an educational strategy designed to redistribute opportunities, especially to the working classes, at the same time as it more efficiently recruited the ablest from all classes for society as a whole. It recognized the innate inequalities which resulted from that relationship, and attempted to operate directly on the school system to: (a) increase the connection between schooling and the 'needs' of an advanced industrial society, while (b) reforming some of its more glaring social-class characteristics. [. . .]

To meet both the redistributive and the efficiency criteria outlined it was necessary to: broaden the base of educational access, *and* improve, refine and elaborate the means of selection. As the occupational strata of advanced industrial societies grew more complex, so education itself – now more broadly available – needed to improve its means of selecting those best fitted for certain required tasks in society. This tended to highlight the grading, streaming, testing, assessing, ability-measuring, scoring, qualifying aspects of the modern school system. Here the school is seen no longer as simply maintaining (or modifying) in a general way the relationship between social class and occupational designation, but as more tightly and closely articulated with the social structure – principally through its selection mechanisms. There is no question that these have been enormously refined in the post-war period in the secondary school system. [. . .] Those most involved in the elaboration of the selective or filtering aspects of schooling were often those most concerned to improve and widen access to education. The IQ test and its prevalence in modern, industrial, capitalist school systems was envisaged, by reformers, as more 'universal' – and, therefore, 'fairer' – than the anachronistic selection mechanism of rich fathers sending their children to privileged schools and thus preparing them for the best, most highly-rewarded jobs.

It is now widely acknowledged that the 'reformist' approach – both in the 'equality of opportunity' or in the 'compensatory education' forms which it later assumed – has met with little success. The research reported by Douglas, among many others, shows how effectively, after a period of supposed reform, 'father's occupation' still served as the best predictor of the kind of job his son or daughter was likely to get.[10] In short, neither the reforming-modifying nor the selection strategies were powerful enough to break the maintenance function [. . .]. Indeed, the stress on the selective and quantifying aspects of schooling undoubtedly reinforced the school's role as a system of maintenance for social class inequalities. In the process, equality of education arguments were transformed into technical-meritocratic ones. Social class → school → social class remained the dominant relationship, i.e. the school as a 'reproducer' of the social-class structure. The judgement of Halsey, who was himself one of the principal architects of the reformist strategy, is definitive:

> The essential judgement must be that the 'liberal' policies failed even in their own terms. For example, when in a large number of the richer countries during the nineteen fifties a considerable expansion of educational facilities were envisaged, it was more or less assumed that, by making more facilities available, there would be a marked change in the social composition of student bodies and in the flow of people from the less favoured classes into the secondary schools and higher educational institutions. This has certainly not happened to the degree expected. While expansion of education was accompanied by some increase in both the absolute numbers and the proportions from poor families who reached the higher levels and the more prestigious types of education, nevertheless progress towards greater equality of educational opportunity as traditionally defined has been disappointing. It is now plain that the problem is more difficult than had been supposed and needs, in fact, to be posed in new terms.[11]

This meant, in fact, that it was necessary to conceptualize the connection or relation between schooling and society in new ways.

One such aspect involved deepening our understanding of the factors that underpin the coupling of schooling to society in ways which are disadvantageous to many, and undermine the efforts of the school to play a moderating influence in the process of reproducing the class structure. This has principally entailed extending the analysis to what might broadly be called *cultural* factors. We might make a distinction between cultural factors in the backgrounds and environments of the school population which are so powerful and deep-rooted as to inhibit and limit the school's 'compensatory' role; and cultural factors in the school itself, which might have the (perhaps unintended) consequence of reinforcing, rather than weakening, the mechanisms which bind the school to the social structure outside it. [...] [These would include] in the *first* range: broken homes, language in the home, the attitudes of teachers towards social, cultural and racial differences, child-rearing practices, and so on. Some of the factors in the *second* range [would be] teachers' perspectives, [pupil cultures and] classroom interactions. But we would have to add here some aspects of the work which really belong to other perspectives: for example, Bernstein's early work on linguistic codes and on modalities of classroom control, and the critically related work of Labov and Rosen [...] and some of Bourdieu's earlier work, for example, the essay, 'The school as a conservative force'. [...] The argument about the 'cultural deprivation' of the working-class child and how the school might serve to reinforce it is admirably caught in Bernstein's remark [...] that 'If the culture of the teacher is to become part of the consciousness of the child, then the culture of the child must first be in the consciousness of the teacher'.[12]

Another approach has been to suggest that, in fact, the failure of the 'compensatory' perspective lies in the inadequate manner in which it has conceived the structural features of contemporary societies with which the schooling process is connected. This is the critique powerfully argued by Bowles and Gintis [...]. They perceive the schooling process as fundamentally determined by and linked to the 'reproduction of the power relations of economic life' in capitalist societies; as mirroring and recapitulating the class structure of inequalities, the hierarchy of authority necessary to capitalist work relations; as fostering the cognitive, physical, psychological and operational skills required by such a society and serving to legitimate its dominant and exploitative structures. Here the connection between schooling and capitalist society goes beyond the general functions of 'maintenance' or selecting and filtering the school population for occupational positions. The terms used in Bowles and Gintis' critique are those of a *direct correspondence* between the two structures – the schooling process is seen as directly replicating and reflecting the wider structures of authority and control, the necessary division of labour characteristic of a capitalist economy. They call this connection, in fact, 'the correspondence principle'. We shall discuss Bowles and Gintis more fully below. But it should be noted here that though the connections are drawn essentially in terms of direct correspondence, this operates in fact, on several different dimensions, and is conceived as a very diffused process.

Yet another approach to the problem of conceptualizing the link between schooling and society tends to fasten on the cognitive or knowledge-dimensions of the relationship. Bowles and Gintis tend to argue that the cognitive functions of the school have been overemphasized; these functions 'by no means exhaust their [i.e. the schools'] social functions'. Whitty, Young and others, however, have argued that this function has not been sufficiently explored; rather, the role of the school in transmitting knowledge has tended to be 'taken for granted' as an un-qualified 'good' in itself, and the structuring of knowledge through the curriculum has been received as an unassailable and transparent 'fact' [. . .]. From this perspec-tive, what the school sees itself as doing (and is seen to be doing) – transmitting knowledge – *is* important, but not in the universalistic way it is conceptualized in ordinary common sense. This is because schools transmit 'knowledge' in a structured form. This approach, then, interprets the schooling-society connection in terms of how what is taught is graded, bounded, classified and framed (to employ Bernstein's terms, which are some of the most powerful in this argument) – how the schools define what passes for knowledge, and who should know what, and the various modalities of cognitively grasping the world and its relationships. Here schooling is understood not as directly replicating the structures of the wider world outside, but as indirectly reproducing, in the very way it transmits and structures knowledge, the division between mental and manual labour in the world of capitalist work and in society generally. The key term for the connection is neither maintenance nor selection, nor even correspondence, but *reproduction* – the parallels between *social* reproduction (of class relations) and *cultural* reproduction [. . .].

On the other hand, if you examine what has been called the 'hidden curriculum' – especially the development of the 'hidden curriculum' in the historical context of the system of mass schooling – and regard the schooling process from the vantage point of the maintenance of discipline, hierarchy and control, and the 'cultivation' of appropriate forms of dominant and subordinate consciousness, then it is this latent but powerful 'message' which provides us with the main mechanism through which class relationships are transmitted and maintained within the schooling process. In these terms, the 'social control' aspects of schooling can be linked to the wider system of the hegemonic domination of the ruling classes, and the corresponding subordination of the dominated classes outside the classroom. Here, the key term is neither correspondence nor reproduction, but domination – *hegemony*.

The legitimating and consensual functions of the school are closely linked to this 'hegemonizing' role, and so (inevitably) are the forms of opposition and resistance which the implantation of a hegemonic domination always awakens as a response. Certain aspects of 'classroom interaction' [. . .] and school-related but extra-classroom cultural manifestations [. . .] can be linked to this kind of analysis. So can the role of 'the intermediaries' – the teachers who, like managers in relation to labour and social workers in relation to poverty, 'manage' the problems of the system on behalf of, without belonging to, the dominant classes. In hegemonic terms, they are what Loren Baritz once called the 'servants of power' (cf. in the American context Karier's important essay [. . .] on 'Liberalism and the quest for orderly change').[13]

I have outlined six basic ways of posing the schooling-society relationship: industrialization, disadvantage, cultural deprivation, correspondence, hegemony, reproduction. [. . .] They represent, obviously, very different ways of making that connection. They emphasize very different dimensions of the schooling-society relationship. They specify very different mechanisms. Of course, 'society' is a short-hand term for a very complex form of social and historical organization; it may therefore be wrong to expect the school-society connection to be operative along one dimension only, through one mechanism only. Indeed, we may have to look at different kinds of connection, and different mechanisms, in relation to different aspects of schooling. It may be too reductive to search for one, overarching 'master connection'.

On the other hand, there may be real – i.e. logical and theoretical – *incompatibilities* between these different approaches. Does schooling, at one and the same time, maintain, select for, apprentice to, correspond with, prepare for, feed into, replicate, reproduce and mirror the dominant class relations and structures of class society? [...] Society is necessarily complex, that is to say, it is composed of different levels and practices, which come together in such a way as to form or compose a unity or 'ensemble'. This 'unity' is not a simple, functional 'fit' between all its parts, but it is nevertheless structured in such a way as to sustain a particular form of material life, a distinctive structure of social relationships, a particular range of cultural and ideological formations. It is not necessarily contradictory to assume that a process like mass-schooling will articulate with different levels of such a social formation, through very different mechanisms, and, perhaps, with very different consequences and outcomes. In addition, we may simply not yet be at the stage of theoretical clarification which would enable us to comprehend the connections and complementary aspects of the schooling-society relationship. [...]

Several of these approaches note that the two structures – schooling and society – exhibit certain parallel features, for example, between the two pyramids of school and occupational inequalities. Others reach for a more causal or transitive connection, sometimes cast in the language of *functions*. But the concept of 'functions' varies, depending on the theoretical paradigm in which it is cast. Generally, a 'functionalist' approach tends to conceive society in terms of the functional interdependence or coherence of its parts, so that society is maintained as an on-going entity, a social order. [...] 'Marxism' shares something of this perspective with functionalism, in that it too sees society as a 'whole' – a unity or totality. But it conceives that 'unity' differently – as, by nature, driven and sustained through contradictions, rather than by means of functional coherences, and maintained through conflict and domination, rather than through a normative consensus and institutional differentiation. For 'functionalism', order is assumed; it is the deviations from order which are problematic. For Marxism, contradiction and conflict are assumed; it is the maintenance of (class) order which is problematic. Thus both paradigms may employ the language of 'function' and 'reproduction', while meaning very different things by it. For functionalism the general function involved is, precisely, that of reproducing society again, one generation after another, more or less in its already existing form; according to functionalism, this is how and why societies continue to exist. When Marxists use the term, they signal the contested reproduction of society's fundamental relations, which enables society to produce itself again, but only in the form of a dominant and subordinate (i.e. antagonistic, not functional) social order. This is not simply a society governed by a ruling class; it is a society whose fundamental structures and relations come together in such a way that an existing mode of production and all the structures necessary to it are maintained, in and through the antagonisms they engender. This is a society that is 'structured in dominance', in Althusser's phrase. Reproduction, in the Marxist perspective, is also the reproduction of that dominance. Whereas for functionalists the prime level of determination which draws the different parts of society into a coherent unity is the 'global functional needs' of social systems to maintain themselves in being, for Marxists it is the mode of material production, its conditions and relations (and the conditions required to reproduce the mode of production) which give the determining shape to, and sustain the determining 'logic' of, the system throughout all its parts.

However, within these broad differences, further, quite fundamental differences of emphasis and stress can be observed. Some kinds of 'structural functionalism' give greatest weight to the established institutional structures of society: the interrelationships between the economic, the political, the kinship, the religious and cultural institutional orders (as, for example, in British anthropology). Others tend to see values and norms – the 'central value system' – as the principal domain of integration (as, for example, in the work of Talcott Parsons). Some kinds of Marxism give considerable weight to the primary determining nature of the economic structure and the relationships directly connected with the production of men's material requirements, treating other spheres – politics, social relations outside production, 'civil society', culture, ideology and consciousness (sometimes called 'the superstructures') – as dependent levels, which are determined either in content or form by the economic structure and reflect the latter in a fairly direct manner. Such variants of Marxism will tend to look for correspondences between schooling and society principally where they relate to these determining economic relationships. They assume a fairly immediate 'reflection' of the economic structure in the superstructures. Pyramid theories, education-and-the-labour-market theories, selection theories, theories of the 'recapitulation' of work processes and work disciplines in the classroom – whether Marxist or not – will tend (we cannot say more than that) to present the argument in this form. For example, Bowles and Gintis seem to look for the clinching arguments principally at this level: 'For the past century at least, schooling has contributed to the reproduction of the social relations of production largely through the correspondence between school and class structure'.[14] But the use of the term 'reproduction' here should warn us against any tendency to reduce their position to a simple economic reductionism. Bearing this important caveat in mind – and simplifying only for the purpose of convenience of exposition – we can call this the *correspondence* paradigm or principle.

Another variant of 'Marxism' attributes the fundamental determination in securing the 'complex unity' of society to the relationships of the economic structure, but regards the so-called 'superstructures' as having vital, critical 'work' to do in sustaining, at the social, cultural, political and ideological levels, the *conditions* which enable capitalist production to proceed. Furthermore, it regards the superstructures as having the role, above all, of drawing society into 'conformity' with the long-term requirements and conditions of a capitalist economic system (for example, in the work of Gramsci). This suggests that, though the superstructures are more determined than determining, the topography of base/superstructure is not so important as the relatively autonomous 'work' which the superstructures perform for the economic structure. This is regarded as difficult, contested 'work', that operates through opposition and antagonism – in short, by means of the class struggle, which is present at all the various levels of society – where simple 'correspondences' are hard to come by. Far from assuming a simple recapitulation between the various structures of society, this approach sees the 'work' which the superstructures perform as necessary precisely because, on its own, the economic system cannot ensure all the conditions necessary for its own expanded reproduction. The economic system cannot ensure that society will be raised to that general level of civilization and culture which its advanced system of production needs. Creating an order of society around the fundamental economic relationships is just as necessary as production itself; the relations of production alone cannot 'produce' such a social order. Here, then, the relationship is not one of correspondence but of *coupling* – the coupling of two distinct, but interrelated and interdependent spheres. Gramsci is one of the outstanding theorists of this position. The nature of the 'coupling' envisaged is described in Gramsci's phrase, the 'structure-superstructure complex'. Again, simplifying, we may call this the paradigm of *hegemony*.

We can identify another, closely related variant of the Marxist approach. While acknowledging that, in a Marxist approach, the economic structure or mode of production must 'in the last instance' determine, this position insists that the 'last instance' is endlessly postponed. It refers to an analytical necessity, not an empirical fact. The 'economic' level is never actually active in society, in history, on its own – outside the other political, cultural, ideological levels. For not only does any feature or relation in society always contain economic, political, cultural and ideological components, but, also, these levels of practice are only very rarely *in correspondence* with one another. Only in moments of fundamental rupture or transition are the levels aligned, and this is not because they all exhibit the same contradictions, developed to the same point, but because very different contradictions, active at the different levels, have fused, condensed into a rupture or 'break'. (This effect of condensation is not determination but what Althusser calls 'over-determination' – see his essay, 'Contradiction and over-determination').[15] Thus, correspondence, 'fit' and identity between the different structures opens – so far as this perspective is concerned – a false and reductive trail. The relations between, say, the economic structure of society and schooling will not be identical – the one replicating or reflecting the other – but necessarily uneven and displaced. In this paradigm, the superstructures have their own 'structure', their own role and function, their own place and conditions of existence, their own effectiveness. The superstructures obey their own 'relatively autonomous' logics, and only analytically 'in the last instance', or in some more formal or global sense, are they given their specific gravity and weight by the economic level. Thus, the different 'tasks' of schooling for capitalist society can (and, indeed, must) be clearly differentiated. The school's function in reproducing the relations of the productive life of capitalist societies must be clearly demarcated from its political function in cementing a particular form of class domination, and this, in turn, must be differentiated from the school's role in cultural or ideological reproduction. In some ways, this approach tends (again, this is an over-generalization) to take the *ideological* functions of schooling as more significant than the functions that the school might perform directly for production. This ideological function is the site of 'reproduction'. School in capitalist society obeys the logic of capitalist class relations, not by mirroring production-relations and labour organization directly in the classroom, but by maintaining its own forms of educational hierarchy, specialization and control.

Generally, this position has been most forcefully advanced by Althusser, especially in his essay on 'Ideological state apparatuses' – of which the education system is one.[16] Here we find the distinction between production and *social reproduction*. In the 'relations of production', society reproduces its material life in capitalist forms. In the superstructures society reproduces the relations of production *outside* production, *for* production. Althusser, in this essay, draws a good deal on Gramsci's formulations, but he takes them a step further along the path to 'reproduction'.[17] But there are other theorists who, also working on the examination of 'reproduction', read the nature of the 'unity' differently from Althusser – for example, Bourdieu and Bernstein [. . .]. Bourdieu conceives the articulation between schooling and society neither as a correspondence, nor as a coupling, but as a 'homology'. A homology is a similarity of structure between two relatively independent fields. Schooling is 'conformed' to capitalism, not because schools are organized like factories, or filter children directly into the occupational system, but because, within its own sphere, education organizes itself in the same way as capitalist relations are organized. Whereas correspondence theories *tend* (remember the caveat) to match one field (education) to another (production) or to look for structural parallels, reproduction theories tend to underline their separateness, their specific nature, their distinctiveness from one another. Schooling can only function on behalf of the system by playing its own role. It supports and reproduces the general structure of class relations by the elaboration of a particular set of 'educational class relations'. Bourdieu and Bernstein, in their different ways, have both advanced this paradigm of the schooling-society link conceived as a set of continuities and discontinuities. Schooling is therefore articulated with capitalist society as much through its differences as through its correspondences. This is one of the most distinctive features of what we shall call, in a very general way, the *reproduction* paradigm.

[. . .]

Schooling and 'reproduction'

Let us turn, finally and briefly, to the *reproduction* paradigm. This, too, is a cluster of approaches, rather than a single approach – as will be obvious if you try to gather together into a single theoretical camp theorists as difficult and different as Althusser, Bourdieu, Bernstein and Freire. [. . .] But there are some common theoretical postulates or positions that distinguish 'reproduction' theories from other paradigms discussed here, and it is important to identify what the essence of this theoretical distinction is.

One way to conceive the approach through *reproduction* is to see it as grounded in an expansion of Marxist theory – not the theory of the early, 'philosophical' Marx which yielded the concept of 'alienated labour', but of the later, more mature Marx, and the substantial work of *Capital*.[18] In *Capital* Marx drew a distinction between the historical stage where capitalist social relations first emerged and began to displace the relations of earlier modes of production, and the later stages where capitalism stood on its own ground, maintaining itself and sustaining its dynamic through its capacity to reproduce itself on an expanded scale. [...] Here Marx was obliged to move away from the production process itself, and examine the ways in which, by combining production with distribution and consumption, capital was able, at one and the same time, to realize itself, to replace itself on an extended scale and to replace all the elements necessary for it to continue its work on an expanded level. In *Capital* Marx's demonstration of this process required the articulation of what he called the different 'circuits' of capital – circuits through which production and reproduction were effectively combined.

[...]

The important point is that, basing his analysis on the conditions of production, Marx was able to suggest what requirements the production process made of relations (for example, consumption) and institutions (for example, the market and the family) which were necessary to it, but not based directly *in* production. For example, unless the family fed, housed and 'reproduced' the labourer, biologically and 'culturally', he (or she) could not provide the production system with productive labour. The material basis of this 'reproduction of labour power', accomplished in the site of the family, was, however, provided by capital itself, in the form of the wage. Hence, the family was an essential part, not simply of production (consuming what production produced) but of the production-reproduction circuit. The same could be said of other institutions, linked with but not directly part of production. The 'reproduction' of the instruments of production, for example, required all those relations which, under modern production conditions, enabled society to apply knowledge, science and technology to the instruments of production (machinery) 'as a material force'. Similarly, the school could be regarded as essential in forming and 'cultivating' the working class and equipping it with skills in a particular form, while not being directly under the command of capital itself.

In *Capital*, the question of 'reproduction' is still examined principally in its structural-economic aspect. But the analysis clearly lays the basis for examining other aspects of the 'reproduction process', in a way that would show both how and why they were separated from production proper, and yet how and why they were linked with and necessary to its expansion. Recently, as attention has shifted to some of these other aspects of capitalist societies – the family, ideology, the legal and political superstructures, the state – so attempts have been made to develop a full theory of 'social reproduction' grounded in Marx's original propositions. One of the most fruitful areas of work in this connection relates 'reproduction' to the role of the family, the sexual division of labour, and the role of women in domestic labour (see, for example, Juliet Mitchell's *Woman's Estate* and *Psychoanalysis and Feminism*).[19] It should be added that since, for Marx, the 'capital-labour' relationship was intrinsically an antagonistic one, its 'reproduction' always involved the reproduction of these contradictions. Capital, in reproducing itself, therefore, also reproduced its own contradictions, and the limits and barriers to its infinite expansion.

Though we have placed Gramsci's work in a different paradigm – that of hegemony – it is clear that many of his ways of conceptualizing the relationship of education and schooling, the state and other political, cultural and civil institutions to production fall into the general framework outlined here, though Gramsci does not explicitly use the term 'reproduction' to describe them. The term is, however, employed in this much-expanded form most powerfully in Althusser's seminal essay, 'On ideological state apparatuses' [...] where Althusser is explicitly working with concepts drawn from Marx's work.[20] In fact, in this essay, Althusser is also very close to Gramsci, though he elaborates his central concepts differently. (For a discussion on the Gramsci-Althusser relationship see 'Politics and ideology: Gramsci', by Hall, Lumley and McLennan).[21]

Althusser's starting point is Marx's argument (in Volume 2 of *Capital*) that 'no production is possible which does not allow for the reproduction of the material conditions of production'. But reproducing the means or instruments of production also entails reproducing the 'forces' of production – labour power itself. This second kind of reproduction is a complex matter, for it means 'producing again' (either in the same generation, daily, or across generations) not only physically and materially, but ideologically and culturally, those who must take their places in, and be 'competent' at, the production process. This means that labour must be 'suitable to set to work in the complex system of the process of production'. For example, labour must be diversely skilled, according to the requirements of the socio-technical division of labour (a task which, as Althusser points out, used to be largely performed within production itself – on the job – but is now increasingly 'achieved more and more outside production, by the capitalist education system and by other institutions and instances'). But it also entails ensuring that labour has 'learned the "rules" of good behaviour', that is, 'the attitude that should be observed by every agent in the division of labour, according to the job he is destined for; rules of morality, civic and professional conscience, which actually means rules of respect for the socio-technical division of labour and ultimately the rules of the order established by class domination'. Althusser sums up this argument by saying that the 'reproduction of labour power requires not only a reproduction of its skills, but also, at the same time, a reproduction of its submission to the rules of the established order'. This is the terrain of *social reproduction* – the process of capitalist production, examined 'from the point of view of reproduction'.

Althusser's essay has had a seminal role in advancing the viewpoint of 'reproduction' with respect to the examination of the school, the family, the media and other cultural institutions, the political parties and trade unions, and other 'ideological state apparatuses'. This is an important, though ambiguous phrase. He terms these institutions 'ideological' because (as in Gramsci's discussion of 'hegemony', on which Althusser draws widely) they tend to 'work through ideology' (or consent), rather than through coercion; and, secondly, because their 'function' is to cement a society or social formation beneath the sway of the dominant ideology. He calls them '*state* apparatuses' (in this he differs from Gramsci, who maintained a distinction between the state and 'civil society') because, under modern capitalist conditions, these apparatuses are now situated within the embrace of a much expanded state. The example of education – the rise of mass schooling, and the placing of the education system in the care of the state – are pertinent examples to which Althusser's analysis can be applied.

However, a number of criticisms of Althusser's work on 'reproduction' need to be borne in mind. (a) His essay is pitched at a high level of generality. The work of showing how any specific ideological state apparatus 'works' to fulfil its function remains to be done. (b) Though drawing directly on Marx, he diverges from Marx's argument in at least two critical directions: he deals exclusively (as Marx does not) with the reproduction of labour-power, or, more accurately, with the reproduction of 'wage labour'; and he deals almost exclusively with the ideological aspect of 'reproduction'. (c) The analysis of 'reproduction' is supplemented by a complex and difficult set of propositions about how 'ideology in general' works. This is an original theory, but it diverges in important ways from Marx's theory of ideology. (d) He tends to see the 'work' of reproduction as proceeding, under capitalism, virtually without limit or contradiction. He recognizes the presence of 'the class struggle', but only peripherally, and very late in his argument. This treatment of 'reproduction' as, essentially, unproblematic for capitalism has led to the charge against Althusser that his theory is really a variant of Marxist functionalism. This charge of functionalism opens up a different and intriguing line of enquiry. For theories of education and schooling based on 'reproduction' can *also* be understood as developing certain insights derived not from Marx but from Durkheim and the school of 'structural-functionalism' which he inaugurated. To this tradition, we could (in very complex combinations) assimilate not only Althusser (and his close follower, Poulantzas), but such theorists as Bourdieu and Bernstein, in his later work, who also make use of the concept of 'reproduction'.

[. . .] Though radically different in many fundamental ways, Marx and Durkheim do share something (as against other schools and theorists) at least in so far as both treat 'society' as a 'whole' or 'totality'. They both regard society as a structure of interconnecting parts. Here, of course, the similarities end. For whereas Durkheim sees the social process as leading towards some sort of 'functional integration', Marx sees society as a structure of contradictory tendencies and forces. However, the attention to societies as 'ensembles' does, under certain conditions, open the way to a sort of *rapprochement* – at least around the question of how societies secure the conditions for their own survival and their 'reproduction'. It is therefore interesting, in this respect, that two other major theorists of 'reproduction' base their work, in different ways, on some combination or synthesis of Durkheimian and Marxist concerns. This is relevant to Bernstein (whose roots in Durkheim and Marx have been openly acknowledged) as well as to Bourdieu (whose range of 'sources' is even wider, and must be held to include, not only Durkheim and Marx, but also Weber and Levi-Strauss. [. . .]

In his book, *Reproduction in Education, Society and Culture*, for example, Bourdieu does not look for or expect to find any direct similarities or 'correspondences', say, between the processes of schooling and those of production – between 'cultural' and 'social' reproduction.[22] He does not deny that schooling has a role in maintaining the domination of the dominant class and its culture, and the subordination of the subordinate class and its culture. He sees classes as 'given' in production, and as rooted in power relations. But schooling does the work – has the effect – of reproducing these 'external' relations of class and power, by performing its own, specific 'pedagogic work' (in the school). Further, precisely because the 'work' of the pedagogic institution and its 'action' is specific, distinct and conducted under the 'neutrality' of the schooling process, it has the additional effect of permitting society to 'misrecognize' the contribution schooling makes towards the maintenance and reproduction of power relations.

[. . .]

For [Bourdieu] schools operate in the field of 'symbolic positions and oppositions', which is, crudely, the field of *culture*. Schools, in their manifest function, reproduce the 'agents' to fill the required 'jobs and posts' in production, by apparently qualifying them according to appropriate criteria. But, through this task of 'inculcation' by means of the school's 'pedagogic action', schools also reproduce the distribution of what Bourdieu calls 'cultural capital'. That is to say, schools both depend on the already-distributed cultural capital in the classes of society, and reproduce that capital by reproducing, through their own actions, class cultures of different indices of strength and power. They thus, also, reproduce the relations of power – of domination and subordination – between the different class cultures. In part, schooling performs this work by the inculcation of a 'habitus' – by imposing certain distinctive ways of perceiving and acting in the world; by administering its own rules of classifying and framing the world; through its own kinds of distinctive cognitive modalities – each appropriate to the cultures of the different classes. Bourdieu speaks of this as the imposition of a 'cultural arbitrary' – or the work of 'symbolic violence'.

For our purposes, the important point is that schooling is linked with classes and with production, not by the fact that the latter are directly mirrored or represented in the classroom (classroom discipline does not equal factory discipline), but only through a series of transformations, which articulate one relatively independent or autonomous 'field' with another (the imposition of a cultural arbitrary with the imposition of class domination). The ruling class – to adapt a current phrase – does not 'rule OK' (but invisibly and surreptitiously) in the classroom. The ruling class can only benefit, in the sphere of power, from the work that schools do (in the sphere of symbolic relations) because, paradoxically, *teachers* 'rule' according to a certain logic and practice, in the classroom. The way education as a field is structured and practised is similar, in form and structure (i.e. 'homologous') to the way classes rule in the power relations of society, and to the way economic capital 'rules' and is reproduced in production. Each structure or field is, therefore, subject to a 'double determination': those determinations internal to its own specific field and practice, and what we can call (the phrase is *not* Bourdieu's) the 'over-determination' of other fields on it. A field, like education, can therefore only sustain other fields and relations external to it because it is capable of sustaining and reproducing its own 'internal' rules and classifications. Bernstein, in a recent paper, which attempts to apply the codes of classification and framing to the relations between education and production, is moving – from a rather different starting point – towards much the same point of theoretical resolution: the stress on the 'relative autonomy of education'.[23]

There are radical points of difference between the approaches to the education-society connection through the perspective of 'reproduction', as adopted by Althusser and Bourdieu. These should not be underestimated. However, it is also possible, tentatively, to establish some common ground between them – at least in contrast with other paradigms discussed in this section. The element we would tentatively fasten upon is this: theories of 'reproduction' present the structures of production and of reproduction (for example, education) as *articulated* together – but *not* because they are the same, or identical, or convergent, or corresponding. In contrast with other paradigms, they constantly expand and extend the differences, the distances which separate and differentiate the two fields. They stress the *specificity* of the institutions or apparatuses involved in reproduction, and the degree of their *relative autonomy* from the sphere of production proper. They thus occupy a theoretical position at absolutely the opposite end of the spectrum from that of Bowles and Gintis' 'correspondence principle'.

Bourdieu, as we have seen, handles the question of the specificity of schooling in a very distinctive way; and although his theory is, at first, hard to grasp, and draws very freely on apparently incompatible theoretical paradigms (Durkheim, Marx, Weber, the structuralists), it has the merit of addressing, directly, features and processes which are specific and peculiar to the field of education as such. But, in their own – and very different – ways, both Gramsci and Althusser are also pointing in the same general direction. Gramsci, whose work is deeply historical and very far from formalist in inspiration, nevertheless escapes from any taint of economic reductionism by his insistence on the absence of any direct, immediate, functional or eternal identity between 'structure' and 'the superstructures'. Althusser, extending Gramsci's 'genial insights' further, within a structuralist framework of argument, insists that we must look for a necessary unevenness, a 'relative autonomy', between the two instances. The ideological state apparatuses, he insists, 'are multiple, distinct, "relatively autonomous" and capable of providing an objective field of contradictions which express, in forms which may be limited or extreme, the effects of clashes between the capitalist class struggle and the proletarian class struggle, as well as their subordinate forms'. If this formulation retains a trace of functionalism, it is not the functionalism of 'integration', nor one powered by the simple action of an 'economic base', but one capable of ensuring, at best, what Althusser describes as 'a sometimes teeth-gritting harmony' between, say, education and the society it 'reproduces'.

None of the paradigms examined [here] are perfectly satisfactory. Indeed, none are fully worked out, even within the limits of their own logics; and none – not even those based on 'cultural disadvantage' – are yet exhausted. Certainly, they are not all compatible. Though the field of educational theory is full of surprising reappearances and echoes of former positions, each paradigm contains a set of originating premises, certain distinctive ways of conceptualizing societies and their relations and structures, which cannot easily be elided into other sets. I hope this commentary and summary has, however, been sufficient to [show that the] problem of 'schooling and society' opens out into a rich field of theoretical and empirical work – work which, because it deals with central and controversial social themes, and is likely to inform real educational practices, is more than 'merely speculative'. Scientific work cannot be absolutely 'free' – it has its own limits and conditions. It remains, nevertheless, an open enterprise, to which, as Marx once remarked, 'there is no royal road'.

Notes and References

1 FINN, D., GRANT, N. and JOHNSON, R. (1977) 'Social Democracy, Education and the Crisis' *Working Papers in Cultural Studies* no. 10 University of Birmingham, Centre for Contemporary Cultural Studies.
2 *ibid.* p. 153.
3 TAWNEY, R.H. (1922) *Secondary Schools for All*, London, George Allen and Unwin.
4 Harold Wilson quoted in FINN, D., GRANT, N. and JOHNSON R. *op cit.*, p. 185.
5 FINN, D., GRANT, N. and JOHNSON R. *op. cit.*, p. 185.
6 *ibid.* pp. 189–90.
7 *ibid.* p. 190.
8 JOHNSON, R. (   ) 'Notes on the schooling of the English working class, 1780–1850' in DALE, I.R., ESLAND, G.M., MACDONALD, M. (Eds) (1976) *Schooling and Capitalism: a sociological reader* London, Routledge and Kegan Paul/The Open University Press, p. 47.
9 *ibid.* p. 48.
10 See, for example, DOUGLAS, J.W.B. (1967) *The Home and The School*, London, Panther; and DOUGLAS, J.W.B., ROSS, J.M. and SIMPSON, H.R. (1971) *All Our Future*, London, Panther.
11 HALSEY, A.H. (1972) *Educational Priority*, Vol 1, London, HMSO, chapter 1, p. 7.
12 BERNSTEIN, B. (1977) 'Education cannot compensate for society' in COSIN, B.R., DALE, I.R., ESLAND, G.M., MACKINNON, D. and SWIFT, D.F. (Eds) *School and Society: a sociological reader* London, Routledge and Kegan Paul/The Open University Press, p. 68.
13 KARIER, C. (1976) 'Liberalism and the quest for orderly change' in DALE, I.R., ESLAND, G.M., MACDONALD, M. (Eds) *op. cit.*
14 BOWLES, S. and GINTIS, H. (1976) *Schooling in Capitalist America*, London, Routledge and Kegan Paul.
15 ALTHUSSER, L. (1969) (trans., BREWSTER, B.) *For Marx*, Harmondsworth, Allen Lane, The Penguin Press, 'Contradiction and over-determination'.
16 ALTHUSSER, L. (1971) *Lenin and Philosophy and Other Essays*, London, New Left Books, 'Ideology and ideological state apparatuses'.
17 The Althusser-Gramsci relationship has been discussed by ANDERSON, P. (1976) 'The antinomies of Antonio Gramsci' *New Left Review*, No. 100 November 1976–January 1977, pp. 5–78; and by HALL, S., LUMLEY, B. and McLENNAN, G. (1977) 'Politics and ideology: Gramsci' in *Working Papers in Cultural Studies*, No. 10, pp. 45–76.
18 MARX, K. (1867) *Capital* (3 Volumes), London, Lawrence and Wishart (1974).
19 MITCHELL, J. (1971) *Women's Estate*, Harmondsworth, Penguin Books Ltd.; and (1975) *Psychoanalysis and Feminism*, Harmondsworth, Penguin Books Ltd.
20 ALTHUSSER, L. (1971) *op. cit.*
21 HALL, S., LUMLEY, B. and McLENNAN, G., *op. cit.*
22 BOURDIEU, P. and PASSERON, J. (trans. NICE, R.) (1977) *Reproduction in Education, Society and Culture*, London, Sage Publications.
23 BERNSTEIN, B. (1977) 'Aspects of the relations between education and production' in *Class, codes and control*, Vol. 3, London, Routledge and Kegan Paul (2nd edn.) Chap. 8.

2 Capitalism, Liberalism and Schooling

David Hogan

Historical analyses of the dynamics of educational change have for the most part assumed that ideological or political forces – whether progressive reformism or the imposition of social control – were the principal sources of educational change in America.[1] Other historians have assumed that the principal source of educational change was the profound and continuous effect of technological change upon the skill levels required of the labor force and the differentiation of the occupational structure;[2] occasionally these assumptions are explicitly acknowledged as derivatives of modernization theory.[3] With the publication of *Schooling in Capitalist America*, by Sam Bowles and Herb Gintis, we get an immensely important effort to provide an alternative conceptualization of the dynamics of educational change along Marxist lines, to lay bare, so to speak, the economic laws of motion of education in American capitalism.[4]

The Functions of Capitalist Schooling

The primary theoretical claim of *Schooling in Capitalist America* is that the nature and functions of schooling cannot be understood apart from the matrix of economic life, specifically the dynamics of capitalism (pp. 224, 284). In Chapter Three ('At the Root of the Problem: The Capitalist Economy'), Bowles and Gintis therefore present a Marxist outline of the political economy of recent American capitalism. They stress in particular the control of the capitalist class over production or work – the 'accumulation' process – institutionalized in various market and property relations (p. 57), and the historical processes through which this control was strengthened: the proletarianization of the labor force – the extension of the wage labor system to ever larger portions of the labor force – and the extension of the hierarchical social division of labor. But because the accumulation process generated class conflict, the reproduction of the social relations of production, particularly the wage labor system necessary to the capitalist accumulation process, has been

Source: This is an abridged version of David Hogan's article in *Theory and Society* 8 (1979) pp. 387–413.

continuously threatened. It is this contradiction between accumulation and reproduction which is the basic dynamic of capitalism: the extension of the wage labor
system and the maintenance of the hierarchical social division of labor 'clashes
with the objective of reproducing the social, political, and economic conditions
for the perpetuation of capitalism as a system' (p. 279, see also pp. 203–4, 213–20,
271–81). During those critical junctures in American history when the process of
capital accumulation was deepened or widened – in the 1830s and '40s with the
emergence and consolidation of the factory system (Ch. 6), in the late nineteenth
and early twentieth centuries with the development of monopoly capitalism (Ch. 7),
and in the 1960s with the expanded proletarianization of white-collar workers,
their integration into the hierarchical division of labor, and the integration of blacks
into the wage labor system (Ch. 8) – the class struggles attendant upon such transformations provoked capitalists and schoolmen to look to the schools as a means
of resolving the conflict between labor and capital. That is, they looked to schools
to eliminate threats to the reproduction of the social relations of production. Bowles
and Gintis argue that each of these periods of acute social conflict was characterized
by: first, the extension and deepening of the process of capital accumulation and
second, a series of deliberate and conscious educational reforms to alleviate the class
struggle between labor and capital.[5] [...]

From this analysis of the dynamics of the capitalist economy, Bowles and Gintis
derive the two 'functions' of schooling in capitalist America: first, the reproduction
of the labor power essential to the process of capital accumulation, and second,
the reproduction of the social relations of production. The first function they define
as the provision of students – future workers – with the 'technical and cognitive
skills required for adequate job performance' (p. 129). Included in these skills
are also 'those personal characteristics relevant to the staffing of positions' in the
hierarchical social division of labor (p. 130). The second function they define as
the reproduction of those 'institutions and social relationships which facilitate the
translation of labor into profits' (p. 129). This is apparently accomplished in
two major ways: first, the 'education system legitimates economic inequality by
providing an open, objective and ostensibly meritocratic mechanism for assigning
individuals to unequal economic positions (pp. 103, 111, 114, 119, 123, 129–300);
and second, schooling reproduces those forms of 'consciousness' – for example,
with respect to the social relations of work, private ownership of the means of production, racism, sexism – that are conducive to the reproduction of the social order,
including 'the stratified consciousness on which the fragmentation of subordinate
economic classes is based' (p. 130).

This formulation of the functions of schooling in capitalist America is intended
to explain the major causal relations between schooling and capitalism. This they
do in Chapters Four and Five. They point out first that 'although higher levels
of schooling and economic success tend to go together, the intellectual abilities
developed or certified in school make little *causal* contribution to getting ahead
economically' (p. 110). The relationship between schooling and economic success,
they argue, is not to be explained in terms of the cognitive skills that schooling
imparts, but by the direct economic relationship among 'four sets of noncognitive

worker traits – work-related personality characteristics, modes of self preservation, racial, sexual and ethnic characteristics, and credentials' (p. 140) developed in schools. Schools inculcate those 'personality traits and forms of consciousness' necessary for successful job performance in the capitalist hierarchical social division of labor (pp. 94–100, 132–141). Schools are economically important to individual success because they socialize future workers into work habits that will successfully integrate students into the work place. Second, they argue that the level of income and the level of education achieved are principally determined, not by 'intelligence,' but by the familial socioeconomic positions of the individual (pp. 30–36, 84–92). Moreover, while inequality in the levels of schooling has declined, it is still substantially unequal and dependent 'upon family background as much in the recent period as it did fifty years ago' (p. 33). Furthermore, income levels have not been equalized despite the reduction of inequality of educational attainment (p. 34). In short, the relationship between schooling and economic success is not meritocratic, nor a question of 'luck' as Jencks suggested, but is systematically class based. Consequently, schools do not create inequality, but only reproduce existing inequalities in the economy (p. 248; pp. 11–12).

Finally, Bowles and Gintis provide an account of the mechanism through which these outcomes occur. Their argument centers upon the notion of 'the correspondence principle,' the claim that 'the major aspects of educational organization replicate the relationships of dominance and subordinancy in the economic sphere' (p. 125), specifically, that 'the social relations of education – the relationships between administrators and teachers, teachers and students, students and students, and students and their work – replicate the hierarchical division of labor' (p. 131). Through the experience of schooling, students are socialized into the habits and personality traits appropriate for their later (alienated) work life in the hierarchical division of labor (pp. 131–41). Thus, on the basis of a correspondence between the social relations of production and the social relations of education, Bowles and Gintis assert the 'ability of the educational system to produce an amenable and fragmented labor force' (p. 125).

The analysis Bowles and Gintis provide of the functions of schooling has much to commend it. First, it thoroughly undermines liberal functionalist-meritocratic explanations of the functions of schooling. Functionalists typically view the school as a market system in which education links the supply and demand for talent: schools are institutions which select and sort people on the basis of ability and achievement. Moreover, the intergenerational transmission of inequality is (allegedly) weakened as educational achievement becomes the principal determinant of success and equality of opportunity is obtained: the educational market is then free of imperfections. Bowles and Gintis demonstrate, however, that the meritocratic assumption that the inter-generational transmission of inequality is weakening is false, that educational achievement is not based on IQ or 'ability', and that the assumption that it is cognitive skills that are crucial to economic success is invalid. Second, Bowles and Gintis for the most part avoid the conceptual traps that plague most analyses of the functions of schooling, whether by historians, economists, or sociologists. Thus they refrain from reducing their analysis of the functions of education to an analysis of the *purposes or intentions* of those who designed or control the school system. Such analyses are analyses of ideologies, and while they are absolutely crucial to understanding how it is schools came to be what they are, and in determining the extent to which schools actually fulfill their stated goals, by themselves analyses of intentions or purpose will not tell us what schools do. Likewise, the analysis of particular educational outcomes – for instance, the unequal distribution of educational attainment between different student groups – is not sufficient by itself or in conjunction with analyses of the ideology of schooling to provide an analysis of the functions of schooling. An argument about the functions of schooling, whether in historical or systemic terms, is an attempt to articulate the nature of the systematic interrelations between different social institutions and processes. Such an account incorporates analyses of the outcomes and ideology of schooling within a general theory about the political economy or the social system; needless to say, such a theory need not be 'functionalist'.[6]

Finally, Bowles and Gintis avoid the mistake of assuming that the analysis of the *control* of schooling is an analysis of the functions of schooling, a major trap of educational historians. The historiography of education is replete with debates about the 'class' composition of school boards, the development of educational bureaucracies, or the professionalization of teachers, as if these issues will unlock the door to our understanding of what schools do.[7] But to assume that analyzing the composition of school boards or boards of regents or the process of decision-making will establish the function of the educational system is only to perpetrate what might be called a 'nominalist fallacy'. Such studies will perhaps tell us who nominally controlled schooling, with what purposes elites viewed schooling, *how* the demands for labor power and control of class conflict emanating from the political economy were translated into educational policy, and the relative importance of the bureaucracies relative to school boards. But they will not tell us what schools *do*, in the sense of either their outcomes or their functions. This conceptual hiatus in educational history is indicative not only of a desperate need to develop a theory of schooling that is cognizant of the instrumentalist-structuralist debate on the theory of power,[8] but also of the failure of education historians – and others – clearly to differentiate class analysis from the analysis of inequality.

Unfortunately Bowles and Gintis do not always sustain this distinction. To argue, for instance, that schools differentially train and insert workers into the social division of labor is to point to the fact that schools are institutional mechanisms that produce a differentiated labor force, a claim that is *not* equivalent to the claim that schooling reproduces inequality. To say, for instance, that schooling reproduces patterns of inequality, is to claim that there is a close association between family socioeconomic status and years and/or type of schooling completed. This claim may be more or less true *independent* of the fact that the schools produce a wage labor force; the reproduction of inequalities is not the same thing as the reproduction of classes, although they are in fact closely related. Likewise, to emphasize the hierarchical nature of the division of labor is to forego what is distinctive about a Marxist analysis of the political economy, namely the analysis of class relations and class formation.[9] While Bowles and Ginits provide us with a lengthy and valuable account of the nature and types of inequality in America (pp. 26–36, 84–100), we do not get a comparable analysis of class formations nor a sufficient explication of class relations. It is not that there are any objections in principle to studying patterns of inequality, whether political, economic, educational, or cultural – indeed it is a task of immense theoretical and political importance – but only that it be remembered that such analyses do *not* constitute what is the core of a Marxist analysis, the analysis of class relations and their reproduction through various mechanisms, political, economic, cultural, or educational.

It was this task, particularly the reproduction of the pivotal class relationship of capitalism, the wage-labor relationship, that was the center of Marx's own research. [. . .]

Marx was interested in explaining *how* wealth and poverty, domination and subjugation, were reproduced over time. That is, he was not primarily interested in *who* was wealthy, or powerful, or mobile, or even in patterns of such inequalities over time, but in the structure and reproduction of social relations that gave rise to these inequalities. The inequalities were to be explained by class relations. In doing so, he focused not on the rich, the wellborn, and the powerful, nor on the poor, the lowly born, and the powerless, but on *capital*, i.e., upon the relations of production (the relation between capitalist and wage earner), and their connection to the productive forces, to the state, and to ideology. The reproduction of capitalist society required at heart the reproduction of the capital relations: 'on the one side the capitalist, on the other the wage laborer'.[10] Accordingly, the historical study of capitalism must have as a primary focus the reproduction of the capital-labor relationship, in particular, the *process* of its reproduction at various levels – economic, political, educational, ideological. Instead of starting with such questions as 'who rules'? or 'who is wealthy'? or 'who is immobile'?, the critical question is the reproduction of the labor-capital relation: what institutions support it? What role does the state, or education, play? How does this happen? How does the class system work? Perhaps no one has made the point clearer than E.P. Thompson in his critique of stratification theorists:

> Sociologists who have stopped the time machine and, with a good deal of conceptual huffing and puffing, have gone to the engine room to look, tell us that nowhere at all have they been able to locate and classify a class. They can only find a multitude of people with different occupations, incomes, status-hierarchies, and the rest. Of course they are right, since class is not this or that part of the machine, but *the way the machine* works. Once it is set in motion – not this interest and that interest, but the *friction* of interests – the movement itself, the heat, the thundering noise. Class is a social and cultural formation (often finding institutional expression) which cannot be defined abstractly, or in isolation, but only in terms of relationship with other classes; and ultimately, the definition can only be made in the medium of *time* – that is, action and reaction, change and conflict. When we speak of *a* class we are thinking of a very loosely defined body of people who share the same congeries of interests, social experiences, traditions and

value-system, who have a disposition to behave as a class, to define themselves in their actions and in their consciousness in relation to other groups
of people in class ways. But class itself is not a thing, it is a happening.[11]

Bowles and Gintis have done much to provide a concrete picture of how American
capitalism works, but, as I shall argue later, they fall short of what is required.

Schooling Viewed Historically

What is to be said, then, of Bowles and Gintis' historical treatment of the functions
of schooling? Three major problems stand out: a failure to develop an historical
account of the functions of schooling over time; a failure to develop a sufficiently
comprehensive theory of reproduction and contradiction; and a misleading account
of educational politics in America.

In Chapters Six, Seven, and Eight, Bowles and Gintis provide an account of
the school as a reproducer of the social relations of production, but not of the
function of the school as a producer of labor power. In effect they do not provide
any evidence that would enable the reader to decide what in fact has been the
historical relationship between the two functions over time. Have they changed
relative to one another? If so, when, why, under what conditions, and with what
implications for their analysis? In other words, Bowles and Gintis do not indicate
whether in fact, and if so, in what manner, and for what reasons, there have been
changes in the ways schools have functioned.

This is an important point, since the relationship between schooling and the
capitalist political economy that Bowles and Gintis describe was not born full-
grown at the time of the Industrial Revolution, but slowly evolved over time with
changes in the accumulation process and the level of class conflict. Before the
Industrial Revolution, and even up the 1880s, almost the exclusive purpose of the
public school system was to insert children into the ideological – particularly
political – practices of the society, what was called 'citizenship', or 'character
training'. Training for participation in the labor force was of secondary importance. Again, universities up to this time were largely finishing schools for the
upper-middle classes; it was not until the twentieth century that they gained their
stranglehold on professional education. Only gradually over time were the schools
and then the universities integrated into the economy as suppliers of differentiated
labor power, and increasingly subject to the central dynamic of capitalist society,
the contradiction between accumulation and reproduction: it was only after the
emergence of monopoly capitalism that educators self consciously made serious
efforts to integrate the schools into the wage labor system as a supplier of differentiated labor power. In effect, American mass education was first established
not so much for industrial as for political reasons under the impact of ideological
pressures from Republicanism and Protestantism in a time of acute social disorder.
[...]

The initial integration of the schools into the political economy during the nine-

teenth century was thus not so much because schools were to function as an economic institution, but because they were designed to integrate children into the
ensemble of class relations – political, economic, cultural – of nineteenth century
American capitalism, and not just the social relations of productions. This suggests
the necessity of distinguishing between the importance and effect of the contradiction between accumulation and reproduction in drawing schools into the political
economy, on the one hand, and the extent to which schooling itself was subject
to the contradiction between accumulation and reproduction, on the other hand.
Not only was the expansion of schooling in the early nineteenth century more an
issue of political reproduction than of economic reproduction, but also it was not
until the early twentieth century that the schools became important institutions
supplying labor power and reproducing the social relations of production. Moreover, it was not until this time that the schools themselves exhibited the impact of
the contradiction between accumulation and reproduction in the form of a conflict
between the demand for differentiated vocationally based schooling (vocationalism)
and the traditional emphasis upon citizenship in common schools.[12] It was only
at this point that the accumulation pressures upon the school reached a level of
such significance that they threatened to overwhelm the traditional political role
of the school. Thus, while capitalists and some educators demanded the integration
of public schooling into the wage labor system through the introduction of vocational and differentiated education, vocational guidance, the junior high school,
and the testing movement, it was a fear that such programs might undermine the
reproduction of the social relations of liberal capitalist society that led other progressive reformers to strenuously oppose such legislation as the Cooley Bill in
Illinois, to support the principle of the comprehensive high school, extra-curricular
activities, activity pedagogies, and to dictate the incorporation of vocationalism
into the ideology of citizenship, in part through redefining the meaning of citizenship, equality of opportunity, and democratic education.[13]

The Correspondence Principle

The second major problem with Bowles and Gintis' treatment of the functions
of education centers upon their concept of the correspondence principle. [...]

In attempting to explain *how* it is that schools carry out their functions, Bowles
and Gintis suggest first that 'the educational system helps integrate youth into the
economic system, we believe, through a *structural* correspondence between its
social relations and those of production' (p. 131, emphasis added), that is, there
is a forward linkage between the school and the economy through a correspondence
of the social relations of production and education. And second, they posit a backward linkage to the social structure via the family by positing a *cultural* correspondence between the institutions of work, family and school such that 'the reproduction
of consciousness is facilitated by a rough correspondence between the social
relations of production and the social relations of family life', that, following Melvin
Kohn, they explain as a consequence of 'the experiences of parents in the social
division of labor' (p. 143).

In explaining the causal mechanisms or processes which create and sustain the correspondence between the social relations of education and production, Bowles and Gintis very carefully emphasize that 'the independent internal dynamics of the two systems (work and schooling) present the ever-present possibility of a significant mismatch arising between economy and education' (p. 236), while yet insisting that the history of education is replete with the efforts of capitalists and reformers to create such a correspondence between the work place and the school, and that in general, and in the long run, through processes of 'pluralist accommodation' (pp. 236–7) and 'concrete political struggle along the lines of class interest' (p. 238), a considerable correspondence has been effected between the work place and the schools. The existence of lags or mismatches does not invalidate this argument, for they can be seen simply as cases where the exceptions prove the rule. [. . .]

If their account of the political processes through which the correspondence between work and schooling is created is cogent and provocative, the explanation they provide of the educational mechanisms sustaining it is suggestive but inadequate. They stress that the mechanism sustaining the correspondence is the experience of schooling itself, specifically the *form* of the social relations of education:

> The heart of the process is to be found not in the content of the educational encounter – or the process of the information transfer – but in the form: the social relations of the educational encounter. These correspond closely to the social relations of dominance, subordination, and motivation in the economic sphere. Through the educational encounter, individuals are induced to accept the degree of powerlessness with which they will be faced as mature workers (p. 265).

This is much too exaggerated. While Bowles and Gintis present evidence of the statistical correspondence between the personal attributes required for success in work and in schools (pp. 131–41), the evidence is at the most only suggestive and requires considerable further research. But more importantly, they neglect mechanisms other than the correspondence between the social relations of production and education. Other features of the educational process besides the form of the social relations of education might also have been considered: Basil Bernstein, for instance, has argued that the form of the relations between curriculum, pedagogy, and evaluation (that is, the nature of the 'classification' and 'framing' of 'educational transmissions') embody important ideological messages and are a critical part of the process of cultural reproduction of class relations.[14] Others have pointed out that the content of the educational process – the 'cultural capital' – is also a significant aspect of the cultural reproduction of class relations.[15] In effect, Bowles and Gintis, by limiting their analysis of reproduction to the correspondence between the form of the social relations of education and production, have a much too restricted theory of the reproduction of class relations through schooling.[16]

The second string of Bowles and Gintis' correspondence theory is an account of the cultural correspondence between the social relations of work, family life and education: experience of the social relations of work strongly affects the social relations of family life which in turn correspond to the social relations of education that the children of the families experience. Drawing upon the work of Melvin Kohn, they describe the cultural correspondences in the 1960s between work and family life; they do not note, however, the considerable cultural conflicts between schools and families, particularly along class and ethnic lines; even more significantly, they do not develop an historical account of the complex cultural *relationships* and conflicts (again along class and ethnic lines) among work, schools, and families,[17] the cultural process of class formation,[18] and the persistent efforts of educational reformers to destroy what they considered to be antagonistic working class cultures.[19] Finally, the explication of the relationship between family culture and school life would have been considerably strengthened by utilizing Bourdieu's theory of 'cultural capital' and Bernstein's work on language and class.[20] In short, subsequent researchers need to develop a more comprehensive theory of the impact of the social structure on education, the reasons for differential educational achievement, and the conflicts and contradictions among work, families, and schooling.

Educational Politics in America

The inadequacies of Bowles and Gintis' theory of reproduction and contradiction is perhaps both cause and effect of a profoundly erroneous application of their theory of educational politics to American educational history. I have already commented that some of the formal claims of this theory – specifically, that the control of the educational system tends to become an overt political issue, occasionally with distinctive overtones of class conflict, in those periods characterized by a serious disjuncture between the schools and the economy, and that for the most part, the correspondence between work and schooling is maintained through a politics of pluralist accommodation within the context of a wage labor political economy – are extremely valuable. But in their application of the theory, they seriously misconceive the relationship between capitalism and liberalism, a fact of both theoretical and political significance since this deficiency seriously impairs the value of *Schooling in Capitalist America* as a history of American education, its ability to function as a starting point for a Marxist research program in the history of education, and its effectiveness as a contribution to socialist political strategy. This failure has two aspects: first, an inaccurate characterization of liberal social theory and educational objectives, and second, a seriously misleading account of the politics and relationship between liberal educational objectives and (capitalist) educational practice.

[...]

Yet despite these limitations, their insistence on class conflict (rooted in the accumulation-reproduction nexus) as the centerpiece of a general interpretation of the dynamics of educational change is a provocative, persuasive challenge to liberal and revisionist interpretations of the history of American education (pp. 129, 148, 175, 228–9, 239–40). Both their substantive historical claims and their methodological injunctions directly undermine the consensus assumptions of liberal historiography. But they are also a challenge to the 'social control' or 'revisionist' historians (Karier, Violas, Lazerson, Spring) who have tended to emphasize class domination, rather than class conflict, by focusing on the ideologies, programs, and activities of élites in education. One can have little quarrel with the 'social control' revisionists' claim that élites have dominated educational reform and policy, but this is not to say that their domination has been unlimited nor uncontested. Clearly it seems reasonable to interpret compulsory education as an attempt to use the coercive power of the state as a means of establishing broad hegemonic control of the social order through the insertion of children into the ensemble of capitalist social relations. And the same can be said of the development of 'industrial intelligence' – specific forms or habits of behavior required for proper job performance and industrial peace – in vocational education programs or career education currently; these programs were and are efforts designed to socialize students into acceptance of the social relations of production. But such explanations need to avoid the trap of viewing these efforts as a process of dissemination downwards from the upper classes to the working class of the ruling class ideology, or as a process of embourgeoisment. Rather, they should be understood as deliberate processes through which élites desired to integrate an often intractable and hostile working class into the ensemble of social relations of liberal-capitalist society.

Not only must the efforts of the hegemonic classes to ensure the reproduction of capitalist social relations be studied, but also the various forms of resistance, passive or active, of the working class. Despite the efforts of the hegemonic classes to incorporate subordinate classes into a particular set of legitimating social practices, the social experience of the subordinate classes was such that it generated counter-hegemonic practices and ideologies. This process was enhanced by virtue of the existence of what Raymond Williams has called 'residual cultures', such that 'some experiences, meanings and values which cannot be verified or cannot be expressed in the terms of the dominant culture are ... lived and practiced on the basis of the residue – cultural as well as social – of some previous social formation'.[21] The exemplary, indeed paradigmatic, analysis of one such residual culture is E.P. Thompson's brilliant account of the making of the English working class, specifically his analysis of the importance of historical artisan political cultures within the process of class formation.[22] Similar research on working class culture has recently commenced in America, but very little research on the educational 'mentalities' of the American working class has been undertaken.[23] [...]

In the same manner, traditional ethnic cultures were a source of counter-hegemonic beliefs (cultural pluralism) and practices (e.g., family leisure and educational behavior) among the immigrant working class. These practices and beliefs were the subject of direct attacks by Americanizers, prohibitionists, and compulsory education reformers, but the attendance of immigrant children at school, and indeed their demand for schooling, even for vocational education, was not so much a victory for 'ideological hegemony' as Michael Katz recently claimed,[24] but principally (apart from the compulsory education laws) the belief among working class people that in a wage labor society and the increasing importance of educational credentials in the division of labor, education was the key to economic survival. Immigrant acceptance of education then was very much a consequence of the immigrants' perception of their class position in a class society: it was structurally, not ideologically, imposed. Within the limits imposed by poverty and the struggle to survive, both unskilled immigrants and skilled workers increasingly sent their children to school as a means of enhancing the value of their children's labor power in the labor market. And as a consequence, they were deeply embroiled in conflicts over the cultural content of schooling.[25]

The existence of such oppositional visions of citizenship and cultural conflicts over the content of schooling suggests the imperative need for extensive studies of overt and covert forms of class conflict over the structure and content of education, of what Bourdieu calls conflicting class 'strategies of reproduction'.[26] With such studies we will be in a much better position to develop an adequate theory of politics, and the manner in which contradictions have been mediated by liberal reformers.

[...]

Conclusion

Clearly, *Schooling in Capitalist America* is not without its limitations. It is characterized by an ahistorical treatment of the functions of education, an economistic conception of social structure, an inadequate theory of reproduction and contradiction, and a seriously inaccurate account of educational politics. Yet despite its problems, *Schooling* is a very important and valuable work. Bowles and Gintis are particularly successful in developing an effective critique of the liberal political economy of education, and a conceptualization of a broad theory of the dynamics of educational change that confounds all previous accounts, whether liberal or revisionist. *Schooling in Capitalist America* is therefore a valuable, if flawed, starting point for a Marxist research program into the history and political economy of education. Its contributions to that research program are significant, and its difficulties instructive. While *Schooling* therefore is not all that one could wish for, it is a significant and provocative beginning. Moreover it is model of engaged and committed scholarship that provides some understanding of what is required for the collective control of the future.

Acknowledgment

In the preparation of this essay, I have benefited from the advice of Sam Bowles, Walter Feinberg, Herb Gintis, Bob Halstead, Jerry Karabel, Clarence Karier, Ira Katznelson, Ralph Page, Jerry Selig, and Paul Violas.

Notes and References

1 See, for example, CUBBERLEY, E. (1934) *Public Education in the US* Boston, Houghton Mifflin; CREMIN, L. (1961) *The Transformation of the School* New York, Vintage Books; KATZ, M. (1976) 'The origins of public education: A reassessment' *History of Education Quarterly* 16(4); KARIER, C., VIOLAS, P. and SPRING, J. (1973) *Roots of Crisis* Chicago, Rand McNally; VIOLAS, P. (1978) *The Training of the Urban Working Class* Chicago, Rand McNally; LAZERSON, M. (1971) *Origins of the Urban School* Cambridge, Mass. Harvard University Press.

2 See CUBBERLEY, E. (1909) Cambridge, Mass. Harvard University Press, pp. 18–19, 53–57; NORTH, D.C. (1971) 'Capital formation in the United States during the early period of industrialization: A re-examination of the issues' in FOGEL, R.W. and ENGERMAN, S.L. (Eds) *The Re-interpretation of American Economic History* New York, Harper and Row, p. 277; HABBAKUK, H.J. (1962) *American and British Technology in the Nineteenth Century* Cambridge, Cambridge University Press p. 25; BRIGHT, J.R. (1966) 'The relationship of increasing automation and skill requirements in the employment impact of technological change' National Commission on Technology, Automation and Economic Progress, Washington, D.C., Government Printing Office, Vol. II, p. 207; TROW, M. (1967) 'The second transformation of American secondary education' in BENDIX, R. and LIPSETT, S.M. (Eds) *Class, Status and Power* London, Routledge and Kegan Paul, p. 438. Additional statements of these arguments appear in CLARK, B. (1962) *Educating the Expert Society* San Francisco, Chandler; KERR, C., DUNLOP, J., HARBISON, F. and MYERS, C. (1960) *Industrialism and Industrial Man* Cambridge, Mass. Harvard University Press; WARNER, W.I., HAVIGHURST, R.J. and LOCH, M.B. (1944) *Who Shall be Educated?* New York, Harper and Bros., Chap. 2; ADAMS, D. (1972) *Schooling and Social Change in Modern America* New York, McKay, Chaps. 1 and 5. For a critique, see COLLINS, R. (1972) 'Functional and conflict theories of educational stratification' in COSIN, B.R. *Education: Structure and Society* Baltimore, Penguin Books.

3 See, for example, KATZ, M. (1975) *The People of Hamilton, Canada West* Cambridge, Mass. Harvard University Press, pp. 5, 6, 7, 18–9, 45, 47.

4 See also BOWLES, S. (1971) 'Unequal education and the reproduction of the social division of labor' *Review of Radical Political Economy* 3(4); BOWLES, S. and GINTIS, H. (1972–73) 'I.Q. in the US Class Structure' *Social Policy* Nov/Dec, Jan/Feb.

5 A number of important issues will not be pursued in this essay. First, Bowles and Gintis fail to describe adequately the relationship between reproduction and legitimation. Thus, for example, they overstate that relationship when they argue that education reproduces inequality because of its meritocratic ideology (p. 123) when it is clear from other parts of their book that schooling is an institution that reproduces the labor power necessary for adequate job performance and differentially integrates workers into different levels of the social division of labor through such devices as vocational education (pp. 191–5), testing and tracking (pp. 195–8) and a differentiated system of higher education (chap. 8). That is, schooling operates as an institutional mechanism to reproduce inequality as well as to legitimate it. For this reason, their argument that educational credentials are merely legitimation devices (p. 202) ignores the importance of credentials as a determinant of the supply and demand of workers. Credentials are not only a certification of the workers' characteristics relevant to worker productivity but also a means of regulating the size of the reserve army, i.e. the supply of labor. The 'great training robbery' and the custodial role of schooling since the 1920s of removing adolescents from the labor market in 'disaccumulationist' capitalism cannot be ignored in a comprehensive formulation of the functions of schooling. See KRUG, E.A. (1972) *The Shaping of the American High School* Vol. 2, Madison, University of Wisconsin Press; BERG, I. (1971) *Education and Jobs: The Great Training Robbery* Boston, Beacon Press. See also CARSON, R.B. (1972) 'Youthful labor surplus in disaccumulationist capitalism' *Socialist Revolution* Vol. 9, pp. 15–44.

Second, from the point of view of systematic Marxist theory, the formulation of the functions of schooling raises an interesting theoretical problem. Insofar as schooling reproduces labor power, is schooling to be viewed as a part of the forces of production (i.e. the base)? Or, insofar as schooling legitimates inequality and reproduces a consciousness compatible with the capitalist social relations of production (i.e. as an institution of the ideological network), is it a part of the superstructure? And if schooling is a part of the base, in what sense does it involve the direct appropriation of children's labor power and of surplus value? It is clear that attention to this problem could throw some light on Marxian political economy of schooling and on Marxist theory in general, by attempting clearer formulations of the meaning of 'reproduction' and of the relationship of the base and the superstructure.

6 COHEN, D. and ROSENBERG, B. (1977) 'Functions and fantasies: understanding schools in capitalist America' *History of Education Quarterly* 17(2) Summer, fails to grasp this point. On the other hand,

GORELICK, S. (1977) 'Undermining hierarchy: Problems of schooling in capitalist America' *Monthly Review* October, pp. 20–36, argues that Bowles and Gintis have failed to extract themselves adequately from a functionalist conceptualization of the relationship between schooling and the economy. For an excellent discussion of the conceptual and epistemological issues involved in functionalist theories, see KEAT, R. and URRY, J. (1975) *Social Theory as Science* Boston, Routledge and Kegan Paul, esp. Chap. 5. See also MORGAN, D.H.J. (1975) *Social Theory and the Family* Boston, Routledge and Kegan Paul, Chap. 1.

7 See, for example, CALLAHAN, R.E. (1962) *Education and the Cult of Efficiency* Chicago, University of Chicago Press; BULLOUGH, W.A. (1974) *Cities and Schools in the Gilded Age* Port Washington, New York, Kennikat Press; KATZ, M. (1971) *Class, Bureaucracy and Schools* New York, Praeger; KAESTLE, C.F. (1973) *The Evolution of an Urban School System* Cambridge, Mass., Harvard University Press; CRONIN, J. (1973) *The Control of Urban Schools* New York, The Free Press; RAVITCH, D. (1974) *The Great School Wars, New York City, 1805–1973* New York, Basic Books; TYACK, D. (1974) *The One Best System: A History of American Urban Education* Cambridge, Mass. Harvard University Press; COUNTS, G.E. (1927) 'The social composition of boards of education: A study in the social control of public education' *Supplementary Educational Monographs* July; *Harvard Educational Review* (Special Issue) Social class structure and American education' 23(4) Fall, (1953).

8 For reviews of the instrumentalist-structuralist debate, see GOLD, D.A., LO, C.Y.H. and WRIGHT, E. (1975) 'Recent developments in Marxist theories of the state' *Monthly Review* Oct and Nov; THERBORN, G. (1976) 'What does the ruling class do when it rules? Some reflections on different approaches to the study of power in society' *Insurgent Sociologist* 6(3). See also POULANTZAS, N. (1969) 'The power of the capitalist state' *New Left Review* 59, and his (1973) *Political Power and Social Classes* London, New Left Books; and the excellent critique of Poulantzas by BRIDGE, A.B. (1974) 'Nicos Poulantzas and the Marxist theory of the state' *Politics and Society* Winter.

9 See GORELICK, S. (1977) *op. cit.* (note 6) for further elaboration of this point.

10 MARX, K. (1867) *Capital I*, New York, International Publishers (1967), p. 578.

11 THOMPSON, E.P. (1965) 'The peculiarities of the English' *Socialist Register* p. 357 (emphasis in the original).

12 In this connection it is worth noting that Bowles and Gintis do not provide clear criteria that would enable the historian to know a contradiction when he sees one: when, for instance, is a conflict a contradiction and not simply a conflict? A useful analysis of contradiction can be found in Michael Carter's essay.

13 See VIOLAS, P. (1978) op. cit. (note 1) Chap. 6; HOGAN, D. (1978) 'Capitalism and schooling: A history of the political economy of education in Chicago 1880–1930' unpublished Ph.D. dissertation, University of Illinois, Chap. 7. It would be interesting to assess whether this shift to vocationalism can be interpreted as a shift from what Basil Bernstein calls 'collection codes' to 'integration codes'. See his (1975) *Class, Codes and Control* Vol. III, London, Routledge and Kegan Paul, pp. 90–111. There is also a sense in which the clash between the 'instrumental order' and the 'expressive order' that Bernstein describes parallels the clash between vocationalism and citizenship. Unfortunately, Bernstein's approach is not historical, although in the revised edition of Vol. III of *Class, Codes and Control* (1977) he offers an analytic framework centering around concepts of education and production codes that might prove useful to an analysis of the changing relationship between the school and the economy.

14 See BERNSTEIN, B. (1975) *Class, Codes and Control* Vol. III, London, Routledge and Kegan Paul; SHARP, R. and GREEN, A. (1975) *Education and Social Control* London, Routledge and Kegan Paul.

15 *ibid.* See also BOURDIEU, P. and PASSERON, J.–P. (1971) *Reproduction*; BOURDIEU, P. (1977) 'Cultural reproduction and social reproduction' in KARABEL, J. and HALSEY, A.H. *Power and Ideology in Education* New York Oxford University Press, pp. 487–511; APPLE, M. (1971) 'The hidden curriculum and the nature of conflict' *Interchange* 2(4) pp. 27–40; SALLACH, D. (1974) 'Class domination and ideological hegemony' *The Sociological Quarterly* 51, Winter; ZEIGLER, H. and PEAK, W. (1970) 'The political functions of the educational system' *Sociology of Education* 43, Spring, pp. 129–42; VIOLAS, P (1978) *op. cit.* (note 1) Chaps. 4, 5, 7; HOGAN, D. (1978) *op. cit.* (note 13) Chaps. 7, 8.

16 See above notes 4 and 5; KARABEL, J. and HALSEY, A.H. (1977) *op. cit.* (note 15) pp. 1–85 'Introduction'; and APPLE, M. and WEXLER, P. (1978) 'Cultural capital and educational transmissions' *Educational Theory* 28(1) Winter, pp. 34–43.

17 See, for example, GUTMAN, H. (1973) 'Work, culture and society in industrializing America, 1815–1919' *American Historical Review* 78, June; DAWLEY, A. (1976) *Class and Community. The Industrial Revolution in Lynn* Cambridge, Mass. Harvard University Press; LAURIE, B. (1974) 'Nothing on compulsion: Life styles of Philadelphia artisans, 1820–50' *Labor History* 15(3) Summer; FALER, P. (1974) 'Cultural aspects of the industrial revolution: Lynn, Massachusetts, Shoemakers and industrial morality, 1826–60' *Labor History* 15(3) Summer; LASCH, C. (1977) *Haven in a Heartless World* New

York, Basic Books; COTT, N. (1977) *The Bonds of Womanhood: Women's Sphere in New England 1780–35* New Haven, Yale University Press; MILLER, D. and SWANSON, G. (1958) *The Changing American Parent* New York, Wiley; ZUCKERMAN, M. (1975) 'Dr. Spock: The confidence man' in ROSENBERG, C. (Ed) *The Family in History* Philadelphia, University of Pennsylvania Press; SEELEY, J., SUM, R.A. and LOOSLEY, E.W. (1956) *Crestwood Heights* Toronto, University of Toronto Press; and GORELICK, S. (1977) *op. cit.* (note 6) pp. 25–7.

18 See, for example, THOMPSON, E.P. (1963) *The Making of the English Working Class* London, Gollancz.

19 VIOLAS, P. (1978) *op. cit.* (note 1) Chaps. 2, 3; HOGAN, D. (1978) *op. cit.* (note 13) Chaps. 4, 5, 6.

20 See BERNSTEIN, B. (1961) 'Social class and linguistic development: A theory of social learning' in HALSEY, A.H. (Ed) *Education, Economy and Society* New York, Free Press, pp. 288–314; BERNSTEIN, B. (1973) *Class, Codes and Control*, Vol. 1 London, Paladin; BERNSTEIN, B. (1977) 'Class and pedagogies: visible and invisible' in KARABEL, J. and HALSEY, A.H. *op. cit.* (note 15) pp. 511–534; SHARP, R. and GREEN, A. (1975) *op. cit.* (note 14); BOURDIEU, P. and PASSERON, J.–P. (1971) *op. cit.* (note 15); KARABEL, J. and HALSEY, A.H. (1977) *op. cit.* (note 15) pp. 52–71 'Introduction'.

21 WILLIAMS, R. (1973) 'Base and superstructure in Marxist cultural theory' *New Left Review* 82, 10.

22 THOMPSON, E.P. (1968) *op. cit.* (note 18).

23 For the most part, even these efforts have simply looked at the educational behaviour of different immigrant groups without analyzing either associated behaviour (home ownership, child labor) or the cultural process of class formation. See, for example, COHEN, D.K. (1970) 'Immigrants and the schools' *Review of Educational Research* 40, Feb., pp. 13–27; GREER, C. (1972) *The Great School Legend* New York, Basic Books, Chaps. 6, 7; OLNECK, M.R. and LAZERSON, M. (1974) 'The school achievement of immigrant children, 1900–1930' *History of Education Quarterly* XIV, Winter, pp. 453–64; SMITH, T. (1969) 'Immigrant social aspirations and American education, 1880–1930' *American Quarterly* XXI, Fall, pp. 523–43. For the two efforts that go beyond these studies, see BODAR, L. (1976) 'Materialism and morality: Slavic-American immigrants and education, 1890–1940' *Journal of Ethnic Studies* 3 (4) Winter; and HOGAN, D. (1978) 'Education and the making of the Chicago working class' *History of Education Quarterly*; and (1978) *op. cit.* (note 13) Chap. 9.

24 See KATZ, M. (1976) *op. cit.* (note 1).

25 HOGAN, D. (1978) *op. cit.* (note 23).

26 BOURDIEU, P. and PASSERON, J.–P. (1971) *op. cit.* (note 15) and DURKHEIM, E. (1938) *The Evolution of Educational Thought* London, Routledge and Kegan Paul (1977).

3 Contradiction and Reproduction in Educational Theory

Herbert Gintis and Samuel Bowles

We are often asked how our ideas on education have developed since the publication of our book, *Schooling in Capitalist America*.[1] More specifically, what would we change if we had it to do over again? We must confess that, due to competing research commitments, we have not submitted this issue to a sustained investigation. Thus in this paper we will limit our treatment to a single question: that of our handling of contradictions within education and contradictions in the capitalist social formation resulting from the specific nature of the educational system. This question is absolutely fundamental. For as we suggested in our book, creating a truly egalitarian educational system geared toward the full development of students' cognitive, critical, and personal powers requires fundamental social change. But such fundamental social change, involving as it does overcoming the inertial tendencies in social development, can be achieved only by understanding and exploiting the contradictions already present and operative in society.[2] We feel that one of the weaker aspects of our book lies in its weak and possibly voluntaristic political prescriptions for educational change. This weakness flows from an inadequate treatment of the systemic contradictions of advanced capitalism. We shall here sketch how this fault might be repaired.

The Correspondence Principle

In *Schooling in Capitalist America* we began by asking what might be expected of an adequate educational system. We found that three goals were central to the traditional liberal conception of the social role of schooling. First, education should be *egalitarian* in the sense of acting as an effective force for overcoming the natural, social and historical inequities that tend inexorably to arise in society. Second, education should be *developmental* in the sense of providing students with the means to develop the cognitive, physical, emotional, critical, and aesthetic powers they

Source: BOWLES, S. and GINTIS, H. (1981) in BARTON, L., MEIGHAN, R. and WALKER, S. (Eds) *Schooling, Ideology and the Curriculum* Barcombe, The Falmer Press.

possess as individuals and as human beings. Third, education should be a means of what John Dewey has called the 'social continuity of life'.[3] That is, education should promote the smooth integration of individuals as fully functioning members of society. We then endeavored to show, using a variety of descriptive, historical, and statistical sources that education in advanced capitalism actually *reproduced* social inequality, rather than attenuating it, and acted rather more as a force for *repressing* personal development than fostering it. By contrast, what the schools seemed to do best was precisely to produce the 'good citizen' – its integrative function.

Why this pattern of success and failure? Is it to be found in the educational system itself or in the articulation of the school system with the social structures within which the schools are located? We concluded the latter. Dewey, in *Democracy and Education*, argued that a prerequisite for education's fulfilment of its egalitarian, developmental, and integrative functions is that society be *democratic*. For in a democratic society, the requirements of the citizenry are the abilities to relate to one another equally and reciprocally in controlling their common affairs. Schools that prepare students for this task of life will be necessarily egalitarian. Moreover, full personal development involves precisely the development of those cognitive and other social powers that allow individuals effectively to participate in democratically constituted collectivities and thereby to control their lives.

The critical problem in the articulation of schooling with advanced capitalism, we suggested, lies in its undemocratic structure of control over the process of production. The capitalist enterprise is not characterized by civil liberties, due process, democratic participation, or guaranteed rights. Rather, it is characterized by rights vested in property rather than persons and the control of the production process by capitalists and managerial personnel, giving rise to a class structure quite inimical to democratic principles.

A main proposition in *Schooling in Capitalist America* held that a major objective of capital, in its interventions into the formation and evolution of the educational system, was precisely the preparation of students to be future workers on the various levels in the hierarchy of capitalist production. Given the quite significant success of capital directly and indirectly structuring schools and in the face of the undemocratic nature of economic life, schools could not fulfill their egalitarian and developmental objectives. We concluded that the only means toward the achievement of progressive educational reform is the democratization of economic life, allowing for a democratic and emancipatory school system which does not conflict with the formation of adults capable of effective participation in the system of production.

We also argued specifically that the current relationship between education and economy is ensured not through the *content* of education but its *form*: the social relations of the educational encounter. Education prepares students to be workers through a *correspondence* between the social relations of production and the social relations of education. Like the division of labor in the capitalist enterprise, the educational system is a finely graded hierarchy of authority and control in which competition rather than co-operation governs the relations among participants, and an external reward system – wages in the case of the economy and grades in the case of schools – holds sway. This correspondence principle explains why the schools cannot at the same time promote full personal development and social equality, while integrating students into society. The hierarchical order of the school system, admirably geared towards preparing students for their future positions in the hierarchy of production, limits the development of those personal capacities involving the exercise of reciprocal and mutual democratic participation and reinforces social inequality by legitimating the assignment of students to inherently unequal 'slots' in the social hierarchy.

The correspondence principle, we believe, makes four positive contributions to progressive educational strategy. First, its explanatory value is great. Despite the considerable skepticism which greeted publication of our book, critics have made little headway in overturning our major empirical conclusions. Indeed the one major subsequent statistical investigation of sources of educational and economic success – Christopher Jencks *et al.'s Who Gets Ahead?* – dramatically confirms our own findings.[4] Second, in an era where the failures of liberal school reform have become increasingly evident to policy-makers and the public, the correspondence principle shows a positive alternative. Egalitarian and humanistic education are not unattainable due to some inherent defect in human nature or advanced industrial society, but to the undemocratic nature of participation in economic life. Educational reform requires at the same time economic transformation towards democratic socialism. Third, our formulation rectifies an earlier preoccupation of both liberal and Marxian analysis with the overt content of schooling. By focussing upon the experience of schooling, the correspondence principle provides a consistent analytical framework for understanding the school as an arena of structured social interaction. Fourth, our formulation of the correspondence principle contributes to a more positive understanding of the goals of socialist transition. In older critiques of capitalist society, almost unique stress was laid on the private ownership of means of production. At least as far as educational reform is concerned, we have been able to show that not *ownership*, but *control* is central to social inequities. Merely passing from private to social ownership without challenging in any substantial way the social relations of economic life, can have no impact on the egalitarian and humanistic goals of progressive educational reform. The correspondence principle then represents a powerful antidote to the authoritarian tendencies all too often found in an otherwise progressive socialist movement.

The correspondence principle is, however, not without its problems. The most critical is simply this: by standing, in our approach, as the *only* structural link between education and economy, and by its character as an inherently *harmonious* link between the two, the correspondence principle forced us to adopt a narrow and inadequate appreciation of the *contradictions* involved in the articulation of the educational system within the social totality. Yet as we have stressed, no political strategy can be developed without due attention to the systemic contradictions that can be exploited towards effective and progressive intervention. It is perhaps for this reason that our approach has been variously termed as 'radically functionalist' and imbued with 'missionary pessimism'.

This is not to say that our educational theory has been devoid of principles of contradiction. Indeed, we went to great lengths to demonstrate the 'lack of fit' between education and society at large.[5] Our major contribution in this respect was what we termed the contradiction between *reproduction* and *accumulation* in advanced capitalism. The educational system, we suggested, contributes to the reproduction and legitimation of the social relations of capitalist production. Yet at the same time the tendency of capitalist production is accumulation – the expansion of the wage labor system and the eclipse of older forms of production. This movement leads inevitably to a re-structuring of the social relations of production and a consequent change in the requirements for their reproduction. The contradiction between reproduction and accumulation thus takes the form of the educational system periodically falling *out of harmony* with the evolving structure of capitalist production relations. We do not think the contradiction between reproduction and accumulation is incorrect. Indeed, it is capable of aiding our understanding of both the striking periodicity of educational reform and of the major periods of educational change – such as the Common School Movement, the Progressive Education movement, and most recent the movement for the reform of higher education in the United States. Let us take the latter case as an example.

Many have wondered why such intense opposition to dominant social institutions in the decade of the 1960s occurred predominantly among students in higher education. Our answer, which we still believe correct, ran as follows. The social relations of higher education were laid down in the United States early in the twentieth century to train a professional, managerial, and propertied élite capable of controlling their own lives as well as the lives of others. With the vast increase in the economy's demand for skilled white collar labor after World War II and popular demand for access to higher education, however, higher education had to fill the gap in training students who, far from constituting a quasi-independent élite, were destined to staff the relatively powerless middle levels of the capitalist hierarchy of production. The norms of liberal education, critical thought, and free space for personal expression, all fostered by higher education, clearly failed to provide an adequate affective, normative, or even cognitive preparation for students *en route* to the fragmented, routinized and closely supervised work life of the salaried worker. Whence the material basis for their revolt: a discrepancy between the social relation of education and social relations of production. Indeed, our analysis of the contradictions of higher education has been substantiated by subsequent events. In the United States the response to the student movement in the decade of the 1970s was the move towards the *vocationalization* of higher education: raising tuitions, promoting two-year vocational as opposed to four-year liberal arts schools, redesigning the curriculum to eliminate 'critical thought' in favor of 'occupational skills', and stressing the commuter campus in contrast to the resident university where an oppositional 'youth culture' might develop.[6]

So-called 'back to basics', while having little rationale in terms of either pedagogical or technological reason, may be understood in part as a response to the failure of correspondence between schools and capitalist production brought about by the dynamics of the accumulation process confronting the inertia of the educational structures. This principle of contradiction, however, is clearly insufficient for effective political intervention. For it is purely inertial and passive: education merely *lags behind* a developing economic system. Such a mode of analysis provides no reasons why anything other than a periodic lagging-followed-by-catching-up dynamic might be present in the educational system. This dynamic is hardly absent: indeed it provides a compelling basis for identifying the quite distinct major epochs of educational reform in the United States. Yet it fails to elucidate the dynamic of change internal to the school system. For this reason it provides no clear-cut method for political intervention in the process we have theoretically isolated.

The task of searching for an adequate principle of contradiction between education and economy to supplement the correspondence principle is hampered, we now believe, by the very methodological stance we adopted in analysing social life. We found ourselves much impressed with the classical Marxian paradigm of base/superstructure, according to which the economic system forms a base of material relations defining the essence of social life, with respect to which such institutions as the family, the state, the educational system, the communications media, and cultural relations in general, appear as mere superstructural reflections. According to this approach contradictions in the economic system can have reverberations in other spheres of social life, but the latter cannot impart any autonomous contradictory effects to the reproduction process as a whole save the inertial non-correspondence which then formed the basis of our reasoning. It is hardly surprising, then, that we failed to locate a central contradiction in the education/economy relationship.

Sites and Practices

If a social formation is not to be viewed as an economic 'base' with a series of social levels successively stacked on top, how should it be conceived? We suggest that society be treated as an ensemble of structurally articulated *sites of social practice.* By a *site* we mean a cohesive area of social life characterized by a specified set of characteristic social relations or structures. These distinct 'rules of the game' regulate the manifold social practices at each site. Thus the state, the family system, and capitalist production are all sites in a capitalist social formation. Briefly speaking, the site of capitalist production is characterized by private property in the means of production, market exchange, wage labor and capitalist control of production and investment. The state is characterized by the institutions of liberal democracy, and the family site by the structure of power and kinship known as patriarchy.

These three sites – state, family, and site of capitalist production – we take as fundamental to the dynamics of advanced capitalist social formations. In the first instance, they define the three major relations individuals have *vis-à-vis* their society; each person has at the same time a specific citizenship, gender, and class status, and none of these can be understood as flowing simply from the others. Again, each of these sites is independently capable of supporting relations of dominance and subordinacy. Indeed, we would characterize the site of capitalist production as the site of dominance of capital over labor and the family as the site of dominance of men over women. By contrast, the state in its liberal democratic form, while required to reproduce the conditions of domination and subordinacy in family and economy, is not itself necessarily a site of domination. This observation will be important for our analysis of contradictions in the educational system.

The dynamics of a site cannot be deduced from its structure – its characteristic social relations – either alone or in relation to the structure of other sites. Rather, we must view sites as merely *structuring the practices occuring within them*. Practices, in turn, must be seen as neither the effects nor the reflection of structures, but fundamental and irreducible elements of social dynamics. The relation of a site to practices occuring with it is analogous to the relation between a language and a conversation: the language *structures* the conversation in terms of syntax and grammar, while exercising only partial control over the content of communicative exchange. But we must be more precise concerning our use of the term 'practice'. By a *practice* in general we mean a social intervention on the part of an individual, group, or class, whose *object* is some aspect of social reality, and whose *project* is the transformation (or stabilization) of that object. We will lay stress on four basic types of practice – appropriative, political, cultural, and distributive. By an *appropriative practice* we mean labor in its usual sense of transforming nature; its object is the natural world and its project is the creation of useful products. By a *political practice* we mean a social intervention geared to changing the social relations of a site – the 'rules of the game'. The object of a political practice, then, is the structure of a site or its articulation with other sites, and its project is the transformation of these social relationships. By *culture* we mean the ensemble of tools of discourse that a group employs towards exchanging information, expressing states of consciousness, forming bonds of solidarity, and forging common strategies of action. A *cultural practice*, then, is one whose object is culture and whose project is the transformation of the tools of discourse on the basis of which the formation and co-ordination of all group practices can be undertaken. Finally, the object of a *distributive practice* is the distribution of power, income and other desirable social prerogatives, and whose object is effecting a change in this distribution.

In summation, then, a social formation is a structural articulation of sites, and a site is a structure articulating the appropriative, political, cultural, and distributive practices occuring within it.

Our next goal will be to argue that in view of the particular nature of state, family, and economy in an advanced capitalist social formation, these sites articulate as a *contradictory totality*, and that the dynamics of the whole derive from the contradictory nature of this totality.

We may characterize the interaction of sites in general in terms of two dynamic principles: *structural delimitation* and the *transportation of practices across sites*. By delimitation we refer to the constraints placed on the development of a site by the very nature of its articulation with environing sites. By the transportation of practices we refer to the fact that groups, in their struggle and confrontations, do not always limit themselves to practices characteristic of the site in which these struggles occur but will under specific circumstances, attempt to 'transport' practices characteristic of other sites. These two processes, we suggest, account for the possibility of sites articulating as a contradictory totality. An example from the education/ economy interaction will serve to clarify these two dynamics. First, it is well known that funding for the educational system and willingness of students to participate depend significantly on its ability to enhance the economic status of its graduates. Thus the requirements for economic success, determined within the site of capitalist production, *structurally delimit* the forms of change open to the educational system, whatever the desires of educational reformers. Indeed, this in part accounts for the very existence of the correspondence principle in education. Conversely, educators intent on improving support for educational expansion, have consciously *transported political practices* from the site of capitalist production to restructure the social relations of education.

These two mechanisms account for the structure of education. We have not characterized the educational system as a site, because rather than exhibiting a uniform set of social relations, schools participate both in the state site and the private economy. By and large, however, the educational system is a sub-site of the state but with radically different principles of internal organization and participation. While the state in general is organized according to the principle of majority rule, the schools are organized according to that of top-down control. The mechanism of structural delimitation penalizes forms of educational change which expose students to political relations not compatible with their future positions as workers by ensuring a limited range of job opportunities for these students. In addition, as Raymond Callahan has shown in *Education and the Cult of Efficiency*[7] educators have not merely passively followed the dictates of structural delimitation, but have actively undertaken the transportation of capitalist practices: they have drawn on the literature and philosophy of business organization to mold the schools into forms favorable to the needs of capital accumulation and reproduction of the subservient position of workers at the site of capitalist production.

These examples, however, take the form of *reproductive* delimitation and transportation. We may equally validly speak of these mechanisms as *contradictory*. In terms of delimitation, contradiction takes the form of distinct sites, developing according to their own internal principles, changing so as to *undermine* the reproduction of the social processes of other sites. Contradictory delimitation in the educational system accounts for many of the concrete ways in which the schools fail to conform to the dictates of the capitalist economy. Let us cite three examples. Two of these relate to the critical location of education as *within* the state yet *serving* the site of capitalist production. First, the formally equal status of women as citizens, gained early in the Twentieth Century, virtually ensures that the state political mechanism will come to supply relatively equal education to men and women. Yet the reproduction of hierarchical relations in the capitalist enterprise has depended on the subordination of women to men. The outcome of this discrepancy is either a delegitimation of the educational system or a delegitimation of the economic subordination of women to men in the economy. Second, a parallel development with respect to blacks and minorities has occurred over the past two decades: their relatively equal position as citizens has produced a great deal more educational equality than the capitalist economy, whose hierarchical relations depend in part on the maintenance of the inferior position of blacks, is capable of matching. Once again, delimitation acts *contrary* to the requisites for reproducing the social relations of capitalist production. A third example of contradictory delimitation has been previously mentioned. The expansion of higher education in the post-World War II period, while serving the needs of the site of capitalist production for white collar wage-labor, has still taken the *form* of traditional liberal arts, quite incompatible with the social relations of the capitalist enterprise. This mechanism, which we previously thought of as simply an inertial dynamic of the educational system, now can be more comprehensively described as a form of contradictory delimitation.

The transportation of practices can also take a contradictory form, through their possible effect of the superposition of practices within a site. In terms of education, as we shall stress in the next section of this paper, contradictory transportation often takes the form of imposing forms of democratic participation in education which have been lifted from the state site, of which the educational system is a sub-site with a distinct structure of social relations.

Before returning to a direct treatment of education, we shall elucidate the two principles of contradictory delimitation and contradictory transportation in terms of the notion of the rights characteristic of the three major sites of advanced capitalist social formation.

Political practices at the site of capitalist production are characterized by *rights vested in property*, the rights being exercised by individuals only insofar as they own property or represent those who do. By contrast, political practices in the liberal democratic state are characterized by *rights vested in persons*, according to which all individuals, as citizens, participate equally (though indirectly through representatives) in the determination of state decisions. Again by contrast, the family site is characterized by *rights vested in adult males* to control the labor and reproduction of women.

The articulation of sites in advanced capitalism as a contradictory totality flows, we maintain, from the discrepancies among these forms of vesting of rights of political participation. This is most evident in the case of the transportation of practices. For instance women, having gained the status of full citizenship in the state site, have struggled in recent years to *extend* rights vested in persons to the family site – in the form of the demand for full equality in family life – where they come into direct confrontation with the principles of patriarchal domination.

Another important instance of the transportation of practices has taken the form of workers demanding, and often succeeding in attaining, the precedence of person rights over property rights at the site of capitalist production. We may cite several types of demands that illustrate this process in the history of the workers' movement from the nineteenth century when even full citizenship rights were only extended to the propertied, to the present. The first is the clear and insistent demands of workers for suffrage: full political participation on the basis of person rather than property or estate. The second is the right of workers to associate and organize common representation *vis-à-vis* employers, superseding the market-mediated confrontation of capital and labor. Third, and manifestly unrealizable under capitalism, is the right to employment, negating the market-determination of rates of unemployment. Fourth, and increasingly important since World War II, has been the demand that the civil rights of equal treatment and due process apply to, and hence dominate, market transactions. Thus the Civil Rights Movement in the United States in the 1960s demanded the equal treatment of blacks and whites by merchants and employers, limiting thereby their powers of unrestricted use and free contract. Similarly, the women's movement in the United States and Europe has demanded equal treatment in the capitalist economy in an attempt to weaken the free exercise of property rights on the part of discriminatory employers. Even workers' struggles for decent occupational safety and health conditions have taken the form not primarily of agreement through collective bargaining but of state regulations governing and restricting all contractual relations. Finally, the increasingly popular social goal of equality of opportunity is simply the application of the liberal concept of equality before the law, but now applied to the capitalist economy itself, where it is manifestly unrealizable within the context of the capitalist class structure.

The positive rights to full participation on the basis of person rather than property has involved as well the demand for *the extension of the spheres of social life governed by formally democratic procedures.* The possibility of popular participation in politics in nineteenth century Europe and the United States rested upon the *laissez-faire* state – the state whose concrete practices and interventions were strictly limited to a restricted range of social decision-making. Indeed, for the 'late developers' in Europe – such as Germany, Italy, and Russia – the reliance on a state actively intervening in the process of capital accumulation increased the stakes involved in the granting of democratic forms tremendously – a fact amply reflected in their twentieth century histories. Yet the *laissez-faire* state could not be contained. In part, of course, capitalists themselves demanded extensions towards economic stabilization and the building of the social infrastructure of capital accumulation. But equally important, citizens have demanded extensions of state practices to cover what were traditionally market-governed determinations.

Three dominant trends have been evident in recent decades. While these recent trends are virtual extensions of the historical logic of transportation of practices, their substance is qualitatively distinct. The first involves the transportation of civil equality to the economic sphere. Equality before the law has been a bourgeois demand since the French Revolution but the right to equal treatment in economic relationships directly expresses the dominance of person over property rights. Yet such have been the explicit demands of women, racial and religious minorities, and immigrant workers. Equally potent, but quite unrealizable under capitalism have been the demands for substantive equality of economic opportunity. A second dominant trend has involved the extension of the concepts of positive right from suffrage and association, won by women and the working class through struggle, to a comprehensive set of minimum rights due an individual by the very fact of citizenship. These demands, which may be called an Economic Bill of Rights, include state-provided services, such as health, education and social security, as

well as interventions into private economic transactions, as in the case of occupational health and safety regulations, consumer protective laws, and life-line utility
guarantees. Finally, demands for the extension of democracy have taken the form
of struggles over the transportation of parliamentary democratic practices to those
most sacrosanct arenas of capitalist control – the production and investment processes. While support for due process and constitutional guarantees have always
formed part of twentieth century worker demands, rebellion against 'checking your
civil rights at the factory gate' has in recent years blossomed into increasingly self-
conscious demands for full work-place democracy and control of investment.

Capitalist social formations, then, are inherently contradictory systems, faced
with the difficulty of maintaining the reproductive boundaries between the spheres
of application of property rights, person rights, and male prerogatives. Nor has it
done an acceptable job of maintaining these boundaries. If our analysis of social
struggles presented above is correct, an Achilles heel of the capitalist system lies in
its characteristic articulation of the state, economy, family totality. The liberal
democratic state is at once the citadel of private property and the instrument of
incursions upon this venerable institution. What E.P. Thompson has called the
'logic of the process' of social struggles has taken in part the form of the demand
for the dominance of person rights over property and male privilege.[8] These
struggles have complemented direct confrontation in family and production sites
and can be expected to form an integral element in any effective socialist movement
of coming years.

Before turning to the implication of this analysis for education, we must stress
one aspect of this dynamic of social struggle: its occurrence wholly *within* the liberal
discourse of natural rights. Workers have opposed the domination of capital not by
moving outside liberal discourse, but by turning one of its internal principles against
another. Socialists have often lamented this tendency of the workers' movement,
seeing in it a lack of workers' consciousness of their class condition. Were workers
adequately attuned to the true nature of their social condition and aware of their
objective interests, it is argued, they would reject liberal discourse in favor of a
Marxian analysis of social life. Workers would then demand an end to exploitation
and alienated labor and strive for a classless society.

This interpretation of liberal discourse is, however, quite inappropriate, and
indeed idealistic. Liberal discourse is not a coherent political philosophy or a set
of ideas. Nor was it the creation of the leading classes in society bent on the legitimation of the exploitation of labor.[9] Liberal discourse is the structure of cultural
practices in advanced capitalist social formations. As a real ensemble of social
relations, it is no more capable of being 'false' or 'true' than is a political or appropriative structure. Rather than reflecting or embodying ideas, it is simply a medium
of communication. Like other structures, it in no way determines the acts of communication which occur through it, though it may delimit the range of communicative forms capable of expression within it. Finally, while liberal discourse
may be criticized, it can only be transformed *internally*, through the conscious
cultural practices of contesting groups. Indeed, this is exactly the way in which
liberal discourse has developed through time. To view this fact in proper perspec-

tive, we must reject the notion that terms of discourse have 'meanings' in favor of the more operational notion of their having concrete *social uses* and specific *ranges of application* determined by modifiable social conventions.[10]

[After a certain point in the industrial revolution, workers ceased operating outside the structure of liberal discourse, and rather began to contest the *use* and *range of application* of its fundamental terms.] The conditions surrounding this transformation of discourse varied from country to country, but they generally coincided with workers' receiving concrete gains in the form of political rights and rights of association in return for their acquiescence to the employment of the liberal tools of communicative discourse. They did not, however, leave these tools intact in their bourgeois form. Thus contemporary liberalism, far from being a unified expression of a political philosophy, is itself an internally contradictory system incapable of reproducing the boundaries between the major sites of the advanced capitalist social formation – state, family, and site of capitalist production. In particular, the essence of the demands for democratic socialism are partly expressible through the tools of liberal discourse. Socialism is in part the application of the principle of rights vested in persons to the major institutions of economic life. Its fulfilment involves two major elements. First, the replacement of the political structure of the production process by a fully democratic system of participation and control. Second, in place of capitalist control of investment and growth, a democratic decision process controlled by the groups and communities affected by investment decisions. Similarly, the essence of the demands for women's liberation are easily expressible through the tools of liberal discourse. The subordinate economic position of women can be overturned by applying the principle of the equal rights of citizens to the area of hiring and promotion, in place of the property norms of free contract and hierarchical authority. Similarly the principle of democracy and reciprocity in personal relations is quite adequate to express the basis for a non-patriarchal reorganization of family life.

[What then are the limitations of operating within liberal discourse? By couching its fundamental concepts in terms of *person* rights, liberal discourse has difficulty in expressing issues of solidarity and co-operation as goals of political practices. The only generalizable form of bonding recognized in liberal discourse is that of nationality based on common citizenship and culture. Similarly, by relying on concepts of rights, whose use is virtually restricted to procedural issues, any assessment of the *substance* of democracy and participation lies outside its purview. For this reason appeals for solidarity and co-operation must and do transcend liberal discourse, drawing on the discourse of co-operative, family, brotherhood, and community. The actual discourse of socialism is thus an amalgam of liberal discourse and these expressions of bonding normally banished to the hinterlands of the political idiom.]

Education and the Contradictions of Social Life

The central contradiction in the educational systems of advanced capitalist society derives from two aspects of its location in the social totality. First, it forms in general a subsystem of the state site, and therefore is directly subject to the principle of rights vested in persons. Second, education plays a central role in reproducing the political structure of the capitalist production process, which in turn is legitimated in terms of rights vested in property. Thus education is directly involved in the contradictory articulation of sites in advanced capitalism and is expressed in terms of the property/person dichotomy: education reproduces rights vested in property while itself organized in terms of rights vested in persons.

We have emphasized that it is the *form* of the educational encounter – the social relations of education – that accounts for both its capacity to reproduce capitalist relations of production and its inability to promote domination and healthy personal development. The actual *content* of the curriculum has little role to play in this process. The contradictory location of the educational system can also be described in terms of its characteristic *form* of discourse, as opposed to the actual *content* of the curriculum. The form is that of the cultural structure of liberal discourse.

That liberal discourse has become the predominant cultural-structural form for the constitution of class and gender demands can certainly not be attributed to the educational system alone. Indeed, we have elsewhere argued that the hegemony of liberal discourse in class and gender struggles depended on an historically specific 'accord', arriving at different times in different countries. By an accord, we mean a mutually accepted joint redefinition and consequent reconstitution of political reality by antagonistic classes or class fragments. Through an accord, class interests are redefined. Class identities are respecified so as to produce a novel logic of social action. An accord is a reorganization of society on two levels: institutions and communicative tools of political discourse. On the institutional level, the accord results in the admission of a new set of organizational forms (associations, unions, commissions, electoral laws and practices, etc.) and corresponding to these a new specification of organizational legitimacy. On the communicative level, the accord results in the creation of new communicative tools which (a) provide a common framework for political discourse across contending groups, (b) express the moral legitimacy of the newly created institutional nexuses, (c) are admitted by speakers and hearers as intelligible and worthy of affirmation, and (d) are affirmed in all the major formal institutions of daily life (media, political speeches, educational institutions, churches, law). In short, it is the coming into being of a new set of 'rules of the game' of political discourse and struggle.

An accord is likely to set into motion a totally new logic of social action and class struggle. On the institutional level, the existence of new organizations implies a redefined distribution of political power and a consequently redefined constellation of viable political strategies available to social groups. The new set of tools of communicative discourse, endowed with a new effectiveness by the very institutional forms they express and legitimate, will tend to force out of the political arena older forms of discourse (in the case of the capital/labor accord, for instance, theological and socialist forms) and the organizations that support them. These new tools will in turn represent the only available means of political communication and, thus, will be the basis for any future expression and organization of political demands (until, of course, the accord is destroyed).

The accords giving rise to the current logic of class struggle in advanced capitalist countries occurred in the first decades of the twentieth century, and took distinct forms in each social formation concerned. In nearly all cases the working class was granted suffrage and the right to form workers' associations; in turn, élites have isolated and eliminated revolutionary socialist alternatives. The results were as varied as the conditions giving rise to the heightening of class confrontation. In Northern Europe, the smooth transition to social democracy resulted; in Germany, Italy, and Eastern Europe, the result was the total rupture of political life and the rise of fascism. In the United States, the Progressive Era witnessed the transition from *laissez-faire* to monopoly capitalism, the rise of 'safe' unionism and the squelching of hitherto growing socialist and populist movements.

Thus while the educational system cannot be cited as the source of the near universality of liberal discourse, it certainly has played a central role in its reproduction. Whatever the actual content of the political philosophy and social theory presented in schools, the educational system in the twentieth century surely has provided students with little facility in any but modes of discourse based on natural rights. This contradictory position of education explains its dual progressive/reproductive role (promoting equality, democracy, toleration, rationality, inalienable rights, on the one hand, while legitimating inequality, authoritarianism, fragmentation, prejudice, and submission on the other) and is, in part, a reflection of the stress in liberal discourse on procedure over substance. But it provides as well the tools by means of which it can be transformed into an instrument in the transition to socialism: the exploitation of the contradictions that have come to inhere in the tools of liberal discourse. The goals of progressive educational reform must be framed within the structural boundaries of liberal discourse, and can be simply expressed as the full democratization of education. These goals can be divided into two complementary projects: the democratization of the social relations of education, and the reformulation of the issue of democracy in the curriculum.

We have stressed in *Schooling in Capitalist America* that the transformation of the schools cannot proceed without parallel developments at the site of capitalist production. Demands for the democratization of the social relations of education therefore are likely to be effective only in the context of workers' demands for the democratization of the production process – in short, for the full development of workers' control. The first step in the democratization of education is a similar move toward teachers' and parents' control of the educational process. For teachers, as workers, will surely be involved in the movement for the democratization of economic life and parents, as community members, will similarly be involved in the extension of the powers of local community decision-making.

Beyond this, the philosophy of education must develop in the direction that personal development through schooling be geared toward rendering students capable of controlling their lives as citizens, family members, workers, and community members. In particular, the educational process must be structured so that students gradually come to control increasingly substantial spheres of their education as they move from early to later levels of schooling. Current theories of progressive education stress that students be given free rein to develop their individual personalities, to be self-motivated and self-actualizing. While the substance of such educational reforms must be conserved, they can be criticized in general for their failure to recognize the inherently *social* character of educational formation. As we emphasized in our book, there is no 'true self' to emerge prior to the concrete social interactions that individuals experience. This is not to say that individuals are infinitely malleable or that they should be subjected to a rigidly conformist schooling. Rather, it is to say that the ineLucibly social impact of education cannot be ignored.

The admirable quality of the self-development philosophy of education lies in the power it draws from embracing a central category of the discourse of rights: the right to freedom from unwarranted interference, of which John Stuart Mill was the most eloquent exponent. Its drawback, of being incurably a-social, is easily remedied by recourse to the communitarian emphasis on joint democratic control of conditions of social life by affected groups and individuals. No doubt there are formidable obstacles in the development of such a philosophy of educational structure and we are not personally equipped to meet this task. But it remains central to the growth of an effective movement toward socialist education.

Finally, progressive educators must exploit the internal contradictions of liberal discourse by developing curricula which dramatize the major oppositions inherent in the joint advocacy of rights vested in persons and property. Moreover, it must emphasize the subordination of property and gender rights to person rights in a just society. This of course does not preclude some emphasis on the proper role for property and gender rights as adjuncts and supports for rights vested in persons – for instance a woman's right to choose when to conceive and bear a child independent of the preference of the natural father, or an individual's rights to personal (not productive) property free from social interference.

Liberalism puts forth a promise it cannot make good. The promise it extends is that of democracy, equality, liberty, and personal fulfilment for all, within the context of capitalism. Unlike traditional theology's balm of beatific after-life, this promise is in the here and now and it is the codification of two centuries of struggles, ideals, and aspirations by oppressed groups in capitalist society. The emptiness of its promise must be exposed and this, indeed, has been the project of socialists over the years. Socialism, should it come to pass in the advanced capitalist countries, will however have little to do with the inevitable process of advancing forces of production bursting asunder their capitalist shackles. Rather, it will be the real fulfilment of the liberal promise, and with it the transformation of tools of communicative discourse of capitalism. Our arguments in this paper are no doubt sitting ducks for misinterpretation and calumny. Are we not justifying liberalism? Are we not advocating socialism as its logical culmination? No. We are arguing that liberal discourse is a fact not a defeat. It is a site of intervention and it embodies the emancipatory achievements of the popular classes. The logical culmination, if it have any, is its own demise. In what way depends on conscious choices of political actors. As soon as democracy shows a disposition . . . to become an instrument of the real interests of the people', as Rosa Luxembourg has noted, 'the democratic forms themselves are sacrificed by the bourgeoisie and their representatives'. Yet for all that, socialism remains the extension of democratic freedoms from civil and political life to economic life itself.

Notes and References

1 BOWLES, S. and GINTIS, H. (1976) *Schooling in Capitalist America* London, Routledge and Kegan Paul.
2 *ibid*. Chap. 11.
3 DEWEY, J. (1966) *Democracy and Education*, New York, The Free Press.
4 JENCKS, C., BARTLETT, S., CORCORAN, M., CROUSE, J., EAGLESFIELD, D., JACKSON, G., McLELLAND, K., MUESER, P., OLNECK, M., SCHWARTZ, J., WARD, S. and WILLIAMS, J. (1980) *Who Gets Ahead?* New York, Basic Books.
5 See especially BOWLES and GINTIS, *op. cit.*, Chap. 9 and 11 (note 1).
6 THE CARNEGIE COMMISSION ON HIGHER EDUCATION, (1973) *Priorities for Action*, New York, McGraw-Hill Book Company. KENISTON, K. AND THE CARNEGIE COUNCIL ON CHILDREN, (1977) *All Our Children*, New York, Harcourt, Brace, Jovanovich.
7 CALLAHAN, R. (1962) *Education and the Cult of Efficiency*, Chicago, University of Chicago Press.
8 THOMPSON, E.P. (1979) *The Poverty of Theory and other Essays*, London, Merlin Press.
9 The analysis of liberal discourse as the outcome of class struggles in the early stages of capitalist development is made in GINTIS, H. (1980) 'Theory, Practice, and the Tools of Communicative Discourse', *Socialist Review*, Spring.
10 This type of analysis of social discourse was first developed by the philosopher Ludwig Wittgenstein, and has never been adequately developed in social theory. See GINTIS, *op. cit.*, (note 9).

4　Do We Need a Theory of the State?

C.B. Macpherson

1 The Question Clarified

My question is not whether we need a theoretical understanding of the political process in modern states, but whether we need a theory of the state in the grand manner of the acknowledged 'great' theories, ranging in modern times from, say, Bodin and Hobbes to Hegel and the nineteenth century juristic theories of sovereignty, and on to the less 'great', but in intention equally grand, theories of Green and Bosanquet and such twentieth century thinkers as Barker and Lindsay and MacIver.

There is, I assume, no question that in order to understand the operation of contemporary states we need theories of the political process in our own liberal-democratic states (and, if we are to be comprehensively informed, in Communist and Third World states as well). [. . .]

My concern is whether we now need something more than theories of the political process. Do we need a theory of the state in the grand tradition? The hallmark of the grand theories is that they all tied the state back to supposed essentially human purposes and capacities, to a supposed essential nature of man. In doing so they were of course both descriptive and prescriptive or justificatory. They sought both to explain what the actual state was, and to show either that it was justified or necessary or that it ought to be and could be replaced by something else. But what I would emphasize is that they did relate the state normatively to supposed essentially human purposes. Do we again need such a theory of the state? To raise this question is of course to assume that we haven't got an adequate one now. I make that assumption, and will support it as I go on.

An answer to this question depends obviously on who 'we' are. I take 'us' to be those living in late twentieth-century liberal-democratic societies, and especially those of us whose vocation is the study of politics. Do we, as so defined, need a new theory of the state? I shall argue that some of us do and some of us don't.

We may, I think, divide this whole constituency into distinctively different parts.

Source: This is an abridged version of MACPHERSON, C.B. (1977) *European Journal of Sociology* (XVIII 2) pp. 223–44.

I suggest that a three-fold classification is appropriate for the purposes of our question.

1. In the first category I put those who on the whole accept and uphold the existing liberal-democratic society and state, with no more than marginal reservations or hopes that they can be made somewhat better, within the same framework, by for instance more informed citizen participation, or less or more welfare-state activity. This category includes the bulk of the contemporary empirical theorists and, at a different level, some normative theorists who may be called philosophic liberals.

2. The second category is those who accept and would promote the normative values that were read into the liberal-democratic society and state by J.S. Mill and the nineteenth and twentieth century idealist theorists, but who reject the present liberal-democratic society and state as having failed to live up to those values, or as being incapable of realizing them. This includes the bulk of contemporary social democrats and those socialists who do not accept the whole of the Marxian theory.

3. The third category is those who reject both the idealist normative theory and the present liberal-democratic society and state, and would replace both of them totally by Marxian theory and practice.

I would not claim that this classification is exhaustive. One might, for instance, make a separate category of those who take a philosophical anarchist position, who need at least a theory of the negative relation of the state of essential human purposes: they need a theory of the state in order to abolish the theory of the state. Nor would I claim that the lines between the three classes are entirely clear and sharp, but I think the classification makes some sense in the context of my question.

2 Negative and Positive Needs for a Theory

I shall now argue that those in the first category do *not* need a grand theory of the state, and that those in the second and third categories *do* need one.

1. The first category, as noted, includes both most of the current empirical theorists and some normative liberal theorists. Their needs may be considered separately.

(a) The empirical theorists generally claim to have abstained from any value judgment about the processes they are analysing. But their theories usually have strong commendatory overtones. If they had really avoided all value judgment they would not only not need a grand theory of the state: they would be incapable of one, for such a theory is always normative as well as explanatory. But since a value judgment is at least implicit in their theories, one might argue that they do need a theory of the state after all: that they need to make explicit and to develop the values that underlie their theorizing (which would enlarge their empirical theory to the dimensions of a theory of the state).

But they cannot afford to do this. Having rejected the 'classical' liberal-democratic model of John Stuart Mill and Green and their twentieth century followers, with its humanistic striving – rejected it as unrealistic (that is, as beyond the capacities of the average twentieth century citizen) – the empirical theorists cannot afford a theory which would tie the state back to some supposed essential nature of man. For to do so would be to reveal that they have reverted to a Benthamist or even Hobbesian model of man as possessive individualist. They have, it is true, come some distance from the Hobbes-Bentham model of society as a series of freely competitive market relations. They have been able to adjust their model of society to some of the realities of managed capitalism. But even managed capitalism presupposes maximizing market man, and they have accepted, even while they have refined, that concept of man. That concept of man has, I believe, become increasingly morally unacceptable in the late twentieth century. Thus for the empirical theorists to go on to a theory of the state would be to expose the inadequacy of their basic assumptions. It would endanger their position as the spokesmen for liberal democracy, since their model of man and society is becoming morally repugnant to increasing numbers of people within the liberal democracies, as well as in the world at large. I conclude that the empirical theorists do not need, at least in the sense that they cannot afford, a theory of the state.

(b) What of the contemporary normative theorists, the philosophers who have concerned themselves with the political, of whom the most influential and widely discussed at present are Rawls and Nozick?[1] They also are working with a market model of man and society. There is of course a sharp difference between them: Rawls is happy with the welfare state encroachments on unalloyed capitalism and can even contemplate their extension, whereas Nozick argues for a return to the minimal state. But they both endorse the fundamental relations of capitalist market society and its property institutions. And since they assume maximizing market man as the norm, they need not go behind that to inquire into the nature or potential of man and to relate that to the state. They need not be concerned with any necessary or historical relation of the state to society or to supposed essentially human purposes or capacities. They do not need a theory of the state, but only a theory of distributive justice, i.e. of the just distribution of 'primary goods' (Rawls) or of 'holdings' (Nozick), or a theory of liberty (i.e. of the allowable or morally desirable amount and kind of individual liberty). The state can be treated as simply an agent which does or should subserve the principles of justice or liberty which the theorist argues for.

It thus appears that the philosophic liberals, like the empirical theorists, do not need a theory of the state. [. . .]

2. Turning to my second category – those who accept the humanistic values read into liberal democracy by Mill and the idealists, but who reject present liberal democracy as having failed to realize those values – it can readily be seen that they do need a theory of the state. For, believing as they do that the state should embody certain moral values which they find not now realized by liberal-democratic states, they are committed to a theory at once normative and explanatory, i.e. to a theory in the grand tradition which relates the state to human needs, capacities, and potentialities. It follows that they need a new theory of the state in the measure that the theory they have inherited from humanist liberals and idealists (ranging from Mill and Green to Barker, Lindsay, MacIver, etc.) is inadequate.

That the inherited theory is seriously inadequate is sufficiently evident from the ease with which it was eclipsed in mid-twentieth century by the empiricists' theories. Its eclipse was due chiefly to the fact that the explanatory or descriptive side of the twentieth century traditional theories was demonstrably inaccurate. Citizens of the Western democracies did not behave like the rational, informed, and even public-spirited citizens postulated by the traditional theory.

The traditional theorists might have defended their position by pointing out that they were not trying to describe and reduce to operative principles the political process in those contemporary states commonly called democracies, but were trying to deduce the essential requirements of democracy from their vision of human needs and capacities. This gave them the concept of democracy as a kind of society and political system which would provide the equal possibility of self-development by all. To complete that defence it would only be necessary to argue, as they did, that people are capable of a degree of rational and moral self-development which would enable them to live in a fully democratic society and to participate actively in a fully democratic state.

But such a two-fold defence could not save their position. For while they were indeed seeking to show 'the essentials of democracy' rather than merely to describe existing democratic institutions, they did present the existing liberal democracies as having met the essential requirements in substantial degree. They did so, it may be surmised, because they were all more or less explicitly concerned to build a case for existing democracies *vs* existing or threatened dictatorships. So they had to argue that the existing Western democracies had the root of the matter in them. To do this they had to examine the existing system of parties, pressure groups and public opinion formation, and argue that it did, however roughly, come up to the essential requirements. So they had to argue not merely that people were capable of the required degree of rational and moral self-development but that they had already reached it or nearly reached it.

They thus came up with a pluralist theory of society and of the democratic state. The democratic state was an arrangement by which rational, well-intentioned citizens, who indeed had a wide variety of different interests but had also a sense of a common interest or even a 'general will'[2] could and did adjust their differences in an active, rational, give-and-take of parties and interest groups and the free press. The empirical theorists were able to show that most citizens of liberal-democratic states were far from being such active rational participants, and were thus able virtually to demolish the traditional theory.

Perhaps the fundamental weakness of the traditional theorists was that they had unconsciously adopted the notion of the democratic process as a competitive market. They did not make the market analogy explicitly, as the empirical theorists were to do. That analogy implies a society made up of narrowly self-interested maximizing individuals and this was incompatible with the traditional theorists' image of man as a moral being whose essence was to be realized only in the self-development of all his human capacities. But their model of a plural society was a market model.

This in itself could not have led to their eclipse by the empirical theories, for the latter were openly based on the market analogy. But it has meant that late twentieth century liberal attempts to revive the traditional theory have run aground. For they have adhered to the pluralist model, while the society for which they are prescribing has become increasingly less plural. As I shall argue,[3] late capitalist society does still exhibit some measure of pluralism, but its amount has shrunk and its character has changed as the corporate-managed sector and the state-operated sector of the economy have encroached on and diminished the competitive market sector.

I conclude that contemporary theorists in my second category do need a new theory of the state.

3. Turning finally to those in my third category, I think it is clear that they also need to develop a theory of the state. Marx's theory was certainly normative as well as analytical, and the role of the state was crucial to his whole theory, yet he did not provide more than fragments of a theory of the state. Lenin did rather more, but however appropriate his conclusions were when he wrote they are not adequate for the late twentieth century. It follows that contemporary Marxists do need a new or more developed theory of the state than they have inherited. And Marxist scholars in the West have in the last decade become very much aware of this and have plunged vigorously into the effort to provide it. [...]

A grand theory of the state, I have said, has to tie the state back to the supposed nature and purpose and capacities of man. At the same time it has to take account of the underlying nature of the society in which that state operates. The contemporary Marxist theorists do do both, though with varying emphasis on the two aspects. Indeed much of the dispute amongst them may be reduced to that difference of emphasis, some of them building on Marx the humanist and some on Marx the analyst of capitalist society. The two can be, and to a limited extent have been, drawn together by the recognition, growing since the publication of Marx's *Grundrisse*, that there is no dichotomy between Marx the humanist and Marx the analyst of capitalism. But there are still deep divisions on how or whether Marx's own position on the role of the state in capitalist society, which he never fully spelled out, can be applied to the relation between state and capital in 'late' or 'advanced' capitalism.[4]

I cannot attempt here either to summarize this body of work or to assess it. But I think it is worth asking its relevance to those who are in my second category: what if anything can be learned from it by those who do not accept, or do not fully accept, the classical Marxian position, and yet do not accept the existing liberal-democratic society and state as morally adequate? I find the question worth asking because I place myself in category 2, and because I believe that some contemporary liberal theorists are inclined to move from category 1 to 2. So I shall in the rest of this paper preach to them. A preacher must have a message. My message is, learn from those in category 3.

3 Contemporary Marxist Lessons for Liberal-Democratic Theory

I think there is a lot to learn from them. For they do see more clearly than most others that what has to be examined is the relation of the state to *bourgeois* society, and they are examining it in depth. In this they are repairing a great defect of the twentieth century traditional liberal theory, which accepted bourgeois society but did not examine the implications of that acceptance.

One characteristic of the grand tradition, if we take it from the seventeenth to the early twentieth century, is its move from a materialist to an idealist view of man and society. One cannot say that that move is the measure or the cause of the twentieth century eclipse of the grand tradition: Hegel's theory of the state is, after all, rather more penetrating than Locke's or Bentham's, for Hegel knew that he was talking about the state in bourgeois society. But one can say that the later idealists increasingly departed from that insight, that they played down or virtually dismissed, or at any rate could not cope with, the fact that it was the bourgeois state, or the state in bourgeois society, that had to be dealt with. They sought to rise above that specific society, not by examining any inherent momentum in it which might be transforming it or leading to its supersession, but on the contrary by reaching for an archetype of all human society.

So they were led to what I have called a bow-and-arrow theory.[5] This is rather like the economic theory which, seeking a similar level of generality, defines 'capital' so broadly as to cover both modern capital and the primitive hunter's bow and arrow. Such a concept of capital is formally intelligible: the bow and arrow and the capital of a modern corporation are both the outcome of their owner's abstinence from immediate consumption of some of what they produce or collect, or, if you like, are both the product of their investment decisions. But such a broad concept misses the difference between the two, a difference not just in degree but in kind, and so obscures some essentials of modern capital.

Here, as in theories of the state, the judgment of what are the essentials – the judgment whether the common features are more important or less important than the specific features – is a value judgment (though the theorists often fail to see that it is). For on this choice depends the extent to which the resulting theory will implicitly justify or criticize the specific modern phenomena. The bow and arrow gives you abstinence as the source of capital and so makes modern capital a wholly admirable thing. Similarly with the state. The common feature may be seen as provision for a human desire for the good life or the full life, or for community: in that case the state, any state, is a wholly admirable thing. Or the common feature may be seen as the need for an authority able to hold in check the contentious nature of man: in that case, the state, any state, is still an admirable thing.

It is true that the twentieth century traditional theorists for the most part offered a theory of the liberal-democratic state rather than a theory of the state as such. But they are still caught up in bow-and-arrow thinking insofar as their argument moves from 'the good state' to the liberal-democratic state, justifying the latter as the best or the nearest possible approach to the former.

In any case the twentieth century traditional theorists have not given much attention to the specific nature of the state in capitalist society. It was easy for then to abstract from the capitalist nature of their society, since the one theory which made that central – i.e., Marxist theory – was, through most of the twentieth century, unsatisfactory in several ways. It was associated with dictatorships. It was doctrinaire. And it took so little account of twentieth century changes in the nature of capitalism that it could readily be dismissed as less realistic than a refined pluralism which talked of 'post-industrial society', countervailing powers, and so on. This refined pluralism is not entirely wrong, but it does distract attention from the fact that the motor of our system is still capital accumulation (as should be evident from a glance at any financial paper). And the presumption must surely be that this is bound to have a lot to do with the nature of the state.

The new generation of Marxist scholars in the West has largely overcome the defects just mentioned. Their work is not doctrinaire, and it is mainly concerned with the changed and changing nature of capitalism in the late twenteith century. They are, that is to say, examining the necessary and possible relation of the liberal-democratic state to contemporary capitalist society, which has changed in significant ways since Marx, and since Lenin.

It seems to me that that relation is crucially important to those of us who want to preserve some liberal-democratic values. And I do not see anyone other than the contemporary Marxist scholars examining it in any depth. That is I think reason enough for us to try to learn from them. Let me draw attention to some of their main theses, and suggest some implications for liberal democracy.

1. They assume, with Marx, (a) that the human essence is to be realized fully only in free, conscious, creative activity; (b) that human beings have a greater capacity for this than has ever hitherto been allowed to develop; and (c) that a capitalist society denies this essential humanity to most of its inhabitants, in that it reduces human capacities to a commodity which, even when it fetches its exchange value in a free competitive market, receives less than it adds to the value of the product, thus increasing the mass of capital, and capital's ability to dominate those whose labour it buys.

[. . .]

The present Marxist theorists of the state start from Marx's ontological and ethical position, and go on to consider where the state fits in to this depiction of capitalism and, given that, what are the prospects that late capitalism (which is supported, but also encroached on, by the state) may be transcended, as Marx believed capitalism would be. In pursuing this inquiry they are naturally concerned mainly with the analysis of late capitalism, taking as given the ethical dimension of the problem. Because of that concern, their work may not appear to be in the grand tradition of theories of the state – may appear, that is to say, not to be relating the state to a concept of essentially human needs and capacities. But this is an appearance only. Their work, no less than Marx's, is designed to serve the realization of the supposed essential nature of the human species. So if, in my ensuing description of some of their leading arguments, I appear to move out of the realm of philosophy and political theory into that of political economy this must not be taken to derogate from their role in the grand tradition.

2. It is assumed that an indispensable job of the state in capitalist society is to maintain the conditions for capitalist enterprise and capital accumulation. This, however, does not imply that the state is the lackey or the junior partner of the

capitalists. Indeed, for reasons that will be mentioned,[6] the state is seen to have been moving away from being a mere superstructure and to have attained a significant degree of autonomy. The point is rather that, given a state's commitment to capitalist enterprise as the mainspring of the economy, the holders of state office must in their own interest maintain and support the accumulation process because the state's revenue, and hence the power of the state's officers, depends on it. Hence in a democratic capitalist society, although the electorate determines who shall hold office as the government, governments are not free to make what use they might like of their constitutional power. The government must stay within the limits imposed by the requirements of the accumulation process, limitations generally imposed on social-democratic governments through the mediation of the permanent bureaucracy and sometimes of the military.

3. The need to promote accumulation has, with the maturation of late capitalism required the state to take on a new range of functions, the performance of which has raised new problems. The change has been from the minimal support provided by the classical liberal state (law and order, contract definition and enforcement, and some material infrastructure – roads, canals, ports, etc.), to what might be called maximal support.

Five areas of new or greatly increased support may be identified, all apparently necessary: (a) the whole apparatus of the welfare state, which, in providing cushions against unemployment and against the costs of sickness, old age, and reproduction of the labor force, takes some of the burden that otherwise would have to be met by capital, or if not so met, would endanger public order; (b) the Keynesian monetary and fiscal management of the economy, designed to prevent wide swings and to maintain a high level of employment; (c) greatly increased infrastructure support, e.g. in technical and higher education, urban transportation systems, urban and regional development schemes, public housing, energy plants, and direct and indirect state engagement in technological research and development; (d) measures to prevent or reduce the damaging material side-effects of particular capitals' search for profits, e.g., measures against pollution and destruction of natural resources. These, like the welfare-state measures (which are designed to prevent or reduce the damaging human side-effects of particular capitals' operations) are increasingly required in the interests of capital in general, but do limit the profits of some particular capitals; (e) a large new apparatus of state-imposed marketing boards, price-support schemes, wage arbitration procedures, etc., designed to stabilize markets in commodities and labour and capital.

It is held that while all those new supports are required, they also in some measure undermine when they are intended to support. The extent to which, and the way in which, each does so is different.

The first does not directly undermine it, but since it has to be financed out of the profits of capital, it reduces accumulation (or at least appears to particular capitals to reduce it, though it does so only in comparison with a wage-capital relation that is now insupportable). And it may be said to reduce it by preventing capital driving such a hard wage bargain as it could otherwise do. The second appears to reduce it by limiting the very swings on which capital had relied to redress in the downswings the gains made by labour in the upswings. This reduction, like the first or even more so, is partly illusory: it leaves out of the calculation the loss of accumulation in prolonged periods of depression. The third, like the first, is very costly, and the cost must be met out of the profits of capital. This is not all loss to capital, since some of these state activities, notably technical education and research and development, do increase the productivity of private capitals. But the balance-sheet is hard to draw. The fourth is a clear interference with the freedom of particular capitals. The fifth is perhaps the most serious, in that it replaces freely-made market decisions by political decisions. Particular capitals (and particular segments of organized labour) are compelled to accommodate their conflicting private interests to public decisions. This erodes the ability of capital to make the most of itself, and reduces its accumulative freedom.

[...] Between them these activities may undermine the accumulation of capital in general: by enlarging the public sector, they take an increasing proportion of the labour force and the capital flow out of the operation of the market, and so may reduce the scope of capital accumulation. But this need not amount to a net reduction in private accumulation. It will not do so insofar as the state is thereby taking over unprofitable but necessary operations and/or is absorbing the cost of looking after that part of the labour-force which technological change has made redundant.

4. The late capitalist economy is seen as consisting of three sectors: (a) the corporate oligopolistic sector, the firms in which are largely able to set their own prices and thus can both invest heavily in technological advances and afford high wages, so that the labour force in this sector is relatively advantaged; (b) the remaining competitive private sector of smaller firms, unable to afford either, so that they can neither accumulate through technological investment nor provide secure wages; which leaves its labour force relatively disadvantaged; and (c) the public sector, the labour force in which – blue and white collar and managerial – has its compensation set by political rather than market bargaining, and which is consequently relatively advantaged: if forty per cent of the whole labour force is employed in the public sector, so is roughly forty per cent of the whole electorate.

5. The combined effect of the increase in the role of the state, and the fragmentation of labour and capital into the three sectors, has been a considerable alteration in the classic capitalist relations of production and the relation of capital to state. The economy has become politicized, reverting in this respect to the pre-capitalist pattern. Yet the state now relies, for its own power, on maintaining capitalist accumulation. And since the state is now democratic it faces two new difficulties: it must reconcile the requirements of accumulation with the demands of the electorate, and it must extract an increasing revenue from capital to finance its support of capital and its response to the electorate.

Consideration of these difficulties has led outstanding contemporary Marxist scholars to develop theories of crisis. Habermas writes of the need for the accumulation-supporting state to legitimate itself to the electorate: this is the 'legitimation crisis'. O'Connor finds a contradiction between the state's need for expanded revenues and the maintenance of capital accumulation: this is 'the fiscal crisis of the state'.

'Crisis' suggests either the impending breakdown of capitalism or, if capitalism is to survive, the breakdown of democracy. Either of these is evidently now possible, but I shall suggest not necessary. Certainly the late capitalist state has a legitimation problem which the earlier capitalist state did not have. Earlier, when the market, not the state, was and was seen to be responsible for the economy and all the recurrently damaging effects of depressions, and when the market allocation of rewards was thought to be either fair or inevitable, the state had no great difficulty about legitimating its existence and its performance of its minimal functions. But now that the state takes, and is seen to take, heavy responsibility for the economy and its side-effects, the state has a serious legitimation problem. And as the state takes on more (and more expensive) support functions, it does run into a series of fiscal crises which could lead to the breakdown either of democracy or of capitalism. The outcome of the legitimation and fiscal crises is indeterminate, since it depends not on objective forces alone but also on conscious political action.

[...]

4 Ways Ahead?

I want now to argue first, that as a result of the changes set out in 3 and 4 above, the nature of the legitimation problem has already been altered; second, that the same changes have set up a new kind of pluralism, a pluralism in reverse; third, that the possibility of saving any liberal democracy depends on a change of consciousness, which depends on a public awareness of the real nature of the new pluralism; and fourth, that this sets an agenda for a useful theory of the state in the late twentieth century.

1. The legitimation problem has changed. For the advanced capitalist state can fairly easily legitimate itself to three very large sections of the public.

(i) The whole personnel of the public sector, who owe their relative job security and relatively higher wages to the state. It is true that increasing numbers of public employees, both blue and white collar, have recently unionized (and some have become quite militant) in order to protect their position against government retrenchment policies, from which they would otherwise be among the first to suffer. But they are still more secure and better paid than employees in the competitive private sector.

(ii) The recipients of welfare-state benefits. These also, especially those most in need, are taking to organizing, in welfare rights groups, tenants' organizations, and community coalitions of various sorts, to secure the benefits that are theirs on paper or to demand further benefits. This makes them seem adversaries of the state. But they are still clients, and the more they win the more dependent they are.

This is not to say that they are inert dependants of the state. No one would doubt that the rise of the elaborate welfare-state in all the Western democracies was due to the political strength of organized labour, whether expressed in trade union pressure on established parties or in the rise to power of social-democratic and labour parties. But to say that it was their power which created the welfare-state, and which requires its continuance, is not to deny that they, as well as the unorganized and redundant labour force, all of whom are its beneficiaries, are now dependent on the state for the continuance of their benefits. The relation is reciprocal: they created the welfare-state, but now they are its creature.

They still indeed have the potential of turning out a government which fails to give them what they have come to count on, but since the failure will have been due to the fiscal crisis of the state this will not improve their position as long as they accept the need for private capital accumulation. So, to the extent that they are kept by the state they will keep the state.

(iii) The strongly-organized part of the labour force in the private sector. They can see quite well that they owe their relatively advantaged position to the state's support and subsidization of their employers' operations, and they consequently can readily accept the legitimacy of the state which so serves them.

Against this it may be argued that they, along with the employees of the public sector, are the first to bear the brunt of the now apparently endemic wage and price controls, and that they have shown by their strenuous opposition to such devices no great affection for the state which imposes them. It must be granted that in the measure that such controls are permanent the state will have more difficulty in legitimating itself to them. But realistic trade unionists in the advantaged sectors can see that in spite of this their gain from the continuing state support and subsidization of their employers outweighs their loss from what they hope will be temporary wage controls.

These three categories together make up a substantial majority of the electorate. As long as the state can find the money, it will have no great difficulty legitimating itself to them.

(iv) But what about the holders and operators of capital? Is not the real crisis of legitimation, now, whether the state can legitimate itself to them, rather than to the electorate? To speak of this as a problem of legitimation is to stretch the concept of legitimation considerably beyond its original and its current Marxist usage. There, it has been a matter of the state, or of a virtual merger of state and corporate capital (which merger is seen as parasitic on the body politic), having to legitimate itself to the body politic by mystifying its true nature.

I do not mean to deny the realism of this position. To have seen the problem of legitimation in this way was a substantial step forward. But I suggest that the problem I have put is also a problem of legitimation. For the state, whether or not it is seen as jointly parasitic with capital, is still sufficiently different from corporate capital to have to justify its activities to the latter. If the state cannot do so, capital can go on strike: can make impossible, or severely reduce, the state's operation of all the mechanisms which now legitimate the state to (i), (ii) and (iii), and can thus accentuate the legitimation problem. This seems to me to be the central problem of the advanced capitalist state. But I think it not insoluble.

The state may be able to legitimate itself to (iv) in either or both of two ways. (a) By persuading particular capitals that the state's support of the interests of capital in general is more to their long-term benefit than would be the state's leaving particular capitals to their own devices. [. . .] (b) By making each of the particular capitals (and the particular segments of organized labour) conscious, if they were not already sufficiently conscious, that each of them, separately (not firm by firm, but industry by industry) owes whatever prosperity it has to the state's continuing subsidization and regulation. In all those industries in which the state has become an indispensable subsidizer (which includes virtually the whole of the big corporate sector), the state has considerable leverage: it can hold them separately to ransom by threatening to reduce or withdraw its support. [. . .]

   2. This treating of particular capitals separately is, I suggest, the heart of the new pluralism of the late twentieth century. The new pluralism both is narrower than the received pluralist model, and embodies a reverse pluralism. Its difference from the presently received pluralist model is evident. It is not the give-and-take between the government and a myriad of voluntary associations and interest groups, which was supposed to give every alert citizen, ranged in one or more of those associations, a fair share of influence on government decisions. The received model was, indeed, never entirely realistic. For, while treating the democratic political process as something like a market (which it was), it abstracted too far from the capitalist nature of the society. It did not recognize that the requirements of capital accumulation set limits to, and set the direction of, the state's response to the plural pressures. And it was inclined to treat all pressures as eliciting from a neutral state responses proportional to their size. But at least the received pluralist theory was, for the era of full market competition, fairly accurate in one respect: the state acted upon pressures, but did not itself do much to interfere with those pressures.

   This, I suggest, is what is now changing. The pressures which now operate effectively on the state are those of particular organized capitals (and particular segments of the organized labour force) each of which depends upon the state for the security and preferential treatment it enjoys. This is what has given the state such relative autonomy from capital in general as it now has. Pluralism, in this respect, has gone into reverse: the state now pluralizes capital, by its ability to reduce or withhold favours to separate particular capitals.

   There is indeed some measure also of what might be called reverse-reverse pluralism. Multi-national corporations can play off particular national states against each other for favours, because of their ability to move their capitals. And in federal nation-states, capitals can play off different levels of the state, i.e. of governments and bureaucracies. But the national state's ability to pluralize capital is still significant.

   It is true that the whole range of interest groups celebrated by the received pluralist theories is still alive, and that it comprises not only corporate producers' interest groups and various levels and segments of organized labour, but also many others – professional groups, women, ethnic minorities, scientists, banks, universities, the performing arts, even publishers, not to mention all the ethical groups concerned with such issues as abortion, capital punishment, marijuana, and privacy. They all engage in lobbying. Their voices are heard, but are they heeded? It is a reasonable presumption that all of the demands of these other interest groups which would cost money will get increasingly short shrift as the fiscal difficulties of the state increase. The interest groups that will remain at all effective will be those organizations of particular capitals (and the parallel labour groups) who can show that the

state's continuing support of them is essential to the maintenance of the capitalist economy. And these are the ones that the state can separately hold to ransom. The undoubted fact of increasing concentration of capitals in particular industries does not affect this: the greater the concentration in any one industry – steel, textiles, wheat, oil, cement, communications – the stronger their lobbies become, but the more they are dependent on the state's favors, and the more they can be held in line.
[...]

There is a historical parallel to this state pluralization of capital. Just as the capitalist state from the beginning expropriated the communal life of earlier society, atomized it, absorbed the powers people had exercised together, and used those powers to rule the people in the interests of capital in general[7]; so now, in advanced capitalism, the state has to add a parallel operation – it absorbs from particular capitals some of their powers (i.e., some of their revenues, and hence of their ability to accumulate) and uses that power, still in the interests of capital in general, to make particular capitals dependent on the state.

It is probable that this reverse pluralism, and the relative autonomy of the state, will increase as the state gets more deeply involved in the management of the economy, the stabilization of markets, and the subsidization of production and prices. And the relative autonomy of the state from capital will also be aided as the public sector expands and moves more of the whole labour force and capital force from market determination to political determination.

There are, however, clear limits to any such increase in relative autonomy, *as long as the electorate continues to support, i.e. not to reject, capitalism*. So long as capitalism is thus maintained, the state is still dependent on the accumulation of private capital: even with the enlarged public sector, the state must still operate within the limits of maintaining capital accumulation in general, however skilful it may be in manoeuvering between particular capitals. The state in a capitalist society cannot be a neutral uncle: it must serve the interests of capital.

3. What becomes of the relative autonomy, how it will be used, depends now, I suggest, on whether, or how rapidly, the public becomes conscious of the real nature of advanced capitalism and is moved to political action to alter it. The relative autonomy of the state, or the reverse pluralism, will not be the spark of any such new consciousness: the spark can only be an awareness of the incompetence of advanced capitalism and of the state which supports and tries to manage it: the relative autonomy of the state is merely the conduit in which the spark may ignite.

There are already some indications of such a new awareness. There is a growing disbelief in technology as the cure-all, in view of the damaging uses to which managed capitalism puts it (pollution and ecological destruction). There is a growing restiveness within the labour force over its subordination to organization and technology (wildcat strikes and shop-steward militancy). And as the state runs into deepening fiscal difficulties, there is likely to be increasing restiveness among some of those sections of the public who were said earlier (above, pp. 70–1) to be fairly easily persuaded of the legitimacy of the state as long as the money held out, i.e. (i) workers in the public sector, as expenditures on hospitals, schools, etc., are cut back, so reducing or cancelling their relative job security, and (ii) some of the recipients of welfare-state benefits, e.g. the unemployed, as budgeting provision for them is reduced.

Such disenchantments with the capitalist state are important, for the maintenance of capitalism requires not only all the legal and material supports which the state now supplies, but also a general acceptance of the rightness of the system, or at least a belief that there is no acceptable alternative. In the earlier days of capitalism, *competition* was presented as 'the natural system of liberty', beneficial to all. In advanced capitalism, *organization* takes the place of competition as the universal benefactor: the 'post-industrial', technological, managed society is presented as the solution to all problems and contradictions.[8] In the measure that this belief in organization crumbles, there opens up a possibility that political action can put human purposes above capital purposes.

This is indeed no more than a possibility. The belief, reinforced as it is by the ubiquitous presence of the corporate sector in our channels of political socialization, may not crumble. And the inherent tendency of the Western party system to obfuscate basic issues[9] works to prevent a public consciousness of the real nature of the political economy of capitalism. But there is at least the possibility that reality will break through.

4. It is here that a realistic and normative theory of the state can contribute, by delineating both (i) the necessary and necessarily changing relation of the state to capitalist society, and (ii) the limits of the possible relation of the capitalist society and state to essential human needs and capacities. The contemporary Marxist theorists are doing a good job on (i), but in most cases to the relative neglect of (ii).

To reinstate the tradition of grand theories of the state, further work on (ii) is now needed. The theory of the state does have to come back from political economy to political philosophy, though it can only come back effectively in the measure that it has probed political economy. It also needs more empirical and theoretical work on human needs, wants and capacities,[10] and a full re-assessment of the behaviouralists' findings about the present processes of political socialization from childhood through adulthood.[11]

[...]

Notes and References

1 RAWLS, J. (1972) *A Theory of Justice* Oxford, Clarendon Press. NOZICK, R. (1974) *Anarchy, State and Utopia* Oxford, Basil Blackwell.
2 MACIVER, R.M. (1926) *The Modern State* Oxford, Oxford University Press, p. 342.
3 See below, pp. 72–3.
4 E.g. the controversy between Miliband R. and Poulantzas, N. and other controversies in the *New Left Review*, 92 and 98, e.g. GOUGH, I. (1975) and FINE, B. and HARRIS, L. (1976).
5 Cf. MACPHERSON, C.B. (1970) 'Bow and Arrow Power', *The Nation* 19 January.
6 See below, pp. 71–3.
7 Cf. WOLFE, A. (1974) 'New Directions in the Marxist Theory of Politics' *Politics and Society*, pp. 145 sqq.
8 Cf. MANDEL, E. (1975) 'Belief in the omnipotence of technology is the specific form of bourgeois ideology in late capitalism' in *Late Capitalism* Schocken, New Left Books, p. 501.
9 Cf. MACPHERSON, C.B. (1977) *The Life and Times of Liberal Democracy* Oxford, Oxford University Press, chap. III, sect. 3.

10 Cf. essays by various authors in FITZGERALD, R. (Ed) (1977) *Human Needs and Politics*, New York, Pergamon.
11 A striking beginning has been made in Wolfe's article, cited above, Cf. WOLFE, A. *The Limits of Legitimacy* (1977) Boston, Beacon.

5 Theses on the Theory of the State

Claus Offe and Volker Ronge

Although important Marxist contributions to the long neglected problem of the state have recently begun to appear, these have often failed to keep pace with the increasing dislocation and crisis of the capitalist state itself.[1] While Miliband's study has taken into account changes in the nature of the ruling class, the absence of a theoretical approach to the social function and organization of the state limits his work to a redirection of the notion of a 'plurality of elites' into a theory of the influence of the ruling class. At the same time, Nicos Poulantzas' notion of the state as an autonomous structure, paralleling the structure of the dominant class, is impaired by structuralist blinders to the extent that it fails to take into consideration either the historical character of the state as a changing entity, or its concrete empirical character within the social totality.

In contrast to these approaches, Claus Offe, whose work has received less attention in the US, has consistently attempted to relate analytical categories of the structure and function of the state to historical changes in the nature of advanced capitalist society, while paying close attention to the empirical characteristics of state activity. His essays have therefore exhibited remarkable development as well as sophistication, while maintaining a close relationship to concrete political changes. In his 1972 book, Strukturprobleme des kapitalistischen Staates *(Structural Problems of the Capitalist State), Offe argued, in explicit contrast to political theories that maintained that the state had produced a crisis-free stabilization and integration of advanced capitalist society, that precisely the expanded function of the state was itself the source of dysfunction and crisis. If the efforts of the state to 'repoliticize' sectors of the private economic sphere had reduced the danger of economic crises injurious to the system, they also result in a rupture between sectors of society 'controlled administratively' and those dominated by the realization of value, thereby producing structural contradictions between stabilizing mechanisms and economic accumulation, ultimately leading to fiscal crises and political and social conflict over state policy. More recently Jürgen Habermas has integrated many of these insights into his* Legitimation Crisis, *although explicitly rejecting the theory of potential political and social conflict at that level.[2]*

In his more recent work Offe has expanded these insights through valuable empirical research into specific aspects of state policy and activity.[3] Despite their tentative character

Source: OFFE, C. and RONGE, V. (1975) *New German Critique* 6 pp. 137–47.

as hypotheses for discussion, these 'Theses on the Theory of the State', reflect the results of this research and represent an important theoretical development. In these notes Offe and Ronge point toward the emergence of a new strategy of capitalist state policy. With the fiscal crisis of the state (O'Connor) and the failure of 'welfare state' policies of subsidizing non-exchange value producing sectors of the economy, the state is now increasingly taking on the function of creating the conditions under which values (especially labor power) can regain their function as commodities. This 'administrative recommodification' consists of policies which do not 'support' or 'ignore' specific sectors of the economy which have ceased to earn value as commodities, but instead seek to restore them to that function. These attempts to stabilize and universalize the commodity form and exchange process by political and administrative means, leads, according to the authors, to a number of specific structural contradictions of state capitalist societies which in turn may become the focus of increased social conflict and political struggle.

The Editors, New German Critique

The following notes give a brief outline of some of the theoretically relevant findings which the authors have made in two empirical studies of reformist state policies in West Germany. These studies were concerned with the reform of vocational training and with a new programmatic approach to research and development policies. We believe that such case studies of certain state policies in specific policy areas are necessary to gain both theoretical understanding and political perspectives which cannot be gained either through deductive reasoning or immediate experience. For the sake of convenience, the organization of the argument is divided into eight points. These remarks are intended to provoke discussion and debate and are, of course, tentative in nature.

1. In Marxist theories of the state, there is a cleavage between two approaches. One approach suggests that there is a particular *instrumental* relationship between the *ruling class* (capital as a whole) on the one side and the state apparatus on the other side. The state thus becomes an instrument for promoting the common interests of the ruling class. We believe that this view is gravely misleading – including the version that is offered in the doctrine of 'state monopoly capitalism' with its stereotyped proposition of a 'merger of the monopolies and the state apparatus'. The alternative view is that the state does not patronize certain interests, and is not allied with certain classes. Rather, what the state protects and sanctions is a set of *rules* and *social relationships* which are presupposed by the class rule of the capitalist class. The state does not defend the interests of one class, but the *common* interest of all members of a *capitalist class society*.

2. The concept of the *capitalist state* describes an institutional form of political power which contains the following four major elements:

(a) Political power is prohibited from organizing production according to its own political criteria; property is *private* (be it property in labor power or property in means of production). Hence, it is not from political power, but from private freedom that decisions over the use of the means of production emerge.

(b) Political power depends indirectly – through the mechanisms of taxation and dependence on the capital market – on the volume of private accumulation.

The occupant of a power position in a capitalist state is in fact powerless *unless* the volume of the accumulation process allows that individual to derive the material resources (through taxation) necessary to promote any political ends.

(c) Since the state *depends* on a process of accumulation which is beyond its power to *organize*, every occupant of state power is basically interested in promoting those conditions most conducive to accumulation. This interest does not result from alliance of a particular government with particular classes also interested in accumulation, nor does it result from any political power of the capitalist class which 'puts pressure' on the incumbents of state power to pursue its class interest. Rather, it does result from an *institutional self-interest* of the state which is conditioned by the fact that the state is *denied* the power to control the flow of those resources which are indispensable for the *use* of state power. The agents of accumulation are not interested in 'using' the power of the state, but the state must be interested – for the sake of its own power – in guaranteeing and safeguarding a 'healthy' accumulation process upon which it depends.

(d) In democratic political regimes, any political group or party can win control over institutional state power only to the extent that it wins sufficient electoral support in general elections. This mechanism plays a key role in disguising the fact that the material resources of state power, and the ways in which these are used, depends upon the revenues derived from the accumulation process, and not upon the preferences of the general electorate. There is a dual determination of political power in the capitalist state: by its institutional *form* access to political power is determined through the rules of democratic and representative government, by its material *content*, the use of political power is controlled by the course and the further requirements of the accumulation process.

3. Is there any method by which these divergent constitutional requirements of the capitalist state can be reconciled through the policies of a particular government? Yes, there is *one*. If the conditions can be created through which *every* citizen becomes a participant in *commodity relationships*, all of the four structural elements of the capitalist state are taken into account. As long as every owner of a unit of value can successfully exchange his/her value as a commodity, there is no need for the state to intervene in economic decision making; there is no lack of material resources needed by the state; there is no problem in maintaining a steady process of accumulation (which is only the net result of equivalent exchange between the owners of capital and the owners of labor power); and there is no problem in maintaining political support for a political party which manages to create this universe of commodities. It is only to the extent that values fail to operate in the commodity form that the structure of the capitalist state becomes problematic. The commodity form is the general point of equilibrium of the capitalist state. At the same time, accumulation takes place as long as every value appears in the form of a commodity. The link between the political and the economic structure of capitalist society is the commodity form. Both substructures depend upon the universalization of this form for their viability.

4. The key problem, however, lies in the fact that the dynamics of capitalist development seem to exhibit a constant tendency to *paralyze* the commodity form

of value. Values cease to exist in the commodity form as soon as they cease seeking exchange for money or other values. To be sure, in an economic world consisting of commodities one can never be certain that one particular item offered on the market for sale will actually find a buyer. But in this simple case the failure of a value offered for exchange is supposed to be *self-corrective*: the owner of the exchange-seeking value will either be forced to lower the price or to offer an alternative good the use value of which does have higher chances of being bought. At least in the world of Jean Baptiste Say, an economy consisting of commodities is self-perpetuating: the failure of a good as a commodity leads to other goods less likely to fail. Similarly, parts of labor and parts of capital which are, as it were, temporarily thrown out of the commodity form in the course of an economic depression, create, through the very fact of their idleness, the preconditions for a new boom (at least if there is downward flexibility of prices). The functioning of this 'healthy' self-corrective mechanism, however, does not seem to be the regular case, particularly in advanced capitalist societies. Marxist economic theory has developed various, though controversial, theorems which could explain such failure of self-corrective mechanisms. For example, it is assumed that monopolization of the economy leads to downward inflexibility of prices on the one side, and, to a constant flow of what Baran and Sweezy have called 'surplus profit' on the other, i.e., monopolistic profits unsuccessfully in search of investment outlets. Another explanation is based on the increasingly social character of production in capitalism. This means increasing division of labor within and among capitalist enterprises, hence increased specialization of every single unit of capital and labor, and hence diminished flexibility and adaptivity to alternative uses. Thirdly it has been argued that the periodic destruction of large parts of value through unfettered economic crises is by itself a healthy economic mechanism which will improve chances for the remaining values to 'perform' as commodities, but that the conflict associated with such 'cleansing off' of superfluous values tend to become explosive to the extent that they have to be prevented by state intervention and Keynesian policies.

Whatever may be the correct and complete explanation, there is plenty of everyday evidence to the effect that both labor and capital are thrown out of the commodity form, and that there is little basis for any confidence that they will be reintegrated into exchange relationships automatically.

5. It is equally evident that the most abstract and inclusive common denominator of state activities and state intervention in advanced capitalist societies is to *guard the commodity form of individual economic actors*. This, again, does not directly mean guarding the general interests of a particular class, but guarding the general interest of all classes on the basis of capitalist exchange relationships ('*Tausch als universale Verkehrsform*'). For instance, it would be mistaken to argue that state policies of education and training are designed to provide the necessary manpower for certain industries, since no one, least of all the state bureaucracy, has any reliable information as to what industry will need what type of skills at what time, or in what numbers. Such policies are instead designed to provide a *maximum of exchange opportunities* to both labor and capital, so that individuals of both classes can enter into capitalist relationships of production with each other. Likewise, research and development

policies designed and funded by the state are by no means directed towards concrete beneficiaries (e.g., industries which can use the resulting technologies, or uses of specific 'civilian' technologies). These policies are designed to open up new markets, to shield the domestic economy against the intrusion of foreign competitors – briefly, to create and maintain the commodity form of value, in whose absence values become non-existent in a capitalist society.

6. The overwhelming concern of all state policies with the problem of guarding the commodity form of value is a relatively *new strategy* which in some capitalist states, like the US, is still subject to substantial political and ideological controversies. What are the alternative strategies open to the state in order to deal with the structural problem of failure of values to perform as commodities? The most 'ancient' method seems to be *inaction*, i.e., hoping for the self-corrective mechanism in the course of which those units of value that have dropped out of the commodity form are supposed to return to the market. The assumption is that the more unpleasant unemployment (of labor or capital) is, the sooner the owners of those values will return to the market-place. The flaw in this logic lies, however, in trusting that owners of values do *not* have another option than to return to the commodity form. They do in fact have such options, of which emigration, delinquency and political revolt are only a few historical examples.

The second method is *subsidies and alimentation*. In this case, those owners of labor power and owners of capital who have lost their chance to participate in exchange relationships are allowed to survive under conditions artificially created by the state. Their economic existence is protected although they have dropped out of the commodity form, or they are prevented from dropping out because they are granted a claim for income derived from sources other than the sale of value. The problem with this 'welfare state' type of dealing with 'decommodified' values is that it becomes too costly in fiscal terms, thus sharpening the fiscal crisis of the state. Subsidizing the owners of values that have become obsolete as commodities is particularly costly for the state because it implies a category of expenditures which are by no means self-financing. They do not increase, but rather diminish the basis of future state revenues.

On the basis of these considerations, we wish to argue that the more and more dominant, more and more exclusive strategy of the capitalist state is to solve the problem of the obsolescence of the commodity form by *creating* conditions under which values can function as commodities. More specifically, these attempts develop in three directions: first, the saleability of *labor power* is enhanced through measures and programs directed towards education, training, regional mobility and general adaptivity of labor power. Second, the saleability of *capital* and manufactured goods is enhanced through transnational integration of capital and product markets, research and development policies, regional development policies, etc. Third, those *sectors of the economy* (which can be specified by industry, by region, by labor market segments) which are unable to survive within the commodity form on their own strength are allowed by plan to fall victim to market pressures and at the same time they are urged to modernize, i.e., to transform themselves into 'marketable' goods. We suggest that the term '*administrative recommodification*' might be an appropriate label for this most advanced strategy of the capitalist state; it is basically different from both the '*laissez-faire*' and 'welfare state-protective' types of strategy sketched out above.

7. Policies which pursue the goal of reorganizing, maintaining and generalizing exchange relationships make use of a specific sequence of *instruments*. These instruments can be categorized in the following way. First, we find *regulations and incentives* applied which are designed to control 'destructive' competition and to make competitors subject to rules which allow for the economic survival of their respective market partners. Usually these regulations consist in measures and laws which try to protect the 'weaker' party in an exchange relationship, or which support this party through various incentives. Second, we find the large category of *public infrastructure investment* which is designed to help broad categories of commodity owners (again: both labor and capital) to engage in exchange relationships. Typical examples are schools of all kinds, transportation facilities, energy plants, and measures for urban and regional development. Third, we find attempts to introduce *compulsory schemes of joint decision making* and joint financing which are designed to force market partners to agree upon conditions of mutually acceptable exchange in an organized way, *outside* the exchange process itself, so that the outcome is reliable for both sides. Such compulsory schemes of mutual accommodation are to be found not only in the area of wage bargaining, but equally in areas like housing, education, and environmental protection.

8. Such attempts to stabilize and universalize the commodity form and exchange process by political and administrative means leads to a number of specific structural contradictions of state capitalist societies which in turn can become the focus of social conflict and political struggle. Such contradictions can be found on the economic, political and ideological levels of society. On the *economic* level, the very state policies which are designed to maintain and promote universal exchange relationships have the effect of *threatening the continuity* of those relationships. For all three of the above-mentioned instruments of economic policy making (regulations, infrastructure and compulsive accommodation) deprive the owners of capital of value to varying degrees, either in the form of *capital* that is just 'taxed away', or in the form of *labor*, or in form of their *freedom* to utilize both of these in the way they deem most profitable. To the extent such state policies of 'administrative recommodification' are 'effective', they are bound to put a burden upon the owners of capital which has the paradoxical effect of making them *ineffective*. Since, in a capitalist society, all exchange relationships depend upon the willingness of owners of money capital to invest, i.e., to exchange money capital for constant capital and variable capital; since this willingness depends upon the expected profitability of investment; and since all observable state policies of recommodification do have the side-effect of depriving capital of either capital or labor power or the freedom to use both in profitable ways, the cure turns out to be worse than the illness. That is to say, reformist policies of the capitalist state by no means unequivocally 'serve' the interests of the capitalist class: very often they are met by the most vigorous resistance and opposition of this class. Social conflicts and political struggles do not, of course, emerge automatically from this contradiction. They are waged by political

forces which are willing and able to defend the reformist policies of the capitalist state against the obstructive resistance of the capitalist class itself.

A second structural contradiction is related to the organizational *power structures* created by such state strategies. It has often been observed by both liberal and Marxist social scientists that those sectors of the economy which are not immediately controlled by market mechanisms tend to expand (both in terms of labor power employed and value absorbed) in advanced capitalist social structures. The most obvious example is public administration and all the agencies that are created and controlled by it (like schools, transportation facilities, post offices, hospitals, public service institutions, welfare bureaucracies, the military, etc.). What is the explanation for the growth of the share of these organizations? In the most simplified form, the state's attempts to maintain and universalize the commodity form do require organizations which cease to be subject to the commodity form in their own mode of operation.

This can be demonstrated in the case of teachers. Although it is true that their labor power is *hired* for wage, it is not true that the *purpose* of their labor is to produce commodities for sale (which is the case in commercial enterprises). The purpose of their labor is, rather, to produce such use-values (skills, etc.) which put commodity owners (e.g., workers) in a position to actually sell their commodities. Therefore, schools do not *sell* their 'products' (which hence do not assume the form of commodities), although they help to maintain and to *improve the saleability* of the commodities of the *recipients* of their products. But to the recipients the products of educational activities (i.e., the work of teachers) are distributed through channels different from exchange. The same is true in such organizations as public housing authorities, hospitals, transportation systems, prisons and other parts of the administrative apparatus. Although we often find nominal *fees* (as opposed to equivalent *prices*) as a mechanism playing a role in the distribution of their products and services, the prevailing mechanisms are by no means *sale* but such things as legal claims, legal compulsion, acknowledged need or simply free use.

One of the most debated and most controversial issues in the fields of liberal public economics and political science is just what mechanism of production and distribution of 'public goods' could be substituted for the exchange mechanism that is inapplicable in the area of public production – an increasing part of production designed to maintain and to universalize the commodity form of property.

This strategy of *maintaining* the commodity form presupposes the growth of state-organized production facilities *exempt* from the commodity form. This, again, is a contradiction only in the structural sense – a source of possible conflicts and destabilizing developments which in turn remain contingent upon political action. This contradiction can give rise to social conflicts and political struggles which try to gain popular control over exactly those 'weakest links' in the world of commodities. Although it is a puzzle to many Marxists who consider themselves 'orthodox', it still is hardly deniable that the major social conflicts and political struggles that have taken place during the decade of the sixties did *not* take place within exchange relationships between labor and capital, but took place as conflicts over the control over the service organizations that *serve* the commodity form without themselves being *part* of the commodity nexus. Conflicts in schools, universities, prisons, military organizations, housing authorities and hospitals are cases in point. We suggest that an explanation of this fact can be based on the consideration that such organizations represent the most advanced forms of erosion of the commodity form within capitalist exchange relationships themselves.

A third contradiction can be located on the ideological level, or in the normative and moral infrastructure of capitalist society. The commodity form does presuppose two related norms with which individual actors must comply. First, they must be willing to utilize the opportunities open to them, and they must constantly strive to improve their exchange position (*possessiveness*); and second, they must be willing to accept whatever material outcome emerges from their particular exchange relationship – particularly if this outcome is unfavorable to them. Such outcomes must, in other words, be attributed to either natural events or to the virtues and failures of the individual (*individualism*).

For a capitalist commodity economy to function, the normative syndrom of possessive individualism must be the basis both of the behavior of the actor as well as of his interpretations of the actual and future behavior of others. Our point is now that the contradiction of state capitalism on the ideological level results in the *subversion* of this normative syndrom of possessive individualism. To the extent that exchange relationships are prepared and maintained through visible political and administrative acts of the state, the actual exchange value any unit of property (be it in labor or capital) achieves on the market can be seen at least as much determined through *political* measures as through the *individual* way of managing one's property and resources. These resources themselves thus come to be seen as something resulting from, and contingent upon, political measures. Whether and at what price one succeeds in selling one's labor power appears, within the prevalent framework of interpretation, no longer as being exclusively contingent upon individual skills and efforts, nor to be primarily contingent upon the 'natural' ups and downs of the business cycle, but rather it comes to be seen as a direct result of the accomplishment or failures of state policies, e.g. economic, vocational training or regional development policies. Similarly, for the owner of capital, his market success does not depend upon his preparedness to take risks, his inventiveness and his ability to anticipate changes in demand, but instead upon state policies in such areas as tariffs, research and development, infrastructure supply and regional development. The structural weakening of the moral fiber of a capitalist commodity society – which is caused by the very attempts to stabilize and universalize the commodity form through policy measures – again does not imply any automatic tendency toward crises or the 'breakdown' of capitalism. It can, however, become the focus of social conflict and political struggle which is oriented towards overcoming the obsolete commodity relationships as the organizing principle of social reproduction.

Notes and References

1 See MILIBAND, R. (1969) *The State in Capitalist Society*, New York, Weidenfeld and Nicholson. POU-LANTZAS, N. (1973) *Political Power and Social Classes*, London, New Left Books; also see POULANTZAS, N. (1969) 'The Problem of the Capitalist State' *New Left Review* 58, pp. 67–78, a review of Miliband; and MILIBAND, R. (1973) 'Poulantzas and the Capitalist State' *New Left Review* 82, pp. 83–92.

2 See OFFE, C. (1972) *Strukturprobleme des Kapitalistichen Staates*, Frankfurt am Main, Edition Suhrkamp. Offe's work in English to date is limited to: (1972) 'Political Authority and Class Structures – An Analysis of late Capitalist Societies' *International Journal of Sociology* 2:1, pp. 73–108; (1973) 'The Abolition of Market Control and the Problem of Legitimacy' *Working Papers on the Kapitalistate* 1, pp. 109–16; (1973–74) 2, pp. 73–5; and (1975) 'A Reply to Müller and Neusüss' *Telos*, Fall. For a discussion of the problem of the state in late capitalism in the work of Habermas see SCHROYER, T. (1975) 'The Repoliticization of the Relations of Production: An Interpretation of Jürgen Habermas' Analytic Theory of Late Capitalist Development' *New German Critique* 5, pp. 107–28; also see HABERMAS, J. (1975) *Legitimation Crisis*, Boston, Beacon Press, pp. 66–70.

3 OFFE, C. (1975) *Berufsbildungsreform*, Frankfurt am Main, Edition Suhrkamp.

6   Lessons from Europe

Max Wilkinson

There is one outstanding difference, of which most Britons are unaware, between the ways in which they and all other European countries educate their young.

The countries of Europe have all articulated detailed national policies about what their children shall learn in school and, in many cases, how they shall learn it; in Britain, the major decisions about content and method of education are left to the head teachers and staffs of 27,000 separate schools.

In Sweden, by contrast, the contents and balance of school courses are hotly debated by politicians, industrialists and teachers in a national forum. In France, the studies of each child are under the direct control of the Minister of Education and his regional representatives.

In Britain, however, control and supervision of schools has been delegated to the 125 local education authorities, although the central government does have a number of specific duties. In practice, the Department hardly ever interferes in the running of school courses, while local councillors lack both the time and expertise to take more than a cursory general interest in how head teachers organize the pattern of studies.

The most important consequence has been that the change of methods and style in many, but not all, of our schools has been far more rapid than in most other European countries, although the revolution has been piecemeal and is far from complete.

For this reason, major changes in the character of British schooling have crept into the public consciousness over the last decade with few clear announcements of public policy to precede them and little organized national debate. The transformation of the education system is the result of thousands of individual decisions reflecting the inspirations, the fashions, the idiosyncracies, the political beliefs and the institutional pressures among teachers. The coherence of these changes depends upon the growth of national consensus. It is, therefore, more elusive than the

Source: An abridged version of WILKINSON, M. (1977) *Lessons from Europe* London, Centre for Policy Studies, Chap. 1 'Introduction', pp. 1–14.

rationale of Continental education which, in theory at least, derives logically from national policy decisions.

[...]

By contrast, the British Labour government's recent Bill on comprehensive schools says nothing about curriculum and very little about organization. The government has confined itself to a brief statement of principle (that children should not be selected for schools by ability) and has left all the details to be worked out by local authorities. It will influence local decisions through circulars, the allocation of money and its power of veto over any plan to change the character of a school, but it will not initiate any coherent national strategy on the form comprehensive education should take.

An important consequence of the British de-centralism is that it is much more difficult than on the Continent to know what is actually going on. Extensive research is required, for example, to find out how many schools are 'progressive' and how many 'traditional', to discover the methods generally used in teaching or the choices of course which children are making. Statistics for the GCE 'O' and 'A' level examinations and for the newer Certificate of Secondary Education for the less able sixteen year-olds give, to be sure, a reasonable idea of the system's output. But, for information on what is happening between the ages of five and sixteen, policy-makers have to rely on a combination of hunch, gossip, sampling and the impressions of the inspectorate.

This is very different from the position in France or Germany, where every year children pass or fail to pass through defined grades of a national curriculum, or in Sweden, where national tests are given regularly to children throughout their careers.

In the 1960s, the British were generally satisfied with their unique method of organized schooling. The freedom given to teachers had allowed the best to flourish unhampered by bureaucratic restraints. The development of new styles of teaching appeared to have enlivened primary schools and to be widening opportunities in the secondary sectors. Meanwhile, standards measured by the university entrance and the examination boards appeared to be rising. The well-publicized successes of the best progressive teachers and the new comprehensive schools led to a general belief that a great leap forward was imminent.

That leap forward has not happened. Indeed, it is now frequently stated that standards are actually falling. A mood of disillusionment and bitterness has replaced the buoyancy of a few years ago. The middle classes who in the late 1950s and 1960s were gradually moving their children away from fee-paying schools, are now returning to them in spite of steep increases in fees. The number of sixth-formers qualifying for university has been considerably lower than expected. The public has been shocked by evidence of a falling standard of basic literacy; the complaints of industrialists have now reached a new stridency.

The crisis of confidence in our education system has arisen when, for the first time since 1945, the average standard of living is falling and the British are slowly awakening to the fact that they are among the poorer countries in Europe.

It is natural, therefore, to look overseas and ask what social and economic qualities have enabled the Germans, Swedes, French and Dutch to develop faster than and, in many respects, overtake the British altogether. It is obvious that, in the long run, the education system must have a major effect on a country's prosperity and well-being. Until recently, most British educationalists have been reluctant to draw any lessons from Europe. Indeed, the traffic has been very much the other way, with experts coming to Britain to study new methods, particularly in primary schools. German schooling has been regarded as too inflexibly traditional, the French as too elitist and centralized and the Dutch system as too peculiar to their religious divisions and trading needs. Only the Swedes, with their comprehensive school system and their search for equality in higher education have provided a popular model for us. However, in some important respects, the Swedish experiment has been misunderstood.

The aim of this study is to compare the developments and aspirations of British education with what has been happening in our nearest neighbours: France, Germany, Holland and Sweden. The method will be, as far as possible, practical with the aim of discussing the qualities and accomplishments necessary to industrial societies if they are to survive and prosper. This approach will immediately raise objections: even to suggest that education is an industrial investment and that pupils are future manpower is to invite protest from the British educational establishment.

For many teachers see, as their main responsibility, the encouragement of individual capacities for personal, academic and imaginative development rather than promoting what they regard as narrow mechanistic skills. Some teachers despise an industrial, materialistic society and conceive their task not as servicing industry's needs but as educating pupils who will change them. This is, perhaps, an extreme statement of the tension between personal, liberal education and the demands of vocational preparation, yet the rapid extension of secondary education and the introduction of comprehensive schooling have brought a new urgency to this issue, although there is little evidence that it is being tackled effectively in Britain.

All West European industrial states are facing a similar problem. The Swedes have, perhaps, been the first to realize the full implications, while the British are the least conscious of it. As Dr Charles Bosanquer said a few years ago when he retired as Vice-Chancellor of Newcastle University: 'We are in danger of producing too many talented consumers and too few producers of wealth'. Many recent trends give added point to his fears and, before considering the position in other European countries, it is as well to look at the grounds for concern in Britain.

First must come the increasing compaints by industrialists of low basic standards of reading, writing and arithmetic. Sir Arnold Weinstock, Managing Director of the General Electric Company reported:[1]

Last year, in more than one of our major industrial cities, the engineering employees failed to recruit as many apprentices as they wanted because not enough school leavers achieved adequate standards. This is a remarkable indictment of our education system and one which raises disturbing questions. The applicants were there; the IQs were there (the tests prove it).

But the basic learned skills of literacy and numeracy were not.
What has gone wrong?

Sir Arnold, strongly criticized teachers for helping to perpetuate unhelpful attitudes towards productive industry and said:

> Educationists in the schools and the teacher training colleges should recognize that they do no service to our children if they prepare them for life in a society which does not exist and which economic reality will never allow to come into existence unless at a terrible price of freedom and liberty of choice.

Sir Arnold's views have wide support in industry. Mr Michael Bury, Director of Education and Training for the Confederation of British Industry, told a conference on training in December 1975:

> The question of the relationship between the schools and employment has led to a great deal of comment from CBI members. They plainly have continuing and serious misgivings about the standards of achievement of many secondary school leavers, particularly the sixteen year olds. Much of the comment we have received can only be described as reflecting a genuine anger not, this time, in terms of the difficulties caused for employers, as on behalf of the young people themselves. The view has been expressed that many of these young people, after one of the longest periods of compulsory education in the world, are leaving school in particularly difficult circumstances, badly handicapped for most forms of employment by their lack of elementary skills in reading, writing, arithmetic and communication.

The Electrical Industries Training Board reported at the same conference that many employers were having to send their apprentices back to college – not for further training, but to re-learn the basic mathematics they failed to master at school.

Mr Bury commented:

> To seek a solution only after the school leaving age by passing remedial function to employers and further education is neither sensible nor appropriate.

The first evidence of lowered reading standards was provided by the survey in 1970 of the National Foundation for Educational Research which concluded that, after a steady rise since the war, standards had fallen after 1968. The subsequent enquiry, under Sir Alan (now Lord) Bullock, concluded that the general level of competence was well below the requirements of society and that improvement was needed.[2]

At the same time, a survey by the Schools' Council[3] showed that a third of teachers believed that the basic processes were being neglected.

The system is also under attack at higher levels for failing to produce enough able and qualified youngsters, particularly in science and technology, who want to go into industry. As a result, some of the science and engineering faculties in universities and polytechnics are now half empty or filled with foreign students and nearly all have empty places.

[...]

The number of first degree graduates in pure and applied sciences is still declining – their proportion is, at present, only one sixth of the total. In the last few years, the Standing Conference of University and Polytechnic Appointments Officers has reported a reluctance by graduates to opt for posts in industry. The proportion of first degree graduates going into industry was only 18.4 per cent in 1973/74, in spite of high demand from firms. In 1975, in spite of the severe recession, industry was offering more jobs to graduates than they were prepared to take. These recent trends must be seen in the light of the broad general prejudice against industry which flourished in universities for many years. Research, the civil service and the professions have, traditionally, had greater prestige and, in many ways, have offered better rewards to graduates. As a result, Britain has suffered a steady drain of much of the best talent away from productive industry. This tendency is in sharp contrast to Japan, where service with a good industrial company brings very high prestige. In Germany and France also, the prestige of engineers has traditionally been much higher than in Britain and it is worth noting that, in Germany and Sweden, the engineering faculties at universities are over-subscribed. It would seem obvious that training of large numbers of highly qualified engineers ought to be a priority in a trading nation like Britain, particularly at a time when many traditional industries are losing their competitiveness, yet there is evidence that the study of science and mathematics in our secondary schools is at a very low ebb.

As long ago as 1968, the report by Sir Frederick Dainton[4] on science education drew attention to the downward spiral by which a shortage of good science teachers produces a shortage of good sixth-formers in the subject, which in turn results in a shortage of scientists among the next generation of teachers. Since the Dainton report, the new styles of science courses developed by the Nuffield Foundation have spread widely in schools. A new type of mathematics, intended to be broader, more attractive and less difficult has been developed by the Schools Mathematics Project and is now used in about a fifth of secondary schools. In addition, a new type of combined science degree has been developed by several universities with the intention of providing less specialized studies in the subject.

In spite of all these efforts, there has been very little improvement: the proportion of GCE 'A' Level entries in science is still declining. In 1950, 54 per cent of all 'A' Level subjects attempted were in science. By 1973, the proportion had fallen to 39 per cent. The proportions of mathematics subjects were: 1955 – 15 per cent and 1973 – 13 per cent.

More worrying, the proportion of teachers who have good science and mathematics qualifications has taken a veritable nose-dive in the last year or two. Government figures[5] show that the number of women graduates going into science teaching fell by nearly half in four years to only sixty. The number of men fell by 45 per cent over two years. In primary schools, the situation is hardly better for, in 1975, over 40 per cent of students accepted for teacher training courses did not even possess a GCE 'O' Level certificate in mathematics. This is particularly disturbing at a time of rapid change of the primary school curriculum, when the new mathematics is introducing quite sophisticated concepts to young children. For it is generally admitted that replacing the old-fashioned chanting of tables and the lists of sums by more flexible teaching puts extra demands on the teacher if it is to be effective.

Professional alarm over the decline in science subjects was expressed forcibly by Mr R. Schofield of the Department of Education, Brunel University. After discussing the difficulties of teaching the subject in mixed ability comprehensive schools, he said:

> Calls are voiced for the need to devise a form of physics curriculum with, at the most, minimal mathematics content. It would not be reasonable to argue that such a subject would not be worth learning but it would be proper to point out that it is unlikely to be suitable for someone proposing to enter physics or engineering as a vocation. In the absence of reliable data, no one is able to comment with authority but I believe we are most likely to find that a lowering of standards has taken place.
>
> For these reasons, I regard it as entirely likely that general standards of physics attainment in schools will drop and the subject even disappear from the curriculum. It is possible that 'honours standard' physics would only be undertaken in the postgraduate schools of relatively few universities.[6]

Some educationists, particularly non-scientists, regard the plight of science with unconcern. This is partly because of the peculiar British snobbery between different subjects resulting from the early specialization required by GCE 'A' Level. The decline of science is regarded with suppressed glee by some quite intelligent people. One former professor of education asked me: 'What is the use of science – does it make you a more effective *operator*?'. Others, more rational, blame the dry conservatism of physics syllabuses which, until recently, were heavily dependent on the rote learning of facts and formal proofs discovered in the nineteenth century.

Now, there are unhappy signs that language teaching, a vital area for a commercial nation, is beginning the same downward spiral as the sciences. A ten-year experiment in the teaching of oral French in primary schools has virtually collapsed.

In her report on the project[7] Dr Clare Burstall concluded that primary school French lessons did little to encourage further study of the language and, in a considerable proportion of cases, it had a negative effect by putting children off the subject. And the failure of the primary schools experiment is the least important.

The number of pupils passing GCE 'A' Level French each year has fallen by 1,400 between 1966 and 1973, at a time when overall passes increased by 20 per cent. Passes in German are also static and the proportion of all passes in a modern language is only 6.9 per cent. At 'O' Level, the number of pupils passing in French, fell by 9,000, or about 10 per cent, between 1963 and 1973.[8] As a result, university and polytechnic language departments are, for the first time since the war, having difficulty in recruiting enough suitable students.

When faced with these trends, it is difficult to resist the view that the unique degree of freedom allowed in the British decentralized system has tended to promote, among teachers and pupils alike, a drift away from the 'difficult' subjects. These are the disciplines and the painful mastery of skills and techniques needed before the higher intellectual or imaginative abilities can take flight. Mathematics and languages, like piano playing, demand long, hard practice before the rewards are tasted. (The playing of musical instruments is also on the decline). By contrast, English and History have always offered more obvious gratification at an elementary level, providing earlier chances for the pupil to 'take-off' into speculation or analysis of his own. The recent trend has been for the development of a whole range of hybrid subjects under such banners as 'integrated courses' or 'environmental studies'. They attempt to combine gratification, often termed 'relevance', with elements of the traditional disciplines culled from formerly different subjects. The inherent danger of this approach is that the mastery of specific skills will either be sacrificed intentionally or, more likely, just lost in the fog.

This raises the central question of how to achieve the right balance of skills, factual knowledge, imaginative endeavour and character training [. . .]

However, before considering what lessons can be learnt from other countries, we should pause to look at two other criticisms of our own schooling which have recently been gaining force and which are both related. The first is that schools are failing to prepare pupils for their future jobs and the second is that they are not giving enough attention to the preparation for future citizenship, that important function which in Communist countries is called ideological training and, in religious communities, moral guidance.

The gulf between schooling and future employment was brought to public attention by the Government's inspectors (HMIs) in a report on schools' careers advice. The reports, from 150 inspectors and a survey of 870 schools, showed only tenuous links with industry. Careers advice to children was inadequate, mainly because schools gave a low priority to this aspect of their work. Careers teachers were often deprived of such elementary requirements as filing cabinets and telephones.

More seriously, the report showed that schools were making little or no effort to plan their courses with childrens' future careers in mind. Only 8 per cent of schools had an 'established and profitable' relationship with local industry and some schools quite simply did not understand the need to help pupils towards future jobs.

This failure by many schools to come to terms with the world of work and its demands may, in some cases, have deep roots in the philosophy of education and social traditions which have developed over the years. A chance remark made by one comprehensive school headmaster illustrates the point. It was made at the rehearsal for an Inner London Education Authority closed circuit television discussion on the effects of raising the school leaving age to 16. As a preliminary to the discussion, the authority recorded a short documentary film of school activities: this showed some 16 year-olds busily engaged in metalwork, while the commentator explained that they were being given a foretaste of the kind of work they would be doing after school.

The headmaster, who is among the city's most respected and influential, demanded, with some passion, that the commentary should be changed: he said that the whole purpose of the modern comprehensive school was to give pupils higher ambitions than this kind of 'routine' industrial work.

'But who is going to do these necessary and important jobs, if your pupils will not?' he was asked. His answer was that industry must be changed so that these dull jobs would be mechanized out of existence.

This brief exchange illustrates a thorough confusion in many schools between the admirable aim of encouraging individual pupils to extend themselves and climb the academic ladder and, on the other hand, the need to be realistic about the jobs which the majority of children are *likely* to fill and, indeed, *must* fill if Britain is to produce the wealth on which education depends.

At some stage in their education, nearly everyone must move from the goals of liberal academic education to the acquisition of specific, often narrower vocational aptitudes. (Teachers have been among the few groups exempted from this rule). It is obvious that a child destined for a manual or semi-skilled job will make the switch earlier than one who is going to be a technical expert or an administrator. But, at what stage, should the changeover take place and what should be its form? Should comprehensive schools provide workshop and other specific training to more pupils and at an earlier age?

Would the less able children be happier and more disciplined in secondary schools if they were spending more time learning the skills which they could believe to be useful? Is learning to be a skilled lathe operator, for example, inherently less valuable or less dignified than learning, say, geography?

The British answer to these questions is a result of drift rather than of any careful strategy. This drift has taken us further away from vocational objectives than other European countries, notably Holland; while in Sweden, the effects of comprehensive schooling and a drive towards equality on vocational training have been considered much more carefully than in Britain.

There are several other reasons for believing that a reappraisal of the balance of our education is now overdue. They can be summarized as:

1. Employers' complaints are broadening from the lack of basic skills to unsatisfactory attitudes towards work which, it is believed, schools are helping to foster.

2. Growing indiscipline reported by all the teachers' unions and, indeed, the subject of a Government enquiry. Social factors outside the control of schools are, clearly, a major cause but there is little doubt that bad behaviour and vandalism are also symptoms of a dissatisfaction by pupils with what the schools are providing. Pupils who feel they are getting somewhere are much less likely to break up lessons, smash windows or resort to arson. Yet these behaviour patterns are increasing.

3. Further evidence of pupils' and parents' alienation from the aims of schools

was provided in an important survey by the Schools' Council[10] which revealed a fundamental cleavage of aspirations. Parents wanted their children to learn basic and recognizable skills like literacy and mathematics and to be prepared by their teachers for earning a living. Pupils generally agreed and put a surprisingly high value on the 'hard' subjects, like mathematics. Teachers, on the other hand, put much greater emphasis on the liberal educational goals of developing creative, personal and moral qualities.

There are, however, several powerful obstacles to any concerted change in Britain and, particularly, to a change in the direction of more vocational emphasis. These are, briefly:

1. The background and training of school-teachers who generally have little experience outside the school and college system, in spite of some attempts by industry and commerce to arrange visits for them.

2. The current preoccupation with equality, especially in the developing comprehensive schools. This makes it difficult for teachers to steer children too decisively away from the main academic streams, for fear of re-introducing the irreversible selection which was such an unpopular aspect of the old eleven-plus exam.

3. Inadequate equipment and staffing of technical and workshop departments in many comprehensive schools. Vocational education is more expensive than most 'liberal' education.

4. Traditional prejudice in favour of 'academic' courses. The academic route with university or college as destination and GCEs as milestones has, in the past, carried the highest social status. It has been the highway to the professions and the escape route for bright working class children from the mines, the docks, the railways and other jobs which, until recently, offered low status and low pay.

5. As a result of this general prejudice, the new development of courses in secondary schools has tended to repeat the old academic pattern. Thus, the rapidly expanding Certificate of Secondary Education offers courses which largely mirror, at a lower level, those provided for the top 30 to 40 per cent in the GCE 'O' Levels. Efforts have been made to make academic subjects more 'relevant' to the experience of lower ability pupils (for example, by focusing combined history and geography on local institutions and 'our town' or by use of the project method). However, the old academic aims of broadening the pupils' intellects and providing a general grasp of facts have not generally been re-examined. This is partly because teachers have seen the ideal of 'secondary education for all' as a chance to free children from the narrow Victorian concept of moulding each youngster for a future station in life. Consequently, teachers have, on the whole, failed to reconsider whether the aims of personal development and equal opportunity could be achieved equally well within a school programme geared more specifically to the world of work. [...]

6. A further obstacle to change in the British system is the sharp division between the schools and the further education provided in the technical colleges. The colleges, covered by different rules, different staffing standards and different conditions of service, have traditionally provided the specific vocational education demanded by industry. As a result, such courses have tended to be excluded from schools, so that a youngster wanting to take a course leading, for example, to the building or engineering trades, must necessarily wait until he (or she) has passed the school-leaving age of 16. This, in itself, may be undesirable, particularly now that the leaving age has been raised. But there is also a built-in incentive for schools to try to retain pupils after the school-leaving age when they would be better off in a technical college. Salaries of school staff, for example, as well as the public esteem of a school, depend partly on the size of its sixth form. Even teachers who are entirely disinterested, as no doubt many are, have a further motive for trying to maintain a large sixth form: more pupils will result in more expert staff being available to improve the teaching of all age groups. In addition, teachers have an understandable desire to inspire loyalty and affection for their school which, where successful, will inevitably encourage youngsters to stay on for an extra year. As a result of these pressures, teachers are now campaigning for the introduction of a new examination to be called the Certificate of Extended Education (CEE) which will, effectively, extend the lower standard of education provided by the CSE course up to the age of 17.

The effect of this examination would be to further institutionalize the type of general education currently offered in our schools and to preempt the demands for a greater emphasis on the vocational skills which are largely taught in the colleges.

At the same time, colleges are, for a variety of reasons, moving more and more into the field of general education and providing an increasing number of GCE 'O' and 'A' Level courses. The division between the schools and technical colleges is, therefore, appearing to be more and more arbitrary, and several influential figures led by Lord Alexander, former secretary of the Association of Education Committees, have proposed a more integrated scheme for the education and training of 16 to 19 year-olds.

[...]

In the end, however, the details of the curriculum and of organization are less important than the attitudes and values which teachers communicate to their pupils. This was recognized historically by the religious foundations which established many of our voluntary schools and it has been the informing principle of many of the great public schools which still couple 'Godliness and good learning' as inseparable aims and lay tremendous stress on methods of character formation.

Recently, however, many of the traditional methods of character training schools have been falling into disuse or, at least, assuming a much less important place. This is partly the result of society's trend towards permissiveness and a questioning of authority, partly because of the development of bigger schools and partly because liberal teachers have stressed personal and intellectual scepticism at the expense of corporate discipline. Thus, organized games, the prefect system, school rules and discipline, uniforms and communal worship are all less highly regarded than they were fifteen years ago. In some comprehensive schools, for example, competitive team games have all but disappeared: in other schools, the minimum provision of the 1944 Education Act for a daily act of worship and regular instruction in religion is evaded or ignored. Intellectual liberalism has, indeed, gone so far that Church interests were able to agree a religious syllabus in Birmingham which includes a section on Communism along with other 'stances for living'.

Individually, these changes may not be of very great significance; after all, there are plenty of arguments for liberalizing discipline and for bringing religious instruction more in line with modern practice. But, cumulatively, the changes, particularly in discipline and 'school spirit', may be effecting a profound shift of attitudes to society and work amongst the present generation of children. This shift, for which television must bear a major responsibility, can be seen in all industrial countries. [...]

In an age of doubt and cynicism, it is, perhaps, expecting too much of teachers to give children firm, moral values. Teachers, no doubt, represent the full spectrum of moral and religious beliefs, as they do political convictions. (A survey for the *Times Educational Supplement* by National Opinion Polls before the February 1974 election, showed that they were about evenly divided between the three parties). Nevertheless, the replacement of old certainties by the principles of freedom and tolerance has allowed into the profession a vociferous minority opposed to our society and even actively wishing to destroy it. These intellectual revolutionaries, mainly clustered around Trotskyite persuasions, have had wide ripples of influence out of proportion to their numbers. They have a considerable minority following within the universities and polytechnics and in a small number of schools, particularly in London, their voice has been dominant. Their reverence for the ideal of the class struggle has led to an attack on scholastic standards (because they provide a ladder for the middle class) and a loathing for vocational courses (because they help the ruling class to exploit the children of the workers). Doubtless, the majority of teachers have no sympathy with the extremists' revolutionary mythology yet many younger teachers find it hard to argue against some of their educational conclusions. For recent research[11] has clearly shown that children from deprived working class homes suffer a predestined disadvantage in a school system which uses traditional measures of achievement. In addition, many teachers are, for reasons already summarized, deeply suspicious of anything which looks like training for jobs.

If the ultra-left have, as yet, little political muscle, the more established Marxists centered on the Communist party, undoubtedly do exert wide influence. The 'militants', led by Communists and Marxist sympathisers have, since 1969, held a powerful, though not always dominant, position within the National Union of Teachers – the largest union. The chairman of their education committee is a Communist and one of their leading thinkers on education matters for the last decade has been Mr Max Morris, who was an executive member of the Communist party. The colleges of education have also had their share of lecturers with beliefs in the hinterland between democratic socialism and communism. They have often formed a loose alliance with those suffering from the least logical mutations of liberalism claiming to be vaguely descended from Rousseau and Dewey.

Union pressure has combined with the writings of distinguished Communist intellectuals like Professor Brian Simon, Director of the Institute of Education at Leicester University and the action research of socialists like Dr A.H. Halsey at Oxford University and Dr Eric Midwinter in Liverpool.

One consequence of this concerted emphasis of the system's obvious short-comings, has been to undermine the confidence of teachers in their traditional values. Secondly, the left-wing lobby has promoted beliefs about equality and equal opportunity which have inherent contradictions and which, in the hasty tempo of staffroom discussion can be muddled and confused. Thirdly, the preoccupation with equality has led to a belief that everyone is necessarily competing in the same academic race. Dr Midwinter did, to be sure, realize the futility of this thesis but his work in Liverpool primary schools ran up a blind alley by trying to redefine the aims of a traditional liberal education in terms of working class language and culture.[12]

The alternative possibility of giving children an early option to develop practical skills and craft training as an integral part of a more general school course has been frowned on by the left and therefore it has not been adequately explored.
[. . .]

In Britain, the case for a thorough re-think has been strongly reinforced by recent trends in the distribution of incomes. At a time when plumbers can earn as much as hospital doctors and more than teachers, failure or lack of interest in the academic hurdle race is becoming less of a disaster. If the trend continues, it may be possible even for socialists to return to the basic premise of the 1944 Act; to accept that people are different and that their different abilities and aptitudes require different types of education if they are to be fully realized.
[. . .]

Notes and References

1 WEINSTOCK, A. (1976) *Times Educational Supplement* 23 January.
2 BULLOCK, A. (1975) *A Language for Life* London, HMSO.
3 SCHOOLS' COUNCIL (1974) *What's Going on in Primary Maths?* London, Schools' Council.
4 DAINTON, F. (1968) *The Dainton Report* 'Enquiry into the flow of candidates in science and technology into Higher Education' London, Cmnd. 3541.
5 DEPARTMENT OF EDUCATION AND SCIENCE (1974) *First Destination of Graduates 1972/73* London, HMSO.
6 SCHOFIELD, R. (1975) *Physics Bulletin* May.
7 BURSTALL, C. (1974) *Primary French in the Balance*. National Foundation for Educational Research. cational Research.
8 DEPARTMENT OF EDUCATION AND SCIENCE (1975) *School Leavers CSE and GCE, 1973* London, HMSO.
9 DEPARTMENT OF EDUCATION AND SCIENCE (1973) *Careers Education in Secondary Schools* (HMI's report) London, HMSO.
10 SCHOOLS' COUNCIL (1968) *Enquiry I* London, Schools' Council.
11 JENCKS, C. (1975) *Inequality* Harmondsworth, Penguin. DES (1975) *Education Priority* (Vol. 3) London, HMSO.
12 MIDWINTER, E. (1975) *Education and the Community* London, George Allen and Unwin.

7 Green Paper: Noise of Crisis

James Donald

The present offensive against education, in fact a tightening of controls within the dominant system itself, cannot be defeated by campaigns alone. What matters, quite practically, is redefining the issues.

Raymond Williams

The particular clashes and skirmishes of the 'Great Debate' may be over now, but it's hard not to hear that the education system is still 'in crisis'. The administrative machinery of funding, examinations and school government is being stripped down and reassembled. The Tory right still raises the occasional brouhaha about 'standards'. Battered groupings of left teachers are renewing their exhortations to rally against the 'attack on education'. Academic observers burrow after the source of the crisis – in the crisis of capitalism, in changes in the labour process and the problems of youth unemployment, in the breakdown of social democratic hegemony. Meanwhile, teachers caught up in all this are liable to lose (at best) their autonomy or (at worst) their jobs. In this hubbub of theoretical debate and political struggle it is difficult to stop and ask the quiet, outrageous question: *what crisis?* I'm not saying that there have not been some fundamental changes; some basic contradictions are now clearly having their effects. The trouble is that 'crisis' is such a loose and baggy notion that it can hold a whole range of undifferentiated changes. That's why I want to ask which things have changed, and how, and why.

Most striking are the changes in state policy on education. These are my concern in this article, particularly as they are embodied in the Labour Government's Green Paper *Education in Schools* (Cmnd 6869) published in July 1977. Just what 'policy' means in this context is not self-evident though. It signifies not only a product (the policy statement), but also two practices – the *formulation* of policy and its actual *implementation*. The relationships between these aspects are not as straightforward as is sometimes assumed. The obvious disparities between what the Department of Education and Science says ought to be happening and what is actually going on in

Source: A shortened and revised version of an article first published in *Screen Education* 30 (1979). This version published for the first time in this volume.

schools are usually explained in commonsensical terms of a time-lag, or of the incompetence and/or obstruction of teachers, administrators and students. Both the formulation of education policy and the workings of schools are, it is true, activities of the state; both work, in general terms, to reproduce and modify existing social relations. But there is also a difference between them. They are specific practices of separate institutions and, before it is possible to see how they fit together, it is this specificity that needs to be studied.

The theoretical importance of such a distinction is fairly clear – the distinction between concept and object is axiomatic. To assume that 'education' – one component within a theoretical discourse, significant only in relation to a set of other concepts like 'the state', 'industry', 'nation' and 'family' – is identical with or simply reflects the actual existence and activities of schools easily leads to confusion about just what is being studied. The political implications may be less obvious. The separation of questions of *knowledge* from those of *power* is deeply ingrained. It is a habit that needs to be broken, though, because there is a relationship between the two which is neither accidental nor simply instrumental. Michel Foucault has made the point that 'there is no power relation without the correlative constitution of a field of knowledge, nor any knowledge that does not presuppose and constitute at the same time power relations'.[1] Implicit in the question of the restructuring of education, then, is the question of how the state exercises and imposes its power in part through the *production* of 'truth' and 'knowledge' about education. Not to challenge this process cedes to the state the power to define the site, the terms and the limits of struggle. It's not a matter of being gullible or cynical, but of reading (in this case) the Green Paper in a way that recognizes this power/knowledge complex and thus may displace other (dominant) readings which block attempts to bring about changes in education and the wider social formation. It may then be possible to produce a different analysis which could further that struggle. This article is, I hope, a contribution to such a radical redefinition of the issues, a salvo in the 'battle of ideas' around the imposition of a new hegemony on education.

At its simplest, it is possible to identify two processes at work in 'the education crisis'. What education is for is being redefined and, at the same time, the institutions of the education system are being restructured to achieve these new goals and to fit new patterns of state expenditure. The problem is to see how these two relate to each other and what are the specific tactics of each. One barrier, I think, has been the failure to grasp just what is at issue in the notion of 'crisis'. Most analyses have so far concentrated on the cuts in expenditure and the attempts to gear education more efficiently to the 'needs of industry'. They have identified quite accurately certain empirical causes of the crisis and some of the consequences of policy changes. That doesn't in itself explain what the changes mean in terms of the exercise of state power. The power of the state is not the property of any group or class. It exists only as it is exercised in what Foucault calls the 'micro-physics of power'. The appropriate model, he suggests, is not a contract but a perpetual battle. Power is 'a network of relations, constantly in tension, in activity, rather than a privilege one might possess.'[2] Focusing just on the centralization of power may show where power lies; it cannot explain how it works.

The basic problem then, is the tendency to jumble together concepts which need to be kept analytically distinct – capital, industry and the state, for example, or state policy and what teachers do in schools. One analysis sensitive to such differences is the essay on 'Social Democracy, Education and the Crisis' by Dan Finn, Neil Grant and Richard Johnson.[3] The authors are careful to specify that they are concerned with ideologies *about* education ('particular versions of what schools are for, of how they work and of what it is possible for them to achieve') rather than the ideological work of schools ('their institutional structures, their disposition of knowledge, their pedagogic relationships, their informal cultures and organization'). They show how the continuous debates about education form part of a general political discourse, that 'they are a regional instance of the process of bidding for the consent of the governed'. They also accept the need to define the specificity of 'ideologies about' education and to look for the ways in which these actually relate to what happens in schools.

> The debate *about* education is often constructed at some distance from the processes it purports to describe. It has, however, through *policies*, a real effect upon the educational system itself.[4]

The distinction they don't make is the one between policy as discourse and policy as the administrative and pedagogic 'micro-physics of power' in the schools. In other words, 'policy' here refers ambivalently to the separation as well as the connection of different practices; it doesn't explain either.

Nonetheless, Finn, Grant and Johnson make a substantial contribution to the understanding of 'power-knowledge relations' by tracing the rise and fall of the consensus which dominated educational theory and policy during the long post-war boom: this was based on an alliance of the Labour Party, the teaching profession and academic sociologists. The usefulness of their evidence makes it important to question some of their explanatory categories. Raymond Williams has pointed out the danger of confusing an historical alliance (which contains not merely contradictions, but alternative forces in conflict within the alliance and having different relative importance at different times) with a fully fledged, coherent ideology (typically containing ideas that educational reform through the organs of the state can lead to social equality or 'classlessness').[5] They also tend to treat the relationship of power to knowledge as an instrumental one. In presenting the connection between the emergence of a specialist sociology of education and Labour's formulation of its post-1944 educational goals, for example, Finn, Grant and Johnson stress that the academics were not *simply* party advisers. Nevertheless, they do imply that Labour used their theoretical work for political purposes. They also suggest that the changing relationships within the alliance can be explained in terms of human agency, whether individual (which intellectual or civil servant had which politician's ear, 'the actual careers of individuals as both sociologists and party advisers') or collective (the Fabian or egalitarian influence, the sectional interests of teachers, the rise of the Tory populists).

To question this approach does not mean that I am writing off human agency. On the contrary, my argument is that to press it into service as an unexamined explanatory category ignores its absolutely crucial political significance. Human agency is something that has itself to be explained, and the way to do that is by examining the processes and struggles which produce both the power-knowledge relation and a position within it for the human agent, a position which sustains the relation. Agency can only be understood (and changed) if it is conceived not just as the source of social change, but above all as an effect of particular social and institutional practices. This would lead to a new range of questions. How were the Labour intellectuals and politicians formed so that they could occupy the positions they did within that specific power-knowledge field? How did these positional forces combine or clash to define that field? What different discourses were at play to give these positions their apparent coherence? How did the discursive and administrative practices of which these agents were the 'authors' resolve certain contradictions by containing them in a relation of precarious congruence? These are questions about the mechanisms of 'hegemony'. They call for answers not in terms of causality, but a conjunctural analysis of the balance of social forces. Part of that is the identification of the penetration and effectivity of what have been called 'discourses in power'.[6] The components of such a 'discursive régime' do in fact seem to be nascent in Finn, Grant and Johnson's constellation of *alliance*, *consensus* and *ideology*. But because they explain shifts in the dominant ways of thinking about education in terms of intellectual influence and pressure group politics, they give little sense of the specific conditions and rules which bring about such discursive transformations.

I would accept the general political orientation of Finn, Grant and Johnson. Their analysis is also illuminating in its detail, rigorous in specifying its object of study and accurate in its periodization of policy transformations. There is, nonetheless, a circularity in their argument: the conclusion of their story is implicit in its starting point. This, I think, explains why the story stops short of an adequate account of the present 'crisis' or of a strategic political perspective on it. They argue, quite correctly, that the crisis is specific to education but also fits into the socio-historical conjuncture. Because they do not identify the specific crisis as a discursive transformation, though, they cannot show *how* it fits. They have to sidestep the problem with a gesture.

> The crisis of the educational sector is bound up with the overall crisis of the economy and the State. But while we recognize that the specific form of the educational crisis has its determinations in the general crisis, we must insist that the educational crisis is *also* a regional one.[7]

It is, in the end, the limitation of their method that they offer useful political ammunition rather than the theoretical basis for an oppositional knowledge.

The Green Paper

To challenge the truth of the Green Paper is not a question of saying it's all lies and mystification, but of showing *how it works* as a text and, so, of questioning the definition and effectivity of its status of knowledge. In the next section I shall examine the institutional context in which it was produced, regulated, distributed and circulated but here (the distinction is made purely for purposes of analysis) I shall try to offer some of the tools for a 'reading' which would go against the grain of the Paper. A proper reading would mean breaking it down into fragments and looking at it 'frame by frame', to use a cinematic analogy, showing its 'truth producing' mechanisms at work. Lacking the space for that,[8] I shall pick out examples of how 'problems' are selected for the political agenda and how 'the State' is constructed as a discursive category.

This last point can be illustrated by investigating the apparently innocent words 'we' and 'our'. In the Paper's Foreword, for example, which is signified as by *the Secretary of State for Education and Science and the Secretary of State for Wales* and signed by *Shirley Williams* and *John Morris*, it is clearly these named people who are the 'authors' of the comment that

> *We* hope, therefore, that those who read this Green Paper will do so against this background of much that is exciting and even outstanding.

Compare this with the concluding remark, though.

> But there are times for self-examination followed by the setting down of new objectives and new ways of reaching those objectives. *We* believe that *we* have now reached such a time, and this Green Paper is a response to it.

The first *we* is quite straightforward; it is still the Secretaries of State. But unless the *self* to be examined is that of *Shirley Williams* and *John Morris* the second *we* cannot simply signify them. The *self* must be the body politic, so that *we* signifies not just the authorial subject but author *and* reader, state and citizen.

'We' and 'our', then, do not refer just to the Paper's authors – it's safe to assume that a fair number of civil servants and politicians had a hand in its various drafts – but to its *notional origin* and to a definitive *relationship* between 'author' and 'reader'. The Green Paper seems to speak to its readers in a single, coherent voice, as if engaging them in argument. But it is important to bear in mind that a reader's engagement is with the text and its linguistic structures, not with the mind of the author. The relationship between the 'speaking subject' of an utterance and the 'reader' it implicitly constructs is, therefore, an *imaginary* one, defined by positions within the text and not with reference to the actual relations between Shirley Williams and any particular reader (you, me, Rhodes Boyson). That's not to say that the 'we' which embodies this imaginary relationship is arbitrary or neutral: its ideological importance – which has implications beyond the confines of the text – lies in the way that it invites certain readings and inhibits others. So, to return to the Green Paper, it is worth asking what subject has the authority to speak of *our society, our educational system, our Imperial past, our people, our boys and girls*. Each has slightly different connotations – *our society* and *our education system*, for example, have a social democratic ring to them: not only is society the totality of all 'citizens', but its institutions belong to all its members. But if *our* signifies the imaginary communality of government and governed, then *our people* would be a tautology. This is not simply a question of logic, though: *our people* is an example of how class relations of domination and subordination can be incorporated into a discursive unity. What gives coherence to these variations on *our*, then, is the concept of the State, which itself contains the incompatible meanings of governmental apparatus, community of citizens and antagonistic classes.)

In all the examples I have quoted, the source of the enunciation is present within the statement – '*We* believe that *we* have *now* reached such a time', for example. At many points in the Paper, however, it is suppressed and the very *Secretaries of State* who are the nominal source become actors within it.

> *2.19* It would not be compatible with the duty of the *Secretaries of State* to 'promote the education of the people of England and Wales', or with their accountability to Parliament, to abdicate from leadership on educational issues which have become a matter of lively public concern.

That is not to say that there is no speaking subject here – as I have stressed, there has to be one for the statement to make sense. And once again in this passage it is the State, although not its temporal embodiments but a sort of Hegelian ideal of the State. It is a moral category (*duty* … *accountability* … *leadership*) which provides the over-arching form of the state: it mediates the two moments of its agency (bureaucracy, policy) and its functionality (reproduction, hegemony), and incorporates both the juridically defined 'state' (Secretaries of State, Parliament) and 'society' (the *public*). Take, as a final example of the significance of the source of the enunciation, the conclusion of the Paper. Here it is acknowledged that 'some anxieties are justified' about education and so the State (as moral category) endorses the actions of the state apparatus.

> *9.2* It is right that the Government should give a lead in making these proposals.

In the final paragraph, though, an overtly ideological *we* reappears. In a fairly safe bet on who will actually be reading the paper, it is defined in a way that pulls all the different *we*'s of the text into an imaginary coherence (and possibly into political collusion).

> *9.3* Each child's education is a unique experience. *We*, the partners in the education service, owe it to *our children* to provide them with the best education our means allow.

I have tried to show how, within the text of the Green Paper, a field is defined on which the positional relationships of author and reader to that text and to each other are charted. In his book *S/Z*, Roland Barthes has designated this the *symbolic*, one of five 'codes' which in their interplay create a sense of reality for the reader of a literary text. Although, obviously, there are fundamental differences between the text which Barthes submits to a 'slow-motion reading' (Balzac's short story *Sarrasine*) and a contemporary government document like the Green Paper, the applicability of the symbolic, which is in many ways the most complex, suggests that the same codes can be seen at work in both. Probably the most straightforward of the five is the *semic* code, which plays on the ascription of characteristics to persons, places, things. Thus teachers may possess *vigour, imagination and talent* (Foreword), they may be more or less *able and experienced* (2.2) or they may be inefficient, incompetent and on the verge of nervous collapse (6.36–38). Parents can be *inadequate or even uncaring* (1.13) or they may be caring and fulfilled (2.31) and *involved* (8.5). Schools can be *exciting* (Foreword), inadequate (1.3) or *overambitious* (1.3). Closely related to the semic is the *cultural* code, through which the text refers outwards to 'reality' and to 'common sense'. It invokes the things that everybody knows: Barthes therefore places it *within* ideology.

> If you collect up all these knowledges, all such vulgarisms, they form a monster, and this monster is ideology. As a fragment of ideology, the cultural code *inverts* its (social and school) class origins into a natural reference, into a proverbial assertion.[9]

The cultural code constructs a familiar 'concrete' world which seems to pre-exist the text, and whose existence justifies and validates it. Thus, in the Green Paper, the idea of a *background* is repeatedly invoked – *the background of much that is exciting and even outstanding* (Foreword), *a background of strongly critical comment in the Press and elsewhere on education and educational standards* (1.2), *the wider background of recent history and social change, responsibilities, resources and aims* (1.6), *the background of the resources available* (1.18). The important thing about this 'background' is that it is conjured within and by the text. That does not mean that nothing exists beyond the discourse or that the relationship between the 'source-of-the-represented' and the representation is arbitrary.[10] The point is that in many ways the accuracy with which the 'concrete' is represented is less important than how it is *used*. It is invoked, in a typical sleight of logic, as both the outside *cause* of the text and also as its *guarantee*. Just as ideology in general does not hide 'the real' but creates 'reality', so the Green Paper does not drown out or hide the noise of a capitalist crisis. On the contrary, it is the orchestration of that noise into a politically coherent dissonance. *Noise* here is not just interference in what would otherwise be 'pure' communication. It is not, as Barthes glosses the term, 'confused, massive, unnameable; it is a distinct 'cacography'.[11] Its main theme in the Green Paper is *lively public concern* (2.19) – the noise of *controversy* (Foreword), *critical comment* (1.2), *unease* (2.4), *misgivings* (6.13) and *genuine anxieties* (9.1) – and it is in this cultural cacography that ideology is written.

Given this background, the forward movement of the text towards its inevitable conclusion is sustained by the *proiaretic* and *hermeneutic* codes. The proiaretic composes the text into already known narrative patterns; the hermeneutic constantly reformulates the problem that is the impulse of the narrative, poses and reposes the teasing enigma which must finally be resolved. In the Green Paper, as for other forms of what Frank Burton and Pat Carlen call Official Discourse, these two codes create a 'discourse of tautology' which appropriates a problem in three stages – (i) it theorises a beginning; (ii) it structures an argument; (iii) it attempts a resolution.[12] This pattern is repeated in the sections on separate topics as well as in the overall structure. BACKGROUND, for example, starts with an 'apposite history' which establishes *when* the debate began and *who* has the authority to initiate it:

    1.1 In his speech at Ruskin College, Oxford on 18 October, 1976 the Prime Minister called for a public debate on education.

In the second stage, a perspective is constructed but as if it were neutral, as a natural emergent from the past or, as in this case, from cultural background noise.

    1.2 Children's standards of performance in their school work *were said* to have declined. The curriculum, *it was argued*, paid too little attention to the basic skills ... Underlying all this was *the feeling* that the educational system was out of touch ...

This allows the state to appear as disinterested and judicious ('*1.3 Some of these criticisms are fair* ... *1.2 Other criticisms are misplaced* ... ') and to establish the central enigma. This is a lack of knowledge which will be resolved by positivist empiricism and a *failure* within schools which will be resolved by piecemeal social engineering.

    1.5 The picture, then, is far from clear. Much has been achieved: but there is legitimate ground for criticism and concern.

A variety of devices are put into play to negate particular problems: straightforward assertion (*It is simply not true that there has been a general decline in educational standards*); empiricist faith (*Recent studies have shown clearly that today's schoolchildren read better than those of thirty years ago*); the isolation of failures as an exception rather than the rule (*A small minority of schools has simply failed to provide an adequate education by modern standards*), the 'fraternal critique' in which human fallibility is mitigated by the recognition of good intentions and/or material constraints (*More frequently, schools have been overambitious, introducing modern languages without sufficient staff to meet the needs of a much wider range of pupils, or embarking on new methods of teaching mathematics without making sure teachers understood what they were teaching* ...) and so forth.

The pattern of origin-cause-negation can also help to explain the Labour Government's broader strategy for redefining and restructuring education. From this perspective, the Great Debate should be looked at not as a 'fraud' or 'a smokescreen to hide the cuts', but as an elegant political and epistemological manoeuvre to create a rationale for fundamental changes in social democratic social policy. It did not and could not produce new knowledge – its purpose was the *validation* of existing knowledges through a sort of populist empiricism. The relentless repetition of the process should therefore be seen as a political tactic. The issues selected for discussion in the document *Educating Our Children* set such a rigid agenda for the conferences around the country that by the time of the Green Paper they had become the unarguable constituents of 'the problem of education'. It is in this sense that Barthes says that 'stereotypes are a political fact, the principal aspect of ideology'.[13]

My argument for the need to pay close attention to the language of the Green Paper is based on the principle that contesting its ideology in practice entails exposing the ways in which the 'knowledge' in the text is given credibility. That is, of course, only a first step. But how is it possible to take this opposition to its 'reality' further without appealing to the 'truth' beyond the text which will expose its falsity? This particular trap can be sprung by accepting the need to *construct* a more coherent theorization than is possible within the Green Paper's own terms, a knowledge produced from a different political position – it is certainly possible to offer accounts of sexual difference and of state expenditure (for example) which expose the partiality and inadequacy of their treatment in the Paper. Whereas the first step is deliberately *formalist*, examining the specific nature of the text as text and the ways in which it institutes a position for its 'speaking subject' (here, I have suggested, the state) and invites or blocks certain readings, the second stage emphasizes that such ideological work actually comes into operation as the text is circulated and consumed. And actual readers, of course, bring to bear a diverse range of knowledges, prejudices and resistances: inscribed subject positions are never hermetically sealed into a text but are always positions in ideologies. All readings are therefore *negotiated*, a conjuncture of two ideological formations, the reader and the text. To see how this process works, it is only necessary to look at some of the ways in which the Green Paper has been read.[14] The Confederation of British Industry and the Trades Union Congress, for example, in their different ways absorb the Paper into their existing political discourses and use it as a pretext for reasserting their already known positions. In many ways the most interesting response has come from the National Union of Teachers, which resists the Paper's implicit threat to the power of teachers by reiterating two basic assumptions – that no improvement in education is possible without more resources and that teachers' professional autonomy must be safeguarded and reinforced. Although the 'knowledge' the NUT invokes may be 'different', however, it cannot oppose the definitions given by the Paper. So firmly bound within those terms of reference is it that the Union actually works through each recommendation and proposal in turn, feebly countering with the discredited stereotypes of the old consensus. Unable to challenge the status of the Paper's truth, reading it as it asks to be read, the Union's discourse is politically ineffective because it has become residual.

The New Settlement

At the heart of the Great Debate was the creation and imposition of a 'new settlement' to replace the old consensus in education. The speed with which the NUT's response was rendered irrelevant suggests that it is in part through its power to define 'truth' and knowledge' that the state is able to secure the ideological conditions of this political settlement – which in turn sustains this produced 'truth'. The NUT's problem was its inability to challenge the Green Paper's *status*. At the same time, though, revealing the discursive mechanisms inscribed in such a text cannot show how and why its discourse – and no longer the Union's – comes to be 'in power'. 'Discourses cannot be reduced to language', the *Ideology and Consciousness* collective stresses; 'the exercise of power is conditioned at one and the same time by determinate discourses and by the practices and institutions in which they are always invested'.[15] This leads back to my original question of what a 'crisis in education' actually signifies. It means looking not only at the internal logic of the Green Paper, but at the *circulation* of its discourse, at its correlation with a range of political and economic practices, at the conditions in which its rules became effective and at the ideological work it is supposed to do in rearticulating the forms of state intervention and political representation.

Tracing the path of the discourse embodied in the Green Paper is not the same as looking for its origin or causes. It is a way of bringing to light some of the institutional conditions which made *this* discourse and not another 'happen' in this particular set of circumstances. Where did the terms and the forms of the new settlement come from? Through what institutional practices – apart from the specific signifying mechanisms – have they been imposed and others resisted? What new patterns of social relations has it helped to secure at the same time as they protect its position of dominance? Perhaps most important in this context is the change in the way that the political forces within education are constituted. The old reformist alliance between Labour and the teaching profession was characterized by a commitment to representative parliamentary democracy and a tendency to professionalism. This dyad is now being replaced, it seems, by a new pattern of *centralized bureaucratic planning* and versions of *participatory democracy*. One key to understanding this conjunctural connection is the organic contradiction between the state's role in reproducing the labour force and the drain on surplus value that this process represents; this leads to a periodic 'fiscal crisis' of the state.

In the 1960s, for example, there was a growing conflict between the need to control costs and the increasing demands for access to education. Planning and corporate management were tactics to solve this dilemma. In 1961 the expenditure plans of the DES (as of all other departments) came under the scrutiny of the Public Expenditure Survey Committee. The election of the Labour Government led to the creation of a Planning Department within the DES in 1967. The Tories wound this up in 1970 and replaced it, first, with Programme Analysis and Review and then, in 1971, with a Departmental Planning Organization. Out of this came the 1972 White Paper *Education: A Framework for Expansion*. This is interesting not so much in itself but for the mauling it received in the Organization for Economic Co-operation and Development's review of *Educational Strategy in England and Wales*.[16] Cynical about the mandarin ideology of civil service neutrality on the social functions of education, the OECD examiners deplored the failure of DES planning to transcend the terms of the old alliance. The 'educational community's "consensus"' (largely formed, no doubt, by the more respectable sociologists) on matters like skewing policy in favour of the disadvantaged was too readily accepted. Adequate methods had not been found for restricting the power of the teaching profession by imposing 'understandings not based on economic and political power plans'. In place of the DES's weak version of planning, the examiners called for two sorts of change. They wanted more aggressive corporate management, 'the use of greater daring in the delineation of new paths of learning and of new institutional and administrative developments which would allow education to respond and at the same time contribute to changes in society'. This centralization of power, they recognized, would provoke resistance: 'It will be a challenge to planning how to reconcile the problems arising from the need for such strengthening of central authority with traditional local autonomy seen as essential to the British way of life and politics'.

This is where participation comes in, as the necessary corollary, of corporatism. As the chief examiner commented in an aside, 'participation is clearly not the fashioning of policy through mass meetings'. It has an openly hegemonic purpose:

> Apart from presenting a strategy for the rational allocation of resources, an educational plan can serve as a 'third force' in situations of conflict, a rallying point around which a measure of agreement, a consensus, can develop. To do so, however, it must be the product of appropriate public procedures.

What these would be is clear in the critique of the DES's 'defensive tactics, excluding an open planning process, public hearings, even participation'. In this move to secure consent at the same time as tightening control, what emerges is the ambivalent significance of the crucial term *accountability* – financial accountability to the Treasury, public accountability to 'consumers' ('employers', 'parents', 'the community'). This analysis begins to make sense of what may at first sight appear a contradiction between the 'functionalization' of education for capital (through centralization of power, standardization, and so forth) and increasing public participation (in the form of the Great Debate, for example, or the proposals of the Taylor Report). It is a pattern repeated at many specific levels within education. In training policy, for example, the rise of the Manpower Services Commission has been accompanied by new forms of involvement of local trade unionists and employers in manpower initiatives. It is also the rationale for the changes in the structure of the Schools' Council.

To recognize within the utterances of the OECD examiners the pattern of the new settlement, though, does not mean that their discourse was immediately and unresistingly accepted. In 1975 it was still emergent, and it became dominant only through a process of political struggle. The year after the review's publication, for example, its criticism was taken up by the House of Commons Expenditure Committee as the starting point for their report on *Policy Making in the Department of Education and Science*. Here again the mutual need for control and consent is highlighted.

> We believe that, within the DES, reforms are necessary. It is no excuse to say that, with an economic crisis on our hands, this is no time to make changes. It is the very time to think ahead. Indeed, with public expenditure on education under severe restriction, it is even more important to create a framework for an informed public debate on priorities.

The point was that the secrecy and conservatism of the DES actually inhibited effective corporate planning: 'it is not so much new consultative machinery which is required as a willingness to open up public discussion on policy issues'. The criticism was not popular within the DES. Maurice Kogan, who was an adviser to the Committee, has noted that 'the Parliamentary study of the DES was briefly dismissed in a departmental reply, and no action on its recommendations taken'.[17] It is clear nonetheless that the circulation of such fundamental criticism of its ways of thinking and acting marked a shift of the balance of power within the DES, later reinforced by changes in personnel. Its policies and its practices are quite different from those in the period of the old consensus. The Great Debate, in the populism of its form and the corporatism that has followed it, can perhaps be taken as the moment of this break.

The discontinuity it represents is implied in Kogan's comment on the Taylor Report.

> If this passes into law, it will go counter to the institutional tradition upheld by such a leading Labour politician as Herbert Morrison. He was determined that institutions should not be run by those who work in them or their immediate clientele, but by the local authority that stands for election by the wider constituency.[18]

In the new settlement the losers – as they have quite rightly recognized – will be the local authorities and the representative bodies of the teaching profession. Just as the NUT's response to the Green Paper expressed their resistance to the intervention of central government, so their response to the Taylor Report tries to counter community participation by harking back to the old alliance.[19] They appeal not only to the shibboleth of professional autonomy, but also to its relation to representative democracy. Thus they argue that 'while society has a clear right to indicate its expectations through participation in local government, governing bodies and other means, teachers cannot be held accountable if they are not able to exercise full responsibility for their organization and expertise'. Or again, 'the Union shares the Committee's belief in the importance of representation of community interest, but considers that this should be achieved by inclusion amongst the local authority nominees'. The strongest dissent within the Taylor Committee came from the Chairman of the Cleveland Education Committee, who objected to the direct participation of teachers. He too invoked representation as the true form of democracy. 'I am a very firm believer in local government and would not wish to see any more authority taken away from the local education authority', wrote Mr. Fulton. 'The majority report, if implemented, will devolve to a non-elected unrepresentative body authority without accountability and in my opinion diminishes the role of the local education authority and the headteacher'.[20] This minority report has been endorsed by the local authorities; their opposition combined with the teachers' unions may actually succeed in blocking the implementation of Taylor's recommendations. Similarly, attempts to introduce corporate planning into the local authorities have so far flopped. At the same time, this community approach does open up spaces for tactical opposition.

There are structural contradictions at issue here, not just the conflict of interests represented in the Green Paper. Although financial control and corporate planning allow for the stricter discipline of state employees, they also create the conditions for trade union militancy among teachers. Indeed, much of the pre-1976 expenditure that has been cut was itself an attempt to 'buy' social stability by offering improved welfare facilities and expanding the apparatuses of control and repression. The relation between administrative control and financial control, then, is not only complementary but also contradictory. In a similar vein, Etienne Balibar sees the 'big bourgeoisie' trapped in a dramatic contradiction.

> On the one hand, its political power depends on the maintenance of its (hegemonic and uneven) alliance with the 'middle layers' of society, including intellectual wage-earners and even a fraction of the working class. On the other hand, it is becoming absolutely essential to suppress anything that, from the point of view of capital, contributes to the massive *faux frais* or 'privileges' of these *same layers*; in other words, it is becoming essential to speed up their *proletarianization*, beginning with an attack on their *security* (both Social Security and job security) and their *qualification* (of which the general cultural level forms an integral part). This contradiction is becoming visible today and is, in the long term, of an explosive character.[21]

In the present critical conjuncture of social relations, this contradiction brings to light what may appear as another paradox – the connection between the promotion of very localized forms of participatory democracy with the strategic internationalization of capital. We are not dealing here just with a *national* state apparatus. What is at issue are the preconditions necessary for the 'internationalized' reproduction of capital. Werner Olle and Wolfgang Schoeller suggest that 'just as the process of constituting a total national capital was the *result* of functions of the national state, so even the *tendency* towards the constituting of a "true historical world capital" logically and historically presupposes supranational statehood'.[22] This supersession of the national state does not result just from some economic mechanism; it can only be achieved by bringing into play all the bureaucratic and ideological mechanisms through which state power is exercised. Nor does it imply a smooth return to equilibrium. Seeing the pattern of the new educational settlement prefigured in the review of the national apparatus by the OECD (itself a powerful supranational state institution) and strenuously fought by national sectoral interests shows something of the actual struggles involved.

It is not only through the circulation of discourses that the new settlement is being achieved. Its dominance is also protected by a restructuring of the state apparatus through which it is imposed. One reason that the DES has changed its ways is that it was simply bypassed in the implementation of the sort of policies outlined in the OECD report on *Education and Working Life*. Instead, new agencies untainted by the old alliance and explicitly committed to the idea of education as training have been created – the Manpower Services Commission, for example, and the Training Services Agency. Other constraints on the national apparatus 'from above' also shape the settlement. Public expenditure cuts, for example, are enforced by the International Monetary Fund as one condition of the national state being given access to the credit necessary, *inter alia*, to meet the costs of reproduction. The problems of social control created by such cuts, I have suggested, have to be tackled by corporate management from the national centre. A similar effect is implied by the dominant themes of 'harmonization' and standardization in the European Economic Community. How the particular 'technology' of its power affects education is rather opaque; it is exercised through extremely general 'umbrella' resolutions combined with detailed discussions in the Education Committee of the Council of Ministers. Its effects can be seen, though, in the moves towards trans-European educational qualifications implicit in the current proposals for reforming the English examination system, the standardization of syllabuses through the 'core curriculum' (an idea which originated in a Council of Ministers' discussion) and even the standardization of record cards for all the pupils in Europe. It is in this context that the Green Paper's harping on mobility and the need to be able to transfer between schools makes sense.

The implication of this analysis is not that these supranational institutions snap their fingers and the national apparatus jumps. Power doesn't just flow from above down through national and local state to the individual school. There is always a struggle. I have tried to assess some of the forces involved in imposing and resisting the new settlement on English education – itself a local tactic in the ceaseless attempts to secure the conditions in which capital accumulation can continue. In part this struggle is about its own forms. Thus corporate management by the state (itself a corollary of internationalization and the restructuring of the labour force) calls forth versions of participatory democracy which opens up new spaces of opposition. Precisely because they are participatory, though, these have to be localized within particular 'communities'. They could thereby actually contribute to the ideological individualization of the 'citizen', the 'parent' and the 'teacher' and so block the construction of a (national and international) *class* opposition. Certainly, the most strenuous resistance has so far come from the sectoral forces dominant in the old consensus. Nevertheless, the settlement I have outlined is still recognizably social democratic – indeed, it highlights many of the contradictions of social democracy in the late Seventies. For example, Labour's control of the state apparatus was originally supposed to reform capitalism in favour of the working class. Education was a major theme in this: it would both equalize opportunities and produce an effective and differentiated work force. In such ways, the state becomes the vehicle of 'the national interest' above class interests. A crisis throws this act off balance: it is on behalf of capital that the social democratic state has to manage the processes of restructuring. Cuts in expenditure, for example, mean that the working class can no longer be incorporated through welfare improvements. The state may continue to expand, but it is to corporatist rather than reformist ends. This opens the ways for a right wing populism which adds to the traditional conservative complaint about the dilution of academic excellence by educational egalitarianism the charge that comprehensivization has produced neither social change nor industrial efficiency. The alternative offered is parental control allied to a radical anti-statist government. Clearly, though, there would be a tension between this and the corporatist form above that I have indicated. The fascination of a Conservative education policy would, therefore, be to see how long the incompatible threads of international corporatism, decimated public expenditure, 'parental choice' and 'standards' could be held together before the whole garment came apart at the seams.[23]

Notes and References

1 FOUCAULT, M. (1977) *Discipline and Punish* London, Allen Lane, p. 27.
2 *ibid*, p. 27.
3 FINN, D., GRANT, N. and JOHNSON, R. (1977) 'Democracy, education and the crisis' *On Ideology*: *Cultural Studies 10* Birmingham, Center for Contemporary Cultural Studies, University of Birmingham.
4 *ibid*, p. 148.
5 WILLIAMS, R. (1978) 'Education and social democracy' paper presented to the Socialist Teachers Alliance Conference.
6 ADLAM, D., HENRIQUES, J., ROSE, N., SALFIELD, A., VENN, C. and WALKERDINE, V. (1977) 'Psychology, Ideology and the Human Subject' in *Ideology and Consciousness* No. 1 May, p. 47.
7 FINN, D., GRANT, N. and JOHNSON, R. (1977) *op. cit.*, p. 190.
8 For a more extensive reading, see the original version of this article in *Screen Education* 30, Spring 1979.
9 BARTHES, R. (1975) *S/Z* London, Cape, pp. 97–98.
10 Cf. TAGG, J. (1978) 'The means of representation may exist distinct from the source-of-the-represented – they may have their "relative autonomy" – but, if the complex process of constitution of the representation neither allows us to identify the content of the representation and the source of the represented nor to compare the representation and this source, no more does it lead us to the view that the "represented has no existence beyond the process which represents it".' ('The currency of the photograph' in *Screen Education* 28, Autumn, pp. 55–6).
11 BARTHES, R. (1975) *op. cit.*, p. 132.
12 BURTON, F. and CARLEN, P. (1977) 'Official Discourse' in *Economy and Society* Vol. 6, No. 4 November. I have borrowed many of their explanatory categories for this analysis – apposite history, the exception rather than the rule, the fraternal critique, etc.
13 Barthes, quoted in COWARD, R. and ELLIS, J. (1977) *Language and Materialism* London, Routledge and Kegan Paul, p. 54.
14 See CBI EDUCATION AND TRAINING COMMITTEE (1978) 'Education In Schools' in *CBI Education and Training Bulletin Supplement* Vol. 8, No. 1; TUC (no date) *Note of Comment on the Government's Consultative Paper 'Education in Schools'* London; NUT (1977) *Education in Schools* London.
15 ADLAM, D. *et al* (1977) 'Debate' in *Ideology and Consciousness* No. 3, Autumn, p. 125.
16 OECD (1975) *Educational Strategy in England and Wales* National Reviews Paris, OECD.
17 KOGAN, M. (1978) *The Politics of Educational Change* London, Fontana, p. 143.
18 *ibid*, pp. 71–2.
19 NUT (1978) *Partnership in Education* London.
20 DES and WELSH OFFICE (1977) *A New Partnership for our Schools* (Taylor Report) London, HMSO, p. 125.
21 BALIBAR, E. (1978) 'Irrationalism and Marxism' in *New Left Review* No. 107, January/February, p. 4.
22 OLLE, W. and SCHOELLER, W. (1977) 'World Market Competition and Restrictions upon International Trade-Union Policies' in *Capital and Class* No. 2, Summer, p. 70.
23 This article was written in 1978. In shortening it for publication here I have not revised it to take account of developments since the election of Mrs. Thatcher's government.

8   Trade Unions, Artisans and the 1870 Education Act

P. McCann

Those for whom popular education is intended have, in the nature of things, seldom been articulate. In most cases we have to rely on the educated for accounts of the reactions of the under-privileged to educational legislation, improvement, or reform. If, in Forster's words, the 1870 Education Act was intended to extend and improve 'the elementary education chiefly of the working classes';[1] what do we know of their attitude to the Bill, the Act, its administration and indeed to education in general? The traditional answer has been that we know very little. It is the purpose of this article to show that the advanced sections of the working class – the trade unionists and skilled artisans and their representatives – took a deep interest in education and played an active part in both the campaigns and the debates that accompanied the passing of Forster's Bill.

This interest in government educational policy was symptomatic of the changed outlook of mid-Victorian artisans as compared with militant Chartists of a previous generation. In 1870 Thomas Cooper, the old Chartist, noticed that the Lancashire working men of the 1830's and '40's, ragged and hungry, eager for political justice and socialism, had been succeeded by well-dressed working men whose main topic of conversation was their shares in Co-ops and building societies.[2] The skilled artisans of the 1860's valued prudent saving, temperate habits, and a conscientious attitude to work. More highly skilled than the mass of 'common labour', comparatively well paid – their average wage exceeded 28 shillings per week – they were often described as the aristocracy of labour. They numbered some 800,000 or 11 per cent of the working class and by and large formed the bulk of the trade unionists.[3] The new model or 'Amalgamated' unions of the 1850's and '60's were stable craft organizations with a centralized administration, paid secretaries, relatively high subscriptions and a wide range of friendly benefits. Their members had a reputation as hard bargainers on wage demands; the strike weapon, though seldom used, was not entirely discarded.

In addition to purely economic issues, the trade unionists of the period interested themselves in a range of social questions, including the extension of the franchise

Source: McCann, P. (1970) *British Journal of Educational Studies* Vol. XVIII, No. 2, June.

(achieved by the great majority of the urban workers in 1867), legal security and a recognized position for trade unionism and an extended and improved system of popular education. Edinburgh Trades Council aptly expressed, in 1863, the aspirations of the artisans of the time; in addition to strong trade unionism, the Trades Council wanted 'good, commodious and open dwellings, to insure good health, and also the entire disuse of intoxicating liquors, and a good general system of instructions (sic) to youths and also to grown up persons'.[4]

This desire for improved instruction reflected the low level of education among the working class as a whole. According to Thomas Wright, 'The Journeyman Engineer', who had extensive experience of workshop life, the educated working man was in a small minority in any place of work. Looked up to as a 'scholard' by his fellow workers, he was constantly in demand to read or write letters, settle disputes, draw up petitions or addresses and act as spokesman in putting forward demands or grievances to the employer. He would be a man of 'tolerably sound education', moderately well read in popular and standard literature, capable of forming opinions on questions that affected him and expressing them in plain and popular language, and difficult to move to action unless his reason had been appealed to.[5]

Politically, men of this type tended to follow the Liberal party or its Radical wing. They were attracted to Joseph Chamberlain's National Education League, a Radical-Nonconformist pressure-group formed in Birmingham in October 1869 to campaign for a national system of free, compulsory and unsectarian education, in opposition to Forster's policy of filling the gaps in the voluntary system by the creation of Board Schools. The Liberal government and the majority of the party were supported on the education issue by the largely Anglican and Conservative National Education Union. 'The League might fairly be called the Reform or aggressive party', explained George Dixon its Chairman, 'and the Manchester Union has taken upon itself to uphold and defend the existing system, seeking merely to improve and amend it.'[6]

Both organizations attempted to enlist the support of trade unionists and artisans, and in this the League were more successful than the Union. The League envisaged, as a spokesman later pointed out, a collaboration between the middle and working classes in order to bring pressure to bear on Parliament.[7] The Union merely attempted to pick up working-class support in areas where conditions were particularly favourable. 'The Union', wrote Chamberlain to *The Times*, '... has nothing to show against the long list of the leaders of working class organizations, and the officers of great trade societies who support the League.'[8] This support was made easier by the fact that trade unions had for some years been speaking and acting on the education question. At the first Trades Union Congress, in June 1868, papers on technical education were read and demands voiced for a national system of primary instruction.[9] In Birmingham and London, committees of artisans campaigned for the provision of technical education[10] and the Amalgamated Society of Carpenters and Joiners had sponsored Institutes in many northern towns to teach the theory and practice of their trade to building workers.[11]

The first trade union official to be enlisted by the League had been Robert Applegarth, general secretary of the Amalgamated Society of Carpenters and Joiners, who was approached by Dixon to join the projected new body at a chance meeting in the House of Commons during the session of 1868.[12] Applegarth, an outstandingly intelligent and effective working-class politician, was a self-educated Yorkshireman without formal schooling who had started work at ten years of age in a shoemaker's shop. Later he had picked up his trade as a joiner and emigrated to the United States. Returning in 1857 he had settled in Sheffield, becoming secretary of the local branch of the Carpenters Union (characteristically moving its meeting place from a public house to a reading room) and in 1862 general secretary of the recently formed Amalgamated Society. In the later 1860's he was a man of some stature. He had impressed the Royal Commission on Trade Unions with his eloquent defence of the 'new model' unions. He was a close friend of A.J. Mundella, M.P., pioneer of Conciliation Boards; he had collected information on the Swiss system of education for Forster when attending the 1869 Congress of the International Working Men's Association at Basle; at this Congress he moved a resolution urging trade unions to agitate for compulsory state education, a project he had previously discussed with Karl Marx at the latter's house.[13]

In the summer of 1869 the Provisional Committee of the League began their campaign to enlist the support of trade unions by formally asking the A.S.C.J. to assist them in carrying out their objects.[14] Some weeks later Dixon approached the second Trades Union Congress with a request that Charles Hibbs, a Birmingham gun-maker, be allowed to put the League case to the delegates. Hibbs made a persuasive appeal, designed to allay any fears the delegates might have on questions of compulsion and sectarian teaching and the Congress carried a resolution urging Parliament to institute a system of national, unsectarian and compulsory education and also one urging individual unions to support the League's policy.[15]

A few weeks later, in October 1869, the National Education League invited a representative number of trade union and working-class political leaders to its first general meeting. Applegarth spoke on behalf of the A.S.C.J. The London Trades Council, unable to send its secretary, George Odger, promised active support.[16] Lloyd Jones, the veteran Owenite and secretary of the Labour Representation League, an organization led by prominent trade unionists, pledged co-operation on behalf of his organization. These and other trade union speakers, whilst making clear that the League's policy did not necessarily meet all their wishes, supported it on the grounds that it stood for a national system, backed by compulsion. 'I am here,' said Applegarth plainly, 'to demand that education shall be placed within the reach of every child, however poor, however degraded', and the policy of the League, he believed, was 'a step in the right direction'.[17] Applegarth and George Howell of the Operative Bricklayers, formerly secretary of the Reform League, were elected to the executive of the League at this meeting.

Before the end of 1869, Applegarth's union was urging the government to bring out an education bill which, it pointed out, was needed not only to secure the industrial position of the nation but also for its moral and social improvement.[18] These sentiments were underlined by Applegarth himself as the author of a leaflet entitled 'To the Members of the Trade Societies of the United Kingdom' which was issued to all the unions in England in December 1869.[19] Nine branches of the A.S.C.J. from London to Bristol, from Birmingham to West Hartlepool, supported the League or became constituent members of it.[20] The League leadership utilized these expressions of support from Appelgarth's union in a circular specially addressed to trade unions, hoping that they would popularize League policy in their reports. In addition a special membership form for trade societies was printed, by which they could affiliate to the League on the payment of any subscription.[21]

Two unions, both in the building trade, formally joined the League as constituent bodies and contributed to its funds – Applegarth's Amalgamated Society of Carpenters and Joiners and the Operative Bricklayers' Society. The latter, more usually known as the Manchester Order of Bricklayers, was urged by its secretary George Housley to participate in the work of the League on the grounds that education was a pressing necessity for the working class. After a favourable ballot vote of the membership the union donated £100 to the League, payable in ten annual instalments.[22] In January 1870, the National Association of Miners passed a resolution at their conference in support of the League, but unlike the Carpenters and Bricklayers they did not join it.[23]

Applegarth himself was much in demand as a League speaker, addressing meetings in various parts of the country. He utilized every opportunity which came his way to put his case, whether at a strike meeting in Glasgow, which he turned into a demonstration of support for his educational principles,[24] or at Downing Street itself, where as a member of a League deputation to Gladstone, he forcibly told the Grand Old Man that as he and his colleagues had worked hard to elect the Government, he expected a thorough-going national educational policy in return.[25]

George Howell's contribution was perhaps a more modest one. In Bristol he persuaded the Operative Liberal Association, the Amalgamated Carpenters and Joiners, and a delegate meeting of all the trades to support the League.[26] His experiences at another meeting he noted in his diary:

> ... at 8 to meeting of Gen. Union of Carpenters and Joiners. All in favour. They will bring the matter before Branches. Some difficulty arose as to compulsion, Bible as a textbook etc., but they melted away. All promised co-operation.[27]

Apparently he found no more difficulty in other towns he visited, for in the early part of 1870 he addressed trade union delegate meetings in Liverpool, Birkenhead, Blackburn, Huddersfield and the Potteries, all of which went on record in support of League policy.[28] Eventually, nineteen local trade societies formally affiliated to the League, including the branches of Applegarth's Union mentioned above. Apart from these affiliations, it was claimed that 'vast numbers' of trade societies supported League policy.[29]

Working-class public meetings on education, often called spontaneously by local trade union organizations, amounted to something like a national campaign during the first six months of 1870. Some of the most important gatherings were held in Leeds (January, March and May), Leicester (January), Edinburgh and Halifax (February), Hanley and Wolverhampton (March), Manchester (April) and Shields

(June), and several in various London boroughs.[30] Not all were held under the auspices of the League. The meeting at Leeds in January was convened by the Trades Council and represented all the industries it covered. Discussion was undertaken 'in an enlightened and temperate spirit' and the meeting concluded with the passing of a resolution favouring national, free, unsectarian and compulsory education. The Edinburgh conference, which supported a similar policy, was called by Scottish trade unions, 20,000 of whose members were represented.[31] On 21 May the North of England Miners held a special meeting on education and voted support of League principles.[32]

Coincident with this union-based activity, a great deal of public campaigning was carried out by Working Men's Auxiliaries, sponsored by both the League and the Union. Undoubtedly the most interesting and important bodies to emerge from the educational ferment of the time, these were *ad hoc* organizations of artisans, organized specifically to stimulate interest in education. They attracted workers outside the formal membership of trade societies, though they were often under trade union leadership. Fifteen auxiliaries were set up by the League, mostly in larger industrial centres,[33] but the Union seems to be the first to have formed one.

As early as January 1870, the Birmingham Working Men's Auxiliary of the National Education Union had been set up under the leadership of David Marks, the local secretary of the Provincial Typographical Society. Marks believed that the education question 'deeply affected every working man in the country' and deplored the fact that it was becoming a party question. At a meeting called by the League on 5 January 1870 he moved a resolution stating that the interests of education would best be served by a meeting between League and Union with a view to amalgamation. This failed to find a seconder and a week later he set up the Union Auxiliary.[34]

It held several meetings during the debates on the Bill. Working men, speakers asserted, would be against paying an educational rate and desired 'religious' rather than 'unsectarian' instruction. The League's use of the latter term, declared the Conservative *Gazette*, a Union supporter, was merely a hypocritical device 'to clothe in lamb-like guise the wolf of Radical iconoclasm.[35] Auxiliaries did not appear to have a high priority in the Union; Manchester seems to be the only other city where its principles found any degree of working-class support. There as in Birmingham the general policy was to support Forster's Bill, attack compulsion and brand League Auxiliaries as Radical or infidel bodies.

The Birmingham League Auxiliary was formed after the local Trades Council had refused to take sides on the education question, remaining neutral between League and Union,[36] despite the Chairman Thomas Green's confident assertion at the League General Meeting four months earlier that the Council's members 'from the Red Republican to the milk-and-water Liberal-Conservative, from the Roman Catholic to the latest discovered sect, the Hallelujah Band' unanimously upheld League policy.[37] Green, with other Liberal working men, set up the Auxiliary in March 1870; it immediately started a membership drive and began issuing leaflets and pamphlets, using the organizational machinery of League headquarters for the purpose.[38]

The League Auxiliary soon showed its strength. At a mass meeting in Birmingham Town Hall on 10 May, delegates from the Trades Council and the local Labour Electoral League were on the platform, together with David Marks of the Union Auxiliary, presumably to demonstrate both the power and the benevolence of the League. The chairman, introducing George Odger and Robert Applegarth, the main speakers, pointed out that the working class no longer discussed the propriety of education but met to consider the best means of securing it. Odger, expounding the benefits of free schools and the need for rating, attacked the rich who had, he alleged, filched the schools from the people of England and now supported these institutions with money left for the education of the poor. Applegarth also dealt ironically with the public schools of the rich, but devoted a large part of his speech to explaining the beneficial effects which improved education would have on the lives of working-class women, a point rarely made by educationists of any persuasion.[39]

If working-class opinion in Birmingham was largely on the side of the League Auxiliary, in Manchester, which lacked the long Radical traditions of the other city, the labour movement was sharply divided by League and Union rivalries. The Trades Council, which had 25,000 members in 60 societies, was led by two Conservatives, W.H. Wood and S.C. Nicholson.[40] It refused to be identified with any political movement and rejected overtures from both the Union and the League on the grounds of not wishing to offend any section of its membership.[41]

Outside the pale of the Council, however, the political rivalry between Wood and Nicholson on the one hand and two prominent Radical members, Malcolm Macleod of the Amalgamated Society of Engineers and Frederick Booker of the A.S.C.J. on the other, produced some violent clashes on the education issue. The first occurred on 11 March, when a League meeting in Manchester Town Hall was brought to an untimely end by Conservative hecklers, among the most prominent of whom was W.H. Wood.[42] A few days later a meeting of Salford Working Men's Branch of the League was broken up by Union opponents fighting, shouting, and singing 'Rule Britannia'. After several supporters of the League had been 'literally chased out of the hall', the water jug and glasses on the Chairman's table smashed, and the reporters' table occupied, the hall was cleared by the police. The local Radical press believed the Orange Lodges were behind the disturbances.[43]

Radical trade unionists rallied to put their case and on 20 April an impressive number of 97 delegates from local organizations assembled in the supper room of the Free Trade Hall. The meeting passed a resolution in favour of the League, but substituted the term 'secular' for 'unsectarian' in the declaration of arms.[44] Though the tenor of the debate was by no means theoretically anti-religious, the word secular gave scope to opponents to attack them as 'infidels'. The Conservatives counter-attacked at a public meeting in Albert Square six weeks later, at which Nicholson decried compulsory education as 'un-English' and forecast that it would be rejected by the independent British workmen, who, he claimed, also stood for religious and Biblical teaching and against the promotion of infidelity. Wood also stressed the importance of what a later speaker called the 'four R's' – reading, writing, arithmetic and religion – and made much of the Bible as 'the secret of England's greatness'. Not surprisingly, the meeting supported Forster's Bill.[45]

In London there were none of the political or religious differences that had shown themselves in Birmingham or Manchester. A Working Men's Educational Committee was set up in May which decided to hold one large central meeting and organize a deputation to Forster.

On 14 June Exeter Hall was, according to an eye-witness, 'literally crammed with working men'. The attendance was estimated at 3,000 and a speaker commented favourably on the large number of 'wives, mothers and daughters' of the supporters who were present. The platform party included well-known London trade union leaders and working men politicians – W.R. Cremer, Daniel Guile, Thomas Mottershead, Benjamin Lucraft and others, and seven Liberal M.P.'s including George Dixon and Henry Fawcett. The Rev. C.H. Spurgeon, the revivalist preacher, chaired the meeting and made a stirring call for a thoroughly national system of education. He was followed by Cremer, who moved the first resolution advocating a universal system of free schools, with compulsory attendance and with optional Bible reading.

Following a lively discussion on the religious issue, in which a secularist amendment against the inclusion of any religious influence in national rate-aided schools received twenty votes, the meeting unanimously approved a resolution in favour of setting up universal school boards with governmental powers to enforce their provision in the event of local deficiency or failure.[46]

Forster himself commented favourably on this gathering in the House of Commons.[47] A few days later he met a deputation from the Working Men's Committee at the Privy Council offices. Cremer, the leader, after outlining the Committee's policy, outspokenly criticized the support which the Bill was receiving from the Tory benches and even implied that the Government had not brought out a stronger Bill because of a compact they had made with the Irish party not to introduce a measure which would prejudice the position of denominationalism in that country. At this point Forster, who was not well known for his tact, put in some plain speaking of his own; such a suggestion, he said, was an utter delusion and altogether erroneous, and the Bill was, in fact, less denominational in character than the existing system in Ireland. Forster also regretted that the delegates, who criticized the Bill mainly on the grounds that it did not make compulsion general nor education entirely free, were disappointed in the measure, and assured them that the conscience clause safeguarded the religious scruples of parents, and that the attendance question would be solved when the provision of schools was sufficient.[48]

The confrontation with Forster was the high point of the widespread movement by trade unionists and artisans to improve and extend the government's measures. Accounts of meetings, however, give an impressionistic rather than a statistical picture. As we have seen, all the important trade union organizations formally supported League policy. Their membership figures and those of affiliated unions, despite a certain amount of overlapping, give a reasonably accurate reflection of the numbers involved.

The 1869 Trades Union Congress claimed to represent a quarter of a million workers.[49] The membership of the London Trades Council stood at 5,000.[50] The A.S.C.J. in 1870 had 10,778 members and the Operative Bricklayers 3,850, reasonably large figures for the period.[51] The numbers involved in the grass roots bodies attached to the League – the Working Men's Auxiliaries and the affiliated trade societies – are unknown, but probably ran into only a few hundreds. Nevertheless, they played a key role in propaganda work in the provinces. The distribution of both the 15 Auxiliaries and the 19 local trade societies shows a similar pattern – a fairly equal division between London, Lancashire and Cheshire, the Midlands and Yorkshire. The trade societies represented mainly the building trades, boot and shoe making and some Sheffield and Birmingham crafts, significant of the skilled artisan orientation of the movement.[52]

Joseph Chamberlain, as early as October 1869, had claimed the support of between 800,000 and 1,000,000 working men for the League;[53] though his figures were broadly coincident with the number of skilled artisans in the country, he gave no evidence in support of what was undoubtedly an exaggerated estimate. Nevertheless, taking into account the propaganda tours, the attendance at meetings and the wide circulation of leaflets and pamphlets, there could have been few socially-conscious artisans in London and the industrial districts who were unacquainted with the working-class case for a national system of education in 1870. Even the delegates of the Co-operative movement, though they took no part in the campaign, heard an eloquent speech from Applegarth on the necessity of national education at their first Congress in 1869.[54]

George Howell, in later years, considered that the participation of the trade unions had added greatly to the fervour of the League's campaign.[55] Its immediate impact was not without effect. Jacob Bright's amendment in favour of undenominational Bible reading in schools scored a moral victory; it received 130 votes, but less than 100 Liberals voted for the government, 133 walking out without voting.[56] The later Cowper-Temple clause, successfully moved by a Union supporter, which prohibited the use of catechism and formulary in religious teaching, embodied the gist of Bright's amendment. It is difficult to imagine the government amendments of May,[57] outside the context of public opinion spearheaded by the League, Francis Adams, the League secretary, in retrospect considered that the final form of the Bill conceded in principle the main aims of the League, which was in itself an achievement.[58]

Despite the general support given to the League's slogan of national, free, compulsory and unsectarian education, it is clear that artisan opinion did not always and entirely endorse it as a complete expression of their aims and that there were conflicting attitudes and varying degrees of acceptance. Not surprisingly, there was little opposition to free schools, though trade union spokesmen felt obliged to answer the allegation, often voiced by middle-class opponents of free schooling, that it would degrade the workers or cause them to undervalue education. Applegarth pointed out that the American workmen with whom he had shared a bench in the USA had not felt degraded by the free education which they had received.[59] Free schools, in Hibbs' opinion, would be valued to the extent that they were worthwhile:

> Was it true, as some said, that they would not value what they got for nothing? The richer classes were not blind to the advantages of a free education for their children. They did not despise it when they could get it.

> The working men prized their free libraries and free parks, and they would
> prize free schools if they were only worth prizing. They did not want
> educating to value school teaching . . . if the schools were really what they
> ought to be – educational institutions – and not miserable dame schools,
> where the 3 R's were merely taught. Free schools of that description
> would not be prized.[60]

Consideration of the religious issue inevitably called into question the position
of the Voluntary system. Only the supporters of Union Auxiliaries were prepared
to defend it. Implicit in the League standpoint was the belief that Voluntaryism
had failed to provide for the educational needs of the working class. Applegarth,
though ready to praise the efforts of 'underpaid curates' who had done 'the real
work in the education of the people,' nevertheless pointed out that the Voluntary
system had left the country with a very unequal distribution of educational facilities;
in addition, for the want of 'that great principle, compulsion' there were no less
than 700,000 'vacant seats' in the nation's schools.[61]

On the question of religious teaching, three trends were discernible. Firstly,
there was the support given by the Union Auxiliaries, chiefly in Manchester and
Birmingham, to religion as an essential element of elementary education. The only
important working-class pamphlet giving the Union point of view was largely
devoted to stressing the belief that religion in education was the only bulwark
'against the approaching tide of scepticism.'[62] Secondly, in opposition to this, there
was a wider trend in favour of making schools completely secular. Applegarth, at
the first League meeting, had shown his distaste for mixing up national education
'with any portion of religion, however small the dose',[63] and he frequently alluded
favourably to the secular schools of Switzerland. G.H. Holyoake, the veteran
Co-operator, and Thomas Green, the chairman of Birmingham Trades Council,
had both spoken in favour of secularism at the same gathering.[64] In most large
working-class gatherings there was usually a current in favour of keeping all creeds
out of the classroom, as the meetings in London and Manchester show. At the
latter a carpenter declared that at school he had been made to repeat the 119th
Psalm till he could say it by heart, but that he would have done much better, and
certainly have been a better craftsman, if he had mastered the 47 problems of
Euclid.[65] A cabinet maker at the Leeds meeting of 1 January felt that clergy always
endeavoured to keep people in the dark; he regretted the number of ministers of
religion in the League ranks, for 'wherever there was theology, tyranny and ignorance always existed'.[66]

On the whole, however, the average working man had no objection to the Bible
being read in schools, in the words of a speaker at the Manchester meeting, 'as
Shakespeare was read'.[67] Apart from the exceptional incidents already mentioned,
the fierce sectarian battles in press and parliament, the complex arguments on the
implications of the religious clauses of the Bill found little place in working-class
life. Applegarth seemed to be summing up the position fairly accurately when he
suggested that the religious difficulty in education had been created for and not
by the working class.[68]

Compulsory attendance at school was, of course, a key issue and Forster's plan to make compulsion permissive by leaving it to school boards was seen by League supporters as inconsistent with the aim of getting all working-class children into schools. A middle-class observer felt that the working class were 'probably' not averse to compulsion, because they had already experienced the principle in various Factory Acts.[69] The League issued Robert Applegarth's pamphlet *Compulsory Attendance at School: The Working Men's View* in 20,000 copies. He contended that the working class had made up its mind on this issue and that it was the chief cause of support given by them to the League, because they knew how the Voluntary system had failed to give them the educational advantages which they desired. He quoted the example of Switzerland and the USA as evidence of the acceptance of compulsion by the people and of the superior education which they enjoyed as a result.[70] Compulsory education, argued Applegarth, answering another charge of middle-class opponents, could be reconciled with personal liberty:

> Our workmen . . . are fast learning that they have duties to discharge, as well as rights to enjoy, and although many of them have as much love for themselves, and stickle as much about their 'rights and liberties' as any of their liberty-of-the-subject friends could desire, yet amongst the great body of our workpeople there is a widespread appreciation of the great moral lesson conveyed in the words 'love thy neighbour as thyself'. They are, therefore, fully prepared to submit to a law which, if it prescribes their personal liberty, will prove a wholesome check on their vices, and confer a blessing on posterity.[71]

Only one notable trade unionist, Robert Last, general secretary of the General Union of Carpenters and Joiners, a loosely organized rival of Applegarth's union, thought that compulsory powers given to school boards could materially interfere with personal and parental liberty.[72]

Widespread working-class support for a stronger educational policy than that of the government raises a query about Forster's compromise proposals. Could he have risked a stronger Bill, closer to the views of those 'chiefly of the working classes' for whom it was intended? Added point is given to the question by the support of articulate artisan opinion for a much wider exposition of the aims and content of elementary education than that of either the government or the League.

One of the weaknesses of both the government Bill and the National Education League's platform was that improved education was seen essentially in terms of a greater number of school places. About what was to be taught in schools little was said, beyond support for the continuation of 'payment by results', the examination-haunted system of rote-learning the basic subjects established by Robert Lowe in 1862. It was precisely on the more fundamental issues – the aims of education for the masses, the content of the curriculum, the place of education in working-class life and aspirations – that the most articulate of the artisan spokesmen, particularly Robert Applegarth and Charles Hibbs, made valuable contributions.[73]

Both accepted the position that, educationally speaking, the working class could be divided into three groups – roughly the top 10 per cent or so of skilled and educated craftsmen, the mass of more or less imperfectly educated workmen and what Hibbs called the 'lower deep within the lowest' – the illiterate, impoverished slum dwellers of the cities. Applegarth often suggested a simpler division – between the 'intelligent and industrious' and 'the idle and the vicious' or between 'the sot, the careless and indifferent man' and 'the better class of working man'.[74] He felt that it was incumbent on the intelligent artisan to speak for the whole of the working class, to agitate for education for all and even to compel the uneducated to recognize the value of education.

Although Applegarth could identify himself with Forster on the need to educate British artisans to compete with foreign competitors in the world market,[75] his main arguments on the need for more education had a social orientation. Because ignorance, crime and poverty were so intimately connected (only 5 per cent of criminals could read and paupers were 'utterly void of learning'), improved education would materially reduce the £10 million annually paid out of taxes (which fell heavily on the workers) for the purpose of punishing crime and perpetuating pauperism. In addition, 'a large portion' of the £10 million annually paid to the revenue by the working class as their share of the levy upon drink should be expended on education, as a positive contribution to the happiness of the home.[76]

In addition, the curriculum needed revision. Thomas Wright had drawn attention to the way in which the short period of school life and the mechanical exercise of memory reduced all subjects to dry technicalities which were soon forgotten by most of the pupils.[77] As Hibbs expressed it, the learning of 'unmeaning' sounds and characters, and the performance of arithmetical operations to instruction meant that 'the metal has not been smelted or refined but only coated with a thin lacquer, which wears off as soon as it comes into use'. Products of such an education became citizens without interests or curiosity, content to have opinions made for them and regarding the operation of government as something beyond their ken.

It was this failure of the educational system to produce socially-conscious citizens that was most disturbing. It raised the whole question of the content and aims of education – what kind of education did the working class need and for what purpose? The realities of working-class life, Hibbs argued, pointed towards the answers to these questions. The average workman's existence was divided between the struggle to earn wages to support his family, and the difficulty of making those wages cover the family's wants. Workers toiled monotonously to keep alive, their utmost hope no more than that they might be permitted to do so uninterruptedly to the end of their lives, with the pit of pauperism ever before them should their health or strength fail.

Education, he believed, could vivify that life. All should have the chance to excel at art or science. Education itself should be treated as a science, so that the mental faculties of the pupils could be awakened, leading to all-round improvement by means of 'the electric action of mind upon mind'. Everyone should receive an education to fit him for three things. Firstly, to perform the public duties of a citizen, so that the political machine might work smoothly and without hitch; for this the citizen would need to know the law of production and distribution, the relation of capital and labour, the nature of commercial operations and the theories of civil government. Secondly, to become an effective producer, for which he needed to master the principles of machinery and the processes involved in his daily work. Thirdly, to discharge the private duties of his life in such a way as to conduce to the welfare of the general community. The duties of individual and domestic life were no doubt part of the private domain, but insofar as education could act beneficially on these dispositions, the community had an interest in education. If these aims were kept in view the working class would develop self-reliance and strength of character and 'all those qualities which make a people great'; or in Applegarth's words, workers would become 'complete men', able 'to enjoy life in its most enlightened form'.

Both Applegarth and Hibbs had a vision of society free from crime, poverty and intemperance, in which the whole of the working class, endowed with skill, intelligence and self-respect, would enjoy the performance of useful labour and play their part as socially-valued citizens. Given minimum political conditions such as an extended franchise, they felt it was in the power of education to bring this society into being. In essence it went no further than the radicalism of the James Mill era, expressed in Mill's belief that if the whole population had the vote and were taught to read 'all would be gained'.[78] It was a retreat from the faith in the power of education to regenerate the whole people, to transform the whole of society which had animated the Owenite co-operators and Rational Religionists in the 1830's and 1840's;[79] the conviction of the London Working Men's Association in 1837 that it was the duty of a popular government 'to establish *for all classes* the best possible system of education' in order to eradicate 'those symptoms which tend to future slavery';[80] above all a descent from the high point of working-class expression in the power of education, Lovett and Collins' *Chartism: A New Organisation of the People*, which advocated 'the regeneration of all' in a classless society, to be achieved by a complete system of common schools, from infant schools to colleges, under democratic control, giving mental, moral and physical training and an encyclopaedic education in the arts and sciences, both practical and theoretical.[81]

The outlook of even the most forward looking of the trade unionists of 1870 seems deficient in vision and self-confidence compared with that of the Chartist era. In the 1830's and 1840's, millions of workers had in effect rejected the existing economic and political structure and hopefully looked forward to social renewal. When this did not come about, the labour leaders of the '60's sought the best possible accommodation within the system to re-establish the position of the working class on what they took to be the most solid and realistic foundations.

If we recognize, however, that the views of the Amalgamated unionists represented a lowering of the curve of working-class educational aspirations, we must allow them the merit of re-establishing the place of education in the social policy of the labour movement. From 1870 it became normal for labour organizations to have an educational policy and to agitate for a variety of improvements in educational provision. Immediately after the Act, trade unionists began to exert pressure on the government to amend its educational policy in a more radical direction.

George Howell, now secretary of the Parliamentary Committee of the Trade Union Congress, declared in 1871 that the League must agitate for amendments to the Education Act, or for a new one, regardless of the result to Gladstone or the Government, for if the latter were not prepared to go with the people, the people should go on and leave the Government behind. Cremer urged trade unionists to put pressure on local M.P.'s who were 'knock-kneed' on the education question.[82] At the same time trade unionists were active in backing 'working men' candidates for the new School Boards, usually as members of Liberal groups. Benjamin Lucraft, a cabinet maker, was elected to the London Board in 1870, and several other working-men candidates were successful in provincial cities. Lucraft was joined in 1873 by George Potter, formerly president of the London Working Men's Association and conductor of the *Bee-Hive* newspaper, and together they pioneered developments in technical drawing classes, agitation for free education and inquiry into the uses of educational endowments.[83] In the later 70's several trade unionists were elected to School Boards as 'labour' candidates, notably W.J. Davis, of the Amalgamated Society of Brassworkers at Birmingham in 1876 and Henry Slatter, general secretary of the Typographical Asssociation, at Manchester three years later.

These successes mark the beginning of a distinctive 'labour' policy on education, free from organizational alliance with the Radical wing of the Liberal Party, which was to be developed in the 1890's into the detailed educational proposals of the Trades Union Congress based on secondary education for all, the direct forerunner of the comprehensive ideal of the twentieth century. This was a far cry from the relatively moderate demands of the artisans of 1870, but to them must go the credit for emphasizing the concern of the labour movement with education and for helping to establish the principle that those who were to receive its benefits had a right to a voice in the kind of schools that were to be built and what was to be taught in them.

Notes and References

1 FORSTER, W. (1870) Parliamentary Debate, 3rd Ser., CXCIX, 454, 17 February.
2 COOPER, T. (1872) *Life of Thomas Copper* London, Hodder and Stoughton, p. 393.
3 HOBSBAWM, E. J. (1964) *Labouring Men* London, Weidenfield and Nicholson, pp. 272–5, 297.
4 MACDOUGALL, I. (Ed) (1968) *Minutes of Edinburgh Trades Council 1859–73*, Edinburgh, p. 115.
5 A JOURNEYMAN ENGINEER [Thomas Wright] (1887) *Some Habits and Customs of the Working Classes*, London, pp. 3–4, 11–12.
6 DIXON, G. (1870) *The Times*, 7 January.
7 WALTON, A. (1871) *National Education League Monthly*, 13 June.
8 CHAMBERLAIN, J. (1870), *The Times*, 1 January.
9 FROW, E. and KATANKA, M. (Eds) (1968) *1868: Year of the Unions*, London, Michael Katanka, pp. 32–4.
10 BIRMINGHAM SOCIETY OF ARTISANS: General Rules (1867) Birmingham (n.d.); Report of the proceedings of the Workmen's Technical Education Committee (1869) London, 2nd Edn.
11 *Royal Commission on Scientific Instruction and the Advancement of Science*, P.P. (1872), XXV, 324–6; *Amalgated Society of Carpenters and Joiners Monthly Report*, (January, February, September, October and December 1868).
12 HUMPHREY, A.W. (1913) *Robert Applegarth: Trade Unionist, Educationist, Reformer*, London and Manchester, National Labour Press, pp. 198–9.
13 HUMPHREY, A.W. *op. cit., passim*; p. 107.
14 Amalgamated Society of Carpenters and Joiners *Monthly Report* (August 1869).

15 The Second Annual Congress of Trade Unions . . . Specially Reported by R.S. Kirk (1869) Birmingham (n.d.), 4, pp. 25–6.

16 London Trades Council, Minutes, (October 1869).

17 Report of the First General Meeting of the National Education League (1869), Birmingham, pp. 60–2; 84; 86–9; 137–8.

18 *Monthly Paper* No. 2, (January 1870).

19 In 'A Collection of Circulars, Leaflets, etc., Relating to the National Education League, 1869–75' (Birmingham Central Library). (Hereafter N.E.L. Collection.)

20 Amalgamated Society of Carpenters and Joiners, Monthly Reports, (December 1869–February 1870) *passim.*

21 These are preserved in the N.E.L. Collection.

22 Friendly Operative Bricklayers' Trade Protection Society, Monthly Report, No. 245, (December (1869); *Monthly Paper*, No. 6 (May 1870).

23 *Monthly Paper*, No. 3, (February 1870).

24 Humphrey, *op. cit.*, pp. 219–20.

25 Verbatim Report of the Proceedings of a Deputation to the Right Hon. W.E. Gladstone, M.P. (Birmingham 1870), pp. 19–20.

26 *Monthly Paper*, No. 1, (December 1869).

27 HOWELL, G. (30 November 1869) MS Diary, Bishopsgate Institute.

28 *Monthly Paper*, No. 3, (February 1870); No. 4, (March 1870).

29 Leaflet of the Birmingham 'Working Men's Auxiliary', Dated 20 April, N.E.L. Collection.

30 *Times, Beehive, Monthly Paper*, (January–June 1870), *passim.*

31 *Times* (3 January 1870); (12 February 1870).

32 *Monthly Paper*, No. 7, (June 1870).

33 League Auxiliaries were established in the following towns and cities: Bristol, Birmingham, Birkenhead, Blackburn, Bradford, Burslem, Chesham, Halifax, Huddersfield, Liverpool, London, Longton, Salford, Stoke, and Hanley and Whitby. (Report of the Third Annual Meeting; *Monthly Paper*, No. 4 (March 1870); No. 21 (August 1871), *passim.*

34 *Times*, (7 January 1870); *Birmingham Daily Gazette* (12 January 1870).

35 *Birmingham Daily Gazette* (12 October 1869); (12 January 1870) (21 January 1870).

36 Birmingham Trades Council Minutes, (11 February 1870); (1 July 1870).

37 Report of the First General Meeting, p. 89.

38 *Times*, (22 March 1870); leaflets of the Birmingham Working Men's Auxiliary of the National Education League, dated 16 March 1870, April 20 1870, N.E.L. Collection.

39 *Birmingham Daily Post and Birmingham Daily Gazette*, (11 May 1870).

40 *Manchester Daily Examiner and Times* (9 November 1870).

41 *Manchester City News*, (7 December 1867); *Manchester Guardian*, (9 November 1870).

42 *Manchester Daily Examiner and Times* (12 March 1870).

43 *Manchester Daily Examiner and Times*, (15 March 1870); (16 March 1870).

44 *Manchester Daily Examiner and Times*, (21 April 1870).

45 *Manchester Courier* (30 May 1870).

46 *Pall Mall Gazette*, (15 June 1870); *Beehive*, (18 June 1870); *Reynold's Newspaper*, (19 June 1870).

47 Parl. Deb., 3rd Ser., CCII (20 June 1870), p. 585.

48 *Beehive*, (2 July 1870); *Reynolds' Newspaper* (3 July 1870).

49 MUSSON, A.E. (1955) *The Congress of 1868: The Origins and Establishment of the Trades Union Congress*, London, p. 42.

50 *London Trades Council 1860–1950: A History* (1950) London, p. 39.

51 WEBB, S. and WEBB, B., (1920) *The History of Trade Unionism*, London, Longmans, rev. edn., App. VI. pp. 744–7. The 28 most important unions listed by the Webbs had, in 1870, a total membership of 142,530. No membership figure is given for the National Association of Miners.

52 The list of trade societies is given in Report of the Third Meeting of Members of the National Education League (Birmingham 1871).

53 Speech at a public meeting in Birmingham Town Hall, 13 October 1869, in Report of the First General Meeting, p. 215.

54 Proceedings of the Co-operative Congress 1869, p. 72.

55 HOWELL, G. (1902) *Labour Legislation, Labour Movements and Labour Leaders*, London, T. Fisher Unwin, p. 473.

56 Parl. Deb., 3rd Ser., CII (30 June 1870) pp. 1270–81.

57 These included the introduction of the cumulative vote in School Board elections to satisfy religious minorities, the imposition of the time-table conscience clause on rate-aided schools and the decision

not to examine the religious teaching of any school.

58 ADAMS, F. (1882) *History of the Elementary School Contest England*, London, Chapman and Hall, pp. 235–6.

59 *Sheffield and Rotherham Independent* (12 February 1870).

60 *Monthly Paper*, No. 7, (June 1870).

61 Report of the First General Meeting, pp. 87–8.

62 BRITTAIN, H. (n.d. but 1870) *Thoughts Concerning Education, by one of the Working Classes*, Birmingham.

63 Report of the First General Meeting, p. 88.

64 *ibid.*, 90, pp. 166–70.

65 *Beehive* (23 April 1870).

66 *Times* (3 January 1870).

67 *Beehive* (23 April 1870).

68 *Sheffield and Rotherham Independent* (8 February 1870).

69 PARKER, C.S., 'Popular Education' in *Questions for a Reformed Parliament* (1867) London pp. 176–85.

70 APPLEGARTH, R. (1870) *Compulsory Attendance at School; The Working Man's View*, Birmingham.

71 *Sheffield and Rotherham Independent* (12 February 1870).

72 Forty-Third Annual Report of the General Union of the Friendly Operative Carpenters and Joiners Society of Great Britain and Ireland, from August 1869 to August 1870.

73 Their most important statements, on which the following paragraphs are mainly based, were: APPLEGARTH, R., 'Education in Switzerland' *Sheffield and Rotherham Independent* 29 January, 1, 5, 8 and 12 February 1870; 30 April, 7 and 28 May 1870; HIBBS, C., 'The Education of the People', *Beehive*, 16, 23 and 30 April, 7 and 28 May 1870.

74 *Monthly Paper*, No. 7 (June 1870); Report of the First General Meeting, p. 87.

75 APPLEGARTH, R., 'To the Members of the Trade Societies of the United Kingdom', N.E.L. leaflet dated December 1869, N.E.L. Collection.

76 *ibid.*

77 WRIGHT, T. (1873) *Our New Masters*, London, p. 123.

78 Cited in MILL, J.S. (1873) *Autobiography*, London, Strahan, p. 106.

79 STEWART, W.A.C., and McCANN, P., (1967) *The Educational Innovators* London, Macmillan.

80 LOVETT, W. (1876) *Life and Struggles*, London, pp. 134–46.

81 LOVETT, W. and COLLINS, J. (1841) *Chartism: A New Organisation of the People*. London, 2nd Edn., *passim*.

82 Report of the Third Annual Meeting of the Members of the National Education League (1871), Birmingham, pp. 49–50, 183.

83 For this and the following cf. my unpublished doctoral thesis 'Trade Unionist, Co-operative and Socialist Organisations in Relation to Popular Education 1870–1902.' (1960) Manchester.

2
Education, the Economy and the Labour Process

9   The Modern Corporation

Harry Braverman

[...] The foundations for the theory of the monopolistic corporation were laid by Marx when he described the tendency of capital to agglomerate in huge units. This comes about in the first instance by the *concentration* of capital, which Marx defined as the natural result of the accumulation process: each capital grows and with it grows the scale of production it carries on. The *centralization* of capital, on the other hand, changes the distribution of existing capitals, bringing together 'capitals already formed', by means of 'destruction of their individual independence, expropriation of capitalist by capitalist, transformation of many small into few large capitals. ... Capital grows in one place to a huge mass in a single hand, because it has in another place been lost by many'.[1] This centralization may be accomplished, as Marx points out, either through competition or through the credit system, whereby many owners make their capital available to a single control.

The scale of capitalist enterprise, prior to the development of the modern corporation, was limited by both the availability of capital and the management capacities of the capitalist or group of partners. These are the limits set by personal fortunes and personal capabilities. It is only in the monopoly period that these limits are overcome, or at least immensely broadened and detached from the personal wealth and capacities of individuals. The corporation as a form severs the direct link between capital and its individual owner, and monopoly capitalism builds upon this form. Huge aggregates of capital may be assembled that far transcend the sum of the wealth of those immediately associated with the enterprise. And operating control is vested increasingly in a specialized management staff for each enterprise. Since both capital and professional management – at its top levels – are drawn, by and large, from the same class, it may be said that the two sides of the capitalist, owner and manager, formerly united in one person, now become aspects of the class. It is true that ownership of capital and the management of enterprises are never totally divorced from each other in the individuals of the class, since both remain concentrated in a social grouping of extremely limited size: therefore, as a

Source: An abridged version of BRAVERMAN, H. (1974) *Labor and Monopoly Capital* New York, Monthly Review Press, Chap. 12.

rule, top managers are not capital-less individuals, nor are owners of capital neces-sarily inactive in management. But in each enterprise the direct and personal unity between the two is ruptured. Capital has now transcended its limited and limiting personal form and has entered into an institutional form. This remains true even though claims to ownership remain, in the last resort, largely personal or familial in accordance with the rationale and juridical structure of capitalism.

To belong to the capitalist class by virtue of ownership of capital, one must simply possess adequate wealth; that is the only requirement for membership in that sense. To belong to the capitalist class in its aspect as the direct organizer and manager of a capitalist enterprise is another matter. Here, a process of selection goes on having to do with such qualities as aggressiveness and ruthlessness, organi-zational proficiency and drive, technical insight and, especially, marketing talent. Thus while the managerial stratum continues to be drawn from among those endowed with capital, family, connections, and other ties within the network of the class as a whole, it is not closed to some who may rise from other social classes, not through the acquisition of wealth on their part but through the co-optation of their talent on the part of the capitalist organization which they serve. In this case the ownership of capital later follows from the managerial position, rather than the other way around. But this is exceptional, not just because top management is drawn as a rule from within the class, but also because the stratum as a whole is not a large one.

While the title of 'manager' is bestowed in various statistical classifications upon a great variety of jobs, the possession of this title has, for most, nothing to do with the capitalist management of the substantial corporations of the country. For example, the Bureau of the Census classified almost six and one-half million persons, out of some eighty million, as 'managers and administrators, except farm', in the census of 1970. But this included perhaps a million managers of retail and service outlets, and as much as another million self-employed petty proprietors in these same fields. It included buyers and purchasing agents, officials and administrators at the various levels of government, school administration, hospitals and other such institutions; postmasters and mail superintendents; ships' officers, pilots, and pursers; building managers and superintendents; railroad conductors; union officials; and funeral directors. Since such categories consume almost half of the entire classification, it is clear without further analysis of the rest that the managerial stratum of true operating executives of the corporate world is quite a small group.

But though proportionately small in the total population, this stratum has become very large in comparison with the pre-monopoly situation. Speaking of the early part of the nineteenth century, Pollard says: 'The large-scale entrepreneur of the day began with very limited managerial, clerical or administrative staff; he wrote his own letters, visited his own customers, and belabored his men with his own walking stick'. The small number of clerks employed even in large establishments did not only bookkeeping but timekeeping, quality control, traveling, and drafts-manship. For years, says Pollard, Watt made all his drawings himself, and he gives this remarkable statistic: 'The Arkwrights, in 1801–4, employed only three clerks to look after 1,063 workers, nearly all of whom, again, were paid by complicated piece rates'.[2] In the United States, Alfred D. Chandler points out:

> Before 1850 very few American businesses needed the services of a full-time administrator or required a clearly defined administrative structure. Industrial enterprises were very small, in comparison with those of today. And they were usually family affairs. The two or three men responsible for the destiny of a single enterprise handled all its basic activities – economic and administrative, operational and entrepreneurial.[3]

The institutionalization of capital and the vesting of control in a specialized stratum of the capitalist class corresponds chronologically to an immense growth in the scale of management operations. Not only is the size of enterprises growing at a great pace – to the point where a few enterprises begin to dominate the productive activity of each major industry – but at the same time the functions undertaken by management are broadened very rapidly. We have already traced this development in the sphere of production. When fully reorganized in the modern corporation, the producing activities are subdivided among functional departments, each having a specific aspect of the process for its domain: design, styling, research and development; planning; production control; inspection or quality control; manufacturing cost accounting; work study, methods study, and industrial engineering; routing and traffic; materials purchasing and control; maintenance of plant and machinery, and power; personnel management and training; and so on.

But if the engineering organization was the first requirement, it was soon outstripped in functional importance by the marketing apparatus. The first great integrated corporations, which began to appear in the United States in the 1880s and 1890s, were constructed on the basis of a new approach to the marketing problem and it is not too much to say that, after the assurance of basic engineering requirements, it was this revolutionary marketing approach that served as the basis for the monopolistic corporation. The earlier pattern had been one of buying and selling through commission agents, wholesalers, and the like. The growing scope of the market, based upon improvements in transport and communications as well as upon the rapid increase in the size of cities created by the growth of industry, showed itself not only through increases in volume but also in geographical dispersion. The fundamental corporate innovation in this area was the national marketing organizations they established as part of their own structures, organizations which were soon to become international.[4]

The transportation network was the first arena for the giant corporation. The railroads and shipping organizations, by virtue of their demand for steel rails, plate, and structural shapes, drew in their wake the steel industry which had just begun to become proficient in the manufacture of steel at a price and quantity that made these developments possible.

Special adaptations of the means of transport to food shipping, in the form of insulated and refrigerated compartments (at first iced, later mechanically cooled), made possible the long-distance movement of the most essential commodities required by the rapidly growing urban centers. The cities were released from their dependence on local supplies and made part of an international market. Gustavus

Swift began in the mid-1870s to market Western meat in the Eastern region, and by the end of the century his organization had become a giant vertically integrated manufacturing, shipping, and marketing empire. This lead was soon followed by a number of other meatpackers, as well as by Andrew Preston who, beginning with bananas in the 1890s, had laid the foundation for the United Fruit Company by the end of the decade.

In general, the industrialization of the food industry provided the indispensable basis of the type of urban life that was being created; and it was in the food industry that the marketing structure of the corporation – embracing sales, distribution, and intensive consumer promotion and advertising – became fully developed. The canning industry had come into being in the 1840s with the development of stamping and forming machinery for producing tin cans on a mass basis. The expansion of this industry to embrace national and international markets did not come, however, until the 1870s, when further technical developments, including rotary pressure cookers and automatic soldering of cans – not to speak of the development of rail and sea transport – made it possible.[5] And soon thereafter, in the 1890s, the automatic-roller process for milling grain formed the basis for the international marketing of centrally produced flour.

Apart from food, various other industries based themselves upon the urban pattern of life that was coming into being. Steel-frame construction in the cities brought about a demand which supplemented and soon replaced the railroads as the prime market for steel. The production of petroleum was perforce localized while its use was international, and the marketing apparatus of the oil industry corresponded to this. The tobacco industry is another example: cigarettes were smoked almost entirely in the cities. The cigarette rolling machine devised in 1881 furnished the technical basis upon which Duke raised a national and international sales organization.

Cyrus McCormick's vast agricultural-machinery enterprise was built upon his own worldwide marketing and distribution organization, as was William Clark's Singer Sewing Machine Company. In these cases, as in the cases of the many machine-building and electrical-equipment companies that came into existence in the early period of monopoly capitalism, the need for a self-operated marketing organization was imposed, in addition to those factors we have already discussed, by two further reasons. First, the orders, specifications, and uses of the products became more technical and complicated, and demanded a specially trained sales organization which could work closely with the engineering division. And second, the new machines could not be sold without the provision of maintenance, service, and in many cases installation. This made it difficult for the manufacturer to be represented on the spot by existing trade facilities. Factors such as the need to provide service and replacement parts virtually dictated to the new automobile industry the construction of its own marketing network.

Thus marketing became the second major subdivision of the corporation, subdivided in its turn among sales, advertising, promotion, correspondence, orders, commissions, sales analysis, and other such sections. At the same time, other functions of management were separated out to form entire divisions. Finance, for example, although not as a rule large in size, became the brain center of the entire organism, because here was centralized the function of watching over capital, of checking and controlling the progress of its enlargement; for this purpose, the finance division has its own subdivisions for borrowing, extending credit, collections, supervising cash flow, stockholder relations, and overall supervision of the financial condition of the corporation. And so on, throughout the various functions and activities of the corporation, including construction and real estate, legal, public relations, personnel and labor relations, etc.

Each of these corporate subdivisions also requires, for its own smooth functioning, internal departments which reflect and imitate the subdivisions of the entire corporation. Each requires its own accounting section, ranging from the complex cost accounting of the manufacturing divisions to the simpler budgeting functions required of even the smallest divisions. Each often controls its own hiring through its own personnel department; many require separate maintenance and cleaning sections, as well as traffic and routing, office management, purchasing, planning, correspondence, and so forth. Thus each corporate division takes on the characteristics of a separate enterprise, with its own management staff.

The picture is rendered still more complex by the tendency of the modern corporation to integrate, vertically as well as horizontally. Thus, by growth and by combination, the manufacturing corporation acquires facilities for the production of raw materials, for transportation, semi-banking institutions for the raising of capital or extending of credit, etc. At the same time, horizontal integration brings together a variety of products under the aegis of a single aggregate of capital, sometimes assembling under one overall financial control products and services bearing no discernible relation to each other except in their function as sources of profit. Each of these massive sub-corporations requires a complete management structure, with all of its divisions and subdivisions.

As Chandler has related, the eventual outcome of this pyramiding was the need for decentralization, and the result was the modern decentralized corporate structure pioneered by Du Pont, General Motors, Standard Oil of New Jersey, and Sears Roebuck in the 1920s, and much imitated since. The essence of the policy has been best explained, in brief form, by Alfred P. Sloan, long-time operating head of General Motors and the person responsible, more than any other, for the adaptation of this method to that corporation. It places, he said, 'each operation on its own foundation . . . assuming its own responsibility and contributing its share to the final result'. The final result is of course the accumulation of capital. Each section 'develops statistics correctly reflecting the relation between the net return and the invested capital of each operating division – the true measure of efficiency . . .' This 'enables the Corporation to direct the placing of additional capital where it will result in the greatest benefit to the Corporation as a whole'.[6]

From this brief sketch of the development of the modern corporation, three important aspects may be singled out as having great consequences for the occupational structure. The first has to do with *marketing*, the second with the *structure of management*, and the third with the *function of social co-ordination* now exercised by the corporation.

The overall purpose of all administrative controls is, as in the case of production controls, the elimination of uncertainty and the exercise of constraint to achieve the desired result. Seymour Melman says:

> The explanation of the rather homogeneous increase in the administrative type of overhead will be found, we suggest, in the growing variety of business activities which are being subjected to controls, both private and public. As administrators have sought to lessen the uncertainty of their prospects, by controlling more and more of the factors which determine the advantage of their plants and firms, they have attempted to control, in ever greater detail, production costs, intensity of work, market demands for products, and other aspects of firm operation. Following this hypothesis, the evolution of the business process towards the expansion of controlled areas of activity by management comprises the basis for the additions to administrative functions, and, thereby, the enlarged administration personnel.[7]

Since markets must remain the prime area of uncertainty, the effort of the corporation is therefore to reduce the *autonomous character* of the demand for its products and to increase its *induced character*. For this purpose, the marketing organization becomes second in size only to the production organization in manufacturing corporations, and other types of corporations come into existence whose entire purpose and activity is marketing.

These marketing organizations take as their responsibility what Veblen called 'a quantity-production of customers'. His description of this task, while couched in his customarily sardonic language, is nevertheless a precise expression of the modern theory of marketing: 'There is, of course, no actual fabrication of persons endowed with purchasing power *ad hoc* ... ; nor is there even any importation of an unused supply of such customers from abroad, – the law does not allow it'. Rather, as he points out, there is 'a diversion of customers from one to another of the competing sellers'. But, from the point of view of each seller, this appears as 'a production of new customers or the upkeep of customers already in use by the given concern. So that this acquisition and repair of customers may fairly be reckoned at a stated production-cost per unit; and this operation lends itself to quantity production'. Veblen goes on to point out that:

> the fabrication of customers can now be carried on as a routine operation, quite in the spirit of the mechanical industries and with much the same degree of assurance as regards the quality, rate and volume of output; the mechanical equipment as well as its complement of man-power employed in such production of customers being held to its work under the surveillance of technically trained persons who might fairly be called publicity engineers.[8]

Moreover, within the manufacturing organization, marketing considerations become so dominant that the structure of the engineering division is itself permeated by and often subordinated to it. Styling, design, and packaging, although effectuated by the producing part of the organization, represent the imposition of marketing demands upon the engineering division. The planning of product obsolescence, both through styling and the impermanence of construction, is a marketing demand exercised through the engineering division, as is the concept of the *product cycle*: the attempt to gear consumer needs to the needs of production instead of the other way around. Thus through the direct structure of the marketing organization, and through the predominance of marketing in all areas of the corporation's functioning, a large amount of labor is channeled into marketing.

Second, the change in the overall structure of management: We have already described the specialization of the management function, and the reorganization of management from a simple *line* organization – a direct chain of command over operations from executive head through superintendent and foreman – into a complex of *staff organizations* suited to a subdivision of authority by various specialized functions. It must now be noted that this represents the dismemberment of the functions of the enterprise head. Corresponding to the managing functions of the capitalist of the past, there is now a complex of departments, each of which has taken over in greatly expanded form a single duty which he exercised with very little assistance in the past. Corresponding to each of these duties there is not just a single manager, but an entire operating department which imitates in its organization and its functioning the factory out of which it grew. The particular management function is exercised not just by a manager, nor even by a staff of managers, but by an *organization of workers under the control of managers, assistant managers, supervisors, etc. Thus the relations of purchase and sale of labor power, and hence of alienated labor, have become part of the management apparatus itself.* Taken all together, this becomes the administrative apparatus of the corporation. Management has become *administration, which is a labor process conducted for the purpose of control within the corporation,* and conducted moreover as a labor process exactly analogous to the process of production, although it produces no product other than the operation and co-ordination of the corporation. From this point on, to examine management means also to examine this labor process, which contains the same antagonistic relations as are contained in the process of production. In the words of one observer:

> The corporation is a society which accomplishes its work through division of labor – a proposition now so much taken for granted that it is surprising to think it once represented a discovery. In the modern industrial corporation, division of labor has been carried to great lengths. Not only are there broadly separate functions tied to classes of individuals – marketing, production, finance, law, accounting, technology, management – but within each of these there are many subdivisions, any one of which may constitute a career. This functionalism rests on the clear description of the varied, interrelated tasks that make up the corporation's work. The 'job description' is a statement of task meant to be independent of the individual who fills the job. Individuals become 'personnel' or 'manpower' in relation to such job descriptions. . . .

In the twentieth century we have become increasingly aware of the tendency of this industrial functionalism to take on the characteristics of the production process itself. Not only is the complex work of the corporation divided into many discrete tasks performed by discrete individuals, but there has been a strong tendency to make these tasks consist of simple, uniform, repeatable elements capable of at least partial mechanization.[9]

[...]

Finally, there is the corporate function of social co-ordination. The complexity of the social division of labor which capitalism has developed over the past century, and the concentrated urban society which attempts to hold huge masses in delicate balance, call for an immense amount of social co-ordination that was not previously required. Since capitalist society resists and in fact has no way of developing an overall planning mechanism for providing this social co-ordination, much of this public function becomes the internal affair of the corporation. This has no juridical basis or administrative concept behind it; it simply comes into being by virtue of the giant size and power of the corporations, whose internal planning becomes, in effect, a crude substitute for necessary social planning. Apart from the federal government, for example, corporations are the largest employing and administrative units in the United States. Thus the five hundred largest industrial corporations employ almost fifteen million persons, or three-quarters of the persons employed by all industrial corporations. The *internal* planning of such corporations becomes in effect *social* planning, even though, as Alfred P. Sloan explained, it is based upon the 'net return' on 'invested capital', which he calls 'the true measure of efficiency'. The rapid growth of administrative employment in the corporations thus reflects the urgency of the need for social co-ordination, the general absence of such co-ordination, and the partial filling of the gap by the corporation operating on a capitalist basis and out of purely capitalist motivations. The expansion of governmental functions of social co-ordination in recent decades is another expression of this urgent need, and the fact that such government activities are highly visible, in comparison with those of the corporation, has led to the notion that the prime exercise of social control is done by government. On the contrary, so long as investment decisions are made by the corporations, the locus of social control and co-ordination must be sought among them; government fills the interstices left by these prime decisions.

Notes and References

1 MARX, K. (1867) *Capital* (Vol. 1) Moscow, Foreign Languages Publishing House (1954), p. 586.
2 POLLARD, S. (1965) *The Genesis of Modern Management* London, Edward Arnold.
3 CHANDLER, A.D. (1962) *Strategy and Structure: Chapters in the History of the Industrial Enterprise* Cambridge, Mass., MIT Press, p. 19.
4 *ibid.* On this, and what follows, I am indebted to the first chapter of Chandler's book.
5 COREY, L. (1950) *Meat and Man: A Study of Monopoly, Unionism and Food Policy* New York, Viking Press, pp. 38–9.
6 SLOAN, A.P. (1965) *My Years With General Motors* New York, Doubleday, p. 50.

7 MELMAN, S. (1951) 'The rise in administrative overhead in the manufacturing industries of the United States, 1899–1947' *Oxford Economic Papers* new series, No. 3, p. 92, quoted in DELEHANTY, G.E. (1968) *Non-production Workers in US Manufacturing* Amsterdam, North Holland Publishing Co., p. 75.

8 VEBLEN, T. (1923) *Absentee Ownership and Business Enterprise in Recent Times* London, Allen and Unwin, (1924).

9 SCHON, D.L. (1967) *Technology and Chang: The New Heraclitus* London, Pergamon pp. 60–1.

10 Scientific management

Harry Braverman

The classical economists were the first to approach the problems of the organization of labor within capitalist relations of production from a theoretical point of view. They may thus be called the first management experts, and their work was continued in the latter part of the Industrial Revolution by such men as Andrew Ure and Charles Babbage. Between these men and the next step, the comprehensive formulation of management theory in the late nineteenth and early twentieth centuries, there lies a gap of more than half a century during which there was an enormous growth in the size of enterprises, the beginnings of the monopolistic organization of industry, and the purposive and systematic application of science to production. The scientific management movement initiated by Frederick Winslow Taylor in the last decades of the nineteenth century was brought into being by these forces. Logically, Taylorism belongs to the chain of development of management methods and the organization of labor, and not to the development of technology, in which its role was minor.

It is important to grasp this point, because from it flows the universal application of Taylorism to work in its various forms and stages of development, regardless of the nature of the technology employed. Scientific management, says Peter F. Drucker, 'was not concerned with technology. Indeed, it took tools and techniques largely as given'.[1]

Scientific management, so-called, is an attempt to apply the methods of science to the increasingly complex problems of the control of labor in rapidly growing capitalist enterprises. It lacks the characteristics of a true science because its assumptions reflect nothing more than the outlook of the capitalist with regard to the conditions of production. It starts, despite occasional protestations to the contrary, not from the human point of view but from the capitalist point of view, from the point of view of the management of a refractory work force in a setting of antagonistic social relations. It does not attempt to discover and confront the cause of this condition, but accepts it as an inexorable given, a 'natural' condition. It investi-

Source: An abridged version of BRAVERMAN, H. (1974) *Labor and Monopoly Capital* New York, Monthly Review Press, Chap. 4.

gates not labor in general, but the adaptation of labor to the needs of capital. It enters the workplace not as the representative of science, but as the representative of management masquerading in the trappings of science.

A comprehensive and detailed outline of the principles of Taylorism is essential to our narrative, not because of the things for which it is popularly known – stopwatch, speed-up, etc. – but because behind these commonplaces there lies a theory which is nothing less than the explicit verbalization of the capitalist mode of production. But before I begin this presentation, a number of introductory remarks are required to clarify the role of the Taylor school in the development of management theory.

It is impossible to overestimate the importance of the scientific management movement in the shaping of the modern corporation and indeed all institutions of capitalist society which carry on labor processes. The popular notion that Taylorism has been 'superseded' by later schools of industrial psychology or 'human relations', that it 'failed' – because of Taylor's amateurish and naive views of human motivation or because it brought about a storm of labor opposition or because Taylor and various successors antagonized workers and sometimes management as well – or that it is 'outmoded' because certain Taylorian specifics like functional foremanship or his incentive-pay schemes have been discarded for more sophisticated methods: all these represent a woeful misreading of the actual dynamics of the development of management.

Taylor dealt with the fundamentals of the organization of the labor process and of control over it. The later schools of Hugo Münsterberg, Elton Mayo, and others of this type dealt primarily with the adjustment of the worker to the ongoing production process as that process was designed by the industrial engineer. The successors to Taylor are to be found in engineering and work design, and in top management; the successors to Münsterberg and Mayo are to be found in personnel departments and schools of industrial psychology and sociology. Work itself is organized according to Taylorian principles, while personnel departments and academics have busied themselves with the selection, training, manipulation, pacification, and adjustment of 'manpower' to suit the work processes so organized. Taylorism dominates the world of production; the practitioners of 'human relations' and 'industrial psychology' are the maintenance crew for the human machinery. If Taylorism does not exist as a separate school today, that is because, apart from the bad odor of the name, it is no longer the property of a faction, since its fundamental teachings have become the bedrock of all work design. 'As a separate movement', says George Soule, 'it virtually disappeared in the great depression of the 1930's, but by that time knowledge of it had become widespread in industry and its methods and philosophy were commonplaces in many schools of engineering and business management'.[2] In other words, Taylorism is 'outmoded' or 'superseded' only in the sense that a sect which has become generalized and broadly accepted disappears as a sect. Peter F. Drucker, who has the advantage of considerable direct experience as a management consultant, is emphatic on this score:

Personnel Administration and Human Relations are the things talked about and written about whenever the management of worker and work is being discussed. They are the things the Personnel Department concerns itself with. But they are not the concepts that underlie the actual management of worker and work in American industry. This concept is Scientific Management. Scientific Management focuses on the work. Its core is the organized study of work, the analysis of work into its simplest elements and the systematic improvement of the worker's performance of each of these elements. Scientific Management has both basic concepts and easily applicable tools and techniques. And it has no difficulty proving the contribution it makes; its results in the form of higher output are visible and readily measurable.

Indeed, Scientific Management is all but a systematic philosophy of worker and work. Altogether it may well be the most powerful as well as the most lasting contribution America has made to Western thought since the Federalist Papers.[3]

The use of experimental methods in the study of work did not begin with Taylor; in fact, the self-use of such methods by the craftsman is part of the very practice of a craft. But the study of work by or on behalf of those who manage it rather than those who perform it seems to have come to the fore only with the capitalist epoch; indeed, very little basis for it could have existed before. The earliest references to the study of work correspond to the beginnings of the capitalist era: such a reference, for example, is found in the *History of the Royal Society of London*, and dates from the middle of the seventeenth century. We have already mentioned the classical economists. Charles Babbage, who not only wrote penetrating discussions of the organization of the labor process in his day, but applied the same concept to the division of mental labor, and who devised an early calculating 'engine', was probably the most direct forerunner of Taylor, who must have been familiar with Babbage's work even though he never referred to it. France had a long tradition of attempting the scientific study of work, starting with Louis XIV's minister Colbert; including military engineers like Vauban and Belidor and especially Coulomb, whose physiological studies of exertion in labor are famous, through Marey, who used smoked paper cylinders to make a graphic record of work phenomena; and culminating in Henri Fayol, a contemporary of Taylor, who in his *General and Industrial Management* attempted a set of principles aimed at securing total enterprise control by way of a systematic approach to administration.[4] The publication of management manuals, the discussions of the problems of management, and the increasingly sophisticated approach taken in practice in the second half of the nineteenth century lend support to the conclusion of the historians of the scientific management movement that Taylor was the culmination of a pre-existing trend:

> What Taylor did was not to invent something quite new, but to synthesize and present as a reasonably coherent whole ideas which had been germinating and gathering force in Great Britain and the United States throughout the nineteenth century. He gave to a disconnected series of initiatives and experiments a philosophy and a title.[5]

Taylor has little in common with those physiologists or psychologists who have attempted, before or after him, to gather information about human capacities in a spirit of scientific interest. Such records and estimates as he did produce are crude in the extreme, and this has made it easy for such critics as Georges Friedmann to poke holes in his various 'experiments' (most of which were not intended as experiments at all, but as forcible and hyperbolic demonstrations). Friedmann treats Taylorism as though it were a 'science of work', where in reality it is intended to be a *science of the management of others' work* under capitalist conditions.[6] It is not the 'best way' to do work 'in general' that Taylor was seeking, as Friedmann seems to assume, but an answer to the specific problem of how best to control alienated labor – that is to say, labor power that is bought and sold.

The second distinctive feature of Taylor's thought was his concept of control. Control has been the essential feature of management throughout its history, but with Taylor it assumed unprecedented dimensions. The stages of management control over labor before Taylor had included, progressively: the gathering together of the workers in a workshop and the dictation of the length of the working day; the supervision of workers to ensure diligent, intense, or uninterrupted application; the enforcement of rules against distractions (talking, smoking, leaving the workplace, etc.) that were thought to interfere with application; the setting of production minimums; etc.. A worker is under management control when subjected to these rules, or to any of their extensions and variations. But Taylor raised the concept of control to an entirely new plane when he asserted as an *absolute necessity for adequate management the dictation to the worker of the precise manner in which work is to be performed.* That management had the right to 'control' labor was generally assumed before Taylor, but in practice this right usually meant only the general setting of tasks, with little direct interference in the worker's mode of performing them. Taylor's contribution was to overturn this practice and replace it by its opposite. Management, he insisted, could be only a limited and frustrated undertaking so long as it left to the worker any decision about the work. His 'system' was simply a means for management to achieve control of the actual mode of performance of every labor activity, from the simplest to the most complicated. To this end, he pioneered a far greater revolution in the division of labor than any that had gone before.

Taylor created a simple line of reasoning and advanced it with a logic and clairty, a naive openness, and an evangelical zeal which soon won him a strong following among capitalists and managers. His work began in the 1880s but it was not until the 1890s that he began to lecture, read papers, and publish results. His own engineering training was limited, but his grasp of shop practice was superior, since he had served a four-year combination apprenticeship in two trades, those of patternmaker and machinist. The spread of the Taylor approach was not limited to the United States and Britain; within a short time it became popular in all industrial countries. In France it was called, in the absence of a suitable word for management, 'l'organization scientifique du travail' (later changed, when the reaction against Taylorism set in, to 'l'organisation rationnelle du travail'). In Germany it was known simply as *rationalization*; the German corporations were probably ahead of

everyone else in the practice of this technique, even before World War I.[7]
[. . .]

Taylor set as his objective the maximum or 'optimum' that can be obtained from
a day's labor power. 'On the part of the men', he said in his first book, 'the greatest
obstacle to the attainment of this standard is the slow pace which they adopt, or
the loafing or "soldiering", marking time, as it is called'. In each of his later exposi-
tions of his system, he begins with this same point, underscoring it heavily.[8] The
causes of this soldiering he breaks into two parts:

> This loafing or soldiering proceeds from two causes. First, from the
> natural instinct and tendency of men to take it easy, which may be called
> *natural soldiering*. Second, from more intricate second thought and reasoning
> caused by their relations with other men, which may be called *systematic
> soldiering*.

The first of these he quickly puts aside, to concentrate on the second:

> The natural laziness of men is serious, but by far the greatest evil from
> which both workmen and employers are suffering is the *systematic soldiering*
> which is almost universal under all the ordinary schemes of management
> and which results from a careful study on the part of the workmen of what
> they think will promote their best interests. . . . The greater part of system-
> atic soldiering . . . is done by the men with the deliberate object of keeping
> their employers ignorant of how fast work can be done.
>
> So universal is soldiering for this purpose, that hardly a competent
> workman can be found in a large establishment, whether he works by the
> day or on piece work, contract work or under any of the ordinary systems
> of compensating labor, who does not devote a considerable part of his
> time to studying just how slowly he can work and still convince his
> employer that he is going at a good pace.
>
> The causes for this are, briefly, that practically all employers determine
> upon a maximum sum which they feel it is right for each of their classes
> of employees to earn per day, whether their men work by the day or piece.[9]

That the pay of labor is a socially determined figure, relatively independent of
productivity, among employers of similar types of labor power in any given period
was thus known to Taylor. Workers who produce twice or three times as much as
they did the day before do not thereby double or triple their pay, but may be given
a small incremental advantage over their fellows, an advantage which disappears
as their level of production becomes generalized. The contest over the size of the
portion of the day's labor power to be embodied in each product is thus relatively
independent of the level of pay, which responds chiefly to market, social, and
historical factors. The worker learns this from repeated experiences, whether
working under day or piece rates: 'It is, however', says Taylor, 'under piece work
that the art of systematic soldiering is thoroughly developed. After a workman has
had the price per piece of the work he is doing lowered two or three times as a result
of his having worked harder and increased his output, he is likely to entirely lose

sight of his employer's side of the case and to become imbued with a grim determination to have no more cuts if soldiering can prevent it'.[10] To this it should be added that even where a piecework or 'incentive' system allows the worker to increase his pay, the contest is not thereby ended but only exacerbated, because the output records now determine the setting and revision of pay rates.

Taylor always took the view that workers, by acting in this fashion, were behaving rationally and with an adequate view of their own best interests. He claimed, in another account of his Midvale battle, that he conceded as much even in the midst of the struggle:

> His workman friends came to him [Taylor] continually and asked him, in a personal, friendly way, whether he would advise them, for their own best interest, to turn out more work. And, as a truthful man, he had to tell them that if he were in their place he would fight against turning out any more work, just as they were doing, because under the piece-work system they would be allowed to earn no more wages than they had been earning, and yet they would be made to work harder.[11]

In this respect, the later industrial sociologists took a step backward from Taylor. Rather than face the fact of a conflict of interests, they interpreted the behavior of workers in refusing to work harder and earn more under piece rates as 'irrational' and 'noneconomic' behavior, in contrast to that of management, which always behaved rationally. And this despite the fact that, in the observations made at the Hawthorne plant of Western Electric from which the 'human relations' school emerged, the 'lowest producer in the room ranked first in intelligence and third in dexterity; the highest producer in the room was seventh in dexterity and lowest in intelligence'.[12] [. . .]

The conclusions which Taylor drew from the baptism by fire he received in the Midvale struggle may be summarized as follows: Workers who are controlled only by general orders and discipline are not adequately controlled, because they retain their grip on the actual processes of labor. So long as they control the labor process itself, they will thwart efforts to realize to the full the potential inherent in their labor power. To change this situation, control over the labor process must pass into the hands of management, not only in a formal sense but by the control and dictation of each step of the process, including its mode of performance. In pursuit of this end, no pains are too great, no efforts excessive, because the results will repay all efforts and expenses lavished on this demanding and costly endeavor. Clearly, this last conclusion depends on Adam Smith's well-known principle that the division of labor is limited by the extent of the market, and Taylorism cannot become generalized in any industry or applicable in particular situations until the scale of production is adequate to support the efforts and costs involved in 'rationalizing' it. It is for this reason above all that Taylorism coincides with the growth of production and its concentration in ever larger corporate units in the latter part of the nineteenth and in the twentieth centuries.

The forms of management that existed prior to Taylorism, which Taylor called 'ordinary management', he deemed altogether inadequate to meet these demands.

His descriptions of ordinary management bear the marks of the propagandist and proselytizer: exaggeration, simplification, and schematization. But his point is clear:

> Now, in the best of the ordinary types of management, the managers recognize frankly that the ... workmen, included in the twenty or thirty trades, who are under them, possess this mass of traditional knowledge, a large part of which is not in the possession of management. The management, of course, includes foremen and superintendents, who themselves have been first-class workers at their trades. And yet these foremen and superintendents know, better than any one else, that their own knowledge and personal skill falls far short of the combined knowledge and dexterity of all the workmen under them. The most experienced managers frankly place before their workmen the problem of doing the work in the best and most economical way. They recognize the task before them as that of inducing each workman to use his best endeavors, his hardest work, all his traditional knowledge, his skill, his ingenuity, and his good-will – in a word, his 'initiative', so as to yield the largest possible return to his employer.[13]

As we have already seen from Taylor's belief in the universal prevalence and in fact inevitability of 'soldiering', he did not recommend reliance upon the 'initiative' of workers. Such a course, he felt, leads to the surrender of control: 'As was usual then, and in fact as is still usual in most of the shops in this country, the shop was really run by the workmen and not by the bosses. The workmen together had carefully planned just how fast each job should be done'. In his Midvale battle, Taylor pointed out, he had located the source of the trouble in the 'ignorance of the management as to what really constitutes a proper day's work for a workman'. He had 'fully realized that, although he was foreman of the shop, the combined knowledge and skill of the workmen who were under him was certainly ten times as great as his own'.[14] This, then, was the source of the trouble and the starting point of scientific management. [...]

Taylor liked to pretend that his work standards were not beyond human capabilities exercised without undue strain, but as he himself made clear, this pretense could be maintained only on the understanding that unusual physical specimens were selected for each of his jobs:

> As to the scientific selection of the men, it is a fact that in this gang of seventy-five pig-iron handlers only about one man in eight was physically capable of handling $47\frac{1}{2}$ tons per day. With the very best of intentions, the other seven out of eight men were physically unable to work at this pace. Now the one man in eight who was able to do this work was in no sense superior to the other men who were working on the gang. He merely happened to be a man of the type of the ox, – no rare specimen of humanity, difficult to find and therefore very highly prized. On the contrary, he was a man so stupid that he was unfitted to do most kinds of laboring work, even. The selection of the man, then, does not involve

finding some extraordinary individual, but merely picking out from among very ordinary men the few who are especially suited to this type of work. Although in this particular gang only one man in eight was suited to doing the work, we had not the slightest difficulty in getting all the men who were needed – some of them from inside the works and others from the neigh-boring country – who were exactly suited to the job.[15]

Taylor spent his lifetime in expounding the principles of control enunciated here, and in applying them directly to many other tasks: shoveling loose materials, lumbering, inspecting ball bearings, etc., but particularly to the machinist's trade. He believed that the forms of control he advocated could be applied not only to simple labor, but to labor in its most complex forms, without exception, and in fact it was in machine shops, bricklaying, and other such sites for the practice of well-developed crafts that he and his immediate successors achieved their most striking results.

From earliest times to the Industrial Revolution the craft or skilled trade was the basic unit, the elementary cell of the labor process. In each craft, the worker was presumed to be the master of a body of traditional knowledge, and methods and procedures were left to his or her discretion. In each such worker reposed the accumulated knowledge of materials and processes by which production was accomplished in the craft. The potter, tanner, smith, weaver, carpenter, baker, miller, glassmaker, cobbler, etc., each representing a branch of the social division of labor, was a repository of human technique for the labor processes of that branch. The worker combined, in mind and body, the concepts and physical dexterities of the specialty: technique, understood in this way, is, as has often been observed, the predecessor and progenitor of science. The most important and widespread of all crafts was, and throughout the world remains to this day, that of farmer. The farming family combines its craft with the rude practice of a number of others, including those of the smith, mason, carpenter, butcher, miller, and baker, etc. The apprenticeships required in traditional crafts ranged from three to seven years, and for the farmer of course extends beyond this to include most of childhood, adolescence, and young adulthood. In view of the knowledge to be assimilated, the dexterities to be gained, and the fact that the craftsman, like the professional, was required to master a specialty and become the best judge of the manner of its application to specific production problems, the years of apprenticeship were generally needed and were employed in a learning process that extended well into the journeyman decades. Of these trades, that of the machinist was in Taylor's day among the most recent, and certainly the most important to modern industry.

As I have already pointed out, Taylor was not primarily concerned with the advance of technology (which, as we shall see, offers other means for direct control over the labor process). He did make significant contributions to the technical knowledge of machine-shop practice (high-speed tool steel, in particular), but these were chiefly by-products of his effort to study this practice with an eye to systema-tizing and classifying it. His concern was with the control of labor at any given level of technology, and he tackled his own trade with a boldness and energy which astonished his contemporaries and set the pattern for industrial engineers, work designers, and office managers from that day on. And in tackling machine-shop work, he had set himself a prodigious task.

The machinist of Taylor's day started with the shop drawing, and turned, milled, bored, drilled, planed, shaped, ground, filed, and otherwise machine- and hand-processed the proper stock to the desired shape as specified in the drawing. The range of decisions to be made in the course of the process is – unlike the case of a simple job, such as the handling of pig iron – by its very nature enormous. Even for the lathe alone, disregarding all collateral tasks such as the choice of stock, handling, centering and chucking the work, layout and measuring, order of cuts, and considering only the operation of turning itself, the range of possibilities is huge. Taylor himself worked with twelve variables, including the hardness of the metal, the material of the cutting tool, the thickness of the shaving, the shape of the cutting tool, the use of a coolant during cutting, the depth of the cut, the frequency of regrinding cutting tools as they became dulled, the lip and clearance angles of the tool, the smoothness of cutting or absence of chatter, the diameter of the stock being turned, the pressure of the chip or shaving on the cutting surface of the tool, and the speeds, feeds, and pulling power of the machine.[16] Each of these variables is subject to broad choice, ranging from a few possibilities in the selection and use of a coolant, to a very great number of effective choices in all matters having to do with thickness, shape, depth, duration, speed, etc. Twelve variables, each subject to a large number of choices, will yield in their possible combinations and permutations astronomical figures, as Taylor soon realized. But upon these decisions of the machinist depended not just the accuracy and finish of the product, but also the pace of production. Nothing daunted, Taylor set out to gather into management's hands all the basic information bearing on these processes. He began a series of experiments at the Midvale Steel Company, in the fall of 1880, which lasted twenty-six years, recording the results of between 30,000 and 50,000 tests, and cutting up more than 800,000 pounds of iron and steel on ten different machine tools reserved for his experimental use. His greatest difficulty, he reported, was not testing the many variations, but holding eleven variables constant while altering the conditions of the twelfth. The data were systematized, correlated, and reduced to practical form in the shape of what he called a 'slide rule' which would determine the optimum combination of choices for each step in the machining process.[17] His machinists thenceforth were required to work in accordance with instructions derived from these experimental data, rather than from their own knowledge, experience, or tradition. This was the Taylor approach in its first systematic application to a complex labor process. Since the principles upon which it is based are fundamental to all advanced work design or industrial engineering today, it is important to examine them in detail. And since Taylor has been virtually alone in giving clear expression to principles which are seldom now publicly acknowledged, it is best to examine them with the aid of Taylor's own forthright formulations.

First Principle

'The managers assume ... the burden of gathering together all of the traditional knowledge which in the past has been possessed by the workmen and then of classifying, tabulating, and reducing this knowledge to rules, laws, and formulae . . . '[18] We have seen the illustrations of this in the cases of the lathe machinist and the pig-iron handler. The great disparity between these activities, and the different order of knowledge that may be collected about them, illustrate that for Taylor – as for managers today – no task is either so simple or so complex that it may not be studied with the object of collecting in the hands of management at least as much information as is known by the worker who performs it regularly, and very likely more. This brings to an end the situation in which 'Employers derive their knowledge of how much of a given class of work can be done in a day from either their own experience, which has frequently grown hazy with age, from casual and unsystematic observation of their men, or at best from records which are kept, showing the quickest time in which each job has been done'.[19] It enables management to discover and enforce those speedier methods and shortcuts which workers themselves, in the practice of their trades or tasks, learn or improvise, and use at their own discretion only. Such an experimental approach also brings into being new methods such as can be devised only through the means of systematic study.

This first principle we may call the *dissociation of the labor process from the skills of the workers*. The labor process is to be rendered independent of craft, tradition, and the workers' knowledge. Henceforth it is to depend not at all upon the abilities of workers, but entirely upon the practices of management.

Second Principle

'All possible brain work should be removed from the shop and centered in the planning or laying-out department . . . '[20] Since this is the key to scientific management, as Taylor well understood, he was especially emphatic on this point and it is important to examine the principle thoroughly.

In the human, as we have seen, the essential feature that makes for a labor capacity superior to that of the animal is the combination of execution with a conception of the thing to be done. But as human labor becomes a social rather than an individual phenomenon, it is possible – unlike in the instance of animals where the motive force, instinct, is inseparable from action – to divorce conception from execution. This dehumanization of the labor process, in which workers are reduced almost to the level of labor in its animal form, while purposeless and unthinkable in the case of the self-organized and self-motivated social labor of a community of producers, becomes crucial for the management of purchased labor. For if the workers' execution is guided by their own conception, it is not possible, as we have seen, to enforce upon them either the methodological efficiency or the working pace desired by capital. The capitalist therefore learns from the start to take advantage of this aspect of human labor power, and to break the unity of the labor process.

This should be called the principle of the *separation of conception from execution*, rather than by its more common name of the separation of mental and manual labor (even though it is similar to the latter, and in practice often identical). This is because mental labor, labor done primarily in the brain, is also subjected to the same principle of separation of conception from execution: mental labor is first separated from manual labor and, as we shall see, is then itself subdivided rigorously according to the same rule.

The first implication of this principle is that Taylor's 'science of work' is never to be developed by the worker, always by management. This notion, apparently so 'natural' and undebatable today, was in fact vigorously discussed in Taylor's day, a fact which shows how far we have traveled along the road of transforming all ideas about the labor process in less than a century, and how completely Taylor's hotly contested assumptions have entered into the conventional outlook within a short space of time. Taylor confronted this question – why must work be studied by the management and not by the worker himself; why not *scientific workmanship* rather than *scientific management*? – repeatedly, and employed all his ingenuity in devising answers to it, though not always with his customary frankness. In *The Principles of Scientific Management*, he pointed out that the 'older system' of management

> makes it necessary for each workman to bear almost the entire responsibility for the general plan as well as for each detail of his work, and in many cases for his implements as well. In addition to this he must do all of the actual physical labor. The development of a science, on the other hand, involves the establishment of many rules, laws, and formulae which replace the judgment of the individual workman and which can be effectively used only after having been systematically recorded, indexed, etc. The practical use of scientific data also calls for a room in which to keep the books, records, etc., and a desk for the planner to work at. Thus all of the planning which under the old system was done by the workman, as a result of his personal experience, must of necessity under the new system be done by the management in accordance with the laws of the science; because even if the workman was well suited to the development and use of scientific data, it would be physically impossible for him to work at his machine and at a desk at the same time. It is also clear that in most cases one type of man is needed to plan ahead and an entirely different type to execute the work.[21]

The objections having to do with physical arrangements in the workplace are clearly of little importance, and represent the deliberate exaggeration of obstacles which, while they may exist as inconveniences, are hardly insuperable. To refer to the 'different type' of worker needed for each job is worse than disingenuous, since these 'different types' hardly existed until the division of labor created them. As Taylor well understood, the possession of craft knowledge made the worker the best starting point for the development of the science of work; systematization often means, at least at the outset, the gathering of knowledge which *workers already possess*. But Taylor, secure in his obsession with the immense reasonableness of his proposed arrangement, did not stop at this point. In his testimony before the Special Committee of the House of Representatives, pressed and on the defensive, he brought forth still other arguments:

I want to make it clear, Mr. Chairman, that work of this kind undertaken by the management leads to the development of a science, while it is next to impossible for the workman to develop a science. There are many workmen who are intellectually just as capable of developing a science, who have plenty of brains, and are just as capable of developing a science as those on the managing side. But the science of doing work of any kind cannot be developed by the workman. Why? Because he has neither the time nor the money to do it. The development of the science of doing any kind of work always required the work of two men, one man who actually does the work which is to be studied and another man who observes closely the first man while he works and studies the time problems and the motion problems connected with this work. No workman has either the time or the money to burn in making experiments of this sort. If he is working for himself no one will pay him while he studies the motions of some one else. The management must and ought to pay for all such work. So that for the workman, the development of a science becomes impossible, not because the workman is not intellectually capable of developing it, but he has neither the time nor the money to do it and he realizes that this is a question for the management to handle.[22]

Taylor here argues that the systematic study of work and the fruits of this study belong to management for the very same reason that machines, factory buildings, etc., belong to them; that is, because it costs labor time to conduct such a study, and only the possessors of capital can afford labor time. The possessors of labor time cannot themselves afford to do anything with it but sell it for their means of subsistence. It is true that this is the rule in capitalist relations of production, and Taylor's use of the argument in this case shows with great clarity where the sway of capital leads: Not only is capital the property of the capitalist, but *labor itself has become part of capital*. Not only do the workers lose control over their instruments of production, but they must now lose control over their own labor and the manner of its performance. This control now falls to those who can 'afford' to study it in order to know it better than the workers themselves know their own life activity.

But Taylor has not yet completed his argument: 'Furthermore', he told the Committee, 'if any workman were to find a new and quicker way of doing work, or if he were to develop a new method, you can see at once it becomes to his interest to keep that development to himself, not to teach the other workmen the quicker method. It is to his interest to do what workmen have done in all times, to keep their trade secrets for themselves and their friends. That is the old idea of trade secrets. The workman kept his knowledge to himself instead of developing a science and teaching it to others and making it public property'.[23] Behind this hearkening back to old ideas of 'guild secrets' is Taylor's persistent and fundamental notion that the improvement of work methods by workers brings few benefits to management. Elsewhere in his testimony, in discussing the work of his associate, Frank Gilbreth, who spent many years studying bricklaying methods, he candidly admits that not only *could* the 'science of bricklaying' be developed by workers, but that it undoubtedly *had been*: 'Now, I have not the slightest doubt that during the last 4,000 years all the methods that Mr. Gilbreth developed have many, many times suggested themselves to the minds of bricklayers'. But because knowledge possessed by workers is not useful to capital, Taylor begins his list of the desiderata of scientific management: 'First. The development – by the management, not the workmen – of the science of bricklaying'.[24] Workers, he explains, are not going to put into execution any system or any method which harms them and their workmates: 'Would they be likely', he says, referring to the pig-iron job, 'to get rid of seven men out of eight from their own gang and retain only the eighth man? No!'[25]

Finally, Taylor understood the Babbage principle better than anyone of his time, and it was always uppermost in his calculations. The purpose of work study was never, in his mind, to enhance the ability of the worker, to concentrate in the worker a greater share of scientific knowledge, to ensure that as technique rose, the worker would rise with it. Rather, the purpose was to cheapen the worker by decreasing his training and enlarging his output. In his early book, *Shop Management*, he said frankly that the 'full possibilities' of his system 'will not have been realized until almost all of the machines in the shop are run by men who are of smaller calibre and attainments, and who are therefore cheaper than those required under the old system'.[26]

Therefore, both in order to ensure management control and to cheapen the worker, conception and execution must be rendered separate spheres of work, and for this purpose the study of work processes must be reserved to management and kept from the workers, to whom its results are communicated only in the form of simplified job tasks governed by simplified instructions which it is thenceforth their duty to follow unthinkingly and without comprehension of the underlying technical reasoning or data.

Third Principle

The essential idea of 'the ordinary types of management', Taylor said, 'is that each workman has become more skilled in his own trade than it is possible for any one in the management to be, and that, therefore, the details of how the work shall best be done must be left to him'. But, by contrast:

> Perhaps the most prominent single element in modern scientific manage-
> ment is the task idea. The work of every workman is fully planned out by
> the management at least one day in advance, and each man receives in
> most cases complete written instructions, describing in detail the task which
> he is to accomplish, as well as the means to be used in doing the work. . . .
> This task specifies not only what is to be done, but how it is to be done and
> the exact time allowed for doing it. . . . Scientific management consists
> very largely in preparing for and carrying out these tasks.[27]

In this principle it is not the written instruction card that is important. [. . .] Rather, the essential element is the systematic pre-planning and pre-calculation of all elements of the labor process, which now no longer exists as a process in the imagination of the worker but only as a process in the imagination of a special management staff. Thus, if the first principle is the gathering and development of knowledge of labor processes, and the second is the concentration of this knowledge as the exclusive province of management – together with its essential converse, the absence of such knowledge among the workers – then the third is the *use of this monopoly over knowledge to control each step of the labor process and its mode of execution.*

As capitalist industrial, office, and market practices developed in accordance with this principle, it eventually became part of accepted routine and custom, all the more so as the increasingly scientific character of most processes, which grew in complexity while the worker was not allowed to partake of this growth, made it ever more difficult for the workers to understand the processes in which they functioned. But in the beginning, as Taylor well understood, an abrupt psychological wrench was required. One must not suppose from this that such a psychological shift in relations between worker and manager is entirely a thing of the past. On the contrary, it is constantly being recapitulated in the evolution of new occupations as they are brought into being by the development of industry and trade, and are then routinized and subjugated to management control. As this tendency has attacked office, technical, and 'educated' occupations, sociologists have spoken of it as 'bureaucratization', an evasive and unfortunate use of Weberian terminology, a terminology which often reflects its users' view that this form of government over work is endemic to 'large-scale' or 'complex' enterprises, whereas it is better understood as the specific product of the capitalist organization of work, and reflects not primarily scale but social antagonisms. We have seen in the simple Schmidt case the means employed, both in the selection of a single worker as a starting point and in the way in which he was reoriented to the new conditions of work. In the more complex conditions of the machine shop, Taylor gave this part of the responsibility to the foremen. It is essential, he said of the gang bosses, to 'nerve and brace them up to the point of insisting that the workmen shall carry out the orders exactly as specified on the instruction cards. This is a difficult task at first, as the workmen have been accustomed for years to do the details of the work to suit themselves, and many of them are intimate friends of the bosses and believe they know quite as much about their business as the latter'.[28]

Modern management came into being on the basis of these principles. It arose as theoretical construct and as systematic practice, moreover, in the very period during which the transformation of labor from processes based on skill to processes based upon science was attaining its most rapid tempo. Its role was to render conscious and systematic, the formerly unconscious tendency of capitalist production. It was to ensure that as craft declined, the worker would sink to the level of general and undifferentiated labor power, adaptable to a large range of simple tasks, while as science grew, it would be concentrated in the hands of management.

Notes and References

1 DRUCKER, P.F. (1972) 'Work and tools' in KRANZBERG, M. and DAVENPORT, W.H. (Eds) *Technology and Culture*, New York, Schoken Books, pp. 192–3.
2 SOULE, G. (1952) *Economic Forces in American History*, New York, Sloane, p. 241.
3 DRUCKER, P. (1954) *The Practice of Management*, New York, Harper, p. 280.
4 See KAKAR, S. (1970) *Frederick Taylor: A Study in Personality and Innovation*, Cambridge, Mass, MIT Press, pp. 115–7; and FAYOL, H. (1916) *General and Industrial Management*, London, Pitman, (1949).
5 URWICK, L. and BRECH, E.F.L. (1945/6/8) *The Making of Scientific Management*, London, Management Publications Trust. 3 Vols.
6 See FRIEDMANN, G. (1964) *Industrial Society*, Glencoe, The Free Press, pp. 51–65.
7 URWICK, L. (1929) *The Meaning of Rationalization*, London, Nisbet and Co. pp. 13–6.
8 TAYLOR, F.W. (1903) 'Shop management' in THOMPSON, C.B. *Scientific Management: A Collection of Articles Describing the Taylor System of Management*, Harvard Business Studies, No. 1; and TAYLOR, F.W. (1911) *Principles of Scientific Management* New York, Norton (1967) pp. 13–4; and Taylor's Testimony in THOMPSON, C.B. (1914) *op. cit.*, p. 8.
9 TAYLOR, F.W. (1903) *op. cit.*, pp. 32–3.
10 *ibid.*, pp. 34–5.
11 TAYLOR, F.W. (1911) *op. cit.*, p. 52.
12 MAYO, E. (1945) *The Social Problems of an Industrial Civilization* Boston, Harvard University, p. 42.
13 TAYLOR, F.W. (1911) *op. cit.*, p. 32.
14 *ibid.*, pp. 48–9, 53.
15 *ibid.*, pp. 61–2.
16 *ibid.*, pp. 107–9.
17 *ibid.*, p. 111.
18 *ibid.*, p. 36.
19 *ibid.*, p. 22.
20 TAYLOR, F.W. (1903) *op. cit.*, pp. 98–9.
21 TAYLOR, F.W. (1911) *op. cit.*, pp. 37–8.
22 Taylor's testimony before the Special House Committee, pp. 235–6.
23 *ibid.*
24 *ibid.*, pp. 75, 77.
25 TAYLOR, F.W. (1911) *op. cit.*, p. 62.
26 TAYLOR, F.W. (1903) *op. cit.*, p. 105.
27 TAYLOR, F.W. (1911) *op. cit.*, pp. 63, 39.
28 TAYLOR, F.W. (1903) *op. cit.*, p. 108.

Athar Hussain

Abstract

The purpose of this article is to analyse the relations between the educational system and economy in capitalist societies. The economy is conceived here in terms of its technical as well as its social relations. The analysis here is centred around the capitalist labour market rather than capitalist technical relations of production as is usual in the literature on the relations between the educational system and the economy. This article is a preliminary attempt to break out of both economistic and sociologistic conceptions which dominate the literature on education.

It is now commonplace to say that the economic performance of a country depends on its educational system. Official reports on education reiterate this theme and economists of education take this for granted. For economists the relationship between the educational system and the economy is a technical one. They start with the assumption that the productive capacity of an economy (the volume of goods and services it can produce) depends not only on its endowment of industrial plants, machines, tools, buildings and natural resources but also on educational training embodied in its labour force.[1] Given this assumption, the educational system is seen as a supplier of a factor of production (namely, the educated man-power), which in its own peculiar way responds to the demand for its product. Peculiar, because educational institutions, unlike firms, are not run on profit-loss principle. It is this view of the educational system which leads economists to see the changes in the distribution of educational qualifications in the labour force in capitalist countries as responses to the change in the structure of occupations in those countries. For example, the increase in the average number of years of education in advanced capitalist countries is sometimes explained in terms of the growing technical complexity of those economies, and the consequent shift from the blue collar to the white collar occupations.[2]

It is not too difficult to discredit the notion that the relation between the economy and the educational system is a purely technical one by examining the relation

Source: HUSSAIN, A. (1976) *Economy and Society* Vol. 5, No. 4, November.

between educational qualifications and occupations.[3] Still, the educational training of a large part of the labour force in advanced capitalist countries consists of not much more than an apprenticeship in three Rs and the inculcation of bits and pieces of general knowledge. True, the elementary education administered to children does play a part in the vocational training of the labour force in that it provides a base, in the form of ability to read, write and calculate, for the acquisition of occupational skills. Nonetheless, the link between the length and the content of the general educational training of the labour force and the kind and variety of work it performs is tenuous. It will, however, be pointed out that not all education is general and unrelated to vocations. Not only that a fair proportion of education in capitalist countries is vocational and professional, but also there has been a marked shift towards this kind of education in those countries. Indeed, the institution of apprenticeship is on the way out. The expansion of vocational education has been general. There has been a proliferation of occupational courses not only at the tertiary level (universities and polytechnics) but also at the secondary level, e.g. colleges of further education. Furthermore, vocational courses are not restricted to any particular group of occupations; they encompass engineering, applied sciences, marketing, management, typing etc. Given the increase in the average number of years of education and the extension of vocational education on the one hand, and technical changes brought about by the application of scientific knowledge and the shift in the composition of the social product away from tangible goods to services in advanced capitalist countries on the other, there is a temptation to see the latter as the cause of the former. This conclusion, it should be noted, is based on the assumption that the work (taken in its technical sense in each case) by itself indicates the educational qualification an individual has to have in order to perform it. It is this assumption which one needs to question. Once this assumption is discarded, it becomes impossible to sustain the argument that changes in the educational qualifications of the labour force are merely responses to changes in the structure of occupations (due to a change in either the composition of the social product or techniques).

It is necessary here to qualify. The argument is not that there is no technical connection between occupations and educational qualifications. Indeed, there is such a connection, especially so in the case of occupations where the performance of work presupposes the knowledge which is exclusively produced and disseminated in educational institutions, e.g. natural sciences. Instead, in general terms the argument is that the relation between educational qualifications and occupations is not purely technical.

This argument is not unusual, most sociologists who write about education subscribe to it. Sociologists focus on what they consider to be the social functions of education. Roughly, the social functions attributed to education are: Education is a means of social control. Education is the bond which holds together the societies which are internally differentiated. Education is a means of legitimation, and, in particular, educational differences are the means for legitimating inequalities.[4] However, the purpose here is not to discuss these functions in detail; but, instead, to point out that sociologists proceed on the assumption that if the link between occupations and educational qualifications is not technical then, *ipso facto*, the link is 'social' rather than economic. In other words, sociologists too identify economic relations with technical relations. It is this premise which sociologists of education share with economists of education. For the most part, the difference between them is that while the former emphasize the social functions the latter focus on the technical functions of education.

The usual literature on education offers a choice between the economist's and the sociologist's perspective of the relation between the educational system and the society of which it is a part. It is this choice that this article wants to avoid. To do so one has to reject the technocratic conception of the economy – a conception which reduces economic relations to technical relations. Once the economy is conceived not only in terms of its technical relations but also its social relations, the relations between the economy and the educational system in capitalist societies appear in a different light.

The capitalist economy and its relation to the educational system

The analysis here is based on the premise that the economy, regardless of whether it is pre-capitalist, capitalist or socialist, is never reducible to the technology it employs to produce goods and services. Production always takes place under definite social relations; and those social relations determine not only how production is organized and how social production distributed but also, at least indirectly, the technology employed in production. Briefly, the economy is conceived here as a combination of social and technical relations of production. The general signification of the technical relations, for present purposes, is clear so we may leave it aside for later discussion. Schematically, the social relations of production are the relations which underlie the distribution of the social product among the members of society, the organization and the purpose of production. The relations governing the distribution are not technical for the reason that technical methods employed to produce goods do not by themselves indicate how and on what basis they are to be distributed. Nor for that matter, do techniques of production by themselves indicate whether production is to be organized in capitalist firms producing commodities for sale, or in socialist enterprises producing goods for delivery to the state or to other enterprises.[5]

This is nothing more than a rough outline of the relations which constitute an economy. The main purpose here is to assert the importance of the social relations of production and to get away from, what may be termed, the technocratic conception of the economy. Instead of starting with either the technical relations of production or the determinants of an individual's income, as is usual in economics of education, the analysis here starts by the following facets of capitalist relations of production, namely: that first, labourers do not own means of production, and second, goods are produced for sale and criteria of profit and loss govern their production. These two are used here to delineate the role and function of educational institutions in the occupation distribution and the training of the labour force.

The immediate corollary of the fact that labourers do not own means of production is that they have to seel their labour in order to procure the goods necessary for their survival. The labour market is, therefore, a necessary feature of capitalist economies. In the case of the occupations directly related to the production of goods and services, the participants in the labour market are, on the one hand, the labourers who do not own means of production and, on the other, those who do (either firms or individuals). The labour market in capitalist societies distributes individuals not only into occupations connected with the production of goods and services but also into occupations not directly concerned with production, e.g. occupation in marketing and finance, in public administration etc. What is of interest for the analysis here are not just the occupations connected with the production and distribution of commodities but all the occupations into which the labour market distributes individuals. In other words, it is the sale and purchase of labour as such regardless of the locus of employment of the purchased labour which is important for the analysis here. The reason is that the role which educational qualifications play in the occupational distribution of the labour force in capitalist societies is not restricted to any particular class of occupations. To restrict the analysis to a particular class of occupations e.g. those connected with the production of commodities, is to neglect what is crucial, namely: educational qualifications determine access to not one but a very wide variety of occupations.

It is through the labour market that one has to approach the relation between the capitalist economy and educational institutions. For the present purpose the important implications of the distribution of the labour force into occupations through the labour market are: First, the division of work into discrete categories of occupations is determined by employers and not by employees; and, second it is employers who decide both the volume of employment and the requirements of entry into occupations. Educational divisions on the basis of the length and the subject of education are pertinent to the distribution of the labour force only in so far as suitability for occupations is defined in terms of educational qualifications. The question is what is the status of educational qualifications when they are used for assessing suitability for occupations?

Educational qualifications and occupational distribution

The category educational qualifications is heterogeneous; it includes both general and professional and vocational educational qualifications. The status of the latter two as qualifications of entry into occupations, at least for the present purpose, is unambiguous in that they are, it could be argued, indices of technical competence for the occupations to which they relate. But what is the status of general educational qualifications *qua* requirements of entry into occupations? Here, one could with justification argue that, in part, differences in occupations are not based on differences in competence required for them; but, instead, on the simple fact of the division of labour and specialization. In other words, competence need not be job or occupation specific. That an individual is competent to perform one kind of work does not exclude the possibility that he can also perform other kinds of work. The implication of the argument is that though general educational qualifications are not geared to any particular occupation, nonetheless they are, and can be taken as, indices of technical competence for not one but a variety of occupations. Moreover, one may add here, they also provide an index of capability to learn from experience on the job. These arguments may seem convincing, but they are inadequate. These arguments are based on the premise that the competence for occupations are determined solely by reference to the technical nature of the work involved. It is this premise which needs questioning rather than whether or not general educational qualifications are satisfactory indices of technical competence.

It is here that the social dimension of the division of work into occupations becomes relevant. Usual discussions of the division of labour take for granted the division into occupations, and they restrict themselves to analysing the effects and implications of that division. A case in point is Adam Smith's famous discussion of the division of labour in a pin factory. Economists analyse the economic implications, efficiency, productivity of labour etc., while sociologists the social implications of the division of labour, the maintenance of social cohesiveness in a society characterized by the division of labour. To take the division of labour for granted is to evade the question what are the factors which enter into the division of work into discrete units of occupations, or the way in which the work is apportioned among individuals. The main point is this: work by itself does not indicate how it is to be divided and assigned to individuals. There is nothing in the mere fact of the division of labour which indicates that mental work should exclude manual labour, or for that matter management and co-ordination should exclude, what is termed, execution. In the literature it is implicitly assumed that the division is technical, or the analysis of work by itself indicates how it is to be divided. Strictly speaking, there is no such thing as a purely technical division of labour. The division of labour takes place in societies and its form is determined by the social relations that characterize that society; in this sense all technical division is at the same time a social division.[6] The social relations affect the division of labour by establishing a hierarachy of work – a classification and ordering of different kinds of work, by defining the criteria of selection and access to occupations. In capitalist societies differences in terms of employment, remuneration, the way remuneration is determined and the way it is revised, are the factors which differentiate one occupation from another. Selection for occupation in capitalist societies is at the same time a process of social differentiation; thus, the requirement of entry into an occupation necessarily involves a comparison with other occupations. What this means is that the factors used to select individuals for occupations have a dual role and function, namely: to determine the technical competence for the work in question and to place the occupation in relation to others. The implication is that educational requirements for entry into occupations need not bear any direct relation to what is technically necessary to perform the work in question; instead their function may just be to place the occupation with respect to others. Those who have analysed educational requirement for entry into occupations point out that in many cases they do not bear any direct relation to the work that is involved. From this observation it is concluded that extraneous factors enter into selection for occupations. But the conclusion is based on the premise that all that is not directly related to work is extraneous. Instead, the argument is that the so-called extraneous factors are not extraneous at all, on the contrary, they are necessary components of the definition of competence for occupations.

A number of conclusions follow from the argument here. Firstly, educational qualifications as requirements of entry into occupations have not one but a number of different roles to perform. Technocratic explanations fail because they treat educational qualifications as indices of technical competence. Sociologistic explanations, on the other hand, suffer from the defect that any requirement of entry into occupation not related to technical competence is treated as extraneous and thus as something whose use as qualification of entry into occupations has to be explained by reference to some social requirement, e.g. legitimation. Secondly, when educational qualifications are used to locate an occupation *vis à vis* others, it is not educational qualifications as such but the distribution of educational qualifications and educational differences which matter. The function of an educational qualification in that case, it should be noted, is to serve as a basis of differentiation, and as a result, the significance that an educational qualification has as a basis of differentiation can only be determined with respect to other educational qualifications and their distribution in the labour force. This argument in particular points to the possibility of a change in educational requirements for entry into occupations as the distribution of educational qualifications in the labour force changes over time.

Educational qualifications and economic inequality

Educational qualifications serve as bases of selection for occupations; but it is not the educational system which actually channels individuals into occupations. The volume, categories and the terms of employment are determined not inside but outside the educational system. Simple and obvious though it is, this point is often overlooked; this oversight is particularly common in the literature on economic inequality and determinants of personal incomes. It is a common observation that the lowest paid are also those with the lowest education (normally measured in terms of the number of years of education) and that the well paid are usually also the well educated. From this observation it is deduced, usually implicitly, that educational inequality is one of the main causes of economic inequality. This then leads to the belief that economic inequality can be, at least in part, reduced by widening access to educational institutions and taking positive measures (e.g. compensatory education) to reduce educational differences.[7] However well intentioned and noble the belief may be it rests on a strange, but unstated, premise that somehow the provision of more education will lead to a disappearance of low paid occupations. The proposals for the reform of the educational system to achieve greater equality are based on two premises, namely: it is possible to reduce educational differences and, second, educational qualifications are not just bases for selecting individuals for occupations but they are actually entitlements to occupations. The second assumption may seem far fetched; but, as we explain later, this is precisely what is assumed when educational qualifications are treated as an important determinant of personal incomes.

To turn to educational differences first: There are a number of dimensions to educational differences, namely: the length of education, the subject of education, the level of academic performance etc. It may be possible to reduce educational differences in one dimension but not in others;-for example, given the regime of universal compulsory education in capitalist countries, it is possible to reduce the differences in the length of education through the simple device of raising the school leaving age, but, at the same time, it is not possible to reduce the differences in the subject and the content of education. On the contrary, the history of education in capitalist countries points out that the increase in the average number of years of education and the correlated reduction in the length of education has been coupled with the widening of differences in other dimensions, e.g. the subject and courses of studies. Without going into the reasons for this, what can be said is that educational differences are inscribed in the very functioning of the educational system. For the discussion here, it is not the educational differences as such, but their significance and role in the occupational distribution of the labour force which is important. Earlier, it was argued that differences in educational requirements of entry into occupations delineate and order occupations *vis à vis* each other. In selecting individuals for occupations it is not educational similarities but educational differences which count. Thus a reduction in educational differences in a particular dimension, say the length of education, may simply signify a shift in the criteria of differentiation and selection rather than the end of differentiation and the equality of opportunity. It is this which is forgotten when education is regarded as a remedy for economic inequality.[8]

Now we turn to the role educational qualifications play in determining personal incomes. Individuals deduce from the fact that educational qualifications serve as criteria for selection that they can move up the income ladder or the hierarachy of occupations by acquiring more education. However, this deduction is valid only if everybody is not trying to do the same. This belief on the part of individuals is a *ceteris paribus* assumption, and, just for that reason, it can not be a valid basis for the generalization that individuals can move up the income ladder by acquiring more education. However, the generalization is, it should be noted, valid if it is assumed that educational qualifications are not merely criteria of selection for occupations but instead entitlements to occupations. The assumption, to say the least, is absurd, because it implies that it is the educational system which determines the volume and the terms of employment. Alternatively, the assumption is that educational qualifications by themselves indicate the terms of employment of their possessers. Nevertheless, economists of education, in effect, treat educational qualifications as entitlements to income when they follow what the literature terms 'The returns to education approach'[9] – an approach which is by no means a monopoly of economists of education. Briefly, the approach consists in this: The differences in the respective earnings of the less educated and the more educated are presumed accounted for by differences in their education. From this premise it is argued that the higher the educational attainment of an individual the higher are his earnings. In fact, what the argument means is that education is in itself a source of earnings and educational qualifications entitlements to income.

The problem with the approach is this: In general terms the positive correlation (by no means perfect) between incomes and the length of education is not in doubt. But what is actually wrong with the approach is that it separates educational qualifications from occupations and treats them as if they were sources of income in their own right. Educational qualifications are treated as if they were bonds (gilt edged one should add) whose possession is a guarantee of continual income. What we must remember is that incomes are attached to occupations and not to educational qualifications. The latter seem to be a source of income because they are used as bases of selection for occupations. But this appearance is misleading; educational qualifications are entitlements neither to income nor to occupations; they do determine access to occupations but they do not guarantee entry to them.

This qualification is necessary. The distribution of educational qualifications in the labour force is for the most part determined by criteria internal to educational institutions (educational performance of students, qualifications of entry into courses and institutions) and not by the requirements of the labour market. In fact the distribution of educational qualifications cannot be completely geared to the requirements of the labour market, because general educational qualifications are by definition not geared to any particular occupation. On the other hand the volume and categories of employment are, as pointed out earlier, determined not within but outside the educational system. Given this, a lack of synchronization between educational qualifications and the categories of occupations to which they grant access is to be expected. What we have done so far is to indicate the role educational institutions play in the distribution of the labour force into occupations and the limits to that role.

The Position of the Family Under Capitalism

So far, it has been assumed without any discussion that educational institutions and workplaces are the two main sites of the training of the labour force under capitalism. It is to this assumption that we now turn. It should be noted that the family is not regarded as important in the training of the labour force. This presumption is contrary to what radical critics of the educational system argue, i.e. the educational performance of children and thus their future occupation is heavily predetermined by their family background.[10] So first we discuss the position of the family and the role it plays in the occupational distribution of the labour force; and then we turn to the factors which determine, so to say, the division of labour between educational institutions and workplaces in the training of the labour force.

It is best to start with the labour market when analysing the economic role and position of the family under capitalism. The labour market exists in both capitalist and non-capitalist societies; what makes the labour market capitalist is, first, the separation of the unit of production from the unit of consumption and, second, the rules and relations which govern the organization of production. It is the first which is relevant here. Under capitalism, the household – a unit built around the relations of maternity and paternity – is the unit of consumption, while the firm – a unit which owns the means of production and produces commodities and whose boundaries are delineated by the commodities it buys and sells – is the typical unit of production. The important feature of capitalism is that the units of production and consumption are distinct and separated from each other, and that the relationship between them takes the form of market relationship. In particular, this separation implies that the upbringing and training of children in the family is not adequate to equip them for any particular vocation or occupation. The family cannot be a site of the training of the labour force because it is not economically self-sustaining, and it has to resort to the market to procure goods necessary for its survival. The purchase of commodities in the market presupposes a source of income. In general terms there are only two sources of income under capitalism, namely, the ownership of property and the sale of labour. Neglecting the income from property, the sale of labour is the condition for the economic survival of the family under capitalism. Once the necessity of the sale of labour is accepted, it is clear that neither the terms nor the nature of employment is determined within the family. In that case, the training of the labour force necessarily means the training for employment outside the family. For purposes of illustration, it is instructive here to contrast the respective economic positions of the family in capitalist and pre-capitalist societies. In peasant agriculture, for example, the family – a unit built around the kinship relations which govern the transmission of land (the principal means of production in that economy) from one generation to another – is both the unit of consumption and the unit of production. The peasant family for the most part consumes what it produces. In a peasant economy, as a result, children are never separated from the process of production, and their upbringing and training in the family is at the same time their apprenticeship in productive work. Moreover in that economy, the family, because it is also the unit of production, is also the locus of the distribution of the labour force. This is in complete contrast to the place and position of the family under capitalism.

Radical critiques of the capitalist educational system assign family ties an important role in the educational performance of children and thus in the occupational distribution of the labour force. It is therefore necessary to say a bit more about the economic role of the family under capitalism. The way children are brought up in families does have an important effect on them and in many cases it influences them for life. It is in the family that children receive their first apprenticeship in the use of language, and it is their competence in the use of language which is an important determinant of their educational performance. But this is not the point at issue. Instead the important question is: why are the differences between families relevant either for educational performance or the occupational distribution, when the family is neither a locus of employment nor a locus of education (in the formal sense)? No amount of research on differences between working class and nonworking class families can, on its own, shed any light on the question. Such researches do nothing more than point out that children are always already differentiated before they enter the school. But to say, as some radical sociologists of education do, that the school merely reproduces the differences among children at the time of their entry to the educational system is to treat the school either as an extension of the family or a 'standards agency' – an institution which classifies the products submitted to it according to their quality and stamps them accordingly. A standards institution has the sole function of declaring the things for what they are, and it exists because it is recognized to be an objective arbiter. But the school cannot be treated as a standards institution for the simple reason that it classifies what it itself produces, i.e. persons with education. If there is a relation between the family and the school it is not because the latter is simply there to vouchsafe the origin and pedigree of children, but because both of them are a part of the same society and their respective places in the society are, in general terms, determined by the same social relations.

The actual locus of social divisions under capitalism is not the family but the school. To shift the discussion to the family is to mask what is crucial about capitalism, namely, the social distribution of the labour force into occupations is based on the relations of competition and concurrence and not on the relations of heredity. The family does have an effect, but the effect it has on the occupational distribution can only be understood by reference to the mechanism through which individuals are distributed into different occupations. Having indicated the limits on the economic role of the family, we now move on to the question why children go to school under capitalism.

Universal Education

For there to be universal education, there must be a childhood separated from life and regarded as a formative phase of life. There is childhood in all societies but its significance differs from one society to another. Children are trained and educated (in a general sense) in all societies but they are not necessarily made to learn how to read and write. The important point about childhood under capitalism is its separation from economic activities. It is important here to emphasize that it is not the capitalist economic relations which separate children from work, they merely explain why the family cannot be the locus of economic activity. Instead, it is the legal injunctions, which forbid the employment of children in factories and other places of work, customs, and religious notions which give rise to the notion of a minor who has to be protected from adult life and trained to read and write, which together create a childhood separated from economic activities. There is nothing specifically capitalist about these factors, and, as a result, universal education is not an institution peculiar to capitalism. Universal education has existed in pre-capitalist societies, for example in eighteenth century Germany. Pre-capitalist universal education was, however, tied to religious instruction in the sense that the main purpose of teaching children to read and write was to enable them to read religious texts, and the pre-capitalist school was in many cases an extension of the church. Moreover, the pre-capitalist school, except in particular cases, did not have any role to play in the occupational distribution of the labour force because that was for the most part determined on the basis of hereditary relations. But what is peculiarly capitalist is the development of secular universal education. Moreover, it is only under capitalism that children get distributed into occupations at the end of the period of schooling rather than before it or independently of it.[11]

The treatment of universal education here is sketchy. The main purpose is to point out that the reasons for the existence of universal education are social. The argument is directed against the idea that universal education exists because education and learning satisfies some inner need of mankind. Alternatively, universal education is not a self evident necessity, it only becomes so under particular social relations. Lastly, though universal education has existed in different types of society, its economic significance and role have not been the same in all cases.

With these general comments on universal education we now move on to a discussion of the factors which determine the division of labour between educational institutions and workplaces in the training of the labour force. This discussion derives its importance from the fact that there has been a shift in the site of the training of the labour force from workplaces towards educational institutions. The reasons for the shift, as we explain later, are not purely technological. The importance of technology and technological factors is not denied, they are discussed in the last section.

The training of the labour force through its participation in work is not peculiar to capitalism, in fact it is common to all types of economies; but it does have a specific character under capitalism. Training through work under capitalism presupposes the sale of labour, and this is important from the point of view of the length and the range of training through work which is actually provided. It implies a cost to the employer in that he pays for the labour of the trainee, and, as a result, he has an interest in minimizing this cost just like any other cost. In particular, he has an interest in minimizing the length of the training and gearing it to his immediate requirements. It is instructive here to contrast capitalist and artisan production; the apprenticeship in the former is specialized and as short as possible, while in the latter it is comprehensive and long. Furthermore, apprenticeship under artisan production is training for what is going to be a life-long occupation of the labourer, while apprenticeship under capitalism may, in actual fact, mean training for an occupation which over time either becomes obsolete (due to technical change) or redundant (due to a change in the composition of production). Both technical change and changes in the composition of the social product are perennial features of capitalist economies, so there exists side by side with the problem of training an additional problem, namely the problem of the retraining of the labour force. The correlate of the problem of retraining is the problem of unemployment, and it is this problem in conjunction with the technical organization of production which explains, first, the division of labour between workplaces and educational institutions and, second, the shift in the site of training from the former to the latter.

Unemployment and its implications

To turn to the problem of unemployment and the role it plays in determining the structure of the educational system. The category of unemployment is the converse of that of employment, and both of them only make sense when there is a market for labour. Under capitalism, labour is sold for a given period of time and the seller of labour, normally, takes that period as an institutional datum. Thus in general the correlate of the sale and purchase of labour is the segmentation of time into periods of work and non-work. The notion of a standard working day is a creation of the capitalist organization of production in factories, and it is this notion which is used to delineate the employed from the unemployed. A labourer is said to be unemployed when he cannot sell his labour for a specific length of time. The yard stick used may be a standard working day, week, month or a year depending on the nature of the labour contract normally made for the kind of work at issue. The cause of unemployment, given the notions of standard working time, is fluctuations in the level of production – a perennial feature of capitalist economies.

Unemployment has existed since capitalism has existed. But what has changed are the remedies for unemployment and the measures taken to alleviate it. The unemployed have always posed political problems under capitalism, but political policies towards unemployment have not always been the same. In nineteenth-century Britain, the policies were more concerned with the effects of unemployment, e.g. poverty, homelessness etc., rather than with the provision of employment or assistance, in the form of either information about vacancies or the provision of training, towards finding employment. It is this change in the political measures towards unemployment which explains the shift towards educational institutions and away from work places as sites of the training of the labour force. It is necessary to add here that the change can only take place provided the educational system is structured in such a way that it can act as a match maker between the demand and supply of different kinds of labour. In this respect, the public control of the educational system in the form of indirect control through the provision of finances or the direct control over the content and the range of educational courses is of special importance, because it provides a means for tailoring the workings of the educational system to the requirements of the labour market.

Since it was argued earlier that educational institutions determine access to occupations but do not guarantee entry to them, it is necessary to indicate more precisely what their actual role is as a match maker between the supply and demand of labour. To start with, we need to distinguish between two categories of unemployment under capitalism, namely unemployment in the aggregate and structural unemployment. The former refers to a situation where the total number of vacancies is less than the total number unemployed. What this means is that unemployment can only be reduced through the creation of more jobs, and the educational system has no role to play in reducing this type of unemployment. No amount of education can bridge the gap between unemployment and vacancies. The second, on the other hand, refers to a situation where there is an overall balance between vacancies and unemployment but a lack of correspondence between the types of labour demanded and the types of labour supplied on the market. Structural unemployment results from the fact that the labour market is not homogeneous but highly differentiated. There are a number of facets to the differences in the labour market, e.g. spatial or regional, the distribution of ability or competence to perform different kinds of work. The educational system has a role to play in alleviating structural unemployment in so far as it is due to mismatching between the skills and abilities demanded by employers and those which the unemployed possess. However, the efficacy of educational institutions depends on the range of vocational training provided in them and the extent to which competence for occupations is defined in terms of educational qualifications. In addition, there is an important limit on the ability of educational institutions to match the demand and supply of labour. This limit is imposed by the fact that it is left to students to decide which courses they follow and educational institutions do not necessarily tailor the numbers entering different courses to the requirements of the labour market.

The shift (by no means complete) in the site of the training of the labour force from work places to educational institutions not only affects the functioning of the labour market but also the structure of the educational system. The main point about vocational and professional training is that it has no specific locus in the educational system; it is, with the exception of the elementary educational stream, provided at all educational levels. Moreover, vocational training is provided in a wide variety of educational institutions. So far as Britain is concerned, vocational and professional training is provided not only in universities and polytechnics (parts of the tertiary level) but also in colleges of further education (in actual fact, off-shoots of the secondary educational stream) and industrial training boards. The last in formal terms are not a part of the educational system; nonetheless, they should be treated as educational institutions because they represent the separation of learning from economic activities. The main reason for the fact that vocational education is provided in a wide variety of educational institutions is that the gradation of vocational education is coupled with the gradation of general education. For example, universities and other institutions of higher education restrict themselves to those vocational courses which are educationally at par with the general educational courses they teach (in terms of the requirements for entry, and the equivalence of the educational qualifications granted at the end). There is a hierarchy of vocational and professional education running more or less parallel to the hierarchy of general education. Given this hierarchy, a widening in the range of vocational education therefore, presupposes either a multiplication of educational institutions or a transformation in the ones already existing. In cases where educational institutions merely provide a substitute for training at the workplace the expansion of vocational education is restricted to the institutions which presuppose nothing more than elementary education on the part of entrants, e.g. colleges of further education, polytechnics, industrial training boards etc. But in cases where the shift is due to the application of an organized body of knowledge to work, e.g. applied science engineering or what is termed management science, the expansion is either in universities or in equivalent institutions. In recent years it is the former type of expansion which has been most important.[12]

Technical Relations

Now we come to the organisation of production under capitalism and its implications for the relation between the educational system and the economy. This discussion has a specific purpose, namely: first to explain why the process of production under capitalism is subject to continual technical change and secondly to point to the link between the educational institutions and the economy which technical change under capitalism presupposes.

Whatever form the organization of production takes, both labour and the means of production participate in that process. But what is different between different modes of production – capitalist, precapitalist, socialist, etc. – is the principle governing the division of technical functions between labour and the means of production. Under capitalism the division of functions between men and machines is determined by the state of technology and, naturally, this division changes with changes in technology. Examples are many: the invention and introduction of mechanical sources of energy meant the replacement of men as sources of energy by machines while the introduction of automative systems, a process currently under way, has meant machines taking over the function of the supervision of the process of production from men. So in general, labour performs those technical functions which either cannot be performed by machines or those which it can perform more cheaply than machines. The division of technical functions between labour and machines in other words is jointly determined by what is technically feasible and what is economically profitable. The point which needs most emphasis in view of the common currency of technocratic explanations of inventions, is that technical change and the introduction of inventions is never solely determined by the considerations of technical feasibility. Factors determining what is technically feasible do nothing more than set a limit to technical change; they cannot determine its precise character. The character and the frequency of technical change under capitalism cannot be adequately analysed without reference to, first, the organization of production and, second, the methods of calculation and accounting used under capitalism.

Changes in technology and consequent changes in the divisions of functions between machines and labourers presuppose in the first place that machines and labourers can be substitutes for each other. The condition for substitutability is that the emphasis should be on functions rather than on who, men or machines, performs the function. The condition in other words is that men and machines should, from the point of view of production, appear at par with each other. It is the way in which the cost of production is computed under capitalism which leads to the satisfaction of this condition. Both labour and the means of production appear as items of costs, and production under capitalism is organized so as to minimize the total cost. In capitalist accounting the cost of labour is at par with the cost of the means of production because both of them are bought in the market.

Not only is there no restriction under capitalism on machines performing the work previously done by labourers, but also the units of production are organized in such a way as to facilitate the introduction of technical change. For example there is no absolute limit on the size of the unit of production under capitalism. This lack of restriction makes it possible to introduce technical change which presupposes production on a large scale. Furthermore, the capitalist firm is not tied to the production of any particular commodity in the sense that there are no restrictions other than economic ones on the range of goods produced by the firm. It is this lack of restrictions which opens up the scope for the introduction of new commodities. In effect, what has been argued so far is that the process of production under capitalism is organized in such a way as to imply a lack of restrictions and barriers to the introduction of technical change either in the form of new products or the substitution of machines for labour.

It is the lack of restrictions on technical change which opens up the scope for the application of the knowledge furnished by sciences to the process of production. The important point is this: it is not sciences and their development, but the rules and relations on which capitalist production is based which account for the application of sciences to the production of commodities. The relation between sciences and technology has not always remained the same. It is well known that very few of the major inventions of the eighteenth and the early part of the nineteenth century were based on sciences. The application of sciences to production took place only after capitalist production had established itself and taken control of the main branches of manufacturing. Not only has the relation between sciences and technology changed over time, but that relation also varies from one invention to another. Whereas some important inventions – like transistors – rely heavily on the latest scientific knowledge, others – like zip fasteners and safety razors– do not. Sciences and technology move on different planes. The direction of inventive activity in the sense of the type of products to be produced and the nature of the problems to be solved are determined by economic factors. On the other hand the direction of sciences is determined by problems and questions internal to sciences and they may or may not be of economic interest. Furthermore, in most cases the knowledge furnished by sciences cannot be directly used in the process of production. This is mainly due to the fact that sciences are segmented into different disciplines on a theoretical basis, and that the problems encountered in the process of production do not lend themselves to the same division as that between different sciences. It is rarely the case that an invention draws on the knowledge furnished by only one scientific discipline.[13]

The application of knowledge furnished by sciences to the production of commodities gives rise to a specific class of occupations connected with it. The important point about these occupations is that training for them has to be provided in educational institutions because the production and dissemination of scientific knowledge, for the most part, takes place in educational institutions rather than in workplaces. It is these occupations which receive most attention in the literature on the economic benefits of education. However, it is necessary to point out that these occupations account for a small proportion of total employment. Moreover, neither the increase in the pace of technical knowledge nor automation on its own leads to a great increase in these occupations. It is, as a result, misleading to use these as the point of reference when analysing the economic role of the educational system under capitalism. As for what has received a great deal of attention in the literature, namely, the effect of technical change, in particular of automation, on the occupational structure of the economy, it must be said that although technical change does affect the occupational structure, the effect depends on the nature of technical change, and so one cannot, for that reason, lay down a general rule. In particular, it cannot be argued that overall automation increases the demand for personnel trained in sciences, technology and skilled labour. Automation has two different types of effect on the occupational structure; on the one hand, it makes certain skills redundant (e.g. skills connected with the supervision and control of machines), but, on the other, it gives rise to a demand for particular types of skills and educational training (e.g. skills connected with the programming and supervision of automative systems). Here, one should distinguish between the type of labour and personnel required for the design and the initial production, and that required for the running, of automative systems. Usually, the former are highly skilled and trained in science and technology but the latter, for the most part, may be unskilled and with nothing more than a general education. Computer designers and operatives provide a good example of the difference. Moreover, the former constitute a small proportion of total employment. So it cannot be argued that, overall, automation increases the demand for labour trained in science and technology.

The most important effect of the application of scientific knowledge to production is that it gives rise to new disciplines and thus new subjects for educational training. In particular it gives rise to disciplines which draw on a number of distinct sciences and which are geared to the solution of practical problems. The boundaries of these disciplines are not determined theoretically, as in pure sciences, but by the practical problems with which these disciplines are concerned. The disciplines in question are engineering, agronomy and applied sciences. The boundaries of these disciplines are not given once for ever, the range and the content of these disciplines change with the change in the practical problems to which scientific knowledge is applied. One may ask here, what are the factors which govern the application of sciences to practical problems? It should be noted that, sciences and scientific knowledge by themselves do not indicate the problems to which they are to be applied. Nuclear physics, for example, does not by itself indicate whether it is to be applied to the generation of electricity or to the manufacture of nuclear bombs. Scientific knowledge may indicate the range of its application, but the actual problems to which it is to be applied are determined by social and economic factors.

The last remark brings us to the issue of the development of technical education in capitalist societies. To start with it should be pointed out that the history of technical education cannot be written just in terms of the development of sciences. There are two distinct sets of factors which govern the development of technical education, namely, the range of occupations open to individuals with technical education, and the possibility of accommodating technical subjects in educational curricula. The relevance of the first derives from the fact that technical education is for the most part vocational – geared to specific occupations; as a result, for there to be technical education there must be a range of occupations for which the competence is defined in terms of technical educational qualifications. For there to be colleges of agronomy or courses in agronomy there must be an agriculture which has a place for agronomists. The relevance of the second on the other hand is due to the fact that educational institutions in their functioning delineate what can be and what cannot be a part of educational curriculum. An educational institution may well be organized in such a way that technical education has no place for them. Technical education in European countries did not initially develop in the institutions already existing but in new institutions geared to the teaching of technical subjects, Grandes Ecoles in France and Technische Hochschulen in Germany.[14]

To end by briefly indicating what has been done in this article and what remains to be done. It is through the capitalist labor market and its implications that we have approached the relation between the economy and the educational system in capitalist countries. The privileged position of the labour market is explained by the structure of the capitalist economy itself. The sale of labour, the terms of its sale and the conditions governing access to occupations, is the locus of social differentiation under capitalism. The principal question, to start with, is how do educational qualifications affect the distribution of the labour force into occupations? It has been argued that educational qualifications are not only indices of technical competence, but also social means for differentiating one occupation from another. Educational institutions and workplaces are regarded here as the two main sites for the training of the labour force under capitalism. The family, on the other hand, is not accorded that status on the grounds that the distribution of the labour force under capitalism is based on the relations of competition and concurrence rather than on the relations of heredity. The latter part of the article can be regarded as an answer to the question what are the factors which determine the division of the labour force between workplaces and educational institutions *qua* sites for the training of the labour force? The question is answered here in terms of the limited role of training on the job, government policies towards unemployment and the technical relations of production under capitalism which opens up the possibility of the application of scientific knowledge to practical problems. Though the argument here is directed against what has been termed the technocratic conception of the economy, technology and technical relations are not considered unimportant. The basic premise here is that the role of technology and technical factors and their effect on the educational system under capitalism cannot be understood except in conjunction with the social relations that characterize capitalism. This article is no more than a first step towards an analysis of the relation between the economy and the educational system in capitalist societies which is not based on the technocratic conception of the economy. We have for reasons of space avoided the analysis of the role of ideological and political factors.

Notes and References

1 DENISON, E.F. and POUILLIER, J.-P. (1972) 'Education and the labour force' in COSIN, B.R. *Education: Structure and Society*, Harmondsworth, Penguin.
2 This is argued by GALBRAITH, J.K. (1972) *The New Industrial State*, Harmondsworth, Penguin. See the excerpts reproduced in COSIN, B.R. (1972) *op. cit.*

3 For a critique of the economist's view of education see COLLINS, R. (1971) 'Functional and Conflict Theories of Educational Stratification' in COSIN, B.R. (1972) *op. cit.*

4 For a general discussion see COSIN, B.R. (1973) 'Education and production' the Open University Course Unit E352 Block 3. The thesis that educational differences are a means of legitimising inequalities is argued in JENCKS, C. (1975) *Inequality* Harmondsworth, Penguin, esp. p. 135.

5 The social and technical relations of production are discussed at length in BALIBAR, E. (1970) *Reading Capital* London, New Left Books.

6 The Marxist literature on the division of labour distinguishes between the technical and the social division of labour. See POULANTZAS, N. (1975) *Classes in Contemporary Capitalism* London, New Left Books.

7 Jencks points out that 'the case for equalising schooling and cognitive skills derives ... from the assumption that equalising schooling and cognitive skills is necessary to equalise status and income'. JENCKS, C. (1975) *op. cit.*

8 Radical authors take the view that the widening of access to education is unlikely to lead to a significant reduction in economic inequalities. See in particular JENCKS, C. (1975) *op. cit.* pp. 221–25.

9 For a general description see BOWEN, W.G. (1963) 'Assessing the economic contribution of education' in COSIN, B.R. (1972) *op. cit.*, pp. 23–37; ATKINSON, A.B. (1975) *The Economics of Inequality* Oxford, Clarenden Press, pp. 79–86.

10 See for example JENCKS, C. (1975) *op. cit.*, pp. 135–45.

11 For a discussion of the attitudes towards the education of children see ARIES, P. (1973) *Centuries of Childhood* Harmondsworth, Penguin, pp. 316–23.

12 For a general account of vocational and technical training and education see HOLMES, HOWE, and LAUWERYS, J.A. (1969) 'Education within Industry' in LAUWERYS, J.A. (Ed) *Education and the Economy* London, Evans.

13 For a discussion of the relation between sciences and technology see BERNAL, J.D. (1953) 'Science and industry in the nineteenth century' in COSIN, B.R. (1972) *op. cit.*

14 On the development of technical education see ASHBY, E. (1966) 'Technology adopted' in COSIN, B.R. (1972) *op. cit.*; and LANDES, D.S. (1969) 'Industry, skills and knowledge' in COSIN, B.R. (1972) *op. cit.*

12   A Recurring Debate: Education and Industry

David Reeder

One of the main purposes of the 'Great Debate', so we are told, is to relate thinking about the curriculum of schools more closely to the requirements of industry. Looking back over the events leading up to the Prime Minister's intervention in current and more widely-based discussions, it seems evident that central government was responding to a groundswell of complaints, emanating from various quarters, not only employers, but professionals in education, about the contribution being made by schooling (at all levels) to industrial development and the quality and attitudes of the labour force. These complaints represent, it will be suggested in this chapter, the most recent phase of a long-standing controversy about the role of schooling in a modern industrial society.

It seems ironical, in a way, that a debate on education and industry should arise in a country whose economic and social development is so closely associated with the provision of education. After all, one of the more important effects of technology on our way of life has been to make the various sub-systems which make up society – political, economic and educational – more and more dependent on each other. Changes in industry, related to an accelerating rate of technological innovation, have led to a much greater premium being put on educated and qualified manpower than at any time in the past. Changes in the education system – the emergence of a differentiated set of institutions – have meant that schools now function to sort and allocate manpower to different occupational levels in the economy.

On the other hand, education and industry have developed as (mainly) independent or autonomous social systems (the autonomy of schoolteachers being delegated to them by government). Each of these systems has a life of its own that expresses the occupational interests of professional groups in relation to different, though possibly over-lapping, goals and objectives. The development of these on-going social systems may become out of step with what are regarded as the economic requirements of the nation.

The question of how, specifically, education might contribute to industrial development is not one that can be easily answered, and the changes which made schooling

Source: REEDER, D. (1979) in BERNBAUM, G. (Ed) *Schooling in Decline* London, Macmillan.

so important to industrial society have brought additional problems and dilemmas. Since the beginning of the nineteenth century, educational reformers committed to various forms of vocationalism have attempted to promote changes in the curricula to bring schooling more in line with the new conditions of industrial society, but they have tended to come up against institutional blockages and, to an extent, ambivalent or hostile attitudes towards industrial culture. Furthermore, the ambitions of reformers have not necessarily corresponded with the perceptions of industrialists about the role of schooling in the preparation of the work force. The historical record suggests that employers as a whole have been slow to formulate their 'needs', and that considerable differences exist within the industrial system about educational priorities and the extent of industrial responsibility for education and training.

This chapter discusses the recurring themes in the debate about education and industry. It sets them out, first, in relation to changing demands for vocational education, and second, in relation to the changing attitudes of industry towards educational progress. A last section brings the account up to date by referring to current anxieties about industrial recruitment and the problems of the transition from school to work. An historical perspective on the issues in the debate may bring us nearer to understanding the genesis of present discontents – at least on the part of those groups who are seeking, through schooling, to maintain and improve industrial capitalism as the foundation of Western democracy.

The issues which determine the character of the debate derive in one sense from the ambiguities and tensions within Western educational thought in a society permeated by technological change. Take, for example, the argument for useful knowledge as the basis of the curriculum. This argument has a very long and respectable ancestry. During the nineteenth century, it was taken over by groups of intellectuals, from the Utilitarians to the Fabians and to the modern philosophers of technocratic society, most of whom supported changes in schooling in order to adapt future generations to the conditions of living and working involved in modern industry. Such views conflicted, however, with ideas about schooling embodied in another tradition of educational thought which rejected, in the main, many features of urban-industrial society. Within that second and more pervasive tradition, schooling was regarded for example as a means of combating the disruptive and dehumanizing effects of technology and 'technicism' in modern industry.

These tensions began to emerge in early nineteenth century debates about education and industry associated with the rise of the factory system. The case for combining manual with intellectual training as the basis for industrial education, for instance, was elaborated by idealistic reformers such as Robert Owen in connection with larger schemes for a schooling that would transform the industrial order, restoring the dignity of labour. In contrast, a case for manual and intellectual training was also made by the defenders of the half-time system of schooling introduced by the Factory Acts, but mainly in connection with the socialization of children from low-status groups – an aspect of the history of vocationalism which is offensive to modern educationists, inclined to judge this (and other) arguments for manual training from the standpoint of modern aspirations for schooling. The ideological conflict, at the heart of the vocational argument, between those concerned with transforming the social order and those concerned with improving its effectiveness, was not peculiar to Britain. It emerged also in another form in the United States, just after the turn of the century, in the debate between the educationist John Dewey and those who expressed the discontents of the American business community by pressing for educational change in the interests of social efficiency. Both Dewey and the philosophers of social efficiency shared the assumption that traditional schooling would have to give way to approaches more relevant to socio-economic conditions; but on one basic point (at least), they disagreed. As Dewey put it:

> The kind of education in which I am interested is not one which will adapt workers to the existing industrial regime; I am not sufficiently in love with the regime for that. It seems to me that the business of all those who would not be educational time servers is to resist every move in this direction, and to strive for a kind of vocational education which will first alter the existing industrial system, and ultimately transform it.[1]

This attitude still persists: it is likely to do so, whilst there are low level occupations arising from the division of labour in industry. The central problem of the vocational educationist, a European working party discovered in 1973, was whether such occupations can represent valid educational goals, so that 'individuals negatively selected for such tasks can be guided into them'. The working party also considered whether there were plausible alternatives, but concluded that despite the promising trends towards polyvalent technical education the full educational potential of vocational preparation could not be achieved within the existing conditions of European society.[2]

The argument for a curriculum based on useful knowledge has been inhibited, then, by dilemmas about the purposes of schooling and the nature of the industrial order, coming up against beliefs in the 'civilizing' and liberalizing mission of schooling within Western European thought. That is one reason why the liberal-vocational studies controversy has arisen and persisted for so long. In addition, the argument for vocational or useful knowledge in some forms has been strongly resisted within the school system, especially in Britain. During the nineteenth century, for example, it came up against the social esteem attached to liberal culture and the liberal professions. Consequently, those who pressed the case found themselves cast in the role of educational reformers, challenging some of the social as well as the educational values of the school system. This point can be illustrated more fully with reference to the late-Victorian movement for scientific and technical education, an episode which is frequently invoked by modern critics of schooling.

The country's deficiencies in scientific and technical knowledge have been, in fact, an important theme in educational debates since the nineteenth century, in so far as these have touched upon the world of business at all. As is well known, concern was frequently shown, in books and speeches, and before various committees and commissions, stretching roughly from the late 1860s to the 1890s. The demands being made were of two inter-related kinds. One was for a *specialized* science education, another was for technical instruction, defined as systematic instruction in the arts and sciences related to specific trades and employments.

An important pressure group formed to advance both these demands was the National Association for the Promotion of Secondary and Technical Education, whose declared object was to 'improve the capacity in a broad sense of all those upon whom our industry depends'. Its members were not only concerned to promote specialist curricula and institutions, but sought, more generally, to modernize schooling in the light of industrial requirements. But this meant doing battle against traditional education, specifically the literary-classical curriculum. As Captain Abney of the Department of Science and Art explained, in response to pressures from the Headmasters' Conference for maintaining the position of secondary as against technical education in the newly formed Board of Education:

> The question to be settled is far too grave for any personal motive to find a place ... It is a question of whether the fruits of the victories of the war waged during the last twenty-five years between modern and literary education shall be disallowed to the former.[3]

Technical educationists were interested in all aspects of schooling. They argued for an elementary schooling, for instance, to prepare children for industrial employment, finding common ground with 'progressive' educationists in proclaiming the educational value of a training in 'hand and eye'. The social basis of this claim was established by Philip Magnus, Director of the City and Guilds of London Institute for the Advancement of Technical Education: 'the real aim of school education', he pointed out, 'should be – to establish such a relation between school instruction and the occupations of life as to prevent any break in continuity in passing from one to the other'. In this view, the 'bookish' courses in the elementary school failed to do that for industrial employment. A similar general claim was made for secondary and intermediate education following from the dilemma of trying to expand educational opportunity whilst retaining the ablest children of the working classes for industrial occupation. The conception of tapping a larger 'pool of ability', involved developing, in the words of Sidney Webb, the Fabian and Chairman of the London Technical Education Board, 'a capacity-catching machine'; but the dilemma was recognized by two Liberal politicians in a survey of London secondary schools, when they remarked on how scholarship children tended to receive the 'stamp of middle-class ideas'. The conclusion, they went on, 'is that a great want exists for more practical and modern curricula, though not necessarily a distinctive technical course of instruction'. The Bryce Commission on Secondary Education (on which National Association members were represented) had formulated a similar conclusion: the solution to the problem of combining secondary and technical education was to regard both of them as elements in a general education whose main purpose was 'fitness for life'.

There are several points to be raised about this late Victorian phase which are relevant to an understanding of the current situation. The first is how to explain the momentum of the campaign. On this, specialist historians have tended to emphasize the role of professional groups, such as the science associations, and the influence of individual scientist-politicians. Thus Professor Meadows, a historian of science, has claimed that the demand for a specialized science education was generated within the profession: it was not really a response to any external influence from industry. Paradoxically, by adopting German models of the university as the rationale for specialized academic study, the late-Victorians laid the basis for what has now come to be seen, in some quarters, as a chief impediment to an industrially related curriculum.[4]

The support for technical education in the late-Victorian period seems to have been rather more widespread, and received national support from some business-men, as for example those who financed the Royal Commission on Technical Instruction and the Moseley Commission to the United States. Such industrialists are frequently described by the specialist historians as pioneers or prophets, in-fluenced by German experiences; and of course they *were* exceptional in being un-usually conscious of the significance of specialized knowledge to industry. There is plenty of evidence to show that many other employers were either indifferent to or ambivalent towards new developments in scientific and technical education. As several economic historians have pointed out, one reason for this was the influence in British industry of the belief in practical experience as the best school of training, a belief which became more pervasive as the industrial-practical man was established in the ranks of mill and factory managers. The problem with this interpretation is to account for the support which urban business communities very evidently gave to a range of schools and colleges founded in the late nineteenth century, whose curricula in many cases (though not in all) were expected to have a general con-nection with local industrial and commerical requirements. There is much that needs to be found out still about the attitudes and motives of local businessmen in this respect, but the historical work so far suggests that no simple explanation is possible, that social and civic aspirations were as important as economic concerns. In some cities metropolitan definitions of culture influenced the aspirations of the founders and supporters of schools and colleges; in other cities, local needs were paramount.

The nature of the support for scientific and technical education is a complex subject, and the wider social penumbra cannot be pursued here. It can be noted in passing, however, how a contemporary sociologist, Emile Durkheim, explained the crisis in French secondary education during the second half of the nineteenth century. In his lectures Durkheim wrestled with many of the problems which vexed counterparts in England, as, for instance, how the new generation of the industrial and commercial work force were to be educated, and what the status of science and technology should be. Durkheim took the view that a divergence had occurred between the occupational interests of teachers in contemporary lycées, 'shut up in their own specialisms', and the interests of other groups in the community. As he then put it:

But that is not all. Secondary education has for more than half a century been undergoing a serious crisis which has by no means reached its conclusion. Everybody feels that it cannot remain as it is, without having any clear idea about what it needs to become . . . moreover the question is not peculiar to France; there is no major European state in which it has not risen in almost identical terms. Everywhere educationalists and statesmen are aware that the changes which have occurred in the structure of contemporary societies, in their domestic economies as in their foreign affairs, require special transformations, no less profound, in the special area of the school system.[5]

In Britain, concern did not become general until the 1890s, when anxieties were developing about the capacity of the nation to sustain an Imperial role and to carry on a war with Germany. Hence the stress placed upon national efficiency (including the idea of expert knowledge) by many people concerned about the country's poor economic and military showing at the turn of the century. These anxieties were also influenced by perceptions of internal stresses, especially fears about the future of youth in an urban society. It is worth emphasizing that in the 1890s many educational reforms were advocated partly because of anxieties about the possibilities of social and economic disorganization, from industrial training for the urban poor, to technical classes in continuation schools for working-class school-leavers. Such fears had contributed to the argument for technical education, which could be regarded as a way of reasserting moral and social controls weakened by the erosion of apprenticeship and the advance of machine processes in industry. They were also to find expression in the demand for raising the school-leaving age and compulsory continued education, demands that were supported by technical educationists as a way of combating the impact on youth of a proliferating number of unskilled and 'dead end' jobs within the urban economy. Again, moral as well as economic considerations entered into the elaboration of a concept of industrial citizenship during and just after the First World War. Moreover industrial citizenship was not only advanced as a way of solving youth's problems: it was linked to aspirations for more social harmony in the post-war world. As H.A.L. Fisher, the author of the Education Act of 1918, told a group of 'paternalistic' employers whose interest in works schools had led them to form the Association for Education in Industry in 1911:

> I have always felt the great problem for the next years is to bring the world of business and the world of education into clear connection. We have the same interests, and I believe that the solution of all the difficulties between capital and labour will ultimately lie, not in the sphere of wages at all, not in any material sphere, but in the kind of improvement in the general condition which is due to the spread of knowledge and intelligence amongst the people and amongst the employers.[6]

This theme of the social purposes of technical education is an important one, which seems to have re-emerged in some recent statements on the role of schooling.

During the inter-war years however, it was not of general interest, being maintained only by a few educationist-politicians, notably Lord Eustace Percy, for a time President of the Board of Education. Eustace Percy was one of the few people at that time to see in the separated development of technical education after the 1902 Act, a potential for educational and social innovation – an alternative route as well as an alternative curriculum, 'a coherent and graduated course of intermediate and higher education'.[7] A contemporary journal put him in the vanguard of an attempt to alleviate industrial troubles, by making the educational content of industrial work more substantial and real. This was in reference to the Board of Education pamphlet no. 64 (Industry Series no. 1), *Education for Industry and Commerce* (1928) in which the preface (written by Percy), adopted the arguments of American vocational educationists, that such studies were a method of democratizing the schools. Percy saw the secondary grammar schools formed after 1902 as inheriting the public school tradition, 'which is really the traditional spirit of the nation planted and acclimatized by the culture of centuries, in the society of the school'. The time had come, he thought, for the industrial and commercial professions to become more highly organized and conscious of their needs, if they were to exert the same influence on the schools as the liberal professions. He believed that the prevailing dissatisfaction and unsettlement in industrial society was largely due to the fact that the worker in industry, the value of whose job entitles him to an equal respect, had behind him no such standard. These are views which form a bridge between the Bryce concept of 'fitness for life' and the development of further technical education, even if a central support, the idea of continuation education for all young workers as of right, was never properly established, then or since. And in practice Percy seems to have done little to influence developments in schooling.

Enough has been said in the preceding section to indicate the ramifications of the vocational argument and the issues raised in the late-Victorian movement for scientific and technical education. Clearly, some of the arguments used then, especially the economic arguments, and the idea of mobilizing talent for industry, have been handed on to become elements in more recent educational policies. On the other hand, some of the objectives of the scientific and technical educationists were not realized in the way they had intended. There are points to be discussed here about the resolution of late-Victorian pressures by the Education Act of 1902, a piece of legislation whose effects are still hotly discussed by historians of education. One point to consider is why the inter-war period became a kind of interregnum in the debate on education and industry.

When technical educationists look back on the inter-war years, they generally take a rather jaundiced view of what actually happened, regarding their predecessors as inhabiting an unfashionable and restricted sector of the system, a kind of institutional rump. The memory of this still influences the rhetoric of present-day arguments. As early as 1938, it was alleged in the Spens Report that the effect of the settlement of 1902 was to remove the practical-technical curricula from the main-

stream of English schooling. Some technical educationists have laid the blame for
that on the officials of the Board of Education, especially Robert Morant, as if they
have not wanted to believe that the tide was turning. Others have recognized that
reactionary forces had built up, taking the view that the advance of science was
held back by class prejudices and then forced into a narrow and class-restricted
channel.[8] Whatever the reasons, the consensus is that after 1902 older ideals and
traditions were drawn back into the system. Consequently technical educationists
have looked sceptically at inter-war statements made in public reports, such as the
Hadow Report to the Board of Education, on the need for practical and realistic
curricula in schools, judging that they were diluted versions of older ideals which in
the event did not come to much. How far this view can be supported is problematical,
because there is little detailed research on schooling in the inter-war years. Two
relevant matters that need looking into especially are, first, the extent to which
the occupational interests of teachers after 1902 were taken up with internal matters,
especially the development of academic examinations, and second, the effects of
the easing of the Board's regulations in 1926, which would have made it more
difficult for any President of the Board of Education to prescribe detailed changes
in the curriculum of the elementary school. In any case, there do not appear to have
been any strong pressures for changing the curricula of schools in the direction of
practical or vocational education from outside interests.

The last point can be gone into more fully with respect to industrial interests, a
chief concern of this chapter. From that point of view, one important interest was
the trade union movement, which evidently did not accept the settlement of 1902
but was not particularly anxious either to promote the more realistic curricula of
the vocational educationists. Trade unions formed a pressure group for extending
educational opportunity in the inter-war years, supporting an education at all
levels which would be broad enough to 'give every worker who desires it a new
sense of understanding and therewith of power to mould the world in accordance
with his human and social ideas'. The conception which trade unionists had of the
need to emancipate workers from a servile view of education, conjoined with
aspirations for extending opportunity, meant that they tended to regard both
continuation education (in the form proposed by Fisher) and vocational or quasi-
vocational education more generally as unduly restrictive and possibly damaging.[9]
In contrast, employers generally seem to have thought vocational studies unnecessary, despite the good opinion held of the relatively few junior technical and trade
schools of the inter-war years. What evidence there is of employers' opinions suggests that they had rather low expectations of elementary schooling. The evidence
given, for example, to the investigation of Higher Elementary Schools in 1906
(as interpreted by the Consultative Committee), indicated that what employers
wanted from these more advanced schools for the children of the working class
was a good character, qualities of subservience and general handiness. As for the
Fisher proposals for extending education, these measures were opposed by representatives of northern textile manufactures (and other industries) and continued
to be resisted by the National Confederation of Employers' Organizations when the
possibility of re-introducing them came up again in the 1920s.[10]

By and large, the settlement of 1902 seems to have established a system which apart from occasional grumbles suited the majority of employers in the sense that developments in schooling helped to sort children into industrial strata for them. The key to the attitudes of 'organized' industry was contained in the first public memorandum of the Federation of British Industries (FBI) to the Board of Education on the Fisher Act of 1918, from which the following extract is the most important section:

> The committee wish to state quite categorically that they consider the extension, and above all, the improvement, of the educational system of the country to be one of the greatest needs of the present time and they will welcome any well considered development of educational facilities for all children without distinction throughout the country. If any of their recommendations fall short of the ideal, it is because they feel at present it is impracticable to obtain all that may be desirable. . . . They have according-ly decided to lay stress in their reports on those reforms which they believe to be the most urgent: firstly, the improvement of elementary education; secondly, the provision of full secondary education for the most able children, *and only after these measures have been taken, an improved general education for the remainder* [italics added].[11]

For the most part, however, our knowledge about industrial attitudes to schooling in the inter-war period is dependent in the main on the way that the Board of Education – in effect 'T' (technological) branch – interpreted the situation. The general view was that many employers were ignorant of the schools and indifferent to the potentialities of technical education. This situation could be improved by better contacts. The question of industry's relations with (technical) education seems to have been a recurring theme – though not followed up zealously – of 'T' branch from Pullinger's time certainly. But as the Board's officers frequently pointed out in various office papers, there were great difficulties in bringing technical education into closer relation because no one, no group, 'speaks for industry'. The Board's representatives recognized that the Association for Education in Industry and Commerce (as it had become in 1926) formed a pressure group within industry favourable to promoting interest in education, including schools, but they were always careful to point out that the Association represented a particularly 'progressive' and relatively small number of employers – and was therefore to be treated cautiously. So in any attempt to follow the policy through they tended to find a lack of response or initiative from employers in the localities, which was reinforced by the economic crisis of the late 1920s and early 1930s, when the various reports instigated by Percy were published.

The most influential of the reports was that of the Malcolm Committee on *Education and Industry* in 1928, coming as it did against a background of complaints in the press about standards of literacy in elementary schools, and an unofficial enquiry on technical education and industry by the ATTI chaired by Lord Emmott, which prodded the Board into a similar action, although this also reflected Percy's interests. The Malcolm Committee helped to establish the official view in their report

(p. 10): 'Industry must define their needs and no other body can do it for them, but if such definition is to be of any use it should be based on a reasonably full and sympathetic knowledge of what the schools are doing and trying to do'.

The point was accepted by the FBI in a memorandum to the Board on *Education for Industry* in 1928, but the response by one of the inspectors throws a rather different light on the Board's conception of what industry might expect from the technical colleges. W.M. Davies remarked in passing on the characteristics of technical education: first, that the schools were 'intrinsically conservative'; second, the teachers had mainly experience of limited technical functions; and third, that students lacked the advantages of a general education and could probably 'derive greater profit from the precise discipline of mathematical and scientific study'.

Representatives of the Board occasionally took the view also that developments in schooling were not understood by industrialists. This is an interesting point which has been reiterated in more recent times because of the way that developments in schooling have tended to reduce the pool of talent available for craft and, to an extent, technical employment. In 1937 R.S. Wood, Principal Assistant Secretary to 'T' branch (1936–40), who went on to make a strong contribution to the reforms associated with the 1944 Act, addressed a conference on 'Education and Industry', pointing our that:

> You get the complaint that the elementary school does not give you the boy as good as he used to be, the complainant being quite oblivious of the fact that the best children have been taken from the elementary school and sent to the secondary school, where the employer does not apply for his labour.[12]

Industrial representatives were complaining at the time not only about 'deplorably low standards in elementary and mental arithmetic': many of them thought schools were not giving a broad enough training for 'general intelligence and adaptability'. This sounds, in retrospect, like a rehearsal for the contemporary dialogue. Certainly, it might be regarded as a prelude; after a period of relative quiet since the early twentieth century, there was now growing pressure for educational reform in the community just before and during the Second World War, one major aspect of which was the resurgence of the criticism that the 'secondary school curriculum . . . had stunted the mind and blunted the character with over much academicism'.[13]

Dr. Gosden's summary of discussions about technical education during the war, and of the criticisms made by industrialists and educationists of the inadequate treatment of technical education in the White Paper, illustrates again the emergence of new tensions, and also introduces a sceptical note on the Board's attitudes to industry in the inter-war years. One particular comment on the Green Paper which Godsen describes is revealing in this last respect. It was made by Sir Horace Wilson, Permanent Secretary to the Ministry of Labour in the 1920s, and consisted of a complaint that the 'aloofness' of the Board had led 'leaders of industry to write off a good deal of the educational system'. This comment, strongly denied of course, is a reminder that relations between the Education and Labour Ministries after 1919 had been strained at times. The fissure in the bureaucratic set-up concerned with juveniles had complicated and confused inter-war policies towards youth unemployment, resulting in short-term expedients such as the juvenile instruction centres.

The most important aspect of the continuing debate about education and industry in the years after 1944 was the way that new groups, within and outside of education, became critical once again of the dominant values and occupational interests of the school system at all levels, and beyond that, of what were considered to be unfavourable attitudes towards industry and the values of industrial culture more generally. The origins of the new phase in the debate can now be traced, focusing first of all on the response of industry to educational progress in the post-war era, but attempting to relate these attitudes to changes in the internal economy. However, the question of what industry as a collective entity regarded as educational priorities is quite difficult to determine and interpret even in more recent times. It has to be borne in mind, going back to an earlier point, that there was no simple relation between technological change and the educational interests of industry. It is worth re-stating that industry, like education, is a complex sub-system, part of a larger network of social relationships, and influenced to that extent not only by occupational interests but also by social and political attitudes. Expressions of opinion on education reflect to an extent the social and political role of representatives of organized industry, and there is the further complication that national bodies may not be wholly representative.

Another more serious problem in discussing industrial attitudes is that of relating expressed opinions to changes in economic and social organization. It seems clear, for example, that attitudes must have been affected by the connection which seems to have been increasingly cemented in the inter-war years, between industry and the public schools. Professor Coleman, an economic historian, has summarized the evidence on the linkage of class, business leadership and education in particular industries, a phenomenon that was growing in strength – at least amongst the bigger companies – from the 1860s to the 1940s, and is still evident in more recent investigations of the recruitment of British managers. Professor Coleman adds the comment: 'It seems likely ... that, during the years, the larger the business the more likely would it be that its leaders had attended Public Schools and the ancient universities'.[14]

On the other hand, the nature and extent of the recruitment of educationally qualified managerial and technical staff must also have been affected by the increasing complexity of industrial processes and organizational changes: the rise of large companies, for example, and the associated development of 'scientific management', along with the growth of industrial research in particular firms during the inter-war years. Michael Sanderson, another economic historian, has emphasized the importance of what he calls the 'progressive connection of industry and the universities', beginning in the later nineteenth century, continuing through the inter-war years, and becoming fully established in the post-war era. The most important factor affecting the situation was the rise of 'new' industries which by their scientific nature required men with higher education. However, the impact of the expansion of universities in the post-war era, and of the increased recruitment of graduates to industry, on the over-all qualifications of British management, is an arguable matter. With regard to large companies, the most recent investigations provide somewhat differing evidence, varying from the 40 per cent of one survey of chief executives who had degrees, to the 80 per cent with degrees (and equivalent qualifications) in another survey of major companies and nationalized industries. But, whatever the precise changes, the number of graduates employed now is considerably more than in the inter-war years, when probably they made up no more than 1 to 5 per cent of the manufacturing labour force as a whole. They were also unevenly spread among different industries. Lord Jackson of Burnley, who had been a university engineer, recalled in 1970 in the inaugural Willis Jackson lecture that:

> At no time prior to the outbreak of the second World War do I remember any discussion or expression of concern about the adequacy or otherwise of the annual supply or active stock of qualified engineering and related manpower to meet the needs of the national situation. What I do remember is that in the late 1920s and early 1930s such engineering graduates as were being produced experienced no small difficulty in obtaining employment and were regarded by many industrial employers as unsuitable recruits.

At the same time, some industries, especially engineering, were beginning in the inter-war years to look for recruits to managerial and technical posts from the technical colleges. 'One of the most striking features of our evidence', the report of the Committee on Education for the Engineering Industry remarked in 1931 (p. 19), 'is the practically unanimous approval of the National Certificate Courses and Examinations by witnesses (from industry) who are acquainted with them'. The growth of National Certificate Courses was the most striking feature of the development of technical education between the 1930s and the 1960s. More generally, there is some evidence that new demands on technical colleges were being made by industry (and commerce) from the early 1930s onwards, especially from industries short of graduate labour and from those industries and those parts of the country where other awkward labour shortages existed, despite over-all high unemployment. The continuing shortage of skilled labour to some key industries probably lay behind the evident growth of day-release students from the 1930s to the 1950s, and the involvement even in the inter-war years of some businessmen in course innovation and design in provincial cities. Such trends suggest that by the later 1930s technical education was 'a service under demand pressure', a state of affairs that seems to have persisted until the mid-1950s.

With this background in mind, we can start commenting on the attitudes of 'organized' industry to educational progress in the post-war years, introducing the discussion with an extract from the report of the FBI on *Industry and Education* in respect of the Butler Act of 1944.

> Education has three closely interrelated aims: to enable the individual to realize for himself the fullest cultural and social life, to enable him to find

his place in and assume an appropriate degree of responsibility towards the community as a whole, and to enable him to earn his daily bread . . . Industry is not only concerned with the effects which education will have on a man's skill in his job. Industrialists are vitally concerned with the first two objects indicated above, *for a properly integrated and happy individual who is also a good citizen is bound to be an asset in industry whatever may be the position he holds* [italics added].

The contrast with the earlier statement on the Fisher Act is interesting. It has to be assessed, of course, in the context of the post-war mood of euphoria, and also perhaps the exceptional concern about youth during the war, and the revelations made then about the working conditions of juveniles in industry. Whatever the reasons for it, the statement heralded a period during which the FBI gave a general approval to policy documents and plans for educational expansion, especially of the universities. The FBI not only supported, for example, the Barlow expansion of the 1940s in the interests of science courses, but also the more general Robbins expansion of the 1960s. In addition, and possibly in reaction to increasing state intervention in industrial affairs, industrialists from time to time came forward to emphasize the wider social and educational responsibilities of industry. To cite just one example, in July 1959, Sir Hugh Beard, President of FBI, in a BACIE memorandum, projected a vision of industry's unaided emancipation: 'Industry has a new role to play . . . to initiate, to sponsor, to finance research and education, the care of youth, and the aged, culture and in fact civilization'.

It became increasingly evident, however, that overall support for public educational policies implied a bargain, a moral contract of a kind, tacitly implied at first, then more openly expressed, that particular support would be given to the promotion of science and technology, increasingly the latter, and that every opportunity ought to be taken to establish direct links between industry, the colleges and the schools. In report after report on conferences organized by the FBI and those of the Association (now the British Association) for Commercial and Industrial Education, repeated calls were made for the orientation of schools towards industry and a better understanding and more active collaboration between local industrialists and the schools. In 1956 the Federation pointed out in *Industry and the Technical Colleges* how they had been following a long-term programme, designed to foster increasingly close links with the schools:

> The Federation's objects are twofold: firstly, to keep the world of education abreast of industry's point of view with regard to current scientific, technical and managerial developments over a whole range of industrial activity, thereby acting as a link between the educationalist and the industrialist, and, secondly, to attract suitable young people by demonstrating to teachers and students alike that modern industry not only offers a worth while career in material terms, but constitutes a creative challenge and a service to the community equal to the best that other careers can give.

Each successive development in educational policy was monitored by relevant committees (education and industry and research), and working parties and standing committees were formed to consider the relationships between industry and education.[15]

The earlier demands for links reflected the sellers' market in graduates up to the mid-1950s, with industry 'courting' the universities, and developing interests in their sources of supply in schools. But the effects of new conditions in the labor market on changing the attitudes of particular industries should not be exaggerated. As P. W. Musgrave pointed out in his study of the iron and steel industry, the demand to the schools, even from this industry with its more sophisticated training procedures, was very much the same as the earlier Malcolm Committee and then the Norwood Committee had found: 'a source of ready comprehensiveness, adaptability, judgement, initiative and the like ... qualities ... best fostered by a broad curricula rather than by ... special studies'. On the other hand, industry had become, in effect, a pressure group for science, although the extent of this in terms of financial support requires investigation. A measure of both the continuing importance of the public school connection, as well as of the new view on education and science, was the success of the Industrial Fund for the Advancement of Scientific Education which gave considerable financial support to the Public Schools.[16]

It should be said here that the emphasis of public policy and public commentaries during the 1940s and 1950s was mainly on the need for science rather than technology as such, which reflected perhaps the influence of the Barlow Committee on Scientific Manpower more than Lord Eustace Percy's Committee on Higher Technological Education, set up in 1945 on the initiative of Lord Butler. The message of the Percy Report on the need for a new class of entrant to the engineering industry was rather lost in the political wrangles about technological awards and the status of technical colleges undertaking 'advanced' work. The clarion call of the need for science came, once again, from professional and scientific groups intent on demonstrating the technical and economic functions of their discipline. These groups included new sections within particular sciences (as the founders of the journal *Chemistry and Industry*), and old established national organizations, such as the British Association for the Advancement of Science: the setting up of a science and education committee in 1952 (reconstituted with the Royal Society of Arts and the Nuffield Foundation as joint sponsors), resulted in three reports eventually which established the real substance of the claim for science as a permanent influence on economic success, provided science was applied not only to the technical operations of industry, but to commercial and management services, as an expression of the whole attitude of the firm. As in the late-Victorian period, the upsurge of science groups contributed to influencing the climate of opinion, and had, in the more recent period, a direct impact on public policy, through the reports of the Advisory Council on Scientific Policy, whose Committee on Scientific Manpower (the Zuckerman Committee), was judged by one group of economists to be a demonstration 'of a science lobby in action'.[17]

On the whole, technology had not the same organizational support as science until the later 1960s, and 'organized' industry, represented by the FBI, was slow to develop any pronounced public interest in the technical colleges until the mid-

1950s, although individual industrialists had become conscious by then of the political implications of neglecting technology. The FBI were also reluctant to express a preference as between the universities and the technical colleges on the development of technology, believing that the resources required to promote the proposed CATs should not be at the expense of existing technological departments or the upgrading where appropriate of existing technical colleges. This rather cautious view contrasts both with the firm advocacy of the CATs by the Institute of Physics, and the alternative solution to the Percy Report's dilemmas held by a body of opinion led by Lord Cherwell (formerly Professor Frederick Lindemann) that wanted to see technological universities established in Britain similar to those at Zurich and Delft. When the FBI did make out a case for technology they expressed it in general terms, arguing for technological education as a necessary part of a general education in an industrial society. The message tuned in with the aspirations of some technical educationists who were caught in the dilemma of supporting the technical schools but sympathetic to the opposition now beginning to develop towards tripartism. The chief impediment to a theory of technical education for all was the kind of psychological assumption about the technical cast of mind which the Spens Report had used, paradoxically, to release technical education from its earlier class-restricted associations. One of the more impressive arguments advanced for technical education in the early 1960s drew on older philosophies of useful knowledge and claimed that:

> The accelerating industrialization of society not only creates directly technical and scientific occupations in ever greater number, importance and variety, but also causes traditional activities of all kinds to become permeated with science and technology ... Thus education is increasingly called upon to produce not only technicians but a population sympathetic to technological advance.[18]

The point was elaborated further by engineer-educationists in the universities who sought the accolade of a liberal education, maintaining that engineering studies united thought and action, the contemplative and the active life, in a way that no other subject does. But it is difficult to say whether the attempt to enhance the academic standing of technology ever came to much or whether this was the kind of argument likely to benefit it most. The practical outcome was a series of experiments in the schools, supported by the Schools Council projects, and the effort made by the Scottish Education Department to suggest ways of integrating technology into the school curriculum.

This brings us to the critical phase in the origins of present discontents with the school system. The attempt to stimulate greater interest in technology was an aspect of mounting anxieties about the difficulties of recruiting to university engineering departments in the late 1950s and early 1960s. Furthermore, trends were setting in which seemed particularly disturbing in the political climate of these years and the international rivalry in science and technology. An acute shortage of mathematics teachers in the schools, the beginnings of the swing away from 'A'-level science, and continuing forecasts of a shortage of scientists and technologists, allied with the effects of the 'brain drain' on the home employment of graduates, formed the background to a rising chorus of complaints about the educational system and those engaged in it. The new critique of schools and universities came from the groups most interested in the development of science and technology. The substance of it was that the autonomous development of the educational system was operating to restrict and distort the flow of more able pupils and students into industrial employment. The strongest and most clear-cut indictment of schooling was contained in the reports of the Advisory Council on Scientific Policy, culminating in the special reports of 1967–68, the Dainton, Swann and Jones reports. The basic argument tying these reports together was that, in effect, teachers and academics were 'locked up' in their specialisms producing thereby a group of narrow specialists for the employment market. The specialized, theoretical education of postgraduate courses was criticized especially, not only because they seemed unrelated to the 'needs' of industry, a point which was not yet generally accepted even among industrialists, but more importantly because these courses seemed to be drawing talent away from employment in British industry. The universities seemed to be feeding off their own products. This analysis was linked to the criticism that the science curriculum of the schools was out of date or intellectually unexciting, charges which came on top of earlier discouraging comments in unofficial reports on the image of technology particularly amongst sixth-form boys.

In his major historical study of industry and the universities, Michael Sanderson calls the period of the 1960s a 'watershed' in their relations. He was not so much concerned with the student unrest of the period, although some of the student polemics were directed against industry, but thought the more serious problem was the evident signs of tension about the nature and control over university courses. This tension affected the school system as well, with 'organized' industry reacting to current trends and contributing further criticisms of the schoolteachers. In 1965 the FBI adopted a more emphatic line in the report, *Industry and the Schools*, which urged the adoption of positive steps to overcome misconceptions. A strong plea was made that teachers should more readily seek to direct the abilities and enthusiasms of abler students towards the applied sciences. The Federation had already participated in 1964 in a Committee on Publicity for Engineering and Technology, and were now to back a new drive, Project Engineers and Technologists for Tomorrow (PETT). This was followed by a joint report with the Schools Council on closer links between teachers and industry and commerce. The British Employers' Confederation then pioneered the 'Introduction to Industry' scheme for student teachers following on the evidence given to the Newsom and Scottish Brunton Reports. More critical attitudes to teachers were reflected in the evidence of the British Employers' Confederation to Newsom (para. 239), reiterating a view formed earlier, that schoolteachers neither knew nor understood the industrial and commercial environment in which most of their pupils would need to work, and for that reason, consciously or unconsciously influenced them away from industrial careers. In the main, however, representatives of industry were still less concerned with specialist education in schools than the attitudes of teachers and pupils towards industry, and beyond that, to what some industrialists thought was the bad 'image' of industry in society at large. These anxieties became more pronounced during the 1960s when the interests of employers' organizations began to switch from earlier concerns with the recruitment of able children to new concerns with the schooling of the labour force as a whole. The emergence, or perhaps re-emergence, of this broader interest was connected with industrial changes, most importantly with the growth and reorganization of training practices within industry. Before making some final comments on the origins of present-day criticisms of schooling, it is necessary therefore, to explain how the improvement of industrial training has had repercussions on the relations between industry, the colleges and the schools.

Relations between industry and the technical colleges have been closer than in other parts of the educational system because of the industrial orientation of college courses and the working relationships established with local firms (and, to an extent, relationships with particular industries, such as aeronautical engineering). On the other hand, the increasing dependence of industry on the technical colleges has tended also to bring latent tensions into the open. The basic reason is not difficult to find: it stems mainly from the historical distinction between education and training characteristic of the concept of industrial education in Britain. The expansion of further education in the post-war years, changes in the industrial system, and the creation of new administrative structures for education and training, have all tended to complicate and confuse long-standing distinctions between the responsibilities of colleges and of industry. A very summary account of these changes may serve, therefore, to illustrate further how institutional developments exposed ideological conflicts about the relations between education and industry.[19]

British further education has grown haphazardly, influenced by the availability of funds for capital expenditure, but dependent also on local and institutional aspirations. A precondition for accelerated growth was the shift in political attitudes towards further education during the 1950s when the drive for expanding highly qualified manpower began to have implications for the number and quality of technical support staff in industry. A heightened political awareness of the potential contribution of technical education to the economy and to the extension of social opportunity (the 'alternative route'), lay behind the call for expansion 'on all fronts' in the White Paper *Technical Education* (1956). This was the decisive turning-point, a preliminary to the subsequent explosion of courses and student numbers. Given more permissive attitudes on the part of governments, the really dynamic factors in the expansion appear to have been generated internally, deriving from the ambitions of principals and the way that colleges were organized. Growth took place without necessarily being related directly to local industrial and commercial needs, although entrepreneurial staffs were shrewd at spotting changes in market conditions. One effect of relatively unrestrained growth was the multiplication of examinations, some of them with ill-defined and overlapping functions, especially in the case of technician examinations which had to be cleared up subsequently and put on a new footing by the Haslegrave report. Furthermore, growth was not concentrated only on industrial courses however widely defined, but took place in areas which gave the colleges new functions (as the teaching of liberal studies, university entrance and other non-vocational courses), so tending to create problems of organizational identity and some internal conflicts between staff who perceived their objectives as 'meeting the needs of industry', and those with more widely educational objectives. In some ways, the development of teacher training for this sector (though still on a voluntary basis) contributed to further extending educational aspirations by emphasizing the generic connections between teaching in the colleges and the schools. In addition, attempts were made to overcome the institutional separation of school and college with the introduction of 'link' courses and the very partial implementation of the concept of the tertiary or junior college for all sixteen- to nineteen-year-old students. Whilst many of these changes were welcomed by industry, they had been very largely autonomous developments rather than overt responses to demands made by local firms.

The growth of training within industry in the post-war years owed little to government intervention prior to 1964, and depended therefore on the attitudes and traditions of particular firms within industry. Hence the response to persistent shortages of skilled men in the post-war period was extremely uneven, the provision of day-release and industrial training varying between different industries and between different firms in the same industry. A contributory factor to this variable response was the persistence of small firms, with low ratios of skilled employees. This is an important point because the opinions of 'organized' industry on technical education, as on other aspects of schooling, probably represented more the requirements of 'big' industry, which may not have been typical. As the National Institute of Industrial Psychology pointed out in a survey of 1956, despite the rising cost of juvenile labour, 'the typical firm had *not* reckoned the cost of *not* training: it had not even got past the starting post of establishing criteria for evaluating the results of training'. Yet changes in industrial processes were making training more necessary as well as imposing new requirements on the courses provided by the technical colleges. The most important changes were the trends towards supervision rather than direct manipulation of processes, and towards skills based on knowledge of plant and equipment rather than manual dexterity. Responses to these trends were not only inhibited by the traditionalism of college courses, but according to a Royal Commission in 1969, by outworn ideas and negative attitudes within industry.

Before 1964 governments were hesitant about interfering with industrial recruitment and training, preferring to concentrate resources on technical education. What interest was shown derived more from demographic than economic trends, as when the Carr Committee was set up in 1954 to consider arrangements for the training of juvenile workers in industry. Anxieties about the effects of the 'bulge' on the juvenile labour market (and also about the 'wastage' of talent from early school leaving), formed the basis for the Crowther recommendations for raising the school-leaving age, and for reviving continuation education, the latter measure having failed to be implemented after 1944. The Carr Committee made no such bold demands, and the attitudes of industrial representatives at the time were mainly in favour of retaining the *status quo*. The approach of trade union representatives was influenced by a general commitment to extending educational opportunity which included support for the Crowther recommendations. Attitudes to technical education as such, and to industrial training, were still ambiguous, the result of inter-war experiences and what one leader called the 'mentality of the craftsman'. Generally, trade union leaders argued for a wider view of education and training as, for example, Harold Clegg, chairman of the Workers' Education Trades Union Committee, when he remarked: 'there have got to be considerations going beyond the individual, beyond the firm, even beyond the industry . . . we have got to get away from the idea that schemes of education and training represent something that a benevolent employer provides for his workers'. The eventual collaboration of the TUC in the reorganization of training was something of an achievement: it reflected the support which Congress gave from the later 1950s to the idea of improving productivity, and to central planning for economic development, including manpower planning. However, the main impetus for legislation seems to have come more directly from a small group of employers, members of the British Association for Commercial and Industrial Education, whose traditional interest and financial outlays in education and training were sufficient to overcome any reluctance about the idea of state intervention. The BACIE conferences kept the subject of training under discussion, and extended the initial conception of it to all levels of occupation including management, a principle embodied in the regulations accompanying the Industrial Training Act of 1964. This Act was, in effect, a compromise between a *laissez-faire* approach to training within industry, and the unification of education and training under the Education Department. There were strong arguments against the latter course, not only from the industrialists, but also educationists, notably from Lady Williams, an influential social economist, who explained the dangers of reversing the traditional idea of training within industry, one of the main reasons being that the alternative of training within an educational institution would be likely to impose its own rigidities. Ironically, criticisms of rigidity were subsequently made of the bureaucratic structure of training boards.[20]

Between 1964 and the early 1970s, the journals serving technical and further education carried many assessments of how the new partnership was working, some of the articles revealing the recriminations and disputes that had arisen about implementing the Act and the consequent revision of technical examinations.[21] The anxieties of some college staffs – not only of the 'intellectuals' imported into the colleges, but of traditional craft teachers – were deeply rooted, stemming from apprehensions about the possibility, whether real or not, of becoming instruments in the making of an industrial helotry. The basic question at issue was whether vocational education was to be revised in the interests of rationalizing productive processes or with the specific educational aim of enhancing the opportunities and self-determination of individuals. In a survey of further education published in 1969, the educationists Cantor and Roberts leaned towards the latter argument, charging the Act with having 'failed to provide for the majority of young people', and having 'institutionalized a position where educational opportunity has become dependent upon the wishes and needs of industry'.[22] The failure of day-release classes to grow in the way envisaged in the government report of the industrialist C. Henneker Heaton provided a further testimony to the educational inadequacies of the Act.

Despite the government review of industrial training in 1973, and a token attempt to bring the training system into contact with the machinery of educational planning, the administrative divisions of the state bureaucracy, and the anxieties of college staffs, have persisted. The new threat, according to staff most sensitive to the traditional educational objectives of the colleges, arises from the activities of the Manpower Services Commission in financing a range of 'training' courses within educational institutions. On the other hand, this development has given strength to more long-standing arguments on the part of both technical education-ists and industrialists that the division between education and training tends to separate the acquisition of technical knowledge from the needs of industrial occupa-tions; and that argument has led to a new demand for a more unified approach, bringing in the schools, so that institutional rigidities do not impede adjustments to changing conditions. The Training Boards, representative of technical educa-tionists and industrial trainers, have charged schoolteachers with not fully appre-ciating the level of theoretical knowledge and technical accomplishment required not only in traditional maintenance crafts but also in many operative jobs. Hence the recent interest in school mathematics. At a national level, several organizations – the Technician Education Council and the Training Services Agency, for example – have been seeking to influence school curricula by general exhortation and support for such new ventures as the 'gateway' courses, and the concept of 'unified vocational preparation'. However, the belief in the autonomy of the curriculum and practices of schooling is sufficiently strong as to make outside interests cautious about bringing too much pressure, avoiding delicate issues of control by coining such phrases as 'the inter-face between school and work'.

Nevertheless, the present demands for improved standards of literacy and numer-acy, should be placed in the context of wider concerns about recruitment to the industrial labour force reflected in the attention currently being paid to the transition, as it is called, from school to work. The 'needs' of industry have not only, or even mainly, been expressed in terms of cognitive requirements, and the interest in pre-employment courses derives also from the more traditional concerns of some employers in the social experiences and welfare of youth, a concern which, in the past, has combined a sense of social responsibility with anxieties about the loyalties and docility of the work force. Industrialists (and trade unionists) have supported the many voluntary organizations set up over the years to mobilize youth and guide them through adolescence, and more specifically those organizations attempting to identify and overcome in practical ways the problems of initial employment, especially in low-level occupations. Industrialists have supported ventures such as Young Enterprise and Trident, and the 'adjustment to industry' schemes of the National Association of Boys' Clubs. They have shown interest in the work of the Industrial Welfare Society on the human problems of industrial society and the inter-relations between industry and the community. They have encouraged the work of the Centre for Applied Research of the Tavistock Institute founded (in

1966 with financial aid from the Baxi Trust) to carry out a research programme which started with investigations of labour turnover and other phenomena in industry, and went on to study aspects of the transition from school to work.[23] Similarly, there has been support and interest in local authority initiatives, such as that of the Leicestershire Education Committee in establishing (about ten years ago) a working party (now a committee) to look at aspects of education and industry and the relationships between them. An initial piece of research, funded from local in-dustrialists as well as the Authority, was transformed into a larger investigation of induction practices with a grant from the Training Services Agency. The research showed, incidentally, considerable variability in the induction practices of local firms, and some examples of mismatch between what employers thought they were offering and what entrants thought they had obtained from various procedures. It is a reminder of the differences which may exist between the general sentiments of industry and the attitudes and behaviour of local firms.

Recent discussions about the transition from school to work indicate, neverthe-less, a coming together of educationists who support Newsom type proposals and of industrialists anxious about recruitment problems and the attitudes of the juvenile work force. The link has been formed by the more general recognition that the stresses of adolescent development may coincide with the 'culture shock' of the transition from school to work. The entry of young people into work is no longer regarded as simply a problem of relating supply and demand. For many social educationists, and members of the careers advisory service, it is an aspect of the personal development and socialization of the young, as well as being the central mechanism by which the work force is renewed. Much current psychological research on these matters implies or contains strong criticisms of the attitudes of teachers, which are based, so it is argued, on misconceptions of the meaning and significance of work, including industrial work, to the young. On the other hand, educationists sometimes claim that a gap exists between the aspirations and expecta-tions of the young and the employment conditions of modern industrial processes, which they are not sure how to close or whether they should attempt to do so. Thus Schools' Council reports based on Newsom ideas about social education have been challenged by philosopher-educationists for skating over the dilemma of how to develop a genuinely educational programme without committing the young to particular social and moral values.[24]

But for some groups in the community such considerations seem rather remote from the social problems of an economy under stress; and recent statements from industrial organizations imply that educational theorizing contributes to forming ideological prejudices. The suspicion that attitudes towards industry are hardening is implied by the recent 'Understanding British Industry Project', whose background statement complains of the 'divorce between academic and industrial society'. It is articulated more forcefully in the reports of a working party, representative of educational and industrial interests, invited by the training board of the Rubber and Plastics Processing Industry to study its problems of recruitment. This group found they were dealing with an aspect of a much larger national problem, the main element of which related to the employment prospects of school leavers with minimal qualifications, no career ambitions and little interest in any job which they find themselves. Faced with an apparently inflexible school system, orientated to academic success, their solution comes near to a modest form of de-schooling: they propose, for example, the development of 'alternative curricular pathways whose goals are located outside of the education system' and which presuppose not only a two-way exchange, but the active participation of industry by the appointment of foremen-tutors.

The sense of frustration evident in these and other comments on the problems of juveniles has been sharpened no doubt by current economic difficulties and rising youth unemployment. The latter is not peculiar to Britain. According to a recent OECD survey, there is evidence in many countries of long-term imbalances between the growing demand for employment for the young and the absorptive capacity of European economies. The point of the survey is to report that although economic recession may have brought the problem of youth employment to the forefront of public attention, the causes of the problem are more long term, related to changes in the structures of growth, particularly changes in the age pyramid of populations and in the nature and composition of labour markets. British commentators have also maintained that youth unemployment is not simply a cyclical phenomenon, to be fought with 'fire-fighting' measures, but an aspect of structural changes in the character and economic organization of cities. Thus the current economic problem of youth simply highlights the deprivation that is characteristic of the inner districts of many British cities. The calls for vocational education and 'alternative curricular pathways' are but instances of a variety of measures being proposed to rescue school leavers from what is known as the 'poverty trap' of the inner city; and such proposals are frequently accompanied by warnings of social disorganization.[25]

Current school practices, so the argument goes, may be actually contributing to social dangers by labelling those who do not achieve academic success as 'failures'. Although historical analogies can be misleading if pushed too far, there are distinct echoes in recent commentaries of anxieties which influenced late-Victorian educational reformers, many of whom, then as now, discerned connections between the employment prospects of youth and the prevalence of street 'hooliganism' in the larger cities. Furthermore, the failure of schooling to become concerned about the 'after-life' of the young was held to be contributing to social problems in both periods.

This brings us, finally, to other complaints being publicized widely in the national as well as the educational press since the early 1970s.[26] Recent statements on higher education, for example, express considerable disillusion with what seems to be a continuing mismatch between educational outputs and the needs of the economy. Many commentators seem baffled by the current statistics of enrolments in arts and social sciences, as well as by the trends in graduate employment. One particularly 'alarming trend' picked out is the apparent failure of industry to increase or even maintain a share of graduate output during the period of expansion. Whereas the Robbins expansion of the universities (and the Crosland expansion of the polytechnics) probably kept pace with the growth of employment in the public sector of the economy between 1960–75, this does not appear to have been the case with private industry, although industrial demands have tended to fluctuate depending on the economic situation. The balance of reasons is not clear, but the facts are: since the peak years of 1968–70, the absolute number and the proportion of all graduates entering home employment who go into manufacturing have both fallen, with the proportion going down from 40 per cent in 1970 to 26 per cent in 1975. Such trends lay behind current demands for new forms of manpower planning, and they are invoked by public bodies critical of how educational and research monies have been spent.

The condition of the engineering industry is a kind of barometer for registering shifts in the climate of opinion: frustrations with past policies are evident here in the renewed debate about the quality of new entrants to management, which is linked to recent trends in engineering education and, so it is claimed, the continuing low status of the mechanical engineer in industry. For some critics, the really 'alarming' trend is the virtual demise of the National Certificate and Diploma courses as an entry to the profession, and, despite repeated attempts at putting elements of practical experience back into undergraduate and postgraduate courses in engineering, there is a distinct sense in public comments that much has been lost in the past few years. One symptom of that is the revival of the argument about whether engineering is an academic discipline, or more realistically, a professional training. Another symptom, perhaps, is the revival of two (apparently contradictory) demands, for the formation of specialist high-level institutions and for the production of what are called 'technical generalists'.

And so the debate goes on. A comparison with the late-Victorian period is instructive, because just as arguments were put forward then by various groups in order to extend and improve education, so the arguments of recent years have been advanced by groups who were optimistic about the benefits of educational expansion – only to find that changes in schooling have not taken place to the extent thought necessary for bringing the 'pay off'. A difference between the two periods, however, is the emergence of 'organized' industry as a critical educational force. It is worth emphasizing too that the character of modern arguments has been shaped by structural changes in the relations between education, industry and the state. The general drift of many criticisms is that economic and social developments affecting education and industry have produced a gap, a divergence, between the occupational interests of teachers and those of industrialists in relation to education and training the work force; and, because of the institutional tensions indicated in this chapter, criticisms are now being made not only of the academicism of schooling, but of the inflexibility and insularity of the *school system*.

The historian must be cautious about making too much of recent statements that are often of an ephemeral character and may be no more than straws in the wind. One of the important questions needing to be explored is whether the views of particular groups, and of the politicians who represent them, can be said to reflect currents of opinion more generally, rather than those of special interests; and related to that question, whether a gap has really opened up between the perceptions and interests of teachers (and academics) and the real processes affecting society. If the debate about education and industry is symptomatic of more broadly-based demands for changes in the relations between school and community, then structural changes may possibly have to be made to resolve the tensions.

But such changes are not likely to resolve the issues underlying the debate. One of the more fundamental issues is that of conflicting priorities, between education's role as a critical force, monitoring social and economic developments, and education's role as an adaptive force, matching these developments. This is an issue which takes the form now of a conflict over the degree of autonomy to be accorded the educational system; and it is symptomatic of the times that autonomous developments in the further education sector can be described pejoratively as examples of 'academic drift'.[27] But the question of the role of education in an industrial society is also one of cultural priorities, and, ultimately perhaps, what should be recognized as culture. Those educationists resistant to socio-economic pressures take a stand on the cultural argument for the intrinsic values of education; whilst the critics of modern education claim that the cultural argument is distorted by the social esteem attached to academic studies, and by the failure to recognize the validity of technical culture. The historian may think that all this has been said before. As one historian points out, recalling the arguments about national and social efficiency at the turn of the century, cultural determinism is always perceptible. So it can be argued that any society which feels itself threatened from without or enfeebled from within is likely to assert the value of useful knowledge and to stress the importance of the extrinsic purposes of education. In that respect, present controversies might be regarded as no more than a particular phase in what has been, and probably will go on being, a recurrent debate.[28]

Select Bibliography of Post-war Reports

Science, technology and industry

Higher Technological Education (Percy Report) (London: HMSO, 1945).
Scientific Manpower (Barlow Report) Cmnd. 6824 (London: HMSO, 1946).
The Education and Training of Technologists (London: FBI, 1948).
CARTER, C. and WILLIAMS, B.R., *Industry and Technical Progress* (London: British Association, 1957); *Investment in Education* (London: British Association, 1958); *Science in Industry* (London: British Association, 1959).
Technology and the Sixth Form Boy (Oxford University Department of Education, 1963).
The Brain Drain (Jones Report) Committee on Manpower Resources, Cmnd. 3417 (London: HMSO, 1967).
Enquiry into the Flow of Candidates in Science and Technology into Higher Education (Dainton Report) Cmnd. 3541 (London: HMSO, 1968).
The Flow into Employment of Scientists, Engineers and Technologists (Swann Report) Cmnd. 2760 (London: HMSO, 1968).
Scottish Education Department, *Technical Education in Secondary Schools* (London: HMSO, 1973).
House of Commons, *Select Committee on Science and Technology*, HoC Paper 680 (London: HMSO, 1976).

Education and industry

Mutual Relations of Education and Industry (London: BACIE, 1944).
Industry and Education (London: FBI, 1945).

Industry and the Universities (London: FBI, 1949).

Industry and the Technical Colleges (London: FBI, 1956).

School and Industry (Nottinghamshire Education Committee, 1956).

Ministry of Labour, *Training for Skill: Recruitment and Training of Young Workers in Industry (Carr Report)* (London: HMSO, 1958).

Central Advisory Council, *15–18 (Crowther Report)* (London: HMSO, 1959).

VENABLES, P.F.R. and WILLIAMS, W.I., *The Smaller Firm and Technical Education* (London: Parrish, 1961).

Department of Education and Science, *Day Release (Henniker – Heaton Report)* (London: HMSO, 1963).

Central Advisory Council, *Half Our Future (Newsom Report)* (London: HMSO, 1963).

Industry and the Schools (London: FBI, 1965).

Education in Transition: Implications for Industry (London: FBI, 1965).

Schools Council, *Closer Links between Teachers and Industry and Commerce* (London: HMSO, 1966).

Technician Courses and Examinations (Haslegrave Report) (London: HMSO, 1969).

Mathematics and the School/Industry Interface (Southend: Institute of Mathematics and its Applications, 1975).

Education, Industry and the Economy (Coombe Lodge: Further Education Staff College, 1976).

Engineering Industry Training Board, *Basic Skills in Mathematics* (London: Shell Centre for Mathematical Education, 1977).

Department of Industry, *Education, Industry and Management: a Discussion Paper* (London: HMSO, 1977).

School and work

Citizens of Tomorrow (London: King George Jubilee Trust, 1955).

The Transition from School to Work: Some Practical Aids (London: Industrial Welfare Society, 1962).

Scottish Education Department, *From School to Further Education (Brunton Report)* (London: HMSO, 1963).

The Training of Young People In Industry (London: Industrial Welfare Society, 1965).

Department of Employment, *Unqualified, Untrained and Unemployed* (London: HMSO, 1974).

Education and Working Life (Paris: OECD, 1975).

The Education/Training of Young People (Brentford: Rubber and Plastics Processing Industry, 1975).

Department of Education and Science, *Unified Vocational Preparation: A Pilot Approach* (London: HMSO, 1975).

Foundation Courses (London: City and Guilds of London Institute, 1976).

Department of Education and Science, *Getting Ready for Work: 16–19* (London: HMSO, 1976).

HILL, J.M.M. and SCHARFF, D.E., *Between Two Worlds. Aspects of the Transition from School to Work* (London: Tavistock Institute, 1976).

KEIL, E.J., *Becoming a Worker* (Leicestershire Education Committee, 1976).

School Curricula for a Changing World (Brentford: Rubber and Plastics Processing Industry, 1976).

House of Commons, Tenth Report from the Expenditure Committee, Session 1976–77, *The Attainments of the School-leaver*, HoC Paper 526–I (London: HMSO, 1977).

DEAN, J. and CHOPPIN, B. *Educational Provision 16–19* (Windsor: National Foundation for Educational Research, 1977).

Manpower Services Commission, *Young People and Work. Report on Feasibility of a New Programme of Opportunities for Unemployed Young People* (London: HMSO, 1977).

The Education, Training and Employment of the 16–19 Age Group (London: NATFHE, 1977).

General Report: Entry of Young People into Working Life (Paris: OECD, 1977).

Notes and References

1 DEWEY, J. (1915) *The New Republic*, 5 May.

2 Harold Silver has commented more than most historians of education on the relations between education and the division of labour in his writings on Robert Owen and in SILVER, H. (1977) 'Ideology and the factory child: Attitudes to half-time education' in McCANN, P. (Ed) *Popular Education and Socialization in the Nineteenth Century* London, Methuen. The issues raised in the USA by John Dewey versus the Social Efficiency philosophers are discussed in *Studies in Philosophy and Education* viii, 3 (1974). The European Report is VISALBHERGI, A. (1973) *Education and the Division of Labour* The Hague,

Martinus Nijhoff. It should be said that criticisms of technology and industrial capitalism can be made from a cultural point of view as in BANTOCK, G.H. (1963) *Education and Industrial Society* London, Faber, or from a social (frequently Marxist) view as in BRAVERMAN, H. (1975) *Labor and Monopoly Capitalism: the Degradation of Work in the Twentieth Century* New York, Review Press.

3 Public Record Office Files, Ed. 24/64, 26 February, 1900. W. de. W. Abney to G. Kekevich, quoted in ROBERTS, K.O. (1969) 'The separation of secondary from technical education: 1889–1903' *The Vocational Aspects of Education* XXI, 49. The reference to Magnus which follows comes from BRABAZON, LORD (1887) (Ed) *National and School Board Reforms* and to the London survey from ACLAND, A.H.D. and SMITH, H.L. (1906) *Studies in Secondary Education* London, Percival. The best account of Webb's influence and ideas is BRENNAN, E.J.T. (1975) *Education for National Efficiency: The Contribution of Sydney and Beatrice Webb* London, Athlone Press.

4 See, for example, MEADOWS, A.J. (1973) 'Specialization – The Recurring Debate' *Chemistry in Britain* ix, 11.

5 DURKHEIM, E. (1938) *The Evolution of Educational Thought* trans. COLLINS, P., London, Routledge and Kegan Paul (1977) pp. 13–14, quoted by SMITH, D. (1977) 'Social conflict and urban education in the nineteenth century: A sociological approach to comparative analysis' in REEDER, D.A. (Ed) *Urban Education in the Nineteenth Century* London, Taylor and Francis.

6 FISHER, H.A.L. (1919) Inaugural address to the Association *Proceedings* 1, May, in the archives of the British Association for Commercial and Industrial Education (hardly yet exploited by historians of industrial education). I have outlined the theme of the social purposes of educational reform in 'Predicaments of city children: Late-Victorian and Edwardian perspectives on education and urban society' in REEDER, D.A. (1977) *op. cit.* The best general account of the theme is SEARLE, G.R. (1971) *The Quest for National Efficiency: A Study of British Politics and Political Thought, 1899–1914* Oxford, Basil Blackwell.

7 PERCY, LORD EUSTACE (n.d. *c.* 1903) *Education at the Crossroads* London, Evans, esp. p. 59. Also the discussion by SIMON, B. (1965) *The Politics of Educational Reform 1920–40* London, Lawrence and Wishart, esp. pp. 85–115.

8 As in Margaret Gowing's lecture to the Royal Society reported in the THES 26 November, 1976. For the broad historical view, see SIMON, B. (1965) *Education and the Labour Movement* London, Lawrence and Wishart, Chap. VI.

9 The general approach of the TUC can be followed in SIMON, B. (1965) *op. cit.* The quotation is from the Annual Conference of 1922; see also the criticisms of vocational education in TUC (1937) *Education and Democracy-TUC Aspirations and Activities* London, TUC.

10 Discussed by THOMS, D.W. (1975) 'The emergence and failure of the day continuation school experiment' *History of Education* IV, 1. For the report on higher elementary schools, see the extract in VAN DER EYKEN, W. (1973) *Education, the Child and Society* Harmondsworth, Penguin, pp. 126–37.

11 The memorandum is unpublished and contained in the PRO Files, Ed. 24/247. For the next section on the Board of Education (and for comments and suggestions on the chapter as a whole) I am most grateful to an ex-colleague, W. Bailey of Garnett College of Education (Technical). I have also consulted PRO files esp. Ed. 24/1879 and 1881.

12 Again from BACIE archives, report of conference, 1937.

13 GOSDEN, P.H.J.H. (1976) *Education in the Second World War* London, Methuen, p. 237 and, for the references that follow, p. 412 and pp. 210–53.

14 In his stimulating article (1973) 'Gentlemen and players' *Economic History Review* XXVI, 1. For the rest of this section on education and economic change I have relied on: SANDERSON, M. (1972) *The Universities and British Industry 1850–1970* London, Routledge and Kegan Paul; and, for technical education, THOMS, D.W. (1976) 'Technical education and the labour supply in England between the wars' *The Vocational Aspect of Education* XXVIII, 70. The remarks of Lord Jackson are quoted from the inaugural Willis Jackson Lecture 'Manpower for engineering and technology' BACIE, (1970) p. 6.

15 For example, Working Party on Industry and the University (1949), Joint FBI-Technical Colleges Committee (1954), Joint Standing Committee of the Federation of British Industries, Headmasters' Conference and Incorporated Association of Headmasters (1963) and the Joint Committee of the CBI (ex FBI) and the Committee of Vice-Chancellors on the Relations of Industry and the Universities (1965). The quotation is from the FBI report *Industry and the Technical Colleges* (1956). All post-war reports are listed in the Select Bibliography at the end of the chapter.

16 Based mainly on MUSGRAVE, P.W. (1967) *Technical Change and the Labour Force* Oxford, Pergamon Press, p. 101.

17 GANNICOT, K.G. and BLAUG, M. (1969) 'Manpower forecasting since Robbins: A science lobby in action' *Higher Education Review* Autumn. The technical criticisms in this piece reflect divisions taking place at the time between investment theory economists and manpower planners.

18 PETERS, A.J. (1963) 'The changing concept of technical education' *British Journal of Educational Studies* 11 May. Other statements were made by PETERSON, A.D.C. of the Oxford Institute and Professor PARKES of the University of Leicester. See PARKERS, E.W. (1963) *The Education of an Engineer* University of Leicester Press.

19 The question of how ideology influences the attitudes and behaviour of teachers in further education is being investigated by George Young, a colleague in the School of Education. The general interpretation which follows is based on the work of another ex-colleague, now at the University of London Institute of Education, TIPTON, B.F.A. (1973) *Conflict and Change in a Technical College* London, Hutchison. See also, SHUTT, W. (1975) 'Organizational Survival and educational adaptation in a technical college' *The Vocational Aspects of Education* XXVII, 66 and BRADLEY, K. and JONES, M. (1975) 'The intellectual in the technical college' *ibid.*

20 For this section on industrial training, I have relied on the information in PERRY, P.J.C. (1976) *The Evolution of British Manpower Policy* London, BACIE, esp. pp. 60–2, 106–7, supplemented by a reading of documents from BACIE archives. I have also consulted the *Royal Commission on Trade Unions and Employers' Associations* (1969) London, HMSO.

21 For example, WILCOCK, R. (1969) 'Troubled techs' *Education* 14 November; METCALFE, F. (1970) 'Partnership between education and industry: Is it working?' *The Technical Journal* VIII, 7; McQUEEN, W.M. (1969) 'Dangerous misinterpretations of the Industrial Training Act' *The Vocational Aspects of Education* XXI, 49.

22 CANTOR, L.M. and ROBERTS, I.F. (1972) *Further Education in England and Wales* 2nd ed., London, Routledge and Kegan Paul, p. 101. This is the best survey.

23 Again, all these reports are listed in the select bibliography at the end of the chapter.

24 PRING, R. (1975) 'Socialization as an aim of education' in ELLIOTT, J. and PRING, R. (Eds) (1975) *Social Education and Social Understanding* London, University of London Press.

25 Some of these arguments are detailed in the two conferences reported in FIELD, F. (Ed) (1977) *Education and the Urban Crisis* London, Routledge and Kegan Paul.

26 Much of the following section is based on a reading of the *Times Higher Education Supplement* for 1975–77. Statistics of graduate employment over the last ten years or so are conveniently displayed, along with other useful material, in DEPARTMENT OF INDUSTRY (1977) *Industry, Education and Management: A Discussion Paper* London, Department of Industry.

27 See, for example, BURGESS, T. (1976) *Education After School* Harmondsworth, Penguin, pp. 27–32.

28 In making the concluding remarks of this section I owe much to a conversation with Dennis Smith of the Department of Sociology, University of Leicester and to a personal reflection on the 'Great Debate' by BRENNAN, E.J.T. (1977) in *The Vocational Aspects of Education* XXIX, 74.

Michael Sanderson

'*One of the many lessons of the Great War was that industry needed all the help that science could give her. That help could best be given through the universities by training experts and conducting research*'.[1]

'Hyman Levy: *So you agree that universities, whatever else they are doing are un-consciously playing their part in assisting industrialists to carry on their business?*

Julian Huxley: *Yes that is so. . . .* '[2]

In the inter-war years the university population of Great Britain stood at around 40,000 in the early and mid 1920s, then rose steadily from 1926 to 1932 to around 50,000 where it remained fairly constantly throughout the 1930s. In contrast to the relative stability of the universities, in a hiatus between the great expansions of the pre-1914 and post-1945 periods, the experience of industry was necessarily far more volatile. Post-war boom gave way to severe slump in 1920, followed in turn by a modest recovery in the later 1920s. This, although less marked than that of other major industrial countries, was yet as powerful as the 1930s recovery in its beneficial effects on graduate employment. The good times of the 1920s were ended by depression initiated by the American crash of 1929 and the crisis of 1931. Recovery followed, notably from 1933, though it was interrupted by the milder recession of 1938. But the broad trends of the movement of the economy masked wide divergences of fortune between the declining basic old industries of the nineteenth century, often located in the North of England, and the rising new industries of the South, highly science-conscious and developing technologies originating from the turn of the century. It is the purpose of this chapter to examine the interplay of the universities and industry in these conditions. We will consider the new factors creating a greater need for graduates on the part of industry and industrial attitudes towards graduates. Then the contribution of the universities to industrial science and business education will be examined. [. . .]

Source: An abridged version of SANDERSON, M. (1972) *The Universities and British Industry 1850–1970* London, Routledge and Kegan Paul, Chap. 9, pp. 243–75.

Many of the new industries of the inter-war years were scientifically very sophisticated. It was a period of the cumulative working out of developments in radio, aircraft, motor vehicles, synthetic fibres, dyes, and so forth, many of which had been virtually created by the needs of war and all of which called for a high degree of scientific and technical expertise.[3] Moreover, many old industries were forced into technical improvement under the spur of depression,[4] and some old industries so changed their techniques as to render the common distinction of 'old' and 'new' industries practically meaningless. Such examples were the application of X-ray analysis to textile fibres and the cold rolling of steel, or the altering of the chemical structure of cotton fibre to render it crease resistant.

While technical change was scarcely new, organized research became one of the leading sources of invention in the inter-war years and this by its very nature required graduate labour. Research became important in the 1920s for a variety of reasons.[5] First, the experience of the war had shown the possibility of universities, firms, and government departments being geared to the solution of specific research problems as a basis for production. Second, in chemical and particularly in mechanical processes, the new mass production conditions of manufacture made research as a distinct activity all the more necessary. Modification on the job became far less possible when vast capitals had been sunk in plant for processes which scarcely allowed any possibility of interference when they were set in train. In these circumstances research in laboratory conditions beforehand became a vital adjunct to test the feasibility of large-scale manufacture.[6] Third, the research department became a useful nursery for introducing into the firm able graduates who may later move to management.[7]

The rapid formation of research departments by firms was a remarkable feature of the years at the end of the war and the early 1920s. Tootal's and Courtauld's began theirs in 1918, and among the electrical firms Metro-Vickers began their laboratory in 1917 and BTH had one by 1919, while the great GEC laboratories at Wembley and those of Siemens in Preston were opened in 1923. Apart from these, by 1922 Lever's, Boots, Kynoch's, Brown and Firth, Brunner Mond, Chance's, Adam Hilger, Nobel's, and Burroughs Wellcome, merely to select some of the main ones, were all undertaking research of first-rate importance.[8] Research within the firm rose markedly during the 1930s from 422 firms spending £1.7 million in 1930 to 566 firms spending £5.4 million in 1938.[9] At the same time research associations undertaking research for whole industries arose under the DSIR, creating yet further demand for the research scientist. Accordingly industry had to turn more to the graduate. The universities in turn, with the impossibility of travel to Germany during the war, had started their own Ph.D. higher research degrees, at the same time providing the new type of advanced graduate for research.

It was not only the increasingly scientific character of industry in these years that created a demand for graduates; it was also felt by several eminent business leaders that management was becoming more difficult and called for better educated and more intelligent minds than before. Part of the difficulty arose from the severe depression of the period which increased the keenness of competition and the dangers of failure. But also the actual performance of the job seemed to many to be becoming more demanding. Sir Robert Waley Cohen of Shell thought that, compared with the past, industry now 'demands exact thought and power to analyse a difficult and complicated situation'.[10] Likewise Sir Kenneth Lee of Tootal's, perhaps the most dynamic figure in the cotton industry, held that higher management needed 'minds trained to appreciate reports on highly specialized and complex matters of production, merchanting and finance and to give sound judgement thereon'.[11] The complexity was both technical and organizational. Not only was research more technical but so also was the management of production, and this called for a massive upgrading of jobs and higher demands on the labour required to fulfil them. R.H. Clayton addressing Manchester businessmen observed that, whereas formerly university men in industry were predominantly researchers, now they had invaded works control, 'the mass of graduates is at the present time employed in controlling works operations previously run by skilled artisans, who are, under the complexities of modern methods, now unable to fill these positions'.[12]

There were also complexities of an organizational kind. Through the process of rationalization and merger several industries became more concentrated, with larger firms and wider integrations that called for a greater degree of administrative ability at the top. This was certainly true in bricks, metal boxes, sugar, soap, steel tubes, and flour milling, for example.[13] T.M. Knox of the Oxford Appointments Board considered that 'the demand for graduates in business is perhaps contemporaneous with the amalgamation of firms into large units, and in fact demand arises in the main from such industrial combines'.[14] Similarly, the Liberal Industrial Inquiry of 1925, after commending a university education as necessary for the higher direction of industry, noted 'the present tendency towards the creation of large industrial units' as 'a particular reason for industry to select administrators of the broadest and most highly educated outlook'.[15] Another change in managerial organization resulting from increased scale was the tendency towards functionalism. In small firms the old style of manager dealt by himself with a wide range of technical and personnel issues, but increased scale had led to increased specialization of managerial functions and consequently greater expertise demanding in turn a higher level of education.[16] A.S. Rowntree, for example, observed that '... today is the day of the specialized. The day of the all round manager is disappearing. Businesses, or at any rate the larger ones, are becoming functionalized'.[17] Both these characteristics of undertaking research and the formation of large units and bureaucratization were especially features of the rising new industries and both created an extra demand for graduates in these years.

Expertise, however, was not enough. It was felt in these difficult times that extra, less definable qualities were necessary, and that they were to be found in the university man, not so much for his skills, as for his wider culture. Sir Kenneth Lee considered 'a bigger outlook is necessary and that is more likely to be produced by a university education', the Liberal Inquiry referred to a 'wider outlook', Knox to a 'broader vision', and the UGC 1925 report to a 'breadth of outlook'. This was all somewhat broad and vague, but the cliché expressed an implied dissatisfaction with the narrowness of the technical college product and the ex-apprentice. There was a belief that the new ideal needed by industry was the graduate with horizons widened through social mixing, sport, the OTC, and travel – the NUS, for example, became very active in student travel in the 1930s. All this produced what came to be called the 'right type' in industrial and careers literature of the period, superseding the 'right stamp' and 'right calibre' metaphors of earlier periods.

There were, however, other less elitereal motives for looking to the graduate that were more important in these years than formerly. First, although the university population rose only modestly, the proportion of university students per head of the population rose fairly markedly from one per 1,146 to one per 929 between 1921 and 1939, a trend encouraged in the lower levels of society by the state scholarships and local authority awards for university entrants. Since intelligent boys were thus more likely to go to university in the inter-war years, firms had less likelihood of picking up the talented youth straight from school, and had instead to wait to catch him at a later stage as a university graduate. Indeed, the depressed state of the economy increased this probability of attending university for two reasons. In the first place, job opportunities and the very prospects of work were greater for the graduate than for even the skilled apprentice, since the former always had teaching as a possible alternative. Second, in depression, as several observers pointed out, a university education was often entered simply to bide time in the hope that conditions would improve.[18] In fact, this seemed to be the case, for it was over the years of depression that the university population climbed from 40,000 to 50,000, whereas in more normal times of the twenties and thirties it was fairly constant. For these reasons firms had now more often to catch young talent at a higher level up the educational ladder.

A further reason why many of the most important firms in British industry turned to the graduate in these years of organizational growth and technical change was the problem of management succession. Part of the problem arose from the war itself. During this time recruitment had ceased in many firms and some of the younger workers who had gone to fight had been killed off, leaving in the post-war years an age structure in the firm divided more sharply than usual into older managers and youthful newcomers. As the older ones came to retire, so they cast an eye vainly over the ex-elementary school and still relatively young labour force or the equally ageing and even worse-educated old style foremen. Consequently, managements thought in terms of bringing in graduates and expecting them to rise to top management within a very short time. Many firms approached the Cambridge Appointments Board with this problem,[19] seeking Cambridge graduates as a solution. For example, at Tate and Lyle's, process work in the 1920s had been managed by relatively uneducated men who had risen within the firm, and it was intended eventually to replace them with twenty or thirty graduates. Graduates were especially necessary for higher sales management. Pilkington's tried selling their luxury Vita glass through ordinary commercial travellers, without success, and then formed a special marketing board for Vita with a picked team of graduates in 1929. In this most pointed way they introduced graduates to sidestep the traditional labour on the sales side. Rural industries like Clark's also found that local labour was not throwing up the higher calibre personnel necessary for a national firm and turned to Cambridge graduates to fill in the gap. What the Cambridge

Appointments Officer noted of Pilkington's was true of all – 'they hope to get men who will fill all the higher posts in the firm. This move represents a quite definite break with previous policy. They are aiming for a higher type altogether'.

However, if many firms turned eagerly to the graduate, yet there was still a body of opinion hostile to his reception into industry. Lord Leverhulme was perhaps the most eminent businessman noted for his scepticism about graduates. He believed that 'the Oxford graduate is not a patch on the "hard knocks" graduate',[20] the grounds of his resistance being that the knowledge of book-trained students was of less value than that of practical craftsmen.[21] That the universities did not teach useful practical knowledge was a prime grievance among businessmen who affected to despise graduates.[22] A second ground of scepticism was the view that universities led graduates to 'hold decided opinions without first giving them the sound knowledge on which those opinions should be based'.[23] A third argument, a curious reversal of the second, was that practical men of business made decisions subconsciously and a university training ruined this facility by replacing it with logical thought without common sense.[24] A fourth argument was that twenty-one, after completing a degree, was too old to start a business career,[25] while a fifth was that the irregular hours induced by university work ruined men for the discipline of business; both Leverhulme and Benn believed this. A sixth ground of suspicion of the graduate was more serious, namely the tradition of irresponsible hooliganism among students in the 1920s[26] and then the notorious 'King and Country' debate in 1933 evoking Churchill's condemnation of university students as 'callow ill-tutored youths'. All this cast doubt on the claims that universities were fit places to train the sober and reliable young men needed to run business concerns. But underlying many of these arguments was a genuine fear that the university graduate, because of his scholastic success, 'pretends to a knowledge and authority which he cannot justify',[27] and this makes him unwilling to settle to the humdrum tasks of business life and, even worse, makes him impossible for others to work with. C.F.G. Masterman considered 'the class instinct of the undergraduate of Cambridge and Oxford makes him difficult and impossible in business and industry'.[28] This was best expressed in a student cartoon from Manchester University in 1924 which depicted an enthusiastic young graduate, hands in pockets, haranguing a dismayed managing director with the words 'moreover I'll soon put this moth eaten old works on its feet for you', to the consternation of his secretary and an ancestral portrait on the wall.[29] It was an amusing caricature, but underneath lay the serious unease that many conventional businessmen felt about graduates and their pretensions.

But whatever the grounds for suspicion against graduates in industry, some having sound foundations and others being merely bizarre, informed opinion tended to move more in their favour as the death of Leverhulme in 1927 removed the last great reactionary. The pro-graduate views of such business leaders as Waley Cohen, Melchett, Kenneth Lee, and David Milne Watson were also in accord with the facts. Industry moved more towards the universities and the universities were more than willing to meet it halfway. We should now turn to examine the universities' half of the link through their development of fields of teaching and research orientated to science in the service of industry.

The response from the universities in developing studies of industrial relevance was considerable, and we are here concerned to highlight specialities and fields which certain universities were particularly prominent in developing for the service of local and national industry.

Cambridge had an unequalled reputation in pure science and especially physics. On the other hand, the great achievements of the Cavendish Laboratory had little effect on industry at the time; indeed some argued that they were diverting attention from traditional industrial themes with positively harmful results for industry.[30] There was, however, no doubt of the importance of industrial backing for the extension of Cambridge science in the inter-war years. Money came from the oil companies for chemistry in 1919, from Mond and Austin for physics, and Sir John Siddeley for aeronautics in the 1930s, and it was in this latter decade that the building expansion of Cambridge physics was most marked.[31] Of immediate industrial application, however, Cambridge was perhaps best known for its engineering school. The professor throughout this time, Sir Charles Inglis, had close contacts with industry as a consultant, especially in bridge and railway work,[32] while aeronautical engineering was a new post-war departure.[33] Low temperature research was another Cambridge forte which had important implications for the food preservation and refrigeration industries.[34] Oxford, by contrast, had little part to play in industrial science at this time. Lindemann revived the Clarendon Laboratory from its abysmal state, and he was on close personal terms with Lord Melchett and Sir Harry McGowan of ICI as well as Nuffield,[35] but, like Cambridge's science, Oxford's was pure rather than applied.[36] Indeed, Tizard, a staunch advocate of science at Oxford, did not consider it wise to develop a large school of applied work.[37] At the end of this period Lord Nuffield sought to link Oxford more closely to the industrial world with grants of money for Nuffield College and for physical chemistry in 1937, to bridge the 'gulf which at present exists between academic studies and practical affairs'. The part-time fellows of Nuffield especially were to enrich the university with the 'fruits of their practical experience ... in industry or commerce'.[38] But for the most part Oxford did not claim to be a technological university and it would be irrelevant to criticize it for not doing what it did not set out to do.

Almost every conceivable science was studied at London University, but here we may isolate certain fields in which it played a special role. London was chiefly instrumental in meeting the shortage of chemical engineers in the inter-war years with the Ramsay Chemical Engineering Laboratory at University College powerfully supported by ICI, Lever's, and Shell. The new professor, E.C. Williams, formerly of the British Dyestuffs Corporation and National Benzol, pointed out that such had been the development in plant that chemical expertise was becoming even more important for the engineers building the plant than for the industrial chemists who used it, hence the necessity for the fusion of the sciences.[39] Industry certainly regarded the department as a success; its graduates were absorbed into industry even before they finished their courses, and as a result of research within the department a new industry was started in Coventry, the production of bi-metallic sheets of nickel and copper by electrolysis.[40] King's College, too, was noted for chemical engineering and also engaged in photochemistry as one of its main lines of research. In physics they made special studies in electricity, radio waves, and thermionic vacuum tubes, claiming that they proved excellent qualifications for men entering industry.[41] Imperial College naturally had a wide range of sciences, but it is worth drawing attention to its particular concern with aeronautics. Sir Basil Zaharoff had founded the chair there with Sir Richard Glazebrook as the first professor in 1919. Within the industry C.R. Fairey and Handley Page took a particular interest in the department, and Zaharoff expected Churchill to keep an eye on it.[42] With good fortune, in 1929 Henry Tizard, celebrated for his aeronautics work during the war, became Rector of Imperial College, further cementing the close links of the college with this new technology.[43] In one or two other areas the college also played an important part in British industrial science. Sir Patrick Linstead's work created the Monastral pigments marketed by ICI in the 1930s,[44] and it was also a leading centre for geophysics and chemical engineering – both areas in which output of graduates was short in the inter-war years.[45]

By virtue of their origins the civic universities of the North of England and the Midlands remained closely linked with local industry at several points. Manchester University science was first-rate; indeed that the university had the services of Rutherford, Bohr, Robert Robinson, Alexander Todd, and Lawrence Bragg within these years indicates its very high importance.[46] On the other hand, the excellence of its physics had already swung this field away from the traditional local industrial interests to which it had related in the nineteenth century.[47] However, there were certain fields in which Manchester and its faculty of technology had valuable vitalizing effects on the new sectors of the Lancashire economy. The electrical industry in particular benefited. Sir Ambrose Fleming recommended Manchester for those seeking a degree in electro-communication engineering [48] and Metro-Vickers of Trafford Park sent its best people there for training. The university also had close links with the Chloride Electrical Storage Company, the largest battery makers in Europe, who drew most of their research staff from there, while the university was associated with the company's metallurgical research.[49] Indeed, metallurgy was one of the growth points of the university in the 1920s.[50] On the industrial chemistry side, Manchester had special facilities for dyestuffs research and close association with the British Dyestuffs Corporation (later ICI) research laboratory at Blackley.[51] Professor Robert Robinson had already worked there before he moved into academic life and Heilbron, who moved to Manchester from Liverpool, maintained the ICI link. Finally, in the 1930s Manchester was rare if not unique in Britain in providing university education for the paper and building industries.[52]

Of particular local maritime relevance, Liverpool University was already by 1920 one of the two main centres of marine engineering education in England, based on the Harrison Hughes laboratories. Also the university developed two specialisms of particular value for the port and its produce. J. Wemyss Anderson was a noted pioneer of refrigeration engineering, putting cold storage on a scientific footing, while Professor Percy Hilditch transformed the chemistry of fats in the twenties and thirties, vital for the West Africa trade and the fat processing chemical industries of the hinterland.[53] Finally, at the local level, the university was the main centre of oceanographic research on the English north-west coast, and in the 1920s it was the professor's stated policy to relate his work to the Irish Sea fishery and the Manx lobster hatcheries.[54] In service of the wide national economy, Liverpool was a major centre of electrical engineering. It had particularly close links with British Insulated Cables and the Automatic Telephone Company, while their Professor of Applied Electricity co-ordinated all experimental work in wireless throughout Britain for the Radio Research Board.[55] In chemistry, the department had very close links with ICI and Lever's who each year made large donations for research, while Sir Ian Heilbron, the Professor of Organic Chemistry, sat on the Organic Research Committee of ICI. It was a fitting and natural relationship with the chemical industry of the Mersey basin. They also helped to fill an important national shortage of scientific expertise by specializing in geology[56] and especially oil from 1919.[57]

In the Midlands, these were the decades of the striking rise of Nottingham University with the outstanding benefactions of Lord Trent. One of their first post-war actions was the establishment of a separate department of textiles in 1922, while the university also served the local coal mining industry, its department being supported by a levy on the coal owners. Sir Jesse Boot's gifts to the college began in 1920 and made possible the building of engineering laboratories between 1930 and 1934 catering for civil and mechanical engineering. Nottingham University, like the city, was thus a mixture of old basic and new industries in the inter-war years. Most of the university's money came from a new scientific industry though its own industrial contribution was chiefly to the old ones of coal and hosiery.[58] Leicester presents an interesting Midlands contrast. A more prosperous town, and more committed to light new industry than its neighbour, its firms were, however, smaller and less able or willing to support the university.[59] Accordingly, while the college developed a normal range of subjects, nothing emerged of special interest to industry.

Birmingham University on the other hand, a much older institution in the heartland of heavy industry, inevitably had much closer links. Here mining remained a particular strength under Sir John Cadman, the cabinet adviser on coal and petroleum and later Chairman of the Anglo-Persian Oil Company. In 1921 the Doncaster Coal Owners' Research Association was moved to the university under Cadman, so that during the inter-war years the mining research laboratory had a mixed university-industrial character. Its members worked on safety and illumination in hot and deep mines and on the Bergius process of hydrogenation of coal, turning it into thick oil under pressure.[60] They also had especially good facilities for coal dressing and preparation for marketing, and for ore crushing and dressing, as well as a working mine under the university grounds itself.[61] But beyond its orthodox mineral mining education, Birmingham was especially valuable in widening its activities into oil engineering, a more promising field in which university expertise and men were lacking.[62] In chemistry, Birmingham was foremost in the development of carbohydrate chemistry in the tradition of Irvine's school at St Andrews, and it was the first university to synthesize vitamin C in 1933.[63] Its brewing work continued and this moved into a £100,000 laboratory block in 1927 with other biological subjects, and was the chief centre for higher scientific biochemistry training in this industry.[64]

The Yorkshire universities were not to be outdone in serving the local economy.[65] At Leeds, mining and geology were important studies, with pioneering work on mapping the concealed east Midland coalfield and on rescue apparatus. Equally significant was the university's contribution to the woollen textile industry of Yorkshire. W.T. Astbury used X-ray techniques to reveal the molecular framework of wool, while the importance of the sulphur linkages in wool fibre and their breaking as a cause of shrinking was for the first time appreciated.[66] Leeds' unique specialism in leather remained strong, dealing with the protein chemistry of skins and the mineral tanning of leather.[67] Lines of research were also developed linking with the new industries, notably aeronautics through Professor Brodetsky, a war-time pioneer of aerodynamics. Sheffield University was somewhat less diversified in industrial research than Leeds though it had close links with local mining and metallurgy. The particular importance of the mining department was its pioneering work on the devising and testing of flameproof electrical equipment for mines; indeed, it was said that 'the extensive use of electrical plant in mines today has been largely rendered possible by the work carried out in the department'.[68] In metallurgy a new laboratory was built with money from Sir Robert Hadfield, the pioneer of manganese and hardened steels, and from 1934 attention was paid to the scientific aspects of metal foundries. In particular, they were pioneers of the cold working of steel, stamping, wire drawing, and cold rolling.[69] Finally, Sheffield was famous for its glass research that we have seen starting during the war under Professor Turner.[70] Their chief work was with container, tableware, and electrical glass, unlike the optics of the London colleges. The sheer change in physical appearance of the humble jam jar between the 1920s and the 1930s, for instance, was but one of the important ways in which this department was helping to change both industry and the amenities it provided. Finally, Hull, emerging as the third Yorkshire university in the late 1920s, shrewdly chose its own specialisms. Principal Morgan planned to link university science with fishing, through marine biology, and to the port, through seed crushing and oil extraction, while of more national importance they also did aeronautics work.[71]

The universities of the South and West more usually found their strengths in engineering, physics and the food industries than in the basic industry technologies of the North of England. From 1928 the college at Southampton was seeking to become an independent University of Wessex providing engineering training and research for a revivified port and city.[72] Internal combustion engineering became a special forte of the college under Wing Commander Professor T.R. Cave-Brown-Cave, especially in problems of high speed engines.[73] He began the work on the suppression of noise that has broadened into one of Southampton's well-known specialisms of the present time.[74] They had close links with local engineering firms Thornycroft's, Avro, and Supermarine Aviation, that were powerful prestige builders for the struggling University College.[75] Bristol University, too, was strong in engineering and maintained pre-war and war-time links with the local aircraft industry, though the chief forte of Bristol in the inter-war years, its physics based on the superb new Wills laboratories, had little immediate industrial significance.[76] On the chemistry side, Leverhulme endowed a chair of physical chemistry in 1919, whose first occupant, J.W. McBain, worked on the colloidal chemistry of soap[77] in the twenties. Less usual in character was Bristol's contribution to the food industry. First, from 1921 they supervised the Campden Research Station, which virtually created canning as a scientific industry in Britain from the mid 1920s.[78] Chivers, Hartley's, and the CWS were among the business interests on the management committee. The other food industry connection of Bristol was with cider and perry manufacture. The Long Ashton station established in 1903 had been part of the university since 1912 and their scientific work developed cider into a national industry as well as creating non-alcoholic apple juice and blackcurrant juice as commercial drinks. Equally important, the discovery in 1924 of potash deficiency as a major cause of fruit failure revolutionized the efficiency of industrial fruit production in England.[79] By contrast, the other two universities of the South and West had little industrial significance at this time. Reading stands apart as being deliberately and wisely orientated towards agriculture and does not concern us.[80] Exeter, young and struggling, intended to become a centre of research for the economy of the far west [81] yet one finds very little evidence of this kind,[82] partly because mining technology was dealt with already at Camborne and marine engineering at the Plymouth Technical College, both of which were better sited for the practical aspects of this work.

Finally, by contrast, Armstrong College, Newcastle, still an offshoot of Durham University, was firmly wedded to the basic industries of the North East.[83] Mining remained its particular strength, and in 1927 various miners' associations made grants for a new laboratory creating one of the finest mining schools in the country. They also did important work on coke for the Durham Coalowners' Association. It's naval architecture department was somewhat stultified by depression though their staff designed the Channel train ferry,[84] and Professor Hawkes became one of the leading authorities on the diesel engine.[85] Electrical engineering being a prominent industry of Tyneside, the university also had a flourishing electrical engineering department which did research on insulators. But the studies of Armstrong and King's College in these years remained rather too committed to old declining industries and they seem to have done little to help the diversification of new scientific industry in the area.

This spread of interests and specialisms prompts comment on a number of points. First, the universities, by dealing with the various forms of engineering, including the newer forms of electrical and petroleum engineering, aviation, the chemistry of fats, dyes, and soaps, the food industries and nutrition, were certainly contributing to the change in industrial structure and the rise of 'new' industries. Second, there was plenty of evidence of close collaboration with industry and firms – the support of the coal owners and brewers for various departments, Manchester and Metro-Vickers and ICI Dyestuffs, Sheffield and Hadfield's, Southampton and Supermarine, Bristol and Chivers, and many others referred to in the preceding pages, not to speak of others too numerous to mention. Third, almost all universities, with the exceptions of Cambridge, Oxford, Exeter, and Leicester, drew much of their strength through their service to local industry as well as national. The interests of local industrial needs and the civic universities were well matched.

But on the other hand, certain criticisms arise. In the first place there did seem to be a great deal of university expertise being lavished on the mining industry. Tizard and the UGC came to think so in the mid 1930s,[86] pointing out that there were ten university schools of mining and that this was probably too many, leading to duplication of effort. This compared with five in Germany, and yet while most of the senior positions in German collieries were occupied by university men, in Britain 'although there is a distinct tendency in this direction progress is slow'.[87] Certainly if anything was satisfactory about this worst of inter-war industries it was its improving technical performance and raised productivity, while the deep mining and electrification that lay behind it was made possible chiefly by the universities.[88] Yet all this expertise yielded but a sorry return in terms of employment, growth, or exports. One or two departments like Leeds and notably Birmingham diversified into oil engineering and also metal mining, which was starved of recruits, but this might have been done with fewer centres. Overall there ought to have been a much more radical shift away from coal mining education to these other forms whose shortages of manpower reflected in the highest salaries of any graduate industrial occupations in these years.

Second, of the new industries, aeronautical engineering seemed to become fashionable in perhaps too many places. Tizard, who often cast an astringent eye over the higher education-industrial scene in these years, thought that at the beginning of the period aero research was rather split up.[89] Similarly, the Air Ministry Committee on which he sat, while admitting that the subject might be taught in various places, insisted that research had to be concentrated at Farnborough and Imperial College.[90] In these circumstances, due to the vast costs involved, it seemed to doom most other centres to teaching without real practical research. To have minor university colleges like Southampton and Hull moving into the field might have seemed inappropriate, had not the energy and qualifications of Cave-Brown-Cave justified the former.

Third, it may be somewhat surprising that electrical engineering does not figure rather more prominently in the preceding paragraphs. It was a common university subject and there was no particular shortage of university electrical engineers, but the universities were not prominent as sources of innovation in the industry in the inter-war years as they had been in the 1890s and 1900s. Innovation moved from the university laboratory to the research laboratory of the firm, especially GEC at Wembley, Metro-Vickers, Siemens at Preston, and BTH, whence came, among much else, strip lighting, continuously evacuated valves, the first provincial broadcasting, the transistor, and the first talking cinematograph apparatus in Britain. It was said with regard to electro-technics just prior to 1939, that 'our research activity in those branches of science likely to affect engineering development at a reasonably early date was on the whole inadequate ... '.[91] This was said at Manchester University, which did more than most in the electrical field. It was only the Second World War, this report thought, that had brought an intimate liaison of industry and university departments in this work. There also seemed to be a gap in the provision of education for metallurgists, with only Sheffield appearing really prominent, and it did lead to a serious shortage of men in this profession. Of the new industries it may be remarked that the universities seemed to do virtually nothing for the motor car industry, a less serious matter since this was a successful industry that arranged its own training and research outside the universities.

Fourth, how far were the universities creating fruitful cross-fertilizations of the sciences from which new industries might be expected to flourish? In one or two fields they were strikingly not doing so. Although chemical engineering was developed at some London colleges in the mid 1920s, not enough was done in this particular field. Also there seemed to be a positive disengagement between physics and engineering in some areas. The predominance of Cambridge theoretical physics, and its migration to most of the chairs in the country, swung the subject, notably at Bristol, Manchester, and Liverpool, away from a concern with matters of immediate potential relevance for engineering. At Cambridge it created a situation of engineers not much interested in research, and of physicists whose work was to have no practical effect on industrial engineering until the nuclear reactors of the 1950s. Perhaps the best example of successful cross-fertilization of physics and chemistry into a new technology, however, was the textile work at Leeds. Consequently chemistry was the predominant industrial science rather than physics, and this temporary disengagement of mainstream university physics from industrial concerns was an unusual interim in the span of industrial science from Watt to the present day.

[...]

Apart from their contributions to technology, the universities continued trying to serve industry in the fields of economics and business training. [...] [This] form of university education became prominent in the 1890s and 1900s, and we wish now to consider how it developed in the inter-war years.

The immediate post-war years saw the extension and creation of economics and commerce courses in universities continuing the trend begun in the 1900s. At the 1921 Congress of the Universities of the Empire, Ashley, his prestige further enhanced by his war work and knighthood, yet again urged the necessity of university commercial education.[92] After the war, Aberdeen and Edinburgh began Bachelor of Commerce courses in 1919,[93] and by the same year Leeds, which had started economics in 1902, had joined commerce to it and had an advisory committee of businessmen.[94] By the time of the Balfour Report in 1927, Reading, Nottingham, and Southampton had followed suit. These were the later workings out of the pre-war movement begun by Ashley at Birmingham. However, perhaps the most important single change was at Oxford which, almost twenty years after the Economics Tripos, came into line with Cambridge by establishing the Honour School of PPE in 1921.[95]

In spite of these developments there were others who remained unsatisfied at the state of economics and business training and who sought to push on even further than Ashley in relating such education to industry by the creation of studies in industrial or business administration. The most lively advocate of this approach was Dr James A. Bowie of Manchester. In 1918 a committee of prominent industrialists in Manchester was instrumental in forming and financing the department of industrial administration in the College of Technology (the faculty of technology of the university). Bowie joined this in 1919 and became its director in 1926.[96] He was critical of the Birmingham and other conventional programmes of commercial education, pointing out that foreign languages, geography, and banking, although academically respectable and closer to business interests than traditional arts subjects, were of little practical use to factory managers. His course, by contrast, would be focused on more immediately vocational matters including industrial finance, costing, business statistics, the study of wages systems, and factory law.[97] He was also the pioneer of the American case study method in Britain[98] and his Manchester department acted as secretary to fifteen firms engaged in management research, thereby keeping the academics in touch with business conditions.[99] This is what he claimed, though Abraham Flexner, who intensely disliked this kind of education, considered that his staff had no practical connection with industry, nor did local businessmen contribute anything to the course. In 1931, Bowie moved to Dundee to establish the Dundee School of Economics.

Industrial administration gained another strong foothold in England at the London School of Economics.[100] In 1929–30 the school was offered £5,000 a year for five years to establish a department of business administration for research and training. After discussion with a wide range of firms, the school accepted the idea in 1930. It is interesting to note that, as with the Manchester scheme, the initiative came from business rather than the university; this indeed was the best augury of success. The plan of study was more avowedly like the Manchester course, including accounting, business statistics, commercial law, marketing, finance, and factory organization and control. Several prominent firms had a right to nominate students to the course as a condition of their support, including giants like ICI, GEC, Imperial Tobacco and stores like Debenham's, Harrod's, Lewis's and Selfridge's. The course was also proving a success in attracting the attention of employers beyond those who sent their own selected students.[101] Evidently this 'industrial' or 'business administration' approach was itself more practical than 'commerce' or 'economics' and was proving attractive to employers.

Perhaps the most extreme development in practical business training in the universities was found surprisingly at Edinburgh University in the 1930s. They had started their B. COMM. in 1919, supported by the Edinburgh Chamber of Commerce, typical of the formation of many such courses at this time. However, from 1935 this development was given an unusual direction by the gift of £10,000 from J. Albert Thomson, a former president of the Scottish Motor Trade Association. This money was used to create the Jane Findlay Thomson Commercial Laboratory in the same year on the astonishing grounds that 'those who aspire to the higher positions in industry should have an intimate working knowledge of all up to date office machinery',[102] and the B. COMM. was revised to include this practical work.[103] They claimed this was a success and that industry was receptive to their graduates.[104] Indeed, in 1939 they considered that even more practical business procedure training was necessary and that all graduates ought to undertake some as a new kind of liberal education.[105] The reception of this essentially empirical office machine and procedure training into a university was all the more remarkable in that the Scottish universities had been cautious and even laggard over starting Ashley-type commerce economics. Now that Edinburgh had veered into this extreme it is difficult to avoid the view that they had moved beyond the pale of genuine university work. That this 'commercial laboratory' opened in 1935 and Keynes's *General Theory* was published in the following year most sharply indicates to what polarized extremes the divergent interpretations of 'economics' as a university subject had led.

Apart from economics and commerce, however, three other adjacent university subjects experienced considerable development in the inter-war years as managerial skills, notably modern languages, industrial psychology, and statistics. Just as we saw earlier that languages were held to be part of commercial education before 1914, so in the 1920s there were important new departures in this field. Sir Stanley Leathes's committee of 1918 had been highly critical of the state of modern languages teaching, and this report and the war especially stimulated some new development. For example, a charter was granted in 1916 to the School of Oriental Studies in the University of London, partly to match the Germans whose linguistic superiority before the war had facilitated their penetration of Far Eastern markets.[106] There was also a much greater concern for the teaching of Russian, especially as she became our ally during the war, and the London School of Slavonic Studies was established following the lines of Sir Bernard Pares's pioneering department at Liverpool. The Liverpool and London schools worked in co-operation and Liverpool was consulted about similar projected developments at Sheffield, Manchester, Nottingham, and Bristol. Pares noted that 'there is also a strong development of Russian teaching in English Schools of Commerce',[107] and that 'the English interest [in Russian] is so largely economic'. The concern to expand language teaching for commerce apart from French and German was evident in a number of universities. At Leeds, departments of Spanish and Russian were begun in 1916; at Birmingham the Russian chair was founded in 1917 by the Chamber of Commerce; at Sheffield Russian was started in 1916 and Spanish in 1918 because Sheffield businessmen were established in the Russian steel industry and interested in the South American trade. It was unfortunate that the new Soviet régime's restrictive view of foreign trade rendered university attempts to widen the teaching of languages for commerce and industry somewhat less effective and relevant than they might otherwise have been.

Also arising from the later years of the war, but having fewer pre-war antecedents than the developments in languages teaching, was the involvement of universities in industrial psychology.[108] Although there had been little interest in British universities in the subject before 1914, it was the war that effectively created the study of industrial psychology in Britain. In 1915 Lloyd George set up the Health of Munitions Workers Committee and this began to study the psychological aspects of fatigue in industrial working. More important, their work led to the creation of two other bodies, the National Institute of Industrial Psychology in 1921 and the Industrial Fatigue Research Board, which were to develop its work in the inter-war years. At a stroke, the universities became deeply concerned with the study. Bernard Muscio of Cambridge published his pioneering lectures on industrial psychology in 1916, and this stimulated the future doyen on the subject, C.S. Myers, also of Cambridge, to turn his own attention to this field. He further aroused the interest of various firms, and as a result the National Institute of Industrial Psychology was formed in 1921 with the backing of Rowntree's, Cadbury's, Tootal's, Cammel Laird, and Harrison and Crosfield's, while Myers left Cambridge to become its director. The Cambridge psychology department ran the important summer school in industrial administration, and Cambridge remained pre-eminent in this field with the work of Sir Frederick Bartlett on fatigue, skills, and incentives. Industrial psychology is an interesting example of a subject of ill-defined limits separating itself from philosophy and the pure arts to become, like economics, its predecessor in the fission, a component of the new industrial administration idea of the 1920s and a new and important point of contact between the universities and industry.

The third special area of higher commercial training developing in the inter-war years was that of statistics. Hugh Quigley noted that in 1932 efficient statisticians were fewer than the posts available, and he noted a change in attitude in favour of the use of statisticians within the firm in recent years. He deplored that probably only about ninety firms in British industry used statisticians, but warned that foreign competitors in Germany, France, and the United States had 'evolved a technique in market research and product control which is rooted in economic analysis'.[109] The idea caught on in the thirties. For example, William Hollins approached the Cambridge Officer for 'an economist who can interpret statistics . . . they have quantities of machines and people to work them but no one really to interpret the results and apply them'.[110] Hollins's concern arose from part of their attempts to improve efficiency in the later 1930s. They began various statistical exercises and charts on costs and profits which was 'something of a novelty in British industry at the time',[111] and clearly needed statisticians to do it for them. On the university side, Oxford set up its Institute of Statistics in the mid 1930s,[112] and another major centre, Egon Pearson's department at University College, London, also began at the same time. Pearson was especially careful to establish contacts with industrial firms 'as the future of its work is most likely to be related to the application of statistical method in industry'.[113] In perspective, only forty-six men gained degrees in statistics between 1925 and 1939 in British universities, but presumably some firms were using pure mathematicians for this, of whom over 2,000 were produced.

These important developments were enthusiastic attempts by universities to cater for the careers of non-scientific graduates in industry. However, there were less encouraging features of this particular liaison, several of which were revealed by the Balfour Committee.[114] It was especially difficult to get qualified teachers in statistics and transport economics, and especially instructors with industrial experience. There was considerable and widespread doubt about the quantity and quality of students choosing such programmes in commerce, and there was little co-operation with commercial interests in planning curricula. What must have been more disheartening were the rather cool and even hostile attitudes towards commerce courses from both industry and universities alike. Lord Leverhulme (II) had no belief in the value of university economics and commerce studies.[115] F. J. Marquis (Lord Woolton) deprecated the university study of commerce, preferring a broad liberal education,[116] and Milne Watson, though a backer of the LSE business administration course, thought that commerce courses could be of only limited use since 'the particular needs of any given commercial concern are too specialized to be served very materially by any general commerce course'.[117] These were far from isolated examples. In 1929, Harold Rostron of Tootal's undertook an enquiry for the AEIC that must have chilled the hearts of commercial education enthusiasts. The general view among their members (which included virtually all the significant firms of British industry) was [118]

> that a degree in arts, science, mathematics, modern languages, etc. gives a man a wider training than that obtained with a degree in economics or commerce – which they regard as a of more technical nature, and as such, is more rightly placed as a course of study to be followed after a general degree course in one of the former subjects . . .

Two years later the Goodenough Committee found the same position, that 'commercial faculties have not so far received any great encouragement from employers' and 'recruitment to commerce of men with commerce degrees was comparatively small'.[119] The same also seemed to be the case in Scotland at the end of the twenties.[120]

However, if this was the position around 1930 there is some evidence to suggest that more firms were becoming slightly more interested in graduates with economics and business degrees in the 1930s than they had been in the 1920s. This was an issue that the Cambridge Officer raised from time to time with the firms with whom he dealt, and from his memoranda (see Table 1) we can see the changing pattern of reception of the idea throughout this time.[121]

Table 1 Firms' stated attitudes to graduates in economic and commerce

Favourable	Opposed
Mather and Platt 1923	
Energen 1930	
Jantzen 1930	
United Steel 1932	
Lamson Paragon 1932	
Sir Alfred Read of Coast Lines 1933	Equitable Life 1933
Hudsons Bay Company 1935	Selfridge's 1935
New South Wales Bank 1936	
J. and P. Coats 1936	
Hollins 1937	

The mass of firms of course were not moved to express strong opinions one way or the other, but it is significant that there did seem to be a drift of opinion in industry moving slightly more in favour of the economics graduate in the 1930s that was not so discernible in the 1920s. And yet we should not exaggerate this for the bulk of firms as a whole. For example, Mr Locke of Rowntree's considered that the view 'common among business people and employers' was that if they had any belief in economics it was only as a study to follow practical business experience.[122] In the important Cambridge survey of 1937–8 it was found that although firms were actually more prepared to use arts men in administration than technical men, yet they did not want such arts men trained in commerce or even in the Cambridge Economics Tripos which they regarded as too theoretical.[123] Finally, in 1939 the Association of British Chambers of Commerce could offer only a gloomy conclusion to the period. The actual intake of commerce graduates by firms, it pointed out, was slight, probably 'well below 100', and in any case 'sporadic and exceptional'.[124] The Chambers of Commerce piously hoped that a larger proportion of graduates would be recruited into commerce, but even by 1939 opinion was against it.

Whatever the scepticism from business, advocates of commercial education faced some hostility from academic colleagues. The Principal of Armstrong College, for instance, frankly admitted that he really thought commerce in universities was 'a bit of eyewash'.[125] At Nottingham, Professor A.W. Kirkaldy, who held strong views that universities should train men for industrial life, ran a three-year commerce course as well as being closely involved with the local Chamber of Commerce. Even in so industrially orientated a university as Nottingham it was felt that 'what he was trying to do was not the proper function of an academic institution ... ', and when he retired in 1931 his chair was not filled.[126] At Oxford, likewise, T.M. Knox of the Appointments Office was publicly hostile to commerce and even economics education for industry as being useless.[127]

The output of men with first degrees in economics in the inter-war years was modest.[128]

Output of economists from British universities

1925–26	60	1932–33	127
1926–27	65	1933–34	126
1927–28	60	1934–35	106
1928–29	82	1935–36	106
1929–30	80	1936–37	99
1930–31	85	1937–38	102
1931–32	81	1938–39	115

It compares unfavourably with a reputed 16,000 students of industrial administration in Germany in 1929, and 80,000 in the United States.[129] By 1938–9, in spite of the expansion evident from the above figures, economics and the social sciences generally were still a markedly lagging sector of British university education, as Sir John Clapham's committee found (see Table 2).[130] By any criterion economic subjects seemed to be underdeveloped, and Clapham noted that his committee 'cannot regard as satisfactory' the situation revealed.

But what happened to graduates in economics and commerce, and did they

Table 2 Findings of Sir John Clapham's committee

	Professors and readers	Expenditure (1938–39)
		£
Arts	463	1,084,873
Pure sciences	296	984,663
Social sciences	52	115,909

filter into industrial posts or not? At the London School of Economics 13 per cent of graduates taking the B.Sc. (Econ.) between 1902 and 1920 went into business, and 16.4 per cent between 1920 and 1932. On the other hand, almost 60 per cent of those taking the B.Comm. went into business between 1921 and 1932. The largest proportion of graduates in the 1920s went into teaching and research. Clearly whatever hopes there had been about the B.Sc. Econ. as a feeder into industry were not well grounded, and it needed the new form of commerce education with the B.Comm. to make a really distinctive change from other arts subjects. With the espousing of business administration in 1930 so LSE courses became more directly related to business and so presumably did its graduates' careers.

What did LSE male graduates do and what sort of firms and industries thought it worth while to absorb men so educated? For the 1920s we can trace 145 graduates going into 102 firms, or 1.42 graduates per firm. It is interesting to note that the market for economics graduates was rather less specialized than that for engineers – the ratio for Liverpool engineers for the 1920s was 2.14 graduates per firm – but slightly more specialized than that for graduates in general – the Sheffield ratio was 1.27 graduates per firm.[131] But while there was a fairly healthy spread of takers for LSE graduates, some were especially keen and repeated employers. Those taking three or more were the Bank of England, Barclay's Bank, Candles Ltd, GWR, ICI, Sir William Crawford, Lever Brothers, Midland Bank, Henry Schroder's Bank, Westminster Bank. We can get some idea of what the graduates were used for in the firms by considering the relative incidence of job specification. The actual work is not always or usually indicated, but from those instances where it is we can obtain some rough idea of what economics graduates were used for. First in importance was statistics. This was quite the most commonly cited use, and bore out Quigley's pleas for more statisticians and the heavy demand for them. Next they were mostly commonly used as accountants, with nine specific cases. Then came various aspects of the sales and distribution side of the firm's work, with five in advertising, four in transport and distribution management, and four including commercial travellers and their organizers. It was in these fields rather than the management of technical production in which men with economics training were most sensibly used. Finally, the areas of business and industry taking most LSE graduates were communications, electricals and banking.

At other universities the fate of their economics students must have given some concern. At Southampton, for example, things seemed to be going wrong even in the buoyant late 1930s. In 1936 and 1937 they produced nine economists, seven of whom became elementary school teachers. They observed jadedly, 'it seems a pity that some more specialized kind of employment should not have been found for them'.[132] At Leeds, likewise, of twenty-three graduates in economics between 1919 and 1930 eleven went into some kind of teaching and only two into firms.[133] At Newcastle, of twenty-six graduates in commerce and economics between 1919 and 1938, only eleven at a generous estimate could be said to be engaged in administration and sales in industry, commerce, or banking. Here again, school-teaching and accountancy were the largest absorbers.[134] Of those for which we have figures, the Aberdeen commerce department seemed perhaps the most successful in feeding its students into business. Of the 117 graduates they produced between 1919 and 1933, forty-three went into business, twenty-one into accountancy, seven into banks, insurance, and telephones, three into the law, two into Inland Revenue, two into railways, two secretarial, and nineteen into teaching.[135] Although the Aberdeen figures are fairly creditable, the experience of the others suggests that the early claims of economists such as Ashley and Marshall that economics was going to be especially suitable as a university training for industry seemed, in the inter-war years, to be largely unfounded. The large numbers still going into teaching suggest that it had not proved itself as distinctively different from any other non-vocational arts subject as its pioneers would have wished.

But how did graduates in commerce and economic subjects fare in comparison with their arts fellows in job satisfaction, employment, and salaries? Only 65 per cent of Birmingham commerce graduates considered that their qualifications were relevant to their work compared with 82 per cent of arts graduates, 75 per cent of applied scientists, and 78 per cent of pure scientists. It was curious that the least practically orientated subjects were those whose practitioners found them most relevant to their everyday work, while those designed to relate most closely to industrial work proved to their practitioners to be less relevant. One suspects the higher figures for arts are due to the fact that arts men were using their subjects by teaching them. However, the point at issue here is that not many fewer than half of commerce graduates did not really find their skills useful in the work they adopted. Commerce graduates were slightly less satisfied with their jobs than their colleagues. Sixty-two per cent were satisfied with their work compared with 64 per cent of applied scientists, 65 per cent of arts graduates, and 58 per cent of pure scientists. On the other hand, commerce graduates' salaries compared well with their scientific and arts colleagues' at various stages of their careers (see Table 3). Generally they compared well but it is worth noting that for those beginning a career in the 1930s with this qualification their salaries were slightly unfavourable. Those who began

Table 3 Salaries in 1938 of men graduates, University of Birmingham (in £s)[136]

Date of leaving university	Commerce	Arts	Applied science	Pure science
1937–38	150–200	150–250	150–200	200–250
1928–33	250–350	300–350	250–350	250–350
1923–28	350–400	300–350	350–450	350–400
1918–23	c. 600	450–500	700–800	400–450

in the 1920s and persevered found their relative salary position improved *vis-à-vis* arts and pure science men.

In summary, the inter-war years saw considerable new developments in commercial higher education, notably the new concept of industrial administration and the rise of such ancillary subjects as languages, statistics, and industrial psychology; though in some cases these experiments proved so radical as to pass beyond what was acceptable as university education. Considerable resistance to graduates so trained persisted in the 1920s, though with some traces of a slightly more favourable drift of opinion in the 1930s. The social sciences remained under-represented and under-financed and their output of graduates was modest. Most, in any case, experienced little career choice different from those who had taken pure arts subjects since most still went into teaching. Commerce graduates were at risk in experiencing low job satisfaction, and in feeling that their training was irrelevant to their future occupations. On the other hand, they were quite well remunerated if they stuck to their posts.

There is not very much about all this that would have gladdened the hearts of Ashley and Marshall had they lived to see it. But the chief developments were not so much the forging of closer links between economics and commerce and industry but the building up of the whole intellectual level and standing of the subject itself in the 1930s. These theoretical accomplishments proved in the long run more important than the excessively practical activities into which Edinburgh had been sidetracked. There are indeed analogies with physics here. In both cases the intellectual developments of the subject by a few people were of vastly greater significance than any short-term immediate services to industry. As these developments came to be appreciated, thus enormously raising the prestige of the subjects, so accordingly there followed at a gap of a generation or so the expansion of the routine output of students to industry – the nuclear physicists of the 1950s and the economists in the 1960s, both of which would have been impossible without the scholarly developments of the 1930s. Thus while the development of closer connections between the universities and industry in economics and commerce subjects seemed to be modest in the inter-war years, the importance of the period lay in the creation of the intellectual seed corn for the post-war years.

Notes and References

1 Pro-Chancellor Alsop of Liverpool University, *Liverpool Courier* 29 November (1918).
2 Conversation of Prof. Hyman Levy and Julian Huxley in HUXLEY, J. (1934) *Scientific Research and Social Needs* London, Watts and Co., p. 22.
3 SAYERS, R.S. (1950) 'The springs of technical progress in Britain, 1919–39' *Economic Journal* June; RICHARDSON, H.W. (1961) 'The new industries between the wars' *Oxford Economic Papers* Vol. XIII.
4 BRITISH ASSOCIATION (1935) *Britain in Depression* London, British Association, pp. 158–9, 257, 276, specifically noted technical improvement spurred on by depression in coal, steel and shipbuilding.
5 SANDERSON, M. (1972) 'Research and the firm in British industry 1919–39' *Science Studies* April, examines this more fully.
6 QUIGLEY, H. (1924) 'Engineering in the economic development of Manchester' *The Woman Engineer* March.
7 FLEMING, A.P.M. (1936) in *Daily Dispatch* – Industrial Survey.

8 FLEMING, A.P.M. and PEARCE, J.G. (1922) *Research in Industry* London, Pitman.

9 FEDERATION OF BRITISH INDUSTRY (1943) *Industry and Research* Report of the Industrial Research Committee, Oct.

10 Report of the Proceedings of the Fourth Congress of the Universities of the British Empire (1931) 'The university graduate in commerce and industry'.

11 Sir Kenneth Lee cited in MILNE WATSON, D. (1934) 'University men in commerce and industry' *Oxford* Winter.

12 CLAYTON, R.H. (1937–38) 'Training leaders for industry' *Memoirs and Proceedings of the Manchester Literary and Philosophical Society* Vol. LXXII.

13 EVELY, R. and LITTLE, I.M.D. (1960) *Concentration in British Industry* Cambridge, Cambridge University Press.

14 KNOX, T.M. (1938) 'Graduates in business' *Oxford Magazine*, 20 January.

15 *Britain's Industrial Future . . . Report of the Liberal Inquiry* (1925) London.

16 URWICK, L. (1933) *Management of Tomorrow* London, Nisbet and Co., p. 164 and esp. part 4, 'Training for management'.

17 The Association for Education in Industry and Commerce Report on Education and Management, (1928) May, p. 5. See DUMMELOW, J. (1949) p. 85 for a good specific example in the case of Metrovickers where in the 1920s some functions of foremen were centralized into a specialized rate fixing department dealing with the works as a whole.

18 DELLER, E. (1933) *Tendencies in University Education* Oxford, Oxford University Press. University of London Institute of Education Studies and Reports, No. 3, p. 10. This was not an uncommon observation; see *University of Liverpool Society Chronicle* (1931) July p. 8 and 'The overproduction of graduates' *The Weekend Review* (1932) July 2.

19 For example, Burmah Oil (1920); Rylands of Warrington (1925); Gas, Light and Coke Co, (1925); Tate and Lyle (1928); J. Dickinson (1928); Tootal's (1929); Pilkington's Vita (1929); C. and J. Clark (1929); Coast Lines (1933); Pilkington's (1933); Ocean Accident and Guarantee Corp. (1933); Rio Tinto (1933); Atlas Engraving Co. (1936); Norfolk Rush and Reed Industries (1938); Longman's (1938); London Passenger Transport Board (1939). These are taken from a collection of several hundred private memoranda of the Cambridge Appointments Board. I am particularly grateful to the board for allowing me to use these documents. Since they were confidential the author will not be cited and on occasion the firm concerned will not be revealed. Henceforth they will be referred to as CAB Memoranda.

20 *Progress* (Lever's house magazine) (1924) October, p. 206.

21 LEVERHULME, LORD (1917) 'Victims of education' in *The Six Hour Day and Other Industrial Questions* London, Allen and Unwin (1918) pp. 221–30. His son noted of him that 'on the whole his prejudices were perhaps against the university man'; *Viscount Leverhulme by his Son* (1927) London, p. 145. Lever's nephew, J.L. Tillotson, sought to overcome his uncle's prejudices against graduates; WILSON, C. (1954) *A History of Unilever, A Study in Economic Growth and Social Change* London, Cassell, Vol. 1, p. 50.

22 See HALL, J. (1928) *Alma Mater, or the Future of Oxford and Cambridge* London, Kegan Paul and Co., p. 89; and BRIANT, K. (1937) *Oxford Limited* London, Michael Joseph, pp. 271–2, for a defence of universities against this attack. The former also included an attack specifically on Leverhulme.

23 ANON (1930) 'Business careers for undergraduates' *Oxford Magazine* 30 January, citing the views of Sir Ernest Benn, the publisher.

24 MELCHETT, LORD (1928) 'The relations of the universities and industry' *The Universities Review* October, cited this argument with which he heartily disagreed.

25 MILNE WATSON, D. (1934) 'University men in commerce and industry' *Oxford* Winter, cited this though he disagreed with it. However, Sir Robert MacAlpine and A.W. Gamage thought this was so: (1927) 'Is the university man a failure in business?' *Evening Standard* 13 January.

26 For example, the Pussyfoot riot at King's, London, 1919; the riot in a theatre by undergraduate ex-servicemen of Liverpool University, 1920; the Phineas War, 1922, between University and King's Colleges, London; the Exeter statue-painting scandal of the early 1920s, and others.

27 MASSON, I. (1935) 'University training and business posts' *Durham University Journal* March, citing E.A. Eaton's Presidential Address to the Durham Union Society.

28 MASTERMAN, C.F.G. (1927) 'The boy, where should he go?' *Evening Standard*, 11 January.

29 'George M' (1924) 'That degree feeling' (cartoon) *The Serpent* (Manchester University) 18 November.

30 HASLETT, A.W. (1937) 'Scientific careers, the next thirty years' *Journal of Careers* June.

31 ROACH, J.P.C. (1959) 'The university of Cambridge' in *Victoria County History of Cambridgeshire* Vol. III 'The city and the university' Cambridge, Cambridge University Press, pp. 295–9.

32 HILKEN, T.J.N. (1967) *Engineering at Cambridge University, 1783–1965* Cambridge, Cambridge Uni-

versity Press, p. 171.

33 CUR 39.54. Professorship of Aeronautical Engineering, Items 1 and 11a.

34 GRIFFITH, E. (1937) 'Refrigeration Engineering' *Journal of Careers* October. Low temperature research at Cambridge was a joint DSIR and university project.

35 The Earl of Birkenhead (1959) *The Professor in Two Worlds* London, Eyre and Spottiswoode, p. 101. p. 101.

36 HINSHELWOOD, C.N. (1939) 'Laboratories and research in natural science' *Oxford University Handbook.*

37 TIZARD, H.T. (1937) 'The needs of Oxford science' *Oxford* (special number) February.

38 *The Times* (1937) 13 October.

39 WILLIAMS, E.C. (1931) *The Aims and Future Work of the Ramsay Memorial Laboratory of Chemical Engineering; University of London, Department of Chemical Engineering,* University of London Press, HALE BELLOT, H. (1929) *University College, London, 1826–1926* London, University of London Press.

40 University College, London Report, 1937–38.

41 CROMER, H.W. (1933) 'Industry and the universities. I-King's College, London' *JC* September. It is a pity that this series was not continued. Annual Reports of King's College, London, 1928–39, *passim.*

42 Zaharoff Chair of Aviation, 1918; 1919–23. File 1120, Imperial College Archives. Letter, Sir Basil Zaharoff to W.S. Churchill, (1919) 18 November.

43 CLARK, R.W. (1964) *Tizard* London, Methuen, Chap. 4.

44 'A History of the Chemistry Department at Imperial College' unpublished typescript in the college, (1963) p. 62.

45 WRIGHT, W.D. (undated) 'History of the Physics Department, Imperial College' and 'History of the Department of Chemical Engineering and Chemical Technology 1912–39' in Imperial College archives, p. 24.

46 BRAGG, W.L. (1938) 'The Physics Department' *Journal of the University of Manchester.*

47 'Put and take', 'An appeal', *The Serpent* (1921) 31 January, for such a complaint about the university's disengagement from local industry. This was the magazine of the Students' Union.

48 FLEMING, SIR AMBROSE (1930) 'Electro-communication as a career' *JC* July–August.

49 'The Chloride Electric Storage Co.' *JC* (1931) July–August.

50 Description of the New Metallurgical Laboratories opened by Sir George Beilby, FRS (Manchester, 1923).

51 'The British dyestuffs industry' *JC* (1926) June. CAMPBELL, C. (1939) 'The chemistry department' *Journal of the University of Manchester.*

52 Manchester Municipal College of Technology Jubilee, 1902–52 (this was the faculty of technology of the university). It is worth noting that the official history – CHARLTON, H.B. (1951) *Portrait of a University, 1851–1951* Manchester, Manchester University Press, – is highly misleading in having virtually nothing on the inter-war years' science of the university.

53 'Thomas Percy Hilditch, 1886–1965' *Biographical Memoirs of Fellows of the Royal Society* (1966) November.

54 Sir D'Arcy Thompson MSS St. Andrew's University. Letter, Jas. Johnstone to D'AT. (1920) 22 January '... it's rather useful that we should deal with the industry ... So I say trawling be it. I'm sure it will be appreciated'. For the lobsters see Vice-Chancellor's Report, 1926.

55 *Liverpool Courier* (1920) 20 January and 4 June.

56 *The Jane Herdman Laboratories of Geology* (1929?).

57 *Liverpool Daily Post* (1919) 3 September and 3 April; the Liverpool Geological Society urged this course on the university because there were then only two schools of petroleum geology in the country.

58 WOOD, A.C. (1953) *A History of the University College, Nottingham 1881–1948* Oxford, Blackwell.

59 SIMMONS, J. (1958) *New University* Leicester University Press, p. 69.

60 Reports on the work of the Mining Research Laboratory, University of Birmingham, 1921–24.

61 University of Birmingham Mining Department, Opening of the Coal Treating Laboratory, (1926) 25 November, Opening of the Ore Dressing Laboratory, (1931) 16 December.

62 Report on the work of the Department of Oil Engineering and Refining, 1926–28.

63 CARTER, S.R. and STACEY, M. (1954) 'The School of Chemistry in the University of Birmingham' Journal of the Royal Institute of Chemistry, August.

64 VINCENT, E.W. and HINTON, P. (1947) *The University of Birmingham, its History and Significance* Birmingham, Cornish.

65 SHIMMIN, A.N. (1954) *The University of Leeds, the First Half Century* Leeds, University of Leeds.

66 KING, A.T. (1937) 'A university's assistance to industry' *Yorkshire Observer Trade Review* 23 January and *Yorkshire Post* 16 November. I am grateful to Professor Whewell for being allowed access to the news-cuttings books of the department.

67 *Department of Leather Industries Prospectus, University of Leeds, 1933.*

68 *Sheffield Telegraph* (1936) 4 November. Reports on research work ... Departments of Mining and Fuel Technology, 1928–37.

69 University of Sheffield, Reports of the Research Department for the Cold Working of Steel and other Ferrous Metals, 1932–36.

70 'William Ernest Stephen Turner 1881–1963', *Biographical Memoirs of Fellows of the Royal Society* (1964) November Vol. X; CHAPMAN, A.W. (1955) *The Story of a Modern University: the History of the University of Sheffield* Oxford University Press. The glass museum within the department at Sheffield well illustrates the comment about jam jars, a tacit tribute to the department's work.

71 MORGAN, A.E. (1927) 'The project of a university college at Hull' *The University Bulletin* April.

72 University of Wessex, an appeal to Southampton, 1928. 'The trend of engineering in the South' *Wessex* (1928) June.

73 CAVE-BROWN-CAVE, T.R. (1931) 'Our engineering development' *Wessex* June, and (1932) 'Progress in engineering' *Wessex* June.

74 Unpublished memorandum by Cave-Brown-Cave, 'Investigations and experimental developments made between 1934 and 1939'.

75 TEMPLE-PATTERSON, A. (1962) *The University of Southampton* The University of Southampton.

76 COTTLE, B. and SHERBOURNE, J.W. (1959) *The Life of a University* University of Bristol.

77 GARNER, W.E. (1954) 'Schools of Chemistry ... the University of Bristol' *JRIC* January. Lever was persuaded to do this by Ernest Wells, an ex-Bristol student and a director of Lever's.

78 *The Campden Research Station* (University of Bristol, 1937).

79 *University of Bristol and the National Fruit and Cider Institute Jubilee Celebrations of the Long Ashton Research Station* (Bristol, 1937).

80 CHILDS, W.M. (1933) *Making a University, an Account of the University Movement at Reading* London, J.M. Dent and sons.

81 *Western Morning News and Mercury* (1925) June 17.

82 University College of the South West of England Annual Reports, *passim*. A possible exception was the work of E.C. Wray, formerly of ICI Dyestuffs, in the new Washington Singer chemistry laboratories.

83 WHITING, C.E. (Ed) (1937) *The University of Durham* Durham, p. 57, and his (1932) *The University of Durham, 1832–1932* London, Sheldon Press.

84 Armstrong College, Reports of the Standing Committee on Research, 1927–38.

85 'History of the Engineering Department of King's College [Newcastle]' in pamphlet *The Stephenson Building* (1951).

86 UNIVERSITY GRANTS COMMITTEE (1935) *Report for the Period, 1929/30–1934/35*, Tizard (speaking 1934) cited p. 40.

87 CROSLAND, J. (1933) 'Organization of the Modern Colliery' *Leeds University Mining Society Journal* September.

88 COURT, W.H.B. (1945) 'Problems of the British coal industry between the wars' *Economic History Review*, Vol. XV.

89 CLARK, R.W. (1964) *Tizard* London, Methuen, p. 65.

90 (1920) IX *Report of the Air Ministry Committee on Education and Research in Aeronautics* (Glazebrook) Cmd. 554

91 *Report on the Extension of Scientific Research in Manchester University, particularly in Relation to the Industries of its Area* (1944) Manchester University, p. 18. The quotation referred to electro-technics.

92 Second Congress of the Universities of the Empire (London, 1921), 'The universities and training for commerce and industry'. Sir William Ashley's contribution was also reprinted as chap. 4 of his book *Commercial Education*.

93 SIMPSON, W.D. (1963) *The Fusion of 1860 ... a History of the United University of Aberdeen, 1860–1960*, p. 35.

94 Department of Economics and Commerce Prospectus, 1919 (University of Leeds).

95 PEARSON, T.H. (1920) *A Plea for the Greater Recognition of Economics in Oxford*. Pearson was a Fellow of Pembroke. CLARK, G.N. (1934) 'Social Studies at Oxford' *The American Oxonian* July.

96 BOWIE, J.A. (1930) *Education for Business Management* Oxford University Press.

97 BOWIE, J.A. (1928) 'Industrial management as a career' *JC* Oct.

98 URWICK, L. (Ed) (1956 and 1963) *The Golden Book of Management* London, pp. 259–262, Bowie is still revered as one of the few British pioneers of management training.

99 BOWIE, J.A. (1931) 'The Manchester experiment' in MACKAY, R.J. (Ed) *Business and Science, the Collected Papers to the Department of Industrial Co-operation at the Centenary Meeting of the British Association*.

100 BEVERIDGE, LORD (1960) *The London School of Economics and its Problems, 1919–37* London, Allen and

Unwin, p. 86. Prospectus of the Department of Business Administration, London School of Economics, 1931. 'Training administrators for industry and commerce' *JC* (1929) May.

101 CAB Memorandum (1934) May 28, on a visit to LSE: 'he [Mr. Menken of LSE] has a good many enquiries for men who have been through the course without being earmarked in advance'.

102 *The Scotsman* (1935) April 2 and 24 October.

103 BAXTER, W.T. (1936) 'Careers for graduates, prospects offered by university training' *The Scotsman* 15 and 16 October.

104 OLIVER, W. (1938) 'The Bachelor of Commerce degree as an aid to training for business' *The Student* (Edinburgh University) 17 May.

105 MACKENZIE, A. (1939) 'The graduate in the commercial world' *The Student* 25 April.

106 (1917) XI *Report of the Board of Education, 1915–16* Cmd. 8594.

107 Sarolea Papers 81/1, University of Edinburgh. Typescript memorandum, Sir Bernard Pares to Charles Sarolea (Professor of French at Edinburgh) (1916) March.

108 HEARNSHAW, L.S. (1964) *A Short History of British Psychology, 1840–1940* London, Methuen.
URWICK, L. and BRECH, E.F.L. (1959) *The Making of Scientific Management* London, Management Publications Trust, Vol. II, Chap. XII.

109 QUIGLEY, H. (1932) 'Where trained economists and statisticians are wanted' *JC* March. WHITE, G.R. (1935) 'Openings for statisticians in industry and research' *JC* September, also noted their increased use in the last ten years.

110 CAB memorandum (1937) 25 May.

111 WELLS, F.A. (1968) *Hollins and Viyella* Newton Abbot, David and Charles, pp. 193–4.

112 LINDSAY, A.D. (1937) 'Social Studies in Oxford' *Oxford* (special number) February.

113 Report of University College London, 1934–35.

114 *Committee on Industry and Trade* (Balfour) (1927) 'Factors in industrial and commercial efficiency', pp. 236–41.

115 Young Men in Industry and Commerce. AEIC Conference at Liverpool, (1930) June, p. 5.

116 *ibid.*, p. 15.

117 MILNE WATSON, SIR D. (1934) *Oxford*, Winter, *op. cit.*

118 Association for Education in Industry and Commerce Report on Education for Higher Positions in Commerce (1929) October esp., p. 20.

119 GOODENOUGH, SIR F. (1931) *Final Report of the Committee on Education for Salesmanship* London, HMSO, p. 65.

120 SCOTT, W.R. (1929) 'Report of the Special Committee on University Training in Industrial Administration' *Monthly Journal of Glasgow Chamber of Commerce and Manufactures* March.

121 CAB Memoranda for firms and dates concerned.

122 CHOSSUDOWSKY, E.M. (1938) 'Graduate employment in industrial management' *The Student* 18 October. This was a report of the main views expressed at the Universities Commerce Association Conference held at Leeds University, March, 1938.

123 *University Education and Business, a Report by a Committee Appointed by the Cambridge University Appointments Board* (Cambridge, 1946). The survey was made in 1937–38 though not published until after the war. It was under the chairmanship of Sir Will Spens.

124 The Association of British Chambers of Commerce Report on the Commercial Employment of Students with Degrees in Commerce, (1939) 11 January.

125 MORISON, SIR T. (1921) 'The universities and training for commerce and industry', Report of Proceedings of the Second Congress of the Universities of the Empire.

126 WOOD, A.C. (1953) *op. cit.* p. 115.

127 KNOX, T.M. (1934) 'University men and appointments in business' *Oxford* Summer, p. 89.

128 Calculated from UGC returns.

129 SCOTT, W.R. (1929) 'Report of the Special Committee' *op. cit.*

130 CLAPHAM, SIR JOHN (1945–46) XIV *Report of the Committee on the Provision for Social and Economic Research* Cmd. 6868.

131 The Liverpool and Sheffield evidence is considered more fully in SANDERSON, M. (1972) *The Universities and British Industry 1850–1970* London, Routledge and Kegan Paul, Chap. 10.

132 Reports of the Secretary of the Appointments Board, University of Southampton, 1937–38, 1938–39.

133 Calculated from *Leeds University Old Students' Yearbook, 1930–31*.

134 Calculated from *King's Old Students' Association Yearbook, 1938*.

135 RITCHIE, D.J.B. (1935) 'The graduate in business, Scottish graduates and business careers' *JC* April.

136 GUILD OF GRADUATES OF THE UNIVERSITY OF BIRMINGHAM (1938) *Graduate Employment, A report of the graduates of the University of Birmingham* University of Birmingham.

Jane Barker and Hazel Downing

The word processor is making an impact on offices all over the country in both the public and the private sectors. The introduction of microelectronically controlled word processors constitutes the first major attempt at office rationalization since the introduction of the typewriter in the 1870s. This paper seeks to chart the ongoing shift in office organization by taking a historical look at the entry of women into the office, the culture of the office and, finally examining the rationale behind the introduction of word processors and their potential impact.

Introduction

The analytical starting point in our examination of this particular labour process is the concept of the move from formal to real subordination of labour which we find useful in understanding current changes in office organization and other applications of micro-electronic technology. We do, however, recognize that there are certain major problems with the wholesale application of marxist concepts onto a labour process which is primarily female and which merit some discussion in this introduction.

Recent feminist studies of women's waged work, correctly point out the importance and centrality of an analysis of the family in its relation to the capitalist mode of production as the starting point for understanding women's work outside the home. We share with these analyses a recognition that where, when and under what conditions women's work is governed by the mechanisms of the family and patriarchal ideology of women as wives and mothers. In other words, all women's work is firmly rooted within patriarchal relations. We would emphasise, however, from the outset that we consider these patriarchal relations to be increasingly firmly rooted in, and defined by, the relations and needs of capital.

[...]

A useful understanding of the 'problem' is that put forward by Zillah Ellenstein[1]

Source: An abridged version of BARKER, J. and DOWNING, H. (1980) *Capital and Class* Spring, pp. 64–99.

'capitalism uses patriarchy and patriarchy is defined by capitalism'. It becomes possible at certain moments, under certain conditions, for patriarchy to be subsumed to the needs of capital and at other times to be given pride of place, such that on the surface each can appear separate and independent, but the two are in effect mutually dependent. In which case, it becomes more realistic to speak of a capitalist patriarchy and to examine the elements of this admixture not only in relation to the where and when of women's waged work but, crucially, to how it operates at the point of production: the culture of, in this case, the office.

Taking our original framework, we understand the mechanism of capital accumulation to involve the move towards real subordination through simultaneously cheapening labour power and by striving for tighter control over the labour process. In the production process proper, this process has occurred historically through the use of machinery and Taylorist methods of rationalisation. Where labour within production processes is primarily female, however, forms of control which are specifically patriarchal function over and above these other forms, as is excellently pointed out by Anne Pollart in her recent study of women workers in a tobacco factory.[2]

[...]

In the office, the extent to which machinery and Taylorism have or, indeed, could be used has been complicated by what appears to be a major contradiction. On the one hand, we have the need for optimum capitalist efficiency, and on the other, a set of relations of control embedded in both patriarchy *and* the ideology of mental over manual labour which actually hinders cost-effective efficiency.

So, we would maintain, patriarchal relations affect the whole of women's lives, including every area in which women are permitted to work, but the office throws up a complicated cross fertilization of the status relations of mental labour and relations of male domination and female subordination.

It is only in recent years and, particularly now with an impending world recession that managements have looked to their administrations as well as their production lines for making economies. The use of patriarchy as a means of control in the office has been dominant over other more strictly capitalist forms of control, until as Braverman puts it:

> Top managers watched this multiplication of secretaries with nothing more than amusement, until it grew to dimensions which threatened the balance sheet.[3]

Faced with such economic problems and with the possibility of transferring control onto a new technological development which is also extremely cheap, it is becoming increasingly necessary for individual capitals to renounce their more direct use of patriarchy in favour of a specifically capitalist means of control.

The Feminisation of Clerical Labour

The introduction of women into offices occured through several isolated but nevertheless related causes. The growing middle class women's movement, especially through the established voice of the Society for Promoting the Employment of Women, aided the entry of women into traditional male preserves but this development was not totally antagonistic to the changing needs of capital. Until around 1871, the absence of women from 'professional' employment was the result of poor education and its ideological underpinning which assumed that the education of women – other than instruction into the essentials of womanhood such as embroidery, music and French – was a waste of money. The middle class woman straddled the uneasy contradiction between, on the one hand, playing the lady of leisure, a role which was designed to shore up the husband's prestige as a reflection of his wealth and ability to maintain a wife and servants, and on the other, justifying this existence in face of the prevailing ethic of work, thrift and abstinence.

At a time when large numbers of eligible young men were emigrating to the newly colonized richness of India or the freedom of the New World, middle class women of marriageable age far outnumbered their male counterparts. Between 1830–75, about five million unemployed, mainly men, left Britain. The census of 1851 showed an excess of women over men between the ages of twenty and forty of 133,654; by 1861, there were 2,482,028 'spinsters' over the age of fifteen, of whom 404,773 lived in London. For such women the choice was simple – work or starve.

Rapid developments in capitalist production and the imperialist penetration of western capital into the newly colonized areas of Africa, Latin America and Asia, resulted in a massive increase in administration and paperwork, and hence, the need for more labour to fill the expanding offices of commerce and industry. The census figures bear witness to the increase in women clerical workers. In 1851, there were 11,755 male commercial clerks, and only 15 women, ten years later there were 274 women. In 1871, however, the number of women had increased to 1,412, the major employer being the Civil Service, and by 1881 with the impact of the typewriter, the figure had reached 5,989 women and 175,468 men.

Clerical work immediately offered a world entirely different from that presented by the other types of work open to middle class women. Nursing offered a world of poverty and extremely bad conditions, as did teaching. And, as the most commonly popular employment for genteel ladies – that of governess – rapidly became saturated and competition keener, even as wages dropped, the field of clerical work was opened up to them. In addition was the fact that office work provided independence from the restrictions of 'living-in' occupations. [...] And of course, the degradation of working for money could be somewhat softened by the fact that the office offered a middle class environment with men of their own class, should they be forced to come into contact with them.

The Prudential Assurance Company which describes itself as one of the first companies to employ 'lady clerks' in 1872, went to great lengths to protect the ladies from the slightest possibility of contact with men and any subsequent loss of respectability:

> A room had to be provided and it was thought more becoming for them
> to lunch on the premises than in one of the coffee houses . . . [The Ladies']

times of arrival and departure were so arranged that they did not coincide with those of the male staff and they entered and left the building by a separate entrance. Under Miss Wood [the superintendent] and her successors, they lived a secluded life of their own, visited a few times a day by a junior clerk who collected the letters they typed and the policies they copied.[4]

Initially, there was considerable moral concern about middle class women entering the business world. The apparent ease with which the all-male office was transformed to accommodate them required a massive ideological shift in attitudes towards middle class women engaging in the sale of their labour on the open market. It was the fact that they were cheaper and more abundant than men which gave that ideological shift its impetus.

The Post Office, the largest employer of women in the Civil Service, initially employed 'lady telegraphists', the advantage being that they had a 'delicacy of touch, are more patient than men during long confinement to one place, and take more kindly to sedentary employment'.[5] The most favourable advantage, however, was their cheapness. Not only were they 'prepared' to accept lower wages than men, but, since it was the policy of the Civil Service not to employ married women (a policy which was not revoked until 1948 and which also affected women teachers and nurses), they were forced to leave on marriage (or hide their marital status) and replacements could be taken on at the bottom of the salary scale. The ideological construction behind this, the 'family wage' assumed (and still does) women's most natural state to be marriage with the husband as the principal wage earner.

[. . .]

When women entered the office, and most particularly when they entered it as 'typewriters', the whole structure of office organization underwent dramatic changes. In the early nineteenth century counting house, which generally consisted of the employer and a small retinue of male clerks, the working relationship was highly personalized and the clerk could labour in the expectation of one day becoming a partner in his employer's firm or even an employer in his own right:

> The dependence of the clerk on a particular employer and the difficulty of mobility between firms once a mature age had been reached, were, in theory at least, counter-balanced by the opportunities for advancement through staying with one firm and gradually 'making oneself indispensable' . . . the particularism of the relationship between clerk and employer, the possibility of rising from one position to the other, and the largely individual and informal training within the counting house, served to strengthen ties between individual clerks and individual employers and thereby weaken the common interests that existed among clerks as a body.[6]

The structure of the apprenticeship of the clerk to his employer enabled him to learn all the ramifications of the business; the division of labour was negligible and generally the clerk gained a complete overview of the whole functioning of the office. With the introduction of the typewriter, it became possible to simplify and routinize tasks by dividing and allocating the various components which made up the processing of information to separate departments and at the same time create a whole new area of 'women's work'.

Before looking at this in detail, an important point must be made regarding the link which exists between the relations which characterized the work of the male counting house clerk and those of today's secretaries and typists; a link which is never made although vaguely hinted at, for instance, by Lockwood:

> The clerical notion of gentlemanly behaviour, at least in its lower middle class admixture with 'respectability' acted as a powerful social control over any intransigence or insurrection on the part of the clerks.[7]

Any deviation from the norm of gentlemanly behaviour could be held in check by the employer's Damoclean threat of the withdrawal of his benevolence in supplying the clerk with a livelihood. Any rupture in the closely personal nature of this relationship would make it unworkable. This enforced loyalty guaranteed by a patrician form of a patriarchal relationship reflects to a certain degree the social relations which govern today's office. *The entry of women, we maintain, was to a certain extent facilitated by this same form of control, mediated not so much through class relations as with the male clerk but through relations of male domination and female subordination* – relations which we define as patriarchal. The strand which runs through both types of relationship is based on the mental/manual division which assumes ideologically that mental labour is more difficult, more demanding, requires a higher educational standard and hence, carried more status than manual labour. Then as now, the status was not accompanied by significantly high pay.

Women were trained as 'typewriters' as they were first known because it was considered that, since they could play the piano, it would naturally follow that they could type[8] – if this was the case, why were there no great women concert pianists?

The advantages of the typewriter, first produced by Remingtons in 1873, were its greater efficiency in terms of cost and time. The *Morning Post* of 30 January, 1889 reported that about £10,000 *per annum* could be saved in and around Whitehall by the employment of women and typewriters, and in the Civil Service, Probate Office, the work of copying titles which formerly cost £3,000 *per annum* by male clerks, could now be done by three women on typewriters at a cost of £300 *per annum*.[9]

The pattern of growth of offices during this period is well illustrated by the Prudential Assurance Company. In 1858 their 'Chief Office' comprised a staff of five young male clerks and less than twenty years later, in 1874, the staff in the same office had increased to a total of 600 males and 200 females.

No longer under these circumstances was there any need for apprenticed clerks. With the increase in the division of labour, specialization and mechanization, the general standards of education required for clerical work dropped and the need for apprenticeships became eliminated. In fact the period saw a growth in what was termed 'commercial education' which effectively replaced the training received during apprenticeship.

Despite the fact that women were 'invading' a strictly all-male workplace, there was no obvious resistance on the part of the existing workforce of the kind we experience today when, as women, we attempt to penetrate traditional 'masculine' areas of work. This anomaly has been explained by the fact that the introduction of the typewriter created a completely new area of work:

> Typing was 'sex-neutral' because it was a new occupation. Since typing had not been identified as a masculine job, women who were employed as typists did not encounter the criticism that they were taking over 'men's work'.[10]

> New technology helped women get to the office, because it provided whole new categories of work that no one, man or woman had ever done, and thus the question of usurpation did not arise. The new machines with the biggest impact were the telephone and the typewriter, both of which are still practically female monopolies.[11]

But this does not take account of the male clerks whose jobs were upgraded as women came in at the bottom rungs to do the routine work. At the same time, some clerks must have been *replaced*. For much of the clerk's work involved the laborious copying of all types of documents, from lengthy conveyances to simple letters in neat copper-plate handwriting – a 'skill' which was gradually replaced by women and typewriters. (Although in fact some solicitors still required that conveyances be hand written in india ink which was considered to last longer than typewriter carbon – a process which went on until into the 1920s.)

A crucial factor, however, was that clerical work during that period was a major growth area and women entered it when there were not enough suitable men to fill the posts: a situation similar in fact to the two world wars, with the exception, however, that this time women stayed in the job because it became feminized from the beginning.

The immediate impact of the introduction of the typewriter was the possibility it created for the diversification of office work into specialised departments, as illustrated again by the Prudential:

> There was an Opening Room for incoming mail and a Postal Department which despatched a prodigious correspondence. The ladies had their own luncheon and rest rooms and a promenade on the flat roof. There was a recreational library, an electric clock, a pneumatic service for sending letters to the Postal Department . . . [12]

In addition, an Actuary's office was established along with a Statistical Department, an Estate Department, and an Audit Department, while the ladies continued undisturbed in the seclusion of their typewriting office.

Although reliable statistics on clerical incomes are not available until 1909–10, evidence from the *Bankers Magazine* suggests that before that period, clerical salaries were in fact being eroded. A letter to the magazine on the 'Prospects of Bank Clerks' in May 1889 states that the starting salaries for bank clerks were between £40–70 *per annum* and that the maximum for 'ordinary clerks' was from

£150–250 *per annum*. The writer expresses concern that there was 'fierce competition' for banking jobs and that because of this 'high salaries except in a few cases, cannot be expected'.[13] The predominance of the practice of saving on wages by dismissing the older clerks and employing younger, junior clerks is also suggested. The figures for 1909–10 suggest that the majority of male clerks were earning less than £160 *per annum* (61/6d per week) while the majority of women clerks received £40 and below, the average salary being £45.

In 1910, a pamphlet entitled *The Clerk's Charter* appeared and offered some interesting explanations for the general fall in clerical salaries. Firstly, the introduction of compulsory education for working class children which produced a flood of potential clerks onto the market, hence depreciating the value of their labour power, as Marx pointed out earlier:

> The universality of public education enabled capitalists to recruit such labourers from classes that formerly had no access to such trades and were accustomed to a lower standard of living. Moreover, this increased supply, and hence competition. With few exceptions, the labour power of these people is therefore devalued with the progress of capitalist production. Their wage falls, while their labour capacity increases. The capitalist increases the number of these labourers whenever he has more value and profits to realize. The increase of this labour is always a result, never a cause of more surplus.[14]

Secondly because of the rapid entry of women into offices who, through lack of choice and organization had to accept low wages. The Charter estimated the number of female commercial clerks at around 100,000 – in fact the census a year later in 1911 revealed the accuracy of this estimate, there were 117,000:

> Thousands [of women] are being turned out every year by business training colleges, schools, typewriter companies and second hand typewriter dealers. One well known firm of the last-named category advertise constantly that they will send out machine and operator for 15s a week. That they sweat their girls is patent by the advertisements appearing in the Daily Mail for girls to come and earn 2s 6d a week, while learning. Having finished such an apprenticeship I have known girls to offer their services through a labour exchange at nothing a week, in order to get into a real office and make a start. At this point the sweating is complete, one cannot go below nothing, but any number of advertisements appear offering from 5s to 15s a week for women clerks and plenty of young women can be found to accept such derisory salaries.[15]

Patriarchal and Capitalist Relations of Secretarial Labour: the Social Office

[...]

As we emphasised in the introduction, all areas of women's waged work are affected by relations of capitalist patriarchy. However, what differentiates office work from other sectors of women's employment is the significant way in which these relations are crosscut by the mental/manual division of labour. Running through our analysis therefore are three conceptually separate but interrelated lines: class, gender and the mental/manual division.

Office work, then, is characterized by a different range of ideologies from other sectors that women are employed in – in comparison with for example shop work where notions of personal service predominate and with factory work. It is within the ideology of mental labour that patriarchal relations find an easy footing and where we find the ideological (not material) justification for office work as clean, glamourous, professional and 'easy'. [...] The whole ethos of working class masculinity which sees male office workers, or pen-pushers, as 'pansies' or not real workers can actually be related to this idea of office work being an easy job – i.e. not hard, dirty or strenuous, but clean, light work. (The ideological division between intellectual and manual labour is well illustrated by Paul Willis' 'lads' in his *Learning to Labour: How Working Class Kids Get Working Class Jobs*.[16]) Health problems which are specifically related to things like bad lighting, heating, inadequate and/or badly designed furniture – especially seating – unhealthy air conditioning systems, exposure to toxic cleaning fluids, etc. which produce such symptoms as headaches, backaches, nausea and tiredness, are not seen as having material bases – rather they are seen (especially by managements) as individual idiosyncratic problems. Office work is, after all, not hard, dirty or strenuous.

Within mental labour, however, there exists a further division, which Poulantzas calls 'a hierarchy within mental labour itself'.[17] Although Poulantzas doesn't make the direct connection, the 'reproduction of the mental/manual labour division within mental labour itself'[18] is in large part guaranteed by the sexual division of labour. The apparent loyalty and passivity of women office workers is enhanced by patriarchal control and, importantly, a place within the hierarchy of mental labour.

The difficulty of attempting to apply strict marxist categories to office work lies in the fact that running through the hierarchy is a concern with status; it is perhaps for this reason that in the past, marxists have been somewhat reticent about theorising the office labour process, except for two notable exceptions. Firstly Poulantzas[19] whose concern however is solely with the class categorization of office workers and secondly, Braverman.[20] Despite his excellent analysis, Braverman tells us little about the culture of the office and, specifically, about subjective experience and forms of resistance, which prevents him from envisaging any struggle amongst office workers. We feel, however, that it is important to come to terms with status through 'intellectual' labour because of the precise way in which this interacts with class and gender to produce the anomaly of the *social office*. And it is precisely the social office which stands in the way of capitalist efficiency and which requires transformation.

Braverman, for instance, recognizes the importance of the social office but fails to develop the contradictions he raises, particularly in relation to the Babbage principle:

Thereafter this system of secretarial assistance spreads to lower ranks as well, as the numbers of managerial and semi-managerial employees increase. Since the Babbage principle operates wherever a mass of work may be subdivided and in its 'lower' portions separated out and delegated, it invades all the realms of paper work performed by executives, assistants to executives, heads of small departments, sometimes consisting of no more than the 'head' and a secretary, professional and even semi-professional employees. *The Babbage principle has here transcended its own limits, especially as social and prestige factors come into play and the personal secretary becomes a perquisite of the privileged job as one of its chief privileges.* (emphasis added)[21]

It is no accident that the majority of office workers and the vast proportion of those in the lower grades, are women. The following, written by a Mr C.C. Harper in 1894, despite its chauvinistic tenor, is worth quoting at length for its 'perception':

If the time is past when women were regarded as a cross between an angel and an idiot, it is quite by her own doing, and if she no longer receives the deference that is due of an angel, nor the compassionate consideration usually accorded an idiot, no one is to blame but herself . . . in the occupations of clerks, cashiers, telephonists, telegraphists, and shorthand writers, they have sufficiently demonstrated their unfitness and only retain their situations by reason of the lower wages they are prepared to accept, in competition with men, and through the sexual sentimentality which would rather have a pretty woman to flirt with in the intervals of typewriting than a merely useful and unornamental man.[22]

A secretary can constitute a perk to a male office worker and in this function she provides management with a useful means for controlling its own lower ranks. At the same time, however, what Harper terms 'sexual sentimentality' is a mirror image of male domination and female subordination within a hierarchy which, to paraphrase Mary Kathleen Benet is more akin to a middle class Victorian household without the children.[23]

Despite differences between different types of organization (private or public sector, manufacturing or professional, multinational or family type firm, metropolitan or provincial) women at the lower ranks of the hierarchy, without the promotion incentives which are presented to male office workers, and employed as a means of securing their loyalty and hence devotion to duty, are encouraged through other ways. Flattery and praise, the engendering of a sense of indispensability, as well as an underlying, albeit sometimes explicit sexual innuendo, are all forms of patriarchal control. As in society generally, they are encouraged to fulfil their roles as 'real women', both as 'office wife', caring and servicing groups of or individual men, and as whore/prostitute, the conventional dolly bird/sex object – and in this latter role, they frequently become the object of sexual harrassment, even if in the guise of a joke. In other words, the organisation, discipline, working and social relations of the office between men and women, women and women, and men and men, are all governed by the patriarchal relations which permeate the whole of capitalist society.

Class and Hierarchy

While typing and shorthand (or audio) are essential qualifications for all secretarial workers, the proportion of time actually spent using these technical skills decreases the higher one ascends the hierarchy of secretarial work itself. The copy typist in the pool will have little or no contact with the originator of the material she's typing, while the secretary (private/personal assistant) will most probably sit in an office adjacent to the boss and her job will involve more personal, servicing duties than that of her colleague in the pool. In other words, although in financial and status terms, the private secretary wins out over the copy- or shorthand-typist, the amount of time spent using her technical skills is much less. Instead she is required to spend much of her time on jobs which, according to standard industrial definitions, would not be considered skilled at all. While typing and shorthand are skills which take years to perfect and build up speeds in, and which can be lost if not regularly used, conventional notions of skill cannot easily be applied to the other aspects of secretarial work. The abilities and qualities necessary for the development of a good working relationship within the confines of the boss/secretary couplet, or even in the office generally, are ones which are *learnt through an apprenticeship in womanhood.*

It is significant in this respect that job descriptions are a rarity for secretarial workers. Where they do exist, then they usually specify: first, shorthand (audio/copy) and typing; second, general office duties; third, *etcetera*. It is the '*etcetera*' which not only permits the gross exploitation of women office workers, but also assumes the naturalness of women performing specifically feminine tasks which involve caring and servicing. This is stated quite explicitly in secretarial manuals:

> In order to stay in the battle and reap a victory, in the form of a top job other far more intangible qualities are required ... These qualities are mainly concerned with dealing with people. They include poise, good manners, tact, sensitivity, and adaptability. They also include good personal habits and the ability to speak well. In short, the top secretary should look the part, sound the part, and act the part.[24]

There are women who make it to the top of the secretarial hierarchy only to find themselves performing more and more of their boss's jobs, but without any appropriate salary increase. An example of this type of exploitation, as referred to above, is that of a large solicitors' practice in the City of London where the secretaries are responsible for the conveyancing and the solicitors merely add their signatures. The problems of high labour turnover and subsequent recruitment costs can be avoided by allowing the women to get to know more about the job, increasing their 'job satisfaction'. [...]

Many working class girls, faced with the 'choice' of factory, shop, or office work, invariably go for the latter, a job which is considered clean, comfortable respectable and glamourous. It is also seen as a means for social mobility, providing an arena for meeting respectable middle class men and hopefully marriage within that class. 'Choice' however is a misnomer. Many women do not 'choose' office work; they fall into it. The responsibility for this lies in large part with the education girls receive. At school, apart from learning the 'obvious' skills of bathing babies, changing nappies, cookery, as well as the application of make-up, the only vocational skills girls learn is shorthand and typing.

> HD: Did you always want to do office work?
>
> J: I couldn't actually decide what I wanted to do when I left school. I thought I'd like to be a teacher when I was younger, but I was put into the commerce stream and learnt shorthand and typing. So I suppose rather than hairdressing which a friend of mine started doing – and she got all sorts of skin problems with the shampoo you know – I thought I might as well do office work.

In addition, secretarial work presents itself as incorporating a straightforward career structure through which the intelligent ones can make it by moving up through the hierarchy from pool typist to executive secretary. If the only requirements were good shorthand and typing speeds, upward mobility would be relatively easy for people like Chris who at 17 was earning £1,700 *per annum* (1977) to type envelopes and operate the franking machine. She was lucky enough to be given day release to learn shorthand, and this she hoped, would enable her to 'get a really good job', which she described as one at the top involving travelling. However, the structure of the hierarchy is deceptive, masking the class nature of secretarial work which ensures that there is no guaranteed move from one level to the next. The illusion of a career in secretarial work is maintained in secretarial manuals, commercial colleges and schools, and by careers teachers. 'A top secretarial position is an excellent stepping-stone to many interesting and remunerative careers in various fields';[25] ' . . . a magic carpet, an open sesame, to a life full of interest – a life with a complete fulfilment'.[26]

Generally, top jobs (which are thought of as involving a varied timetable, a pleasant office, an IBM golf ball typewriter, a personal telephone, as opposed to one shared with four other people and, of course, a relatively high salary) go to women graduates who leave university armed with a degree only to find they are unemployable and are encouraged to do a secretarial course – until the right job comes along.

But although those in top secretarial posts are given the opportunity to work on their own, using their initiative (whatever that means), the difference between them and those employed as shorthand/copy/audio typists is nominal. The status of a secretary within a particular organization is dependent not so much on her level of 'skill' and ability to work to a high degree of efficiency using her own initiative, but on the status of her boss and concomitantly on her ability to manipulate modes of femininity which are specifically middle class.

Quite often working on one's own amounts to no more than the execution of routine administrative tasks, such as filling in holiday charts, typing memos to accounts departments when a member of staff is ill, handling the petty cash tin, and paying milk bills. Status is *the* decisive factor in the hierarchy. The secretary to the director is guaranteed a much higher place in the hierarchy than the secretary to a mere manager.

[...]

The type of women who make director-level secretary, particularly in large firms where being a director carries more status than in small firms, require the kinds of qualities which come from a solid middle class upbringing and/or education. (In a West End stockbrokers and financial advisors, where the clientele is specifically middle if not upper class, all the secretaries had been to finishing school!) For working class girls to be accepted into this type of world they have to learn to develop middle class ways of operating within their femininity: a 'natural' telephone voice, a perfect dress sense, perfect grooming, etc. What this means is fitting 'submissively' into the gentlemanly professional atmosphere of serious business – displaying the correct attitude of deference to the big decision makers – playing the whiter than white Madonna. The other side of the couplet – the whore – is more befitting the inhabitants of the typing pool where the girls can 'have a laugh' when (usually only when) men aren't around.

[...]

The idea of 'professionalism' which reinforces the importance of submissiveness, is clearly not just a problem for women, but one which exists in the 'paperworld' as a result of the mental/manual division of labour and which also affects men in the lower ranks – albeit in different ways. In relation to women, one can see a certain exchange of class for status. The male boss acquires a certain status by virtue of having a secretary and the secretarial worker, in turn, acquires a higher class position – a relationship of dependence almost, and one which enhances loyalty to the company from both sides. Despite the proletarianization of many office jobs, office work is still seen by office workers as a middle class occupation. The early women's clerical associations (particularly the Association of Women Clerks and Secretaries) were extremely élitist and clearly reflected the effectiveness of the mental/manual division in their proneness 'to asserting their superiority over those in less well-paid, manual occupations'.[27] Despite the vast increase in numbers of working class women, especially since the second world war, this ideology still persists and is perpetuated by patriarchal forms of control.

The Alienation of the Office

After a few secretarial jobs, a pattern begins to emerge in the work of secretarial workers – boredom. Maybe one firm wins out over the other because one can make personal phone calls without the switchboard operator continually monitoring them ... While it's true that women who are skilled typists take a certain pride in producing a well set-out piece of work with few, or if possible no mistakes, there is no intrinsic satisfaction in typing itself. With shorthand too, there is a certain pride in being able to read back and transcribe correctly, but there is also the constant fear, especially at the beginning of the job when the terminology is not familiar, of having to go back to the dictator and admit to not being able to read a particular shorthand outline and feeling humiliated.

It's easy then to understand why many women admit that what keeps them in any one job for any length of time is the company of the other women for, after all, this is where they spend the majority of their waking hours. Sue, for instance, left a well paid job because of constant arguments with an older woman who was in fact her junior. This is not to suggest, however, that women only change jobs when they don't get on with the other women. It is quite common for, especially, young unmarried secretarial workers to make a career of changing firms looking for that perfect secretarial job – which they soon discover doesn't exist – and because for many this is the only way they can increase their salary; and in a bad working environment 'handing in one's notice is ultimately the only effective short-term response to a collective problem where there is no developed collective solidarity'.[28] To move upwards, women must learn to isolate themselves from their workmates, distancing themselves from the 'girls' and for many women, especially if they are married, without the inclination to change jobs every six months or so, it is rarely the content of the job which holds them in any one company, but the company of the other women.

[. . .] The secretary needs to develop a certain loyalty to her boss and when this is achieved, it means that she finds herself even further distanced from her workmates, for her adherence now is to the side of management away from the other workers and is enhanced by virtue of the confidence and secrecy involved in dealing with, for instance, information on wages, and other personnel matters, or even with the company's proposed take-over bid. She is encouraged then, to develop a cool, but friendly relationship with those in the lower ranks in order also to maintain their respect, for part of her job may, by virtue of her higher status, involve their supervision.

[. . .]

To a certain extent the rationalization of office organization through the application of Taylorist techniques has undermined the effectiveness of this form of control. In large corporations for instance, where fragmentation of tasks is most economical, there has been the development of large numbers of workers whose sole duty is the processing of one minute piece of information, the development of company loyalty becomes problematic. In small firms where the secretary can have a total overview of the business of her employer, she probably derives some satisfaction from knowing something about what is going on, and following the process through from beginning to end. [. . .] Although she has at least a sense of indispensability, even if she doesn't really understand the technicalities of her firm's products or business, she ultimately has no real interest in the company, since she has no real control over what it does and reaps no financial incentives at the end of the day other than her wage. Her loyalty begins at nine and ends at five.

In large companies, the tasks of the small office are fragmented and placed into the hands of small separate departments (post room, filing room, stationery supplies, reprographics departments, accounts departments, etc.) and increase the feeling of merely being a number on the payroll and of not being of any real value, thus increasing alienation. The possibility of the lower grades in the hierarchy developing a sense of loyalty to the Du Ponts, ICIs and GECs of the multinational world are remote. Lower management who effectively have no control over company policies (although they can live in hope of becoming managing director), can be 'bought off' through the trappings of secretarial prestige; secretaries can direct their loyalty to the man they work for, and where this one-to-one relationship doesn't operate and the shorthand/copy typist works for several men, she may select one she prefers. And in the 1950s at least there was evidence to show that typing pools rarely operate in a totally dehumanizing manner, with no personal contact between typist and author. Lockwood cited a contemporary study which showed that:

> Typing pools have motivational disadvantages which are not always taken into account at first when assessing their economic advantages ... many executives preferred to have a particular typist of their own and ... many typists preferred to be attached to a particular officer.[29]

However, as we go on to show, there is now a case for arguing that there is increasing militancy among these levels of workers which is forcing managements to look around for other forms of control.

Word Processing: the Transformation of Patriarchal Relations of Control

Where forms of resistance other than direct strike action, such as absenteeism, high labour turnover, sabotage, lateness, are taken seriously, it is always in relation to men – as if women weren't capable of resistance. However, our extensive experience of secretarial work points up how women have developed a culture of resistance which is peculiar to them as women, within the patriarchal relations of control of the office.

Workers have almost always attempted to find ways of getting some time for themselves when confronted with boring, alienating work. It is, however, usually only the visible signs of resistance which are recognizable – such as pacing their work, or finding an excuse to stop the line.

It is within the invisible culture of the office that we find the development of forms of resistance which are peculiarly 'feminine'. It is a culture which is contradictory, appearing oppressive but at the same time containing the seeds of 'resistance'.

Because the work in the office is boring and alienating, and because 'work', that is waged work, is not traditionally seen as being central to women's lives by both employers and women themselves, it is not surprising that women tend to bring their domestic lives into work with them. Thus, the stereotyped roles of women as wives and mothers is perpetuated. In a business world which is totally devoid of meaning, a sense of purpose and meaning is created in the culture which women create for themselves, and which in effect reinforces their subordinate position. The image of the secretary filing her nails all day is, despite the sexist assumptions on which it is based, often not that far from reality. [. . .] The following is also worth quoting in full:

> Five of us 'secretaries' sat in an expensive West End office and knitted

patiently until our bosses rang for us (usually around 4.30 p.m.). Small wonder that after a few months of this we began to feel put out when we were disturbed from our knitting. 'Let him wait', we would mutter crossly as we counted our stitches. All the girls in that office were engaged to be married and I soon joined them; indeed we had nothing else to think about but men and home-making. Inevitably we progressed from knitting to making curtains and fine embroidered table cloths and secretarial work became more and more of a tiresome interruption. As my wedding day approached I could stand the office no longer and gave in my notice. My boss was disappointed and sighed over the necessity of losing me just as I was 'getting to know the work' – I assured him he would find someone else who could manage it and he pressed a large wedding cheque into my waiting palm. We parted the best of friends.[30]

Conversations in offices are invariably personalized – i.e. rarely about events, political or otherwise, which do not affect them or the people they know personally. Not surprisingly, their conversations rarely concern the subject matter of the things they are typing – it is quite difficult to construct much of a conversation around an invoice. Rather conversations centre around personal, domestic concerns, such as families, weddings, children, cooking, knitting, marriage, boyfriends and clothes, etc. It is in fact a world which is quite difficult to inhabit comfortably if one chooses not to marry.

[...]

The significance of the culture we have attempted to describe is that it is indeed a factor in the reproduction of women's oppression, but it can also be seen as the development of an informal work culture which cannot be penetrated by 'masculine' work standards. In other words, it constitutes a world which the males bosses (and their underlings) cannot penetrate, thus allowing the women to get away with doing certain things which cannot be controlled.

[...]

Because conventional typewriters rely on the control of the typist, she can adopt any number of methods to break the routine of typing: she can sit on her work and pretend to look busy to have a chat, she can drop a paper clip in the basket of her typewriter and wait around for the mechanic to come, she can run out of stationery and then with an excuse for being out of the office, go off and visit someone in another office. It the work is late then 'the ribbon got stuck' or she had to phone a company to get Mr So-and-So's correct title and 'it took ages getting through'. In addition, those duties which are auxiliary to typing, such as filing, or even photocopying, enable her not to be tied to the typewriter all day – thus she has a certain amount of control over her space and movements.

Then, of course, there are those little jobs which women are expected to perform just because they are women: such as making the tea, watering the plants, organizing leaving/wedding/birthday presents, going out of the office on errands for the boss, all of which, while on the one hand reinforcing their ideological role as 'office wife' *can be used to create space and time away from the routine of typing*. (When working as a secretary one of us had to take a week off work – on full pay of course – to look after the boss's dog while he was at a conference). Automation is designed to change the office in very radical ways to eliminate this non-productive time, as Braverman notes when writing of the USA:

> Among the subsidiary benefits management expects to derive from (office automation) is the reduction and thus cheapening of the skills of adminis-trative employees, and *not least the squeezing out of the minutes and hours of labor power lost in the personal relations and contacts among secretaries and between secretaries and their 'principals'* – which is what they mean when they speak of the 'end of the social office'.[31]

Word processors are an attempt to achieve this by the replacement of patriarchal forms of control by more direct capitalistic forms of control: the move towards the real subordination of office workers.

Briefly, a word processor consists of a keyboard, a visual display unit (VDU), a memory, a mini- or micro-computer, plus printing facilities. The image of what is 'typed' into the memory (not onto paper) is displayed on the VDU. Only when the display shows that the memory holds the information in the correct form is the text printed onto paper – and it is printed extremely fast. These elements of a word processor can be arranged either as a 'stand alone' model, i.e. they are all combined on a desklike unit, or as 'shared logic' work stations – several desks, each with a keyboard and a VDU linked up to a larger computer, thus enabling access to greater computing power which can also operate print machines and telecommunications systems. Printing facilities here are usually separate from the work station, often in a different room. A word processor costs between £7,000 and £45,000.

Before looking in detail at the actual and potential impact of word processors, we will make a few general statements about why such microelectronically based equipment is being introduced *now*.

The Economic Crisis

The continuing existence of the capitalist mode of production depends on the constant accumulation of capital. The current economic crisis, with the huge drop in the overall rate of profit in 1974, challenges this accumulation process and demands that capital find ways of stabilizing its position. Historically this drive for accumula-tion has depended on the continual reorganization of the labor process in order to cheapen the price of labour and also on attempts to take control of the labour process out of the hands of the individual worker and transfer it into the realm of management.

This process of stripping workers of control is dependent upon changes in the means of production – the introduction of new forms of technology into the work-place as part of the trend towards the real subordination of labour to capital in the form of machinery. It is within this overall context that we must view the introduc-tion of word processors and other microelectronically based office equipment into offices – not as part of a technology which is autonomous, driving itself forward by its own momentum, but related to and influenced by and crucially part of capital's strategy to continually reproduce itself.

Just as management's strategy of control over individual workers in the office reflects and embodies the social relations of women's subordination to men, word processing technology reflects and embodies the social relations of capital's dominance over labour. However, we would emphasise that historically, previous technological innovations into the workplace have not operated solely in the ways managements have anticipated – workers *have* responded to and undermined attempts by management for increasing their control.[32] However ultimately, these have constituted defensive responses to retain a level of existing control, rather than aggressive attempts to obtain *more* control.

[...]

A factor in the growth of office workers as a major sector of employment has been capital's attempt to restructure and reorganize labour involved in the production process proper. Now the office has become a major bottleneck in the accumulation of capital. The recent Civil Service dispute showed how much power can be concentrated in the hands of very few workers. Out of a total membership of several thousand CPSA and SCPS members, only a couple of hundred on strike was necessary to cause severe disruption.

The period since the end of the second world war has seen a growth in the paid employment of women, who now constitute 41 per cent of the UK workforce, compared to only 32 per cent in 1951.[33] As we have shown, it is no accident that this increase has been on that side of the sexual division of labour which has traditionally been allocated to women, so that now two in five, (40 per cent) of all waged women are employed in the clerical sector, within which they represent 70 per cent of all clerical workers, and 98.6 per cent of secretaries and typists.

Overall, the clerical and administrative sector has grown rapidly as a proportion of the UK workforce. In the 12 years between 1964 and 1976, it has increased from 30 per cent to about 45–50 per cent; a growth which has been due to the restructuring and reorganization throughout the post war boom of the British economy, not only in relation to the further development of the financial sector, and increased state intervention in both production and reproduction, but also to changes in production. The takeovers and mergers of this period have resulted in larger plants and sites with a need for planning both individual factories and overall corporate strategy – requiring, thus, increasing numbers of clerical workers. Also, the spreading of Taylorism and moves towards the real subordination of labour in the production process itself, requires first of all, capital's acquisition of knowledge about all the human actions within the labour process. *Only then can machinery be designed to pace or replace those human motions.*

This need for knowledge and, hence, control, has resulted in more and more workers being involved in the acquisition, storage, tranformation and presentation of this information for capital, with a declining proportion involved at the actual point of production. Whereas, in 1949, only 17.9 per cent of the workforce in manufacturing consisted of clerical workers, by 1976, this proportion had increased to 30 per cent. So that now, half the operating costs of all US corporations is expended on running offices – 80 per cent of this figure being spent on clerical wages.

Although attempts were made in the 1910s and 20s to increase productivity in the clerical sector, this was achieved primarily through office reorganization and fragmentation of tasks, and to a lesser degree by technological innovation, i.e. the use of adding machines and dictaphones (and in the 1950s the computer). While Lockwood could write in 1958 that:

> Mechanization, though comparable in its most advanced effects to factory mechanization is, on the whole, a factor affecting the social relations of office work to a much smaller extent than is often imagined.[34]

and with this statement, effectively dismiss Klingender's earlier assessment (1935) that it is the process of mechanization 'which completes the technical proletarianization of clerical labour',[35] he could not foresee the development of a technology which could effectively and very radically transform those very social relations of office work which preclude its comparability with factory work.

Overall increases in productivity in the blue collar sector have not been paralleled by similar increases in that of office work; whilst the former has risen by 200 per cent in the last decade, the latter has only increased by 4 per cent. In part, this is attributable to the fact that the largest single category within it, secretarial workers (of whom there are about a million, and whose numbers have recently grown rapidly) have been working with the same type of machine for the last 100 years – the typewriter.

[...]

Militancy at the Typewriter

As we have already described, both the technology of the typewriter and the organization of the office have allowed women the space to develop specifically 'feminine' forms of resistance. However, not only are the patriarchal relations of control being resisted, but they are also beginning to be directly attacked by women themselves.

Throughout the last decade, the women's movement has attacked patriarchal capitalism in its many forms. Women have criticized and challenged not only the categorisation of paid work into men's jobs and women's jobs, but have also struggled against sexism generally. In the office the direct challenge to patriarchal control has taken various forms – from a secretarial worker no longer being prepared to service her boss to the same degree as before (for example, not making her boss coffee) to some typists refusing to do anything other than type. [...]

A lot of these women would not see themselves as part of the women's movement. However in spite of the attempt by the media to undermine the women's movement by ridicule, they have begun to express their dissatisfaction with sexist hierarchies. There is a sense in which ideas of women's equality have now seeped into the common consciousness of many women who are consciously refusing to comply with expected modes of behaviour.

This, in turn, has been a factor in the unionization of the white collar sector, of whom obviously a large proportion are clerical and administrative workers. A recent publication gives the following figures – ASTMS has over 440,000 members, APEX 150,000, TASS 178,000, NUPE 117,000, ACTSS (TGWU white collar sector) 122,000 with, in the public sector, the Civil Service unions having 530,000 members and NALGO 709,000.[36] This sector as a whole has begun to show levels of militancy especially (of particular relevance) the Civil Service 1979 dispute and more recently the strike of the clerks in the Magistrates Courts – workers, who a few years ago would themselves have been surprised at the thought of engaging in such militant activity. In the winter of 1978–79 typists working for the London Borough of Camden struck for two months in order to pursue their demand for upgrading. This growing resistance sporadically breaking out into militancy has contributed to increased office costs at the same time as threatening management's control.

Manna from the Multinationals – Microelectronics

The present possibility for the transformation of patriarchal relations of control by the automation of the office rests on the development of microelectronics. In the 1950's and 60's, the development of the transistor meant that computers could be made smaller and more reliable and that the labour costs of their production could be reduced. Manufacturers consciously sought out new markets for their computers in addition to scientific establishments – i.e. businesses and state departments. Microelectronics, initially developed for the USA Defense Department, consist basically of a chip of silicon on which complex electronic circuits have been etched, and drastically reduces the labour costs in the production of the central processing unit and memory of the computer. Now computers are more flexible and reliable, they are smaller, and importantly much cheaper than ever before. In this period of high inflation, the cost of computing power has fallen more than a thousand fold over the last few years. Chip production is capital intensive. For such mass production to be profitable new markets for microelectronics must be found. The earliest markets were the application of microelectronic technology to already existing consumer products, for example, digital watches and cash registers. Markets for capital goods with computers as the control unit are now following – and the office is the prime target.

> Two years ago, the Chairman (sic) of IBM told shareholders that 'Office systems is *the single biggest business opportunity* facing the corporation'. The rationale for this is simple but compelling. Some 40 per cent of the workforce in both the USA and Europe work in offices. Yet the average capital investment in office equipment is only some £2000 compared with the £10,000 behind each worker in manufacturing. Multiply the office work force by that investment gap and a figure, for the UK alone, of some £100,000,000,000,000 emerges.[37]

Mackintosh Consultants have estimated that in 1983 the European market for word processors alone will be approximately £430 million after an annual growth of 27 per cent, whilst for office computers the market is expected to be more than £1,500 billion after growing at a rate of 49 per cent per year.[38]

Until now office equipment for 'information workers' has consisted of typewriters, traditional dictation machines, copiers/printers and filing cabinets. However the efficient office of the not too distant future could contain word processor systems linked via computers and advanced telecommunications systems; telex, data and text processing systems will be linked together. The office is intended to be the repository of a convergence of the hitherto separate technologies of computing, traditional office systems and telecomms. Already the existing manufacturers of these separate technologies are diversifying and competing in the office system market.

Although in this paper we are specifically concerned with the impact of word processors on secretarial workers, we must stress that *microelectronically based 'office systems', of which word processors are only a component, are aimed at increasing the productivity of all office workers – clerical workers, professionals and especially management.*

Pointing out that the cost of secretarial workers accounts for a relatively low proportion of the office wage bill (estimates vary between 10 per cent and 15 per cent), the manager of Business Strategy for the British state-funded NEXOS office systems supplier stated in 1979:

> To be of real value, 'office systems' development must focus on the effectiveness of the manager/professional. This will require a much more comprehensive technical solution than simple word processing – and customers are beginning to demand it now.[39]

[...]

Although a detailed analysis of this trend has yet to be undertaken it appears that the beginnings of a proletarianization of lower management is occurring. Parelleled to the breaking up of skilled jobs into simpler repetitive tasks and the growth of large units of production and state bureaucracies has been the growth and stratification of management. Many of the lower ranks, particularly those in the public sector are already in trade unions.

> ... so many studies (in the quality of working life) and other indicators, like managerial membership of trade unions, indicate a growing disenchantment with many managers failing to find in their work those motivations that we are so busily trying to inject into the lives of those engaged in demonstrably prosaic work.[40]

We have already mentioned that patriarchal relations in the office are not only a form of management control over subordinate women workers but are a form of control over lower management. If our overall thesis is valid, transformation of such relations of control contributes to the need for different techniques for controlling lower management – 'office systems'. This could lead to a possible contradiction. *The Financial Times* of 23 October, 1978 had this to say:

> The computer in the office is going to close off employment opportunities

by a massive improvement in office production capability. And it will not do it without stress and strain, some of which is as yet unimagined. A girl (sic) may now be given the opportunity to handle four or five drafts in a day and still get it out before working hours are over. But are the people who are preparing the drafts capable of handling that number of drafts?

One or two executives have already discovered that, whilst they approve of increased productivity below them, they are not quite so sure when it reaches their own level.

However, the 'foot in the door' towards the electronic office are word processors with the initial impact on clerical and secretarial workers.

Word Processing – An Attempt Towards the Real Subordination of Typists

Word processing and auxiliary office equipment are intended to increase productivity by an average of 100 per cent by radically changing the relation between capital and labour due to the conscious application of science and technology to office work. Capital is attempting to gain greater control over the relationship between labour and the means of production leading to de-skilling and the subsequent cheapening of labour.

A reading of any document by manufacturers of the new office equipment regarding the possible installation of word processors will show that the primary initial task of management is a detailed study, of amongst other things, type of document produced, work input and output i.e. productivity rates. The introduction of automatic equipment into offices will mean that such information about typists' productivity can be readily available; the attempt to get greater control over typists will be incorporated into the machinery owned by capital.

This reading of the adverts and sales brochures from word processor manufacturers clearly shows the basis on which such equipment is sold and bought. Obviously, though, these tend to over-estimate the equipment's capabilities and underestimate workers' ability to struggle against it. Already word processor operators have discovered that coffee 'accidentally' spilt into the machine can stop it functioning – and if the word processor has 'key pressing monitoring devices' incorporated in them, that by keeping on pressing the backspace key, the operator can stop working and talk without it being apparent. However as we have already stated this is a defensive response which is only effective for some of the time – snatching a few minutes for herself.

As usually occurs whenever new equipment is introduced into workplaces, a new terminology describes the new job content and the new worker. Those who work with word processors are no longer referred to as typists but as word processor operators. With word processors the tasks of a typist are fragmented – no longer does she press keys to print information onto paper rather she simply presses keys to feed information into a memory. The printing is done separately. Thus a word processor operator (WPO) 'keyboards' or 'keys in'. The separation of keyboarding and printing enables productivity to be increased as follows. It has been estimated that a typist will spot about 87 per cent of errors within typing the next six characters and so, to reduce the time taken for corrections, when the WPO makes an error, all she has to do is backspace, key in the correct word over the error and it is the correct word which is retained in the memory. Only when the WPO has checked that all the correct words have been keyboarded in will the text be printed.

Many documents go through several drafts before being finalized and the use of word processors eliminates the need for each draft to be completely retyped. Since the original is stored in the memory and word processors have editing facilities, any deletion or addition to the original draft can just be keyboarded in. Standard sentences, paragraphs, letters, address lists *etc.* can also be stored, recalled and displayed on the VDU by keying in their reference number. They can then be automatically printed. This is likely to lead to a trend towards greater standardization of documents. As standard sentences, paragraphs *etc.* are stored on the machines, output from document authors will have to be standardized if the equipment is to be utilized to the full. This is already happening in the USA where journalists have to produce their copy using specified sentences to describe particular events.

The memory is usually floppy discs, which as the name implies are like flexible gramophone records. A floppy disc can store about the equivalent of 100–120 A4 pages of information. Not only does this have implications for the amount of work for filing clerks but also eliminates an auxiliary skill of a secretary. (A secretary told us that one way of becoming 'indispensible' is to organize the filing so that only she could understand it.)

This fragmentation of operations augments productivity even further by the possibility of one printer being fed from several workstations via a mini computer. The printing is done at a much faster rate than the most efficient typist who can manage speeds of 70 w.p.m., or using conventional automatic memory typewriters can manage about 150 w.p.m. The new Siemens laser printer marketed by ICL 'prints' at 2000 *lines* per minute. As WANG, a manufacturer of word processors, states:

> Input and output at the same time … simultaneous input and output
> allows your typist to continue creating (sic) or editing work in the work
> station while the printer automatically plays out completed documents.
> Your typists become more efficient and productive.

This enables cheaper labour to be employed. When Bradford Metropolitan Council fragmented the production of printed documents in its Jacob Well office, by having a separate print room from the word processing work stations, they were able to employ a school leaver as print controller at a lower rate than they had previously paid a shorthand typist.

The move to word processing removes the need for skill in producing neat, well set out work. The machines can indent, centre, justify margins and tabulate, which, together with touch typing are crucial components of any typing course and basic requirements for RSA typing examinations. In removing the need for these skills, word processing effectively removes an area of control which the typist has over both her work and her typewriter; through choosing how to lay out a particular document, the typist is instructing the machine on what to do, her skill and initiative are guiding the machine through its various functions. With word processors control is limited to pressing the appropriate button and letting the machine do the rest.

Since documents are stored in the memory, the WPO can theoretically work continuously in front of the machine without ever needing to leave her seat, for example, to look up documents in a file. Word processors will, according to Monotype who manufacture them, increase operator efficiency thus:

> Costly and energy wasting procedures are abolished: the walking, waiting, filing, correcting updating and supervision go, and are replaced by a system that does what you want it to do.
>
> From a secretarial station all work is productive and done on the spot. No waiting, walking and wondering.

An important part of a word processor is access to computing power other than the memory. In shared logic work stations, a control unit (sic) can continuously feed in dictated work to the word processor operator in an attempt to obtain continuous output. With conventional centralized dictation, the author dictates into a specially wired conventional telephone and records onto a machine in the typing centre. However, this is superseded by the direct link method. Here a telephone is still used, but the dictation goes via the control unit which examines each word processor operator's backlog of work and keying in speeds before deciding to which operator the work should be allocated.

Apart from these aspects of monitoring and control, some manufacturers offer 'additional' explicit supervision and control devices. WANG states:

> Monitor your workload: And finally a built in reporting system helps you monitor your work flow. It automatically gives the author and typist's name, the document's number the date and time of origin of last revision, the required editing time, and the length of the document.

Dictaphone have recently introduced two systems designed to measure performance of word processor centres. One is called 'Timemaster' and the other 'Mastermind' since, presumably, as a spokesperson for the company said:

> they give all that a good supervisor would know – but now electronically. You couldn't fail to get work in on time.

Proponents of word processing put foreward the two common myths about automation – that word processors will free secretarial workers from boring and soul-destroying jobs and allow them to engage in more interesting work. However in light of the above, word processing could lead to work becoming more boring, intense and alienated.

As we have pointed out previously, conventional notions of skill and deskilling cannot be applied to a predominately female labour process because the very fact of a job being labelled 'women's work' brings in enormous ideological determinations which enable its skill content 'somehow' to be devalued. Apart from high speeds in shorthand and typing, secretarial workers require special qualities which can only be learnt through an apprenticeship in womanhood and in this sense the notion of 'deskilling' takes on a different tone.

Despite this, we would argue that typing is a 'skill' which together with shorthand takes time and training to perfect. The need for shorthand – the one area where personal contact with the boss could be ensured even for those working in a pool – has been gradually eroded since the first dictaphone machines at the beginning of the century. Its replacement by that most de-humanizing task, audio-typing, has been first on the check-list of most efficiency minded managements, anxious to save the extra wasted time which dictation involves. Now with word processing, the ability to type is becoming eroded, and recent developments in voice printing, suggests that the need for operators themselves will be reduced. Indeed this ties in with our earlier comment on how office systems are an attempt to increase manager/professional productivity. Reporting on a study to 'investigate require-ments for an integrated office communications system and to provide a framework for developing a prototype of such a system' a recent IBM systems Journal stated:

> The often-asked question, 'Will the principal (author) use an electronic work station which involves a keyboard?' was addressed. We found the answer to be affirmative if individual benefits are perceived by the in-dividual.[41]

Apologists for word processing argue against any notions of deskilling, but suggest instead that new skills are being created. Doris Lenson, consultant to the Automobile Association which has had automatic typewriters for almost 15 years, in a paper presented at a conference held in October, 1978 by Information Studies Ltd., suggests that:

> as the operation of word processing machines requires special training, an extra skill is acquired – the staff selected must have logical and sometimes imaginative minds.

The logic and imagination is presumably required to understand the 'screen prompts' and to recognize which key to press. Whereas typing and shorthand take some time to perfect and work up really high speeds, the word processor requires the minimum of familiarity with a keyboard. A representative of UDS, a word processor manufacturer, informed us that to learn the whole complex of operations which the word processor can perform would take a qualified typist three to four days. An unqualified typist could learn the most basic procedures in half a day. Jean Manning, who supervises the typing centre at the Central Electricity Gener-ating Board in Bristol concludes in *System: A Journal for Word and Data Processing* May 1977:

> A less experienced typist is able to produce the same quality of work as a really skilled girl (sic) and almost as quickly.

A report on the effect of the introduction of new technology on clerical work by the Insurance Training Council and Training Agency in 1976 said of future recruitment:

> Many firms are rethinking their recruitment policy and are considering recruiting school-leavers with *lower* level educational qualifications but still with the desirable personal characterisics likely to produce accurate, dependable and stable employees. (emphasis added)

As for being freed to go on to do more interesting work, if we think back to the pyramidal nature of secretarial work, it becomes obvious that word processors will be part of the complete restructuring of this hierarchy. As the sub-division of the labour process continues with increased rationalization and the repetitive typing becomes allocated to the word processor operators located in their work stations, the gap between the few super secretaries at the top and those who were always in any case destined for the lower, routine jobs will become visible. Promotion will not become limited, but its limitations will become more manifest and the class nature of secretarial work more distinct.

The following description from an 'unofficial' report by Bradford NALGO Action Group (1977) on the introduction of word processing in Bradford Council is worth quoting in order to understand what secretarial workers' experience of word processors already is.

> The machines are in constant operation, and are programmed by the rate material comes in. The workers have one ten minute break in the morning and afternoon, and otherwise have no contact with other workers during office time. All new work comes in through a special anti-static glass box, and no non-section workers enter the room. The operator has almost no contact with the finished product . . . . The existing tenuous relationship between a typist and her work is finally broken altogether – there is no sense any longer in which it is her work.

Needless to say when the council tried to introduce word processors throughout, the typists who would be affected by this went on strike.

An additional feature of word processing is the changes it can mean in office hours. Because of pressure by management to get the maximum possible use out of them, there are moves in some firms to eliminate the dubious advantage of flexitime and move into shift work. That shift work is generally associated with deskilled work is also not simply a coincidence. The 'twilight shift' has existed for some time, for instance in mail order firms in Bradford, but the trend is likely to spread, particularly with the use of special GPO telephone lines which can transmit typed copy from one word processor to another and which is cheaper to use in the evenings. Logica have had an additional evening shift from 6 p.m. to 10 p.m. for about 18 months.

Associated with the move towards real subordination are new health and safety risks which, regarding word processors, are primarily linked to the VDU. Word processor operators are likely to suffer from some of the following if they operate the machine for any length of time – headaches, nausea, eyestrain, dizzyness *etc.*

Although we are not dealing with this aspect in any detail whatsoever, we wish to point out that the only research on the long term implications of working with VDU's was undertaken for the military and is therefore classified information. In spite of this, health and safety has been an area of trade union struggle around the introduction of word processors and VDU's with local branches blacking their introduction until certain requirements are met and trade unions at a national level putting forward recommendations for the maximum time spent per day in front of a VDU.

Although the initial concern of this section is the transformation of patriarchal relations of control by the move towards real subordination with the introduction of word processors into offices we wish to locate it in the wider political context of the present high unemployment level in Britain where, bearing in mind that two out of five waged women are clerical workers, we see it as a specific attack on women's waged employment.

As far as job loss is concerned, various estimates have been made. For instance, the Nora report by the French government calculated that modern computing technology in banking over the next ten years could reduce staff in this area by 30 per cent. Similar figures apply to the insurance industry. It also suggests, as far as the general office environment is concerned, that many of France's secretaries and typists could be replaced by word processing systems. Similarly, a recent estimate by Siemens, the large West German electrical manufacturer, suggests that by 1990, 40 per cent of present office work could be carried out by computerised equipment; the German Trade Unions translated this into figures and have calculated that this will mean a staggering loss of two million out of West Germany's five million secretarial and typing jobs. As far as Britain is concerned, ASTMS have forecast that 2.6 million of the wider category of 'information' workers could lose their jobs by 1985, whilst APEX has calculated that a quarter of a million secretarial jobs could be lost by 1982.[43]

[. . .]

Conclusion

We have tried to show in this paper that traditional, previously effective forms of control in the office which have their roots in patriarchy are, within the context of the present crisis in the accumulation process, becoming redundant. Microelectronically based equipment is seized by capitalists as a solution offering a new form of control which enables them to cheapen labour and intensify productivity.

We do not see word processors as being liberating for typists. Although they do eliminate boring retyping, other aspects of word processors could lead to more boring, more intense and more hazardous work. The continued existence of the tedious job of a typist is not due to the lack of automation until now but its very creation and continuation is due to the sexual division of labour incorporated into the capitalist mode of production.

The attempt to introduce word processors into offices represents a specific attack on the employment of women. Already there are over two million people unemployed in Britain if we include those whose employment depends upon direct state subsidies – TOPS, YOPS *etc.* and many married women who are ineligible for benefits and those who just don't register. In such a period, the resurgence of the ideology of a woman's place being in the home has already started. Lord Spens in a recent outburst in the House of Lords referred to the home as being women's rightful place to which they should return. And perhaps more politically significant is the recent statement on Radio Four by the Social Services Secretary, Patrick Jenkin, when, in a discussion about state provision of nurseries, he agreed that although waged women made a contribution to the British economy, in this period of high unemployment 'the balance between the national need [for women's directly productive work] and the need for them to look after their family is now shifting'.

[...]

Acknowledgements

This paper was initially written in December 1978 for discussion with the CSE Microelectronics Group. It has been expanded and re-written in the light of subsequent discussions and comments from many individuals, and especially the CSE Microelectronics Group and the *Capital and Class* editorial group. We would like to thank the CSE Microelectronics Group for providing the original impetus for this paper and encouragement to publish it. We are also indebted to both the CSE and the London Microelectronics Group for the wide ranging discussions on research and information presented by other people which has helped in our understanding of what we see as one of the crucial political problems facing the working class today.

Notes and References

1 ELLENSTEIN, Z. (1979) *Capitalist patriarchy and the case for socialist feminism* New York, Monthly Review Press, p. 28.
2 POLLART, A. (1979) in *Socialist Review* No. 13 July–August.
3 BRAVERMAN, H. (1974) *Labor and Monopoly Capital* New York, Monthly Review Press, p. 342.
4 BARNARD R.W. (1948) *A century of service: Prudential Assurance Company, 1848–1948* London (Times Publishing).
5 SILVERSTONE R. (1976) 'Office work for women: a historical review' in *Business History*, (January Vol. 19, Part I, p. 101).
6 LOCKWOOD D. (1958) *The blackcoated worker*, London, Allen and Unwin, p. 22.
7 *ibid.*, p. 29.
8 BENET M.K. (1972) *Secretary: An enquiry into the female ghetto*, London, Sidgwick and Jackson, p. 39.
9 SILVERSTONE, R. (1976) *op. cit.*, p. 105.
10 DAVIES, M. (1974) 'Woman's place is at the typewriter: the feminisation of the clerical labor force' in *Radical America* Vol. 8, No. 4, July–August, p. 9.
11 BENET, M.K. (1972) *op. cit.*, p. 39.
12 BARNARD, R.W. (1948) *op. cit.*, p. 31.
13 KLINGENDER, F.D. (1935) *The condition of clerical labour in Britain,* London, Martin Lawrence.

14 MARX, K. (1894) *Capital* London, Lawrence and Wishart (1974) Vol. III, pp. 300–1.

15 KLINGENDER, F.D. (1935) *op. cit.*, p. 22.

16 WILLIS, P. (1978) *Learning to labour: how working class kids get working class jobs*, Saxon House.

17 POULANTZAS, N. (1975) *Classes in contemporary capitalist society* London, New Left Books, p. 256.

18 *ibid.*

19 *ibid.*

20 BRAVERMAN, H. (1974) *op. cit.*

21 *ibid.*, p. 342.

22 Cited in SILVERSTONE, R. (1976) *op. cit.*, p. 108.

23 BENET, M.K. (1972) *op. cit.*

24 BOSTICCO, M. (1975) *How to be a top secretary* London, New English Library, p. 149.

25 *ibid.*, p. 9.

26 HARDWICK-SMITH, S. and ROWE, B. (1958) *The private secretary* London, Museum Press, forward.

27 LEWENHAK, S. (1977) *Women in the trade unions*, Ernest Benn Ltd. p. 94.

28 PURCELL, K. (1979) 'Militancy and Acquiescence amongst women workers' in BROWN, S. (Ed) *Fit work for women* London, Croom Helm, p. 128.

29 LOCKWOOD, D. (1958) *op. cit.*, p. 93.

30 Letter to *Honey* (1975) October, p. 85.

31 BRAVERMAN, H. (1974) *op. cit.*, p. 347.

32 Cf. BROWN, G. (1977) *Sabotage* (Spokesman).

33 For a detailed analysis of women's paid employment see BRUEGEL, I. (1979) *Women as a reserve army of labour: a note on recent British experience* Feminist Review, No. 3.

34 LOCKWOOD, D. (1958) *op. cit.*, p. 94.

35 KLINGENDER, F.D. (1935) *op. cit.*, p. 61.

36 JENKINS, C. and SHERMAN, B. (1979) *White Collar Unions: the rebellious salariat*, Routledge and Kegan Paul.

37 ELLIS, C.W.H. (1979) *Office systems and convergence*, Conf. Proc.

38 *Financial Times* (1979) 10 July.

39 ELLIS, C.W.H. (1979) *op. cit.*

40 COOPER, C. and TORRINGTON, D. (1979) 'Strategies for relieving stress at work' *Personnel Management* June.

41 ENGEL, G.H., GROPPUSO, J., LOWENSTEIN, R.A. and TRAUB, W.G. (1979) 'An office communications system' in *IBM Systems Journal*, Vol. 18, No. 3.

42 APEX Word Processing Working Party (March 1979) *Office technology: the trade union response.* ASTMS (1979) *Technological change and collective bargaining.* See also AUEW-TASS (1979) *Computer Technology and Employment*, (National Computing Centre).

15   The Class Significance of School Counter-Culture[1]

Paul Willis

The existence of anti-school cultures in schools with a working-class catchment area has been widely commented upon.[2] The raising of the school-leaving age has further dramatized and exposed this culture, often in the form of a 'new' crisis: disruption in the classroom. Teachers' unions are calling more and more vehemently for tougher action against 'violence' in the classroom, and for special provision for the 'unruly' minority. The 'reluctant fifth', difficult 'RSLA classes' and young, 'always in tears' (usually female) teachers, have become part of staffroom folklore.

The welter of comment and response, has, however, served to conceal certain crucial features of this culture: the profound significance it has for processes of job selection, and its relation to the wider working-class culture. In what follows I want to draw attention to these omissions. Concretely I want to make two suggestions. First, counter-school culture is part of the wider working-class culture of a region and ultimately of the nation, and, in particular, runs parallel to what we might call shop-floor culture. Second, the located anti-school culture provides powerful informal criteria and binding experiential processes which lead working-class lads to make the 'voluntary' choice to enter the factory, and so to help to reproduce both the existing class structure of employment and the 'culture of the shop floor' as a segment of the over-arching working-class culture. My argument is, then, that the stage of affiliation with the counter-school group carries much more significance than is usually acknowledged. I therefore go on to examine, in the latter part of this chapter, when, how and why this process occurs. I will conclude with some comments on the meaning and status of this general class culture, of which the school and factory variants are part.

[...]

My own research suggests that there is a direct relationship between the main features of working-class culture, as it is expressed in shop-floor culture, and school counter-culture. Both share broadly the same determinants: the common impulse is to develop strategies for dealing with boredom, blocked opportunities, alienation

Source: An abridged version of WILLIS, P. (1976) in HAMMERSLEY, M. and WOODS, P. (Eds) *The Process of Schooling* London, Routledge and Kegan Paul.

and lack of control. Of course the particular organization of each located culture has its own history and specificity, and worked-up institutional forms. The institution of the school, for instance, determines a particular uneven pattern of extension and suppression of common working-class themes. In one way a more protected environment than the shop floor, and without the hard logic and discipline of material production, the school is nevertheless a more directly face-to-face repressive agency in other ways. This encourages an emphasis on certain obvious forms of resistance specific to the school. In one sense this is simply a question of inverting the given rules – hence the terrain of school counter-culture: smoking, proscribed dress, truancy, cheek in class, vandalism and theft.

At any rate, the main cultural and organizational aspects of shop-floor culture (at least in the Midlands industrial conurbation where I did my research), and for the moment ignoring the range of historically and occupationally specific variants, bear a striking similarity to the main features of school counter-culture. [. . .]

The really central point about the working-class culture of the shop floor is that, despite harsh conditions and external direction, people do look for meaning and impose frameworks. They exercise their abilities and seek enjoyment in activity, even where most controlled by others. They do, paradoxically, thread through the dead experience of work a living culture which is far from a simple reflex of defeat. This is the same fundamental taking hold of an alienating situation as one finds in counter-school culture and its attempt to weave a tapestry of interest and diversion through the dry institutional text. These cultures are not simply foam paddings, rubber layers between human and unpleasantness. They are appropriations in their own right, exercises of skill, motions, activities applied towards particular ends.

More specifically, the central, locating theme of shop-floor culture – a form of masculine chauvinism arising from the raw experience of production – is reflected in the independence and toughness found in school counter-cultures. Here is a foundry-man talking at home about his work. In an inarticulate way, but for that perhaps all the more convincingly, he attests that elemental, essentially masculine, self-esteem in the doing of a hard job well – and to be known for it.

> I work in a foundry . . you know drop forging . . . do you know anything about it . . no . . . . well you have the factory know the factory down in Bethnall Street with the noise . . . you can hear it in the street . . . I work there on the big hammer . . . it's a six-tonner. I've worked there 24 years now. It's bloody noisy, but I've got used to it now . . and it's hot . . . . . . I don't get bored . . there's always new lines coming and you have to work out the best way of doing it . . You have to keep going . . . . and it's heavy work, the managers couldn't do it, there's not many strong enough to keep lifting the metal . . . I earn 80, 90 pounds a week, and that's not bad is it? . . . it ain't easy like . . you can definitely say that I earn every penny of it . . . you have to keep it up you know. And the managing director, I'd say 'hello' to him you know, and the progress manager . . . . they'll come around and I'll go . . 'all right' (thumbs up) . . . and they know you, you know . . . . a group standing there watching you . . . . working . .

I like that . . . . there's something there . . . watching *you* like . . working
. . . . like that . . you have to keep going to get enough out.

Here is Joey, this man's son, in his last year at school, and right at the heart of the
counter-culture:

> That's it, we've developed certain ways of talking, certain ways of acting
> and we developed disregards for Pakis, Jamaicans and all different . . , for
> all the scrubs and the fucking ear – 'oles and all that (. .) There's no chivalry
> or nothing, none of this cobblers you know, it's just . . if you'm gonna fight,
> it's savage fighting anyway, so you might as well go all the way and win
> it completely by having someone else help ya or by winning the dirtiest
> methods you can think of like poking his eyes out or biting his ear and
> things like this.

There's a clear continuity of attitudes here, and we must not think that this distinctive
complex of chauvinism, toughness and machismo is anachronistic or bound to
die away as the pattern of industrial work changes. Rough, unpleasant, demanding
jobs *do* still exist in considerable numbers. A whole range of jobs – from building
work, to furnace work to deep sea fishing – still involve a primitive confrontation
with exacting physical tasks. The basic attitudes and values developed in such jobs
are still very important in general working-class culture, and particularly the
culture of the shop floor. [. . .]

The other main, and this time emergent, theme of shop-floor culture – at least in
the manufacturing industries of the Midlands – is the massive attempt to gain a form
of control of the work process. 'Systematic soldiering' and 'gold bricking' have been
observed from the particular perspective of management from F.W. Taylor[3]
onwards, but there is evidence now of a much more concerted – though still
informal – attempt to gain control. It does happen, now, sometimes, that the men
themselves actually run production. Again this is effectively mirrored for us by
working-class kids' attempts, with the resources of their counter-culture, to take
control of classes, insert their own unofficial timetables, and control their own
routines and life spaces.

> *Joey*: (. .) of a Monday afternoon, we'd have nothing right? Nothing
> hardly relating to school work, Tuesday afternoon we have swimming and
> they stick you in a classroom for the rest of the afternoon, Wednesday
> afternoon you have games and there's only Thursday and Friday afternoon
> that you work, if you call that work. The last lesson Friday afternoon we
> used to go and doss, half of us wagged out o' lessons and the other half go
> into the classroom, sit down and just go to sleep, and the rest of us could
> join a class where all our mates are.
> *Will*: (. .) What we been doing, playing cards in this room 'cos we can
> lock the door.
> *PW*: Which room's this now?
> *Will*: Resources Centre, where we're making the frames (*a new stage for
> the deputy head*), s'posed to be.

PW: Oh! You're still making the frames?
Will: We should have had it finished, we just lie there on top of the frame, playing cards, or trying to get to sleep.
PW: What's the last time you've done some writing?
Will: When we done some writing?
Fuzz: Oh ah, last time was in careers, 'cos I writ 'yes' on a piece of paper, that broke me heart.
PW: Why did it break your heart?
Fuzz: I mean to write, 'cos I was going to try and go through the term without writing anything. 'Cos since we've cum back, I ain't dun nothing.
(*It was half-way through term.*)

Put this against the following account from the father of a boy who was in the same friendship group as the boys talking above. He is a factory hand on a track producing car engines, talking at his home.

Actually the foreman, the gaffer, don't run the place, the men run the place. See, I mean you get one of the chaps says, 'Allright, you'm on so and so today'. You can't argue with him. The gaffer don't give you the job, the men on the track give you the job, they swop each other about, tek it in turns. Ah, but I mean the job's done. If the gaffer had gid you the job you would ... They tried to do it, one morning, gid a chap a job you know, but he'd been on it, you know, I think he'd been on all week, and they just downed tools. (....) There's four hard jobs on the track and there's dozens that's, .. you know, a child of five could do it, quite honestly, but everybody has their turn. That's organized by the men.

Of course there is the obvious difference that the school informal organization is devoted to doing nothing, while in the factory culture, at least, 'the job's done'. But the degree of opposition to official authority *in each case* should not be minimized, and production managers in such shops were quite as worried as deputy heads about 'what things were coming to'. Furthermore, both these attempts at control rest on the basic and distinctive unit of the informal group. This is the fundamental unit of resistance in both cultures, which locates and makes possible all its other elements. It is the zone where 'creative' attempts to develop and extend an informal culture are made, and where strategies for westing control of symbolic and real space from official authority are generated and disseminated. It is the massive presence of this informal organization which most decisively marks off shop-floor culture from middle-class cultures of work, and the 'lads'' school culture from that of the 'ear-'oles' (the name used by the 'lads' of my research to designate those who conformed to the school's official culture).

The solidarity, and sense of being 'in the group', is the basis for the final major characteristic of shop-floor culture that I want to describe here. This is the distinctive form of language, and the highly developed humour of the shop floor. Up to half the verbal exchanges are not serious or about work activities. They are jokes, or 'piss-takes', or 'kiddings' or 'wind-ups'. There is a real skill in being able to use this language with fluency: to identify the points where you are being 'kidded' and to have appropriate response in order to avoid further baiting.

This badinage is necessarily difficult to record on tape or represent, but the highly distinctive ambience it gives to shop floor exchanges is widely recognized by those involved, and to some extent re-created in their accounts of it. This is a foundry-worker talking at home about the atmosphere in his shop:

> Oh, there's all sorts, millions of them (*jokes*). 'Want to hear what he said about you', and he never said a thing, you know. Course you know the language, at the work like. 'What you been saying, about me?'; 'I said nothing', 'Oh you're a bloody liar', and all this.

Associated with this concrete and expressive verbal humour is a developed physical humour; essentially the practical joke. These jokes are vigorous, sharp, sometimes cruel, and often hinge on prime tenets of the culture such as disruption of production or subversion of the bosses' authority and status. Here is the same man:

> They er'm play jokes on you, blokes knocking the clamps off the boxes, they put paste on the bottom of his hammer you know soft little thing, puts his hammer down, picks it up, gets a handful of paste, you know, all this. So he comes up and gets a syringe and throws it in the big bucket of paste, and it's about that deep, and it goes right to the bottom, you have to put your hand in and get it out (. . . .) This is a filthy trick, but they do it. (. .)
> They asked, the gaffers asked – to make the tea. Well it's fifteen years he's been there and they say 'go and make the teas'. He gus up the toilet, he wets in the tea pot, then makes the tea. I mean, you know, this is the truth this is you know. He says, you know, 'I'll piss in it if I mek it, if they've asked me to mek it'. (. . . .) so he goes up, wees in the pot, then he puts the tea bag, then he puts the hot water in. (. . . .) – was bad the next morning, one of the gaffers, 'My stomach isn't half upset this morning'. He told them after and they called him for everything, 'you ain't makin' our tea no more', he says. 'I know I ain't not now'.

This atmosphere of rough humour and horseplay is instantly recognizable among the 'lads' in working-class schools, and obviously missing from the more hesitant 'polite' exchanges amongst the 'ear-'oles'. The ethnography of school cultures is full of similar – virtually interchangeable – incidents. There is the same felt desire to brighten grey prospects with a 'larf'. Certainly for the group of 'lads' who were the focus of my 'main' case study, reliance on the group, verbal humour and physical trickery, was the continuous stuff of their informal relations.

> *Joey*: You know you have to come to school today, if you're feeling bad, your mate'll soon cheer yer up like, 'cos you couldn't go without ten minutes in this school, without having a laugh at something or other.
> *PW*: Are your mates a really big important thing at school now?
> – Yeah

– Yeah

– Yeah

Joey: They're about the best thing actually.

Spanksey: You like to come to school, just to skive, 'cos you get bored at home. You'd rather come here and sit in the Youth Wing or summat.

Joey: (..) You'm always looking out on somebody (*when skiving*) and you've always got something to talk about, .. something.

PW: So what stops you being bored?

Joey: Talking, we could talk for ever, when we get together, it's talk, talk, talk.

There is no space to pursue the point any further, but in more detailed ways, from theft, vandalism and sabotage to girlie books under the tool-bench or desk, it is apparent that shop-floor culture and school oppositional culture have a great deal in common.

The parallelism of these cultures suggests, of course, that they should both be thought of as aspects of the larger working-class culture, though a fuller account would obviously further differentiate regional, occupational and institutional variations. The fundamental point here is to stress that anti-school culture should be seen in the context of this larger pattern, rather than in simple institutional terms. This wider connection has important and unexamined implications for the school's management of the 'disruptive' minority. Put at its most obvious, strategies conceived at the institutional level will not overcome problems arising from a profound class-cultural level. In fact the concerned teacher may be effectively boxed in, since the undoubted level of institutional determinancy – which I am not denying – may well block those strategies which do take into account the wider working-class culture. I mean that the teacher who tries to use working-class themes or styles may be rejected because he's a teacher: 'there's nothing worse than a teacher trying to be too friendly', and that a teacher who innovates organizationally – destreaming, mixed ability groupings, etc. – can never prevent the emergence of oppositional working-class themes *in one form or another*. It is the peculiarly intractable nature of this double determinacy which makes this form of working-class culture present itself as a 'crisis'. It shows up in high relief some of the unintended consequences and contradictions inherent in the state's ever-expanding attempts to make inroads into located working-class culture.

I do not wish, here, to go into the complex questions concerning what makes working-class culture – in all its variety and sectionalism – what it is. Nor – having, I hope, established the similarity between shop-floor and anti-school culture – do I want to claim any simple causation between them. My aims are more limited; my immediate text is that of job choice among working-class lads. What I want to argue about the parallelism I have described is that it accomplishes – in practice – a continuity between the two cultures, between work and school, in terms of the experiential passage of the working-class individual and his group. Processes within the school culture generate unofficial and deeply influential criteria which guide kids to similar, though expanded, situations: i.e. the shop floor. These unofficial criteria make a much more compelling case for particular job choices than does any amount of formal guidance.

Before looking at these located criteria, though, let us look at the manner in which the counter-school culture blocks, or reinterprets, the formal information concerning work with which it is saturated. All official communications about careers and work are importantly filtered through the group. By and large what might be termed as the *denoted*[4] messages from teachers and careers officers are most heavily filtered. This is the manifest content of particular communications concerning either the practical details of specific jobs or general principles about the best form of approach to work. Unless an individual has already decided to do a certain specific job, information about it is simply not taken in. It is certainly not true that new information is fed into a rational grid system which matches job profile with ability profile, or lifestyle/with/job/ambition profile. If things are remembered, they are picked up by some highly selective living principle of the counter-cultural school group. [...]

In terms of actual 'job choice', it is the 'lads'' culture and not the official careers material which provides the most located and deeply influential guides for the future. For the individual's affiliation with the non-conformist group carries with it a whole range of changes in his attitudes and perspectives and these changes also supply over time a more or less consistent view of what sorts of people he wants to end up working with, and what sort of situation is going to allow the fullest expression for his developing cultural skills. The located 'lads'' culture supplies a set of 'unofficial' criteria by which to judge not individual jobs or the intrinsic joys of particular kinds of work – indeed it is already assumed that all work is more or less hard and unrewarding – but generally *what kind* of working situation is going to be most relevant to the individual. It will have to be work where he can be open about his desires, his sexual feelings, his liking for 'booze' and his aim to 'skive off' as much as is reasonably possible. It will have to be a place where people can be trusted and will not 'creep off' to tell the boss about 'foreigners' or 'nicking stuff' – precisely where there were the fewest 'ear-'oles'. Indeed it would have to be work where there was a boss, a 'them and us', which always carried with it the danger of treacherous intermediaries. The experience of the division 'ear-'ole'/'lads' in school is one of the most basic preparations for the still ubiquitous feeling in the working class proper that there is a 'them' and an 'us'. The 'us' is felt to be relatively weaker in power terms, but also somehow more approachable, social, and, in the end, more human. One of the really crucial things about the 'us' which the 'lads' wanted to be part of was that they were in work where the self could be separated from the work task, and value given to people for things other than their work performance – the celebration of those independent qualities which precisely the 'ear-'oles' did not have. Generally, the future work situation would have to be one where people were not 'cissies' and could handle themselves, where 'pen-pushing' is looked down on in favour of really 'doing things'. It would have to be a situation where you could speak up for yourself, and where you would not be expected to be subservient. The particular job would have to pay good money fairly quickly and offer the possibility of 'fiddles' and 'perks' to support already acquired smoking and drinking habits. Work would have to be a place, most basically, where people were 'all right' and with whom a general culture identity could be shared. It is this human face of work, much more than its intrinsic or technical nature, which confronts the individual as the crucial dimension of his future. In the end it is recognized that it is specifically the cultural diversion that makes any job bearable. Talking about the imminent prospect of work:

> *Will*: I'm just dreading the first day like. Y'know, who to pal up with, an er'm, who's the ear-'oles, who'll tell the gaffer.
> *Joey*: (..) you can always mek it enjoyable. It's only you what makes a job unpleasant, .. I mean if you're cleaning sewers out, you can have your moments like. Not every job's enjoyable, I should think. Nobody's got a job they like unless they're a comedian or something, but er'm .., no job's enjoyable 'cos of the fact that you've got to get up of a morning and go out when you could stop in bed. I think every job's got, has a degree of unpleasantness, but it's up to you to mek .. to push that unpleasantness aside and mek it as good and as pleasant as possible.

[...]

Altogether, in relation to the basic cultural ground-shift which is occurring, and the development of a comprehensive alternative view of what is expected from life, *particular* job choice does not matter too much to the 'lads'. Indeed we may see that, with respect to the criteria this located culture throws up, most manual and semi-skilled jobs *are* the same and it would be a waste of time to use the provided middle-class grids across them to find material differences. Considered, therefore, in just one quantum of time – the last months of school – individual job choice does indeed seem random and unenlightened by any rational techniques or end/means schemes. It is, however, confusing and mystifying to pose the entry of working-class youth into work as a matter of *particular* job choice – this is, in essence, a very middle-class construct. The criteria we have looked at, the opposition to other more conformist views of work, and the solidarity of the group process, all transpose the question of job choice on to another plane: these lads are not choosing careers or particular jobs, they are committing themselves to a future of generalized labour. Even if it's not explicitly verbalized, from the way many of the kids actually get jobs and their calm expectation that their jobs will change a lot, they do not basically make much differentiation between jobs – *it's all labour*. [...]

Shop-floor culture has, as we have seen, an objective dimension which gives it a certain strength and power. Now this quality chimes – unexpectedly for some – with the criteria for acceptable work already thrown up by the counter-school culture. The young adult, therefore, impelled towards the shop floor, shares much more than he knows with his own future. When the lad reaches the factory there is no shock, only recognition. He is likely to have had experience anyway of work through part-time jobs, and he is immediately familiar with many of the shop-floor practices: defeating boredom, time-wasting, heavy and physical humour, petty theft, 'fiddling', 'handling yourself'.

There is a further, perhaps less obvious, way in which the working-class boy who is from the 'lads' is drawn in to the factory and confirmed in his choice. This is in the likely response of his new employer to what he understands of the 'lads'' culture already generated at school. The reverse side of the 'them' and 'us' attitude of the 'lads' is an acceptance by them of prior authority relations. Although directly and apparently geared to make some cultural interest and capital out of an unpleasant situation, it also accomplishes a recognition of, and an accommodation to, the facts of power and hierarchy. In the moment of the establishment of a cultural opposition is the yielding of a hope for direct, or quasi-political, challenge. The 'them' and 'us' philosophy is simultaneously a rescue and confirmation of the direct, the human and the social, and a giving up – at any conscious level – of claims to control the under-workings of these things: the real power relationships. This fact is of central importance in understanding the peculiar density and richness, as well as the limited-ness and frequent short-sightedness, of counter-school and shop-floor culture.

[...]

What is surprising in this general process of induction into the factory is the voluntary – almost celebratory – nature of the 'lads'' choice. The recognition of themselves in a future of industrial work is not a question of defeat, coercion or resignation. Nor is it simply the result of a managed, machiavellian process of social control. It is a question, at any rate in part and at least at this age, of an affiliation which is seen as joyous, creative and attractive. This fact is of enormous importance to us in understanding the true complexity of the reproduction of our social order: there is an element of 'self-damnation' in the acceptance of subordinate roles.

It is the partly autonomous functioning of the processes we have been considering which surprisingly accomplishes the most difficult task of state schooling: to 'direct' a proportion of kids to the unrewarding and basic tasks of industrial production. The word 'direct' is carefully chosen here since it need not have connotations of coercion, but it does make the unequivocality of the destination clear.

Pierre Bourdieu[5] argues that it is the exclusive 'cultural capital' – among other things, skill in the symbolic manipulation of language and figures – of the dominant groups in society which ensures the success of their offspring and so the reproduction of their class privilege. This is because educational advancement is controlled through the 'fair' meritocratic testing of precisely these skills which 'cultural capital' provides. We can make a bleak inversion of this hypothesis and suggest that it is the partly 'autonomous' counter-cultures of the working class at the site of the school which 'behind the back' of official policy ensure the continuity of its own under-privilege through the process we have just been considering. This process achieves the reproduction of under-privilege much more systematically than could any *directed* state policy. Of course state policy *says* it is doing the opposite. In this case, then, 'autonomous' working-class processes achieve the 'voluntary' reproduction of their own conditions *in spite of* state policy. We cannot unravel this complex knot here, save to observe that the widespread *belief* in the egalitarian-ism of state policy – not least among teachers themselves – may be an essential prerequisite for the continual functioning of those *actual* processes which are working to the opposite effect.[6]

We have looked at aspects of the process whereby some typical working-class kids come to regard their future in the factory as natural, inevitable, and even freely chosen. We have seen the pivotal importance of the 'lads'' counter-school culture in this process. Analytically, therefore, the most basic parameter in terms of so-called 'job choice' is affiliation or non-affiliation with this group, rather than the more or less random (correctly recorded in the major studies) influences – official and other – operating during the specific period of the actual passage from school to work. From my own work it is perfectly clear that this affiliation with the counter-school group can happen at any time from the second year onwards. I want to term this important process of affiliation *differentiation*: the separation of self from a pre-given system.[7]

Even where there had been some form of social division in the junior school – and there is plenty of evidence in 'ragging of teacher's pets', that there was, – in the first years of the secondary school everyone, it seems, is an 'ear-'ole'. Even the few of those who come to the school with a developed delinquent eye for the social landscape behave in a conformist way because of the lack of any visible support group. On 'coming out' as a 'lad':

> *Spike*: In the first year ... I could spot the 'ear-'oles'. I knew who the fucking high boys was, just looking at 'em walking around the playground – first day I was there (. . .) I was just, was just quiet for the first two weeks, I just kept meself to meself like, not knowing anybody, it took me two years to get in with a few mates. But, er . . . after that, the third years was a right fucking year, fights, having to go to teachers a lot.

Still, whether the process is resumed or starts from afresh in later years, what can we understand of its elements and nature? Basically I suggest that we should understand *differentiation* not as some quality or change within the individual but as a *change in the relationship* – at a greater or lesser speed – between staff and pupils. The founding relationship between teacher and pupil in our society, and one which can endure for the entire pupil career of some individuals, is of superior/inferior established in the axis of institutionally-defined qualities – knowledge, development, effort, probity – and on the destruction, suppression or suspension of 'private' or 'other' axes of knowledge and control. This is something of an ideal type, and has been hardened here for the sake of clarity. Certainly some reformists might argue that there is more now allowed under the school roof than a conventional model of this type. Be that as it may, in terms of how schools are *actually* run in working-class areas, and certainly the ones I saw, this axial definition gives us the most useful paradigm for understanding actual behaviour. In a very obvious sense, despite much vaunted curriculum reform, teachers control what is taught in classes – most certainly in the early school years. This model, and especially what it tells us about the attitude to privacy, becomes most valuable, however, when we come to look at face-to-face relationships – and remember that the school is the agency of face-to-face control *par excellence*. The stern look of the inquiring teacher; the relentless pursuit of 'the truth' set up as a value even above good behaviour; the common weapon of ridicule; the accepted arrangements for tears after a caning; the stereo-typical deputy head, boy poised, head lowered, finger jabbing the culprit; the unexpected head bearing down on a group in the corridor: 'Where's your tie, think you own this place?' are all tactics for exposing and destroying, or freezing the private. What successful conventional teaching cannot tolerate is private reservation. And in the early forms in virtually any school it's plain to see that most kids are reciprocating in this relationship. The eager first-form hands reaching and snapping to answer first are all seeking approval from an acknowledged superior in a very particular institutional form. And in the *individual* competition for approval, the possibility of private reservations becoming *shared* to form any oppositional definition of the situation is decisively controlled. The teacher is given formal control of his pupils by the state, but unless he can exert his social control through an *educational* paradigm, his position would become merely that of the prison guard.

For the members of the 'lads'' culture, of course, that is exactly how the teachers are seen and, for the teacher, the change in relationship this implies makes his situation increasingly untenable and one of survival rather than of education. *Differentiation* is where the teacher's superiority is denied because the mode in which that superiority is expressed is delegitimated – there are *other* ways of valuing oneself. This valuation comes from those 'private' areas, *now shared* and made visible, which were held in check before. These resources are mobilized to penetrate the nature of the teacher's previous authority and to develop forms of resistance. [. . .]

During this period of *differentiation* and after, one really decisive way of blocking the teacher's attempts to penetrate that which is private and informal is to be 'ignorant': to be uninterested in what the teacher has to offer. In a system where knowledge, and the educational paradigm, are used as a form of social control, 'ignorance' can be used in the same way as a barrier to control. The traditional notions of the causality of counter-school culture in low (measured) intelligence would, perhaps, be better reversed.

If the conventional paradigm of the teaching relationship is expressed powerfully in face-to-face situations, so is the differentiated resistance of the 'lads'. There is a particular overall style which communicates quite clearly to any teacher that 'this guy is not going to be pushed about'. It's a surly, disdainful look; a way of standing in the corridor as an obstruction though it could never be proved; a foot-dragging walk; an over-friendly hello; an attention on ties, fingers, shoes, books, anything rather than the inquiring eyes of the teacher which might penetrate too far.

For those involved the process of becoming a 'lad', is seen as a definite step towards maturity; it's 'coming out of your shell' or 'losing your timidity'. Diligence, deference, respect – these become things which can be read in quite another way.

> *PW*: Evans (*the careers master*) said you were all being very rude, (. .) you didn't have the politeness to listen to the speaker (*during a careers session*). He said why didn't you realize that you were just making the world very rude for when you grow up and God help you when you have kids 'cos they're going to be worse. What did you think of that?
> *Joey*: They wouldn't. They'll be outspoken. They wouldn't be submissive fucking twits. They'll be outspoken, upstanding sort of people.
> *Spanksey*: If any of my kids are like this, here, I'll be pleased.

[...]

Attempts to uncover the basic determinants of school counter-culture are fraught with difficulties. It is here that we skirt the deep waters of the determinacy of basic class cultures. Certainly we should be wary of simplified causal explanations. We can, however, suggest some of the possible factors which first break the individual from the mould of the conventional teacher/pupil paradigm – and once opposition is born it is amplified through group processes and staff reaction, and ultimately becomes self-justifying.

Though it is only rarely verbalized, and though it is finally expressed only at the level of action and cultural involvement, we can discern at the heart of the 'lads'' culture a fundamental assessment of the real conditions facing them. At some basic level they weigh up and compare the likely outcomes of the possibilities facing them. Now since many of the boys involved enjoy a considerable native intelligence, we cannot assume that the outcome of taking the 'conformist road' is reckoned to be academic failure and obloquy. There is, therefore, at some level, an estimation of how even the *successful* outcome of the 'conformist road' – CSE, perhaps GCE passes and an office job – measures up to the results of taking the 'non-conformist road' – independence, social collectivity, celebration of direct experience. In one way these are, of course, the obvious and immediate pay-offs, the 'instant' as against 'deferred' gratifications. It *seems to be* these interests, as such, which win the day. In a discussion on 'ear-'oles':

> *Joey*: (...) We wanna live for now, wanna live while we're young, want money to go out with, wanna go with women now, wanna have cars now, and er'm think about five, ten fifteen years' time when it comes, but other people, say people like the 'ear-'oles', they'm getting their exams, they'm working, having no social life, having no fun, and they're waiting for fifteen years' time when they're people, when they've got married and things like that. I think that's the difference. We are thinking about now, and having a larf now, and they're thinking about the future and the time that'll be best for 'em.

However, I want to argue that this is not the thick-headed animal choice for the nearest bale of hay but the result of a collective and individual cultural process of some maturity which takes a sensible wager on the meaning and pay-offs of *several* possibilities over time.[8] The possibility of reaching up to the highest strata of employment through the school system as it confronts them in the working-class area seems to be so remote as to be meaningless.[9] The route of *relative* success – an office job – through conformism is more possible. Such an achievement, however, is viewed in a very ambivalent light. The 'real world', they felt in their bones, was not quite like the school account of it. The institution might give you a few CSEs but what did that matter if you were an 'ear-'ole'. 'Immediate gratification' might be the basis for the development of highly necessary *long-term* skills. It does not pay to be too 'timid' in the strange, modern, industrial metropolis. In a discussion of 'ear-'oles':

Spike: Well, they've got no push, I tell yer. Jones, Percival, or . . . , they've got nothing inside 'em to get up there, (. .) If they've got nothing inside 'em – no spunk to give 'em the push – they've gotta have somebody behind 'em to push 'em all the time, and that's no good. You can't survive like that.

In a specifically *cultural* mode, then, I am suggesting that the 'lads' make some basic assessment of their situation: most obviously of where their *immediate* interests lie, but also of the distinction between 'how things really work' and how the state institution of the school says they work;[10] of how actually to survive in the society which *they know*. Their own analysis is, in many ways, superior to that given to them by their teachers, and it clearly exerts a determining pressure upon the extent of allegiance to the 'lads'.

[. . .]

The preceding has over-neatly divided the two categories of conformist and non-conformist. Any living school year is a complex mixture of individuals some-where between these two points. Furthermore, it is also true that staff do not necessarily rate *very* conformist behaviour highly. Their own institutional axis of approved values registers a certain kind of obedience as 'girlishness', so that they often see a watered-down 'lads'' influence in a positive light. Certainly, there is a very important zone between the 'ear-'oles' and the 'lads' not dealt with in this paper, where the staff are able to control a certain independence, with its roots in the 'lads'' culture by the exercise of curriculum areas and practices which include elements of both the conventional teaching paradigm and the oppositional culture. Sport is the obvious example here, and the following extract comes from a boy who is precisely on this middle ground.

If it was true I wouldn't mind admitting I was an ear-'ole, but I think I come somewhere in between . . I suppose in the first year I was a bit of an ear-'ole, you know, and, like more, I've got on with the sports teachers, because I enjoy me sport and I've progressed, because I don't mind having a joke. I don't take it too serious but sometimes I crack a joke about the teachers, you know to their face sort of thing, and they see the funny side of it all. They don't seem to have relationship like that with the ear-'oles. They teach 'em, nice, good lads. They seem to treat me as somebody to talk to like.

I have been stressing the 'cultural level' and the way in which 'semi-autonomous' processes at this level have profoundly important material outcomes. In order to do this I have necessarily emphasized the 'creative', independent and even joyous aspects of working-class culture as it is, anyway, for the 'lads' during the 'transition' – they may well have different views a few years *into* work. Certainly we need to posit the attractiveness of this culture to avoid simple determinist and economist views of what makes kids go to the factory, and to establish properly the level of the 'voluntarism' by which these lads go to a future that most would account an impoverished one. However, we should be careful not to lionize or romanticize our concept of working-class culture. School counter-culture and shop-floor culture are fundamentally limited and stop well short of providing any fully worked-out

future which is an alternative to the one they oppose. Indeed, in certain fundamental respects, we are presented with the contradiction that they actually – in
the end – *do the work of bringing about the future that others have mapped for them*. The
basic shortcoming of these cultures is that they have failed to convert *symbolic*
power into *real* power. The real power thus still creates the most basic channels
along which symbolic meanings run so that the symbolic power is used, in the end,
to close the circle the *actual* power has opened up, and so finally to *reinforce* the real
power relationships. The insistence of a human meaning which must justify its
situation, but which does not have the *material* force to change its situation, can
simply operate all too easily to legitimate, *experientially*, a situation which is fundamentally alien to it. To put it more concretely, the school counter-culture, for all
its independence, accomplishes the induction of manpower 'voluntarily' into the
productive process, and its mate, shop-floor culture, encourages an accommodation
to, rather than a rejection of, the *fundamental* social relations there.

Something in the spirit of betrayal implicit in this kind of powerful and intensive,
but formally limited, cultural organization is often caught in the semi-mythical,
apocryphal, cultural folk wisdom of the shop floor. The following is an explanation
of why young lads want to go on the shop floor given to me by a middle-aged worker
in an engineering factory.

> I was thirteen, like, an impressionable age, I s'pose, and this is something
> I've never forgotten. I was with my old man and we were at the zoo, and
> we saw a crowd up on the 'ill like, people were clapping, and all crowding
> around a gorilla's cage. We pushed to the front, like, Dad was more curious
> than me, like, he got right to the front, and there was this gorilla clapping
> and stamping, and lookin' around like, havin' a good time. All the people
> were clapping, egging him on like. Then he suddenly come to the front of
> the cage and spat a mouthful of water all over our old man. He'd been goin'
> to the back of the cage, like, gettin' a mouthful of water, comin' forward,
> clapping like, then spitting the water out all over 'em.
>
> My old man stood back really shocked like . . . then he went back in the
> crowd and waited for some other silly buggers to push forward. I didn't
> realize then, like, I was only a kid, what it meant like . . . , but I do now.
> We don't all grow up at once, see, that's life, we don't grow up at the same
> time, and when you've learnt it's too late. It's the same with these kids
> comin' in the factory, every time, they think it's great. 'Oh, what's this, I
> wanna be there', y'know what I mean. You'll never change it, it's the same
> with everything, comin' to work, getting married, anything – you name it.

There is a fairly clear theory here about what makes kids want to start work, as well
as a long-suffering, half-amused, typical working-class fatalism. There is also the
ironic dynamic of the morality play. What is most noticeable, however, is a
naturalized sense of timelessness: 'life's like that'. It's nobody's fault, nobody's
failure, that makes the gorilla spit, or shop-floor life kill with monotony, or the wife
nag to an early grave. It's simply the grim reality that humans have *always* faced.
The same principle of the treacherous appearance disguising – and leading to an

entrapment in – the real situation below is common to many aspects of working-class culture, and particularly in people's attitudes to the main transitions of life: birth, death, marriage, retirement, religious conversion. Even sometimes, it seems, death will turn out not to have been worth the trouble, though of course, the compelling unity of the drama means that the full ritual of the funeral cortege, plus cars bigger than ever were ridden in during life, must be gone through. We may suggest, however, that this final powerlessness before nature might be less of a universal law, and more a product of a specific, historic and continuing failure of working-class culture to achieve a basic modification of the conditions which brought it in to being. For all its symbolic resistance, the moving spirit of working-class culture till the present has been accommodation to a pre-given reality, rather than an active attempt to change it.

The reasons for this basic limitation stretch right back to the history of the world's first industrial proletariat and we cannot go into them now, but two contemporary factors might be mentioned specifically in relation to shop-floor culture. The trade union is the institutional extension of the culture of the workplace, the form in which culture and its meanings might have become more visible and the vehicle through which really concrete attempts have been made to transform *symbolic* into *real* control.

Trade unions, however, can be seen in their modern function merely as a mediation between shop-floor culture and the dominant managerial culture. Unionism negotiates the space between them and, in this negotiation, gives up much that is really central to the shop floor for what is often simply an accommodation in managerial interests. The nature of unionism and its organization is not, however, evenly textured. While the union bosses adopt a form of managerial culture and join the main industrial establishment,[11] the shop stewards and local organizers are still very much of the local culture. While trying to achieve union and organizational aims, they use specifically cultural forms of communication – spectacle, bluffs drama, jokes, sabotage, to mobilize the men.[12] The union structure, then, is a complex and varied institution which strikes different degrees of appeasement at its various levels. The power of shop-floor culture determines at least the *form* of union activity at plant level, but the higher administrative level has completely lost that detailed binding-in with the lived culture of the work-place which was the original guarantee of true representativeness. To put it another way, the unions have lost touch with, even betrayed, the real roots of working-class radicalism – the culture of the shop floor.

From the side of capital, one of the most important controls on the power of shop-floor culture to challenge its own conditions is the practice of management science and human relations. Under the banner of a 'neutral' humanization of the work process, it has been one of the most formidable techniques of social control ever developed. Essentially, human relations rest on a simple and obvious discovery: informal groups exist. This is precisely, of course, the area covered by the culture of the shop floor. Hard on the discovery of this territory came techniques for colonizing it. Techniques of 'employee-centred supervision', 'consultation', 'open door relations' can neutralize oppositional shop-floor culture on its own grounds by claiming the informal group for management ideology. This can unbend its springs of action. The sense of control given to the workers by these techniques is usually illusory – the basic structures of power remain – and yet the located, rich, potentially dominating culture of resistance is being destroyed.

Whatever the final balance-sheet drawn of strengths and weaknesses in shop-floor and working-class cultures,[13] the point of this article has been to stress the continuity of school culture with the wider class culture, and to draw attention to the deep-moving processes of regeneration among this class – some of the most important of which occur at the site of the school. These processes should not be mistaken, in the sociology of education, for mere institutional flux or localized disturbance. What is *not supposed* to go on in school may have more significance for us than what is *supposed* to go on in school.

Key

( )	background information
(inaudible)	part of sentence inaudible
/ /	description relating to collective activity
. . . .	long pause
. . .	pause
. .	short pause
. . ,	phrase incompleted
, . .	phrase completed, then pause
(. .)	phrase edited out
(. . .)	sentence edited out
(. . . .)	passage edited out
–	speaker interrupting or at same time as another speaker
- - -	transcription from a different discussion follows
—	speaker or name not identified

Notes and References

1 This article is based on the findings of a project at the Centre for Contemporary Cultural Studies between April 1973 and June 1975, financed by the SSRC, on the 'transition from school to work' of white working-class average to low ability boys in a Midlands industrial conurbation. It used intensive case-study methods and participant observation based on a number of schools and factories in this region. The 'main' case study was of a friendship group of twelve boys as they proceeded through their last four terms in a single-sex secondary modern school (it was twinned with a girls' school of the same name). The school was adapting itself organizationally – mixed ability groupings, time-table blocking, destreaming, etc. – in preparation for an expected redesignation as a comprehensive school which finally occurred only after the case study group had left. All of the parents of the lads were interviewed in depth, and a period of participant observation was spent with each of the lads at some point in the first six months of their respective work situations. The full results of this work will be available in *Learning to Labour: How Working-class Kids get Working-class Jobs*, (1977) Saxon House.

2 HARGREAVES, D. (1967) *Social Relations in a Secondary School* Routledge and Kegan Paul; SHIPMAN, M.D. (1968) *Sociology of the School* Longman; KING, R.A. (1973) *School Organization and Pupil Involvement*

Routledge and Kegan Paul; YOUNG, M.F.D. (1971) *Knowledge and Control* Collier-Macmillan; LACEY, C. (1970) *Hightown Grammar* Manchester University Press.

3 TAYLOR, F.W. (1947) *Scientific Management* Greenwood Press (1972).

4 For a fuller explanation of this concept and its relation to the 'connoted', see BARTHES, R. (1972) *Mythologies* Cape, (1967) *Elements of Semiology* Cape. Basically the difference between *denoted* and *connoted* refers to the difference between the direct and intended message of a particular communication and the direct, often unintended messages which are communicated at the same time through such procedures as association, generalized suggestion and use of available cultural stereotypes. I consider the important 'connoted' level of careers information elsewhere, see *Learning to Labour* (note 1).

5 BOURDIEU, P. and PASSERON, J.-P. (1971) *La Réproduction: Eléments pour une Théorie du Système d'Enseignement* Editions Minuit.

6 *Learning to Labour* deals more fully with these questions.

7 I argue elsewhere that this is a fundamental principle of working-class culture in general: 'Human experience and material production: the culture of the shopfloor' University of Birmingham, Centre for Contemporary Cultural Studies (mimeograph).

8 A mathematician could tabulate these possibilities in the form of a non-zero-sum-game and come up with very similar results.

9 And surely figures for university entrance amongst the working-class proper support them in this.

10 This bears an interesting relationship to the Marxist distinction between the 'state' and 'civil society', as does the 'lads' *cultural* concept of generalized labour to the notion general labour power, and as does the folk wisdom notion of false appearances (described later) bear a relationship to the Marxist notions of real relations/phenomenal forms. I develop the meaning of these 'coincidences' for a notion of advanced proletarian 'consciousness' in *Learning to Labour*.

11 LANE, A. (1974) *The Union Makes Us Strong: the British Working Class, its Politics and Trade Unionism* Arrow Books.

12 BEYNON, H. (1973) *Working for Ford* Allen Lane.

13 These questions are taken up more fully in *Learning to Labour*.

3
Education and National Development

16 Some Comparative Principles of Educational Stratification

Randall Collins

[...]

What determines the structures and contents of educational systems? A great deal of research in the sociology of education has taken an existing structure and its content for granted and concentrated on describing the social processes that occur within it. We are left with the question of why a given educational system exists – what conditions or forces produce it, sustain it, change it, or even abolish it. This theoretical question has often been answered from a functionalist or social-order perspective, which explains education by citing its contributions to the integration or productivity of society. Alternatively, education may be explained as a weapon in the struggles for domination that make up the phenomenon of stratification, whether considered from the viewpoint of Marxist theory, Weberian theory, or some mixture of the two.

The social-order approach, long accepted rather uncritically by many American social theorists, has a number of crucial weaknesses. In its most general formulation – that education socializes young people into the existing social order[1] – the theory is causally underdetermined. Its apparent truth is tautological. The proposition justifies *any* educational structure after the fact; it does not explain why one particular structure exists rather than some other, and therefore it is not subject to empirical validation. Some functionalist theorists have attempted to evade this difficulty by formulating more specific kinds of social demands that education fulfills: they assert either that education provides specific technical skills or that educational history follows an empirically demonstrable series of stages which evolve from primitive to advanced forms. The evidence usually cited for the first model is the rise over the last century in a given Western country's educational attendance; for the second model, the standard evidence is a set of educational-attendance figures for societies differing on a measure of economic productivity such as *per capita* gross national product.[2] The two specifications of functionalist theory often overlap, since many evolutionary models posit that schooling expands to meet the increasing need for

Source: An abridged version of COLLINS, R. (1977) *Harvard Educational Review* Vol. 47 No. 1, pp. 1–27.

technically skilled workers in industrial and especially in advanced or 'post-industrial' societies.

These efforts to salvage functionalist theory are not very successful, in my opinion. A close look at the evidence indicates that schooling does not supply specific technical skills, as functionalists contend.[3] Furthermore, as we shall see, historical patterns of educational development have been caused by factors other than increasing sophistication of industrial techniques.

These problems with the functionalist viewpoint lead me to believe that the most fruitful new developments in the attempt to explain the evolution and change of educational systems involve the stratification or domination approach. Like the functionalist approaches, the approaches to education which focus on domination have also varied. The Marxist approach has several versions. In the *Communist Manifesto*, Marx and Engels demanded free and universal access to education, a theme that has persisted in liberal as well as radical critiques of class differences in educational access and attainment. More sophisticated Marxist positions have emerged in recent years. Louis Althusser theorizes that education is a mechanism of domination that reproduces the unequal relationship of capitalist production.[4] Samuel Bowles and Herbert Gintis, arguing from a detailed empirical basis, stress education's role in producing a compliant labor force.[5] Standing at least one tenet of Marxism on its head, Alain Touraine interprets the class struggle of each historical period as a conflict between the ruling class, which controls productive skills, and the subordinate classes, which possess only labor power.[6] In this view, education is the basis of modern class domination, and struggles over educational access become the new focus of class struggle.

These Marxist approaches thus include a simple view of education as an unequally distributed good, a sophisticated view of education as a mechanism of domination, and a technocratic, evolutionary view of educationally derived skills as the prime basis of modern stratification. In my view, exponents of the domination approach are on the right track. Althusser's theory, however, shares functionalism's weakness of treating education as part of a given structure without showing, by empirical detail or historical comparison, the conditions for one sort of education rather than another. Bowles and Gintis provide the most specified and empirically bolstered theory, but their single causal dynamic, I shall argue, needs to be incorporated into a larger set of stratifying processes.

Although the Weberian approach rejects the Marxian emphasis on the causal preponderance of the economic structure and its historical evolution, the Weberian approach is, to a degree, a sophisticated version of the Marxian tradition. That is, Weberians do see economic interests based on property divisions as key bases of group organization, of intergroup conflict, and of historical change.[7] But, in contrast to Marx, Weber also pointed out that organizational resources, especially those of state and private bureaucracies, and cultural resources, above all religious traditions (but also secular ones such as education), can create and channel additional interest groups and conflicts.[8] Three lines of societal division – economic, organizational-political, and cultural (or in Weber's terms, 'class', 'party', and 'status') – mesh, so that economic classes or organizational politicians are stronger if they also possess the unity that comes from common cultural resources. But the three types of resources may be differentially distributed; strong ethnic, national, religious, or other cultural divisions can shape struggles for economic or political domination into patterns very different from those emerging along class lines. There are many kinds of stratification systems, and with the proper conceptual tools one may show the conditions for each.

My approach may be broadly characterized as Weberian. I see education as part of a multi-sided struggle among status communities for domination, for economic advantage, and for prestige. This approach allows the incorporation of a multiplicity of particular causes into an overall explanation, since it regards social structure as the result of the mobilization of a variety of resources and interest groups within a common arena. It even permits us to salvage the main intellectual contribution of the social-order tradition as it applies to education – Durkheim's theory of education as an agent of moral socialization and hence as the secular equivalent of religion in modern society.[9] Durkheim shows that participation in rituals – whether religious, political, or educational – promotes group identification, and that myths or symbols that are the focus of rituals become marks of membership in distinctive social groups and the referents of moral legitimacy. Put in this fashion, the Durkheimian theory points the way out of its own major weakness, its obliviousness to the stratifying effects of education and to the social struggles that surround it. For procedures inculcating social membership can be used by particular groups in a stratified society both to cement their own boundaries and to morally legitimate themselves in the eyes of others.[10] In its overgeneralized form, the Durkheimian theory simply asserts that education integrates entire, undifferentiated societies; in a more limited form, it is useful in showing education's contribution to integrating particular groups in situations of conflict and domination. This version of Durkheim fits naturally with the Weberian concept of stratification through status groups.

In what follows, I will attempt to show how the positive insights of the Durkheimian, Marxian, and even practical-skills approaches to education may contribute to a multidimensional Weberian model of stratification. I will also try to specify the types of educational systems of which each approach applies. My overall concern will be with the interaction of the economic, organizational, and cultural aspects of stratification; I shall attempt to show that in the long run the interaction of these spheres generates a market-like structure. Since this pattern is difficult to see except at a macroscopic level, a word about comparative historical evidence and method is in order.

The Uses of Comparative Evidence

The wealth of historical information about educational systems throughout the world in the last three thousand years or more is crucial for building a theory of the evolution and change of educational systems. Historical materials reveal a range of educational structures within which modern ones fall as special types, and this range of structures allows long-term processes to be put in a comparative context that permits causal generalizations about their dynamics.

We can take a comparative vantage point on education in half a dozen major civilizations (Chinese, Japanese, Indian, Islamic, Greco-Roman, and northern European), as well as in a number of tribal societies and early literate civilizations (such as the Egyptian and Mesopotamian). Our information is not equally good on each of these. There is good documentation on the structure, content, and clientele of education in the more centralized periods in China and Japan and in most of Mediterranean and European history since the rise of the Greek city-states. Much less research has been done on education in the Islamic world, and Indian educational history is a matter of somewhat distant inference. For the early literate civilizations, surviving documentation is limited to certain aspects of the education of scribes. Yet, overall, we are in a favorable position to establish general outlines of the main types of education and of the social processes that condition their existence as institutions. Analysing education from a general perspective helps us to move with greater confidence in historical areas where information is sketchy; patterns found in the whole body of evidence allow us to make sense of facts that otherwise might not rise to the level of hints.

The disadvantages of the comparative historical approach lie in researchers' distance from their subjects. In some areas even the main outlines are unclear, and almost everywhere detail is less available and sampling less controllable than in contemporary research. These problems are not insurmountable. An interest in structures directs us to the most often repeated aspects of human behavior; greater detail is not always necessary, and, in the absence of an overview, detail might well obscure the very structures that most call for explanation. Empirical evidence, whether contemporary or historical, detailed or summarized, is meaningful only in the context of theoretical propositions, and the value of these propositions can be established only by their capacity to order a whole range of materials. In this sense, the coherence among theoretical propositions and pieces of evidence is the test of any empirical method. By the same token, contemporary data do not lose their relevance; they are available to test further, or suggest extensions or alternatives to, the models arising from historical materials. Comparative historical analysis and contemporary research are not only complementary but are parts of the same enterprise.

I shall deal with the historical evidence under three main headings, each of which is associated with different demands for education – practical skills, status-group membership, and bureaucracy. In a conclusion I shall discuss how these types of educational demands combine and what their long-term dynamics are. The three categories may be thought of as corresponding in spirit with Weber's three bases of stratification – class, status, and party. Education has been part of struggles for practical economic skills, for cultural integration and prestige of particular associational groups, and for political control by and within formal organizations. I shall attempt to show that education for *practical skills* has largely involved informal procedures of work apprenticeship or family settings; such training has included formal credentials and ceremonial procedures only if a skilled group has had the political power to create a monopoly. Education for *status-group membership*, on the other hand, has been characterized by ceremonies dramatizing the unity of the educated group and its status *vis-à-vis* outsiders; the content of such education has been based upon cultural ideals, usually of an explicitly impractical sort, which reflect the ethos of the particular kind of status group involved. Education which has arisen as part of the process of *bureaucratization* has been shaped by efforts of élites to establish impersonal methods of control; the content of education here is irrelevant (and hence a variety of contents can be incorporated), but the structure of grades, ranks, degrees, and other formal credentials is of central importance as a means of discipline through hierarchy and specialization.

Finally, I shall examine the combinations of these demands that have emerged in particular historical periods. Because education can meet several demands simultaneously, we find some historical cases appearing under a number of headings. In the long run, these three kinds of demands for education may be seen as interacting with various sources of supply so as to constitute a market. Within this market we can note dynamic processes of inflation and deflation in the value of educational credentials. The long-range historical perspective on education leads us to a conceptualization of social stratification in which struggles for domination resemble an economic system not only in the material base but also in the cultural superstructure.

Practical Skills

The most common modern interpretation of the role of education is that it meets the demand for technical skills. Most contemporary evidence, however, contradicts this interpretation.[11] The content of most modern education is not very practical: educational attainment and grades are not much related to work performance, and most technical skills are learned on the job. Although work skills are more complex in *some* modern jobs than in most pre-industrial jobs, in many modern jobs they are not. Similar patterns appear in an overview of societies throughout history. [...]

Most practical education has involved students working as assistants to experienced workers.[12] Schools have sometimes been established in cases where the fundamental components of a practical skill could be learned by repetitious drill, such as in the acquisition of literacy and arithmetic skills. Usually such schooling has been unritualized and aimed at developing proficiency in the most efficient manner. This has been particularly true where dominant social classes have had a ritualized form of education and practical work has been relegated to unprivileged middle or lower classes. At times, though, powerful groups have incorporated practical education into a ritualized educational system. In the United States, for example, a formal structure surrounds elementary education, which alone among all levels of modern education bears a clear relationship to economic productivity.[13] The more elaborate organizational form, though, must be explained by factors other than the demand for practical skills, and to these social factors we now turn.

Status-Group Membership

Weber defined a status group as a community based on a common culture that provides a consciousness of membership (and hence of the boundaries with non-members) and, usually, some claim to prestige and legitimacy in the social order.[14] The key resource for the creation and maintenance of such communities, then, is a common culture. It should be borne in mind that Weber acknowledged the importance of both status-group and class stratification. Cultural resources frequently are stratified by economic class and are one of the weapons that classes can use to become powerfully organized. Cultural resources may also produce status-group divisions within classes or even across them, most notably in the forms of nationalism and ethnicity. In every case, we should remember that cultural resources are *means* and that groups organized on their basis may have a variety of *ends*: groups are not confined to struggling for prestige but may also try to use their culturally based organization to monopolize economic and power positions.

In historical perspective, education has been used more often for organizing status groups than for other purposes. Since the defining locus of status-group activity is leisure and consumption, status-group education has been sharply distinguished from practical education by the exclusion of materially productive skills. Because status groups have used a common culture as a mark of group membership, status-group education has taken the form of a club and has included much ceremony to demonstrate group solidarity and to publicly distinguish members from non-members. This club aspect characterized the activities of Chinese gentlemen who met for genteel conversation and poetry writing, as well as the periodic festivals put on for the Greek public by students, an elite sector of the population.[15]

Status-group education, then, has been ceremonial, aesthetic, and detached from practical activities. Its rituals rarely have dramatized rankings within the group; formal grades, competitive examinations, and degrees usually have been absent. Where competitions have occurred, as in the games and contests of the Greeks, they have shown the group as a whole and have emphasized the leisure of group members and spectators. The main distinctions have been between insiders and outsiders, not among members of the group. Frequently, there have been no formal attendance requirements, and the absence of formal degrees has reflected the fact that acquisition of the status group's culture is the object of education. In contrast with bureaucratic forms of education, the test has come in one's participation in the leisure activities of the status group, and the organization of the schools has been only incidental to that end.

Status-group education has predominated in societies controlled by aristocracies and other wealthy, leisured classes. [...] Well-organized status groups have not been confined to the upper classes, however. Under conditions of an expanding commercial economy and a political system with some dispersion of authority, less dominant classes have been able to claim greater prestige and to organize their communities more strongly by developing their own cultures. Such middle-class education (as among the 'merchant princes' of the Renaissance) sometimes has emulated the aesthetic culture of the upper class, but more usually it has taken a religious form. Examples of the latter were the academies of dissenting Protestant sects in England and Germany during the early Industrial Revolution.[16] We can even see this religious form in the educational movements of the English working class during the nineteenth century – the Sunday schools and Workingmen's Improvement Associations.[17] The workingmen's movement was oriented towards enhancing its discipline and used rituals to increase its social respectability. Education in the movement was used not to enhance work skills, but to make a claim for higher social status and even to assist in political organizing. Similarly, in Islam, the upper-class education provided by the *ulema* – the teacher-judges who interpreted the holy law and were patronized by the wealthy – was challenged by the mystical Sufi cults among metal workers, rug makers, and other urban artisans.[18] These Sufi secret societies, which combined craft apprenticeship with religious learning, were often vehicles for political opposition to the dominant classes, and in Baghdad in the eleventh century they discredited and destroyed the secular, aesthetic culture of the courts.

There have been times when a rebellious class, sensing a shift in the resources that underlie the organization of power, has gone to the extreme of developing a culture which is the opposite of the existing dominant culture. Thus the *philosophes* of eighteenth-century France mocked the traditional religious culture and the classical culture and promoted in their stead the ideal of a modern culture based on science and technology.[19] This cultural ideal appealed to a new status group, which included the emerging administrators of the state, especially members of the new technical branches of the military. This group provided the organizational basis for the revolution of 1789–1800. In England, the utilitarians espoused a similar ideal, although less successfully; their technocratic ideology, although embodied in a number of schools, failed to overthrow the traditional culture of the élite. Still, technocratic ideology has remained a unifying theme in middle-class and, to some extent, labor politics since the early 1800s.[20] This ideology has influenced Communist doctrine, as shown in the Soviet educational system's emphasis on technical education as the sole legitimate qualification for dominant positions.[21]

The contents of status-group education, then, vary predictably with the class situations of the groups that espouse them. We find aesthetic education, often combined with games and a reverence for tradition, in the status cultures of privileged upper classes. Moral respectability, usually in the form of religious doctrine, has been the cultural ideal of moderately aspiring middle classes or upper working classes. Rising classes in revolutionary periods have often taken practical and scientific education as their cultural ideal. Perhaps, though, we are generalizing about rebellious groups from a set of cases that is too historically limited; the more universal principle might be that revolutionary groups draw on whatever cultural form can be claimed to be both progressive and sharply distinct from traditional status claims.

Bureaucracy

Bureaucracy is a style of organization based on rules and regulations, written reports, and files of records. The use of such written materials tends to make control

appear abstract and generalized; bureaucracy makes possible the separation of the individual officeholder from the powers of the position. Bureaucracy helps to solve the crucial problem of rulers and other leaders of organizations: the tendency to lose control of subordinates because they appropriate their positions as their own and thus become independent of their chiefs. Other characteristics of bureaucracy also serve the purpose of control. The specialization of tasks limits the individual's powers and makes him or her more dependent on the co-operation of other specialists. The multiplication of ranks and the setting of regular career sequences with limited periods in each office keep officials concerned with their organizational futures and motivated toward higher offices. Formal examinations maximize the impersonality and competitiveness of the system when they are the basis for entrance into the bureaucracy or promotion within it. Not all bureaucratic organizations have used all these control devices, however. There have been many quasi-bureaucracies which have mixed bureaucratic controls with mechanisms of hereditary aristocracy, purchase of position, or various informal arrangements; research tends to confirm that no organization is without some informal structure.[22]
[...]

In general, any strong, centralized state or church tends to be bureaucratically organized; the bureaucratic control devices themselves are the prime basis of its centralized authority. Such a state or church provides a demand for education, but the relationship between the state or church and the educational system may take several forms. In the weakest form, the state or church simply provides a market for schools that spring up independently, as in many Islamic states, the medieval papacy, and the Chinese Empire. The Ottoman and late Roman empires represent an intermediate form, in which the state oversees and offers some financial support for existing educational institutions. State influence on education is fairly strong where examinations are required for entrance to government office, as in Imperial China, Germany after 1800, and Britain after 1870. The state is most deeply involved in education where it requires school attendance. Attendance was compulsory for aristocrats in Tokugawa Japan and in Russia, but only in the last few centuries has it been required of the general population, beginning with Germany in the eighteenth century, followed by the United States, France, Japan, Italy, and Russia in the nineteenth and by England and other countries in the twentieth.

It is here that the recent Marxist argument – that schooling is used as a device for ensuring labor discipline and, hence, is developed by the dominant class in its own interest – takes on great relevance.[23] Clearly, this argument applies only to modern mass education, not to the elite education that characterized most pre-modern educational systems and that continues to comprise the elite stratum of modern educational systems. With this specification, the labor-discipline argument does find empirical support. Consider, for example, the conservative and conformist values expressed in school texts throughout the period of mass education, and the efficacy of primary schools in inculcating unreflective political loyalty.[24] Yet although modern education does discipline the lower social classes, the demand for labor discipline *per se* does not explain why some industrial societies have large mass-education systems and why some have small ones. For example, the educational system is huge in the United States, relatively large in Russia and Japan, and tiny in Britain, France, and Germany, even though the need for labor discipline is presumably the same in all industrial societies. (Compare the figures from the early 1960s shown in table 1.) Nor does the demand for labor discipline explain the existence of segregated class systems in some societies but not in others.

Table 1

	Percent completing secondary school	Percent attending university	Percent graduating from university
USA	75	39	18
USSR	47	19	9
Japan	57	11	11
France	30	11	—
England	12	6	5
West Germany	11	6	—

Sources: Torsten Husen, 'Social Structure and the Utilization of Talent', in *Essays on World Education*, ed. George Z.F. Bereday (New York: Oxford Univ. Press, 1969), p. 80; Philip J. Idenberg, 'Europe: In Search of New Forms of Education', in *Essays*, ed. Bereday, p. 281; Nicholas De Witt, 'Basic Comparative Data on Soviet and American Education', *Comparative Perspectives on Education*, ed. Robert J. Havighurst (Boston: Little, Brown, 1968), pp. 55–56; John E. Blewett, trans. and ed., *Higher Education in Postwar Japan: The Ministry of Education's 1964 White Paper* (Tokyo: Sophia Univ. Press, 1965), pp. 113, 118, 122, 158–9.

Historical evidence indicates that mass, compulsory education was first created not for industrial, but for military and political, discipline. The first compulsory, state-supported elementary schools were established in the early eighteenth century by Denmark and Prussia, and later by Japan, to accompany the creation of mass conscript armies.[25] In England, where a highly traditional military organization and the aristocracy's near deadlock on political power survived until the late nineteenth century, it was only with military and political reforms and the concomitant organization of a powerful working-class party that a compulsory school system was envisioned.

Capitalists' interest in using education to ensure labor discipline may have been a force behind the development of mass, compulsory education in some of these countries, but it was not the central motive: Prussia and Japan established compulsory schooling well before extensive industrialization, and England long after. The safer generalization is that bureaucratic states impose compulsory education on populations which are seen as potential threats to state control, and that these economic classes which are influential in the state will help define the nature of the 'threat'.

Finally, it seems clear that the initial impetus behind the development of bureaucratized schooling did not come from the bureaucratization of business enterprises. Bureaucracy within private business organizations developed quite late. There are few examples of it before the late nineteenth century in the United States.[26] The industrial organizations of England, France, and Germany in the early and middle nineteenth century did make considerable use of record keeping, and some of these organizations were large enough to have a degree of specialization

and of administrative career hierarchy, but educational requirements and examinations were not part of this structure. Most nineteenth-century British or German
clerks were trained through work 'apprenticeship' after elementary schooling in
literacy. Even in the twentieth century, managers in Britain and Germany have
tended to have had little formal education, because the higher schools have been
connected with careers in government and the élite professions.[27] The civil-service
exams for which students prepare have reflected the culture of the elite status group,
exemplified in England by knowledge of the Greek and Latin classics and in
Germany by knowledge of philosophy and law. Where industrial and commercial
bureaucracies have emphasized educational requirements for employees – above
all in the United States, Japan, and Russia and to a lesser degree in France – the
educational system has taken the lead and business has responded.[28] This has
resulted in a tendency for formal requirements to increase in both spheres.

Conclusion: Towards a Theory of Cultural Markets

We have seen that there are different types of education, each with its own determining conditions. Several of these conditions may operate simultaneously, resulting
in a variety of types of education that coexist or even combine into a single, complex
system. This is especially the case in the modern industrial world, where a great
many interests in education have been mobilized. Sometimes these interests have
conflicted, but they have nevertheless collectively resulted in a larger system of
educational stratification. This system, I would suggest, is a market for cultural
goods in which various sources of demand mesh with sources of supply. The effects
of this market are usually not foreseen by the individual parties involved. Among
these effects are changes in the rates of growth of educational systems, in the price
and purchasing power of educational credentials, and in the structure of educational
systems. Finally, crises may arise as the parties react to the unforeseen outcomes of
the cultural market.

We have examined three types of education. Training in practical skills exists
in any economy but is usually built informally into the work process. The practical
skills of literacy and numeracy have been especially demanded, and sometimes
provided by special teachers, wherever there has been literate administration or
the development of commerce. Education in the leisure culture of a status group
has prospered in relatively peaceful periods during which there is decentralized
competition within a wealthy aristocracy, within a prosperous bourgeoisie, or
within a rising working class; the nature of the status culture has varied with the
groups involved. Highly formal educational systems with specified time sequences,
examinations, and elements of compulsion have developed as bureaucratic devices
are used, especially by centralized states, to control officials, feudal aristocracies,
or, in modern periods of mass political mobilization, the general population.

Historically, these types of education have sometimes combined. To be sure,
some of them are theoretically incompatible; for example, aristocratic status
education has emphasized aesthetic and leisure themes that are explicitly intended

to oppose both practical training and the narrower specializations of thoroughly bureaucratic education. But in practice, these seemingly incompatible types of education have appeared in combination. For example, familiarity with the status culture of the aristocracy has often been used as a criterion for selection of government officials in bureaucratic systems. The Chinese examination system tested the genteel skills of poetic composition and use of literary allusions, just as the British civil-service examinations tested knowledge of the literary classics. In modern times, bureaucratic and compulsory mass education has incorporated elements of practical education by training students in literacy and arithmetic. Similarly, secondary schooling, which developed in post-Renaissance Europe as a support for the status cultures of the prosperous classes, has been incorporated into a standard sequence of educational levels leading up to the university.

Bureaucratization has been the principal means for combining different types of education. The essence of bureaucratic controls is a stress on the keeping of formal regulations and records; any content, whether it be originally aesthetic, religious, legal, scientific, or practical, may be fitted into this system. Thus we find strong bureaucratic states and churches emphasizing various kinds of educational contents: the Chinese classics and the martial arts of Tokugawa Japan, the rhetoric of the late Roman Empire, the dialectics of the medieval university, the inflexible legal canons of Islamic culture, the Greek and Latin classics of British and German elite education, and the sciences of the elite schools in France and the Soviet Union. What all these educational programs have in common is structural formality: grades, examinations, required sequences, and set time periods for instruction that are absent from the pure forms of practical and status-group education. In bureaucratic structures, however, students know that the content of education is arbitrary: even if education is ostensibly aimed at cultivating practical skills, relatively few of these skills, at least in the modern world, seem to stay with students once they have passed through the system and received their credentials.

The various kinds of demand for education – practical, status-group, and bureaucratic – may be viewed more broadly as part of a *cultural market* in which social actors simultaneously attempt to attain certain goals. The interest of government in bureaucratic control over particular classes may mesh with the interest of these very classes in improving their cultural attainments for the sake of status. Thus, we find a symbiosis between the control interest of the Chinese emperors and the status interest of the gentry and, more ironically, between government concern for compulsory educational indoctrination of the modern masses and some interest in status mobility on the part of those masses. The interest of capitalists in ensuring labor discipline adds yet another demand to this market,[29] as does the interest of a particular ethnic group in maintaining its opportunities *vis-à-vis* other ethnic groups.

The extent to which education develops in different societies and historical periods varies according to the nature of their cultural markets. Abstractly, we may see that cultural markets require a common currency and independent sources of supply and demand for cultural goods.

A *common cultural currency* derives from an elite culture, which has undisputed dominance because it legitimates a wealthy and powerful group.

The *supply of cultural goods* (or cultural capital, in Pierre Bourdieu's term[30]) is determined by the availability of teachers, of material resources for schools, of sufficient economic productivity or stratification to permit leisure for cultural activities, and of methods for producing (and especially mass-producing) books and writing materials.

The *demand for cultural goods* is determined by the number of individuals or groups who feel there is a potential payoff from education and by the economic and political resources they have to make their demands effective. The interests motivating these demands can be of all three types discussed above – practical training, status-group training, and bureaucratic control. Since, in principle, the demand for training in practical skills can be satisfied on the job, such training has been demanded in the form of schooling only where occupations and professions have been monopolistically organized through a formal credential system. The desire for training in the culture of a status group has been a stronger source of demand for formal education. Competition over status-group membership or group prestige has been strong during periods of political decentralization or political instability under a unified market economy. It has been even stronger when many culturally distinct ethnic groups live within a common system of economic or political stratification. Situations of ethnic competition have tended to increase the salience of the cultural sphere, first, because the basis of ethnic differences has been cultural and, second, because particular ethnic groups have attempted to use devices for cultural inclusion and prestige as crucial weapons for controlling top economic and political positions. Thus we find in India that the market for status-group education was largest during prosperous, politically decentralized periods when the extraordinary range of ethnic groups was channeled into the occupational monopolies of the caste system. Similarly, status-group education was particularly important in the Hellenistic empires built by Greek conquest of the culturally distinct Middle Eastern and Mediterranean states; in the ethnically diverse Islamic empire; in medieval Europe when an ethnically heterogeneous people were united by the papacy; and in the United States since the immigrations of the mid-nineteenth century.

The demand for cultural goods has also depended on the extent of political opposition to the dominant classes. Where governments have faced only a small politically mobilized class in the population, their demand for education as a bureaucratic control has been quite limited. Where a large population has been mobilized, however, the control interest of bureaucratic elites has been correspondingly large.

The development of a complex school system may itself create an additional demand for employees socialized by its own procedures. Furthermore, due to internal struggles for control, a school system may bureaucratize the careers of its own teachers.

Finally, a source of increases in demand has been population growth, if it has been connected with an existing interest in education. For example, as the Chinese population grew from the sixteenth century onward and as economic changes mobilized an increasing proportion of that population, the number of aspirants for government positions increased steadily. Similarly, population growth played into a mobilized interest in education to create the college-attendance boom of the United States in the 1960s.

What may this market model explain? The ramifications, I believe, are numerous; here it is possible to mention only a few. The varying rates of growth of educational systems (including negative rates) are, in principle, calculable from such a model. And the rate of growth relative to the availability of payoffs in the surrounding society will determine the purchasing power of education for those who acquire it. For example, the demand for education in China increased from the sixteenth through the nineteenth centuries, but the number of government positions was kept virtually constant. Thus, the cultural price of education increased: the examination system was gradually elaborated, resulting in a series of examinations that might take a scholar thirty years to complete.[31] In all educational systems there have been similar processes in which the demand for educational credentials has increased without a commensurate increase in payoffs. Oversupply of graduates may result in upper-level unemployment where job requirements remain constant, as occurred in Germany in the 1920s and in many Third World nations in the 1960s.[32] Where credential seekers are mobilized and able to put pressure on the government to expand the educational system, as in modern democracies, the cultural market adjusts by increasing the formal-training requirements for any given position and, sometimes, by increasing the number of positions for which such formal credentials are required.[33] The situation is analogous to inflation of a monetary currency, which results in a decrease in purchasing power.

The parties that enter the cultural marketplace usually are involved in social conflicts of some sort – whether struggles by economic classes for domination, revolution, or self-improvement, or the more complex conflicts that result when class struggle meshes with the prestige struggle of ethnic or other status groups. The differences among the main types of educational structures in the modern world can be explained by differences among lineups of contending interests.

The most prominent difference is between 'sponsored-mobility' systems, such as those of Britain and most other Western European countries, and 'contest-mobility' systems, such as those of the United States and the Soviet Union.[34] In the former type, children's careers are determined early, usually at the end of primary school. Some children proceed into elite university-preparatory schools stressing traditional high culture; others enter terminal vocational schools; and still others end their education at the elementary level. The group that enters the elite track is virtually guaranteed admission into and graduation from each succeeding level. For this group, mobility is said to be sponsored. In a contest-mobility system, there is no single decision point. Nearly all students are channeled into comprehensive secondary schools, and there is continuous attrition and competition for admission to each higher level.

Class-segregated, sponsored-mobility systems have emerged where there has been a radical mobilization of the middle or working class that has resulted in cultural polarization around distinctively commercial and technical educational ideals, but the upper class has nevertheless managed to maintain power. When such a social division occurs, educational systems have split, too: the middle and working classes are given distinctive educational enclaves while careers in the dominant occupations and political institutions remain monopolized by those who have moved through an elite educational system that maintains the traditional high culture. Contest-mobility systems, on the other hand, have emerged in industrial societies where class conflict has been submerged within a single market for cultural respectability. This may occur, as in the United States, where class differences are subordinate to divisions among many competing ethnic groups, or, as in the Soviet Union (which is also a multi-ethnic society dominated by a particular ethnic élite), where organized class conflict was eliminated, leaving only a single cultural standard for competition.

Conflict over economic interests is not eliminated in multi-ethnic situations, but it is fragmented among a much larger number of contending groups. This leads to greater competition for cultural credentials. Economic outcomes are not necessarily affected by whether class conflict is fragmented in this way; rates of mobility seem to be quite similar in societies with both sponsored and contest structures of education and seem to be quite stable over time when either type of system expands. The differences lie, rather, in the political and cultural spheres: the sponsored-mobility structure keeps class cultures quite distinct and fosters class-based ideological parties, while the contest-mobility structure seems to blur class identification in politics. In sponsored-mobility systems, a sharp split is maintained between élite culture and low culture, while mass, popular cultural movements seem more prevalent in contest-mobility systems.

Inflation of educational credentials is especially likely in contest-mobility systems. For example, the United States has experienced this kind of educational inflation since at least the middle of the nineteenth century. From 1870 to 1970, school-attendance rates rose dramatically at every level, and higher levels were created and expanded as the lower ones filled up. At the same time, educational requirements for employment at all levels increased correspondingly, adjusting to the inflated supply of cultural currency. Such an inflationary process does not necessarily go on indefinitely; the downturn in educational attendance since approximately 1970 and the cultural revolution of student-protest movements and dropout culture of the 1960s are instances of reactions that may occur when a culture-producing system has been expanding in an inflationary way for some time.

An inflationary system, even if it merely expands the supply of currency while leaving the rest of the stratification system in a state of dynamic equilibrium, nevertheless affects cultural consciousness by mobilizing increasing proportions of the population in struggles for control of the stratification system. Such mobilization can become politically dangerous to an authoritarian government, which may react by cutting down the educational system. There are a number of instances of this in Chinese history (most recently in the 1960s) and in nineteenth-century Russian history. Or disillusionment may set in among the purchasers of cultural credentials. This was behind the precipitous drop in European university enrolments in the period after the Reformation, and something similar seems to be developing in America today. Finally, the currency itself can break down. The prestige of a particular élite culture and that culture's accompanying political and organizational domination may give way to independent currencies, as when the separate national cultures of early modern Europe replaced the old international culture of the medieval church. Although it would be hazardous to predict a future change of this magnitude for the United States, we certainly see a trend in this direction in the recent attacks on Anglo-Protestant cultural domination and the efforts towards a new cultural pluralism.

Our understanding of such possibilities depends on the construction of a workable theory of cultural markets. As yet, we are only beginning to see what such a theory would include and what it might explain. Its prospects are extensive. If we have come to see education as basic to our current system of stratification, an exploration of this phenomenon which moves beyond a naïve, functionalist view suggests a major reformulation of all stratification analyses. For the interaction of cultural organization with the material economy is the key to all structures of domination, and the concept of the cultural market may provide a means of encompassing multifaceted interests and conflicts within a single explanatory structure.

Notes and References

1 DREEBEN, R. (1968) *On What Is Learned in School* New York, Addison-Wesley, is a recent formulation of this problem.

2 Use of the second type of evidence involves the fallacy of assuming that static cross sections present a historical sequence actually followed by all societies; the historical approach shows that this assumption is not justified. See BELL, D. (1973) *The Coming of Post-Industrial Society* New York, Basic Books; and HARBISON, F. and MYERS, C.A. (1964) *Education, Manpower and Economic Growth* New York, McGraw Hill.

3 COLLINS, R. (1971) 'Functional and conflict theories of educational stratification' *American Sociological Review* 36, pp. 1002–19.

4 ALTHUSSER, L. (1971) 'Ideology and ideological state apparatuses' in *Lenin and Philosophy and Other Essays* London, New Left Books, pp. 123–73.

5 BOWLES, S. and GINTIS, H. (1976) *Schooling in Capitalist America: Educational Reform and the Contradictions of Economic Life* New York, Basic Books.

6 TOURAINE, A. (1973) *Production de la Sociétié* Paris, Editions du Seuil.

7 See WEBER, M. (1968) *Economy and Society* New York, Bec.minster Press esp. pp. 932–37 and 998–1002.

8 Pierre Bourdieu develops this tradition in a highly original manner. He views the realm of symbolic status as a market for cultural capital in which social struggle is shaped not only by the various competing classes but also by the autonomous structure of the cultural marketplace itself. BOURDIEU, P. (1972) *Esquisse d'une Théorie de la Pratique* Geneva, Droz, pp. 227–43.

9 DURKHEIM, E. (1925) *Moral Education* New York, Free Press (1961).

10 This process is explained in COLLINS, R. (1975) *Conflict Sociology* New York, Academic Press, Chaps. 2–4.

11 COLLINS, R. (1971) *op. cit.*

12 This has been the case not only for heavy manual pursuits, but also for the skilled crafts and administrative and ritual skills. The training of priests in both Eastern and Western religions has historically been primarily by apprenticeship, even in the case of the literate churches. See MARROU, H.I. (1964) *A History of Education in Antiquity* New York, New American Library, pp. 419–51; and SPIRO, M.E. (1970) *Buddhism and Society* New York, Harper and Row.

13 COLLINS, R. (1971) *op. cit.*, p. 1006.

14 WEBER, M. (1968) *op. cit.*, pp. 926–39.

15 WEBER, M. (1951) *The Religion of China* New York, Free Press, pp. 119–33; MARROU, H.I. (1964) *History of Education*, pp. 147–64.

16 HANS, N. (1951) *New Trends in Education in the 18th Century* London, Routledge and Kegan Paul.

This disciplined, upward-striving tone of the German dissenting academics is noted by WEBER, M. (1904) *The Protestant Ethic and the Spirit of Capitalism* New York, Scribners (1930).

17 THOMPSON, E.P. (1968) *The Making of the English Working Class* Harmondsworth, Penguin Books.

18 ARBERRY, A.J. (1940) *Sufism: An Account of the Mystics of Islam* London, Allen and Unwin; and LEWIS, B. (1937) 'The Islamic Guilds' *Economic History Review* 8, pp. 20–37.

19 BEN-DAVID, J. (1971) *The Scientist's Role in Society* Englewood Cliffs, N.J., Prentice Hall, pp. 88–97; and KINCH, J.K. (1960) *The Story of Engineering* New York, Doubleday, pp. 137–8, 159–60.

20 HALÉVIE, E. (1955) *The Growth of Philosophical Radicalism* Boston, Beacon Press; and ARMYTAGE, H.G. (1965) *The Rise of the Technocrats* London, Routledge and Kegan Paul.

21 GRANT, N. (1968) *Soviet Education* Baltimore, Penguin Books; GRANICK, D. (1960) *The Red Executive* New York, Doubleday, pp. 46–73; and BRZEZINSKI, Z. and HUNTINGTON, S.P. (1965) *Political Power: USA/USSR* New York, Viking Press, pp. 129–90.

22 WEBER, M. (1968) *Economy and Society*, pp. 956–1110; and Collins, R. (1975) *op. cit.*, Chap. 6.

23 BOWLES, S. and GINTIS, H. (1976) *op. cit.*

24 CHARMS, R. DE and MOELLER, G.H. (1962) 'Values expressed in American children's readers' *Journal of Abnormal and Social Psychology* 64, pp. 36–142; and HESS, R.D. and TORNEY, J.V. (1967) *The Development of Political Attitudes in Children* Chicago, Aldine.

25 BENDIX, R. (1964) *Nation Building and Citizenship* New York, Wiley, pp. 89–93. Japan created a universal, compulsory elementary school system as part of its program of military reform, as it moved from relying on exclusively samurai armies to mass-conscript ones, according to DORE, R.P. (1964) *Education in Tokugawa Japan* Berkeley, University of California Press, pp. 222, 250–1, 297–8.

26 CHANDLER, A.D. (1968) 'The coming of big business' in VANN WOODWARD, C. (Ed) *The Comparative Approach to American History* New York, Basic Books, pp. 220–37; and BENDIX, R. (1956) *Work and Authority in Industry* New York, Wiley, pp. 198–253.

27 GRANICK, D. (1960) *The European Executive* New York, Doubleday, pp. 240–300; and LEWIS, R. and STEWART, R. (1961) *The Managers: A New Examination of the English, German and American Executive* New York, New American Library, pp. 58–75.

28 COLLINS, R. (1971) *op. cit.* pp. 1003–4; AZUMI, K. (1969) *Higher Education and Business Recruitment in Japan* New York, Teachers College Press; and BOURDIEU, P., BOLTANSKI, L. and SAINT MARTIN, M. DE (1974) 'Les stratégies de reconversion: les classes Sociales et le Système d'enseignement' *Social Science Information* 12, pp. 61–113.

29 BOWLES, S. and GINTIS, H. (1976) *op. cit.* similarly suggest that an impersonal market mechanism can bring about the creation of a school system in response to the predominant demands in the class structure.

30 BOURDIEU, P. and PASSERON, J.-P. (1970) *La Réproduction* Paris, Les Editions de Minuit.

31 CHANG, C. (1955) *The Chinese Gentry* Seattle, University of Washington Press; FRANKE, W. (1960) *Reform and Abolition* Cambridge, Mass., Harvard University Press.

32 KOTSCHIG, W.M. (1937) *Unemployment in the Learned Professions* London, Oxford University Press; and HOSELITZ, B.F. (1965) 'Investment in education and its political impact' in COLEMAN, J.S. (Ed) *Education and Political Development* Princeton, N.J. Princeton University Press, pp. 541–65.

33 Weber noted this inflationary tendency in bureaucratic employment requirements in Europe in his day. WEBER, M. (1968) *Economy and Society*. Another period of credential inflation occurred in Germany around 1800, when a mass of applicants for government positions crowded the universities, producing a reform which consisted of an extension of educational requirements to more positions. See BRUFORD, W.H. (1935) *Germany in the Eighteenth Century* Cambridge, Cambridge University Press, pp. 248–68; BRUNSCHWIG, H. (1947) *La Crise de l'Etat Prussien* Paris, Presses Universitaires de France; ROSENBERG, F. (1958) *Bureaucracy, Aristocracy and Autocracy* Cambridge, Mass., Harvard University Press; SCHNABEL, F. (1959) *Deutsche Geschichte im Neunzehnten Jahrhundert* Freiburg, Verlag Herder, 1, pp. 108–57. Inflationary phenomena have been especially noticeable in the expansion of American education since the late nineteenth century, as well as in France since World War II. William G. Spady shows that the relative gaps in education among American social classes have remained constant throughout the twentieth century despite mass increases in the *absolute* level of schooling, SPADY, W.G. (1967) 'Educational mobility and access: Growth and paradoxes' *American Journal of Sociology* 72, pp. 273–86. Similar results for France are reported by BOURDIEU, P. and PASSERON, J.-P. (1964) *Les Héritiers* Paris, Les Editions de Minuit, and in *Lá Réproduction*.

34 The distinction is originated by TURNER, R. (1960) 'Sponsored and contest mobility and the school system' *American Sociological Review* 25, pp. 855–67. Turner bases his distinction on the supposed primacy of the value of ascription or achievement. In my view, however, such values (if in fact they exist outside the mind of the analyst) result from social structure rather than *vice versa*.

17 Comparative Historical School Change: Newfoundland, Southern Ontario and New England

Alan Pomfret

The Problem

The problem of historical school change – by which I mean the origins, develop-ment, and consequences of mass, bureaucratic, state schooling – has been the subject of an unprecedented amount of intensive scrutiny over the past several years.[1] One result is the development of a number of reasonably explicit, coherent, competing theories purporting to explain historical school change in general; another is an expansive, wide open debate not only about what best explains certain aspects of schooling, but also over what aspects deserve explanation. How did schools get started? Who advocated and opposed them and why? How and why have schools changed historically? What relationships have existed among school, state, and society over time? All these issues, and many others as well, remain contentious. Clearly, this is an intellectual terrain where those seeking empirical and causal generalizations had best tread gingerly – if they dare enter at all.

Nevertheless, I should like to propose here a general model for the study of historical school change, one which combines Collins' (1977) notion of cultural markets for schooling with Wallerstein's (1974) modern world-economy concept.[2] The intent is to delineate the relationships among, first, an area's position in the modern world-economy, second, the characteristics of its cultural markets for schooling, and third, its pattern of historical school change. This model is more comprehensive than existing ones, which have been developed to explain develop-ments in what Wallerstein terms 'core-states' and 'semi-peripheral' areas, and which do not adequately account for historical school change in the 'periphery'. To illustrate the potential usefulness of the proposed model developments in the New England states, Southern Ontario and Newfoundland are examined. Let us begin by taking a closer look at the existing models.

Source: A much revised version of a paper presented at the 1977 Annual Meeting of the Canadian Sociology and Anthropology Association, Fredeiction, New Brunswick first published in *Canadian Journal of Sociology* (1979) 4(3), pp. 241–55.

Existing Models: Overview and Critique

Existing models can be classified as either 'liberal' or 'revisionist'. Revisionists reject the earlier liberal perspectives, which have been trichotomized by Bowles and Gintis[3] (1976) as follows: first, the 'democratic imperative' interpretation, which views schools as part of the inevitable, evolutionary advance of freedom (e.g. Butts, 1947);[4] second, the 'popular demand' theory, where schools represent the victory of the common man over the privileged (e.g. Cubberley, 1934; Carleton, 1911);[5] and third, the 'technological' or 'functional imperative' model, linking the social need for improved skills with the growth of schools (e.g. Clark, 1962; Trow, 1966).[6] All revisionists agree that schools control more than they liberate; are middle-class, not working-class, institutions; and exhibit either a miniscule (Collins, 1971) or a negative (Johnson, 1976) relationship to the need for and improvement in skills.[7] Following Sutherland (1975),[8] one can further distinguish between moderate revisionists (e.g. Bailyn, 1960; Cremin, 1977)[9] who fault the liberals' exclusive focus on schools and argue for a very much broader concept of education, and radical revisionists (e.g. Katz, 1971),[10] who contend that schools reflect and reproduce undesirable patterns of social stratification. I will focus on the radicals' models because, more so than the moderates, the radicals deal primarily with historical school change and their models provide the framework for the current debate on historical school change.

Although all radicals focus on the relationships between school and society, not all work with the same conception of society. Some (perhaps most) conceive of society as an urbanizing, industrializing process and attempt to situate historical school change, especially its origins, within that context (e.g. Houston, 1975; Katz, 1971; Lazerson, 1971; Prentice, 1977).[11] I shall refer to this as the urban-industrial model. This model has been extensively criticized (Ravitch, 1977).[12] For my present purposes, however, the important point about such criticisms lies not so much in their details as in the extent to which they accept the model's overall framework. That is to say, although critics may disagree with the revisionists over which aspects of society relate to which aspects of schooling, or to education in general, few if any would dispute the broad contention that ' . . . processes such as industrialization, urbanization and bureaucratization are the context in which mass systems of formal education have emerged in *all* societies . . . ' (Smith, 1976: 75, my emphasis).[13] This, as I hope to show with reference to Newfoundland, is simply not so. To the extent that Newfoundland's experience as a peripheral society is representative of other peripheral areas we can claim that existing urban-industrial models cannot explain developments in the periphery.

While the urban-industrial model does not ignore the uniquely capitalistic features of society, neither does it give these characteristics analytical priority. Other radical revisionists work explicitly with what can be termed a capital accumulation model. They start with the notion of capitalist society, attempt to identify its key features, and examine the relationships of these features to historical school change (e.g. Bowles and Gintis, 1976; Johnson, 1973; Schecter, 1977).[14] For example, Bowles and Gintis (1976) link the early American school reform movement to the need to discipline labour and otherwise contain the changing social contradictions associated with the evolving wage labour system accompanying *factory*-based industrial capitalism. Although Schecter (1977 my emphasis)[15] notes that '... school reform *preceded* industrialization in Canada ... ', he maintains both that ' ... the reforms were designed to discipline the nascent labor force for industrial capitalism' and that such ' ... reforms would have been impossible had capitalism not already been an international system'. Katz (1978),[16] however, rejects equating the origins of institutional change with either urbanizing industrialism or industrial capitalism. He outlines an alternative framework based upon ' ... the spread of wage-labour and the values associated with capitalism rather than urbanization and industrialization' (Katz, 1978) for understanding the origins of institutional change, including historical school change.

Collins (1977)[17] identified a number of weaknesses in the capital accumulation model when it is linked to the notion of *industrial* capitalism. He first points out that, although Denmark, Prussia and Japan established their school systems *prior* to industrialization, England's developed only well *after* industrialization. Second, ' ... mass, compulsory education was first created not for industrial, but for military and political, discipline'. Third, the labour-discipline argument ' ... does not explain why some industrial societies have large mass-education systems and why some have small ones'.

Existing accounts of historical school change in specific societies are not able to satisfactorily explain, or even identify, developments in other societies. A more general model is needed, one that can resolve disputes between competing explanations and incorporate as yet unaccounted for developments. Special attention must be paid to the fact that existing models have been constructed in relation to developments in the core-states and semi-periphery of the modern world economy; experiences in the periphery are ignored. Chirot (1976)[18] has convincingly argued that '[g]eneral evolutionary laws of human development do not work well for peripheral societies', and we would do well to heed his comment in constructing a comprehensive model which can explain historical school change in the periphery as well as in semi-peripheral and core areas. Let us now consider some of the components of such a model.

An Alternative Model

The model I propose is derived from Randall Collins' (1977) notion of cultural markets and Wallerstein's (1974) world-system perspective.[19] Collins' main concern is to present a clear-cut alternative to functional theories of schooling. Consequently, he outlines a theory of cultural markets for schooling that draws heavily upon his interpretation of Max Weber's conflict sociology (Collins, 1975).[20] Within the market, various combinations of power, status, and material interest groups contend for or demand various kinds of education – practical, status-group, and bureaucratic. Collins hypothesizes that the ' ... extent to which education develops in different societies and historical periods varies according to the nature of their cultural markets'. It is plausible that the ' . . . differences among the main types of educational structures in the modern world can be explained by differences among lineups of contending interests' (Collins, 1977).[21] Still, in Collins' model, the markets are 'given'. There is no attempt to *explain* the composition and workings of the markets themselves, and how and why markets change historically. More specifically, do the 'lineups' vary in some systematic way among different *types* of societies and historically within single societies? If so, is there any way of characterizing and accounting for these differences? To answer these questions we must briefly examine Wallerstein's notion of world-systems.

Wallerstein (1974)[22] has recently postulated that truly isolated subsistence economies and world-systems are the only real social systems, (a postulate that prohibits labelling tribes, communities, and nation-states as total systems or proper units of analysis). He distinguishes between two types of world systems: world-empires, based primarily on political linkages, and world-economies, based primarily on economic linkages. At any given point in time each area of a world economy can be classified as core, semi-peripheral, peripheral, or external.[23] The core-states of a world-economy are ' . . . the advantaged areas of the world-economy . . . ' and are characterized by ' . . . a strong state machinery coupled with a national culture . . . '. 'The semi-periphery is a necessary structural element in a world economy', analogous to ' . . . middle trading groups in an empire', and semi-peripheral areas ' . . . are collection points of vital skills that are often politically unpopular'. The periphery ' . . . of a world economy is that geographical sector of it wherein production is primarily of lower-ranking goods (that is, goods whose labour is less well rewarded) but which is an integral part of the overall system of the division of labour, because the commodities involved are essential for daily use'. Finally, the external arena of a world-economy consists of those other world-systems with which a given world-economy has some kind of trade relationship, based primarily on the exchange of preciosities, what was sometimes called "rich trades"'.

Wallerstein (emphasis in original) reasons that '[i]f world-systems are the only real social systems (other than truly isolated subsistence economies), then it must follow that the emergence, consolidation, and political roles of classes and status groups must be appreciated as elements of this *world*-system'. An interesting injunction, especially since Collins (1977)[24] portrays the cultural market for school systems as ' . . . a multisided struggle among status communities for domination, for economic advantage, and for prestige'. Can the groups or communities Collins identifies as components of the market be conceived of as elements of Wallerstein's world-system?

Any attempt to relate the two frameworks must be sensitive to the fact that Collins differentiates classes and status groups using a greater variety of criteria[25] than is found in Wallerstein's writings. Any attempted synthesis or integration must not assume a total of unproblematic congruence between the two perspectives in terms of concepts, variables, postulates, or hypotheses. The identification is problematic because Wallerstein and Collins are not *always* writing about the same groups or classes. Wallerstein distinguishes among classes and groups in terms of their relationship to the production and control of economic surplus. Collins

(1977),[26] drawing on Weber, recognizes ' . . . economic interests based on property divisions as key bases of group organizations, of intergroup conflict, and of historical change' but does not focus exclusively on social relations of production. Instead he argues that ' . . . organizational resources, especially those of state and private bureaucracies, and cultural resources, above all religious traditions (but also secular ones such as education), can create and channel additional interest groups and conflicts'. 'This approach', Collins feels, 'allows the incorporation of a multiplicity of particular causes into an overall explanation, since it regards social structure as the result of the mobilization of a variety of resources and interest groups within a common area'.

These difficulties not withstanding, some sort of synthesis appears to be useful because, once combined, the two perspectives may provide the basis for a more powerful explanation of historical school change than either would if used singly. While cultural markets may explain historical school change, Wallerstein offers the possibility of explaining variations in markets in terms of an area's relationships within a world-system. On the other hand, Collins' markets do permit more explicit explanatory linkages to be made between first, variable stratification patterns in the various areas of world-systems and second, the origins, developments, and current features of each area's school system. For example, does the composition of an area's cultural market for schooling vary systematically with an area's position in the periphery, semi-periphery, or core? Are the purposes of schooling in an area related to its position in the modern world-economy? The general question is whether historical school change varies systematically between and within areas depending upon their relationships within (or to) a particular world-system.

One of the key topics in historical school change is the origins of schooling. Consequently, we begin with this issue as it is presented by urban-industrial and capital accumulation analysts of New England and Ontario. Some of the similarities between the two societies are noted in order to highlight certain features of the Newfoundland experience and some of the key differences among the three areas. Both the similarities and differences are explained by the combined cultural market – world economy model. Denominationalism is the second topic discussed. For both topics the analyses focusses upon Newfoundland since the main contention is that unlike the proposed model neither the urban-industrial nor the capital accumulation interpretations explain developments in the periphery. Moreover, existing accounts of the Newfoundland experience are also inadequate as explanations of historical school change in Newfoundland (Pomfret, 1977),[27] a state of affairs that supports the case for a new approach.

The Origins of Schooling

The data which I should like to employ in order to illustrate the utility of the model sketched above are drawn primarily from three areas: Newfoundland, southern Ontario and New England. One reason for selecting these areas is the abundance of secondary studies on New England and Ontario. Another more compelling, rationale is that each area represents a different type of society. During the nineteenth and twentieth centuries the north eastern United States moved from semi-peripheral status to that of a core-state within the modern world-economy (Chirot, 1977).[28] Meanwhile, Ontario moved from peripheral status in the early and mid-nineteenth century to a semi-peripheral status at the turn of the twentieth century, to marginal core-state status by the end of the Second World War.[29] Newfoundland, however, maintains its peripheral status even today,[30] although unsuccessful attempts have been made to achieve semi-peripheral status.[31]

According to proponents of the urban-industrial model of historical school change, the origins of schooling in New England were embedded in the changing social conditions that accompanied urbanization. For example, Houston (1975)[32] contends that in Upper Canada schools were one way ' . . . the middle classes met the problems of rapid social change at mid-century with solutions appropriate to an urban commercial society'. Similarly, Prentice (1977)[33] maintains that ' . . . the promoters of mass public schooling in Upper Canada . . . ' believed that ' . . . rapid growth and change, immigration and urbanization were the root causes of apathy and social disorder in the province . . . '. For New England, Lazerson (1971)[34] notes that '[a]mbivalent about industrialism and hostile to the city . . . [late nineteenth-century reformers] . . . turned to the school to preserve the social and moral characteristics they thought existed at an earlier period'. Schooling, or rather the demand for it, was a response to the way in which middle-class school promoters perceived the changing conditions and problems unique to a society urbanizing under the impact of industrialization. The perceived problems varied: immigration, vagrant children, a permanent poverty class, crime, labour productivity, social and moral fragmentation and general decay.

Bowles and Gintis (1976) are perhaps the best known of the capitalist accumulation theorists. They argue that the process of capital accumulation, manifested in the rise and spread of the factory system, changed the structure of society (especially contradictions in the wage-labour system) in such a way as to mobilize various, conflicting class based demands that account for the origin, spread, and outcomes of different types of school reforms. By insisting that the ' . . . analysis of the process of educational reform must consider the shifting arenas of class conflict . . . ',[35] they appear to be appealing to Collins' notion of cultural markets although they may not be considering the range of groups and outcomes of interest to him. Hence they refer to 'arenas of class conflict' while Collins talks more generally about cultural markets. At the same time by representing class conflict as ' . . . arising from . . . [the] continued widening and deepening of capitalist control over production . . . '[36] they appear to be trying to explain the changing nature of the cultural market by examining, implicitly at least, the United States' changing relationships in the modern world-economy. Since they are essentially dealing with a specific society during a specific period of time, their study is best seen as a case study which applies a combined world-systems and cultural markets approach. Collins (1977)[37] treats them as such in terms of cultural markets but ignores their attempt to ground the markets in the changing nature of the political economy.

For Ontario, the analyst who comes closest to the conceptualization used by

Bowles and Gintis is Leo Johnson (1973).[38] Johnson's study is valuable for two main reasons. One is the analytical framework he develops. More important, perhaps, is the issue he confronts. The study is of a rural area near Toronto. Consequently, Johnson deals more exclusively and clearly than others with the urban-rural reaction to various school reforms. However, he is less concerned with the origins of schooling and more concerned with how institutions that were developed as unique responses to perceived urban problems were imposed in a substantially unaltered form upon a very different rural milieu. The response he gives to this issue can without too much difficulty be restated in a form similar to that provided by Bowles and Gintis. In Johnson's rural area the opponents of the school promoters were ' . . . the independent-minded farmers and craftsmen . . . and the rich property-owners, urban and rural . . . '.[39] Supporting the school promoters were the ' . . . new urban industrial and mercantile elite of the growing towns . . . '.[40] In addition to an increasingly dominant position in the economic, political, and social life of the rural communities, these 'new men' could also draw upon a set of provincial incentives, laws and regulations that facilitated the spread of schooling. Thus, by gaining control of the state machinery, the school promoters in the larger urban centres, particularly Toronto, were able to create conditions that assisted their more rurally based allies who were a product of spreading industrial capitalism.

Despite the difference in framework and topic with urban-industrial analysts of Ontario, Johnson appears to give the same impression as they do of historical school change: that it was a fairly successful attempt by a small but active middle class group to acquire the resources to impose in a variety of ways their definition of problems and solutions on other groups. One gets the same impression of New England from reading Lazerson (1971) and Katz (1971).[41] On the other hand, Bowles and Gintis contend that the ' . . . impetus for educational reform and expansion was provided by the growing class consciousness and political militancy of working people' and that despite initial employer resistance the ' . . . school was increasingly looked to by the capitalist class as an institution which could enhance the labour power of working people and at the same time reproduce the social conditions for the transformation of the fruits of labour into capitalist profits'. More generally, they argue that ' . . . the spread of mass education can best be seen as an outcome of the class conflict, not class domination'.[42] In explaining the Ontario case, Schecter (1977)[43] goes one step further. While maintaining the integrity of the capital accumulation model (' . . . schooling must . . . be seen as an ongoing dialectic between educational reform and the transformations of capitalism . . . '), he denies the possibility of dividing historical school change as Bowles and Gintis do ' . . . into discrete periods in which a conservative education system is wrenched into line, following the lead given by underlying economic transformations'. Instead, he argues *à la* Weber, that ' . . . educational reform has its own dynamic relative autonomy . . . '.

Numerous features about the origin of historical school change in Newfoundland become notable when examined from the perspective of the preceding account. One is that the movement for schooling started in Newfoundland about the same time as it did in New England and Ontario. After creating a state Board of Education in 1837, Massachusetts had its legislation well advanced with an 1852 compulsory education bill. By 1880 ' ... American education had acquired its fundamental structural characteristics, and ... they have not altered since' (Katz, 1971).[44] Although Upper Canada passed school acts as early as 1807 (for grammar schools) and 1816 (for common schools), the system was not firmly established legally until the acts of 1850 and especially 1871, the latter of which contained a proviso for compulsory school attendance for all children of certain ages. Newfoundland's first school act was passed in 1836, only four years after the colony had acquired a governmental structure empowered to pass such legislation. By 1874, the denominational system was firmly established and has remained intact despite major reorganizations in 1920 and 1968. However, Newfoundland did not pass a compulsory school attendance law until 1943.

Consider the types of concerns that the school promoters in the three societies felt they were addressing. From the beginning in New England, for school promoters '[w]hat was wanted was a general schooling, common to all men, whatever their future plans or hopes' (Prentice, 1970).[45] Not so for Upper Canada and Newfoundland. In both societies the earliest school promoters directed their efforts to a very specific segment of the population: the children of the poorest classes, who, unless something was done to break the poverty cycle, threatened to form a permanent poverty class with all that implied for social disorganization. Note also, however, that in Upper Canada, school promoters soon ' ... offered schooling as an almost certain avenue to upward mobility, to individual as well as class betterment';[46] by way of contrast, in Newfoundland the original emphasis on the poorest classes persisted well into the late nineteenth century. Moreover, schooling was seen at best as an avenue of limited mobility for the children of the poor. It was primarily a way of acquiring the skills and manners appropriate to one's station in life.[47]

Still, despite the changing emphasis in the school promoters' ideologies, a striking similarity exists in the language used by the earliest school promoters in Ontario and Newfoundland to describe the social conditions they wanted to eradicate. Both wanted to help the children of the poorest classes and, in so doing, to eliminate alcoholism, crimes, sloth, and a host of other social ills. What makes these similarities so striking is that they exist at the same point in time in two societies experiencing very different socio-economic conditions. Newfoundland was experiencing neither the process of factory based capitalist industrialization that New England was, nor Ontario's commercial (later industrial) urbanization. On the contrary, while its population increased greatly in the first quarter of the nineteenth century, partly in response to the development of the inshore fishery, settlement occured mainly in rural areas. Moreover, Newfoundland experienced an economic slump, not growth, after the Napoleonic wars ended. Yet Newfoundland hosted a process of historical school change that manifests many of the very features considered unique to urbanizing (capitalist) industrial societies. Why?

The response to this question points to one of the key differences in historical school change among the three societies: the composition of their respective cultural markets for schooling. Plainly stated, for New England it is quite possible to construct an explanation of historical school change by appealing to the workings of a cultural market composed entirely of groups, classes and resources indigenous to the New England states. For Ontario, a similar accomplishment becomes possible as the province's status changes from peripheral to semi-peripheral, that is (at the risk of simplifying the situation to the point of distortion), as the indigenous Ryerson replaces the imported Strachan. For Newfoundland, however, just the opposite is the case: it is impossible to construct an explanation of historical school change unless an appeal is made to a cultural market for schooling that is composed of groups, classes, and resources *external* to the area.

Certainly the early Newfoundland school promoters were individuals from areas outside the colony, usually the British Isles, who had institutional connections with the colony through various commercial and religious organizations. For example, one of the first school promoters, Samuel Codner, was an English merchant from Devon who started the Newfoundland School Society in 1823 (which in 1846 changed its name to 'The Church of England Society For Educating the Poor of Newfoundland and The Colonies'). The support for the Society came from ' ... merchants trading to or based in Newfoundland; Evangelicals, both clerical and lay, of the Church of England; and ... the British government'.[48] Although the most important, this was but one of many external denominationally based societies that promoted schooling. Almost all of them drew their main objectives, financial support, and teaching personnel from organizations outside the colony.

Some evidence for this early period suggests that a few Newfoundlanders were also demanding schooling. Remarkably little is known about the exact identities of the indigenous school promoters although all the evidence in Barnes (1917)[49] indicates that they were merchants or other relatively well placed individuals. But the only direct intervention by indigenous individuals in this early period appears to have occured between 1799 and 1802 when some of the wealthy in St. John's attempted unsuccessfully to establish a secondary school for their children (Barnes, 1917). Generally, the impetus for schooling came from outside the colony.

Historical school change in Newfoundland was then initiated in response to the conditions and concerns of organizations external to the colony, although their efforts gained support from certain elements within the colony. For example, with respect to the bases of support for Codner's Newfoundland School Society, McCann contends that it represented ' ... a tradition of missionary and educational activity in the colonies, particularly in those where the Anglican Church was relatively weak ... ' and ' ... where civil order seemed least stable'. Moreover, by the 1820s, 'Newfoundland merchants ... ', McCann tells us, were worried that the ' ... growth of population, especially by immigration, had created a large unskilled labor force, illiterate or semi-literate, given to intemperence ... '.[50]

Once established, this pattern of externally directed intervention became difficult to alter given Newfoundland's continuing membership in the periphery, a relationship that facilitated the original establishment of the pattern. It was the poverty and weak state structure resulting from Newfoundland's peripheral status that first attracted the external organizations. And it was the continuing poverty and weak state structure resulting from Newfoundland's continuing role as part of the periphery that enabled the external organizations to maintain their influence once they had established it. As such, these organizations remained important contenders in the cultural market for schooling in Newfoundland.

Church, State and Schools

Most of the early school societies in Newfoundland were sponsored by one or another religious denomination that was 'international' in scope. The representatives of these denominations in Newfoundland were usually full-time organizational members. Consequently, their primary commitment was to their respective organizations rather than to Newfoundland itself. Thus, historical school change in Newfoundland had to be shaped to meet the objectives of these various organizations – objectives that were defined within an 'international', not just a Newfoundland context. This, I think, explains the continued attempts of certain denominations[51] to retain considerable direct control over schooling when confronted with repeated, vigorous efforts from the 1830s to the 1870s to situate control in the state.

Still, while the preceding discussion does provide in a general way some indication of why the struggles took the form they did, it does not account for the outcomes: who won and with what consequences? More specifically, why were the denominations successful in retaining effective, direct control over the decision-making process? That is, how were they able to remain crucial contenders in the cultural market? Ontario, in contrast, developed a state run, financed, and controlled school system, except for an initially, relatively weak separate Catholic school board. New England's schools were also non-denominational. Why were the promoters of state run schooling not similarly successful in Newfoundland?

Any satisfactory response to this question must consider a complex set of factors, and only the rough, initial outline of an answer can be given here. Certainly the fact that denominational representatives wanted to maintain control does not explain fully why they were able to do so, although the existence of such an orientation is part of the answer. Hamilton (1970) and Rowe (1964)[52] identify another factor: only with church financial aid could the state meet the operating costs of the system; the price of such assistance was continued church control. But both these conditions were embedded in a more basic fact: Newfoundland's peripheral status. This status was characterized by a political economy retaining relatively little of the surplus from the production of lower-ranking goods, a state of affairs that resulted in a weak state structure. The state was weak not only in the important sense that it lacked financial resources, but also in the sense that it lacked potential allies in the non-state sectors of the political economy. Such allies were lacking because, as is typical of all peripheral societies, the types of material conditions and processes that would produce them were absent. There were thus very few supporters of state schooling.[53] Newfoundland's position on the periphery deprived the state of both its surplus and potential allies. Consequently, the churches' meagre resources were still powerful enough to maintain their position with respect to the state. One result was a continued emphasis on schooling the poor for their station in life within a denominational framework. During the nineteenth century New England

and Ontario came to see schooling as a weapon in the international struggle for economic supremacy among nations, a struggle which necessitated the mobilization of the entire population. In Newfoundland the full emergence of such an orientation had to wait until the provincial state was able to draw upon some of the resources of the federal state after Confederation in 1949.

School attendance patterns provide another example of the consequences of a weak state structure. Newfoundland's 1943 compulsory attendance law, lacking enforcement machinery, remained relatively ineffective until Newfoundland was able to enlist the power of the Canadian state after 1949 in the form of family allowance payments. Moreover, the attendance laws themselves were passed under the Commission of Government (1932–49), during which time Newfoundland was run by six commissioners appointed by the British government. Three were from Britain and managed the colony's external and financial affairs. Three were Newfoundlanders and managed various internal affairs, including education. One purpose of the Commission was to establish a stronger state structure, mainly by regulating finances. But I think it is significant that two key features of a state run school system were established during this time: compulsory attendance in 1943 and a formal tracking or streaming system in 1936–37.[54]

Conclusions

In this paper I have attempted to demonstrate in a general way the value of combining the notions of world-systems and cultural markets as a way of describing and explaining historical school change. The notion of cultural markets is analytically useful in that, through it, explicit explanatory linkages can be made to different types of school structures and contents. However, if the markets are taken simply as 'given' they have limited value for explaining historical school change. What is required is a way of explaining the markets, that is, why they work in the ways that they do, and how and why they change historically. To assist in this task I have enlisted the notion of a world-system, specifically the idea of a modern world-economy. By itself, the notion appears too grounded in concerns other than historical school change to be of much use: its emphasis is on the material conditions and processes generating class and status group conflict in relation to the transformations of the political economies of the various areas making up a world-economy. But it may also be useful for explaining the class and group processes that comprise the cultural market for schooling. After all, we need to know not only which classes and groups were contenders in the market, but the quantity of resources they were able to bring to bear in their struggles, and the opportunities they had to employ them. These, surely, are determined in substantial measure by the nature of the political economy.

This perspective also raises the question of whether historical school change varies systematically as a result of various areas' relationships with a world-system. The data examined in this paper, drawn as they are from only three areas in the modern world-economy, do not allow us to make *any* firmly grounded generalizations. Still, a few hypotheses can be formulated. One is that the more peripheral an area, the more likely it is that groups external to the area will be contenders in the cultural market for schooling and the less likely it is that indigenous groups will be able to prevail over external groups. Another is that the more peripheral an area, the more likely it is that non-state controlled school structures and contents will arise. Moreover, the more peripheral an area, the more likely it is that its school system will be controlled by religious denominations and the more likely it is that the content of schooling will be directed at a specific segment of the population and stress schooling for a low, but respectable, station in life. Finally (and this is a very tentative hypothesis) the more peripheral a society, the more likely it is that the origins and development of historical school change will be located in the attempts of a higher class or group to impose a system of social control upon a lower class or status group. We are obviously dealing with a high level of generality here. Still, these hypotheses do indicate some of the potential linkages that may be made.

Acknowledgements

I am very much indebted to Bob Brym, Lawrence Felt, Carolyne Gorlick, Eric Jarvis, Ralph Matthews, Ken Walker, Gordon West and the anonymous CJS reviewer for their comments on earlier drafts. I wish only that I could have responded to all the issues they raised.

Notes and References

1 See CLIFFORD, G.J. (1977) 'Education: Its History and Historiography'. SHULMAN, L.S. (Ed) *Review of Research in Education 4.* Itasca, Illinois: Peacock F.E., pp. 210–67; COHEN, S. (1973) 'New Perspectives in the History of American Education, 1960–70'. *History of Education 2,* pp. 79–98; KAESTLE, C.F. (1972) 'Social Reform and the Urban School'. *History of Education Quarterly.* XII, pp. 221–8; ROOKE, P. T. (1975) 'From Polyanna to Jeremiah – Recent Interpretations of American Educational History', *Journal of Educational Thought.* 9(1), pp. 15–28; SLOAN, D. (1973) 'Historiography and the History of Education'. in KERLINGER, F.N. (Ed) *Review of Research in Education 1.* Itasca, Illinois: Peacock, F.E., pp.239–69; and WILSON, J.D. (1977) 'Historiographical Perspectives on Canadian Educational History'. *Journal of Educational Thought.* 11(1), pp. 49–63.
2 COLLINS, R. (1977) 'Some Comparative Principles of Educational Stratification'. *Harvard Educational Review.* 47, pp. 1–27; WALLERSTEIN, I. (1974) *The Modern World-System: Capitalism Agriculture and the Origins of the European World-Economy in the Sixteenth Century.* New York: Academic Press.
3 BOWLES, S. and GINTIS, H. (1976) *Schooling in Capitalist America: Educational Reform and the Contradictions of Economic Life.* New York, Basic Books, pp. 225–30.
4 BUTTS, R.F. (1947) *A Cultural History of Western Education.* New York: McGraw Hill.
5 CUBBERLY, E.P. (1934) *Public Education in the US* Boston: Houghton-Miffin; CARLETON, F.T. (1911) *Economic Influences upon Educational Progress in the US 1820–1850.* Madison: University of Wisconsin Press.
6 CLARK, B.R. (1962) *Educating the Expert Society.* San Francisco: Chandler; TROW, M. (1966) 'The Second Transformation of American Secondary Education'. In BENDIX R. and LIPSET, S.M. (Eds) *Class, Status and Power: Social Stratification in Comparative Perspective:* New York: The Free Press, pp. 437–49.
7 COLLINS, R. (1971) 'Functional and conflict theories of educational stratification' *American Sociological Review* 36, pp. 1002–19. JOHNSON, R. (1976) 'Notes on the schooling of the English Working Class, 1780–1850'. in DALE, R., ESLAND, G. and MACDONALD, M. (Eds) *Schooling and Capitalism: A Sociol-*

ogical Reader. London: The Open University Press, pp. 44–54.

8 SUTHERLAND, N. (1975) 'Introduction: Towards a History of English-Canadian Youngsters' in KATZ, M.B. and MATTINGLY, P.H. (Eds) *Education and Social Change: Themes from Ontario's Past*. New York: New York University Press, pp. xi–xxxi.

9 BAILYN, B. (1960) *Education in the Forming of American Society*. New York: Vintage Books; CREMIN, L.A. (1977) *Traditions of American Education*. New York: Basic Books.

10 KATZ, M.B. (1971) *Class, Bureaucracy, and Schools: The Illusion of Educational Change in America*. New York: Praeger.

11 *ibid*; HOUSTON, S.E. (1975) 'Politics, Schools, and Social Change in Upper Canada'. in KATZ, M.B. and MATTINGLY, P.H. (Eds) *Education and Social Change: Themes from Ontario's Past*. New York: New York University Press, pp. 28–56; PRENTICE, A. (1977) *The School Promoters: Education and Social Class in Mid-Nineteenth Century Upper Canada*. Toronto: McClelland and Stewart.

12 RAVITCH, D. (1977) *The Revisionists Revised: A Critique of the Radical Attack on the Schools*. New York: Basic Books.

13 SMITH, D. (1976) 'The urban genesis of school bureaucracy: a transatlantic comparison'. in DALE, R., ESLAND, G. and MacDONALD, M. (Eds) *Schooling and Capitalism: A Sociological Reader*. London: The Open University Press, pp. 66–77.

14 BOWLES, S. and GINTIS, H. (1976) *op. cit.*; JOHNSON, L.A. (1973) *History of the County of Ontario 1615–1875*. Whitby: Corporation of the County of Whitby; SCHECTER, S. (1977) 'Capitalism, class and educational reform in Canada' in PANITCH, L. (Ed) *The Canadian State: Political Economy and Political Power*. Toronto: University of Toronto Press, pp. 373–416.

15 SCHECTER, S. (1977) *op. cit.*, p. 379.

16 KATZ, M.B. (1978) 'Origins of the Institutional State'. *Marxist Perspectives*. 1(4), pp. 6–22.

17 COLLINS, R. (1977) *op. cit.*, pp. 20–1.

18 CHIROT, D. (1976) *Social Change in a Peripheral Society: The Creation of a Balkan Colony*. New York: Academic Press, pp. 163.

19 COLLINS, R. (1977) *op. cit.*; WALLERSTEIN, I. (1974) *op. cit.*

20 COLLINS, R. (1975) *Conflict Sociology: Toward an Explanatory Science*. New York: Academic Press.

21 COLLINS, R. (1977) *op. cit.*, p. 23, 26.

22 WALLERSTEIN, I. (1974) *op. cit.*, pp. 301–2, 349–50, 351.

23 Actually Wallerstein refers to core areas as core-states because one of the characteristics of core areas is a strong state structure. External areas are termed arenas and are not actually 'within' or 'of' the world system of interest although they maintain trade relations with it.

24 COLLINS, R. (1977) *op. cit.*, p. 3.

25 COLLINS, R. (1975) *op. cit.*, Chaps. 2 and 6.

26 COLLINS, R. (1977) *op. cit.*, p. 3.

27 POMFRET, A. (1977) 'Historical School Change in a Peripheral Society: A Working Paper on Newfoundland'. A paper presented at the annual meetings of the Canadian Sociology and Anthropology Association, Fredericton, New Brunswick.

28 CHIROT, D. (1977) *Social Change in the Twentieth Century*. New York: Harcourt, Brace, Javanovich.

29 *ibid*., Chaps. 2 and 7; JOHNSON, L.A. (1974) 'The Political Economy of Ontario Women in the Nineteenth Century'. in ACTON, J., GOLDSMITH, P. and SHEPPARD, B. (Eds) *Women at Work: Ontario, 1850–1930*. Toronto: Women's Educational Press, pp. 13–31; CUNEO, C.J. (1978) 'A Class Perspective on Regionalism'. in GLENDAY, D., GUIDON, H. and TUROWETZ, A. (Eds) *Modernization and the Canadian State*. Toronto: Macmillan, pp. 132–56.

30 ALEXANDER, D. (1977) *The Decay of Trade: An Economic History of the Newfoundland Saltfish Trade, 1935–1965*. St. John's: Institute of Social and Economic Studies, Memorial University of Newfoundland; CUNEO, C.J. (1978) *op. cit.*, p. 151; NOEL, S.J.R. (1971) *Politics in Newfoundland*. Toronto: University of Toronto Press, Chaps. 11, 12, 15.

31 GWYN, R. (1972) *Smallwood: The Unlikely Revolutionary*. Toronto: McClelland and Stewart, Chaps. 15, 20, 27; INNIS, H.A. (1978) *The Cod Fisheries: The History of An International Economy*. Toronto: University of Toronto Press, Chaps. 12, 14.

32 HOUSTON, S.E. (1976) 'School Reform and Education: The Issue of Compulsory Schooling, Toronto 1851–71'. Toronto: Mimeo, pp. 28–9.

33 PRENTICE, A. (1977) *op. cit.*, p. 59–62.

34 LAZERSON, M. (1971) *Origins of the Urban School: Public Education in Massachusetts, 1870–1915*. Cambridge, Massachusetts: Harvard University Press, ix.

35 BOWLES, S. and GINTIS, H. (1976) *op. cit.*, p. 235.

36 *ibid*., p. 234.

37 COLLINS, R. (1977) *op. cit.*, pp. 20, 23.

38 JOHNSON, L.A. (1973) *op. cit.*

39 *ibid.*, p. 265.

40 *ibid.*, p. 278.

41 LAZERSON, M. (1971) *op. cit.*; KATZ, M.B. (1971) *op. cit.*

42 BOWLES, S. and GINTIS, H. (1976) *op. cit.*, pp. 234; 239–40.

43 SCHECTER, S. (1977) *op. cit.*, p. 381.

44 KATZ, M.B. (1971) *op. cit.*, xix.

45 PRENTICE, A. (1970) 'The American Example'. in WILSON, J.D., STAMP, R.M. and AUDET, L.–P.
    (Eds) *Canadian Education: A History.* Scarborough, Ontario: Prentice-Hall, pp. 41–68, esp., p. 54.

46 PRENTICE, A. (1977) *op. cit.*, p. 66. See also HOUSTON, S.E. (1976) *op. cit.*; and SCHECTER, S. (1977)
    op. cit.

47 BARNES, A. (1917) *The History of Education in Newfoundland.* New York: Unpublished Doctor of
    Pedagogy Thesis, New York University; McCANN, P. (1976) 'The Newfoundland School Society,
    1823–36; Missionary Enterprise or Cultural Imperialism?' St. John's: Memorial University of New-
    foundland. Mimeo.

48 McCANN, P. (1976) *op. cit.*, p. 8.

49 BARNES, A. (1917) *op. cit.*, pp. 68–72.

50 McCANN, P. (1976) *op. cit.*, pp. 3, 4, 9.

51 The fight over denominational control in Newfoundland was essentially a struggle among the Pro-
    testant denominations. The Catholics had won the right to their own school system in the 1850s.
    The remaining conflict was between the Anglicans, who wanted denominational control, and the
    other Protestant denominations, which did not. The Anglicans managed to pass a denominational
    law in 1874 because their party had won a majority of seats in the legislature in the 1873 election.

52 HAMILTON, W.B. (1970) 'Society and Schools in Newfoundland' in WILSON, J.D., STAMP, R.M. and
    AUDET, L.–P. (Eds) *Canadian Education: A History.* Scarborough, Ontario: Prentice-Hall, pp. 126–142;
    ROWE, F.W. (1964) *The Development of Education in Newfoundland.* Toronto: The Ryerson Press.

53 The situation changed in the twentieth century. Consider Rowe's (1976, pp. 23–4) observation con-
    cerning amalgamated school, '... whereby two or more boards of education, with the approval of
    their respective religious authorities, could operate a joint service. These schools originated in the
    industrial areas of the Province where paternalistic companies agreed to support education on the
    condition that the Protestant schools, at any rate, would get together to operate a joint service. The
    success of these schools led to a steady increase in their numbers and, perhaps more than any other
    factor, influenced the major Protestant churches to integrate their educational services in the 1960s'.

54 O'BRIEN, G. (1964) 'History of Education in Newfoundland, 1930–49'. St. John's: Memorial Uni-
    versity of Newfoundland. Mimeo.

Additional Bibliography

CASEY, G.J. (1964) 'Education in Newfoundland During Commission of Government'. St. John's:
    Memorial University of Newfoundland. Mimeo.

KING, R. (1970) *A Comparative Analysis of the Evolution of the Education Systems of Guyana and Newfoundland:*
    Halifax, Nova Scotia: Unpublished M.A. Thesis, Dalhousie University.

PARSONS, L. (1964) 'Newfoundland's Struggle to Develop a System of Education'. St. John's: Memorial
    University of Newfoundland. Mimeo. and (1975) 'Political Involvement in Education in Newfound-
    land 1832–76'. St. John's: Memorial University of Newfoundland. Mimeo.

ROWE, F.W. (1976) *Education and Culture in Newfoundland.* Toronto: McGraw-Hill Ryerson.

18   Non-Formal Education and Occupational Stratification: Implications for Latin America

Thomas J. La Belle and Robert E. Verhine

In many parts of the world a combination of social pressures and financial constraints has made it necessary to look beyond the formal school as the only widely accepted means of organized education. Discussions of educational alternatives are now commonplace and nonformal education has emerged as a popular alternative. Defined as ' . . . any organized, systematic, educational activity carried on outside the framework of the formal system to provide selected types of learning to particular subgroups in the population, adults as well as children',[1] nonformal education can include out-of-school programs in such areas as agricultural extension, community development, family planning, technical or vocational training, literacy and basic education and so on. In the Third World, these programs are primarily directed toward youth and adults for whom formal education has been either inappropriate or unavailable.

It is widely assumed that nonformal education can transmit new skills and values effectively and inexpensively, thereby contributing to national development and enhancing the status and income levels of marginal groups. Yet our contention is that these groups are disadvantaged not so much because of their lack of skills but, in part, because they lack the formal school credentials which are necessary for advancement. If this is true, can nonformal education – education without formal credentials – change occupational levels and raise standards of living? We believe not. Our hypothesis is that unless there are concomitant changes in the values and institutions associated with a society's occupational stratification process, nonformal education cannot achieve its long-term goal of greater social and economic equality. [. . .]

Education and Occupational Stratification

Proponents of nonformal education believe that it, either alone or in consort with other educational efforts, can transmit the skills and values necessary for raising status and income levels. Moreover, it is claimed that nonformal education

Source: An abridged version of LA BELLE, T.J. and VERHINE, R.E. (1975) *Harvard Educational Review*, Vol. 45 No. 2, May.

can be particularly successful in accomplishing this for economically marginal groups formerly denied educational opportunities. All of this assumes a relationship between educational and occupational attainment, regardless of whether the education is formal or nonformal. While empirical data on the effectiveness of nonformal education are scanty, because of this assumption, we can look at the general relationship between education and occupational stratification.

A great many sociological studies have attempted to determine the relative importance of ascribed and achieved personal attributes to occupational position (measured by income and/or status) and mobility (measured intergenerationally and/or intragenerationally). Although these studies differ in methodologies, variables and sample populations, they consistently have found that formal educational attainment strongly influences occupational attainment, with a much greater influence on initial employment level than on subsequent promotions. Numerous economic studies also show that education is a major determinant of income growth and differentiation for both individuals and nations. Although most of these studies were done in the United States, recent sociological and economic studies conducted in various Latin American countries have produced similar results. Research by Jacobsen and Kendrick (1973) in Puerto Rico, La Belle (1975) in Venezuela, Carnoy (1964, 1972b) in Mexico and Puerto Rico, Holsinger (1974b) in Brazil, and Roberts (1973) in Costa Rica has indicated that formal education – at least in the urban areas of Latin America – has a significant impact on income and status.[5]

Despite the consistency of these results across national boundaries, there is evidence suggesting that the impact of schooling on occupational attainment is positively related to an area's level of socioeconomic development.[6] Studies of labor market demand and supply show that modernizing economies tend to witness rising educational requirements at all levels of the job hierarchy.[7] Thus, despite the growth of popular demand for formal educational opportunities and an increasingly better educated work force, educational expansion has failed to produce any significant decline in social inequality.[8] As individuals in modern society attain higher levels of schooling, the value of that education is deflated by rising job requirements. Consequently, people must acquire more schooling simply to attain the same levels of social reward. Boudon's argument implies that increasing educational attainment in areas with high levels of socioeconomic development does not necessarily change the social and occupational stratification system.

Presumably, there would be a greater correlation between schooling and occupational level if one could distinguish the aspects and kinds of training which are job or income related.[9] Research conducted in the United States by Blum (1972) and Coleman (1972)[10] took an important step in this direction by considering as two separate variables the education acquired before and after entering the job market. Both studies found that education acquired after job-entry has a greater impact on status and income than does any other post-job-entry variable tested. However, it has significantly less influence than pre-employment educational attainment. Unfortunately, Blum and Coleman did not distinguish between formal and nonformal education in the post-employment education variable.

[...]

One major reason for the failure of nonformal education to increase job attainment may be that employers do not value such credentials when compared with those offered by formal schools. Indeed, the important role of academic credentials in the stratification process is well documented in developed countries. Studies show that degrees and diplomas alone, independent of years in school or cognitive achievement, command additional income and status in the job market.[11]

[...]

Why are formal school credentials more influential in the job market than those offered by nonformal education programs if they both transmit the same skills and values? Two theories have been advanced to explain this. The technical-function theory asserts that education provides the specific skills and/or general capabilities that are required for employment. Educational requirements for jobs tend to rise as technological change steadily creates a need for more highly skilled workers. Thus, school credentials constitute proof that an individual possesses the skills and knowledge necessary for economic production. The status-conflict theory, on the other hand, proposes that formal education socializes individuals and confers elite status or respect for elite status. According to this theory, rising educational requirements for employment are a result of the competition among status groups who use education to dominate the job market by imposing their cultural standards on the occupational selection process. This theory suggests that credentials are more a mark of membership in a particular status group than proof of technical skill or achievement.

Before continuing our discussion of education and stratification, it should be stated that these theories allow us to place the diversity of research cited here in a framework. Many of the relevant sociological and economic studies mentioned here are context-specific and thus may not always be applicable to Latin America. Though these studies have found that apparently most people receive some status and income benefits from formal education, it is clear that the magnitude of these benefits differs substantially between race and sex groups,[12] between regions,[13] and between countries.[14] Moreover, in concentrating on employee attributes and/or income flows, these studies fail to focus on the total occupational selection process. Many do not consider, for example, the structure and requirements of the job market, the quantity and nature of schooling opportunities, and the attitudes, perceptions and behavior of employers. Thus, an additional problem with these studies is that while they posit that people benefit from formal education, they fail to account for such interrelated factors as the dominant cultural values, the rigidity of class and status lines and the linkage of occupational hierarchies to social stratification. However, if they are placed within a theoretical framework which explains in general how educational attainment is related to occupational attainment, these studies can be applied to Latin America. The technical-function and status-conflict theories allow us to do that.

The Technical-Function Theory

The first assertion of the technical-function theory is that skill requirements in an industrial society steadily increase because of technological change. This notion is supported by manpower studies conducted in numerous countries. The early stages of development appear to create a particularly strong demand for middle-level technicians and managers.[15] In Brazil, for example, despite the rapid increase in enrollment, the demand for middle-school graduates is nearly one and one-half times the supply.[16] However, studies conducted in the United States suggest that the upgrading of job skill requirements as a result of technological change cannot account fully for the increasing impact of educational attainment on occupational attainment. Folger and Nam (1964)[17] report that only fifteen per cent of the increase in educational levels in the United States in the twentieth century can be attributed to shifts in the occupational structure – a decrease in the proportion of low skill jobs and an increase in the proportion of high skill jobs. Moreover, investigations of the links between schooling and job skills by Berg (1970), Eckhaus (1964), Horowitz and Hernstadt (1966), and Jaffe and Froomkin (1968)[18] have established that educational requirements for jobs have risen at a faster rate than the actual skill requirements for these jobs. Hence, more and more Americans are and will be in jobs which require less education than they have. Although these findings may not be applicable to Latin America, where the level and accessibility of schooling are relatively limited and the processes of industrialization are relatively new, they nevertheless indicate that the first assertion of the technical-function theory may not be universal.

The second assertion of this theory is that formal schooling transmits the specific skills and/or general knowledge necessary for more highly skilled jobs This presupposes a type of schooling which teaches and selects for skills and qualities leading to occupational success in an industrial economy. However, such schooling may not be prevalent in Latin America. For the most part, Latin American formal education continues to reflect the values of a traditional, aristocratic society. Most schools are academic and emphasize preparation for fields which offer high status but are not directly productive in an economic sense.[19] Indeed, they often foster a disdain for manual work and for those who perform it.[20] Of course, many educational systems in Latin America are in the process of altering their goals and operations in accordance with the economic and social demands of modernization. But even when schools are geared specifically to an industrial economy, it is not clear that they successfully transmit the necessary skills and knowledge, at least if one assumes that people with these skills are readily employable. For example, in several developing countries, economic studies of the returns derived from voca-tional/technical secondary schools demonstrate that with the existing labor market setting, these schools are poor private and public investments.[21] In addition, investigations in the United States have determined that graduates of vocational programs are no more likely to be employed than are high school dropouts.[22]

In contrast, economic cost-benefit analyses indicate that on-the-job training is a relatively sound investment. Mincer (1962)[23] found that the rate of return on selected investments in on-the-job training, such as apprenticeships and medical specializations, is indistinguishable from the rate of return on total college education costs. Machlup (1970)[24] examined the demand and cost considerations of formal education in relation to schooling alternatives and concluded that both on-the-job training and adult education programs have greater short-term economic returns than formal schooling, despite the latter's far greater rate of return over a lifetime. These results support the report by Clark and Sloan (1966)[25] that most manual workers in the United States acquire their skills on the job or casually. The evidence attesting to the higher short-term returns for on-the-job training, coupled with the research showing low economic yields from vocational secondary schools, casts some doubt on the assertion that schools contribute to occupational stratification through the transmission of necessary job skills.

The importance of formal education to nonmanual job skills is also questionable. Soderberg (1963)[26] notes that approximately 40 per cent of the engineers in the United States during the early 1950's lacked college degrees. Hargens and Hagstrom (1967)[27] report that educational quality has little effect on the subsequent productivity of research scientists. Studies conducted in São Paulo, Brazil, show that 40 per cent of the technical or professional employees over age 35 have had no more than a primary school education.[28]

Although it is debatable whether or not formal education is necessary to transmit manual and nonmanual job skills, proponents of the technical-function theory might argue that schooling is important because it provides the basic knowledge necessary for workers to benefit from further training. This contention is supported by time-lag correlations between education and economic growth suggesting that the main contribution of education to economic development occurs at the level of mass literacy (Peaslee, 1969).[29] Thurow (1970)[30] emphasizes the complementary nature of formal education and specific skills training and asserts that the benefits from training and education taken together will be larger than the benefits from formal education and experience taken separately. On the other hand, Berg (1970)[31] questions the assumption that formal education contributes to worker trainability. His careful evaluation of training programs conducted by the United States Armed Forces indicates that discrete measures of aptitude are generally much better predictors of trainee performance than educational attainment.

Proponents of the technical-function theory could also argue that schooling is important because it fosters attitudes conducive to economic production. Indeed, Myrdal (1968)[32] suggests that schools may play an important role in the creation of more modern attitudes toward life and work (for example, punctuality, ambition, readiness for change). This contention receives support from a large body of empirical research, including Holsinger's longitudinal study of primary schools in Brazil.[33] However, the results of modernization studies must be judged in light of other investigations, including many conducted in Latin America which indicate that schools tend to reflect and perpetuate rather than change the sociocultural milieu in which they function.[34] For example, Nash (1965)[35] concludes from his study of schooling in Central America the '[l]ocal schools tend to be conservative agents, transmitting by means that reinforce local tendencies toward stability. Education becomes a force for social change only when the process of social change is well underway'. Thus it is possible that schools do not so much initiate attitude change as they support and accelerate changes emerging from modernization.

David O'Shea[36] (1974) persuasively argues this point, reasoning that students probably acquire attitudes favorable to modernization from their parents prior to entering school. Ironically, it should also be noted that insofar as schools do succeed in fostering attitudes conducive to modernization, they may be raising expectations and aspirations to a level beyond fulfillment and thus serve to retard economic output. Studies conducted in the United States[37] and Africa[38] have demonstrated that educational achievement is associated with the frustration, alienation and oppositionism of workers.

An evaluation of the technical-function theory should also consider the relationship between mental ability and occupational attainment.[39] This relationship would be positive if rising educational requirements for jobs reflect employers' desire to hire more mentally able workers. While older studies appeared to confirm this expectation,[40] more recent research challenges this contention. In his analysis of the economics of education, Becker (1964)[41] reveals that although there is a positive association between mental ability and educational attainment, the latter accounts for much more of the variance in earnings. Using a complex recursive model, Sewell et al. (1970)[42] find that job status, while strongly associated with years of schooling, is correlated only weakly and indirectly with mental ability.

While these studies cast doubt on the validity of the second component of the technical-function theory, economic research seems to offer strong evidence that formal education provides the capabilities needed in an industrial society. Macro- and micro-economic studies uniformly have shown that investment in education, whether made by individuals or by nations, yields substantial returns in income.[43] As a result, many economists now view human resources as a form of capital, a means of production, and the product of investment in education. However, a careful look at these economic analyses suggests that their findings are not as convincing as they appear at first glance.

The much touted residual studies,[44] for example, are arbitrary in attributing the observed difference between the rate of growth of GNP and the rate of increase in measurable inputs to the effects of education. In fact, the residual may result from the improved quality of capital assets rather than from education. Moreover, these studies fail to account properly for on-the-job learning, nonformal training and the effects of worker attitudes and motivation.[45] Inter-country correlations,[46] a second group of economic studies, are similarly limited because they do not consider causality. Though high correlations are reported between enrollment ratios at all levels of education and GNP per capita, it is unclear whether investments in education contribute to economic growth or *vice versa*. The issue is confused further by the fact that educational expansion is often the product of political demand, resulting in the overproduction of educated personnel in many countries.[47]

Micro cost-benefit studies also suffer from severe limitations. When taken together they offer strong support for the notion that education is an economically productive endeavor in most every region of the world.[48] However, when examined individually each is deficient in some aspect of its research design.[49] Moreover, these studies are suspect because of their reliance on the neo-classical marginal wage theory which assumes an economically rational world in which employers allocate human resources for maximum production and pay workers in accordance with their real output. The questionable basis of this theory, especially in the Latin American context, will become clear later in this paper.

Therefore, the various economic studies do not necessarily prove that formal education provides the capabilities required to augment economic production. In fact, there is some evidence that educational attainment, though associated with income levels, does not correspond closely to worker productivity. Berg (1970),[50] in his summary of research dealing with the direct influence of education on individual productivity, concludes that in general, better-educated employees were often less productive than the blue- and white-collar workers, managers and professionals in the sample. He suggests that schooling corresponds to wage differentials, not because education contributes to productivity, but because it helps a person to obtain a better paying job in the first place.

One might argue that the technical-function theory fails to account adequately for the evidence because employers are misinformed; they erroneously believe that in demanding higher levels of education for employment, they are hiring more capable, trainable, and productive workers. At the same time, however, one might argue that employers are not as concerned with the economic productivity of their workers as is generally believed. For example, it appears that employers have imprecise conceptions of skill requirements for jobs, and that they rarely collect or analyze data pertaining to worker productivity or the contribution of education to such productivity.[51] Furthermore, organizations generally do not force employees to work at maximum efficiency. Procedures or personnel are changed only when performance falls noticeably below the minimum levels set for workers.[52] Research shows that employers in Latin America may be even less likely than their North American counterparts to base decisions on rational economic criteria. Studies of the attitudes and behavior of Latin American entrepreneurs confirm that they place little emphasis on bureaucratic and competitive norms; personal characteristics and family origins are valued more than technical or organizational abilities.[53]

The Status-Conflict Theory

An alternative explanation for the role of formal education in social and occupational stratification is provided by the status-conflict theory, largely derived from Max Weber (1968).[54] It has been examined carefully in North America by Randall Collins (1968, 1971),[55] and in Latin America by Martin Carnoy (1972a).[56] According to this theory, society is characterized by a continual struggle among cultural groups for wealth, power and prestige. Membership in these groups gives individuals a fundamental sense of identity; they generally accept one another as status equals. The theory further maintains that status groups use the schools to preserve and strengthen their relative positions in society, and that the primary function of schools is to teach and select for particular status groups by imparting the values, manners, interests, tastes and experiences associated with the group in control of the educational system. Educational requirements for employment, rather than flowing from functional economic demands, enable the particular status group controlling schooling to control the work place as well. By basing occupational attainment on educational attainment, the élite status group assures the selection of higher level employees from its own membership and lower level workers who at least have been indoctrinated to respect its cultural superiority. The status-conflict theory suggests that educational requirements for employment tend to rise over time in response to the increasing supply of educated persons. As other status groups, particularly the middle class, demand the education that will enable them to compete with elites, more and more people will want to become educated. Thus, employers raise educational requirements to maintain both the relative prestige of their own managerial ranks and the relative respectability of the middle ranks.[57]

Lending support to the status-conflict theory are a number of historical and descriptive studies which indicate that schools are founded by powerful and autonomous groups either to provide exclusive education for their children or to promote respect for their cultural attributes. In the United States, for example, historical research shows that a major reason for the rapid proliferation of schools during the colonial period was the competition among communities and religious groups for power and prestige.[58] Moreover, it appears that the impetus for the public school system in the nineteenth century came from a white, Anglo-Saxon élite who wished to propagate Protestant, middle-class standards.[59] Studies in Latin America have pointed to the historic role of formal schooling in the formation of élites.[60] As education evolved from being a function of the church to a function of national governments, it continued to serve two basic functions: to prepare elites for high status and leadership positions and to incorporate non-elites into the lower strata of the social system. Although the highest social classes reserved the upper levels of education for themselves, 'schooling was expanded to socialize marginal groups into the portion of the economic structure controlled by the liberal élite and under a set of rules developed by the ruling group and transmitted through the school'.[61] Education in Latin America today, especially on the secondary level, still bears the mark of centuries of domination by a landed elite. It continues to place emphasis on the borrowed European aristocratic tradition of academic, humanistic learning that is deemed appropriate for preparing a select few for leadership roles.

Additional support for the notion that schools provide training and respect for the elite culture comes from anthropological studies of schools in both developed and underdeveloped regions of the world.[62] They show that the language, values and cognitive styles promoted and reinforced in the school are those associated with the cultural group controlling the school. Thus, it is implied that when the referent culture of students differs from that of the school, their chances of success in school are seriously jeopardized. This implication is particularly relevant to rural Latin America where the school has been described as 'an exotic and sickly import from the cities, deriving from national policy rather than local demands'.[63] Moreover, case studies of formal education in rural Latin America suggest that high dropout and nonattendance rates are consequences of a type of schooling that has little meaning in the rural milieu.[64] The match between the culture of the schools and the culture of the status group may explain why sociologists and economists find that social origins tend to act as a strong predictor of both years of schooling completed and achievement scores.[65]

Hence, those who succeed in formal schools and thereby gain access to high status and income appear to come from families already enjoying these benefits. This suggests that the democratization of schooling opportunities accompanying modernization in Latin America has not given everybody an equal chance to acquire élite status. Schools continue to function on the basis of culturally determined merit which favors the ruling group, whether that group is traditional or modern. As in the case of the occupational marketplace, schools tend to reward individuals who come from middle-and upper-socioeconomic class backgrounds and so constrain those individuals who do not.[66]

Carnoy (1972)[67] has used these conclusions to develop a dynamic model which explains the role of education in developing economies and which supports the status-conflict theory. The model attributes two distinct functions to formal schooling: socialization and elite formation. In the lower grades, the school's primary purpose is socialization. The students in these grades are from heterogeneous socioeconomic backgrounds. But at a certain level, the school's role changes from socialization to selection and élite formation. For the most part, students in the upper grades are either those born into the upper strata of society or those who have acquired elite characteristics. Carnoy's model also proposes that as enrollments in the lower levels of schooling increase in response to the popular demand for more educational opportunities and the economic need for highly skilled labor, the point at which rigorous selection takes place moves to higher and higher grade levels. Using economic rate of return data, Carnoy posits that those levels of schooling to which élites maintain exclusive access are those which yield the highest economic returns. Therefore, élites are able to satisfy the popular demand and economic need for more schooling in developing economies without giving up their own economic and policy-making power. Carnoy's reasoning is similar to Boudon's argument suggesting that the expansion of formal educational opportunities will not be accompanied by significant change in the structure of the stratification system.

[...]

It can now be asked whether employers actually use education as a means of selection for cultural attributes. The preceding analysis of the technical-function theory has suggested that they do; for example, educational requirements for jobs tend to rise faster than the skill demands of those jobs, and employers do not seem to be as concerned with the economic productivity of their workers as is commonly believed. More direct support for the status-conflict theory concerning the United States comes from a large body of sociological literature showing that background factors have a major impact on job selection and attainment.[68] For example, 60 to 70 per cent of American business leaders come from upper- and upper-middle-class families,[69] and such factors as religion, race, ethnic heritage, sex, accent, name and manners have a significant impact on an individual's employment opportunities.[70]

Job market research conducted by Collins (1968, 1971)[71] is particularly relevant in determining the validity of the status-conflict theory. For example, those organizations which are clearly dominated by the white, Anglo-Saxon Protestant upper class also tend to be those organizations which set the highest educational requirements for employment. In addition, Collins finds that educational requirements for white-collar workers are highest in organizations which place the strongest emphasis on normative control of their employees. In testing the relative impact of technical change and normative control of employees on educational requirements for employment Collins' findings show that although both conditions affect educational requirements, those associated with the status-conflict theory are more significant than those associated with technical change.

[...]

Given the adherence to particularistic and ascriptive values by the Latin American élite, and given that formal schools select for élite cultural characteristics, the status-conflict theory provides an especially powerful explanation for occupational stratification. The fact that the status-conflict theory is also applicable to an industrialized society such as the United States suggests that as Latin America continues to move from an agrarian to an industrial economic base, the significance of the status-conflict theory is not likely to diminish greatly.

Implications for Nonformal Education

The foregoing analysis of the technical-function and status-conflict theories makes it possible to speculate on the probable role of nonformal education in developing societies. The technical-function theory suggests that industrialization leads to an upgrading of job skill requirements and that formal schools do not appear to be efficient transmitters of job-related skills and knowledge. This suggests that nonformal education can make a significant contribution to economic growth. Such nonformal programs are likely to be successful at skill training because they can be: first, skill specific and based on practical learning, second, adaptable to the needs and problems of particular groups, and third, relatively inexpensive because of their short duration and informal setting.

The analysis of the status-conflict theory, however, indicates that skill attainment is not the central ingredient in the occupational stratification process. Employers are concerned as much with the social and cultural attributes of their employees as with their level of technical skills or knowledge. Therefore, formal academic credentials are important in occupational selection because they are symbols of an elite-oriented and dominated socialization process. Especially in Latin America, with its industrial and agrarian elites, it is unlikely that nonformal education can provide significant status or income benefits. As nonsanctioned efforts directed at non-élite groups, nonformal education programs are incapable of validating or legitimatizing their experiences. As demands for attainment through the formal system escalate, such programs appear destined to remain at the bottom of the educational status hierarchy.

[...]

Acknowledgements

This article is based, in part, on La Belle, T. J. and Vernine, R.E. (1975) 'Education, social change and social stratification' in La Belle, T. J. (Ed.) *Educational Alternatives in Latin America* Los Angeles: Latin American Center, University of California. We wish to thank the Latin American Center at UCLA for financial assistance in the preparation of this article. Portions of this article were written while Professor La Belle was on sabbatical leave from UCLA and receiving fellowship support from the Inter-American Foundation.

Notes and References

1 COOMBS, P.H. and AHMED, M. (1974) *Attacking Rural Poverty: How Non-ducation Can Help* Baltimore, Johns Hopkins University Press, p. 8.

2 See, for example, SHEFFIELD, J.R. and DIEJOMAOH, V.P. (1972) *Non-formal Education in African Development* New York, African American Institute; WOOD, A.W. (1974) *Informal Education and Development in Africa* The Hague, Netherlands: Institute of Social Studies.

3 See BERG, I. (1970) *Education and Jobs* New York, Praeger; BLAU, P.M. and DUNCAN, O.D. (1967) *The American Occupational Structure* New York, Wiley; BLUM, D. (1972) 'White and black careers during the first decade of labor force experience. Part II: Income differences' *Social Science Research* 1, (3) pp. 271–92; COLEMAN, J.S., BLUM, Z.D., SORENSON, A.B. and ROSSI, P. (1972) 'White and black careers during the first decade of labor force status' *Social Science Research* 1, (3) pp. 243–70; DUNCAN, O.D., FEATHERMAN, D.L. and DUNCAN, B. (1972) *Socioeconomic Background and Occupational Achievement: Extension of a Basic Model* New York, Seminar Press; DUNCAN, O.D. and HODGE, R. (1963) 'Education and occupational mobility: A regression analysis' *American Journal of Sociology* 68, pp. 629–44; ECKLAND, B.K. (1965) Academic ability, higher education and occupational mobility' *American Sociological Review* 30, pp. 735–46; ELDER, G.H. (1968) 'Achievement motivation and intelligence in occupational mobility: A longitudinal analysis' *Sociometry* 31, pp. 327–54; HALLER, O.A. (1968) Education and the occupational achievement process' in US NATIONAL ADVISORY COMMISSION ON RURAL POVERTY *Rural Poverty in the United States* Washington, US Government Printing Office; PERRUCCI, C.C. and PERRUCCI, R. (1970) 'Social origins, educational contexts and career mobility' *American Sociological Review* 35, pp. 451–63; SEWELL, W.H., HALLER, A.O. and OHLENDORF, G.W. (1970) 'The educational and early occupational attainment process: Replication and revision' *American Sociological Review* 35, pp. 1014–27.

4 See summaries in BOWEN, W. (1964) *Economic Aspects of Education; Three Essays* Princeton, N.J. Industrial Relations Section, Department of Economics, Princeton University; BOWMAN, M.J. (1966) 'Human investment revolution' *Sociology of Education* 39, pp. 111–37.

5 JACOBSEN, B. and KENDRICK, J.M. (1973) 'Education and mobility: From achievement to ascription' *American Sociological Review* 38, pp. 439–60; LA BELLE, T.J. (1975) 'The impact of nonformal education on income in industry: Ciudad Guayana, Venezuela' in LA BELLE, T.J. (Ed) *Educational Alternatives in Latin America: Social Change and Social Stratification* Los Angeles, Latin American Center, University of California; CARNOY, M. (1964) 'The cost and return to schooling in Mexico: A case study' unpublished doctoral dissertation, University of Chicago and (1972b) 'The rate of return to schooling and the increase in human resources in Puerto Rico' *Comparative Education Review* 16(1) pp. 68–84; HOLSINGER, D.B. (1974b) 'Education and the occupational attainment process in Brazil' Chicago, Comparative Education Center, University of Chicago, mimeograph; ROBERTS, C.P. (1973) 'The economics of education in Costa Rica: Effects on earnings of family background, school performance and occupation' unpublished doctoral dissertation, University of California.

6 See DUNCAN, O.D. and HODGE, R. (1963) *op. cit.*; BOUDON, R. (1973) *Education, Opportunity and Social Inequality: Changing Prospects in Western Society* New York, Wiley.

7 For a discussion of rising educational requirements, see, for example, BERG, I. (1970) *op. cit.*, BOUDON, R. (1973) *op. cit.*; FAURE, E. (Ed) (1972) *Learning To Be* Paris, UNESCO.

8 BOUDON, R. (1973) *op. cit.*

9 ANDERSON, C.A. (1961) 'A skeptical note on the relation between vertical mobility and education' *American Journal of Sociology* 66, pp. 560–70.

10 BLUM, D. (1972) *op. cit.*; COLEMAN, J.S. *et al* (1972) *op. cit.*

11 BERG, I. (1970) *op. cit.*; ECKLAND, B.K. (1964) *op. cit.*; HANSEN, W.L. (1963) 'Total and private rates of return to investment in schooling' *Journal of Political Economy* 71, (2) pp. 128–41.

12 See BLAIR, P. (1970) 'Rates of return to schooling of majority and minority groups in Santa Clara County' unpublished doctoral dissertation, Stanford University; BLAU, P.M. and DUNCAN, O.D. (1967) *op. cit.*; COLEMAN *et al* (1966) *op. cit.*; HANOCH, G. (1967) 'An economic analysis of earnings and schooling' *Journal of Human Resources* 2(3) pp. 310–29; HINES, F., TWEETEN, L. and REDFERN, M. (1970) 'Social and private rates of return to investment in schooling, by race, sex groups and regions' *Journal of Human Resources* 3, pp. 318–40; WELCH, F. (1967) 'Labor market discrimination: An interpretation of income differences in the Rural South' *Journal of Political Economy* 75(3) pp. 225–40.

13 BLAU, P.M. and DUNCAN, O.D. (1967) *op. cit.*; HINES *et al* (1970) *op. cit.*

14 ANDERSON, C.A. (1961) *op. cit.*; PSACHAROPOULOS, G. (1972) 'Rates of return to investment around the world' *Comparative Education Review* 16(1) pp. 54–7.

15 HARBISON, F.H. and MYERS, C.A. (1964) *Education, Manpower and Economic Growth* New York, McGraw Hill.

16 HAVIGHURST, R.J. and GOUVEIA, A.J. (1969) *Brazilian Secondary Education and Socio-economic Development* New York, Praeger.

17 FOLGER, J.K. and NAM, C.B. (1964) 'Trends in education in relation to the occupational structure' *Sociology of Education* 38, pp. 19–33.

18 BERG, I. (1970) *op. cit.*; ECKHAUS, R.S. (1964) 'Economic criteria for education and training' *Review of Economics and Statistics* 46, pp. 181–90; HOROWITZ, M.A. and HERNSTADT, I.L. (1966) 'Changes in the skill requirements of occupations in selected industries' in National Commission on Technology, Automation and Economic Progress *Technology and the American Economy: Employment Impact of Technological Change* Appendix. Vol. II. Washington, D.C., US Government Printing Office, pp. 225–87; JAFFE, A.J. and FROOMKIN, J. (1968) *Technology and Jobs: Automation in Perspective* New York, Praeger.

19 LIPSET, S.M. (1967) 'Values, education and entrepreneurship' in LIPSET, S.M. and SOLARI, A. (Eds) *Elites in Latin America* New York, Oxford University Press.

20 FERNANDES, F. (1963) Pattern and rate of development in Latin America' in DE VRIES, E. and ECHEVARRIA, J.M. (Eds) *Social Aspects of Economic Development* Paris, UNESCO.

21 AL BUKHARI, N. (1968a) *Issues in Occupational Education and Training: A Case Study in Jordan* Stanford, Stanford University and (1968b) *Issues in Occupational Education and Training: A Case Study in Tunisia* Stanford, Stanford University; BOWLES, S. (1965) 'Efficiency in the allocation of resources in education: A planning model with application to Northern Nigeria' unpublished doctoral dissertation, Harvard University; CALLAWAY, A. (1973) 'Unemployment among African school leavers' *Journal of Modern African Studies* 1, pp. 351–7; FOSTER, P.J. (1966) *Education and Social Change in Ghana* Chicago, University of Chicago Press, and (1971) 'Presidential address: The revolt against the schools' *Comparative Education Review* 15(3), pp. 263–75.

22 PLUNKETT, M. (1960). 'School and early work experience of youth' *Occupational Outlook Quarterly* 4(1), pp. 22–7; DUNCAN, B. (1972) 'Dropouts and the unemployed' *Journal of Political Economy* 73, pp. 121–34.

23 MINCER, J. (1962) 'On-the-job-training: Costs, returns and implications' *Journal of Political Economy* 70, (5, part 2), pp. 50–79.

24 MACHLUP, F. (1970) *Education and Economic Growth* Lincoln, University of Nebraska Press.

25 CLARK, H.F. and SLOAN, H.S. (1966) *Classrooms on Main Street* New York, Teachers College Press.

26 SODERBERG, R.C. (1963) 'The American engineer' in LYNN, K.S. (Ed) *The Professions in America* Boston, Beacon Press.

27 HARGENS, L. and HAGSTROM, W.O. (1967) 'Sponsored and contest mobility of American academic scientists' *Sociology of Education* 40, pp. 24–38.

28 HAVIGHURST, R.J. and GOUVEIA, A.J. (1969) *op. cit.*

29 PEASLEE, A. (1969) 'Education's role in development' *Economic Development and Cultural Change* 17, pp. 293–318.

30 THUROW, L. (1970) *Investment in Human Capital* Belmont, Wadsworth.

31 BERG, I. (1970) *op. cit.*

32 MYRDAL, G. (1968) *Asian Drama: An Enquiry into the Poverty of Nations* New York, Twentieth Century Fund.

33 ARMER, M. and YOUTZ, R. (1971) 'Formal education and individual modernity in an African society' *American Journal of Sociology* 76, pp. 604–26; HOLSINGER, D.B. (1974a) 'The schooling environment as a context for individual modernization' Chicago, University of Chicago (mimeograph) and (1974b) *op. cit.*; INKELES, A. (1969) 'Making men modern: On the causes and consequences of individual change

in six developing countries' *American Journal of Sociology* 75(2), pp. 208–25.

34 HENRY, J. (1963) *Culture Against Man* New York, Vintage; COMITAS, L. (1967) 'Education and social stratification in contemporary Bolivia' *New York Academy of Sciences, Transactions, Series II* 29(7), pp. 935–48; STIMSON, J. and LA BELLE, T.J. (1971) 'The organizational climate of Raraguayan elementary schools: Rural-urban differentiation' *Education and Urban Society* 3(3), pp. 333–49.

35 NASH, M. (1965) 'The role of village schools in the process of cultural and economic modernization' *Social and Economic Studies* 14(1), p. 143.

36 O'SHEA, D. (1974) *Education, the Social System and Development* Denver, University of Denver.

37 BERG, I. (1970) *op. cit.*

38 CASH, W.C. (1968) 'A critique of manpower planning in Africa' in BLAUG, M. (Ed) *Economics and Education* Baltimore, Penguin Books; ADAMS, D. and BJORK, R.W. (1969) *Education in Developing Areas* New York, McKay.

39 Ability here refers to mental intelligence as measured by scores on a standardized aptitude test. Conclusions from these studies must be viewed with caution since they consider only one component of ability.

40 ANDERSON, C.A., BROWN, J.C. and BOWMAN, M.J. (1952) 'Intelligence and occupational mobility' *Journal of Political Economy* 60, pp. 218–39; BOALT, G. (1954) 'Social mobility in Stockholm: A pilot investigation' *Transactions of the Second World Congress of Sociology* Vol. 2 London, International Sociological Association.

41 BECKER, G.S. (1964) *Human Capital* New York, Columbia University Press.

42 SEWELL *et al* (1970) *op. cit.*

43 See summaries in BOWEN, W. (1964) *op. cit.*; BOWMAN, M.J. (1966) *op. cit.*

44 DENISON, E.F. (1962) *The Sources of Economic Growth in the United States and the Alternatives Before Us* New York, Committee on Economic Development; SCHULTZ, T.W. (1963) *The Economic Value of Education* New York, Columbia University Press.

45 HARBISON, F.H. and MYERS, C.A. (1964) *op. cit.*

46 *ibid.*; GALENSON, W. and PYATT, G. (1964) *The Quality of Labor and Economic Development in Certain Countries* Geneva, International Labor Office.

47 CALLOWAY, A. (1973) 'Frontiers of out-of-school education' in BREBECK, C. and THOMPSON, T.J. (Eds) *New Strategies for Educational Development* Lexington, Mass. Lexington Books, p. 15.

48 See summaries in CARNOY, M. (1967) 'Rates of return to schooling in Latin America' *Journal of Human Resources* 2(3), pp. 359–74; PSACHAROPOULOS, G. (1972) *op. cit.*

49 BERG, I. (1970) *op. cit.*

50 *ibid.*

51 *ibid.*

52 DILL, W.R., HILTON, T.L. and REITMAN, W.R. (1962) *The New Managers* Englewood Cliffs, N.J., Prentice-Hall; MARCH, J.G. and SIMON, H.A. (1958) *Organizations* New York, Wiley.

53 CARDOSO, F.H. (1967) 'The industrial élite' in LIPSET, S.M. and SOLARI, A. (Eds) *op. cit.*; LAUTERBACH, A. (1962) 'Managerial attitudes and economic growth' *Kylos* 15, pp. 374–400; LIPSET, S.M. (1967) *op. cit.*

54 WEBER, M. (1968) *Economy and Society* New York, Bedminster Press (1968).

55 COLLINS, R. (1968) 'A comparative approach to political sociology' in BENDIX, R. *et al* (Eds) *State and Society* Boston, Little, Brown, and (1971) 'Functional and conflict theories of educational stratification' *American Sociological Review* 36, pp. 1002–1019.

56 CARNOY, M. (1972a) 'The political economy of education' in LA BELLE, T.J. (Ed) *Education and Development: Latin America and the Caribbean* Los Angeles, University of California.

57 BOWLES, S. (1971) 'Cuban education and the revolutionary ideology' *Harvard Educational Review* 41, pp. 472–500; COLLINS, R. (1971) *op. cit.*

58 BAILYN, B. (1960) *Education in the Forming of American Society* Chapel Hill, University of North Carolina Press.

59 CREMIN, L.A. (1961) *The Transformation of the School* New York, Knopf; CURTI, M. (1935) *The Social Ideas of American Educators* New York, Scribners; KATZ, M.B. (1971) *Class, Bureaucracy and Schools* New York, Praeger.

60 CARNOY, M. (1974) *Education and Cultural Imperialism* New York, McKay; HAVIGHURST, R.J. and MOREIRA, J.R. (1964) *Society and Education in Brazil* Pittsburgh, University of Pittsburgh Press; THUT, I.N. and ADAMS, D. (1964) *Educational Patterns in Contemporary Societies* New York, McGraw-Hill.

61 CARNOY, M. (1974) *op. cit.*, p. 160.

62 GAY, J. and COLE, M. (1967) *The New Mathematics and an Old Culture: A Study of Learning among the Kpelle of Liberia* New York, Holt, Reinhart and Winston; KING, A.R. (1967) *The School at Mopass: A Problem of Identity* New York, Holt, Rinehart and Winston; ROSENFELD, G. (1971) *Shut Those Thick*

Lips! A Study of Slum School Failure New York, Holt, Rinehart and Winston.

63 UNITED NATIONS (1968) *Education, Human Resources and Development in Latin America* New York, United Nations Commission for Latin America, pp. 67–8.

64 HORST, O.H. and McCLELLAND, A. (1968) 'The development of an educational system in a rural Guatemalen community' *Journal of Inter-American Studies* 10, pp. 474–97; NASH, M. (1965) 'The role of village schools in the process of cultural and economic modernization' *Social and Economic Studies* 14(1) pp. 131–43; REICHEL-DOLMATOFF, G. and REICHEL-DOLMATOFF, A. (1961) *The People of Aritama: The Cultural Personality of a Columbian Mestizo Village* Chicago, University of Chicago Press.

65 AVERCH, H.A., CARROLL, S.J., DONALDSON, T.S., KIESLING, H.J. and PINCUS, J. (1972) *How Effective is Schooling? A Critical Review and Synthesis of Research Findings* Santa Monica, Rand; COLEMAN, J.S., CAMPBELL, E.Q., HOBSON, C.J., McPARTLAND, J., MOOD, A., WEINFELD, F.D. and YORK, R.L. (1966) *Equality of Educational Opportunity* Washington, US Government Printing Office; JENCKS, C., SMITH, M., ACLAND, H., BANE, M.J., COHEN, D.K., GINTIS, H., HEYNS, B. and MICHELSON, S. (1972) *Inequality: A Reassessment of the Effect of Family and Schooling in America* New York, Basic Books; SEWELL, W.H. (1971) 'Inequality of opportunity for higher education' *American Sociological Review* 35, pp. 1014–27.

66 UNITED NATIONS (1968) *op. cit.*

67 CARNOY, M. (1972) *op. cit.*

68 See, for example, BLUM, D. (1972) *op. cit.*; BLAU, P.M. and DUNCAN, O.D. (1967) *op. cit.*; COLEMAN *et al* (1972) *op. cit.*

69 See, for example, BENDIX, R. (1956) *Work and Authority in Industry* New York, Wiley; MILLS, C.W. (1963) *Power, Politics and People* New York, Oxford University Press; NEWCOMER, M. (1955) *The Big Business Executive* New York, Columbia University Press; WARNER, W.L. and ABEGGLEN, J.C. (1955) *Occupational Mobility in American Business and Industry: 1928–1952* Minneapolis, University of Minnesota Press.

70 See, for example, BLAIR, P. (1970) *op. cit.*; BLAU, P.M. and DUNCAN, O.D. (1967) *op. cit.*; HINES, *et al* (1970) *op. cit.*; LANDINSKY, J. (1967) 'Higher education and work achievement among lawyers' *Sociological Quarterly* 8, pp. 222–32; NOLAND, E.W. and BAKKE, E.W. (1949) *Workers Wanted* New York, Harper; NOSCOW, S. (1956) 'Labor distribution and the normative system' *Social Forces* 35, pp. 25–33; TAUBER, A.F., TAUBER, K.E. and Cain, G.C. (1966) 'Occupational assimilation and the competitive process: A reanalysis' *American Journal of Sociology* 72, pp. 278–85; TURNER, R.H. (1952) 'Foci of discrimination in the employment of non-whites' *American Journal of Sociology* 58, pp. 247–56; WELCH, F. (1967) 'Labor market discrimination: An interpretation of income differences in the Rural South' *Journal of Political Economy* 75(3), pp. 225–40.

71 COLLINS, R. (1971) *op. cit.*

19   National Education Systems and the International Context: The Case of Ireland

Ann Wickham

The most common unit of analysis in any empirically based discussion of educational systems is the nation-state. It is at the national level that educational systems are described, that data are collected and organized, and that the boundaries of the system are conceptualized. However, this paper will argue that a national education system cannot be understood by reference to the nation-state alone but has to be situated within its international context. Taking the international context seriously will allow a discussion of the issues involved in the whole notion of the state. The resulting arguments will then be applied empirically in an analysis of the external determinants of educational change in the Republic of Ireland.

State Theory and International Context

Much of the work on the theory of the state has been developed on the Left[1] and starts from the assumption that the state has a class basis which its institutions somehow represent. The state is here seen as performing certain tasks which are both necessary for the functioning of capitalism and which cannot be achieved if they are directly associated with the interests of capital within production. While the actual definition of the extent of the state has provided much controversy,[2] in fact, the main problem has been the lack of theoretically informed analyses of the specificities of individual nation-states.

One branch of state theory starts from the abstract formal level of the capitalist mode of production and deduces from this certain essential features of the capitalist state. However, it has proved very difficult to systematically link such essentially logical arguments with the empirical world of different states with their concrete forms and effects. As a result, analyses of national education systems that have drawn on such works have tended to leap immediately from the theoretical identification of the state and its needs and functions to relating particular educational systems (such as the English one) directly to the requirements of the 'state' and

Source: WICKHAM, A. (1980) *Comparative Education Review* October.

'capital' *per se*. Consequently no account is taken of the particular concrete form of the individual state. A second branch of theory starts from the assumption that one particular state (often Britain) can be taken as immediately revealing the essential nature of the capitalist state. Whereas the first approach appears to be too abstract, this approach appears to be too concrete, for here state theory is so tightly tied to one particular nation-state that it is closer to description than theory.

In both cases, therefore, the theoretical object of 'the state' becomes equated with a specific empirical nation-state. By contrast, I wish to argue that the international context is vital both to any understanding of nation-states in general and to the analysis of particular national forms. Within any particular state, foreign and domestic forces interact together, so that its policies and its institutions can only be adequately understood by taking this dialectical interplay into account. Educational systems and policies are just one area of state activity where such arguments apply, but the usually insular understanding of the way that state provision of education has developed makes it particularly important to explore such an argument here.

Conventional understandings of educational development in Western Europe and North America – areas usually seen as advanced capitalist economies – in fact rest on assumptions similar to those of 'modernization theory'[3] as used in the analysis of Third World countries. Modernization theory takes as its unit of analysis a particular society or nation-state and then explains the course of social change largely by reference to internal factors. For more than a decade this approach has been challenged by dependency theory, explaining underdevelopment of the Third World as constructed and reconstructed through its relationship with the advanced core areas of America and Europe.[4] This dependent relationship of the 'periphery' on the 'core' allows education to be discussed by reference to external forces, whether these are overtly colonial or more diffuse or cultural.[5]

Such arguments can be used to rethink Western European educational systems as also not explicable solely by reference to internal forces. While the political autarchy of an individual nation-state does vary historically, in fact, all nation-states are in an international context, and therefore their relations to external forces (forces which themselves alter, change, and contradict) are always part of the conditions of existence of their various 'domestic' practices and interventions. The specific institutions or activities of a nation-state that are most open to external influence will differ in different conjunctures; similar external influences will not have the same effects within different nation-states, *inter alia* because the way that such forces are taken up and articulated with national interests will vary. External influences must always then be considered in relation to institutions and policies that are defined as part of the state at a national level, and this will apply whether that nation is within an advanced capitalist economy or an 'underdeveloped' area.

Irish Education in 1945

This general argument can now be applied and developed in relation to the educational system of one particular nation-state in one particular period of time, namely, the Republic of Ireland in the post-World War II decades. I wish to focus particularly on the influence of international organizations, for their importance is consistently neglected in analyses of education in Europe. This narrowing of focus is necessary in a short paper, but it is not intended to deny the impact of other forms of external influence on Irish educational development.[6] This choice of period also avoids a concentration on forms of influence which are too easily identifiable with the unique and troubled historical relationship between Ireland and Britain.

At the beginning of the post-World War II period, Ireland had a three-tier educational system: a 'national' or primary-school sector, a postprimary sector, and a tertiary sector containing universities and colleges. Education, including the universities, was overwhelmingly denominational: in a country where the majority of the population is Roman Catholic, this meant that the education system too was predominantly Catholic.

In the primary sector, education was mainly provided in national schools (descendants of the mass schooling system set up by the British government in 1831), and day-to-day running of the schools was in the hands of the managers, usually the local parish priests.

At postprimary level there were two sets of schools – secondary and vocational. Secondary schools attracted the most pupils and were owned and controlled by the religious orders, who also provided most of the teaching staff. Vocational schools, on the other hand, were public schools run by local Vocational Educational Committees (VECs) and were mainly financed from local rates.

The tertiary sector was dominated by the two universities: the University of Dublin (Trinity College), which Catholics were forbidden to attend unless they had the permission of their bishop, and the National University of Ireland.

The state provided some form of financial assistance for all three levels of the educational system, and schools prepared pupils for national examinations set by the Department of Education. However, through the National School managers and the religious orders, the Catholic Church retained close control over most of the school system.

Such a description does not reveal the extent to which the educational system also expressed social divisions, especially at postprimary level. Secondary schools were associated with an academic form of schooling and access to higher education; vocational schools were seen as more practically oriented and provided no means of access to further education. Vocational schools therefore lacked status and pupils flocked to the secondary schools. However, the fact that most postprimary schools charged fees barred many from this level of education.

In national and secondary schools the notion of a specifically Catholic form of education was strong. This presented the principal purpose of primary and secondary schools as moral instruction. Together with celebration of the national identity, religious education was seen as by far the most important area of the curriculum, and other school subjects also had to be imbued with religious rationale.[7] In Ireland secular bodies concurred with this view: the Council of Education agreed in 1954 that 'the first purpose of the primary school was to train children in the fear and love of God', and in 1960 the council declared that the main purpose of the secondary schools was 'the inculcation of religious ideals and values'.[8] The focus on moral issues in education overrode the rights of parents, for although the 1937 Irish Constitution emphasized the primary duty of the family to provide for the education of the child, these parental powers were taken over by the church: 'Parents have a most serious duty to secure a fully Catholic upbringing for their children . . . only the Church is fully competent to declare what is a fully Catholic upbringing . . . accordingly in the education of Catholics every branch of human training is subject to the guidance of the church'.[9]

The educational activity of the state was therefore seen as a source of assistance to the family and, above all, to the church. This notion of Catholic education had implications for the form of teaching, since the intention was to mould children rather than bring out their inherent capacities.

Foreign Influences on Irish Economic Development

Acceptance of this form of educational provision initially seemed widespread. However, in the postwar period we can trace the emergence of ideas which were to affect both the structure and the content of the Irish educational system, particularly at the postprimary level. Such ideas were part of a radical reshaping of notions of economic and social development in Ireland which, as this section will show, was in fact greatly influenced by international organizations.

One reason for Irish participation in the Marshall Aid Plan and in the Organization for European Economic Co-operation (OEEC) was the economic difficulties of the immediate postwar period: 'The effort to overcome the shortage of houses, fuel and manufactures caused by the war, together with the natural impulse of consumers to buy greedily whatever was available, had combined together by 1947 to produce a major financial crisis. In consequence Ireland soon found herself in the queue for Marshall Aid and, on receiving it, was inexorably caught up in the machinery of European economic reconstruction, becoming in due course a member of the Organisation for European Economic Co-operation'.[10]

One of the conditions for Marshall Aid was that explicit plans for economic recovery be set out. Although direct economic planning by the Irish state was never made openly until 1958 (and even then was couched in neutral terms such as 'programme'), within the OEEC and later in the Organization for Economic Development (OECD) there was a consistent emphasis on planning for economic growth. This emphasis derived from US policy in Europe, reflecting not just American capitalists' desire for a prosperous European market or the attempt to build a bulwark against the onslaught of Communism, but also domestic American notions that class conflict could be resolved by greater material advantages for all rather than by the elimination of inequality.[11]

Nonetheless, despite Marshall Aid, the immediate postwar period was 'a period of unprecedented gloom and depression. No longer could the state of the economy be attributed to colonial misgovernment or war-time restrictions. Economic growth was non-existent, inflation apparently insoluble, unemployment rife, living stand-ards low, and emigration approaching 50,000 a year, a figure not far below the birth rate'.[12] American-style emphasis on economic growth through trade liberalization only slowly replaced protectionism as the key factor in economic policy in Ireland. In the pre-World War II period Irish protectionism had been acceptable in an international context in which, in the aftermath of the Depression, each country followed its own perceived national interests in isolation. In the postwar era this was no longer the case. The OEEC aimed at 'the achievement of a sound European economy through the economic co-operation of its members'.[13] There were now pressures pushing any Irish government, of whatever party, toward a change in economic policy in order to remedy the desperate social and economic situation. The shift, although drawing on existing policies and institutions, was expressed most clearly with the production of the First Programme for Economic Expansion in 1958, a programme that gave for the first time a commitment by the state to a 'comprehensive and rational plan for the economy as a whole'. The extent to which this programme was in fact a determinant of the economic growth that did follow in Ireland is debatable, but it was interpreted as a psychological turning point for the nation in general.[14] As a result a second and then a third programme followed in 1963 and 1969.

Although the emphasis in the First Programme was on the agricultural sector, it was industry that proved to be the major source of growth. Far from relying on protectionism, during the 1960s industrial development was based on the attraction of foreign investment to Ireland with the aid of a substantial state incentive scheme. With the reassessment of the nature of economic growth, the need to be competitive in a free-market situation, and the increased emphasis on industrial development, it now made sense to reassess education in economic terms, to stress the importance of scientific and technical education, and to prepare schools for a new European context.

International Organizations and the Transformation of Irish Education

One essential element in ideas of planning for economic growth was the notion of manpower planning. This, of course, had educational ramifications, for it posited direct links between the education system and the labour market – the first was to prepare for the needs of the second. However, this clashed with the existing Irish educational emphasis on religious and moral issues as the central themes in edu-cation. With the emergence of the OECD from the OEEC the stress on educational development grew stronger. Education and science were felt to have 'crucial roles in creating technologies and raising productivity' and became a clear focus of interest and then of activity.[15]

Irish representatives participated in the 1961 OECD conference on educational targets for the 1960s. Ireland was the first member of the OECD to take up the conference's suggestion that members should undertake surveys of their educational systems in terms of their adaptation to the future requirements of 'scientific progress and economic growth'. The end result was a document that was to be of central importance in Ireland: *Investment in Education* was published in 1966 and was the first statistical and factual analysis of the Irish educational system. The report discussed educational issues in terms of human capital – the notion that investment in education brought both personal and public returns. It assumed that the main issue was how to 'reconcile a search for the best balance between the needs of the economy and the "output" of the educational system with the concept of the maximum amount of education according to aptitude for all young people'.[16]

In fact, educational changes based on such assumptions had already begun. In all of them there can be seen an overriding concern with people as a productive resource and with education as a prerequisite for economic growth. In 1963, a year after the Investment in Education team was appointed, the then Minister of Education, Dr. Hillery, instituted plans to ensure that there was some form of post-primary provision for all children through the construction of comprehensive schools in areas where postprimary facilities were still insufficient. In addition, plans were formulated for Regional Technical Colleges to supply technical skills to the economy.

The controversy that grew up around these and consequent changes can only be understood by referring back to the denominational nature of the educational system as it existed in the immediate postwar period:

> ... Church and State in Ireland seemed to develop a happy identity in the matter of education, some would claim because of the supine posture of the state in the matter. The schools were small, independent and tightly under church control. The national examinations and the curricula were adminis-tered by the Department of Education in such a clear and rigid way that each school had a feeling of considerable autonomy, since there could be no interference except in accordance with rule. In such a steady state the education system in the nineteen fifties saw its own reflection and was well pleased.[17]

Any move by the state in terms of access to schools, their form, and their provision was a challenge to the *status quo* and indeed was interpreted by many members of the religious orders as a direct assault on their position in the educational system. In 1968 Sean O'Connor, Assistant Secretary in the Department of Education, wrote of his own personal belief that 'no-one wants to push the religious out of education; that would be disastrous in my opinion. But I want them in as partners, not always as masters'.[18] This was seen by many as epitomizing the state's new strategy, which was characterized by the Teaching Brothers' Association as 'nation-alization by stealth, whereby property is not taken over but management is'.[19]

From 1963 onward under a series of ministers of education there emerged a succession of major schemes for educational change, many of which were to deal with the postprimary sector. The *Investment in Education* report provided the factual basis for these developments by highlighting some of the major deficiencies in the existing system: problems of access to postprimary education, regional differences in the provision of schooling, social differences in participation, and inadequacies in the variety and content of the curriculum.

> The mere list of the major schemes emanating from successive ministers from about 1963 onwards conveys something of the atmosphere of urgency that has suddenly pervaded this hitherto quiescent area of Irish life. The list, then, includes a much more determined drive than hitherto, to consolidate and amalgamate the small or rural schools; the building of comprehensive schools designed to combine both grammar school (secondary) and vocational courses for scattered communities; a massive development of vocational education in general, with particular emphasis upon the establishment of regional Colleges of Technology; the provision of free secondary education, though on terms that make the participation of Protestant schools difficult, and also of free transportation; the allocation of much larger funds for scholarships, especially to the universities, and the revision of the Leaving Certificate syllabus to allow of greater specialization.[20]

The fact that the state implemented such numerous changes does not necessarily mean that the Catholic Church has lost control of the school system. Although management of national schools has changed, with a move from a single manager to a board of managers, the patron of the school (usually the bishop) has a clear majority of nominees on the board. Comprehensive schools (i.e., schools providing both academic and vocational education within the same institution) are specifically denominational. Although the first comprehensive schools were managed by a committee representing the Vocational Education Committee, the religiously controlled secondary schools, and the Department of Education, the fact that a local clergyman usually dominates the Vocational Education Committee has meant that the church has automatically gained a majority on the comprehensive-schools committees. In this way it has kept control of the schools while not having the same financial problems as it would if it were solely responsible for the schools.

In 1970 a new type of school was suggested, the community school. Community schools are comprehensive in that they provide a combination of academic and technical subjects, but are also broader: 'The Community School was to be a comprehensive school, but firmly founded in the local community and serving all the needs of the local community. Community Schools were to provide a wide programme of adult education as well as ordinary secondary schooling: they were to have large sports complexes, including swimming pools which were to be used by the local community. The community was to be represented in their management; the schools were to be a local point of community life with the buildings being used by the local residents and other voluntary associations'.[21] The whole concept of community schools has become a very contentious issue within Ireland, and this is especially true in relation to the forms of management and deeds of trust for the schools. However, what concerns us is the question of finance and the role of international organizations in this respect.

The changes that were initiated in the educational system in the 1960s had the desired effect of increasing participation. With the introduction of free postprimary education in 1967, schools reeled under the influx of numbers. Secondary-school admissions went up by 15,000 and enrollments in vocational schools by approximately 3,000.[22] This rapid expansion of the educational system brought increasing financial problems. More pupils meant more teachers and salaries, and more pupils also meant larger capitation grants, while an increased emphasis on technical and scientific subjects necessitated a greater expenditure on facilities and equipment. More pupils also meant, of course, more buildings. It is apparent that a massive new financial burden was emerging for all parties concerned in educational provision.[23]

One solution to this problem has been external sources of finance. The *Investment in Education* report was itself possible because the OECD put up half the cost. One other source of capital in the early 1970s proved to be the World Bank, and the republic received loans of $13 million and $25 million in 1972 and 1974, respectively.[24]

Much of this money was to be used for the expansion of the technical sector, but some of it was also to be used in the construction of community schools. Much of the current controversy in Ireland about these schools centres not on the content of the schools but on their control and management. Despite accusations that community schools represented the establishment of a general system of state schools, it is clear that in fact the religious are not being driven out. Indeed, it has been argued that the religious orders are guaranteed preferential treatment in the schools, and that the basic rules and regulations (the 'Deeds of Trust') could affect the autonomy of lay teachers within such schools. The religious orders have little to lose and a lot to gain from participation in the community schools. For many, especially the unions: '... the religious are in fact, implementing the famous FIRE Report (Future of Religious in Education). This report was never officially published but its contents are widely known. The major recommendation was that religious orders in a dilemma over dwindling vocations, should concentrate their numbers and energies in big urban population centres ...' and as one union member said: 'I know we may sound paranoid but we just get the feeling that the religious orders are coming from all over the Country, and just closing in on the Community Schools'.[25]

Although there are many advantages for the religious orders in the construction of schools where their members would have guaranteed posts and where 90 per cent of the funds would be provided by the state, there has also been considerable questioning of the role of the World Bank in influencing this new form of educational provision. Such suspicions range from the mass-conspiracy theory of the pamphlet *Have the Snakes Come Back?* which sees community schools as part of a plot by UNESCO to destroy Catholic morals in Ireland,[26] to the more measured suspicions of the Provincial of the Marist Order that the World Bank has insisted on the 'size, control and multidenominational aspects' of the scheme.[27]

The World Bank had a very clear educational policy and did indeed lay down certain conditions for its loans. The bank's policy reflected a concern for economic growth, but whereas previous attempts by aid organizations to stimulate such growth by inputs of capital had failed, the bank placed an emphasis on human resources as the key to development. The bank operated mainly in Third World areas, and indeed it was only Ireland's position in the European economic periphery that enabled it to qualify for a loan at all. From the bank's perspective, the stress was mainly on education for a modern services and industrial sector and above all on the production of manpower: 'The Bank and IDA, should be prepared to consider financing a part of the capital requirements of priority education projects designed to produce, or to serve as a necessary step in producing, trade manpower of the kinds and in the numbers needed to forward economic development in the member country concerned. In applying this criteria the Bank and IDA, should concentrate their attention, at least at the present stage, on projects in the fields of first, vocational technical education and training at various levels, and second, general secondary education'.[28] Following this policy, 72 per cent of the bank's educational loans to various countries between 1963 and 1971 went into intermediate education and 23 per cent of the loans into higher education. Primary and basic education received only 5 per cent of the available loans.

The bank also stressed the priority it gave to the notion of equality of opportunity: 'In the interest of both increased productivity and social equity, educational opportunities should be equalized as fully as possible'.[29] The bank was accordingly committed to forms of comprehensive schooling, that is, schools that had no selective entrance policy. It would appear that in Ireland it was less a case of the bank enforcing its own policies than of a similarity in ideology of both government and bank as to the purposes of schooling. It was the notion of comprehensive access that stimulated the adoption of community-school forms rather than any notion of a particular state-controlled form of education:

> In its negotiations for the first loan the Department proposed a programme of school development based largely on the statistics, forecasts and arguments contained in the 'Investment in Education' report. The emphasis, as the Bank requires was on developing the technical and vocational side of the system, meeting manpower needs, and rationalizing to the maximum possible extent the existing school facilities. According to the Department the Bank expressed no interest in the form of management of the schools. They did not require Government or local authority control, and expressed no feelings either way about the joint public private management boards eventually agreed for the Community Schools. One thing that they did take into account, however, was the Department's assurance that the schools would have an important role in providing facilities for adult education. This apparently was a major part of the deal and one incidentally that has yet to be fulfilled to the extent envisaged at the time of the loan. . . . Another thing that would interest the Bank would be the terms of admission to the school. Entrance to such schools would have to be freely available to all the pupils of the area, and there could be no question of selection examinations or of segregation by religion.[30]

The bank therefore determined that the community schools could not be identified with particular religious interests as the earlier comprehensive schools had been. In practice, as we have seen, this did not necessarily lessen the grip of the Catholic Church upon the school system. What is important about the whole issue is that the availability of finance from external sources made the expansion of educational resources in under-supplied areas possible at a time when continued reliance upon the private resources of the church and parish could not have coped with the demand. Furthermore, the money also made possible the very emphasis on technical as well as on academic subjects that the state was pursuing in its policy of investment in human resources. Outside financial sources made it possible both for educational provision to expand and at the same time to follow the more expensive pattern a technical emphasis demands: 'One of the strongest recommendations of Community schools is that money for their construction is readily available and that they can be built and equipped within a relatively short space of time. Schools financed by the VECs or indirectly by the Department have to wait their turn in the queue and very often have to fight for the facilities included without argument in these Community Schools'.[31]

In this case, then, external forces provided ideological and financial support for government policy on the future of educational provision in Ireland. In the course of these changes, the content of Irish education has come to be seen no longer in purely moral terms, but at the same time the Roman Catholic Church has maintained considerable organizational control.

It must be continually stressed that educational changes, whether in the structure and form of education or in its content, are an articulation of internal and external forces and pressures and not merely the result of one or the other. What is fascinating about Ireland in this period in educational terms is not just the nature of the changes that were introduced but the political basis on which they were made. Similar changes occurred throughout the rest of Europe in the same period, but in many areas, especially in Britain, these changes were introduced on an explicitly social democratic basis. There were, of course, national variations, but all over Europe social democratic notions of equality of opportunity conceptualized the existing unequal access to education in terms of social class and all proposed remedies supposedly attuned to working-class demands.

In Ireland these same notions were taken up but without there being a large working class in the traditional sense of an industrial proletariat. In the Republic of Ireland in 1966, 15 per cent of the economically active population was employed in manufacturing as salaried employees, as against 36 per cent for the same period in Britain. Further, there is in Ireland no clearly identifiable social democratic party, that is, a party closely connected to the unions and articulating working-class demands. The closest would be the Irish Labour Party, but this is small, traditionally drawing its support from rural laborers, and in the postwar period has been ineffectual. The other two main parties, Fine Gaél and Fianna Fáil, are the parties that have really dominated politics in Ireland – indeed, Fianna Fáil has had almost a monopoly of government office since 1932. Although their support was certainly originally class based, the ideological differences between them are rooted in constitutional issues deriving from the Civil War of 1922–23. Thus Fine Gael derives from those who accepted the Treaty of 1922, which partitioned Ireland into a 26 county state with political independence and a remaining six counties still united with Britain; Fianna Fáil by contrast has its origins with those who took up arms against the treaty and the new Irish government. The two parties were above all else pro-treaty or anti-treaty parties. This meant that as they developed (with Fianna Fáil originally drawing support from the lower middle classes and workers and Fine Gael from the middle class), rather than deepening their support along class lines, they tried to broaden its basis. Given the historical importance of nationalism, the parties competed with each other to become *the* national party. As Kircheimer points out:

> National societal goals transcending group interests offer the best sales prospect for a party intent on establishing or enlarging an appeal previously limited to specific sections of the population.[32]

Fianna Fáil presented the economic policy it developed in the 1950s and 1960s on a national basis as something almost above politics. Similarly, equality of opportunity, more access, more provision, more technical subjects were for the 'nation' and not for one class. This does not, of course, mean that such changes cannot be analyzed as benefiting distinct class groups, but that they were introduced through a populist rather than a class-based ideology. Certainly international organizations outside Ireland provided theories of educational change, just as they also provided financial resources with certain policy implications. Nonetheless, such external influences could only actually operate within Ireland because they could be utilized by Irish political parties for their own purposes. There is a dialectical interplay between the forces internal and external to the nation-state boundaries.

The EEC and Irish Education

So far we have seen that Irish education has been powerfully influenced by international bodies such as the OECD and the World Bank. Such organizations are essentially intergovernmental: their policies are arrived at by consensus among participating states and, crucially, depend on persuasion and at most financial inducements for their implementation by individual governments. However, since 1973 the Republic of Ireland has also been a member of the European Economic Community (EEC), and this has involved the possibility of rather different forms of external influence. Above all, the EEC has legal tools, such as regulations and directives,[33] through which its decisions can be enforced.

Although in the 1960s there was an unwritten taboo on the discussion of education in the EEC, because 'education seemed to be at the very heart of public sensitivity about national autonomy',[34] many of the Articles of the Treaty of Rome, on which the EEC is based, had educational implications. This is especially true of those dealing with the movement of labour, for this involved the question of mutual recognition of qualifications. An EEC education programme was finally produced in 1976. Directives related to this programme, such as one on immigrant children, have begun to appear. There are, as well, proposals covering areas such as equality of education for women, proposals which one Irish paper interpreted as a 'threat to girls only schools' (most postprimary schools in Ireland are single-sex schools).

There are also limited financial resources available. Money has come into Ireland through the European Social Fund (ESF), a fund originally set up to finance training to cope with the effects of the transition to a full European market. However, the money has gone not only to AnCO (the Industrial Training Authority) but also to finance courses in Regional Technical Colleges, saving money in local Vocational Education Committee budgets.[35] The EEC money has also been available to finance curriculum-development projects.

Both the legal and financial aspects of the European Community make it increasingly likely that the impact of European membership will continue to be felt on education in Ireland. However, it is an interesting contradiction that, while in the early 1970s Ireland profited by her relatively peripheral economic status to obtain World Bank loans, she now gains extra financial resources from membership in what is essentially an organization of more developed economies.[36]

Conclusion

The example of the Republic of Ireland has been used to illustrate the argument advanced at the start of this paper that policies and ideologies operating in and transforming institutions at the nation-state level cannot be understood solely by reference to forces confined within nation-state boundaries. The paper has attempted to show the manner in which educational changes in the republic were initiated in the 1960s and 1970s in such a way that reference to external forces, whether these are political, institutional, or financial, has to be made if any adequate account of the changes is to be produced. Yet at the same time the paper has stressed the extent to which this does not involve any direct external manipulation or conspiracy and has emphasized the importance of understanding the specificity of political forces inside the republic.

This argument raises substantive questions in terms of state theory. The confusion of the theoretical notion of the state with the concept of the concrete nation-state is common, and linguistic usage makes it a difficult problem to avoid. Nonetheless, there is nothing in theories of the state, however these are formulated, which necessarily demands that 'the state' should be identified with the 'nation-state' form. In other words, theories of the 'state' turn out to analyze not the relationship between specific political institutions and specific economic interests confined within one legally defined geographical area, but rather the interrelationship between politics and economics in general. Once we move from such abstract considerations to analysis of individual nation-states we cannot assume that either all the relevant political institutions or all the relevant economic interests will in fact be located within the particular territorial area with which we are concerned.

Not only is any discussion of education which focuses on the nation-state as some form of expression of the concept of 'the state' *per se* incorrect, but it may also be time to move away from the belief in a unitary state form. In the future a more viable and pertinent mode of analysis will be one that attempts to come to terms with the specificity of the forces at work. It will not be tied to attempts to seek out a unitary policy functioning for capitalists but rather one which allows some room for the consideration of the effects of international practices and forces such as those I have delineated in one concrete example.

Acknowledgements

I would like to thank Dr I.R. Dale, Mrs R. Pollard and Dr J. Wickham.

Notes and References

1 An outline of various theories of the state can be found in JESSOP, R. (1972) 'Recent theories of the capitalist state' *Cambridge Journal of Economics* 1, No. 4 (December) pp. 353–73.

2 For example, in ALTHUSSER, L. (1971) 'Ideology and ideological state apparatuses' in ALTHUSSER, L. *Lenin and Philosophy and Other Essays* London, New Left Books, pp. 121–73, the state contains any institution considered to be a factor in social cohesion.

3 For a good outline of modernization theory, see TURNER, B. (1975) *Industrialism* London, Longmans.

4 One example of such an approach would be the work of FRANK, A.G. (1969) *Latin America: Under-development or Revolution* London, Monthly Review Press.

5 THOMPSON, A.R. (1977) 'How far free? International networks of constraint upon national education policy in the Third World' *Comparative Education* 3, (October) pp. 155–68.

6 See the suggestion in BELL, R. (1973) 'Ireland – A case study' in *Education, Economy and Politics* (E352) Milton Keynes, Open University Press, Block 5 (pt. 3) pp. 36–41.

7 KING, J. (1971) 'The attitude of the Roman Catholic Church towards participation in state systems of education: The Irish case' Ph.D. dissertation, University of Wisconsin.

8 AKENSON, D. (1975) *A Mirror to Kathleen's Face: Education in an Independent Ireland* London, McGill, p. 98.

9 *ibid.*

10 LYONS, F.S.L. (1971) *Ireland Since the Famine* London, Weidenfeld and Nicholson, pp. 589–90.

11 MAIER, C. (1977) 'The politics of productivity' *International Organization* Vol. 31, (Autumn) pp. 607–33.

12 MURPHY, J. (1972) *Ireland in the Twentieth Century* Dublin, Gill and MacMillan, p. 142.

13 Quoted in BLACKSELL, M. (1977) *Post War Europe* Folkestone, Dawson, p. 35.

14 FITZGERALD, G. (1968) *Planning in Ireland* Dublin, Institute of Public Administration. For a discussion of the political issues involved see, WICKHAM, J. (1980) 'The politics of dependent capitalism: international capitalism and the state' in MORGAN, A. and PURDIE, B. (Eds) *Ireland: Divided Nation, Divided Class* London, Inklinks.

15 AUBREY, H. (1967) *Atlantic Economic Co-operation: The Case of the OECD* London, Praeger, p. 93.

16 OECD (1969) *Reviews of National Policies for Education: Ireland* Paris, OECD, p. 8.

17 McCARTHY, C. (1973) *The Decade of Upheaval* Dublin, Institute of Public Administration, p. 200.

18 O'CONNOR, S. (1968) 'Post-primary education now and in the future' *Studies* 57, (Autumn) pp. 233–51.

19 The Executive of the Teaching Brothers' Association (1968) 'Comments on S. O'Connor's "Post-primary education"' *Studies* 57 (Autumn) p. 282.

20 LYONS, F.S.L. (1971) *op. cit.*

21 *Irish Times* (1978) May 4.

22 RANDLE E. (1975) *Post-Primary Education in Ireland* Dublin, Veritas, p. 277.

23 In 1978 a report produced by an American researcher, Dale Tussing, while working at the Irish Economic and Social Research Institute, made controversial proposals on education finance. It suggested that all state finance for educational provision after the age of fifteen be withdrawn and that a system of scholarships and above all loans should provide access for the less well off. See TUSSING, D. (1978) *Irish Education Expenditures – Past Present, and Future* Economic and Social Research Institute General Research series No. 92. Dublin, Economic and Social Research Institute.

24 WORLD BANK (1974) *Education: Sector Working Paper* Washington, D.C. World Bank.

25 *Irish Times* (1977) July 28.

26 *Have Snakes Come Back?* Dublin, Vera Verba (n.d.).

27 Statement by Declan Duffy, Provincial of the Marist Brothers, *Education Times* (1974) March 21.

28 WORLD BANK (1974) *op. cit.*

29 *ibid.*

30 *Irish Times* (1974) March 18.

31 *ibid.*

32 A quote from Otto Kircheimer is used to this effect in CHUBB, B. (1970) *The Government and Politics of Ireland* Oxford, Oxford University Press, p. 76.

33 Regulations have the direct force of law in every member state. Directives detail the result to be achieved but leave the means to the discretion of national authorities.

34 *Irish Times* (1978) June 8.

35 Union of Students in Ireland, Internal Officers Report, November 1975.

36 Ronan Fanning comments that in 1973 by transferring from Part II to Part I membership of the International Development Association (the World Bank agency which makes loans on preferential terms), Ireland chose to be grouped with economically more advanced, as opposed to developing countries. See FANNING, R. (1978) *The Irish Department of Finance* Dublin, Institute of Public Administration, p. 614.

20   *Democracy and Socialism in Education in Portugal*

Stephen R. Stoer

There have been present in Portugal in the period following the military coup of 25 April, 1974, two major educational ideologies. One of these may be termed, in some sense, *democratic* in nature, and the other, in some sense, *socialist*. In addition, there have been present remnants of Salazarist educational ideology, an educational ideology distinctly 'feudalist' in flavour (as Maria Filomena Mónica has demonstrated in her analysis of the construction and articulation of Salazarist ideology in the primary school sector during the years 1926 to 1939[1]), but only as rather plaintive echoes of an era that is now most decidedly in the past. The main objective of this article is to explore what democracy has meant for the 'democratic' educational ideology, and to explore what socialism has meant for the 'socialist' educational ideology. We will also examine how education and development were related in Portugal during the decade of the 1970s.

A Brief Background

Both democracy and socialism in education in Portugal were articulated during the period of the First Republic (from 1910–26), the former in a comprehensive way, the latter only hesitantly. The First Republic saw the 'great watershed in Portuguese education reform'[2] (although Manuel de Silva Passos – 'Passos Manuel' – the leader of the Nineteenth Century September Revolution had largely prepared the path for the reforms to come in the Republican period). The main objectives of the 1911 reforms were the decentralization of primary education (centralized once again, however, in 1918), the extension of primary education to the countryside, increased salaries for teachers (teachers were central to Republican education policy which conceived of them as a force capable of achieving social change by supplanting, or at least rivalling, the traditional leadership of the local priest in small communities), and the general increase of all sectors of education. In a nutshell, educational opportunities were to be spread to ever-larger numbers of the population. Also during the Republic Period the Portuguese Communist Party (founded in 1921) and the anarcho-sindicalists, through their mouthpiece 'A Batalha', produced some of the first important articulations of the relationship between education and work.

On 28 May, 1926, the Republican period dramatically came to a close with the seizure of power by the Armed Forces. This allowed the comprador fraction of the bourgeoisie to maintain its economic dominance while political power fell into the hands of Dr. António de Oliveira Salazar, the Finance Minister called in to take drastic measures along classical economic lines (i.e. balanced budget, a build-up of gold reserves, salary freezes, etc.) to solve the continuing economic crisis ushered in with the Republican period.[3] Salazar became Prime Minister in 1932 and remained in power until 1968.

In terms of educational reform between the period stretching from the late 1920s to the late 1960s, 'Salazar's Portugal' was relatively unique – instead of going forward, it went backwards. The period can be divided into two parts: a first part from 1930 to 1950 centered on an all-pervading ideology – which explicitly politicized education and which closely linked education with political power; and a second part, from 1950 to 1973, where education began to develop a certain autonomy due, paradoxically, to the construction of a very complex repressive state apparatus.[4] Naturally, only during the second period did oppositional ideologies of education become apparent in the social formation.

Salazarist educational ideology centred itself on the principle of 'Deus, Patria, Familia' (God, Fatherland, Family) and may be typified by the following fundamental line of future educational policies of the 'Estado Novo' (the 'New State', set up by the 1933 Constitution) as set out by the First Congress of the National Union (1934, the 'União Nacional' was the only political party allowed by the Constitution). In education there should be:

> A reduction of programmes to allow for concentration on 'fundamentals', and an emphasis on 'applied knowledge' [this meant on design and manual work for boys and domestic activities for girls] and 'all principles are to indicate ideas of country, family and the love of birthplace'.[5]

To illustrate the effects of educational policies of the 'Estado Novo', one can turn to any educational sector, but perhaps the sector of teacher training is most illuminating. In 1936 the 'Escolas do Magistério' (teacher training colleges for primary school teachers) were *closed*, on the grounds that a training programme centred on 'pedagogical objectives' for teachers of primary schools was a waste of time, money, and intelligence. The schools were later reopened, in 1942, but the course was reduced from three years to two years. In the meantime, 'regentes escolares', that is, 'teachers' with only primary school education (four years of schooling) were called in to fill the places of trained teachers, thus providing an economic means of teacher supply. The programmes, i.e. curricula, of the Magistérios were approved in February, 1943 and remained in effect until October, 1974. An idea of the nature of these programmes can be gained from an extract from the section on 'pedagogy and general didactics':

> What is needed to be taught in this first part (pedagogy) is of little impor-

tance and shouldn't occupy more than a quarter of a semester (a little more than a month) of the professor's time.

... one shouldn't allow in the Escolas do Magistério Primário any discussion of the ultimate ends that inform the process of formation of human beings in their growing phase. Students don't possess, on the one hand, the cultural formation necessary to treat such intricate problems; and one doesn't find, on the other hand, in our country a state of critical indecision regarding the conception of life and the values of society. We are oriented today with values perfectly defined ... [6]

There is little doubt that education, mass education, played a predominantly repressive role during most of the Salazarist period, carrying out functions which during the latter part of the period became part of the role of an elaborate repressive state apparatus, including political police, para-military organizations, special laws giving special powers to the police, etc.[7] Mónica refers to the Salazarist school as a school which tried to 'form' children rather than 'educate' them.[8] The 'Estado Novo' essentially wanted to 'disarticulate' ideas and practices initiated during the time of the First Republic, to challenge notions of social mobility in the name of order and established hierarchy, and thus to undermine the emphasis which the Republic had put on such values as equality and liberty.

The Veiga Simão Reform

Following the incapacitation of Salazar in 1968, and after several years of colonial warfare, a period of 'liberalization' of the repressive regime set in. One concrete manifestation of this came in 1971 in the shape of a crucially important educational reform, known as the Veiga Simão Reform (after the then Minister of Education, Professor Jose Veiga Simão). This reform was a key expression of almost two and a half decades of popular democratic struggle against a very élitist and out-moded corporatist state educational structure, and the culmination of a gradually closer integration of Portugal into the Western mainstream.[9] It did not, of course, resolve the contradictions present in the Portuguese social formation. Rather it can be argued that, as part of the process of liberalization/democratization of an hierarchical authoritarian state system, it merely helped to widen the already considerable gap between the 'people' – a loose alliance of the domestic and petty bourgeoisies and the working class (urban and rural) – and the ruling sectors, which eventually led to the explosion of mass popular discontent which is now synonymous in Portugal with the Revolution of the 25 April, 1974.

The Veiga Simão Reform was the concrete indicator of the collapse of the dominant educational ideology of the Salazarist era. In the wider context, it was one more, very important, indicator of the collapse of the ruling alliance of the comprador bourgeoisie, large landowners (latifundia element), and certain sectors of the Armed Forces. It was, thus, symbolic of the breakdown of the pervasive ideology that had bound together the education system, political system and apparatus of the state, an ideology of 'traditionalism' based on an essentially mercantile, com-prador-bourgeois *weltanschauung*, combined with strong elements of 'ruralism'. It may be argued that the decline of this ideology had long been evident through the need of the regime for a strong repressive state apparatus; the Veiga Simão Reform was only the confirmation of a rupture that had first shown its 'inevitability' with the Delgado Presidential Campaign, in 1958.[10]

The fact that the Portuguese state, certainly during the second part of the Salazarist regime (i.e. 1950–74), ruled by repression rather than by consent has had important implications. For a long time it played an important economic role; there was in Portugal no period of *laissez-faire* capitalism. This, together with Portugal's periph-eral status, means that it is not possible to talk about the 'interventionist' state in Portugal in the same way as one does in advanced industrial countries. Naturally, the process of *restructuring* the state, and the *redefinition* of education in Portugal has had its own specificity.[11] Specifically, the recent restructuring of the state in Portugal has involved the institutionalization of representative democracy; the redefinition of education has meant, on balance, the institutionalization of equality of opportunity (still a long way from realization) and the development of 'profes-sionalism' (through the construction of a union structure providing slowly in-creasing autonomy for teachers). Rather than a move *towards* centralized bureaucratic planning and versions of participatory democracy, as Donald argues has occurred in Britain, there has been a move *away* from them.[12] These two forms of state power are found, not as modes of state intervention to deal with crises in the accumulation of capital, but as articulated in educational ideologies and concretized in the form of programmes and pedagogy at various levels in the educational apparatus. This aspect will be developed further below.

The Veiga Simão Reform, then, expressed two different forms of conflict. On the one hand it was part of the struggle for a hegemonic rather than repressive state, for rule by consent, for guarantees to prevent power holders from exploiting power for their own private interests, in short, for democracy. In terms of the Reform this meant, in effect, greater equality of opportunity in education, in terms of access, in terms of quantity of education, in terms of region and in terms of gender. On the other hand, it was about a new path to development, a project of *modernization*. In other words, the Veiga Simão Reform expressed more than just demand for access to education, it also implied basic changes in the orientation of the economy. To the extent that ideologies are shaped by what they are *against* as well as by what they are *for*, the Veiga Simão Reform, while not the *cause* of the restructuring and redefining process, did have the effect of specifying the problem. It articulated, in a relatively dogmatic way (considering the obvious limits on its chances of being implemented), the objectives of the 'Developmentalists', a group of economists who through their model of economic development challenged the hegemony, social and political, of the 'Traditionalists', a group largely composed of lawyers.[13] This explains why, as will become clearer later in this article, current educational policy, in its technocratic, human-capitalist form, may be seen as a continuation of the process initiated by the Veiga Simão Reform before the Revolution on the 25 April, 1974.

The international context was, and still is, a vital element in the determination of national education policies in Portugal. The policies and ideologies operating on and transforming institutions at nation state level cannot be understood solely by reference to forces confined within nation state boundaries. Contributing to the discourse for a new orientation of the economy in Portugal, and thus indirectly, or even directly, affecting the advent of the Veiga Simão Reform, were such organizations as the OECD, EFTA, and, of course, the EEC, in the sense that it was towards Europe that the new orientation was directed. Institutionalized in important policy-making entities such as the OECD, UNESCO, USAID, the major foundations, especially Ford and Rockefeller, and particularly the World Bank, was the human capital and economics of education approach. What the Veiga Simão Reform involved was entirely consonant with the educational planning objectives of the human capital model, although by no means reducible to them. Hans Weiler has made explicit some of the notions underpinning the objectives of such educational planning: 'the role of education is to contribute to economic development through fulfilling the manpower needs of the labour market', to plan education therefore is to 'maximize its contribution to economic growth through assessing the adequate supply of employable people'.[14] As Weiler suggests, the assumptions behind such objectives, i.e., first, that education is a motor of development (especially economic development), and second, that the future development of education is foreseeable and manipulable, are dangerously simple assumptions, assumptions that, in their exclusive concern with economic considerations, deny the more complex reality of interrelations between economic interests, social structure and political power.

Concretely, the reforms of the Veiga Simão Reform were as follows: the increase of compulsory attendance from six to eight years; a post-compulsory four years of education – eventually in polyvalent schools; the reform of higher education; the reform of teacher training through the creation of higher teacher training schools and graduate departments of education in universities. The dominant principle throughout is the principle of 'equality of opportunities in education', as may be seen from the programme of 'General Reform of Education in Portugal', presented by Veiga Simão in a broadcast to the nation on 6 January, 1971:

> The programme of projected reform expresses a philosophy of education which would embody the double principle that the education of the individual is the main aim of the educational system and that all, on the basis of equal opportunities, should find in any such system the paths that will guarantee their inalienable rights to be educated. From this we may conclude that the educational system should not be directly subordinated to the demands of economic development.[15]

However, in spite of Veiga Simão's conclusion, a conclusion that, it may be argued, clearly articulates the forms of popular democratic struggle referred to above (the effects of which helped sustain the Reform when other 'liberal' policies began to be distanced from governmental policy-making as the liberalization period retreated in 1973[16]), the principle of equality of educational opportunity does express very clearly an economic goal. Finn, Grant, and Johnson, for example, have argued very strongly that the principle is:

> Based on a conception of education as a 'good' which ought to be more fairly shared, the use and consumption of which has pertinent economic effects. The ultimate point of reference ... has been an essentially liberal conception of society as a market, within which individuals compete. The point according to this 'philosophy' is to allow them to compete more fairly.[17]

Developing a critique of this argument, Raymond Williams has suggested, however, that for many people the principle has represented, (and this is its popular-democratic appeal), expansion of educational resources and expansion of educational opportunities.[18] Indeed, seen in this light, there is a reductionist tone about the Finn, Grant, and Johnson conception of the principle which James Donald insists upon when he argues that they cannot specify the educational crisis' articulation with the 'socio-historic conjuncture'.[19] Nevertheless, and this is the important point for our purposes, Finn, Grant, and Johnson do draw attention to the strong relationship of the principle of equality of opportunity in capitalistic societies, with its inherent notion of meritocracy, to market forces. This enables us to place the 'humanistic' discourse of Veiga Simão in perspective; that is, it can be placed in the overall context of a country located on the periphery of capitalist Europe attempting, during the early seventies, to develop both economically and politically, and thus struggling to shed nearly half a century of repressive dictatorship.

Post 25 April, 1974

Discussion of the period after the coup of 25 April, 1974, up to the oft-termed 'counter-coup' of 25 November, 1975,[20] has frequently centred on the question of whether or not there existed a 'revolutionary situation' at any time during that period, i.e. 'were conditions available for a seizure of power that could have produced a radical break with capitalist relations of production and led to the installation of socialist relations of production?'. This discussion, complicated by the active role of the Armed Forces in the Portuguese Revolution, begs a whole series of questions about certain concepts and their interpretation, some of which will be discussed further below. We would argue that by far the more revealing question for the area of ideologies of education is the one that has been posed, by Poulantzas for example, in the following manner:

> Was the coup itself and the struggle which followed simply another manifestation of that problem which has plagued the bourgeoisie in Portugal ever since it came into existence, namely its inability to establish a bourgeois ideological discourse with a hegemonic character which would enable it to have secure forms of political organization?[21]

It is clear to most observers that the hegemony and leadership of the democratization process in Portugal, several months after the coup, was in the hands of the popular masses. There was no uniform articulation of this process, and the divisions that existed were most clearly manifest at the level of the Armed Forces Movement (the 'MFA'). After the 25 November, 1975, the situation changed quite dramatically; the 'domestic bourgeoisie'[22] managed to take over the leadership of the process, completing the move towards dominance that it had begun before the 25 April during the 'liberalization' process. Perhaps 'dominance' is the wrong concept to employ, however, for up to the present conjuncture no fraction of the bourgeoisie has been able to unify the bourgeoisie in a way that would enable it to hegemonize general political discourse, and thus give itself security.

Forms of political organization now appear to be relatively secure, after the turbulence of the revolutionary period, and in spite of the shadow of military intervention that persists in making itself an important determinant of the future of Portuguese development. The international conjuncture, the strategic importance of Portugal to the West, and the popular support for democracy in Portugal will probably make it possible for the bourgeoisie to maintain its rule without another major 'rupture' in the near future. Of course, the effects of the period of leadership by the popular masses are still very much present in the social formation. This can be felt at many levels, for example, in the mass media, in the forms of democratic organization and evaluation in the schools and universities, and at a more abstract level, in the manner in which the effects of the period are articulated in the *Constitution of the Portuguese Republic*. In terms of the latter, witness the first two articles of the *Constitution* which came into effect in 1976:

> 1 – Establishes a Republic 'sovereign, based on the dignity of the human person and popular will and pledged to the transformation of present society to a society without classes';

> 2 – Defines as an objective of the Portuguese State, securing the transition to socialism by way of the creation of conditions for the democratic exercise of power by the working classes.[23]

As a result of the fact that a hegemonic state was absent in Portugal for some decades, and as a result of the instability of the new hegemonic state, ideological struggle is understandably fierce in the social formation. This is particularly true in educational institutions, which necessarily have a specific effectivity of their own. Educational policy, therefore, finds varying degrees of acceptance and implementation at all levels of education. This fact has largely constituted the 'crisis' in education in Portugal over the last two or three years. Gradually, however, as a 'consensus' in education develops (with recent reverses, however, in governmental strategy, it is debatable whether or not such a consensus will indeed continue to develop), that 'crisis' comes to be seen more in economic, and therefore 'traditional', terms.

The new Constitution expresses precisely the struggle for hegemony that has been taking place in the Portuguese social formation since the 25 April, 1974. To that extent it may be seen as a kind of link between what was a more general struggle at the level of general political discourse before the taking of power by the First Constitutional Government (1976),[24] and the phase of struggle in educational institutions after that act of power-taking. One consequence of the Constitution's attempt to articulate different, and essentially conflicting, educational ideologies has been ambiguities in its interpretation. Nevertheless, it has been very widely considered to be a 'Left' Constitution, with some sectors defining it as 'the most progressive Constitution in Western Europe'. Its reform is now practically taken for granted by most sectors of the political spectrum, mainly to bring it into line with the new dominant (though unstable) political discourse (recently certain political forces bemoaned the fact that the Constitution was 'unacceptable' for Portugal's entry into the Common Market). The following four articles are from the section that concerns education:

> *Article 73* – 'The State will promote the democratization of education and conditions that will permit education to contribute to the development of the personality and progress to a democratic and socialist society';
> *Article 74* – 'Guarantees all citizens the right to education and to "equality of opportunities" in education';
> *Article 75* – Suggests positive discrimination to socially dominated groups – the State must 'stimulate the formation of scientists and technicians from members of the working classes';
> *Article 76* – And further, access to the university should 'stimulate and favour the entrance of workers and the sons of the working classes'.[15]

Education and Democracy

The Portuguese Constitution effectively tries to articulate conceptions of democratic and socialist education. Democratic education means essentially a meritocratic education system. Socialist education means, in Portuguese terms, 'alfabetização' (alphabetization), that is, mass literacy campaigns, and, in general, an 'opening up of the schools to the masses'. It also means more profound notions of democracy expressed essentially through the concept of 'poder popular' (popular power).

Democratic education represents, above all, a continuation of the aforementioned Veiga Simão Reform. In the late 1970s this 'continuation' has been achieved through the concepts of 'normalization' and 'efficiency'. 'Normalization' and 'efficiency' are concepts found not only in the discourse of government ministers, but also in the international reports prepared by such agencies as SIDA and the Stockholm Institute of Education and the World Bank,[26] reports prepared specifically for the Portuguese Ministry of Education. In these reports we generally find, in spite of lip service to social dimensions, (i.e. greater mass participation, greater access and equality), what has been termed a 'banker's approach to educational development'.[27] Thus, what is, in fact, a conservative philosophy suppresses political and ideological considerations in order to grant education a principal role in the productive process, a role as a sector of both public and private investment. The 'aid' of international organizations is, indeed, enlisted for purposes of such investment in education. Education is conceived mainly as an agent of economic, and consequently, social change. Education provides human capital.

Both 'normalization' and 'efficiency' have, of course, been conceived in relation to the steering agent of equality of opportunities. More specifically, 'normalization' of schooling in Portugal has meant a return to a certain order and hierarchy in the school and in the classroom, the signalling of the end of the revolutionary conjuncture when political debate was vital twenty-four hours a day to define and concretize new values and practices. It has also meant the revision of certain programmes and courses. For example, both sociology (without much of a tradition in Portugal prior to the 25 April, 1974, but initiated in secondary and university education shortly after) and the introduction to politics course have both been eliminated from secondary education. Certain forms of 'contact activities' (periods of extended activity with local populations in rural areas) in the Escolas do Magistério Primário (Teacher-training Colleges) have been eliminated from the curriculum. In brief, both in terms of courses and pedagogy there has been a return to more subject-based curricula – thus marking an end at attempts to 'open up' the curriculum through expansion into new areas and through forms of interdisciplinarity – and to more traditional forms of pedagogy. In Bernstein's terms, there has been a return to strong classification and strong framing.

Changes in personnel, the result of 'normalization', have also had serious effects in the schools and colleges. In 1976 new sorts of qualifications were required to obtain certain teaching posts. Particular qualifications, nearly always traditional ones, were determined to be of more value than others. Thus, many teachers with more radical conceptions of pedagogy had to make way for teachers with more 'banking-like' conceptions. This process of changing teachers was especially crucial in the important sector of teacher training. In effect, 'normalization' has meant a return to a more 'individualized' hierarchical education system, at the expense of attempts to create a more 'collectivized' form of education. We shall see what the latter has meant in more detail in the next section of this paper.

'Efficiency' has meant above all *'numerus clausus'*, the attempt to link numbers for entry into the education system directly with places available in the labour market, or with places available in the education system itself. It has also meant evaluation of the education system, at the micro-level, in terms of internal efficiency, and at the macro-level, 'in terms of the product of the school system in relation to the society's demands in terms of priorities in national development, the structure of the labour market, and the ideological and cultural aspirations of the country'.[28] It is at this latter level that recent educational planning has come unstuck.[29] At the heart of the problem is the attempt, in spite of the rhetoric, to orient planning purely in terms of economic and administrative rationality. This means, inevitably, a neglect of political and cultural factors, such as the neglect of the interior part of the country which is demanding compensatory investment in its struggle for equality with coastal regions. Portugal is marked by contrasts (geographical, historical, political) that play a significant role in the efforts made to establish a general political discourse hegemonic in the social formation.

It is the increasing domination by economic and administrative rationality of educational development in Portugal that makes Veiga Simão himself very critical of current educational policy and planning. This is true in spite of the fact, as we have argued above, that the dominant educational ideology above all represents a continuation of the Veiga Simão Reform. He is critical because he sees a *de facto* erosion of the principle of equality of educational opportunities; as he puts it, the principle is not applied rigorously enough.[30] As a result, the popular element of the Veiga Simão Reform, based on the universal principle of equality, no longer carries much weight in relation to the practical measures the Reform proposes, all of which are oriented to the development of economic production. This is so mainly because with the 25 April revolution the Veiga Simão Reform was overtaken. Its popular echoes took on new forms through the attempts in Portugal to create socialist forms of education.

Education and Socialism

As part of the process of popular democratic struggle, articulated in the sphere of education before the 25 April, 1974 through the principle of equality of opportunities in education via the Veiga Simão Reform, there occurred after the 25 April an expansion and democratization of the Portuguese education system. Thus, the following measures were embodied in the programmes of such political forces as the Socialist Party, the Communist Party, and the parties of the revolutionary Left: first, the establishment of free expression, meeting and association in schools and throughout society generally; second, the realization of school assemblies governed by democratic procedures; third, the formation of student's associations and the creation of autonomous teacher's unions in the various zones of the country; fourth, the 'defascistization' of school curricula; fifth, the institutionalization of 'humanist' pedagogy; sixth, the general actualization of reforms conceived prior to the 25 April that would provide for expansion in every sector of the education system; and seventh, the comprehensivization of Portuguese secondary education.[31]

Of course, wanting to carry the process of change further than the creation of pluralist democracy, socialist ideologies also attempted, in different ways, to articulate the integration of the 'world of work' with the 'world of education', under the hegemony of the proletariat (rural and urban), in order to abolish the 'classic' division between manual and mental labour.[32] In fact, this process of change was articulated in mainly two ways: first, through an emphasis on the 'opening up' of the Portuguese education system, i.e. opening it up to the masses, and second, through specific notions of popular power, i.e., broadly, through decentralization, stimulation of local cultural forms, etc.

The emphasis on 'alfabetização', that is, on mass adult education, on literacy campaigns, by certain political forces, through an expansion of the education system, and through a campaign for general educational reform, including the increase of compulsory schooling from six to eight years, the creation of a study-grants system, the elimination from the labour market of persons under fourteen years of age, and, and, above all, the creation of nursery school education (absolutely crucial in educational terms to fight selection and to disarticulate Salazarist ideology), expressed, in essence, the desire to rid Portugal of an élitist class-ridden educational system. The Portuguese Communist Party, and its allies, conceived a programme of expansion and reform within a general framework of democratic – i.e. consultative – educational planning. The fundamental obstacle to the integration of education and work, and thus to the eventual end of the mental/manual split, was seen to be the continued existence of a long-since out-moded anti-democratic state apparatus that was incapable of promoting real educational reform. Thus, the apparatus had to be destroyed to create a 'new apparatus serving the cause of democracy'.[33]

Underlying the analysis that called for a new state apparatus lay a particular analysis of change in Portugal. Álvaro Cunhal, General Secretary of the Portuguese Communist Party, and also its principal theorist, concluded that within the Portuguese social formation after the 25 April, 1974 (in actual fact, later, after the revolutionary movement had achieved its zenith), 'capitalist relations of production are still predominant but not determinant'.[34] Thus, the essential problem concerned the lack of articulation between the major economic changes brought about by the 25 April and the school system. The question was: how can the education system rid itself of the 'privilege of the bourgeoisie'? How can education be made to serve, as the Constitution later came to say it should, the interests of the mass of the people?

Of course, merely expanding an educational system does not by itself necessarily mean changing its nature. Educational expansion does not necessarily mean greater equity in the distribution of income, goods, and statuses. It may merely contribute to reproducing and further consolidating the inequalities already existing in a given society. It is at this level that groups representing the revolutionary Left in Portugal raised their objections to what were termed 'reformist tendencies'. Such tendencies, it was argued, fail to grasp the nature of the capitalist reproduction process; they view the school as a 'service' and not as a site of cultural expression and production; they negate its political nature. Thus, reformist programmes of educational change emphasizing modes of access, planning, and mass schooling are incapable of affecting, and in the end, altering, the class nature of schooling in Portugal. In contrast, such groups argued, the school must be viewed as a site of class struggle where, in order to construct the 'socialist school', first, one recognizes the possibility of 'democratizing the school' within the confines of capitalist society, i.e. without transforming capitalist social relations, however, and second, only in a socialist society is a school *necessarily* democratic, in the sense that it is a direct expression of the transformation of productive relations.

Therefore, a 'revolutionary' strategy works towards the following goals: first, the creation of a school which produces the instruments of criticism that permit the working class to exercise its control over the school, in effect allowing it to define its action; second, the linking of the school with production, not in the perspective of technocracy but in the perspective of the destruction of the capitalist school; and third, the total eradication of capitalist social relations within the interior of the school.[35]

Effectively, the revolutionary Left did not recognize the 'non-determination' of capitalist relations of production as proposed by Álvaro Cunhal. Thus, what was for the Communist Party a struggle for the construction of a socialist state was seen by the revolutionary Left as a mere 'occupation' of the state apparatuses.

Contrasting the two positions in terms of particular practices illustrates their different conceptions of socialist construction. We can see, for example, that in terms of union struggle the revolutionary Left called for the decentralized union (termed the distinction between the 'autonomy of the union' and 'partidarização', i.e. 'partisan politics'), whereas the Communist Party, and its allies, argued for a central union, united, and able to promote the autonomy of the teaching profession (after so many years of degrading treatment). In terms of the democratization of the school, popular power advocates consistently demanded the autonomy of the school through the 'AGEs', 'Assembleias Gerais da Escola' (General School Assemblies), whereas the Communist Party insisted on the need to create a new democratic state apparatus. Rogério Fernandes, of the Portuguese Communist Party, and Director-General of Elementary Education at the time, termed the position of the 'autonomous school' as one which would simply turn the Ministry of Education into an accounts department paying bills.[36] Members of CEC, 'Contra a Escola Capitalista' (Against the Capitalist School), on the other hand, argued that the 'reformist' position was one of 'centralization, bureaucratization, and assault on the state apparatus'.[37]

The area of greatest agreement between the two positions was the area of pedagogy and curriculum. Both conceived pedagogy and curriculum as 'operating to life, participation and co-operation'. Of course, it is understandable that, initially at least, there should have been considerable agreement in this area for the prime objective of both positions was the disarticulation of Salazarist ideology. In addition, there was the mutual objective of instilling notions of democracy, i.e. making students aware of basic facts concerning the society in which they lived, of the relationship between education and work, of the child as a being with rights, etc. After the repressive school of the Salazarist era, where for the mass of the population there was either no education or a total disjuncture work-school, it was predictable, considering also the traditions of the First Portuguese Republic[38] and the total absence of disciplines such as sociology and psychology, that there should be intense efforts to create, through a humanist pedagogy (child-centered) and through a curriculum stressing new socialist ideology, a link between the community and the school.

To accompany, or rather, to *dynamize*, the process was, of course, the 'revolutionary pedagogue', conceived as a missionary-like figure, ready to transform consciousnesses, and thus society. It is interesting to note that the Left in general conceived the teacher in this 'romantic' fashion in Portugal, that it supported and practised pedagogies termed both in capitalist and socialist societies as 'anarchic' and 'utopian'. Portugal's revolutionary period, at least to this extent, repeated the pattern of the Russian, Chinese, and Cuban revolutions – i.e. education was conceived by the Left as a principal agent in changing social relations. Of course, in Portugal's case, this period was a relatively short one – education's principal role had become that of an agent to increase production.

The 'Reorganization' of Education

With the taking of office by the First Constitutional Government, a 'reorganization' and 'regionalization' (so-called – no real progress towards decentralization has yet been made) of the Ministry of Education was carried out by the new Minister of Education, Sottomoyer Cardia (a member of Portugal's Socialist Party). We have already referred to the manner in which the concepts of 'normalization' and 'efficiency' were employed to articulate a 'democratic' educational reform, a reform aimed at improving standards that had depreciated considerably, at training technicians and technocrats much needed to develop the Portuguese economy, and at improving, in general, the efficiency of an out-dated and over-politicized education system. The devices used to execute this reform such as *numerus clausus*, the limitation of the internal democracy of the school, and the hierarchization of academic degrees, challenged directly, and indeed, halted, efforts either to construct the 'socialist school' or to use education in the construction of a socialist society.

The Communist Party, and its allies, saw the process of 'reorganization' as an attempt to contain productive forces, rather than expand them. The restraint on productive forces, it was argued, would increase contradictions between sections of the superstructure and its economic base, thus effectively destroying that newly created in Portugal, and contributing directly to the restoration of capitalist relations of production. Naturally the demands made on the Portuguese Government by the International Monetary Fund, so that Portugal could obtain what was said to be a vital loan to 'stabilize' the economy, thus putting a break on expansion of the economy, were seen as a confirmation of the attempt to restore capitalist relations of production.

For groups comprising 'poder popular', the 'reorganization' was the logical consequence of the restoration of the dominance of capitalist relations of production that occurred with the 'counter-coup' of 25 November, 1975. Thus Cardia's measures were seen as simply 'pre-revolution', designed to return education to notions of schooling isolated from life, to authoritarianism, to forms of hierarchization, to the recreation of a reproductive apparatus of dogmatism, etc.

Conclusion

With the Revolution of 25 April, 1974, the pre-revolution Veiga Simão Reform in education was overtaken. During the period from the date of the Revolution to the investiture of the First Constitutional Government, the popular masses gradually took charge of the democratization of education in Portugal creating, through the political forces that represented them – the Armed Forces Movement (the 'MFA') and the political parties – and through organizations developed at local level – neighbour commissions, housing associations, factory councils, etc. – forms of democratic schooling that had the effect of extending and further developing the notions of democracy contained in the Veiga Simão Reform, and initiated drives for a mass literacy campaign in the name of equality of educational opportunities.

Attempts were made to use education – via changes in curricula, new forms of pedagogy and organization of the school – either to aid the construction of a socialist society or to create the 'socialist school'. Both the extension of the Veiga Simão Reform and the attempts at new forms of socialist education were articulated in the new Portuguese Constitution, which appeared in 1976.

In this article we have attempted to delineate the interpretations that were given to democratic and socialist forms of education. Also, we have argued that the redefinition of education after the revolutionary period has involved a penetration of education by forms of administrative and economic rationality that effectively were predominant in the Veiga Simão Reform and the development of education in Portugal *before* the 25 April, 1974.

In summing up, we would like to agree with the remark made by Professor Veiga Simão, that in the final analysis expresses the outstanding advances made in education in the period after the 25 April, 1974, and which at the same time points to the dangers inherent in a form of democracy that is too closely tuned to the demands of market and administrative forces:

> The advances and retreats [since the promulgation of the Veiga Simão Reform] gave origin to a situation in which the management ['gestão'] of the schools went beyond the Reform, but the structural development of the educational system and the application of the principle of equality of opportunities suffered a dangerous retrogression.[39]

Of course, the retrogression Veiga Simão is referring to is the one he sees in terms of his own Reform, which became Law in 1973. However, as is apparent throughout this article, we would rather see the retrogression in terms of the moves backwards that have occurred since the taking of office by the Socialist Party Minister of Education in 1976. The Communist Party, in a major educational document produced in 1978 at a special conference on education, defines those backward moves in terms of a 'crisis' in Portuguese education. It consists of the following four points:

> First, the persistence of a class system of education; second, an imbalance between education and the new economic and social relations of the country; third, the progressive degradation of scientific quality and educational pedagogy; and fourth, the adoption of the education administration of an authoritarian and centralized policy.[40]

Thus, the 'crisis' in Portuguese education is not about a retrogression in terms of the Veiga Simão Reform, which, in any event, in concrete terms was only just beginning to be implemented at the time of the Portuguese Revolution; rather it is about *a return to that reform*, not in terms of the popular interpellations which it was capable of articulating during that particular conjuncture, and which it certainly is incapable of articulating in the present one, but in terms of the deeper structural characteristics of the Reform, which represent a particular route to the *modernization* of Portugal, a route about which even Veiga Simão himself has recently expressed doubts.

Notes and References

1 MONICA, M. F. (1978) *Educacão e Sociedade no Portugal de Salazar*, Editorial Presenca.
2 KEITH, H.H. (1973) 'Point, Counterpoint in Reforming Portuguese Education, 1750–1973' *American Studies Centre*, p. 8.
3 For the argument on the importance and function of the military see STOER, S.R. (1978) 'Ideology and the Specificity of the Portuguese State', M.A. Dissertation, Institute of Education, London; and PIMLOTT, B. (1977) 'Socialism in Portugal: Was it a Revolution?' *Government and Opposition*, Vol. 12, No. 3, Summer.
4 Paradoxically, that is, until one considers the contradictions that largely were the cause of the appearance of the repressive apparatus.
5 CABRAL PINTO (1977) *Escolas do Magistério, Reforma e Contra-Reforma*, Cadernos 'o professor', p. 13.
6 *Ibid.*, p. 15.
7 See MARTINS, H. (1968) 'Portugal: Part I', in WOLFF, S.J. (Ed) *European Fascism*, Larder, Weiderfeld, and Nicholson.
8 MÓNICA, M.F. (1978) *op. cit.*
9 MIRANDA, S. (1978) 'Portugal e a OCDE: Expansão Económica e Planificacão Educativa' *Vértice*, Vol. XXXVIV, no. 408–9, May/June and to be published in DALE, R. DA MIRANDA, S., STOER, S. and WICKHAM, A. *Making the World Safe for Capital*.
10 General Humberto Delgado ran for President in 1958 creating a focal point for mass political action that hadn't been present in Portugal since the time of the Republic. Salazar abolished direct suffrage for the Presidency after the campaign (Decree-Law no. 43528) and Delgado was later murdered by the PIDE, the Portuguese Secret Police.
11 Schmitter P. has argued that there has been a move in Portugal from a predominantly 'state-corporatist' form of state to a predominantly 'societal-corporatist' form. However, the definition of Portugal's state as a form of societal corporatism, i.e. a 'concomitant component of the post liberal, advanced capitalist, democratic welfare state' hardly seems to fit! See SCHMITTER, P. (1975) *Corporation and Public Policy in Authoritarian Portugal* London, Sage; and MAKLER, H. (1976) 'The Portuguese industrial élite and its corporate relations: A study of compartmentalization in an authoritarian regime' *Economic Development and Cultural Change* 24, 3.
12 In terms of the latter, particularly since the 25 November, 1975 (see note 19).
13 See SACUNTALA DE MIRANDA, (1978) *op. cit.* Miranda also points to the important role of the OECD in influencing Portuguese educational policies in the 1950s and 60s.
14 WEILER, H. (1978) 'Towards a Political Economy of Educational Planning', *Prospects*, Vol. VIII, No. 3.
15 VEIGA S.J. (1971) 'The General Reform of Education in Portugal', Broadcast to Nation, 6 January, in *Western European Education*, Spring–Summer, 1972.
16 PEREIRA, J.M. (1979) *Pensar Portugal Hoje*, Dom Quixote.
17 FINN, D., GRANT, N. and JOHNSON, R. (1977) 'Social Democracy, Education and the Crisis' *Working Papers in Cultural Studies 10*, p. 184.
18 WILLIAMS, R. (1978) 'Education and Social Democracy', paper prepared for the Socialist Teacher's Alliance Conference, London.
19 DONALD, J. (1978) 'Green Paper: Noise of Crisis' re-printed in this volume.
20 The date of the suppression of a Left-wing armed revolt, small in scale, and some say provoked by the Right to end the 'deadlock' of the 'hot summer' of 1975 when the country was close at times to civil war. See FAYE, J.P. (1976) *Portugal: The Revolution in the Labryinth*, Spokesman Books.
21 See POULANTZAS, N. (1976) *The Crisis of the Dictatorships* London, New Left Books.
22 Poulantzas' term, which is an attempt to distinguish a home bourgeoisie which is not completely independent from foreign capital from one that is, i.e. a 'national bourgeoisie'. Nevertheless, since the domestic bourgeoisie is interested in industrial development and extension of the home market, it tends to be polarized against the exploitation of the country by foreign capital. POULANTZAS, N. (1976) *op. cit.*, p. 43.
23 *The Constitution of the Portuguese Republic*, 1976.
24 A government constituted almost entirely of members of the Portuguese Socialist Party.
25 *The Constitution*, 1976.
26 SIDA (1977) There have been several World Bank Reports, during 1977 and 1978. At present the World Bank is largely financing the project of Polytechnic Education in Portugal.
27 ABRAHAM, A.S. (1976) 'Aid to Education: to Change in Order to Preserve', *Prospects*, Vol. VI, No. 2.
28 SIDA Document – from the introduction.

29 As a justification for polytechnic education, Marcalo Grilo, the Director-General of Higher Education at the time, made the following comment in a newspaper interview:

> Still, the factor which most justifies this form of education (polytechnic education) cannot be said to be unemployment, but rather the necessity of the country for technicians absolutely essential to economic development'. (*Diário de Noticias*, 17 May, 1979)

Several days later the polytechnic education programme suffered a setback when the Portuguese parliament (Assembleia da República) heavily passed a motion to elevate the status of 'Institutos Técnicos (Technical Institutes), located in the interior of the country, to 'Institutos Universitários' (University Institutes), thus conceding to the demands of political forces in the interior.

30 In a recent interview in *O Jornal da Educacão*, April 1979. See also VEIGA, S.J. (1972) 'Projected Educational System', Ministry of National Education (Portugal), in *Western European Education*, Spring–Summer.

31 TEODORO, A. (1978) *A Revolucão Portuguesa e a Educacão*, Editorial Caminho; CEC (Contra a Escola Capitalista) (1978) *A Politica na Escola*, Editora: O Armazen das Letras; Socialist Party Programme, 1976.

32 Rogerio Fernandes, Director-General of all Elementary Education, challenged the 'Plano Melo Antunes', a plan of democratic reform, arguing that it aimed at 'bettering the education system without changing it'. Fernandes, 1976.

33 TEODORO, A. (1978) *op. cit.*

34 CUNHAL, A. (1976) *A Revolucão Portuguesa*: *O Passado e o Futuro*, Edicões Avante; p. 36.

35 CEC (1978) *op. cit.*; NAMORADO, R. (1973) *Educacão e Politica*, Centelha.

36 FERNANDES, R. (1977) *Educacão: Uma Frente de Luta*, Livros Horizonte.

37 CEC (1978) *op. cit.*

38 The Liberal Republicans had libertarian conceptions of education – the child was conceived as a flower that should be cultivated and given space to grow so that it would blossom into an autonomous individual.

39 Professor J. Veiga Simão, in an interview published in *O Jornal da Educacão*, April 1979.

40 Portuguese Communist Party Document – *Ensino para a Democracia, Democracia para o Ensino* (1978).

Additional Bibliography

CUNHAL, A. (1977) *A Questão do Estado: Questão Central de Cada Revolucão*, Edicões Avante.

DALE, R. (1978) 'Education in the Crisis and the Crisis in Education', unpublished paper.

MELO, A. and BENAVENTE, A. (1978) *Experiments in Popular Education in Portugal 1974–76*, UNESCO, Ed. Studies and Documents no. 29.

SCHULTZ, T.W. (1972) 'Investment in Human Capital', in *Power and Ideology in Education*, KARABAL, J. and HALSEY, A.H. (Eds), New York, Oxford Press.

SEERS, D., SCHAFFER, B. and KILGIINEN, M.L. (1979) (Eds), *Underdeveloped Europe: Studies in Core-Periphery Relation*, Harvester Press.

SOBEL, I. (1978) 'The Human Capital Revolution in Economic Development: its Current History and Status', *Comparative Education Review*, June.

Newspapers: *Diário de Noticias*, 17 May, 1979.
   O Jornal da Educacão, April 1979.

21 Education, Inequality and the Question of a Communist 'New Class'

Adam Westoby

When the Paris Commune took the management of the revolution in its own hands; when plain working men for the first time dared to infringe upon the governmental privilege of their 'natural superiors', and, under circumstances of unexampled difficulty, performed their work modestly, conscientiously and efficiently – performed it at salaries the highest of which barely amounted to one-fifth of what, according to high scientific authority, is the minimum required for a secretary to a certain metropolitan school-board – the old world writhed in convulsions of rage at the sight of the Red Flag, the symbol of the Republic of Labour, floating over the Hôtel de Ville.[1]

Marx's enthusiastic description of the first, short-lived 'workers' state' has little application to today's Communist societies. They seem to have settled into a more traditional mode, in which the educated emerge on top.

This paper consists of three sections. The first recalls the fact that Communist countries have inequalities of social class and educational opportunities not dissimilar to those to be found in developed capitalist societies, and suggests that education is an important part of the reproduction of social differentiation from generation to generation. The second section recalls that there is also a long tradition of social theory and comment arguing that the abolition of private property would not necessarily end social inequality but might usher in an educated/political/managerial/scientific 'new class'. The final section comments on some more recent writings which have build education into theories of an hereditary 'new class'.

Education and inequalities in Communist countries

Put extremely simply, we may think of the connections between individuals' social and/or economic level, and education in two 'stages': the connection of family background and educational level with childrens' educational achievement; and the connection of education with occupational status and, thereby, with the social level achieved by the next generation.[2] At both of these stages there exist marked associations. In the Soviet Union in the 1960s, despite Kruschev's policy of 'proletarianization'[3] children of the 'intelligentsia', or 'specialists' (and, to a lesser extent, those of 'skilled workers') had a much higher chance of staying on to the upper classes in secondary school (and, from there, of course, of going on to full time higher education).[4] The children of non-manual 'employees' had a three to four times better chance of going on to higher education than those of manual workers or peasants.[5] 'Specialists' formed, in the late 1960s, around 12–13 per cent of the Soviet work force.[6] But, by the time students leave secondary school, their social composition has been markedly 'enriched'; the children of 'specialists' accounted for almost 30 per cent of secondary school graduates.[7] Even after Kruschev's reforms, therefore, the social composition of students in tertiary education remained markedly slanted in favour of non-manual and 'specialist' families.

Within higher education children of the intelligentsia and those in the highest occupations were more likely, by better qualifications, or in some cases, through wire-pulling, to get into the highest status institutions.[8] Within the institutions they were less liable to be victims of the (appreciable) level of dropout.[9] The long-term effect is to place them higher in the professions they eventually enter.[10] Selectivity is less than in Western Europe.[11] Nevertheless manual workers and peasants, comprising perhaps three quarters of the Soviet population, claim little over a third of full time higher education places. While at one end of the same scale peasants are the most powerfully disadvantaged, at the other end the intelligentsia's children form a sizeable majority of students in the best higher education institutions.[12]

This pattern is fairly general to today's Communist societies. And even in 1938, in the heyday of Soviet stalinism, non-manual occupations conferred broadly similar educational advantages.[13] While the situation in the Soviet Union may have altered since the 1960s it has done so only marginally.[14] The same basic patterns occur in the Communist states of eastern Europe: the cases of Hungary[15] and Poland,[16] for example, have also been widely commented on in western studies.

In Communist states, private property in the means of production is largely eliminated and, where it exists, it is on a relatively small scale. Occupation, therefore, is the main factor shaping economic rewards and social status. The *general* connection between education and subsequent employment is one with which we are familiar in the West. The higher the level of occupation (and the greater the salaries and other rewards that go with it) the more years of schooling its incumbents will (on average) have.[17] Graduates are systematically recruited (occasionally compulsorily placed) into the initial stages of careers in skilled occupations.[18] The result of this link, added to the preceding one between family background and education, is that there is a pronounced correlation between the occupational levels of fathers and their children. A local study in the Soviet Union illustrates this: over 70 per cent of the children of 'intelligentsia' fathers become 'intelligentsia', compared with less than a third of manual workers' children.[19] It is also true for example in national data for Hungary where, in 1973, 54 per cent of the men whose fathers had been 'managers and professionals' in 1938 were in that same category, compared with 6.3 per cent for the population as a whole.[20]

Statistical evidence is not easy to come by for China. But during the Cultural Revolution Maoists pointed to very similar social selection, extending down from higher education to special 'collective boarding schools' for children of cadres (i.e. Party officials). According to a Red Guard article of April 1967 'capitalist roaders'

> energetically peddled the black goods of revisionist education, and led these collective boarding schools for children of cadres gradually onto the road of 'schools for aristocratic children' of the British and Soviet types.
>
> . . .
>
> . . . Over many years Liu Shao-ch'i, Teng Hsiao-p'ing, and Lu Ting-i have utilized powers which they usurped to promote energetically in the domain of education a bourgeois educational line in opposition to Chairman Mao's revolutionary line, and they have taken the frontline of education as a position for fostering their successors . . .
>
> . . . They have spread the absurd idea of being 'born Red', rejected the necessity of ideological reform among the children of the cadres, and infused into them the reactionary feudalist 'theory of lineage' by saying that 'the children of the cadres are the successors of lineage to our proletarian revolutionary cause'.[21]

The Cultural Revolution did not eliminate the problem. In September 1979 there were demonstrations by students in Peking against the preferential treatment of cadres' children in admissions to university.[22]

Higher education was considered normal in the Soviet Union, for the upper levels of the party and state, by the 1960s; it is also the usual gateway towards the several hundred thousand posts in party, state and economic administration which form the governing stratum of society, as it is to virtually all scientific and technical posts (though many of these are not particularly elevated) and to many literary and 'creative' ones.[23]

In very broad terms[24] the hierarchies of income difference (and of consumption patterns) appear to correspond to those of occupation in similar ways in both Communist and developed capitalist societies. Of course the differences of *total personal incomes* in Communist countries are less than those in capitalist ones, where concentrations of private wealth enlarge and extend the upper part of the distribution[25] but differentiation of *earned incomes*, though less than that in capitalist societies (and though, in the Soviet Union for example, it has fallen since the late 1950s[26]) remains of a comparable order of magnitude. In the upper part of the range there are many officials, administrators, academics, and so on, getting perhaps four or five times the average wage,[27] and a small group have incomes from nine or ten to perhaps hundreds of times the average.[28]

The connected links: education → occupation: and occupation → income imply a pronounced association of individual income with level of education. This has not received the detailed and specific attention it has in the West, where it forms one of the main interests of economists of education. But we know, for example, that the earnings ratio of Polish 'graduate specialists' to secondary school leavers in 1972 was approximately $1\frac{1}{2}:1$.[29]

Most of the illustrations we have taken come from the Soviet Union. And we have not mentioned many, potentially important, secondary factors: mother's educational/occupational level, part-time study and consequent promotion, for example. Our sketch is therefore extremely broad-brush. But is it grossly exaggerated? The answer is, I think, 'no', for two reasons.

1. The figures we have used (apart from 'guesstimates' of the very highest incomes, which are secret) are based on official sources. Yet marked social inequalities, and their transmission, tend to contradict official claims. In the Soviet Union, for example, it is only in the last 15 years that empirical sociology has revived, and it remains far from unconstrained. It is more likely that official sources play down, than that they exaggerate, inequality.

2. We have so far spoken only of *money* income. But for the higher levels in Communist societies non-monetary official benefits are very important: priority with housing and cars (in some cases provided free); special retail and food stores with better quality and/or imported goods, often subsidized; 'reserved' clinics and holiday resorts; priority for transportation and theatre tickets; easier overseas travel. These types of (tax free) benefits considerably raise the standard of living of those in higher occupations.[30]

Educational differences, therefore, form an important element within a system of substantial and institutionalized inequality. And the system is strongly transmitted from generation to generation. For the top 15 per cent or so of Soviet society the chances of their children finding occupations at the same 'intelligentsia' or equivalent level were two or three times those of the children of manual workers. And even for the children of the intelligentsia who were initially employed in 'lower non-manual' occupations these jobs very often represented a stepping stone (together with part-time further education) in reascent towards their parents' social level.[31] In other words, there exists a social layer which, most of all through family and educational advantage, reproduces its position across generations in a comparably strong way to the middle classes in developed capitalist societies, who have appropriated to themselves the lion's share of the benefits of expanded higher education.

The official images of Communist states do not, of course, recognize this. They do, however, both recognize and support differentiation of salaries according to education. 'From each according to his ability; to each according to his work' is a clause in virtually all contemporary Communist constitutions[32] (it originates in Stalin's 1936 constitution) and 'according to work' is understood to refer largely to the levels of education or skill involved.

This pattern is true also of those countries sometimes thought of as most egalitarian. Le Duan sketched the pattern for North Vietnam in 1962, and some of the problems it provoked:

> A family with two skilled workers can earn about two hundred dongs, or as much as a minister. The lowest wage of a worker is 27 dongs, that is roughly one fifth of the highest wage. This is a feature particular to our country. But the income of a peasant seems low in comparison to that of a worker. The *per capita* income of peasants being only about 10 dongs a month . . . they wonder whether they are making sacrifices to build their future or to let others enjoy higher wages. This is a complicated problem. During the Resistance War, as everyone got nearly the same wage, our ideological work was easy. Now our explanations to the effect that everyone should accept sacrifices is a very hard job . . . We must say unequivocally that there are high and low wages, otherwise socialism could not be built. If a man who works harder than another and whose technical ability is higher, is not better paid, then we cannot encourage him to study and raise his technical level, thus hindering technological revolution. A distribution equal for all is unjust and irrational.[33]

But it is fair to add that this is not how Engels saw the place of more skilled ('compound') labour in building socialism:

> How then are we to solve the whole important question of the higher wages paid for compound labour? In a society of private producers, private individuals or their families defray the costs of teaching the trained worker; hence the higher price paid for trained labour-power accrues first of all to private individuals; the clever slave is sold for a higher price, and the clever wage-earner is paid higher wages. In a socialistically organized society, these costs are defrayed by society, and the fruits, the greater values produced by compound labour, therefore belong to it. The worker himself has no extra claim.[34]

Early views of an educated 'new class'

The existence of inequalities in Communist countries is, by now, generally recognized. Indeed there exists a fairly long line of argument and writing predicting or commenting on the fact that ending private property would not necessarily mean the end of sizeable, institutionalized social inequality. And among such arguments the role of education has quite often been important in explaining how, in the absence of private property, a social élite would nonetheless be formed.

I summarize some early examples, both to recall that these ideas go back some way and perhaps also to prompt some questions about contributions which social scientists of education might make to understanding the social structure of contemporary Communist societies. But the selection is neither comprehensive, integrated, nor a fragment of intellectual history. It is essentially a list of summaries and quotations – ranging in viewpoint from radical to conservative, and in tone from theoretic to polemical. Among them recur two ideas:

1. That with the elimination of private property and inherited wealth (for example, by social revolution) the educated, exploiting their greater culture and capacity for organization, will take over control.

2. That, in the longer term, selective education will act to reproduce substantial social and political differences.

While we may conceptually distinguish these ideas (and the empirical sketch in the first section bears essentially on the latter) they are, of course, not mutually exclusive. And they are not always clearly separated by the writers concerned. In some cases, too, discussion of the functioning of the education *system* as such is slight or inexplicit; the emphasis is on the rule of leaders and managers *by virtue* of their intellectual training or expertise.

One of the earliest (and still one of the most striking) opinions was that of Marx's great political and personal rival, Bakunin. Even if private property were abolished, he warned in 1869, education would still recreate exploitation and oppression:

> Is it not clear that, as between two men, gifted with more or less equal intelligence, he who knows more, whose spirit has been more widened by science, and who, having better understood the interconnections of natural and social facts, or what one calls the laws of nature and of society, is it not clear that he will more easily and fully grasp the situation in which he finds himself, that he will feel himself freer within it, and that he will feel more practically able and more powerful than the other? He who knows more will naturally dominate him who knows less; and if there existed to begin with between two classes only this difference of teaching and education, this difference would very soon produce all the others, and the human world would find itself again at its present state, that is to say that it would be divided again into a mass of slaves and a small number of rulers, the first working, as today, for the second.[35]

Bakunin saw revolution led by Marxist intellectuals as a dangerously probable route to such a state, leading him to predictions – in *Statism and Anarchy* (1873) – which are, perhaps, worth quoting in full:

> But in the People's State of Marx there will be, we are told, no privileged class at all. All will be equal, not only from the juridical and political point of view, but also from the economic point of view. At least this is what is promised, though I very much doubt whether that promise could ever be kept. There will therefore no longer be a privileged class, but there will be a government and, note this well, an extremely complex government. This government will not content itself with administering and governing the masses politically, as all governments do today. It will also administer the masses economically, concentrating in the hands of the State the production and distribution of wealth, the cultivation of land, the establish-

ment and development of factories, the organization and direction of commerce, and finally the application of capital to production by the only banker – the State. All that will demand an immense knowledge and many heads 'overflowing with brains' in this government. It will be the reign of *scientific intelligence*, the most aristocratic, despotic, arrogant and elitist of all regimes. There will be a new class, a new hierarchy of real and counterfeit scientists and scholars, and the world will be divided into a minority ruling in the name of knowledge, and an immense, ignorant, majority. And then, woe unto the ignorant ones!

Such a regime will not fail to arouse very considerable discontent in the masses of the people, and in order to keep them in check the 'enlightened' and 'liberating' government of Mr Marx will have need of a not less considerable armed force. For the government must be strong, says Engels, to maintain order among the millions of illiterates whose mighty uprising would be capable of destroying and overthrowing everything, even a government 'overflowing with brains'.[36]

This was no isolated prediction; it is echoed several times in Bakunin's polemics against the Marxist 'state socialists' in the 1870s.

Marx's reactions also bear recalling. Painfully translating *Statism and Anarchy* from the Russian, he emitted a string of infuriated marginalia: 'quelle reverie!', 'democratic twaddle', 'political drivel', 'asinine!'[37] It is, of course, not easy to evaluate the status of these texts or their structure as discourse. But it is clear that Bakunin's intuitions touched a nerve.

Starting about the turn of the century Bakunin's conceptions were developed by the Pole J.W. Makhaisky.[38] The European social democratic parties and their Marxist leaders were not heralds of socialism, he argued, but of the growing educated middle class, now aspiring to become a new ruling class by riding the working class to power in the name of socialism. Bourgeois society, 'after the suppression of the capitalists [would] continue to be an oppressive society, as before, that of the cultivated rulers and governors, the world of the "white hands" . . . this system preserves and reproduces itself from generation to generation'.[39]

It is, indeed, growing up within bourgeois society. The intellectuals receive their income because they are the hereditary owners of

> all knowledge, culture and civilization. This condemns the majority of humanity to live as a race of slaves, inferior and uneducated. This state of affairs is deliberately camouflaged by the teachings of socialism, according to which the owners of factories and land are the sole exploiters, while the intelligentsia lives only by its own work. Behind the shield of socialist science the most modern form of exploitation of all sprouts.[40]

Makhaisky's theories gained broad currency among Russian social democrats at the turn of the century; it drew the polemical fire of several prominent Bolsheviks. A parallel current also developed among more conservative thinkers. Pareto's theory of the 'circulation of élites' and Mosca's concept of the 'ruling (or political) class' both argue the necessary social re-exudation of a controlling and privileged layer in society. Specialized education is (at least in modern societies) an important avenue for recruitment to the élite, giving 'its possessors affluence, prestige and power'.[41] More specific is Moscas's prediction that 'while today instinct causes owners to leave their wealth to their children, in a collectivist regime it would cause the rulers to engineer the careers of their sons, and with the immense powers they would have, they would have the means to succeed and equality would always remain an empty word'.[42]

This line of thinking connects into Michels' discussion of the tendency to oligarchy in political parties, especially socialist ones:

> ... long experience has shown that among the factors which secure the dominion of minorities over majorities – money and its equivalent (economic superiority), tradition, and hereditary transmission (historical superiority) – the first place must be given to the formal instruction of the leaders (so called intellectual superiority). Now the most superficial observation shows that in the parties of the proletariat the leaders are, in matters of education, greatly superior to the led.[49]

Michels (a disappointed social democrat, who deplored the tendency to an edu-cated oligarchy) was thus led reluctantly to agree with Mosca that even after 'a successful attempt to deprive the bourgeoisie of power . . . always and necessarily there springs from the masses a new organized minority which raises itself to the rank of a governing class'.[44]

> The administration of an immeasurably large capital, above all when this capital is collective property, confers upon the administrator influence at least equal to that possessed by the private owner of capital. Consequently the critics in advance of the Marxist social order ask whether the instinct which today leads the members of the possessing classes to transmit to their children the wealth which they [the parents] have amassed, will not exist also in the administrators of the public wealth of the socialist state, and whether these administrators will not utilize their immense influence in order to secure for their children the succession to the offices which they themselves hold.[45]

Michels had no preventative for this process. But he suggested as the best palliative 'the great task of social education, to raise the intellectual level of the masses, so that they may be enabled, within the limits of what is possible, to counteract the oligarchical tendencies of the working-class movement'.[46]

Michel's comments (like Makhaisky's) refer to the social democratic leaders of the early 1900s in general; it would be an anachronism to see them as warnings specifically about the Bolshevik current in the Russian social democracy.

With the events in Russia in 1917–21,[47] such debates promoted themselves from the speculative to the concrete. Initially, of course, the focus was on the positions and functions occupied by the existing educated classes from the old regime, not on the long term effects of the Soviet education system. Again, libertarians were in the van in detecting a 'new class'. The anarcho-syndicalist Gregory Maximoff was warning, in September 1918:

> the proletariat is gradually being enserfed by the state. The people are being transformed into servants over whom there has risen a new class of administrators – a new class born mainly from the womb of the so-called intelligentsia.
>
> Is not this merely a new class system looming on the revolutionary horizon? Has there not occurred merely a re-grouping of classes, a re-grouping as in previous revolutions when, after the oppressed had evicted the landlords from power, the emergent middle class was able to direct the revolution towards a new class system in which power fell into its own hands?
>
> The resemblance is all too striking. One cannot deny it. And if the elements of class inequality are as yet indistinct, it is only a matter of time before privileges will pass to the administrators. We do not mean to say that this inequality and these privileges are arbitrary, or that the Bolshevik party set out to create a new class system. But we do say that even the best intentions and aspirations must inevitably be smashed against the evils inherent in any system of centralized power. The separation of management from labour, the division between administrators and workers, flows logically from centralization. It cannot be otherwise. There are no other words to the song. The song goes thus: management implies responsibility, and can responsibility be compared with ordinary labour? Responsibility demands special rights and privileges. Such is the source of privileges and of the new anti-socialist morality. Thus we are presently moving not towards socialism but towards state capitalism.[48]

Similar criticisms came later from currents closer to the Bolshevik leadership, especially with the increased reliance on 'experts' under the New Economic Policy (1921 onwards). The Workers' Opposition of 1921 protested against 'specialists, technicians, engineers, and former managers of financial and industrial affairs, who by all their past experience are bound to the capitalist system of production', and who were taking advantage of their positions to recover their former prosperity.[49]

Slightly earlier (1920–21) Bukharin, the Bolshevik leader with the most interest in contemporary sociology, reverted to Michels' prediction, but only to dispute it:

> ... what constitutes an eternal category in Michels' presentation, namely the 'incompetence of the masses' will disappear ... it is likewise a product of the economic and technical conditions, expressing themselves in the general cultural being and in the educational conditions. We may state that in the society of the future there will be a colossal over-production of organizers, which will nullify the stability of the ruling groups.

This applies to developed communist society. But, in the transition period, Bukharin allows a crucial concession:

There will inevitably result a *tendency* to 'degeneration', i.e. the excretion of a leading stratum in the form of a class-germ. This tendency will be retarded by two opposing tendencies; first, by the *growth of the productive forces*, second, by the abolition of the *educational monopoly*. The increasing reproduction of technologists and of organizers in general, out of the working class itself, will undermine this possible new class alignment. The outcome of the struggle will depend on which tendencies turn out to be the stronger.[50]

Karl Kautsky, once Lenin's hero, but now a 'renegade', commented on the same problem. His *Terrorism and Communism* (written 1918–19) deplored the coercion of the intelligentsia, but agreed with Lenin on the need to pay 'experts' more. But

We now see what are the elements which are to become leaders of the Socialist production in the Soviet Republic. On the one side a few old conspirators, honourable fighters of blameless intentions, yet in matters of business merely inexperienced novices; and on the other side numerous educated men who, against their own convictions, either as mere seekers try to adapt themselves to the new power, as they would adapt themselves to any other power, if occasion arose, or who are driven through fear and hunger and punishment; or, finally, such men as allowed themselves to be bought by high wages.[51]

The result is, says Kautsky, that they 'gather together in their hands the beginnings of a new capitalism'.[52] Russia was not 'ripe' for the abolition of capitalism; the attempt has merely meant that, now in the hands of experts and officials, 'industrial capitalism, from being a private system, has now become a state capitalism'.[53]

During the 1920s and 1930s similar ideas were developed by other critics of the Soviet Union, for example the French social democrat Lucien Laurat. Adapting Marx's schema of the distribution of the social product, Laurat saw the 'bureau-technocratic oligarchy in the USSR', as being paid extra out of a portion of surplus value. 'The development [in Laurat's view, progressive] towards a more and more controlled economy creates, together with the necessary control organs, the technicians capable of using them', but a 'small minority controls these levers and ministers this collectivized property exclusively in its own interests'.[54] Nevertheless,

the labour of superintendence and direction is better paid because it is more highly qualified labour, and it will remain so even without constraint and without dictatorship as long as the requisite qualifications are rare. All attempts at excessive levelling in this respect would endanger the smooth working of the economic system so long as . . . the requisite qualifications have not been obtained by a growing number of people, thereby losing their rarity . . . here we have the famous 'apprenticeship fees' of which Lenin spoke and which the workers are obliged to pay to their specialists as long as the latter succeed in maintaining their cultural monopoly.[55]

Nonetheless Laurat feared that the collectivist state 'may easily grow into a forcing house for a class of exploiters'.[56] His view is also interesting as an early example of theories of 'convergence': that both Communist and capitalist societies – in which the state apparatus is increasing its weight and interpenetrating the economy, reinforcing and enriching an educated state bureaucracy – are tending along different routes towards a common type of social structure (in Laurat's view to the collectivized economic premises of 'evolutionary socialism').[57]

A similar idea, but bolder and more pessimistic, appears about the same time in Bruno Rizzi's *The Bureaucratization of the World* (1939)[58] the state bureaucracy is forming itself into a new, exploiting and privileged class. It is more progressive than the classical, competitive capitalist class since it is largely formed by skill and merit, and because it has the advantages of central economic planning. It owns the means of production, through the state, as a 'bureaucratic collectivity'. The USSR represents its most advanced form, but Nazi Germany, New Deal America, Italy, Japan, are all tending in the same direction.

More famous is James Burnham's *The Managerial Revolution* (1941). The separation of legal ownership from control in large scale private capitalism (in the USA, for example) is shifting real 'ownership unambiguously to the new controlling, new dominant class'. This is coalescing with another part of this 'new class', being formed in the state bureaucracy:

> A clear witness to the truth of this last observation is provided by the growth in the number of 'bright young men', of trained and educated and ambitious youth, who set out for careers in the government, not as politicians in the old sense, but as managers in the various agencies and bureaux in all the myriad fields where they now operate. A generation ago these young men would almost all have been headed for private enterprise, with the goal of making a name for themselves in business, industry or finance, and perhaps of finding a place in the charmed ranks of the upper *bourgeoisie*. More and more of them understand now that security, power, or simply the chance to exercise their talents are not to be found in the old ways, but must be sought elsewhere. The young men thinking and acting in this way include, significantly enough, many of the children of the capitalists themselves, who perhaps sense that the dominion exercised by their parents as capitalists can be continued by the children only through giving up capitalism.[59]

In Burnham's view, like Rizzi's, Russia is nearest to the 'system of managerial economy'[60] in which the new class will reproduce itself, through education, from one generation to the next:

> ... the managers will exploit the rest of society as a corporate body, their rights belonging to them not as individuals but through the position of actual direct responsibility which they occupy. They, too, through the possession of privilege, power, and command of educational facilities will

be able to control, within limits, the personnel of the managerial recruits; and the ruling class of managers will thus achieve a certain continuity from generation to generation.[61]

Burnham's theory has been very widely influential and has generated numerous descendants. The idea of a 'new class' ruling Soviet and other Communist societies has become a sociological commonplace. It would, of course, be wrong to suppose too close an identification of view among writers who merely use the same term. The sense given to 'class' varies enormously: for example from denoting the cohesive possession of political power on the part of a governing group, to a sense approximating to that of a range in distributions of income or standards of living. It would be very difficult to give a comprehensive review of the post-war sociological literature in which theories of a new class, formed in part through education, make an appearance. But such ideas have been in circulation a long time.

Some more recent theories

Finally, this section looks at a few recent, Marxist or marxisant, writings which bear on the question whether, and in what sense, it may be possible to conceive of a Communist ruling/governing/dominant/exploiting/privileged and educated 'new class'.

It is cautious to disaggregate the question. And it would be futile to embark on a discussion of theories of 'bureaucratic collectivism', 'managerial power', 'state capitalism' and so on, or of the general question of what is, or should correctly be, meant by the notion of social class. I suggest only that we exclude *purely distributive* definitions, for which the members of classes are simply those occupying a certain (and necessarily arbitrary) range of, for example, income. Because of the criteria for membership such notions have little explanatory purchase.

Eclecticism with regard to notions of class sometimes brings the reproach that the existence or not of social classes (unlike their characteristics) cannot be matters of degree. I do not think we should worry too much over this. It may be that we have to do with classes in the process of formation or gestation. Certainly if there are new forms of ruling class in contemporary Communist states, they cannot have existed, at least in most of their present, national, forms, for more than about three decades. Identification of the early bourgeoisie as a class/social type is a notoriously difficult problem for social historians, and they have a much longer retrospect from which to take advantage of hindsight. 'New' classes do not, by definition, first appear fully grown and intact, and with their organs of reproduction already functioning. And in this case it is possible that we have to do with classes still in an embryonic form.

It is perhaps useful to bear in mind a distinction (important, I think, to many historians) between:

    a. classes *in* themselves, defined essentially by their social relations to the means of production, and

b. classes *for* themselves, as they come to see themselves as having a common identity, common interests and a common fate.

As far as socially exploiting or ruling classes are concerned the class *in* itself has most usually been defined by its ownership of a particular form of private property, which serves at the same time as means for the appropriation of a social surplus. Property ownership gives class membership a certain independence of the personality, education and abilities of the individual. The class is composed of people but it exists, in an important sense, *through* the property and not the people. However, in the case of contemporary Communist states, there is no large-scale property in the means of production and what small-scale private production does exist is undertaken by groups who are not particularly powerful and often not particularly affluent either. Ownership of private property will be of only marginal help to us in analyzing the class structure of these societies, probably of even less use in identifying a 'new class'. Is it possible that education, or more precisely the linked effects of education – in particular higher education – and occupation, play, in communist societies, a role analogous to that of property?

Education could enter into the life of a 'new class' in a variety of ways:

i. as a means of equipping its members for power-wielding jobs – for example, in politics and state administration, in scientific and technical work, in the armed forces, in the higher literary or 'creative' occupations, and in the education system itself. The rest of society tends to be excluded from power, and its concomitant privileges, because they lack the educational pre-requisites of these sorts of jobs.

ii. insofar as more skilled occupations or those requiring higher education get higher rewards education becomes an essential element in economic differentiation.

iii. because of the educational advantages from which the children of the highly educated benefit education may be an important part of the mechanisms transmitting social differentiation from generation to generation. Evidently it is necessary that, in addition to any 'self-transmitting' effect of higher education, it also should tend to confer social advantages on those who possess it.

iv. Education (or some aspects of it) may be essential to a ruling class acting as a class, to its attaining the necessary, and partly collective, self-consciousness and abilities to secure and perpetuate its social position.

v. Conversely education (or some parts of it) may also be essential in procuring the subordinacy or acquiescence in the social structure of those (or some of those) outside the ruling class (what we may call the 'ideological' function of education?).

vi. Insofar as such a ruling class is not composed only of an hereditary membership the selective processes of the education system may provide a means whereby a ruling class identifies and recruits into its ranks young people from other sections of society.

vii. And, aside from the question of 'external' recruitment the education system may provide an equally important part of the means whereby individuals are selected to higher or lower, more or less powerful or appropriate, positions within the ruling class. One of the important advantages of a ruling class not based on hereditary private property is that its internal structure is not tied to accidents of birth, talent or upbringing.

Each of these aspects (which, while distinct, are in general not separate) are potentially of importance. Several of them occur in various recent critical writings on Soviet and eastern European societies.

Rudolf Bahro's study *The Alternative in Eastern Europe* sees, rather than discrete divisions into classes, a continuum both of distribution and in the social division of labour, in which the competitive strivings of individuals are sharpest at the stage of initial formal education:

> ... competition for the appropriation of activities favourable to self-development, for appropriate positions in the multi-dimensional system of social division of labour, becomes the specific driving force of economic life characteristic of actually existing socialism. It is not by chance that competitive behaviour between individuals in our system is so strongly focussed on the phase of education, in which access and admission to favourable positions in the system of overall social labour is determined, with those strata who have already acquired education and influence holding the centre of the stage. This struggle has a marked political character, summed up in the question whether social advance is to be won in a 'pure' competitive struggle, or whether this should be half-heartedly and superficially corrected by the application of social and political discrimination in favor of those strata who are disadvantaged in the division of labour, not to mention also by extensive bureaucratic and unofficial corruption. In any case, care is taken that sons and daughters of cadres never do too badly: they 'belong to the working class' because daddy or mummy works in some ministry or other.[62]

Formal equality within the educational system itself becomes institutionalized *in*equality through the different impacts and cultures of family life: 'In this respect, individual opportunity in our society is on the whole *just* as unequally distributed as in capitalist society . . . '.[63] This is one of the main reasons sustaining the family as a conservative social influence; Bahro's proposals for the reform (the 'Cultural Revolution') of Soviet-type societies consist essentially of a three-pronged attack – on educational specialization, on the division of labour, and on the confinement of the family. In general, Bahro understands these societies as modern versions of Marx's 'asiatic mode of production', ruled by a hierarchy of professional function-aries whose position is not connected with personal property. He does not treat higher education as a new form, or analogue, of property; the social divisions he perceives are stratification divisions, not class divisions.

Ivan Szelenyi and George Konrad, on the other hand, see one primary (though still emerging) class division – between the intelligentsia and the working class.[64] The intelligentsia exploits through control of direct re-distribution, a control which it holds because educated expertise has a monopoly in setting and supervising economic goals: 'If the law of capitalism consists in the striving for more profit, the law of state socialism consists in the striving for the maximization of re-distributive power, and from this point of view the teleological re-distributor with, of course, evangelistic zeal – will be as ruthless as any capitalist could ever be'.[65] A problem here is the sense in which 're-distributive power' can be the possession of individuals. Szelenyi stresses a distinction between the intelligentsia class as a whole and the powerful political or bureaucratic élite drawn from it; he sees many political events (Stalin's purges, and the later 'reform' movements, for example) as struggles over power-sharing between the intelligentsia as a whole and its 'own' political élite. The intelligentsia, at present at least, is a 'non-inheritance class', but this is so only in the weak sense that high political position is not specifically trans-mitted from one generation to the next. (He does not comment on the straight-forward nepotism to be found in, for instance, Rumania, China or North Korea.) But, in a more general sense, Szelenyi recognizes the increasing 'closure' of the intelligentsia as a whole, with downward mobility out of it negligible and upward mobility into it becoming more and more restricted.

Marc Rakovski makes a similar point: 'with steadier industrial development the dominant class has become able to fill management positions by internal repro-duction'.[66] Higher education has thus become a necessary, but not sufficient, condition of membership in it; political activity and personal connections are also required. With industrial development the social weight of the new class rises, while the permeability of the social structure falls.

What Bahro and Szelenyi share is the attempt to find the reason for education's importance for political dominance and economic exploitation (or, at least, privilege) within social relations of production. And, in this respect, their answers are rather similar. Education has a necessary technical significance within production in mod-ern industrial societies: labour is increasingly differentiated, increasingly requires formal learning; and an increasing proportion of the labour force comes to be in-volved in 'creative labour' in which synthesis and organization (whether of a social or a technical character) is the key element, and for which a high level of literacy and culture, together with complex specialist skills, are necessary. These technical conditions of production – which are shared by Communist and capitalist economies – are combined with specialization and selectivity in the education system. In the absence of private property they concentrate the directing (and therefore privileged) functions of production in relatively few hands (or heads). In this facet of their arguments Bahro and Szelenyi return to a view recognizably similar to Michels'.

Hillel Ticktin's writings on Soviet society argue – it is their fundamental method-ological point – that descriptive sociology is not sufficient and that analysis of social relations must start from specifying the basic economic laws of motion.[67] The ruling élite controls and disposes of the social surplus *via* two, conflicting, principles: centralized organization of production (officially described as, but not amounting to, 'planning'); and, continually limiting and frustrating this, the atomized self-interest of individual bureaucrats outside the centre, a statised analogue of the market's individualism. The 'élite', in which the distribution of substantial privilege and political power approximately coincide, is a much narrower group than the 'intelligentsia', which Ticktin equates (in the USSR) with the (approximately 9 million) higher education graduates. Nowadays, however, entry to the élite is almost invariably through higher education.

The internally divided and atomized character of the élite is important. Its self-renewal takes place through internal competition and this, in turn, is largely focused in the education system:

> . . . in the USSR, because the élite does not control the means of production, its control over appropriation is imperfect. On the one hand the élite allocates privileges to itself. On the other hand it has to hide them and distribute them in non-monetary form. As a result the inheritance of élite status and privilege is also rendered more difficult. Since this must be arranged in large part through the educational system it normally involves acting illegally to ensure an obstacle-free path for the children of the élite. The result, not surprisingly, is that such efforts cannot be guaranteed success. The situation is made worse by the fact that different sections of the élite will have greater or less difficulty and individuals may be more or less competent in the task of pushing their offspring. Worst of all it is a tedious and humiliating process. It is not the form that they would have dictated themselves, but one which corresponds to the original contradiction between their dependence on the working class and their antagonism to it.[68]

Ticktin sees education as the main means of selection and renewal of the élite (because of its internal divisions and lack of solidity, he does not call it a class) but he does not analyse it as entering in a fundamental way into the relations of production. The élite, who have the most direct control over distribution, direct the lion's share of privileged incomes towards themselves; among the 'lower' intelligentsia there is, consequently, an endemic yearning for a free labour market, which would *better* reward their education and skills.

In certain respects education is given a more fundamental place in the (assertory but irresistibly provoking) theses of Alvin Gouldner's *The Future of Intellectuals*. Gouldner's view of the Soviet-type intelligentsia is only a particular case within a more general 'convergence' type of theory. He perceives the global rise of a 'new class', characterized by, equipped with and cohering through its 'culture of critical discourse' (CCD), and formed in the – necessarily public and secular – system of education which is its essential organ of self-reproduction. As far as Soviet-type societies are concerned Gouldner draws a key distinction between the technical intellectuals of the 'new class', still in process of advancing their rule, and the main part of the political bureaucracy, the 'old line bureaucrats', from among whose ranks they mainly emerge, but who form a barrier to their rise. The intellectual equipment and outlook of 'old line bureaucrats' is generally routinist, conservative and parochial; that of the technical-intellectual 'new class', pragmatic, iconoclastic, task-orientated. The latter, consequently, is the universal and more progressive class. It is destined to inherit the earth.

Gouldner's 'theses' are full of interesting suggestions and *apercus*. One could quibble with many of them. For example, he suggests that the high proportion of graduates and intellectuals in their leadership expresses the fact that the major communist – led revolutions have been an avenue for the ascent of the 'new class'.[69] This is difficult to reconcile with the fact that the 'old line bureaucrats' have inexorably taken hold of these parties once they are come to power, the 'Cultural Revolution' notwithstanding. Nor does he explain how a class whose being is organically dependent on its intellectual advantages and its 'culture of critical discourse' can exist and prosper with world-views as widely different as, say, American liberal pragmatism, and state-Marxist orthodoxy.[70]

But it is surprising that one of the ideas Gouldner uses has not been more widely explored elsewhere. Economists of education have been prolific in applying to both industrialized and underdeveloped capitalist economies the theory of 'human capital': the idea that additional education, by raising the productivity of an individual's labour, acts as an accumulation of capital, providing extra income (higher wages) throughout his working life. But (as far as I know) economists have not systematically attempted to apply this concept to the associated differences of earnings and education that persist even where, as in Communist economies, most saleable physical capital has been eliminated.

Gouldner does precisely this. The 'new class' is

> a new *cultural* bourgeoisie whose capital is not its money but its control over valuable cultures. A systematic comparison of the New Class and the Old Class would ultimately require analysis of different forms of capital, or stocks of culture versus stocks of money. *Both are forms of capital as each is a source of an ongoing stream of income.* What is needed for the systematic analysis of the Old and New Class is a *general theory of capital* in which moneyed capital is seen as part of the whole, as a special case of capital. Conversely, what is required for the understanding of culture as capital is nothing less than a political economy of culture. (my emphasis)[71]

In beginning to sketch such a 'political economy of culture' Gouldner diverges from both Marx and from most economists of education. Capital (including 'cultural' or 'human' capital) is defined *purely* as a socially enforceable claim on future income and not necessarily as a factor of production.[72]

Economists of education normally consider education, and the expenditures of money and time on it, under two heads: as increasing the future productivity of individuals' labour (*'investment'* in 'human capital'), and as undertaken because it is either enjoyable or compulsory (*'consumption'* of education). Gouldner would, presumably, wish to add a third distinction: as giving access to rights of (unproductive) exploitation, in Soviet-type societies *via* the state apparatus.

Lastly, let me offer a suggestion-cum-speculation, and some questions. Perhaps there is latent in Gouldner's version of 'cultural capital' a view of the social power associated with higher education more closely akin to Marx's concept of capital. Capital may be seen as a claim upon future income. Or it may be seen as a social relation through which the surplus product is accumulated and employed to raise the productivity of living labour. A ruling class is, in general, one in whose hands lies control of surplus product. A rising proportion of the surplus product in most industrialized societies today is devoted to education: the proportion of GNP spent on education has shown an impressive upward tendency. Today's surplus product (tomorrow's 'dead labour') raises the productivity of tomorrow's living labour not just through machinery and physical equipment, but, increasingly, through improving the quality and capacities of labour directly. Since it is neither physical nor saleable this 'cultural capital' cannot take the form of property. But it is an essential part of the means of production. And in Communist societies it remains, like the physical means of production, alienated – in the sense that first, much of it is concentrated in a fairly narrow section of society, and second, control over its production, distribution and use lies with a social élite.

If we were to try to conceptualize today's communist societies within Marx's framework we should (I expect) at least agree that two changes relative to capitalism-changes that Marx held would coincide – have proved in fact to be separable. First, private property in the major means of production has been abolished (and with it the social role of the classical bourgeoisie). But second, the social surplus and the means of production remain out of the control of the large majority of producers, and in the hands of a ruling élite.

As Bakunin and Makhaisky predicted the education system plays a crucial part in this monopoly over the surplus product, and especially its cultural component. The specific education of the élite prepares them for the central oversight of production (including the production of the skills which enter production more directly), and for the political tasks of rule. The ideology under which they rule is perpetuated in the general education of the people. Control over the education system gives control over types and quantities of education within the 'cultural' surplus produced. But, as the instrument of an élite, it must necessarily be selective, concentrating much education – and the controlling types within that – in few heads.

In the absence of private property, control of the education system takes on greatly added importance. It provides the necessary and general conditions for membership of the élite. It becomes a key line of control over the national means of production as a whole. It is *the* mechanism for the specific forms of 'permeability' of the social structure. Gouldner and Szelenyi both stress that an élite which essentially forms itself by education can, by this means, co-opt the potential 'organic intellectuals' of lower classes, thereby doubly strengthening its own relative position.

The notion of alienated production of culture and of a cultural surplus as one of the primary instruments of a 'new class' offers, at least in principle, to bring together some of the different facets mentioned above. Especially, it may help to integrate the places of education in first, 'techniques' of production, second, social relations of production, and third, the formation and reproduction of a ruling minority. And it may help circumvent (by seeing it as a red herring) the vexed question of whether or not, in the absence of property, there can be such a thing as a Communist '*new* class'.

Acknowledgements

I am indebted to those who commented on an earlier draft of this paper, and especially Madeleine MacDonald and Hillel Ticktin.

Notes and References

1 Marx, K. (1871) *The Civil War in France.*
2 Of course these can be broken down into much more detailed stages. But it seems best to focus on the outline picture.
3 See 1958 speech quoted in MATTHEWS, M. (1972) *Class and Society in Soviet Russia* London, Allen Lane, p. 294.
4 *ibid.*, Table 106, p. 265.
5 MATTHEWS, M. (1976) 'Educational Growth and the Social Structure in the USSR' in FIELD, M.G. (Ed) *Social Consequences of Modernisation in Communist Societies* Baltimore, p. 140.
6 YANOWITCH, M. (1977) *Social and Economic Inequality in the Soviet Union* London, Martin Robertson, p. 111.
7 *ibid.*, p. 68.
8 *ibid.*, pp. 83–5; see also SIMIZ, K.M. (1977) 'The Machinery of Corruption in the Soviet Union, *Survey*, Vol. 23, No. 4, Autumn.
9 11 per cent for full-time higher education courses in the mid 1960s, higher under Kruschev. See MATTHEWS, M. (1976) *op. cit.*, p. 299, footnote 16.
10 HUSZAR, T. (1978) 'White-collar Workers, Intellectuals, Graduates in Hungary' in HUSZAR, T., KUKSAR, K. and SZALAI, S. (1978) *Hungarian Society and Marxist Sociology in the Nineteen-Seventies* Budapest, Corvina Press, pp. 164–5.
11 YANOWITCH, M. (1977) *op. cit.*, pp. 87–90; PARKIN, F. (1971) *Class Inequality and Political Order* New York, Praeger, p. 110.
12 YANOWITCH, M. (1977) *op. cit.*, pp. 87–90.
13 MATTHEWS, M. (1976) *op. cit.*, Table 110, p. 219.
14 YANOWITCH, M. (1977) *op. cit.*, p. 95.
15 See LANE, D. (1971) *The End of Inequality?* Harmondsworth, Penguin, p. 116.
16 *ibid.*, p. 110.
17 MATTHEWS, M. (1976) *op. cit.*, Table 42, pp. 143–55. Notice the parallel association in the table with the proportion in Party membership.
18 *ibid.*, Chapter 12.
19 YANOWITCH, M. (1977) *op. cit.*, p. 117.
20 ANDORKA, R. and ILLES, J. (1978) 'Changes in Intergenerational social Mobility' in HUSZAR *et al*, *op. cit.*, p. 202. Of course, in Hungary, the data do not refer to a generation completely brought up in a Communist country.
21 The Chingkangshan Fighting Corps of Peking Normal University for Smashing the Collective Boarding Schools for Children of Cadres, and the Liaison Center for Smashing the Collective Boarding Schools for Children of Cadres, 'On Collective Boarding Schools for Children of Cadres', *Spring Thunder* (Peking Red Guard paper), April 13 1964, translated in NÉE, V. (1969) *The Cultural Revolution at Peking University* New York, Monthly Review Press, pp. 75 et seq.
22 *The Guardian* (1979) 11 and 21 September.
23 See MATTHEWS, M. (1976) *op. cit.*, p. 143; LANE, D. (1971) *op. cit.*, p. 122.
24 Some general exceptions should also be mentioned. In the Soviet Union and eastern Europe, at least,

the generality of white collar workers ('employees') often earn less than manual workers; the effect is to reduce the average of *all* non-manual incomes close to, or below, that for manual workers. And certain highly educated professions (such as doctors and teachers) are much lower on the income scale than in most western countries (they are largely staffed by women). For examples of exceptions, see MATEJKO, A. (1974) *Social Change and Stratification in Eastern Europe* New York, Praeger, pp. 16–8, 21, 50, 159–63; YANOWITCH, M. (1977) *op. cit.*, pp. 30, 34–5, 39; MATTHEWS, M. (1976) *op. cit.*, p. 90; LANE, D. (1976) *The Socialist Industrial State* London, Allen and Unwin, pp. 179–80.

25 See, for general discussion WILES, P.J.D. and MARKOWSKI, S. (1971) 'Income Distribution under Communism and Capitalism' *Soviet Studies*, Volume 22; and WILES, P.J.D. (1974) *Distribution of Income: East and West* Amsterdam, North Holland Publishing Company.

26 McAULEY, A. (1979) *Economic Welfare in the Soviet Union* Wisconsin, pp. 220–4.

27 For the Soviet Union see YANOWITCH, M. (1977) *op. cit.*, pp. 30, 39–40; for China see HOWE, C. (1973) *Wage Patterns and Wage Policy in Modern China* Cambridge, Cambridge University Press, pp. 36–41.

28 LANE, D. (1971) *op. cit.*, pp. 73–5; MATTHEWS, M. (1976) *op. cit.*, pp. 90–93; see also MATTHEWS, M. (1978) *Privilege in the Soviet Union* London, Allen and Unwin; McAULEY, A. (1979) *op. cit.*, pp. 66–7, 232–41.

29 MATEJKO, A. (1974) *op. cit.*, pp. 21–2.

30 See MATTHEWS, M. (1978) *op. cit.*, which also contains some details on eastern Europe.

31 See YANOWITCH, M. (1977) *op. cit.*, Chapter 4.

32 See TRISKA, J.F. (1968) *Constitutions of the Communist Party-States* Stanford, Hoover Institution. The clause derives from the famous expression in MARX, K. (1875) *Critique of the Gotha Programme*: 'From each according to his ability; to each according to his needs' London, Martin Lawrence (1933).

33 LE DUAN, (1965) *On the Socialist Revolution in Vietnam* Hanoi, Foreign Languages Publishing House, Vol. 3, pp. 34–5.

34 ENGELS, F. *Anti-Duhring* Peking, 1976, pp. 357–8.

35 BAKUNIN, M. (1911) OEUVRES, M. Vol. 5, Paris, pp. 134–68 (my translation).

36 BAKUNIN, M. (1873) *Statism and Anarchy* translated in DOLGOFF, S. (Ed) (1973) *Bakunin on Anarchy* London, pp. 318–9.

37 MARX, K. 'Conspections of Bakharin's Statisim and Anarchy'; in MARX, K. *The First International and After* Hammondsworth, Penguin Books (1974) pp. 336–7.

38 A useful account of, and extracts from, this neglected thinker are in MAKHAISKI, J.W. (1979) *La Socialisme des Intellectuels*, textes choisis, traduits et présentés per Alexandre Skirda, Paris, Senil Skirda's introduction distills and adds to the available writing on Makhaisky.

39 MAKHAISKY, J.W. (1905) *The Intellectual Worker* excerpted in MAKHAISKY, J.W. *op. cit.*, pp. 131–2.

40 *ibid.*, p. 163.

41 Cited in MEISEL, J.J. (1958) *The Myth of the Ruling Class – Gaetano Mosca and the 'Elite'* Ann Arbor, University of Michigan Press, p. 18.

42 MOSCA, G. (1902) 'Risposta ad un'inchiesta sul Socialismo' in MOSCA, G. (1959) *Cio che la Storia Potrebbe Insegnare. Scritti di Scienza Politica* Milano, Giuffre, p. 655.

43 MICHELS, R. (1959) *Political Parties. A Sociological Study of the Oligarchical Tendencies of Modern Democracy*, New York, Dover, p. 80.

44 *ibid.*, p. 390.

45 *ibid.*, p. 383.

46 *ibid.*, p. 391.

47 That is, the February and October revolutions, the civil wars and the sweeping elimination of private property in the period of 'war communism'.

48 Quoted in AVRICH, P. (1973) (Ed) *The Anarchists in the Russian Revolution* London, Thames and Hudson, pp. 123–4.

49 KOLLONTAI, A. (1921) 'The Workers' Opposition' in KOLLONTAI, A., (1977) *Selected Writings*, edited by Alix Holt, London, Alison and Busby, pp. 164–9. In 1923 similar criticisms came from the linked opposition groupings 'Workers' Truth' and 'Workers' Group', who asked whether the working class might not be 'compelled once again to start anew the struggle – and perhaps a bloody one – for the overthrow of the oligarchy'. See CARR, E.H. (1969) *A History of Soviet Russia. The Interregnum, 1923–1924* London, Penguin, pp. 88–93, 277–8.

50 BUKHARIN, N.I. (1969) *Historical Materialism: a system of Sociology* Michigan, University of Michigan Press, pp. 310–1.

51 KAUTSKY, K. (1920) *Terrorism and Communism: a contribution to the natural history of revolution* London, George Allen and Unwin, p. 195.

52 *ibid.*, p. 195.

53 *ibid.*, pp. 201–2.

54 LAURAT, L. (1940) *Marxism and Democracy*, London, Gollancz which summarises views developed earlier). See p. 212.
55 *ibid.*, pp. 218–9.
56 *ibid.*, p. 216.
57 *ibid.*, p. 213.
58 RIZZI, B. (1939) *La Bureaucratisation du Monde*. Paris.
59 BURNHAM, J. (1945) *The Managerial Revolution or What is Happening in the World Now* London, Penguin, p. 83.
60 *ibid.*, p. 95.
61 *ibid.*, p. 108–9.
62 BAHRO, R. (1978) *The Alternative in Eastern Europe* London, New Left Books, p. 212.
63 *ibid.*, p. 179. It is interesting that Bahro stresses not the cultural and literary advantages available to children in the families of the non-educated but the obstacles to educational development among children of the lower strata due, for example, to the atomised, disintegrated and purposeless 'time perspective' of the families in which working class children grow up.
64 SZELENYI, I. and KONRAD, G. (1979) *Towards the Class Power of the Intelligentsia* Brighton, Harvester 1979), The basic ideas are summarised in Szelenyi's 'The position of the Intelligentsia in the class structure of state socialist societies' *Critique* Nos. 10–1, Winter–Spring (1978–79) pp. 51–75.
65 SZELENYI, I. (1978–79) *op. cit.*, p. 71.
66 RAKOVSKI, M. (1977) 'Marxism and the Analysis of Soviet Societies', *Capital and Class*, No. 1, p. 101.
67 The basic ideas are set out in TICKTIN, H. (1973) 'Towards a Political Economy of the USSR' *Critique* No. 1, Spring, and (1978) 'The Class Structure of the USSR and the Elite' *Critique* No. 9, Spring–Summer.
68 TICKTIN, H. (1974) 'Political Economy of the Soviet Intellectual' *Critique* No. 2, pp. 15–6.
69 GOULDNER, A. (1979) *The Future of Intellectuals and the rise of the New Class* London, Macmillan, pp. 53–7.
70 For some (I think unsuccessful) points on this kind of objection see *ibid.*, pp. 81–2.
71 *ibid.*, p. 21.
72 *ibid.*, p. 23.

22 Socialist Ideology and the Transformation of Cuban Education*

Martin Carnoy
Jorge Werthein

One educational leader at the Ministry of Education, Abel Prieto Morales, said that when he was in Italy, someone at an education conference asked him: 'Is the school in Cuba an instrument of the State?' His answer was, 'Yes, of course, just as it was before the triumph of the Revolution, and as it is in the present day in Italy.'[1]

In Cuba the State ideology is anti-capitalist and anti-imperialist, and promotes collective action rather than individual initiative. This ideology as it is taught in the school is summarized in an official report by the Cuban government to the UNESCO Conference on Education and Economic and Social Development held in Santiago, Chile, in 1962.[2]

> The bourgeois ideology regarded education as a phenomenon isolated from its economic basis. In fact, however, education is an ideological superstructure and is closely linked with the means of production – that is to say, with the productive forces and the relationships of production.
>
> Throughout the whole history of human society education has been a product of the social classes which dominated at each stage. The content and orientation of education are therefore determined by the social classes which are in power.
>
> In Cuba, those in power are the workers, the peasants, the progressive intellectuals and the middle strata of the population, who are building a democratic society in which group and class privilege are disappearing and in which private ownership of the basic means of production is being eliminated. If anyone wishes to know the aims of our education, they should study the interests of the workers, peasants, intellectuals and the middle strata of the population and they will find their answer. It is these which determine the purpose, the objectives, the orientation, the content and the methods of education in our country.

The document goes on to describe the development of education in Cuban society and the goals of education under the Revolution. Some of the goals stated are the following:

Source: An abridged version of CARNOY, M. and WERTHEIN, J. (1977) in KARABEL, J. and HALSEY, A.H. (Eds) *Power and Ideology* New York, Oxford University Press, pp. 573–89.

... Stress must also be laid on the importance of education for socialism and on the value of science in economic social cultural development.

... They (the pupils) must be brought to have a high sense of duty to work; that is to say, they must be taught to abandon the false notion of work as a punishment and they must be taught the necessity of work.

... They must be taught the value of emulative work and the difference between capitalism and socialism as being based on the difference between competition for private gain and emulation for the sake of increasing the output of the community.

... At the same time, since another of the aims of education for socialism is that of providing the necessary technical and scientific training to produce workers who are capable of directing and increasing production, and since the means of production are in the hands of the State, it is logical that, for many different ideological, practical, and pedagogic reasons, education should be linked with productive labor.

... Our plans and programmes aim at the elimination of verbalism and learning by rote and making education a living matter, in which theory is identified with practice and linked with social labor.

... Here we see two basic aims of socialist education: *the linking of education with productive labor as a means of developing men in every aspect*. Educating in productive labor, making the students familiar with the details of production through practical experience, enabling them to learn its laws and organization as processes; that is, educating them in the very root of all cultural, technical and scientific progress, and giving them ideological and moral training leading to an all-around education.

The relationship between the change in ideology between 1958 and 1961 and the *content* of school curriculum under the reform could not be more obvious. In practice, the implementation of this new ideology in the schools is found in a more technical and scientific orientation, a much closer connection between schooling and work, and a greater emphasis on *collective* work in the schools rather than on individual achievement.

Specifically, ideology is reflected in a number of places in the educational system:

1. One of these is the relationship between *schools and work*. The first clear-cut effort to integrate school and work actually took place during the literacy campaign, when thousands of students went into the countryside to teach people how to read. But beginning in 1966, in part as a response to the shortage of agricultural labor, the first experiment took place. [...] The students were to carry out productive work while keeping up their studies at the same time. For this, the schools, professors, teachers, students, and employees, as well as all the necessary teaching equipment, were relocated in the countryside on various farms or recently constructed school installations. Students and teachers organized themselves in different productive units of the National Institute for Agrarian Reform. We shall discuss these schools further below, showing that this particular form of education corresponds to important economic changes that took place in Cuba after 1964.

However, the point to be made here is that the 'school to the countryside' (*escuela al campo*) movement fits directly into the ideological context of the emphasis on work stated in the 1962 document.

A second manifestation of the work (1) school integration in addition to the universities becoming almost entirely oriented to technical subjects, was that university students after the Revolution could no longer separate themselves from the day-to-day productive activities of the economy.

> The old idea of the classic university will disappear as a concept and as an institution that belongs to a superseded society. And so, production itself, the productive processes, will constitute the material base, the laboratory, where in the future all workers will receive their higher education.[3]

The university reform of 1962 began to carry out this idea of work/study for university students. Students began to move out of the classroom: for example, medical students had to work in hospitals from the beginning of their third year of study; humanities students began to develop social work programs in agricultural development plans; civil engineering students went to the mountains and co-ordinated and combined their studies with agricultural production in the area.

Beginning in 1971–72, it was decided that students must work twenty hours a week in direct production as part of their university studies. In their first two years in the university, students work in unskilled jobs. In their third year, they begin specialized work, whenever possible in workplaces that are connected with the student's speciality. Large-scale programs were also started in the early seventies to bring workers into the university for technical training.

2. In addition to the schools moving to the workplace, Cuba's production system has been integrated into the curriculum of the high schools. This integration was accomplished through the *círculos de interés*. An 'interest circle' is a group of students led by a technical advisor who programs specialized activities in order to promote interest in science and technology, especially in those branches that are most important to economic development in Cuba. These circles are analogous in many respects to extracurricular activities in US high schools, but are organized exclusively around productive activities – animal science, soil chemistry, and oceanography are typical subjects for interest circles. The circles were started in 1963–64 and have been developed extensively as a program aimed at bringing together students of similar interests. They also seem to break away from the traditional scholastic system and to use the rich experience of the community to benefit student learning. The number of these circles has grown every year since their inception: in 1966, 9,000 circles were organized; in 1967, there were 17,000; and in 1973, there were 20,000, with a total membership of 300,000 students. An important aspect of the circles is the development of a close association between the activity of future scientists and technologists and the national organizations and institutions that provide resources for their work. Students studying science lack resources such as pure breeding stock, surgical instruments, mobile weather stations, and land for agricultural experimentation, but through the sponsors they get to use these resources and have a chance to participate in the production sector.

Ideally, the interest circles are a bridge between the school curriculum and the student's later life and productive activity.

> By tying the educational experience more closely to the economy the *circulos de interés* perform a very important function. A society which has foregone the use of wage incentives needs an alternative means of encouraging young people to enter occupations in short supply. Thus, the *circulos de interés* provide a means of informing young people about the content of various occupational pursuits, while at the same time stimulating student interest in careers likely to make a major contribution to national development.[4]

3. After the Revolution, students were encouraged *to study in groups rather than to study as individuals*. As a reflection of the system of socialist emulation being practised in the productive sector, the process of expanding knowledge and competence was seen as a group effort, and elements of competition in the classroom were greatly reduced. Although under the economic strategy of the late sixties and early seventies individual study has been reemphasized,[5] the monitor program continues to emphasize the collective spirit in the classroom. In the program, which draws on a type of mastery learning concept, each school class selects a student or a group of students in each subject to help the rest of the class with their studies. The role of these monitors is primarily to lead group discussions among students and to help individual students who are having difficulty; they take charge of classes being taught by educational television and perform other similar duties.

4. A crucial ingredient in utilizing the schools for propagating the new ideology was the development of a *teacher* corps with new values and skills. The elements of this development were the shift of teacher training from an urban to a rural orientation and the inculcation of socialist values into these rural cadres.

While dependent capitalist countries have great difficulties in 'convincing' teachers to go into rural areas and, indeed, have a 'surplus' of teachers in urban areas (although their student/teacher ratios do not decline even in urban areas), socialist countries like Cuba count on non-market incentives to move teachers into rural schools. Teachers trained to work in rural areas are depicted by the government as an *élite corps* serving the Revolution. Teaching in a rural area is not a second-class job (in which the teacher is penalized by having access neither to further education nor to promotion in the educational system); rather, teaching in a rural primary school is often required service in order to get promotion and access to university education.[6]

The Revolutionary government moved to expand teacher training greatly for both primary and secondary schools, and reduced student/teacher ratios significantly in the decade after 1959, despite a very rapid increase in the number of students enrolled. Furthermore, the new system of teacher preparation (which in this particular form remained in effect until 1968–69) took students who had completed the sixth grade and put them in a five-year course that included a first year in the mountain school of Minas de Frio and a final two years in a training school in Havana.

This type of training program stresses two important features of the Cuban educational reform. The first is the special attention given to the particular problems and discouragements of teaching in rural areas. The second is the view of work and co-operation that we have discussed in the previous paragraphs. Teachers are trained to work alongside their pupils in the fields and to serve as examples of Revolutionary fervor.

The importance of teacher training in a society in the process of ideological transformation and simultaneously trying to increase the technical skills of its labor force is crucial to both these goals, and the Cuban leadership therefore put great emphasis on teacher training and teaching as a service to the Revolution.

5. According to Leiner, '*Boarding schools* are considered by educational leaders to be a key to creating the new Cuban man. First, boarding school students live together and develop attitudes and values consistent with Cuban Revolutionary goals. Secondly, they provide a full curriculum which includes physical education as well as academic subjects, for the training of the whole body and mind. Thirdly, students from rural isolated areas develop skills in arts, science, and technical areas in urban centers. Fourth, the new *semi-internado* (semi-boarding) schools become part of a central town development which consists of the school, a polyclinic, a social center, and new housing for the *campesinos* (peasants).'[7]

[. . .]

6. Ideological socialization is also carried out in *day care centers* (see Table 1). Leiner stresses the ideological importance of these programs both for young children and for adults. Apparently, the first priority in organizing nurseries and kindergartens was and still is the liberation of Cuban women in order to enable them to participate in the labor force. Thus, the day care centers perform an important economic function, in releasing women to work in the labor-short economy. But at the same time, by allowing women to work outside the home, the centers help reduce *machismo* (the Latin variety of male chauvinism), a specific aim of the Revolution since its initial period.

Further, the nursery schools are not merely day care centers to serve mothers, they also provide a structure in which children are trained toward collective consciousness even as little babies:

> When a Cuban baby is placed in a playpen, he is put into no standard United States model with only room enough for himself – or at most two toddlers. The Cuban playpen – or more appropriately, 'corral' – permits at least six infants to play together in a space equal to the size of a small room . . .
> Far more rationally designed than the American playpen, it avoids the tedious efforts of adults in attendance to bend to floor level to assist children . . . Group play as distinct from individual activities takes precedence. . . . Encouraged to design activities to stimulate group play, *asistentes* in the *Circulos* lead children into social and play patterns to help them develop collective attitudes. *Asistentes* are to make special efforts to see to it that all children participate in the program designed for the collective.[8]

Table 1   Cuba: Day Care Centers (Circulos Infantiles) 1961–70

Year	Centers
1961	37
1962	109
1963	144
1964	157
1965	166
1966	194
1967	262
1968	332
1969	381
1970*	430

Source: Marvin Leiner, 1974.
*through November 1970

Educational Reform and Changes in Cuban Economic Strategy

Overall, there can be little doubt that it was the change from dependent capitalism to socialism that had the greatest impact on educational institutions in Cuba. But it is important not to lose sight of the fact that many Cuban educational reforms also took (and continue to take) place within the context of the Revolutionary ideology and overall development policy *in response to changes* in particular economic strategies. One of the most fascinating aspects of Cuban educational reforms is that a number of significant changes in the educational system took place *after* the initial and overwhelming commitment of incorporating the masses into economic development through adult education and the enormous expansion of primary and secondary schooling. These later changes reflected the various attempts to solve the economic growth problem within the constraints of the egalitarian and mobilization goals set by the Revolution. The Cuban government *continuously adapted the educational system to fit their strategies for increasing output per capita and making the socialist economy viable.* At the same time, the underlying earlier Revolutionary theme that education was a *right* to be available for everyone also continued as a foundation of educational policy.

Technical Education

Perhaps the first major change to occur in the Cuban development plan was the de-emphasis in 1963–64 of industrial development in favor of the expansion of the agricultural sector. By that time, there had been large-scale migration to urban areas, and agricultural development had become hampered by a shortage of rural labor as well as by its low productivity.

Education responded to this emphasis on agricultural development. After 1963 there was a rapid growth of middle-level technical education in agricultural schools with a temporary decline in industrial technical school enrollment. University enrollment in agricultural sciences also increased rapidly after 1963. The emphasis on agricultural development thus had an important effect on the orientation of technical and scientific training.

With its pressing need for rural labor and the emphasis on agricultural production, the Cuban economy turned, beginning in 1966, toward moral rather than material incentives, and to the development of the new socialist man. The concept of socialist emulation had been present in the ideological basis of the economic structure since the early years of the Revolution, and it was translated in the schools into a stress on collective work rather than individual achievement. With the advent of moral incentives, a greatly *increased* emphasis was placed on the relationship of schools to work and on teaching young people in schools to behave in a collective, unselfish, and altruistic manner.

Schools to the Countryside

The educational reform that reflected the need for agricultural labor and the development of the new socialist man was 'schools to the countryside'. The first experiment of moving a school to the countryside took places in 1966. The objectives of these schools were defined around the social ideal of the formation of the 'new socialist man', and they were aimed at eliminating the differences between city and country, establishing close bonds between the school and daily life, and educating the new generation in and for work. Apparently, the project had positive results in contributing to the growth of a real awareness among students of farming and related industry. Furthermore, by living together for about seven weeks in the countryside, students were introduced to the mechanics of organization and self-government based on group co-operation and work, thereby developing and understanding collective action. During the work/study period, both teachers and principals lived together with students in dormitories and worked with them in the fields. These activities – students and teachers alike working side-by-side with peasants – probably contributed greatly to the obliteration of class lines based on the manual versus non-manual work distinction. Furthermore, as Bowles points out,

> In the *escuela al campo* program, the leadership of the camp often goes to those who work well, not to the monitors or to others who excel at intellectual tasks. The occasional inversion of the hierarchy of the school's social system itself teaches an additional lesson for equality.[9]

But the 'schools to the countryside' movement also met at least part of the need for additional agricultural labor. In the 1972–73 school year almost 200,000 students were still involved in part-year production through the program. [. . .] Thus, the 'school to the countryside' program not only was consistent with the development of the 'new socialist man' but corresponded to the need for volunteer rural labor in solving significant shortages of agricultural workers.

Nevertheless, the slow growth of agriculture (in comparison with the continued growth of industry), and the dynamic role that agriculture had and has to play in Cuban development, brought out one of the fundamental economic difficulties faced by Cuban leadership: the overall achievement of equalization of incomes and the almost complete elimination of open unemployment seemed to have reduced productivity in rural areas. Even before the difficulties of the 1970 sugar harvest,

Cuban leaders were beginning to reject the concept of moral incentives as a way out of the productivity dilemma and beginning to look for other solutions.

In its effort to increase economic growth the government was also faced with the diversion of large amounts of public funds into schooling. The percentage of investment going to schooling, health, and other social services declined over the decade; nevertheless, the necessary further expansion of the industrial and agricultural sectors needed not only skilled labor, but also enormous investment in machines. A way had to be found that would *reduce the cost of schooling* to the economy at the same time that it lowered dropout and repetition rates in school.

With the attempt to solve these difficulties, 'schools to the countryside' began to be de-emphasized after 1970 for three reasons: first, it became clear that the voluntary labor system in rural areas would not solve production problems; second, students were losing an average of about forty-five days a year working in the countryside, and, although they were supposed to be studying at the same time they were working, 'by nearly everyone's admission, not much serious study goes on in the work camps or other non-classroom activities'[10] and third, during the rest of the year, the schools were largely traditional in their mode of operation and their cost.

Schools in the Countryside

To solve all these difficulties, the school to the countryside was replaced by the school *in* the countryside; the schools *in* the countryside are junior high schools (seventh, eighth, ninth, and tenth grades) catering primarily to urban students and combining work and study in the countryside on a year-round basis.

> There will no longer be the school to the countryside: there is now the school in the countryside. No longer will there be five weeks, six weeks, 40 days, 50 days, in which students leave studies and do work in the countryside. No. We will combine systematically study and productive work daily. What does this permit us? It permits us to create an *economic base from this educational plan*. Because we understand that the production of these schools will cover the schools' investment costs and expenditures. If this is so, then *we will be able to construct schools of this type without limit.* If this is so, we will be able to continue expanding and developing these plans. This type of school combines two factors: First, an ideal educational type of a socialist education, a Communist education with the necessities of our own economic development. At the same time, this kind of school is not a drain on the economy but contributes to the economy and to the development of the country. Thus, we can continue to construct this type of school until we have all our students in secondary schools of this type. Because of this we consider that for the conditions of our country this is the ideal type of school. (emphasis added)[11]

In the 1972–73 school year, the junior high schools in the countryside were attended by about 11 per cent of the students enrolled in the first cycle of the secondary educational system. The schools have their own distinct organizational characteristics. The students, most of whom come from urban areas and board at the school, maintain contact with their families by normally spending weekends at home. Moreover, the school systematically combines study and work during the *entire school year*, producing goods that are part of the economic development plan.

The new program tries to raise *collective consciousness* in students through the organization of study and work; in this way, the school is similar to its predecessors. But, unlike other schooling concepts, this type of educational institution is built around plans for agricultural production (citrus, coffee, and vegetable): the group responsible in each school for productive activity is involved in the administrative council of the agricultural plan. Also, this new school is different in that it tries directly to relocate future workers from the city to rural areas, preparing urban young people to be skilled agricultural workers. Finally, the idea that schools should actually finance themselves by producing goods worth as much as the schools cost to operate is a total departure from standard educational practice and new even to Cuba.

The schools in the countryside, like secondary schools in the previous organization of education, use student monitors and have science and technology circles to promote student interest and to offer the students the opportunity to broaden their theoretical and practical studies in specified fields. Furthermore, although moral incentives have been de-emphasized in production, the schools in the countryside through the work process and heavy emphasis on Revolutionary ideology are attempting to build a level of consciousness that will make moral incentives in production more possible in the future. Despite the increased use of material incentives in factories, the schools are completely organized around socialist emulation, mass participation, and moral incentives. The schools represent a profound reform in the Cuban educational system, a reform that is a response to low productivity in the countryside in the 1960s, to the shortage of rural labor, and to the commitment of Cuban leadership to agricultural development as the lead sector in economic growth.

At the same time that the high school system is being developed along the lines of the schools in the countryside, the primary school and the university are also being transformed under this same concept. [...]

University Education

As far as the university is concerned, the new depersonalization of planning and the move to decentralize somewhat the management of production have contributed to a rapid increase in the growth of the university system. Furthermore, there has apparently been much greater commitment to a university enrollment increase now that the period of using educational expansion primarily as a means of achieving social and economic egalitarianism is over. The new emphasis on economic growth and the development of higher-level management and technical capability as a *primary* concern (it was always an important goal of the Revolutionary leadership) has been a major factor in the allocation of more resources to the university, particularly in higher technical skills.

> While the overall emphasis in educational resource allocation bespeaks a strong commitment to equality, and perhaps even a desire to thwart the development of a technocratic élite, other policies seem to run against the commitment. In a society committed to rapid scientific and technological advance from a position of educational backwardness, the need to fill high level scientific positions has posed a temptation to give special educational opportunities to especially talented students. A secondary school for an intellectual élite has been established in Havana, and as of 1969, plans were under way to establish others in the remaining provinces. Students at this school are chosen primarily on the basis of their scholastic performance.[12]

Despite this tendency toward élitism through selection based on scholastic achievement for special secondary schools which then lead to university, it should be re-emphasized that students in these élite secondary schools must engage in productive work while studying and that the university student must also work concurrently with his or her studies and must be in a producing situation throughout the university stay. Furthermore, there is now increased control of the *kinds* of studies that can be undertaken at the university level, control directly related to professional manpower needs according to the development plan. Until 1969–70, the choice of university career was up to the individual student, which produced rapid increases in prestigious occupations like medicine, but not rapid enough growth in other disciplines like the agricultural sciences. In 1970, the university began to co-ordinate admissions into programs with the manpower plan, limiting access to programs that historically had relatively high numbers of graduates, and attempting to expand others viewed as crucial for future economic development.[13]

Thus, while the investment patterns and selection system in Cuban education seem to reflect an increased élitism intended for increased economic growth, the curriculum at all levels, also designed to integrate schools and students into the production system, is oriented toward moral incentives, the new socialist man, and the attempt to revitalize Revolutionary ideology of love of work and the integration of manual labor and intellectual activity.

The Consequences and Problems of Cuban Educational Reforms

What have all these reforms achieved? We know that the changes in education did *not* produce more equal income distribution or lower levels of unemployment. Those economic reforms resulted from direct intervention in the economic system; indeed, the nature of educational expansion in Cuba reflected the same ideology that produced economic intervention for greater income equality and full employment. As far as growth of output is concerned, *in the short run* it probably suffered from the heavy investment in education and literacy during the early sixties; non-productive investment in 1961 was almost one-half of total investment (not including earnings foregone), and though a substantial portion of this was in adult education most adult training in that period was for literacy and basic cognitive skills. In the longer run, the concentration on education *probably did* contribute to economic growth, particularly in the industrial sector and in those parts of the agricultural sector, like citrus growing, where other constraints did not impede increased production (sugar, for example).[14] Educational investment contributed to mass mobilization, a key element in the Cuban socialist development model.

While we can say little about the growth contribution of educational investment, we can be much more concrete about the delivery of social services: Cuba was able to replace, in a relatively short period of time, the doctors, teachers, and engineers who left after the Revolution. Education and health care are supplied in much greater quantity and in much higher quality in the 1970s for the mass of population than they were in the 1950s (see Table 2). Furthermore, almost no one is illiterate

Table 2 Cuba: Estimated Educational Pyramid 20–29 Year Old Group 1953 and 1973 (Per cent)

Level of schooling	1953 Educated in 1930s and 1940s	1973 Educated in 1960s
No Schooling	20	0
Primary	72	70
Secondary (Academic and Vocational)	6	20
University	2	10

Source: 1953 – Jolly (1962)[15]
 1973 – Estimated from figures in text on dropout rates for 1965–66 cohort.

in Cuba, and reading material is available in much greater quantities now than it was before the Revolution. In part, it is through mass education that people in rural areas have been brought into the mainstream of Cuban development.
[...]

There was, and perhaps still is, a serious dropout problem in schools. Taking first-grade enrollment cohorts for 1958–59 to 1965–66, Dahlman[16] reports (based on data provided by Nelson, 1971)[17] that the first post-Revolutionary cohort (1958–59) had 38.1 per cent reaching the sixth grade, but thereafter the percentage fell to about 20 per cent, rising with the last cohort to 32 per cent. Among those who reached the sixth grade, only about 70 per cent managed to graduate. Furthermore, although nationally 21.2 per cent of the 1965–66 cohort graduated in 1971, the rate for urban elementary schools was 34.2 per cent while that for rural schools was just 11.7 per cent. At the junior high level, of the 59,000 students who entered the seventh grade in 1966–67, only 29 per cent (or 17,000) reached the tenth grade and only 47 per cent of those (or 8,000) passed that grade. This low success rate helps explain the small enrollment in senior high schools and technological institutions. Apparently there is a serious repeater problem in Cuba, which in turn is linked to the problem of those teenagers who, because of high dropout rates, are neither in school nor working.

Castro analyzed these problems of the educational system in a speech at the Second

Congress of the Young Communist League on 4 April, 1972.

> What factors cause these difficulties? There are quite a few. For example, the material resources: school installations, the materials available for study, the difficulties involved in going to school in the mountains, the distance, the isolated school, the poor school, the school in a hut or the school with a roof of thatched palm. There are other problems: the environment, the cultural level of the population, a persisting lack of awareness about the importance of schooling and education, of the need for discipline, regular attendance in school and parental co-operation with the school. Another important aspect is the quality and efficiency of educational personnel in the schools. Out of 79,968 teachers, only 24,265 have graduated from teacher training; in other words, 30.4 per cent of the teachers have graduated. In the elementary schools, 61.3 per cent of teachers are non-graduates and in the junior high schools, 73.7 per cent are non-graduates.

The shortage of qualified personnel is greater at the junior high level because of the bulge of elementary school graduates entering junior high in the late 1960s and early 1970s. It has been estimated that between 1972 and 1976, 22,427 junior high school teachers would be needed, but in this period only 1,990 new teachers will graduate. Although 2,000 more will be available from those working as practice teachers, this will still leave a deficit of more than 18,000 qualified teachers.

Castro also pointed out that the high dropout rate in the lower levels of schooling led to low levels of enrollment in technical and professional education: in 1972, only 24,000 students were enrolled in industrial and agricultural schools.

> If we consider the fact that this country must live off industry and agriculture and that every improvement in our standard of living and in our economy depends on industry and agriculture and their development, 23,960 seems like a figure for Luxembourg or Monte Carlo, but not this country. This doesn't seem to be a Cuban figure.[18]

In order to solve these problems, several measures have been taken and others are in the process of implementation. One such measure, which depends on the development of new schools, is the establishment of special schools in the countryside for 13- to 15-year-old students at the elementary level. These schools are similar to the junior high schools in the countryside that we have described. The students will proceed with their elementary training, separate from the 6- to 10-year-olds. Average junior high students are sent to the polytechnical schools. The solution thus assigns students to schools according to education and age level.

The quality of teaching is to be raised through the 'guerrillas of education' movement, which will try to get more young people to enroll in teacher training schools, and through refresher courses for non-graduate teachers. The number of teachers is low, especially in the junior high schools in the countryside. A movement among junior high school graduates to enroll in teacher training has been started. In 1972, 20,000 students were in the tenth grade; some of these students will be teaching under the supervision of more experienced teachers and will be enrolled in the Pedagogical Institutes. Thus they will be able to go to the junior high schools in the countryside, work with experienced teachers, and get their pedagogical training right there in the school.

> At present there simply isn't any other formula except to go to our tenth-graders and recruit at least 2,000 of them this year, at least 5,000 next year, and so on.[19]

These problems indicate that while the achievements of the Cuban educational efforts have been remarkable, particularly in adult education and in the rapid expansion of primary and secondary school and the extension of schooling into rural areas, such educational expansion even in a society as committed to education as Cuba is fraught with difficulty in a country where the availability of highly-trained teaching personnel is limited (for example, by the conditions of under-development that preceded the Revolution). The shortage of educational personnel also reflects the overall shortage of skilled labor in the economy, and the shortage of adequate facilities in the schools reflects the overall shortages of material goods. Furthermore, as the figures indicate, one of the principal reasons that there are great difficulties in providing schooling in Cuba is the Revolution's commitment to rural areas, areas where the population is thinly spread and transportation not particularly well-developed, and where a culture of traditional values inherited from the pre-Revolutionary social and economic structure is still deeply ingrained.

Castro summarized the situation in the following way:

> We face a really special situation in the coming years. Why? Because we are living through a transitional situation. We still don't have the new man and we no longer have the old one. The new man doesn't exist yet.[20]

[...]

Notes and References

1 LEINER, M. (1973) 'Major developments in Cuban education' in BARKER, D. and MANITZAS, N. (Eds) *Cuba: the Logic of the Revolution* Andover, Mass., Warner Modular Publications, p. 6.
2 For the entire document see SEERS, D. (1964) *The Economic and Social Revolution* Chapel Hill, University of North Carolina Press, pp. 348–51.
3 Fidel Castro, 13 March, 1969. See CASTRO, F. (1974) *La Educacion en Revolucion* Havana, Instituto Cubano del Libra. This volume contains all of Castro's speeches related to education.
4 See BOWLES, S. (1972) 'Education and socialist man in Cuba' in CARNOY, M. (Ed) *Schooling in a Corporate Society* New York, David McKay, pp. 290–1.
5 *ibid.*, p. 291.
6 While the training program provided the means for greatly expanding rural schools, it apparently did not solve the dropout and repeater problem in rural areas. In the late sixties and early seventies, the solution to that problem was sought partly through the boarding and semi-boarding schools in rural areas.
7 LEINER, M. (1973) *op. cit.*, p. 6.
8 *ibid.*, pp. 10–11. Leiner reports that he tried to determine what effect the official ideology was having in the classroom by using the fairly simple technique of the open-ended question. One composition topic he offered to a number of calsses in the upper grades was *If I Had Five Wishes*. He argued that in

the answers to this question 'the themes of commitment and sacrifice are repeatedly expressed in the composition. "To go where the Revolution needs me" is a most frequent expression' (pp. 5–6).

9 BOWLES, S. (1972) *op. cit.*, p. 296.

10 *ibid.*, in 1971, delegates representing teachers, educators, scientists and cultural agencies and institutes participated in the First National Congress on Education and Culture. Among other recommendations, they criticized the *escuelas al campo* on the ground that the time lost from formal schooling was having negative effects on the academic work of students and that the activities of the program had been poorly integrated into the formal school system. See DAHLMAN, C. J. (1973) 'The nationwide learning system of Cuba' Princeton, N. J., Woodrow Wilson School, Princeton University. Mimeograph.

11 Fidel Castro, 25 April (1971). See Note 3.

12 BOWLES, S. (1972) *op. cit.*, p. 301. Bowles in referring to the Cento Vocational School, which was originally created in the school year 1966–67, and which is today the Lenin Vocational School, recently built for the 1972–73 school year. This school, the only one of this kind in Cuba, with a capacity for 4,500 high school and pre-university students, is twenty-three kilometers from the center of Havana and occupies 84,000 square meters of land. This is a school for study and industrial work, primarily in electronics. Besides annual agricultural production exceeding 500 quintals, students at the Lenin School have produced 50,000 battery-operated radios, manufactured goods and sports equipment valued at 1,000,000 pesos, and thirty electronic computers, which have been assembled for use in instruction at the center and in industrial installations elsewhere in the country. The organization cell of the Lenin Vocational School is made up of 120 science and technology circles, encompassing all fields. These circles guarantee a large university enrollment emphasizing technological, scientific and agricultural occupations. (In the past school year, eight-five per cent of the graduates entered careers related to their circle.)

The work of the Lenin Vocational School is divided into agriculture, in which nearly 3,000 high school students participate, and industrial work, in which 700 pre-university students take part. The rest – students, professors, instructors, and pedagogic assistants – do community and service work.

The selection process for the Lenin School is very restrictive; only those pupils who get very high grades in the last three years of primary school are accepted. In 1972–73, the average primary school grade average of students in the first year of the School was 85 per cent, and in 1974 95 per cent. Dropouts from the School represent only 2 per cent of the cohort. (*Granma* special issue on the Lenin School, February, 1974).

13 The selection system works in the following way: information on the high priority careers is passed on to the students in the last year of pre-university training and in the worker-peasant university. The student selects the career he or she wants to follow and is accepted, or not, on the basis of the number of places available and the students grades in the last three years of secondary school. If a student is not selected for the career he wanted he can apply to another career where there is a greater opportunity for admission. In the case of medicine, for example, the situation in 1970 was a relative saturation of the career in terms of the country's needs. Entrance to the study of medicine is now severely restricted through an examination; as a result, enrollment in that field fell from 8,773 students in 1970 to 8,393 students in 1972, while every other faculty's enrollment rose rapidly in the same period. Even so, those with the best grades may still end up in the most prestigious careers.

14 Although there was little *per capita* economic growth in Cuba in the 1960s (see RITTER, A. (1974) *The Economic Development of Revolutionary Cuba*, New York, Praeger) the situation apparently changed markedly after 1970. In his staff report to the Committee on Foreign Relations of the US Senate, Pat Holt said that the *per capita* income in Cuba in 1974 was about $1,600. See HOLT, P. (1974) 'Cuba' Staff Report prepared for the Committee on Foreign Relations of the US Senate. US Government Printing Office. Although this seems high in terms of what Cubans can consume, Holt concluded that 'the Cubans are on the verge of constructing a socialist showcase in the Western Hemisphere' (Holt quoted in ZIMBALIST, A. (1975) 'The development of workers' participation in socialist Cuba' Paper prepared for presentation at the Second Annual Conference on Workers' Self-Management, Cornell University, 6–8 June.

15 JOLLY, R. (1964) 'Education' in SEERS, D. (Ed) *Cuba: The Economic and Social Revolution* Chapel Hill, University of North Carolina Press.

16 DAHLMAN, C. J. (1973) *op. cit.*, pp. 116–21.

17 NELSON, L. (1971) 'The school dropout problem in Cuba' *School and Society* 99, April, pp. 234–5.

18 Fidel Castro in a speech at the Second Congress of the Young Communist League on 4 April, 1972.

19 *ibid.*

20 *ibid.*

Additional Bibliography

ALLEN, G. (1974) 'Education in revolutionary Cuba' *Education Digest* 40, October.

BARKIN, D. (1973) 'Cuban agriculture: A strategy of economic development' in BARKIN, D. and MANITZAS, N. (Eds) *Cuba: The Logic of Revolution* Andover, Mass., Warner Modular Publications.

BENDER, L. (1975) *In the Politics of Hostility: Castro's Revolution and United States Policy* Hato Rey, Puerto Rico, Inter-American University Press.

BERNARDO, R. (1971) *The Theory of Moral Incentives in Cuba* University, Alabama, The University of Alabama Press.

BOORSTEIN, E. (1968) *The Economic Transformation of Cuba* New York, Monthly Review Press.

BOWLES, S. and GINTIS, H. (1975) *Schooling in Capitalist America* New York, Basic Books.

CARNOY, M. (1974) *Education as Cultural Imperialism* New York, David McKay.

CARNOY, M. (1976) 'The role of education in a strategy of social change' in CARNOY, M. and LEVIN, H. (Eds) *The Limits of Educational Reform* New York, David McKay.

CARNOY, M. (1975) 'University education in the economic development of Peru' Consejo Nacional de la Universidad Peruana. Mimeograph.

CARNOY, M. and LEVIN, H. (1976) *The Limits of Educational Reform* New York, David McKay.

CARNOY, M., SACK, R. and THIAS, H. (1976) *The Payoff to 'Better' Schooling: A Case Study of Tunisian Secondary Schools* Washington, World Bank.

CARTER, M. (1975) 'Contradiction and correspondence: An analysis of the relation of schooling to work' Palo Alto, Cal., Center for Economic Studies. Mimeograph.

CUBA, MINISTERIO DE EDUCACION *La Educacion en Cuba* La Habana.

FAGEN, R. (1969) *The Transformation of Political Culture in Cuba* Stanford, Cal., Stanford University Press.

FAGEN, R. (1975) in GOODSELL, J.N. (Ed) *Fidel Castro's Personal Revolution in Cuba: 1959–1973* New York, Knopf.

FAGEN, R., BRODY, R.A. and O'LEARY, T. (1968) *Cubans in Exile: A Demographic Analysis of Social Problems* Stanford, Cal., Stanford University Press.

FERRER, R. (1973) *Convergence* 6, No. 1, Toronto.

FOSTER, P. (1964) 'The vocational schooling fallacy' in BOWMAN, M.J. and ANDERSON, A. (Eds) *Education and Economic Development*.

GILETTE, A. (1972) 'Cuba's educational revolution' *Fabian Research Series* No. 302, June, London.

GINTIS, H. (1975) 'The new working class and revolutionary youth' in CARNOY, M. (Ed) *Schooling in a Corporate Society* New York, David McKay (2nd ed).

JOLLY, R. (1971) 'Contrasts in Cuban and African educational strategies' in LOWE, J. (Ed) *Education and Nation Building in the Third World* New York, Barnes and Noble.

LEINER, M. (1974) *Children Are the Revolution: Day Care in Cuba* New York, Viking.

LEVIN, H. (1976) 'The meaning of educational reform' in CARNOY, M. and LEVIN, H. (Eds) *The Limits of Educational Reform* New York, David McKay.

MANITZAS, N. (1973) 'The setting of the Cuban revolution' in BARKIN, D. and MANITZAS, N. (Eds) *Cuba: The Logic of the Revolution* Andover, Mass., Warner Modular Publications.

MESO-LAGO, C. (1972) *The labor force, employment, unemployment and underemployment in Cuba: 1899–1970* New York, Sage (Professional Paper).

MESO-LAGO, C. (1974) *Cuba in the 1970s* Albuquerque, N.M., University of New Mexico Press.

NEWMAN, P. (1965) *Cuba Before Castro, An Economic Appraisal* New York, Foreign Studies Institute.

PAULSTON, R. (1971) 'Education' in MESO-LAGO, C. (Ed) *Revolutionary Change in Cuba: Economy, Polity and Society* Pittsburgh, University of Pittsburgh Press.

RITTER, A. (1974) *The Economic Development of Revolutionary Cuba* New York, Praeger.

SWEEZY, P. and HUBERMAN, L. (1969) *Socialism in Cuba* New York, Monthly Review Press.

THIAS, H. and CARNOY, M. (1972) *Cost-Benefit Analysis in Education: A Case Study of Kenya* Washington, World Bank.

WILLIAMS, B. and YATES, M. (1974) 'Moral incentives in Cuba' *Review of Radical Political Economics* 6, No. 3. Fall, pp. 86–90.

YGLESIAS, J. (1968) *In the First of the Revolution: Life in a Cuban Country Town* New York, Vintage Books.

*The research reported here was carried out persuant to a grant from the International Bank for Reconstruction and Development. However, opinions expressed do not necessarily reflect the position or policy of the International Bank for Reconstruction and Development, and no official endorsement by the International Bank should be inferred.

List of Contributors

Jane Barker works at the Centre for Alternative Industrial and Technological Systems.

Samuel Bowles is professor of economics at the University of Massachusetts.

Harry Braverman was president of Monthly Review Press.

Martin Carnoy is professor of education and economics at Stanford University.

Randall Collins is professor of sociology and member of the Center for Advanced Study at the University of Virginia.

James Donald was editor of *Screen Education* and is now lecturer in the Faculty of Educational Studies at The Open University.

Hazel Downing is a research student at the Centre for Contemporary Cultural Studies, University of Birmingham.

Herbert Gintis is associate professor of economics at the University of Massachusetts.

Stuart Hall is professor of sociology at The Open University.

David Hogan is research associate and lecturer in the Graduate School of Education at the University of Pennsylvania.

Athar Hussain is lecturer in economics at the University of Keele.

Thomas La Belle is professor of education at the University of California.

P. McCann is lecturer in the Department of Educational Foundation at the Memorial University of Newfoundland.

C.B. Macpherson is professor of political science at the University of Toronto.

Claus Offe is professor of political science and sociology at the University of Bielefeld.

Alan Pomfret is lecturer in sociology, King's College, University of Western Ontario.

Contributors

David Reeder	is senior lecturer in education and urban studies at the University of Leicester.
Volker Ronge	is director of research at the Munich Institute of Survey Research.
Michael Sanderson	is senior lecturer in economic and social history at the University of East Anglia.
Stephen Stoer	is lecturer in sociology of education at the Instituto António Aurélio da Costa Ferreira, Portugal.
Robert Verhine	is a doctoral candidate in the School of Education at the University of California.
Jorge Werthein	is research associate at Instituto Interamericano de Ciencias Agricolas, OEA, Rio de Janeiro.
Adam Westoby	is senior lecturer in the Faculty of Educational Studies at The Open University.
Ann Wickham	is research assistant in the Faculty of Education Studies at the Open University.
Max Wilkinson	was education correspondent of *The Daily Mail* and is now deputy news editor of *The Financial Times*.
Paul Willis	is research fellow at the Centre for Contemporary Cultural Studies at the University of Birmingham.

Author Index

Index

Braverman, H. 202, 230, 236, 244, 255, 256
Brebeck, C. and Thompson, T.J. 319
Brennen, F.J.T. 202, 203
Briant, K. 225
Bridge, A.B. 43
Bright, J.R. 42
Brittain, H. 129
Brown, G. 256
Brown, S. 256
Bruegal, I. 256
Bruford, W.H. 292
Brzezinski, Z. and Huntingdon, S.P. 292
Bukharin, N.I. 318, 359, 370
Bullock, Sir A. 90, 98
Bullough, W.A. 43
Burgess, T. 203
Burnham, J. 361, 362, 371
Burstall, C. 92, 98
Burton, F. and Carlen, P. 105, 113
Butts, R.F. 294, 304

Cabrel, P. 349
Callahan, R.E. 43, 51, 59
Calloway, A. 319
Cantor, L.M. and Roberts, I.F. 195, 203
Cardia, S. 347
Cardoso, F.H. 319
Carleton, F.T. 294, 304
Carnoy, M. 308, 313, 315, 317, 319, 320, 385, 387 (*see also Thias and Carnoy*)
Carnoy, M. and Levin, H. 387
Carnoy, M. Sack, R. and Thias, H. 387
Carson, R.B. 42
Carter, C. and Williams, B.R. 200
Carter, M. 387
Carter, S.R. and Stacey, M. 226
Casey, G.J. 306
Cash, W.C. 319
Castro, F. 383, 384, 385
Cave-Brown-Cave, T.R. 213, 215, 227
Chamberlain, J. 116, 122, 127
Chandler, A.D. 135, 137, 140, 292
Chang, C. 292
Chapman, A.W. 227
de Charms, R. and Moeller, G.H. 292
Charlton, H.B. 226
Childs, W.M. 227
Chirot, D. 295, 298, 305
Chossudowsky, E.M. 228
Chubb, B. 334
Clapham, Sir J. 221, 228
Clark, B.R. 42, 304
Clark, H.F. and Sloan, H.S. 311, 318
Clark, R.W. 226, 227
Clayton, R.H. 207, 225
Clifford, G.J. 304
Cohen, D.K. 44 (*see also Jencks et al*)
Cohen, D.K. and Rosenberg, B. 42
Cohen, S. 304
Coleman, J.S. 187, 292, 308, 318

Coleman, J.S., Blum, Z.D., Sorenson, A.B. and Rossi, P. 317
Coleman, J.S., Campbell, E.Q., Hobson, C.J., McPartland, J., Mood, A., Weinfeld, F.D. and York, R.L. 320
Collins, R. 42, 176, 291, 292, 294, 295, 296, 297, 298, 305, 313, 316, 319, 320 (*see also Lovett and Collins*)
Coombs, P.H. and Ahmed, M. 317
Cooper, C. and Torrington, D. 256
Cooper, T. 115, 127
Corey, L. 140
Cosin, B.R. 175, 176
Cosin, B.R., Dale, I.R., Esland, G.M., Mackinnon, D. and Swift, D.F. 29
Cottle, B. and Sherbourne, J.W. 227
Counts, G.E. 43
Court, W.H.B. 227
Coward, R. and Ellis, J. 113
Cremin, L.A. 294, 305, 319
Cromer, H.W. 226
Cronin, J. 43
Crosland, J. 227
Cubberley, E. 42, 294, 304
Cuneo, C.J. 305
Cunhal, A. 345, 346, 350

Dahlman, C.J. 383, 386
Dale, I.R. 350 (*see also Cosin et al*)
Dale, I.R., Esland, G.M. and MacDonald, M. 29, 304, 305
Dale, I.R., Miranda, S., Stoer, S. and Wickham, A. 349
Davies, M. 255
Dawley, A. 43
Dean, J. and Choppin, B. 201
Delehanty, G.E. 141
Deller, E. 225
Denison, E.F. 319
Denison, E.F. and Pouillier, J.P. 175
Dewey, J. 46, 59, 98, 178, 201
Dill, W.R., Hilton, T.L. and Reitman, W.R. 319
Dixon, G. 116, 117, 121, 127
Dore, R.P. 292
Donald, J. 338, 340, 349
Douglas, J.W.B. 17, 29
Douglas, J.W.B., Ross, J.M. and Simpson, H.R. 29
Dreeben, R. 291
Drucker, P.F. 143, 144, 157
Dummelow, J. 225
Duncan, B. 318 (*see also Duncan et al*)
Duncan, O.D., Featherman, D.L. and Duncan, B. 317
Duncan, O.D. and Hodge, R. 317
Durkheim, E. 26, 27, 28, 44, 181, 202, 279, 291

Eckhaus, R.S. 310, 318
Eckland, B.K. 317, 318
Elder, G.H. 317

392